The Derry Anthology

The
Derry Anthology

edited by
SEAN McMAHON

THE
BLACKSTAFF
PRESS

BELFAST

First published in 2002 by
Blackstaff Press Limited
Wildflower Way, Apollo Road
Belfast BT12 6TA, Northern Ireland

Supported by the National Lottery
through the Arts Council of Northern Ireland

The acknowledgements on pages 417–425 constitute
an extension of this copyright page

Typeset by Techniset Typesetters, Newton-le-Willows, Merseyside

Printed in Ireland by Betaprint

A CIP catalogue record for this book
is available from the British Library

ISBN 0-85640-726-7

Contents

Introduction

THE EXISTENCE OF SUCH A BOOK as *The Derry Anthology* might justifiably inspire two pertinent questions: Why Derry? Why me? The first, however, had better not be uttered aloud until one is safely out of the jurisdiction, say passing Toomebridge or Aughnacloy. Otherwise a hoarse and menacing roar from the citizens of the most chauvinistic town in Ireland might hasten departure. My fellow citizens have many and plangent virtues but self-criticism is not one of them. With more instinctual certainty than historical precision they could (and would) tell you that Derry was a city when Dublin was a ford with hurdles and Belfast the mouth of a sandy inlet, as their Gaelic names connote. It had walls when Belfast had barely a castle and a full-blown siege when the fishing-port on the Lagan had only a few streets. Its own arboreal name, both before and after the coming of Colum Cille, was more elegant than that of either of the comparable settlements, and the founding in 546 of the Columban monastery did establish it as no mean city.

Celtic monasteries contained in miniscule within their security palisades rudimentary examples of the elements that go to make a city. There would have been a church, a hospital, a school (sometimes providing third-level education), workshops, a market-place and lay housing. The Latin words *civitas* (townsfolk) and *urbs* (walled city) have given modern English the ideas of civilisation and urbanity, and though it required a significant evolution from the church-centred monastic precinct to the recognisable medieval city, the roots of urban civilisation were, we like to think, well seated on the 'island' of Derry, bounded by the famous Foyle and the even more famous bog, 'most commonly wet' as it was described by the city's modern founder Sir Henry Docwra (d. 1631). (It was he who graphically pictured the place as 'in form of a bow bent, whereof the bog is the string and the river the bow.')

The original Columban foundation, with its centre the Dubh-Regles (Black Church), suffered through the centuries as did most other parts of the 'distressful country'. The Vikings, with their navigational genius, found the lough and river irresistible and set up a maritime fort at Dunalong, eight miles to the south of the settlement. There was not much in the way of pick-ings in the pocket monastery but they avenged their naval defeat in the Foyle in 833 by burning the town in 997. Since they were the original city-makers of Ireland we might regret their lack of interest in settling in any considerable numbers, but they did bequeath to Derry one of its commonest surnames, McLaughlin. This lack of interest was maintained by the Vikings' colonial descendants, the Anglo-Normans, who preferred to build Northburg at Greencastle, at the mouth of the lough, rather than risk the tedium of defence of Derry against the O'Cahans to the east, the O'Dohertys to the north and the O'Donnells to the west. Derry continued to have an ecclesiastical existence, and in its glory days in the twelfth century under the great abbot Flaithbertach Ó Brolcháin, it could boast of its 'great church' or Tempull Mór, which became the cathedral of the diocese and gave the name to the parish of Templemore. It survived until its destruction in 1567.

Derry's true urban existence did not begin until 1604 when James I decided to establish it as 'a town of war and a town of merchandise'. He obtained the reluctant help of the burghers of the City of London in 1613 and Derry acquired a contentious and awkward prefix, and the beginnings of a chronic dual personality. The famous walls, since more sinned against than sinning, were completed in 1618 and the city's cathedral, dedicated to the founder St 'Columb', opened its gothic doors in 1633. The Free School also set within the walls and founded by Matthias Springham, The Honourable The Irish Society's man in the city, completed the urban quota. There was, then, much justice in the inscription on the stone still preserved in the cathedral porch:

> If stones could speake
> Then Londons prayse
> Should sounde who
> Built this church and
> Cittie from the grounde.

London-derry was to gain its greatest pre-twentieth-century historical fame eighty-four years later with its heroic but slightly bizarre siege. The story has been told many times, with strong-stomached schoolchildren relishing the details of siege fare and the going rate for vermin. Every visitor since has found it necessary to consider the siege and most of those who later published their impressions gave a version more or less coloured by their sources or historical bias. The successful resistance to the motley Jacobite forces outside the permanently rainswept walls made the 'maiden' city a Protestant icon. This symbolic position was easy to maintain until the mid-nineteenth century, when population increase and Donegal famine swelled the numbers of the 'mere Irish' now residing in the drained bog. Sporadic sectarian tension was the inevitable result, and when the city and county were included in the new political unit of Northern Ireland in 1921, it took a great deal of conscientious ward maintenance to preserve a Protestant majority in the corporation of a city which had a majority of Catholics.

Until the dire shadow of Partition fell about Derry, it had promised well. It had been a thriving market and port, and had even built a few ships. It played its part in both eighteenth- and nineteenth-century emigration and remained until the early twentieth century the main departure point for the Donegal seasonal workers as they went 'tatty-hokin'' in Scotland. Its shirts were worn all over the world and it was the *entrepôt* for the whole of north-west Ireland from Coleraine to Sligo. Deprived of the safety of Lough Swilly as a naval ground because of the same Partition, Britain made the less suitable Lough Foyle a premier base during World War II, with Derry as its centre of operations, and the dehydrated and economically deprived city of the twenties and thirties blossomed again. It was unlikely to settle back in a post-war brave new world to its former bleakness, and it too was required to play its awful part in the Troubles that have bloodied the last three decades.

Derry's story is fixed in the world's mind by its two violent dramas, the siege and the events of 30 January 1972. Acres of paper, gallons of ink and now microchips galore have been used in the relentless chronicling of these events. It is perfectly appropriate that this should be so. Yet there is much more to the history of any city than the depiction of its blackest hours. People have lived and loved on both sides of the Foyle for nearly two thousand years and, even if this book were a history, too much emphasis on the apocalyptic side of its story would cause a grave imbalance. It isn't meant to be a history, although sociology, politics and economics must play their informal parts in its composition. It isn't even a portrait since it is necessarily idiosyncratic and incomplete, not to say partial, in the paltering sense. Perhaps mosaic is the best term to describe its impressionistic character, the tesserae found by truffling in printed books and pamphlets. All selection is bias and the view of Derry in as many aspects as I could find in literary representation is ultimately mine, and I take the responsibility for what I hope is not too eccentric a portrait.

To break a seamless chronological continuity and avert the possibility of lumpiness in the mixture, I have chosen thirteen representational categories – no triskaidekaphobe I! They are not mutually exclusive; several of the entries might reasonably have been located elsewhere but there is, I hope, sufficient relevant material in each to merit primary inclusion. The labelling of the categories may seem somewhat riddling but each heading is a quotation from one of the included pieces. 'Our Small City' is a collection of short entries that is meant as a sampler for the book as a whole; 'A Schooling' is the title of a poem by Seamus Deane and the section contains accounts of childhood, education and the sense of growing up in Derry. 'Stroke City', Gerry Anderson's brilliant coinage, is about Derry's dualism and the pains and pleasures of intercourse between the two sides of the 'house' or alternative digging feet. 'A Green Hill Far Away', the title of the hymn by Cecil Frances Alexander (1818–1895) who was the first Protestant to be buried in Derry Cemetery in a grave marked by a cross, contains pieces that might be called devotional or ecclesiastical. It is appropriate in that the cue for recalling to the poet the green hill outside Jerusalem was the green hill of Creggan seen from the rear window of the episcopal palace on (where else?) Bishop Street Within.

'Carlisle Road on a Saturday night' is about entertainments and pastimes, the title coming from a kind of weekend *ramblas* of young people that had persisted for at least a hundred years and only evaporated with the coming of the Troubles. 'A Lumpy Uneven Kind of City', the trenchant description by William Bulfin (1862–1910), the returned gaucho and vocal nationalist who cycled all over the country in 1902, is essentially a Derry visitor's book complete with comments. Thackeray came twice to Ireland in the 1840s, calling himself 'Michael Angelo Titmarsh', and illustrated his *Irish Sketch Book* (1843) with comic drawings. Thomas Carlyle, the Sage of Ecclefechan (1795–1881), found relief in a tolerably prosperous town from the miseries of the Famine which so harrowed him on his visit in 1846. And Sean O'Faolain paid the city the ultimate compliment of wanting to set a novel there.

'A Maiden Still' is the peroration by 'Charlotte Elizabeth', the Protestant laureate, in one of her poems about the siege, and the section contains contemporary and retrospective accounts of either Derry's finest hour or a tiny incident in the War of the Three Kings, depending upon your viewpoint. HMS Marlborough *Will Enter Harbour* is the title of a novella by Nicholas Monsarrat, who wrote *The Cruel Sea* (1951) and knew Derry as a naval officer during World War II. The section contains accounts of what life was like here during the two declared wars. 'Derry is Different' is a kind of city ragbag down the years and 'A Place of Wheels and Looms', a line from the poet Francis Ledwidge who was stationed in Ebrington Barracks in 1917 before being shipped back to Flanders and death, says something about Derry's limited industrial life. 'A Barrage of Stones' tells its own story; and it is something of a relief to return to happier moments in the contemplation of the lordly Foyle, Docwra's bow, in 'A Very Fine and Broad River'. Finally 'The General Witchery' is essentially topographical, showing a proper regard for the magic of particular names and places.

As for my own qualifications, I was born here in 1931 and, apart from four years of frivolity as a student in Belfast, have lived here all my life – so far. A Westbanker – though we did not use the term – I made full use of Derry's seven cinemas, including the Opera House which burned down early in the war. As a child the Waterside seemed to me a remarkable place, with its even steeper streets, its Midland cinema where you could catch up on films you had missed in the city side, and the NCC station, the gateway to summer holidays in Portstewart. The broad-gauge engines with their smell of oil and soot were so much more impressive than the little puffers that went to Buncrana. As one grew up one realised that this east side of the river was subtly different and that a whole drift of fascinatingly unfamiliar females could be met at céilí-and-old-time's in the Pat's Hall of a Friday night. I was also aware from an early age, however retarded other aspects of my aesthetic education, that the Foyle was as *soigné* a river as any Stephen Foster wrote about.

I took the persistent rain in my stride and was slightly shocked when, during the war, I heard the civilian technicians and the armed forces complain about it, as they wondered aloud why they didn't pull the plug and let the (expletive deleted) place sink. On the whole the British and American visitors seemed to like the place, though in a movie called *The Gift Horse* about a lease-lend corvette, a young Richard Attenborough opined: 'Londonderry? No matelot's paradise!' In any case, it was a commonly held belief that the rain was responsible for the marvellous singing voices of the citizens, especially the women, though it did not explain why the accents were generally incomprehensible. On one notable occasion, when a film was made showing some of the work of Paddy Doherty, one of the city's true benefactors, subtitles were found to be necessary. The yearly feis was truly a feast of music and dancing, but to us adolescents it was our best chance of seeing, talking to and, with luck, leaving home marvellous Derry girls.

Derry we accepted, with its rain and its unemployment, its amateur theatre and its gentle humour; and when the just demand for civil rights turned sour, we bore the 'bother' as stoically and as cheerfully as we could. There are many possible Derry anthologies; this one I have tried to make as representative of the city's long pageant as possible. As for my own involvement in its story, I cannot do better than to quote another Ulsterman, Louis MacNeice:

> I cannot deny my past to which my self is wed,
> The woven figure cannot undo its thread.

I take this opportunity of thanking many people who have helped me in various ways with this project: Kathleen Barr, Sam Burnside, Art Byrne, Frank D'Arcy, Mary Delargy, Richard Doherty, Liam Galbraith, Seamus Gallagher, John Killen, Pat McCafferty, Tomás Ó Canainn, the staffs of the libraries in Derry (including that of the University of Ulster at Magee College), Letterkenny and Limavady, and the Linen Hall Library in Belfast, Ken Thatcher, Paul Wilkins, the Reverend John R. Walsh PP; and finally Anne Tannahill and the rest of the peerless staff of Blackstaff Press.

SEAN McMAHON
DERRY
JUNE 2002

· *Our Small City*

THEN FOLLOWED THE IDYLLIC DAYS. Where Maeve went I went, and merely to be with her and with Gortin Lass was heaven. Everything in our small city became intimate and beautiful then as I learned how to count spoons and in any spare moments walked with her in holy purity, far from the sweat and sighs of Dublin Lass, far from the fancies with which Lucy's presence used to fill my mind. This truly was laburnum and lilac love. We were as pure, believe it or not, as any ideal the gregarious preacher could hold before the young men and women of Ireland.

Everything, I said, in our small city became intimate and beautiful then, and one noticed with a stab of affection, like someone seeing the gestures of his father in his son or the deepening of lines on a known face, even the bright saddles on low window-sills in by-streets where lazy men sat and spat and sharpened clasp-knives. In the drowsy lunch-time lull old people that one never saw at any other hour of the day rested without words, under the protection of the Virgin Victory, on seats in the Diamond. The uncanny comparative silence of that hour seemed broken only by the voice of the man selling apples near the arch of the Guildhall Gate (the old walls still preserved rings to which marketing men had once hitched horses) or the limping, peg-legged rattle of looms from a small shirt factory. A few sailors, early on shore, peacocks in bright, ill-creased, foreign suits, looked speculatively at everything in skirts, took a solemn, academic interest in the protruding balloons of bums of the afternoon's young matrons gabbling on circular swivel stools in the hotel bar. Brown eyes in lean, tanned faces were the eyes of children wondering about toys in shop windows. It was a religious little city just as Ireland is a religious little country. Those hilly streets ascended always to steeples and bells, and most of us climbed up to pray whether we meant it or not. But, being a seaport and a garrison town, it had for centuries its proud tradition of depravity, and reckless soldiers and sailors sought fun, and fought, in the pubs of the Fountain Lane gridiron under one corner of the walls, where even the white-putteed shore police, by gentlemanly agreement, left them to their recreations. On the walls and along the docks, dying slowly because it was a small, decaying port, Maeve and myself found two favourite places in the city for hand-in-hand walks.

This (I read from a plaque in a corner of the walls sheltered by a high, brown-brick gable) was Cowards' Bastion.

1

'Being most out of danger,' said the plaque in the grave tones of the seventeenth century, 'cowards resorted here.'

She sat on the butt of a siege gun, wearing the wine skirt to please me, and, her toes straining towards the sandy ground, bent herself at right angles, her shoulders on the barrel, her coppery head towards the embrasure. Bending down quickly, Owen Rodgers, *trouvère*, kissed her lightly on the forehead, then on her warm, dry lips. To preserve us from temptation and recall us to time, the Guildhall clock chimed the quarter. She leaped up laughing, hugged me, danced around me in that corner where cowards had gathered to be away from cannon balls. Cowards in congress, what could their talk possibly have been about?

BENEDICT KIELY, *The Captain with the Whiskers*, 1960

AMERICAN PASSENGER OFFICE, LONDONDERRY

PASSENGERS CONTRACT TICKET

LONDONDERRY, 18TH MAY, 1844

Ship 'Provincialist' of 880 tons Register burden will sail from Londonderry for Philadelphia on the 18th day of May 1844.

———————

We engage that the parties herein named, will be provided with a steerage passage to Philadelphia in the Ship 'Provincialist' with not less than 10 cubic feet for luggage for each adult, for the sum of £4 : 0 : 0 including head money, if any, at the place of landing, and every other charge, and we hereby acknowledge to have received the sum of £2 : 0 : 0 in part payment.

Names.

Ann McElkinney   11 years

Balance to be paid at the office of Wm. McCorkell & Co., on the 16th May, 1844.

Water and provisions according to the annexed scale will be supplied by the ship as required by law, and also fires and suitable hearths for cooking. Bedding and utensils for eating and drinking must be provided by the passenger.

(A ticket for the *Provincialist*, from Londonderry to Philadelphia)

EDWARD LAXTON, *The Famine Ships*, 1996

DERRY IS BUILT ON A HILL which it almost covers, and around a large portion of the hill flow the waters of Lough Foyle. Look now at your map, that you may better understand the situation of the town, and its fitness to endure the siege. The appearance of Derry, even at the present day, is very imposing. The houses rise in tiers one above another, and the lofty spire of the old cathedral tops all. The thick high wall and well preserved towers look even now capable of defence. There is a broad walk on the walls neatly gravelled.

MRS THOMAS GELDART, *Stories of Ireland*, 1851

FROM A DISTANCE, DERRY was lovely and familiar. It looked like a mill-town in Massachusetts – churches and factories piled up on both banks of a river, the same sort of tenements, the same sleepy air of bankruptcy. But up close, Derry was frightful.

PAUL THEROUX, *The Kingdom by the Sea: A Journey Around the Coast of Great Britain*, 1982

ALIO IN TEMPORE QUIDAM BAITANUS, gente Nepos Niath Taloirc, benedici a Sancto petivit, cum ceteris in mari eremum quaesiturus. Cui valedicens Sanctus hoc de ipso propheticum protulit verbum, 'Hic homo, qui ad quaerendum in oceano desertum pergit, non in deserto conditus iacebit, sed illo in loco sepelietur ubi oves femina trans sepulcrum eius minabit.' Idem itaque Baitanus, post longos per ventosa circuitus aequora, eremo non reperta, ad patriam reversus, multis ibidem annis cuiusdam cellulae dominus permansit, quae Scotice Lathreginden dicitur. Iisdemque diebus accidit, quibus, post aliqua mortuus tempora, sepultus est in Roboreto Calgachi, ut propter hostilitatis incursum vicina ad eiusdem loci ecclesiam plebecula cum mulieribus et parvulis confugeret. Unde contigit ut quadam die mulier deprehenderetur aliqua, quae suas per eiusdem viri sepulcrum nuper sepulti oviculas minabat. Et unus ex his qui viderant sanctus sacerdos dixit, 'Nunc prophetia sancti Columbae expleta est, multis prius divulgata annis.' Qui utique supra memoratus presbyter mihi haec de Baitano enarrans retulit, Mailodranus nomine, Christi miles, gente Mocurin.

On one occasion a man named Baitan, a descendant of the family of Niath Talorg, sought the saint's blessing when about to set off with some others in search of a place of retreat out in the seas. As he said farewell to him the saint made this prophecy: 'This man who now goes to seek a place apart in the ocean will not lie in death in such a retreat but he will be buried in the place where a woman will drive sheep over his grave.' And it so happened that Baitan sailed for a long time over the stormy seas without finding a

3

place of refuge, and then returned to his own country where he remained for many years as head of a little monastery in a place called in Gaelic Lathreginden.

In due course he died and was buried in the Oakgrove of Calgach. About that time the placed was attacked by enemies, which led the local people to seek refuge with their wives and children in the church of the place. Thus it came about that one day a woman was seen driving her lambs over the grave of the recently buried Baitan.

A holy priest was amongst those who saw it and he said: 'The prophecy of the saintly Columba made public many years ago has now been fulfilled.' The same priest told me these things about Baitan. He was a soldier of Christ called Mael Odhrain, of the Mocu Curin.

ADAMNÁN, *Vita Columbae, c*. 697
(VERSION BY FRANK D'ARCY)

ONCE OR TWICE AS I HAVE GONE about the circuit of Ireland I have noted down something like this: 'A setting for a novel.' Youghal was one, Clonmel another, and I would now add Derry, or Coleraine. What I meant by that, I think, was that something in the atmosphere of these places – indefinable, impalpable – clustered life into articulate and significant relationships. Perhaps it was the atmosphere of history; or that the people have adopted a certain kind of position, almost a pose, appropriate to the dramatic meaning of their own kind of life; and this had gone into the very stones of the town, all its ways and outer signs, as the face and body of a man reveals his inner nature. Why should it not be so? We say of a man that he has a strong personality. Why may we not say it of a town?

SEAN O'FAOLAIN, *An Irish Journey*, 1940

'I DID FIND IT QUITE IRONIC that The Undertones couldn't even give away records. Maybe the people who liked The Undertones never really had enough money to buy our records. It might have just been a case of pure and hard economics – the starving student brigade!'

FEARGAL SHARKEY, quoted in
Tony Clayton-Lea and Richie Taylor, *Irish Rock*, 1992

OF SOME INTEREST IN THIS CONNECTION is the situation at Pennyburn, Londonderry, where a windmill and a watermill occupying adjacent sites are recorded as working, on average, the windmill twenty-six weeks, the watermill thirty-four weeks in the year. If this is a true reflection of the availability of power it shows wind power at a disadvantage compared with a very significant stream. (1834)

H.D. GRIBBON, *The History of Water Power in Ulster*, 1969

AWAY FROM BELFAST, the most serious incident occurred at Londonderry where 15 civilians were killed when two parachute mines, apparently dropped by the same aircraft, fell on the Derry to Buncrana Road at 0012 hours. A report made by a local ARP officer recorded that there was a 'fairly strong breeze from the north-west' and that 'it was a dark night with intermittent showers and some heavy clouds'.

There is no authenticated explanation for the attack on Londonderry nor does any German record throw any light on the subject.

TREVOR ALLEN, *The Storm Passed By*, 1996

This were pleasant, O Son of God,
   with wondrous coursing
to sail across the swelling torrent
   back to Ireland.

To Eólarg's plan, past Benevanagh,
   across Loch Feval,
and there to hear the swans in chorus
   chanting to music.

ANONYMOUS (TRANSLATION BY JAMES CARNEY),
'Colum Cille's Exile', *Medieval Irish Lyrics*, 1967

SINCE THE BESIEGED STILL MAINTAIN a bold front and since there is a report current that another fleet will come to force through, at whatever cost, relieving supplies for this town and for the Enniskilling area, M. Rosen [Marshal Conrad von Rosen, Jacobite general] decided this morning to issue you a declaration. You will find a copy attached in which you can see, Monseigneur, his plan to force the rebels of Dery [sic] to surrender by sending into them all their relations who will help eat up all their remaining food – unless they choose rather to let them die of hunger. If this does not have the effect he intended, he will destroy all the countryside, as he says in his declaration, in order to deny all means of subsistence to the rebels and to any relieving force from England. Either no money has yet been sent to us or there is not a penny left, for I have had to advance sixty pistoles of my own money to a regiment which wanted to give up completely if there was further delay. The troops here are very tired and many are falling sick. They have been four months on campaign without tents and in a countryside where there is no cover and where it is almost always raining and where the nights are extremely cold.

Letter from M. FUMERON, MILITARY COMMISSARY TO LOUVOIS
(Louis XIV's Minister of War), 30 June 1689,
in *Negociations de M le Comte d'Avaux en Irlande, 1689–90*, 1934
(TRANSLATION BY FRANK D'ARCY)

LOCALITY. — THE CITY OF DERRY, OR LONDONDERRY, is in latitude 54° 59′ N., and longitude 7° 19′ W. Its distance from Dublin by the present mail-coach road is nearly 144 miles. It is in the diocese of Derry, and the N. W. circuit of assize.

The city is placed on the western or Donegal side of the Foyle, about 5 miles above the junction of that river with Lough Foyle, and 14 below Lifford. This situation is equally remarkable for its distinguished local advantages and picturesque features, being a hill nearly insulated by a broad and navigable river, and commanding on every side views of a country, rich in natural and cultivated beauty. This hill, which in troubled times was selected as the natural *acropolis* of the North, comprised till lately within its limits the whole of the city and suburbs; but Londonderry, in its days of prosperity and peace, has spread beyond its natural military boundary, and is now rapidly extending northerly towards the lough, along the bank of the river.

THOMAS COLBY (Colonel, Royal Engineers),
Ordnance Survey to the County of Londonderry, 1837

I WENT TO A PICTURE-HOUSE IN DERRY to see a film I'd also seen in Dublin. I found that the Free State's care for my morals had been carried to an amusing length of prudery. The film dealt with the adventure of a young couple – one of the two unmarried – who being stranded and penniless through the breakdown of a night bus were, among other things, forced to sleep in the same room. But they hung a quilt between the beds, and behaved with almost incredible propriety. The Southern censorship had cut all this part out, and that in a city where a display of revolvers is far more infectious than a display of lingerie. I drew comparisons favourable to

Derry; but too soon. Next day an official of a dramatic society in Derry regretted that the society couldn't used a play of mine because one of the scenes was laid in a public-house. Yet if you wanted to find a public-house in Derry you wouldn't need to put in a ferret.

I went to see the Saturday night parade in Ferryquay Street. The footpaths and the street were filled with a cheerful laughing crowd of young men and women. There was a pervading air of high spirits, almost of carnival, except at the entrance to a side street, where a young lay-preacher was addressing a ring of earnest hearers. A Royal Ulster Constabulary man twiddled the lanyard of his revolver and gazed sardonically at the throng. It was for the most part the unbent bow he was witnessing, mill-hand or shirt-worker relapsing into naturalness after a week of irksome restraint. I talked to the RUC man about it all. He opined that 'some of them lassies should be skelped and sent home to bed'; but he smiled as he said it, and wasn't altogether unsympathetic. We stood awhile and looked on at the swaying, swirling crowd. The whole street as far as the eye could carry was palpitating with humanity – youth, and hot blood, and adolescent impulse, and laughter, and folly, and life let off the chain.

LYNN DOYLE, *The Spirit of Ireland*, 1935

Columba's Derry!
  ledge of angels
radiant oakwood
  where the man dove
knelt to master
  his fiery temper
exile chastened
  the bright candle
of the Uí Néill
  burns from Iona
lightens Scotland
  with beehive huts
glittering manuscripts
  but he remembers
his secret name
  'He who set his
back on Ireland.'

JOHN MONTAGUE, *from* 'A New Siege', in *The Rough Field*, 1989

7

As I was walking round the streets of Derry
I saw old Hobbits
Looking very pleased.
He was wearing a policeman's hat
And about six watches
On his arm.
On his bicycle was
Half a landrover,
And in his hand
A bottle of wine.
I got to thinking there was a riot
And it looked as if old Hobbits had won.

ARTHUR McVEIGH, 'Thought on the Derry Riots' in *A Rage for Order*, 1992

WITH NOTHING BETTER TO DO on my next run ashore I found myself eating beans on toast at the Salvation Army canteen. A large hearty man was busy by the cash till counting the money; he looked up and caught my eye. A short time later he walked over and we exchanged the usual type of pleasantries; cashing-up at some of the canteens I learned was one of his contributions towards the charities concerned.

He asked me if I would like to visit his home.

'It's nothing grand but there'll be a warm welcome from my wife and a warm fire to sit beside.'

We walked up to Pump Street, in the shadow of the Cathedral, and I found a second home.

Fortune smiled on me that evening; he was right about the warmth, I could never visit Derry again without visiting Pump Street and the Bell family. They were my first contacts with all those people of Londonderry whose warm hearts and unfailing kindness came to mean so much to me.

FRED KELLETT, *A Flower for the Sea – A Fish for the Sky*, 1995

FOR THE CAR WHICH CARRIED ME TWO MILES the landlord of the inn made me pay the sum of five shillings. He is a godly landlord, has Bibles in the coffee-room, the drawing-room, and every bedroom in the house, with this inscription –

UT MIGRATURUS HABITA.
THE TRAVELLER'S TRUE REFUGE.
Jones's Hotel, Londonderry

This pious double or triple entendre, the reader will, no doubt, admire – the first simile establishing the resemblance between this life and an inn; the second allegory showing that the inn and the Bible are both the traveller's refuge.

In life we are in death – the hotel in question is about as gay as a family vault: a severe figure of a landlord, in seedy black, is occasionally seen in the dark passages or on the creaking old stairs of the black inn. He does not bow to you – very few landlords in Ireland condescend to acknowledge their guests – he only warns you: – a silent solemn gentleman who looks to be something between a clergyman and a sexton – 'ut migraturus habita!' – the 'migraturus' was a vast comfort in the clause.

It must, however, be said for the consolation of future travellers, that when at evening in the old lonely parlour of the inn, the great gaunt fireplace is filled with coals, two dreary funeral candles and sticks glimmering upon the old-fashioned round table, the rain pattering fiercely without, the wind roaring and thumping in the streets, this worthy gentleman can produce a pint of port-wine for the use of his migratory guest, which causes the latter to be almost reconciled to the cemetery in which he is resting himself, and he finds himself, to his surprise, almost cheerful. There is a mouldy-looking old kitchen, too, which, strange to say, sends out an excellent comfortable dinner, so that the sensation of fear gradually wears off.

WILLIAM MAKEPEACE THACKERAY, *The Irish Sketchbook*, 1842

ROMAN CATHOLICS came out to watch the parades and traders brought their stalls to sell refreshments to the Orangemen or Apprentice Boys along the parade route. Roman Catholic pubs were also kept busy after the parade. Parades were generally regarded as folk occasions.

Indeed, it was not unknown for the lending of instruments to take place between Green and Orange bands before a parade of either community. I have heard of the appropriate insignia being painted on a borrowed drum and the original repainted when it was returned, and there were occasions, I am told, when bandsmen were also borrowed across the divide to stand in for those prevented by illness from parading.

This lending a hand to all and sundry in times of need irrespective of religion or politics was second nature to the Derry people. A prominent parishioner of mine described an incident which took place during the Troubles around 1921 or 1922. He was an officer in what were known as the 'B Specials', a constabulary organised on a part-time basis to assist the RUC, and one evening came across a leading IRA man from Derry endeavouring to drill a squad of volunteers on the strand near Fahan, Co. Donegal, and making a very poor fist of it. Becoming suddenly aware

9

of the Specials officer surveying the scene from the cliff above and knowing he was an expert in military drill, the IRA man shouted up, 'For God's sake will you come down here and lick this crowd into shape.' So down went the 'B' man and drilled the IRA volunteers on Fahan strand. Politics were temporarily forgotten. All that mattered was to extend a helping hand to a fellow Derry man in difficulties and to take pride in a job well done.

(DEAN) VICTOR GRIFFIN, The Mark of Protest, 1993

IN THE DIAMOND I JUMPED AT A SHOUT. But it was only an instructor in the Xtress gym club on the corner, marshalling twenty assorted women in leotards. The statue at the little square's centre was a magnificent montage of Republican heroes – Michael Collins, Patrick Pearse, Daniel O'Connell, Wolfe Tone, Dermot MacMurrough. Of course not. It was a maiden with a sword and a wreath: 'To our honoured dead and those who served 1914–1918, 1939–45.' At her feet a soldier far more mature and aggressive-looking than the lads on the armoured car plunged his bayoneted rifle downwards.

At the bottom of Waterloo Street a blue-grey RUC van cruised slowly past (a 'pig' as the locals call it). The gang of youths on the corner (who on Tory Island would have been illegally catching salmon) yelled loud, expletive-rich abuse at its meshed and darkened windows.

MARK McCRUM, The Craic, 1998

DERRY'S FIRST WALLS were earthwork defences thrown up in 1566 by Colonel Edward Randolph and again in 1600 by Sir Henry Docwra. They were not sufficient to withstand the attack of Sir Cahir O'Doherty in 1608 and in consequence were rebuilt with a stone face between 1613 and 1618. In 1619 Captain Pynnar records the city surrounded with a strong wall 'excellently made and neatly wrought' of rubble limestone. Its circumference was $284\frac{2}{3}$ perches, its height 24ft, and there were four battlemented gates, two of which had drawbridges but no portcullises and were not normally used as entrances to the city. What Pynnar describes is shown in 'The plat of the Cittie of Londonderrie' prepared with other plans of the London Companies' estates by their overseer Sir Thomas Phillips for his Survey of 1622, and what Phillips's map shows is still, with the exception of a part of the East Wall and the exact gates, intact.

Derry's walls are the most extensive early C17 fortifications in the British Isles. They were designed by *Captain Edward Doddington* and built by *Peter Benson*, a grantee of 1,000 acres in Co. Donegal. The core of the rampart is of earth, faced with split-stone rubble laid in lime mortar. The height varies from 20 ft to 25 ft and the breadth from 14 ft to 30 ft. The faces of the walls have a steep batter rising usually to a string course, above which a straight wall-head with embrasures for artillery rises to breast height. The copings are often of dressed sandstone. The town has long ago encroached on all these walls, built up now on the inside and now on the exterior. Something of the historic huddle can still be appreciated on the lower sections to the NE from Butchers' Gate down Magazine Street to Shipquay Place, but the nicest and in many ways the most evocative sections about the wall – Fountain Street, Albert Place, Bishop Street Without, and Nailer's Row – have now been ruthlessly cleared of their little streets and houses as part of an ill-conceived redevelopment plan for Derry.

The walls at the top of the hill today stand bleak and exposed. If this is a questionable way to treat a historic fabric, it does at least serve to emphasize the danger inherent in manning the walls in the C17. They withstood three sieges: first in 1641, next in 1648 and 1649, when the Parliamentarians held out against the Royalists, and lastly in the famous siege of 1688–9 that lasted 105 days against the forces of King James II.

ALISTAIR ROWAN, The Buildings of Ireland: North West Ulster, 1979

Derry, Londoned Derry, jerrybuilt
and gerrymandered – yet turning
to sky and mountains a profile spiritual
as one of its dark appealing ghetto faces.

Close-up eruptions of disease,
on dank walls, broken gable-ends:
UP PAISLEY, BRITISH MURDERERS, FUCK THE POPE.
What flowers among this detritus?
slashing at nettles, a child runs barefoot begging.

ANDREW WATERMAN, 'Derry Images 1968–1971',
in Collected Poems 1959–1999, 2000

1627 Jan. 19. Madrid. The Duke of San Lucar to the Infanta.

The Irish archbishop of the Order of St Francis who recently came here from those states (Flanders) has given me the enclosed memorial ...

Enclosed (a) Observations presented by the Irish archbishop.

Donegal Bay is the most beautiful bay in the kingdom of Ireland and it divides the two provinces of Ulster and Connaught ... The port of Londonderry, which also is in Tyrconnel, fifty miles from Killybegs by land, is well known. The city of Londonderry is small but beautiful and wealthy. It is inhabited by the English only, and is situated in an island in Lough Foyle, which is an arm of the sea running for miles to the said city, and continuing for many miles further.

Queen Elizabeth was never able to conquer the province of Ulster, nor weaken the forces of the Earls until she sent a royal fleet to this port, and fortified it and founded the city there; after which she made gradual progress with the war. Whoever shall win that port, with the port of Killybegs will easily rule the whole province of Ulster and the province of Connaught, which are easily the two strongest provinces of the kingdom of Ireland. And as the port of Londonderry is very near the Scottish islands of the Hebrides, these would immediately arm themselves against the English. The city has good walls but for its defence it has not more than one piece of artillery, unless some pieces have been placed there recently.

BRENDAN JENNINGS (ed.),
Wild Geese in Spanish Flanders, (translated from the Spanish), 1964

DERRY BEING A VERY FRIENDLY PLACE, it's not surprising there's a Chinese family here called O'Doherty. One of the Chinese O'Dohertys drives a taxi.

Ming is quite a common name here, too. Charlie Ming used to be the supervisor at the William Street swimming baths.

One of the Mings hired a taxi the other week for a trip down to Donegal. A soldier at the Buncrana Road checkpoint demanded the names of driver and passenger.

'O'Doherty,' said the Chinaman.

'Ming,' said the Derryman.

They were let go after an hour.

EAMONN McCANN, War and Peace in Northern Ireland, 1998

A Schooling

Ice in the school-room, listen,
The high authority of the cold
On some November morning
Turning to fragile crystals
In the Government milk
I was drinking and my world
All frost and snow, chalk and ice;
Quadratic equations on the board
Shining and shifting in white
Isosceles steps. In that trance
What could I know of his labour?
I, in my infinitesimally perceptive dance,
Thought nothing of the harbour
Where, in his fifth hour,
Waist-deep in water,
He laid cables, rode the dour
Iron swell between his legs
And maybe thought what kind of son,
An aesthetician of this cold,
He had, in other warmth, begot?
But there's ice in the school-room,
Father. Listen. The harbour's empty.
The Government's milk has been drunk.
It lies on the stomach yet, freezing,
Its kindness, inhuman, has sunk
In where up starts the feeling
That pitches a cold in the thought
Of authority's broken milk crystals
On the lips of the son you begot.

SEAMUS DEANE, 'A Schooling', *Rumours*, 1977

M Y LAST YEAR AT SCHOOL was respectable, uneventful and cost a lot of my fellow pupils money in lost bets. There was a tradition in the school called the Lists. On the first Sunday of each year the entire school would assemble in the chapel, and the principal would read the rules and announce the list of prefects. There were 10 of these functionaries, all final year pupils, all enjoying considerable authority and quite a few privileges. For example, a request to go out to the pictures on a Saturday afternoon was always granted to a prefect and automatically denied to everyone else.

In the first days of the year, therefore, the gamble was to predict the correct 10 candidates. You submitted your 10 choices and a shilling bet to one of the self-appointed bookies and an all-correct forecast earned you 10 shillings.

Every year one or two punters would come up with a correct list but there were no winners in my last year. The first eight or nine were reasonably predictable and there was a certain hopeful restlessness among the congregation as the principal folded up his notes before delivering himself of the last name.

'Library prefect, Owen Kelly,' he said and walked out.

If he had announced the excommunication of the entire school he couldn't have got a more stunned reaction. Your man Kelly, him that got thrown out twice and kept back that Hallowe'en? The fellow that was caught coming out of the Strand Cinema with a girl from Thornhill one Saturday last year? Nobody was more stunned than I was. It took us all quite a while, and me longer than most, to spot that what the man was doing was turning a poacher into a gamekeeper. I met Father Coulter in the corridor a few minutes later. He gave me a conspiratorial wink. 'Some people just have to be saved from themselves,' he said enigmatically and passed on.

This shrewd appointment didn't have any appreciable effect on anybody's behaviour except my own. I suppose the principal thought that to take one setter of bad example out of circulation was bonus enough for the school. Of course I never once failed to apply to the dean for permission to go to the pictures on Saturdays but I have to admit the crack had gone out of it entirely.

There wasn't much excitement in rambling through the city knowing that I had every right to be there. I even contemplated admitting to the dean that I had borrowed his bike for a visit to Creggan during the previous year, just to see what his reaction would be. After due consideration I abandoned the idea. There's a limit to the extent you can test people's endurance and live to talk about it.

The examination timetable for that year meant that I was one of the last half-dozen still in residence at the end of the following June. When I walked out into Bishop Street for the last time I saw one of the lay teachers approaching on the far side and I particularly wanted a word with him.

Now that it was safe to do so, I wanted to ask why he hadn't reported me the year before when he saw me coming out of the Strand Cinema with the girl from Thornhill, at a time when I was supposed to be in the college attending to my studies. Before I drew level somebody on the other side stopped to talk to him and he didn't see me pass. And that's how my grammar school career ended. Not with a bang, not even with a whimper.

OWEN KELLY, Hens' Teeth and Other Rarities, 1990

His nights in the aunts' house, their talk and tea:
who can trace a line back like they can?
They cover the district faster than Tarzan
family tree to family tree

and keep track of their own who're away
– Father Tim's tapes from the Far East:
It's O'Doherty's mince I miss most.
Laughter. Shrieks. It's as good as a play.

They prefer it like this, indoors, the fire on
with their three-tiered cakes stands for three-course snacks
legs apart, enjoying the crack
(he fancies the youngest one).

'Don't be getting an eye for the girls whatever you do.
Get all your degrees
and they'll be running after *you*.'
They give him a briefcase for getting an A and two Bs.

Are there men by any chance?
The men doze in chairs
while the women sort out their affairs
– an extreme case of aunts-in-the-pants.

And in summer the big two-car day trips
aunts crammed in the back, at the wheel glum men.
The men have no say in destination or stops.
They have to bolt their ice cream and drive on again.

MICHAEL FOLEY, 'A Provincial Adolescence',
The GO Situation, 1982

OUR VISITS TO DERRY were chiefly to the dentist, dear old Mr Williams. My mother brought us up to regard this as a treat. She would say: 'If you are good, I will take you tomorrow to the dentist.' We thought the drill great fun, and Mr Williams used to let us mix the fillings with the pestal and mortar, and shake out the mercury. Then he gave us chocolate when we left. But what made the day was going for tea at Fosters. This was about the only teashop in the North West, and we adored the triangular soda scones with butter, and the wonderful selection of iced cakes. My favourites were called German biscuits. But after the start of the 1914 war the name was changed to Belgian biscuits. We drank chocolate with cream on top; and occasionally, in the height of the summer, Bridget the waitress would tell my mother: 'We have ices today, Madam.' This was about the only time we ever did see ices, perhaps once a year. Not like today when every little sweetie shop has them. There was in fact an old man known as Thomas Kindness, who used to push a little cart with ice-cream round Strabane. But we were never allowed to go near him, as we were told he kept the ice-cream under his bed. We sometimes drove to Derry but generally went by train. We used to take one of the old horse-trams from the GNR station to the Guildhall. We sometimes had a meal in Mrs McMahon's Hotel, which was on the 'walls' below the YMCA. She had real silver on the table, left to her by someone for whom she had once been cook.

REX HERDMAN, *They All Made Me*, 1970

In my memory, I will always see
The town that I have loved so well,
Where our school played ball by the gas-yard wall,
And we laughed through the smoke and the smell.
Going home in the rain, running up the Dark Lane
Past the Jail and down behind the Fountain,
Those were happy days, in so many, many ways
In the Town I Loved So Well.

In the early morning the shirt factory horn
Called women from Creggan, the Moor and the Bog,
While the men on the dole played a mother's role
Fed the children, and then walked the dog.
And when times got tough, there was just about enough
And they saw it through without complaining.
For deep inside was a burning pride
In the Town I Loved So Well.

There was music there in the Derry air
Like a language that we all could understand.
I remember the day that I earned my first pay
When I played in a small pick-up band.
There I spent my youth, and to tell you the truth
I was sad to leave it all behind me.
For I'd learned about life, and I'd found a wife
In the Town I Loved So Well.

But when I've returned, how my eyes have burned
To see how a town could be brought to its knees
By the armoured cars and the bombed-out bars,
And the gas that hangs on to every breeze.
Now the Army's installed by that old gas-yard wall
And the damned barbed wire gets higher and higher.
With their tanks and their guns, Oh my God, what have they done
To the Town I Loved So Well?

Now the music's gone, but they carry on
For their spirit's been bruised, never broken.
They will not forget, but their hearts are set
On tomorrow and peace once again.
For what's done is done, and what's won is won,
And what's lost is lost and gone forever.
I can only pray for a bright, brand new day
In the Town I Loved So Well.

PHIL COULTER, 'The Town I Loved So Well',
in *There Was Music in the Derry Air* (ed. A.M. Murray), 1989

FIRE

June 1949

IT WAS A CITY OF BONFIRES. The Protestants had more than we had. They had the twelfth of July, when they celebrated the triumph of Protestant armies at the Battle of the Boyne in 1690; then they had the twelfth of August when they celebrated the liberation of the city from a besieging Catholic army in 1689; then they had the burning of Lundy's effigy on the eighteenth of December. Lundy had been the traitor who had tried to open the gates of the city to the Catholic enemy. We had only the fifteenth of August bonfires; it was a church festival but we made it into a political one as well, to answer the fires of the twelfth. But our celebrations were not official, like the Protestant ones. The police would sometimes make us put out the fires or try to stop us collecting old car tyres or chopping down trees in preparation. Fire was what I loved to hear of and to see. It transformed the grey air and streets, excited and exciting. When, in mid-August, to commemorate the Feast of the Assumption of Our Lady into heaven, the bonfires were lit at the foot of the sloping, parallel streets, against the stone wall above the Park, the night sky reddened around the rising furls of black tyre-smoke that exploded every so often in high soprano bursts of paraffined flame. Their acrid odour would gradually give way to the more fragrant aroma of soft-burning trees that drifted across the little houses in their serried slopes, gravelled streets falling down from the asphalted Lone Moor Road that for us marked the limit between the city proper and the beginning of the countryside that spread out into Donegal four miles away. In the small hours of the morning, people sitting on benches and kitchen chairs around the fire were still singing; sometimes a window in one of the nearby houses cracked in a spasm of heat; the police car, that had been sitting in the outer darkness of two hundred yards away, switched on its lights and glided away; the shadows on the gable wall shrivelled as the fires burnt down to their red intestines. The Feast of the Assumption dwindled into the sixteenth of August, and solo singers began to dominate the sing-along chorusing. It marked the end of summer. The faint bronze tints of the dawn implied autumn, and the stars fainted into the increasing light as people trailed their chairs reluctantly home.

The dismembered streets lay strewn all around the ruined distillery where Uncle Eddie had fought, aching with a long, dolorous absence. With the distillery had gone the smell of vaporised whiskey and heated red brick, the sullen glow that must have loomed over the crouching houses like an amber sunset. Now, instead, we had the high Gothic cathedral and its parochial house, standing above the area in a permanent greystone winter overlooking the abandoned site that seemed to me a faithless and desolate patch, rinsed of its colour, pale and bald in the midst of the tumble of small houses, unpaved streets and the giant moraine of debris that had slid from the foot of the city walls down a sloping embankment to where our territory began. In the early winter evenings, people angled past like shadows under the weak street lights, voices would say goodnight and be gone.

There were two open spaces near our house. Behind our row of houses, the back field sloped up towards the Lone Moor Road; it ended in a roadway that curved down towards Blucher Street and then straightened towards the police barracks, three hundred yards away. The roadway was flanked by a stone wall, with a flat parapet, only five feet high on our side, twelve feet high on the other. On the other side was Meenan's Park, although the older people still called it Watt's Field, after the owner of the distillery. We could climb the wall and drop down on the other side; but the wall ran past the foot of the streets – Limewood, Tyrconnell, Beechwood and Elmwood – pierced by a rectangular opening at each street that led to a flight of railed steps down to the park. A line of air-raid shelters separated the top section of the park from the open spaces beyond, where we played football. At night, the field and the park were pitch-black. The only street light was a single curved lamp, eight feet high, at the end of each street. We were told never to play in the park at night, for Daddy Watt's ghost haunted it, looking for revenge for the distillery fire that had ruined him. Those who saw him said he was just a black shape that moved like a shadow around the park, but that the shape had a mouth that opened and showed a red fire raging within.

SEAMUS DEANE, *Reading in the Dark*, 1996

SINGING WAS ALWAYS IMPORTANT IN OUR HOUSE, as far back as I can remember. My mother sang and everyone in our family had a gift for singing – all of them better at it that I was! I learned a lot from their singing of the songs they had got at school, with the Mercy nuns up in Francis Street, beside the Cathedral. In fact there were two schools there – what we called the 'wee nuns', which was on the lower side of the street and a much bigger building opposite, that we knew as the 'big nuns'. It wasn't that the nuns in one building were bigger than those in the other, but that the school on the lower side catered for infants only, while the other one, which was a girls-only institution, catered for students up to leaving-school-age, which in those days was fourteen.

I went to school at four years of age to the 'wee nuns' and stayed there until first class. Boys had to leave the 'wee nuns' and find another school when their infant training was done, whereas the girls could cross the road into the 'big nuns', as all my sisters did.

One of my teachers in the wee nuns was Sister Laurence, a big kindly person who used to keep drums, whistles and basic musical instruments, suitable for children, on top of a high cupboard: she would bring them down and let us play them as a special favour, when we were good. Mrs McCabe, who, I discovered fairly recently was the mother of Cathal McCabe, Director of Music in RTE, was, like her colleague Miss Durnin, another inspiring teacher. We were lucky students, for whom nothing was left to chance – I remember Sister Laurence bringing unconsecrated hosts from her convent in Pump Street, where they were made, so that we would know exactly what the real thing would feel like on the tongue on our First Communion day in the Cathedral. We were strictly cautioned not to mention it outside the school, in case of misunderstanding or of giving scandal. Look at that now! I have let the cat out of the bag at last, but I hope Sister Laurence, God be good to her, is in a forgiving mood!

Allowing the host to drop from your tongue onto the floor in those pre-Vatican Two days was almost enough to cause an international incident! I am a little ashamed to admit it, but my big memory of First Communion day – or could it have been Confirmation day, I don't remember – was of getting a new shiny twelve-sided threepenny bit as a present. That was big stuff in those days and the coin, still relatively unknown then, had a solid, comforting feel, squeezed into the palm of my hand, pushed deep down into the trouser-pocket of my new velvet suit.

At the age of twelve I left to go to the Christian Brothers' School on the Lecky Road, which was known as 'The Brow of the Hill', and had a reputation for good teaching and firm discipline. Going to the Christian Brothers involved a big decision, as all my male cousins had gone to Rosemount School, which was nearer, but my mother thought I would do better in the CBS environment. To get to the Brow of the Hill, I had to take a halfpenny ride on the Strand Road bus as far as Great James' Street and walk for something less than a mile along Rossville Street and Lecky Road. It was new territory for someone who had never ventured much beyond Barry Street, Meadowbank and Richmond Crescent. I got on well at the 'Brow', as we called it, and was lucky to have Barney Doherty as my first teacher there. Barney, a popular teacher and a Derryman whom everyone liked, wore plus-fours, which, in case some of my readers may not know, were the baggy trousers, tucked into socks, that golfers still sometimes wear. I remember my mother giving me a new tie to present to him when he was getting married. I still remember the first poem he taught us. It was no gem, but was typical of his approach, which was about enjoyment in education. Stand back – here is the long-remembered masterpiece:

> Loofah the bull had two-and-six
> To spend all on his own:
> He did not care for toffee-stick,
> Nor yet for buttered scone;
> And so he bought a fishing net
> To keep his tail from getting wet!

TOMÁS Ó CANAINN, *A Lifetime of Notes*, 1997

STRAND HOUSE SCHOOL as I remember it in Asylum Road was a wonderful place, so big and rambling. What fun we had playing in the open underground part below the KG at the side of the large garden, and the great excitement and daring when we ventured to go along the narrow dark passage lined on either side with boarders' trunks, or to hide in some of the small dark rooms; there were the unlit underground cellar parts of the extensions. One day at play-time we even had a bonfire by the trunks! The gym had a beautiful parquet floor; we used to come back early after lunch, slip in and swing on the trapeze and ropes, or climb the horizontal ladder –

with no adult present of course. The only thing that seemed (to us at any rate) to worry Miss Deane was whether or not we were on that floor with heavy shoes, if so we were chased out!

During the morning 'Recess' the big girls walked round the very large lawn. To me they seemed like ladies with their long navy skirts, long black stockings, white blouses, their hair in great 'bangs' in front and at the sides, and either tied back with a huge bow or actually 'up'! Skirts prior to that must have been even longer, for about 1905 an Official Hockey Rule stated that 'all skirts must be not less than five inches from the ground, so that the ball be not so frequently lost to view'! About the same time the wearing of white lace petticoats for hockey was discouraged as they tended to get muddy! What would have been thought of our modern shorts and bare knees?

MABEL R. COLHOUN, in *Londonderry High School Old Girls' Association Magazine*, Summer 1960

I NEVER THOUGHT OF BETHEL HOUSE as an orphanage at the time I was living there. The word seemed too old-fashioned, like some place in the novels the teacher used to make us read at school. It brought to mind pictures of skinny youngsters shivering with fear and hunger, which was a far cry from the way things really was. I never wanted in Bethel House. At least, I never went cold nor hungry. But I'll tell you this much, my mind took fifty years to get free. Many as grew up with me wasn't near as lucky. Like the bulk brought up in institutions in my time, 'specially institutions run by the Catholic Church, they never managed to escape; not really. We were made to feel we didn't belong in the outside world from the start. Nothing was said to us, but it was got through our heads some way or another we weren't fit to be wives and mothers. As far back as I can mind, I had the notion marriage was a bad thing. Marriage was for other women, outside the House, and men. It's hard to believe now, but this was happening in the Fifties, when the way you looked was everything.

The Sisters ran the primary school in Bishop Street, and Thornhead School – for girls – where I went after that. They were aye scrounging money off relatives to build extensions. I felt a wild pity for the relatives for they couldn't rightly refuse when asked bare-faced like that. The two schools took in youngsters from outside the House as well as us from inside, but it was at Thornhead I got my first real taste of the outside world. I was singled out from the beginning, and pestered and bullied. The ringleader among the bullies was Magdalene Cooke, a big, beefy girl with a plain face and mousy hair. It occurred to me at the time her parents must've been terrible disappointed with Magdalene, for she was the only girl they had and I guessed by her name they had high hopes for her. Her best friend was

Mary Healy. Now, Mary Healy would've slit her own wrists if Magdalene Cooke had asked her to. She was that scared Magdalene would take up with somebody else instead of her. The reason for this was her da had run off to Liverpool with another woman, you see, and Mary stuck like glue to people for fear they'd go away and leave her too. She took it out of Magdalene sometimes, I could see that – the way she hung round her neck. In looks, Mary was awful peaky. She had this thin skin the colour of rice-paper, and freckles just like a wee fella, and pooky hair that aye stood on end even when it rained. Then there was Bernie Sheedy, the pretty one among them. The low, sneakin' sort she was, Bernie Sheedy only ever joined in when the others had the better of me. The second Bernadette was Bernadette Ratty. (There was four in the class on account of a diocesan pilgrimage to Lourdes the year we were all born.) Bernadette Ratty had sticking-out teeth and eyes that nearly met in the middle of her face. Like the others, this one had it in her to be vicious, but she didn't have the gumption to lay into me on her own. As much as she could do was call me names. She was a hanger-on. And there was others too. But these four give me the hardest time.

KATHLEEN FERGUSON, *The Maid's Tale*, 1994

S HE WARMED HER HEART, as she trotted along, with memories of other Christmas expeditions made years ago when she'd been a wee lass, dodging along through the rain in her mother's wake. It had always been this time of day, when the light was beginning to go. Out they'd set to buy a scarf for a present for Daddy, oranges for stockings for the wee ones, maybe a silver star for the tree. And she'd never minded the rain then, not a bit of it – for in the half-light it had decorated the town with coloured reflections of shop windows and streetlamps. It had splashed and puddled brightly underfoot, and fell in gleaming splinters of haphazard light. And she'd never minded, either, the gathering darkness – for it foreshadowed the magic darkness of long-awaited Christmas Eve, when the very blackness of night vibrated with expectation.

The same childish exaltation came back to her now as she bobbed through the wet Christmas crowds, and here before she expected it was the shop where Christmas trees lay in a soaking pile under the falling rain.

MARILYN McLAUGHLIN, 'The Tree', in *A Dream Woke Me*, 1999

T HE DERRY RELATIVES WERE, without any doubt, more stimulating than the Greenisland lot. Their vibrancy was often of a somewhat bizarre nature, and my interest in the unconventional, macabre or slightly sinister was aroused by hearing about some of my ancestors – the Stevenson

equivalent of Auntie-Gertie-who-ran-away. There was 'Uncle Willie drowned in t'Foyle': someone, my father I suspect, made a sort of Stanley Holloway farce out of what must, after all, have been a family tragedy. I do not know when the event occurred but it appears he was on a bicycle and missed the way. Then it was revealed that Grandma's only sister, who appears in the family album wearing a crinoline, ringlets and lace pants, had been 'put away' in Letterkenny Asylum. Political correctness being unheard of then, such places were often referred to as the 'loony bin'. She had been a member of a party, led by Grandfather David, which went on a trip to Paris before the First World War, and there were vague whispers down the years about her incautious intake of French wines and unbridled behaviour, which had marred the holiday. Sadly, it seems, there may have been another alcoholic lurking in the woodwork.

Then there was Uncle John, who was held to be 'a little simple', but there is no indication of what form his simplicity took. He was not a sufferer from Down's syndrome; indeed, the sepia photograph shows a classically even-featured man with a goatee beard and benign expression. His hobbies were fox-terrier breeding and shooting in County Donegal, so presumably he was considered trustworthy with a gun. Poor thing, he was a frequent target for Madam's outbursts of vitriol and was known to have been reduced to tears at meal-times, the dining table being a favourite setting for scenes of family conflict. My mother, whose reticent nature was often affronted by the tirades of personal recrimination which ricocheted around the table, was always astonished at how quickly the air cleared for those directly engaged in battle – mostly Grandma and my father. The more sensitive onlookers were left feeling grazed, so to speak, by the flying glass.

One particularly poignant incident involved the unfortunate John, who had reached an age when nightly rising was a necessity. For some reason connected with hygiene and the breathing of 'pure air', Madam forbade the use of chamber pots, and it was a long, dark, cold linoleum walk from John's room to the bathroom. A greenish stain had been detected running down the roughcast wall just under John's bedroom window. With the opening of Madam's enquiry into the origins of the stain, 'All hell was let loose over the dinner table', and John was reduced to tears and admission of culpability. His last few years passed in peace and tranquillity, when my mother, who did not disallow chamber pots, moved in, and Madam moved out of the Collon House.

ELIZABETH McCULLOUGH, *A Square Peg*, 1997

TOWARDS THE END OF THAT SUMMER when I was twelve, my mother took me on the bus into Derry one Saturday in order to purchase the necessary attire and accoutrements for my new school. Just the two of us.

There were items like knickers and a first brassière, and some roll-ons to keep the stomach in and the stockings up should the garters fail – articles of apparel quite unmentionable in our household. The males, therefore, including my father, were left behind to look after the house. My mother's bras and pants had never been seen by anyone, except sometimes me and, one presumes, her husband. The other washing flapped away merrily on the line day and night, but the secret stuff, hers and mine, she dried in the dark of night, arranging it neatly on brown paper on the open oven door.

We'd had a list of the mandatory requisites for the school uniform, a most lengthy list upon the sight of which my mother had had a fit. *Six* pairs of navy wool knickers, *six* pairs of long black stockings, *six* vests ...

'What do they think we're made of?' she'd cried. '*Six!* Do they think we're right eejits or something?', taking a pencil and substituting in a singularly determined fashion a three for every six. 'We'll soon see about that, we will ... *six*.'

She persisted in her invective, shaking the head disbelievingly. I was distraught. If they said six, they meant six. I'd be mortified, be seen to be the pauper I was. I'd be made an example of, sent home. I started to cry, my lovely new life suddenly in tatters around my feet.

'There, there,' she said. Soothing. 'It'll be all right, pet. We'll just get these for the moment. If you need more we'll buy them. See how it goes ... there, there.'

I knew then she was going to miss me. Even if only a little.

We had to buy the uniform at a particular store. I tried it on. The navy gymslip was far too long but that was because she was going to take it up and let it down by bits as I grew. A royal-blue girdle. White blouse and tie. Black stockings to be held up by the roll-on or garters or both. The school blazer, also royal, with the Alma Mater crest on the pocket. The turned-up pudding of a hat. The outdoor shoes. The indoor shoes. The gym shoes. Poor woman. She it was who carried the household purse. My father never had a penny in his pocket. No need. She purchased his simple pleasures for him – the fags, the tobacco, the pipe cleaners. Today the domestic purse was a deal lighter. A *great* deal. But she didn't seem to mind. She hummed a cheerful little tune to herself and swung the bags nonchalantly, in harmony with the dancing earrings, all the way back to the bus depot.

I hugged my delight to myself. Sweet, sweet loveliness! In the long shop mirror, I had looked upon a different person. I was *somebody* now. A somebody to be reckoned with. No longer the plain little shy body from the bog.

Alleluia! Utility Liz was dead!

The day I left for the convent, the whole family came along. It was a day of extremes, a day of excitement, a day of celebration. And a day full of tears. We saw Patrick off first, at St Columb's for the start of his second year, my mother sobbing herself to distraction as she fluttered the fine lawn handkerchief in a last farewell from the big iron gates. Then we took another bus out on the road towards Donegal, through the setting sun, along the banks of the lovely River Foyle. The convent was some five miles out and stood in its own majestic grandeur amidst sweeping lawns inlaid with flower beds and darkening swathes of rhododendron and azalea. Everywhere there were trees. Big ones, pine, cypress, oak, reaching way up into the sky. I had never seen any place so beautiful.

The convent itself was very old, grey chipped stone, with tall thin windows and turrets and statues and minarets and a belfry – straight out of my story books, indeed, but even better! I was enraptured. But also, suddenly, very afraid. I was being set down amongst strangers, far away from the comforting familiarity of the old bog road. We all started crying again. The good nun who'd received us took over.

'I think it's time you went now,' she murmured gently to the parents. 'It's best you don't loiter. I'll take her up to the dormitory and she'll meet some of the other girls. She'll be as right as rain in a minute ...'

Along a shiny, lofty hall with holy pictures hanging, the Crucifixion, Saint Teresa of Avilà – my favourite saint. Past an open door with clattering of kitchen things, a statue of the downcast Virgin on a far shadowy corner pedestal, freshly flowered, a mellow light unfolding the slender blue fall of her mantle. Up two flights of stairs, round and round, the heavy black serge of the nun's skirt swirling over the polished smooth heels of her shoes.

The dormitory was at the very top of the house, plain white beds up both sides, a handful of girls sitting or standing around, some weepy, others laughing, talking. Clothes everywhere.

'This is yours, Mary,' the nun said, indicating a middle one. 'And this is your locker.' That was it.

At the door, she turned.

'Supper will be ready in half an hour, girls,' the voice cut through the chatter. 'I'll send the Prefect to fetch you. And punctual, please.'

Sister Gertrude, the head nun of the boarders.

I placed my new cardboard case on the counterpane and, looking up, caught the eye of the girl next door. Crystal shining blue eyes, wide friendly smile in a face the prettiest I had ever seen.

'I'm Patsy,' she said, coming over and sitting down on the bed. 'Do you need any help?' She didn't look as though she had the energy to lift a finger, a big girl with an easy languorous grace. I liked her immediately.

'I'm so frightened,' I whispered. 'I've never been anywhere.'

She laughed, a low, warm, cuddling chuckle. 'Neither have I,' she said. 'But my older sister's here, so it's not so bad for me.'

She was from Dungiven, so we were nearly neighbours. At least no distance from each other that a bike couldn't handle.

Together we went down to the refectory and together we joined the other first-years at one of the long wooden tables. I looked around at the faces. Round, square, pretty, not so pretty, cheerful, nervous, chatty, lost. But all of them – every single one – acceptable as potential friends by my parents.

MARYANNE KERR, *Over the Mountain*, 1996

1936 WAS THE YEAR MY FAMILY came to live in 41 Bridge Street. I don't remember much about coming to the street for the first time with my sister Ruby. It was in this house in this street that I was to live for the next 24 years, on and off. I grew up in that street. Well like most young people in those days I had to leave home to try and better myself. Times were very hard then, there were no two or three suits hanging in the wardrobe, or no six or seven pairs of shoes, no fancy track suit hanging over the chair. You were lucky if you had a chair, you just had to do with what you had.

But I enjoyed my young life in that old street, what with its smells and its back lanes and the old air raid shelters, the old tenements with their broken windows and their red oakum paint. Even the rats were a common everyday sight. You could sometimes see a cat carrying a rat out of an old house. The smell of Biggers, and the smell of the old air raid shelters. Then there was the old Bloods ban shed, which we adopted as somewhere else to play. We would play marbles, skipping, and football at Bigger's Gate down the lane, or just swing on the two lamps in the street, those at big Tommy McSherry's shop at the top of Mattie's Lane and down between Neil Murray's yard and Johnny Kilkie's shop.

My mother was left a widow at the age of 39. To be left a widow at this age was bad enough, but to bring up nine kids as well, it must have been really tough. At that time there was a thing called Outdoor Relief, and I think she got seven shillings a week from that. Then there was the old soup kitchen, where you could get the old jug of soup for a tanner. Many's the day it fed us. The St Vincent de Paul were good to her too, you nearly always got a few bob off them on a Saturday night. But at school, we as orphans got free boots, free books and free soup, so all in all, it wasn't too bad. But I must say, we often wore the boots out as fast as we got them. So most of the time you ran around in your bare feet. I often went to school in my bare feet, hail, rain or snow.

Going to school for me was a great thing, but it was after school that I enjoyed myself most. It was then that I had the whole of St Patrick's to myself. As my mother was one of the ladies who looked after and cleaned the school along with her friend, Sarah McCloskey. My mother used to take me with her to help with the cleaning. My job was to see that the fires were cleared out and set for the next day.

DESSIE MOORE, 'Growing Up in Bridge Street', *Derry Journal*, 25 April 2000

I   In the Afterlife

It will be like following Jim Logue, the caretaker,
As he goes to sweep our hair off that classroom floor
Where the school barber set up once a fortnight,
Falling into step as he does his rounds,
Glimmerman of dorms and silent landings,
Of the refectory with its solid, crest-marked delph,
The ground-floor corridor, the laundry pile
And boots tagged for the cobbler. Was that your name
On a label? Were you a body or a soul?

SEAMUS HEANEY, 'In the Afterlife', *from* 'Bodies and Souls', *Electric Light*, 2001

Well, as Kavanagh said, we have lived
In important places. The lonely scarp
Of St Columb's College, where I billeted
For six years, overlooked your Bogside.
I gazed into new worlds: the inflamed throat
Of Brandywell, its floodlit dogtrack,
The throttle of the hare. In the first week
I was so homesick I couldn't even eat
The biscuits left to sweeten my exile.
I threw them over the fence one night
In September 1951
When the lights of houses in the Lecky Road
Were amber in the fog. It was an act
Of stealth.
              Then Belfast, and then Berkeley.
Here's two on's are sophisticated,
Dabbling in verses till they have become
A life: from bulky envelopes arriving
In vacation time to slim volumes
Despatched 'with the author's compliments'.
Those poems in longhand, ripped from the wire spine
Of your exercise book, bewildered me –
Vowels and ideas bandied free
As the seed-pods blowing off our sycamores.
I tried to write about the sycamores

And innovated a South Derry rhyme
With *hushed* and *lulled* full chimes for *pushed* and *pulled*.
Those hobnailed boots from beyond the mountain

Were walking, by God, all over the fine
Lawns of elocution.
                    Have our accents
Changed? 'Catholics, in general, don't speak
As well as students from the Protestant schools.'
Remember that stuff? Inferiority
Complexes, stuff that dreams were made on.
'What's your name, Heaney?'
                              'Heaney, Father.'
                              'Fair Enough.'

SEAMUS HEANEY, *from* 'The Ministry of Fear',
from 'Singing Schools', *North*, 1975

IT WAS WHILE JAMES WAS AT COLLEGE that I was sent to a Young Ladies' Academy in Derry. I was entered three weeks before the end of term, two weeks before the term's examinations, which were a test for the Intermediate Examinations to be held later. This was a Protestant school under the direction of three very distinguished and brilliant sisters, the Misses MacKillip. They were not very interested in me, a little girl who had arrived at the wrong end of the term. They were absorbed in the progress of their examinations. I was classified according to my age which put me into the grade of a girl from Sligo who was the pride of the school. Her name was Charlotte Warner and she moved in an aura of scholarships. She had a magnetic effect upon me. She dispensed an electric atmosphere that excited me. I was drawn towards her by a quickening process that scattered my own darknesses. We sat in desks at right angles so that I was able to squint at her when I wished, which was often. She was quite unaware of me, taken up with urgent matters which entailed her complete attention. I, alone, was conscious of the miracle that *together* we attained some fusion. I did not know what it was. I only knew that it glowed like light, and that we both stood in it and generated it. I have always been conscious of people's brains. I was aware of Charlotte's because of its bright functioning at that time. She was magical to me. I was supported by her presence.

The mathematical Miss MacKillip discovered that I was deficient in Euclid. The only thing I knew about it was that Euclid himself has sat in the sand, mystifying scholars with his symbols. I was given the first two sections of Euclid to work upon as a preparation for my work during the following term. It was only as a pure matter of routine and as a sort of courtesy that I was allowed to participate in the examinations. It was easier to have me in than have me out. I stepped into classes that were in a test state and where all questions were sharpened. I had the advantage of freshness. It was all a wonder and of the deepest interest from the brightness of the girls' faces to the tones of their voices and the quality of their answers. I was astonished by an accuracy that could mean nothing; it was quite tasteless. It was the sober truth, a statement of facts, and it was absolutely dead and left me then and for always puzzled by its worth. The author in the literature class was Washington Irving. It seemed the purest waste of time to deal with him or give him thought. I read the textbook through from beginning to end in a fever to discover one gleam that would alleviate his tedium and I did not find it. I did not understand. Who and what was he that he could be chosen to exercise the mind? Two sisters in the long desk behind me answered all the questions correctly. Their truth was not my truth. Their names were Gladys and Kathleen Scott and they wrote magnificent essays. I made every effort to appreciate what drew out their values but I failed to find it. I was more interested in them than in Washington Irving. Gladys had strong raven-wing hair that rippled from her like a mane. Kathleen's hair was curly. They had dark, wide-spaced eyes and the sort of skin that made you think of damsons. I used to wonder if they liked Washington Irving. They were such fine specialists in his meaning. I never dared to ask. I never became intimate with them. I remained an outsider − with them when recess came but not of them, as was Laura Gailey. Laura, who knew nothing about Petrarch or *his* Laura who, also, wore a green dress. Laura Gailey's dress was not embroidered with violets nor did she walk in the valley of Avignon. She hardly ever walked at all. She skipped and danced and there was about her a brown velvet liveliness that made me think of goats and pansies somehow combined. The only discipline that was in her blood was that which went to music.

There was an older girl whose name I never remembered. She had a desk by an open window in a classroom through which I had to pass. Her face was always in profile against branches of trees laden with spring blossoms. Her auburn hair flowed in waves against a breeze. She had a complexion of cream and roses and there was about her an air of such delicacy that she seemed poised as an angel upon the pink-white light of the flowers. I never seemed able to think of her feet in shoes. They were always bare and white as alabaster with pearls for her toenails. Girls said in hushed voices: 'Isn't she lovely?' She was the school beauty. It was true, but she was only an aspect to me. I was not aroused by her as I was aroused by Charlotte Warner with her strong features and her eyes as clear and hazel as mountain water. Nobody ever said Charlotte was a beauty. She was too grave.

These girls became everlasting. They are with me to this day as in a dream, as visions upon a field one was obliged by some hazard to cross. They have the haze of eternal youth and have remained unspoilt by any circumstance. Everything about them and surrounding them is preserved and perfect. They were companions in an hour that had its own splendour. They came in like the sea on that shore by the Bay of Shadows and went out again. It is what they did not leave that has stayed. It is their intention, their unfulfilled promise that has remained.

During the Easter holidays the senior Miss MacKillip came to call upon my mother. They were closeted in the drawing room and I was not brought in to share their testimony. I was shut out, troubled vaguely in spirit – as one who had sinned in ignorance. Miss MacKillip departed without seeing me and I was told that, for some reason or other, I was not going back to that school. It appeared that Miss MacKillip had wished for me to return. The examinations in some strange fashion had brought me out level with Charlotte Warner and Miss MacKillip had implored Mother to give me to her as a pupil. The terms were evidently not within Mother's means or outside her pride. Whatever the excuse was, it shut the door. I was touched for the briefest instant by a scholastic yearning, by the flags of recognition, then it all vanished and became nothing. It was Charlotte I missed. It was Charlotte I longed for. I was convinced that her companionship was a necessary requisite for my best attainment. She was an urgency in my personal integrity. We had some cathodic power in common that would have enabled us to perform miracles in darkness. I never saw nor heard of her again. I was born under stars and made schools as fleet as comets. They trailed across my sky in sudden and unlasting glory.

KATHLEEN COYLE, *The Magical Realm*, 1943

Sweet babe! a golden cradle holds thee,
And soft the snow-white fleece enfolds thee;
In airy bower I'll watch thy sleeping,
Where branchy trees to the breeze are sweeping.
　　　　　Shuheen, sho, lulo lo!

When mothers languish broken-hearted,
When young wives are from husbands parted,
Ah! little think the keeners lonely,
They weep some time-worn fairy only.
　　　　　Shuheen, sho, lulo lo!

Within our magic halls of brightness,
Trips many a foot of snowy whiteness;
Stolen maidens, queens of fairy –
And kings and chiefs a sluagh-shee airy,
　　　　　Shuheen, sho, lulo lo!

Rest thee, babe! I love thee dearly,
And as thy mortal mother nearly;
Ours is the swiftest steed and proudest,
That moves where the tramp of the host is loudest.
                    Shuheen, sho, lulo lo!

Rest the, babe! for soon thy slumbers
Shall flee at the magic koelshie's numbers;
In airy bower I'll watch thy sleeping,
Where branchy trees to the breeze are sweeping.
                    Shuheen, sho, lulo lo!

EDWARD WALSH, 'The Fairy Nurse', *Irish Popular Songs*, 1847

'Frankie McMahon, you're Bassanio.
Irwin, Launcelot Gobbo. Bredin, Portia.'
That was the cast, or some of it; the scene,
The right-hand side of Gallagher's low desk,
A nowhere where the three caskets were placed
In dumb-show. And off we went again. (And yes,
Of course, Irwin the fabulous
Who'd walked out of the gates on the first day
Was typecast as the runaway apprentice.
And Cassoni the Italian as Lorenzo).
But who was Jessica?
                    Unforgotten,
Out of this world, the start of Act Five, Scene One.
'*In such a night –* continue, please, Cassoni!'
'*– Stood Dido with a willow in her hand
Upon the wild sea banks.*'
                    In summers's language.
In 1954. In the sun-thwarted
Glass and steel of those new showpiece classrooms.

                    ★

Then say *chameleon*. And the boy-men reappear
Who's-whoing themselves like changelings.
                              So will it be
Ariel or the real name, the already
Featly sweetly tuneful Philip Coulter?
Or his brother Joe as Banquo, dressed in white,
Wise Joe, good Banquo, fairest of the prefects?

Aura and justice, soul in bliss or torment,
Ghost on cue at the banquet, entering
And entering memory like mitigation –
The table on stage a long, formica-topped
Table for fourteen, on loan from the refectory
Where we, in fourteens, moon-calves, know-nothings,
Stood by our chairs and waited for the grace.

SEAMUS HEANEY, 'The Real Names', *Electric Light*, 2001

THE TEACHING SYSTEM USED by the first brothers in Derry was the one devised by Brother Rice for his school in Waterford. Each class was divided into groups of twelve, or twenty-four, supervised by a 'monitor'. This was a young man, who had completed his education, and was employed to supervise a small group of boys. The brother taught the lesson at the start of each period to the whole group, and then the monitors supervised and helped the boys in the smaller groups, as they learned their reading or put into practice what they had been taught in arithmetic or writing. Before the school day began the brother met the monitors to instruct them in what he wanted. As the day progressed he went from group to group to check on how they were getting on, and to assist with further teaching. At twelve o'clock each day he drew the whole class together again and the monitors were free while he instructed the boys in religion. The system seemed to work well, and it was for many years the only way of coping with the large numbers they inevitably had to deal with even up to the end of the century. All this was in operation long before Joseph Lancaster of London who invented a similar system, the Lancastrian system, visited Ireland. Along with the monitorial system, Brother Larkin also had a system of 'premiums', that is, weekly prizes, designed to encourage good attendance and hard work. As the 'Manual of Education', published in 1845 for the use of the young brothers starting teaching, said: 'Premiums are productive of much good, causing great regularity, industry, and attention on the part of the children; creating an interest in the school in the minds of the parents; and begetting a kindly feeling between master and scholars.' The same Manual tells us what a typical day would be like in the Brow-of-the-Hill School in 1854. The boys arrived at nine o'clock and spent half-an-hour revising what they had learnt the previous day, or stood round the room in groups studying the maps hung round the walls. (The school had 'a full set of large maps, viz. – the World, Europe, Asia, Africa, America, Ireland, England, Scotland, Palestine, and Australia'. For the senior boys there was also 'a pair of globes (and) a set of solids for the use of boys learning mensuration.') During this time the brother instructed the monitors in what he wanted during the day.

At 9.30 a.m. there was morning prayer, followed by geography or grammar until 10 o'clock. Then the monitors took over, until 10.20. At that time there was an inspection for cleanliness, with prizes for the best three boys. At 10.30 the boys commenced writing under the care of the monitors and reading began at 11 a.m. At 12.00 the brother took over the whole group for religious instruction, until 12.30, when there was a break. In the afternoon there was arithmetic, with geometry or mensuration for the senior boys, followed by dictation, with book-keeping for the senior boys, 'or whatever else the master may deem necessary.' This was followed by prayer at 2.45 and the boys departed at 3 p.m.

In addition, the brothers ran night classes for two hours for apprentices and others who wished to learn and who could not attend during the day, and on Sundays they gave religious instruction in the church for one hour.

The income for the four brothers who formed the Brow-of-the-Hill community came from the annual charity sermon preached in the Long Tower church. Records show that this amounted to £150 in each of their first four years in Derry. The brothers were forbidden to accept fees or reward from the pupils or their parents for their teaching – indeed Edmund Rice made this an extra vow for his brothers when he started – so the sermon was their sole source of income. When one compares Goldsmith's famous curate a hundred years before, when the value of money was less, who was 'passing rich at forty pounds a year' their income is seen to be moderate, though it was as much as those in the Bogside could afford. Edmund Rice has also made it a rule 'that no pupil is to be excluded from the school because of the inability of his parents to pay fees'. Voluntary donations were permitted from the parents and in the case of Derry this amounted to about £35 a year. Any money that came from pupils, however, was spent exclusively on the school – usually on food and clothing for poorer boys, and on paying for slates and pencils, since such equipment was always provided free.

On an income of £150 a year for four brothers, the food and clothing of the community was not very much better than that of the pupils they were teaching – or, indeed, of many of the priests of Derry at the time. Father Kenny, Vice-President of Maynooth, preaching one of the charity sermons, reported that, 'fasting with the brothers is not infrequently a virtue of necessity imposed by the poverty of the community; these brothers live on food which even the poorest peasant of the land would consider meagre and rough. One morning I found the brothers and their Superior sitting down to a breakfast which a common labourer would reject, and this was their usual fare.'

Account books of the time show that dinner was potatoes and vegetables and nothing else. Meat was rarely available. Breakfast was cocoa, bread and butter and occasionally an egg. Tea was bought only rarely and rice and cheese were rare also. Even at Christmas and Easter there was little change in the diet. Since the brothers could not afford to pay a cook, between 1855 and 1857, the senior boys took it in turn to make the dinner. The 'green coats' of the brothers were a constant source of wonder to the people in the Bogside. Their poor-quality black clothing turned green with age and they could not afford to buy new coats so, perforce, they paraded in the old.

Their day too was a long one, since they rose at 6 a.m. for an hour's prayer together, before attending Mass in the Long Tower church. After breakfast, each brother went to his classroom, a large room, crammed with a hundred children, poorly heated by an open fire at one end, and lit by hissing gas lamps. After school they had half-an-hour of prayer together and then spent an hour and a half preparing the following day's work and then had two hours evening class with the apprentices. After night prayers, they went to bed by the light of a candle. It is not surprising to read in the Annals of the house that many brothers had to leave Derry because of ill-health. Even in 1884, they could still only afford to spend £40 on supporting a brother for a year and as the charity sermon approached in that year the total funds of the community amounted to one pound and seven pence.

Living quarters were primitive. The Bishop had intended that they would spend only a few months at the Brow until he provided new accommodation. Financial constraints intervened however and in the event, the brothers lived there until 1970. The house was almost two hundred years old by then, without any architectural merit and totally unsuited to their needs. It was poky and ill-lit and several brothers had to sleep and study in badly-ventilated attics under the roof. For most of that period the sole heating was a fire in the sitting room and the only washing facilities were a jug and basin in each room.

There is no hint of recrimination or complaint in the records of that time at the grim living conditions – after all they were no worse off and, in many cases, better than the mass of the people on the Bogside whom they served and whose condition was so wretched. And they had the consolation of knowing that they were beginning to work a change for the better among the boys of Derry – those attending the 'Brow' were no longer running wild and untameable and the improvement in their manners and conduct was soon noticed on the streets of the city. For the first time, a class of boys was emerging who had pride in themselves, a good education, the ability to earn and keep a job, and – most important in the eyes of the brothers – a good knowledge of their Catholic religion and a commitment to live it. Dr Kelly was delighted with what the school was doing and often visited the school during lessons to talk to the boys and to observe the improvement – he was frequently seen around the Brow. His visitors were usually brought to see the school and to see the good being effected. Among these was Cardinal Cullen, Archbishop of Dublin, who noted afterwards how impressed he was. Dr Kelly frequently praised the school in public and his successor, Dr Eoin O'Doherty was equally pleased. 'The Christian Brothers' School,' he said, 'has a special place in my regard for the good it has effected among the Catholic youth of this city; the change is marvellous indeed.'

(BROTHER) JOHN LEDWIDGE, *The Brow, the Brothers and the Bogside*, 1990

WHEN I FIRST CAME TO DERRY I was propped up between my father and a pile of boxes on the front seat of an old van belonging to a pig-dealer from Donegal. The van had been borrowed and converted for the day into a removal van by a liberal strewing of straw on the floor. Our possessions were piled high in the back, even the old wooden tumble churn that would never be used again. Or at least it was never used to make yellow butter. After a time I rescued it from the back yard of our new house and used it as a rabbit hutch. I bred white rabbits there and sold them to the city boys for a shilling each. It was the farming instinct, my father said, and he then began to take a great interest in my rabbits, something he had never done when we lived on the farm. Eventually he bought a couple of pigeons himself and built a loft for them, much to the annoyance of the neighbours.

We had a house in the Waterside part of the city, away up on top of the hill. It was a small terraced house with a view down over the River Foyle and out across the city-side to the blue of the Donegal hills. At dusk we could see the dished valley dissolving into shadow, and then blackness, and finally into nothingness: later it would break into life again, pimpled with white lights as people flicked their switches in kitchens and sculleries. It was all new and strange to us. Back home we knew every face behind every window, and the lights were soft and yellow and came floating out from oil-lit rooms.

SAM BURNSIDE, 'The Field', *The Blackstaff Book of Short Stories*, 1988

THERE IS AN INCREDIBLE RUMOUR THAT, finally shocked by the half-crazed brutes it is sending out into the world, the College has hired an elocution teacher to convert its older pupils into passionate debaters and eloquent after-dinner speakers. Stranger still, it is said that this stupendous task of animal training has been *entrusted to a woman*.

Not even the most credulous believe the second half of the story. Nevertheless there is a full turnout for the opening class whose membership is as novel as its subject matter, arrogant demigods of science mingling with arts riff-raff. Scarcely has Ward got used to the novelty of sitting once more beside arts-man Shotter, than he is astounded to see enter the room a middle-aged woman with a perm and tweed costume in the style of his Aunt Collette but wearing high red stilettos which Collette would find impossibly common and exuding an aura of vestigial glamour resisting surrender to the nullity of age.

He is not surprised when she reveals that she has been on the stage and intends to teach them how to enunciate and project; her own speech another revelation – rich, honeyed, precise and detached, with none of the och-sure-now familiarity and ingratiation of local women her age ('Like diamantine pearls the notes of her voice welled from her resonant larynx and resolved their personalities into a vibrant aggregate' – Lautréamont). And for those in the front rows there is the further alarming perturbation of an elusive and sophisticated scent. Her presence in the shabby classroom is like that of a sailing ship in a bottle – no one can imagine how the feat was achieved but the incredible reality may not be denied.

However, novelty and an exquisite speaking voice are not enough to subdue brutes. Already she has made the fatal error of permitting a third of the class to loll in postures of provocative indolence. Instead of snapping at them to sit up straight like Christians she distributes brochures with speaking exercises and leads the group in a chant:

> The early bird shall get the worm.
> This proverb always makes me squirm.

She looks pointedly at Shotter. 'Not Squuurrrum ... *squirm.*'

'*Squirm,*' Shotter repeats in a high piping tone with a skilful light patina of impertinent parody.

A low chuckle goes round the room – but again she takes no action.

> The early worm, for being *first,*
> Does not *deserve* to be so *cursed.*

Now there is open laughter. Ignoring it, she gets each of them to read. When it comes to Ward's turn Shotter kicks him under the desk. Suppressing a snigger, Ward begins, 'Two tired toads trotting to Tewkesbury,' then, at another kick, breaks down into laughter immediately shared by the rest of the group.

By the end of the period everyone is sprawling in near-helpless mirth.

Yet there is also much anger. The scientists, confirmed in their scorn for the arts, are furious at this waste of precious time. And the arts men are furious at being associated with absurdity and pretension.

In the storm of contempt and abuse it is difficult to acknowledge tender emotions.

'But she's not all that bad-looking,' Ward suggests diffidently to Shotter. 'For her age, like.'

'That auld *puke!*' Shotter sneers. 'Fuckin' cobwebs on it. And *no wonder.* Be like pushin' a chipolata up the fuckin' Mersey tunnel. That auld sickener'll never see fifty again.'

'Ah but ... not bad legs ... ye wouldn't keek her outa bed.'

Shotter composes his disgusted expression into a grimace of terminal rejection. 'She couldn't give a hard-on to the Boston Strangler.'

Next time she has abandoned the elocution books for a stack of modern poetry anthologies — but her pupils are even more derisive and insolent. Ward can see her wince and quiver as scorn is poured on her beloved poets. One of the scientists declares outright that Wallace Stevens is a load of crap. Tremulous, wounded, a doe at bay, she suggests that they take the anthologies home and choose their own poems for recital.

Ward, who has never been exposed to modern poetry, reads the book from end to end and suffers a queer ebriety at an unlikely poem with an unlikely title: *The Love Song of J. Alfred Prufrock*. Again and again he is drawn back to this piece which, by some form of sorcery, persistently lures him and subtly insinuates itself into his mind. Despite its length there is no need to memorise. Trying to escape its spell is the problem, and the thought of reading it in front of the teacher makes it difficult to concentrate on his maths. Never before has he had trouble with maths. Something strange is muddying the limpid waters of the intellect.

The following weeks she asks Shotter to commence with his chosen poem.

'Hadn't time,' he says with that aggressive assurance that has always been his hallmark. 'Too much other work.'

The next boy takes the same line ... and the next ... and the next. Then Hinds, renowned for his shrewdness and cunning in evading the impositions of authority, surprises everyone by rising. She smiles in pathetic relief — but what he recites, with a knowing smirk at his resourcefulness in choosing the shortest poem in the book, is Pound's two-line image of the faces in the Metro. At once there is a great roar of laughter and approval — for nothing is more appreciated than an expression of insolence within the rules. This is more fun than a simple refusal and so the next boy rises to recite the same two-line poem. Likewise the next ... and the next ... By the time it is Ward's turn she is once again trembling on the verge of collapse. In the eyes that meet his there is no longer hope — only a plea for compassion and mercy. He rises, brimming with tenderness and poetry. But this is the love that dare not speak its name. Here, no love could dare speak its name. The best he can offer is a coded noted of apology in his delivery of the two-line poem.

In a broken despairing voice she announces the exercise for the following week — a speech of explanation by any well-known historical character.

By this time Shotter has compiled a profile of the woman.

'She's come home to look after her auld mother ... think the mother had a stroke or somethin'. She was probably too auld to get work as an actress anyway ... who wants mutton dressed up as lamb? They have one of those massive old houses in West End Park ... you know, full of shabby genteel ... pukes that think they are somebody but haven't a bean. She probably went round the schools begging them to let her do this eejit work – *two fuckin' tired toads trottin' to fuckin' Tewkesbury.*' Shotter pauses to light a cigarette, inhales deeply and blows his smoke into the sky with fierce dismissive satisfaction. 'Thought ye were goin' to recite a poem ... what ye' call it ... that thing ... Alfred Poppyfuck ... or whatever?'

Ward laughs at such a ludicrous notion. 'Nah.'

But all week he works secretly on a monologue for Judas Iscariot in which the much-maligned apostle explains that he did not betray for money ('Bah! Barely enough for wine and a clean whore') but to prevent the inevitable disillusion when Christ's human failings are revealed to his followers. And has the betrayal not been vindicated? His heroic and selfless action has been the making of Christ the Messiah although also the breaking of Christ the Man. The true sacrifice was not that of the Cross but that of the thirty pieces of silver.

Of course Ward could not possibly read this in class. Instead he waits in the school car park and approaches the passenger window of her Mini. She leans across to wind it down with a plump quivering arm, the tight skirt of her suit riding up a little. In the back are her suit jacket, handbag and a pink cardigan, on the passenger seat a box of fluffy pink tissues and on the floor below the passenger seat, temporarily replaced by flat driving shoes, the red stilettos which Ward suddenly longs to seize and bear off to the farthest corner of the school grounds, there to crouch behind the bushes crushing them against his breast forever. However, as he bends to the window he is vanquished by the scent that envelops him ('More laden with oblivion than the fragrance of cedar slivers cloven by magicians amongst the groves of the gardens of Baghdad to shame the flowers of paradise' – Villiers). It feels as though he is entering her boudoir rather than talking into her Mini.

'Why didn't you wait to show me this in class?'

He shrugs, slightly impatient. Surely that is obvious.

Instead of reprimanding him she reaches back for the handbag and withdraws a pair of reading glasses, a revelation of a secret failing that would have torn from his lips a sob of compassion had not enchantment robbed his body of all power except that required to climb into the back seat and curl up with the pink cardie over his head.

'It's very *deep*,' she says at last, peering gravely at him over the rim of her spectacles. 'But terribly *cynical*. You're very cynical for one so young.'

MICHAEL FOLEY, Getting Used To Not Being Remarkable, 1998

PART OF THE PROBLEM WAS GENETIC. By birth and upraising I was an Anglo-Tewtomic-Russian-Menshevik-Agnostic-Jew, and pretty much typical of the type. Born in London, weaned in Scotland and South Africa, I didn't arrive in Ireland till past my fifth birthday, and somehow I never fully acclimatized. Certainly not in native eyes, at any rate. My father wrote books about heretics, my mother had an accent, and I myself was neither Protestant nor Catholic, not Irish but nothing definable else. In the context of Derry, and in particular of Foyle, the moth-eaten Presbyterian shrine in decline where I went to school, I might as well have come from Mars – the man who fell to Earth and, abysmally, failed to bounce.

Magee completed the curse. In theory it was a training school for Calvinist ministers; in reality, with its high stone walls and imported tutors, more like an unarmed encampment; and its isolation from the town was absolute. Dimly one was conscious of the hatred outside, with its perpetual roundelay of Catholic ambuscades and Protestant reprisals, Black Masses and Orange parades. But they seemed to carry no reality. Even when I was blown out of my bed by the concussion of a detonated radio tower, or when a pitched battle raged at the army camp and an RUC (Royal Ulster Constabulary) sergeant had the lobe of his left ear shot off by an IRA sniper, it felt like some yarn out of *Hot Adventures*. If it had not been for Tiggle, the aforesaid janitor, my only link to life as endured beyond Magee's walls, I would hardly have been aware that men, when shot, did actually bleed.

Always the key was that I myself took no part. From my very earliest remembrance, in which my twenty-month self enticed a five-year-old gardener's daughter into climbing up a tree and getting stuck – thus allowing me to study from below the effects of light and shade on her sky-blue knickers, her sweating spun-gold legs all covered with scabs, ripe and pickable as currants baked into damp bread, also the way in which her screams caused her thighs to shimmy and shudder like blancmange in a gale – intuition told me that my best role was not to perform but always to watch, preferably from a safe distance.

The was one exception. At Magee, down by Tiggle's cottage and the tennis court where he died, there was an outhouse with a long and flat cement exterior wall and up against this wall, every rainless afternoon after school, I used to bat a tennis ball. Sometimes I would hit it with a rot-gutted racquet as flaccid as a butterfly net, sometimes with a sawn-off broomstick or the flat of a cricket bat, and sometimes, when times were tough, with a cabbage-stalk soaked in brine; and as I hit, I counted.

The formula never varied. First I would attempt to execute one hundred strokes on my forehand, then another hundred backhand, then forehand again, then backhand, and so interminably on, until at last I miscued, at which point I'd go back to the beginning, start over from Stroke One.

What was the use? I couldn't have explained it then; I'm still not sure today. No special target was involved, no astronomical figure whose attainment would somehow release me. Equally, there was no question of athletic prowess. On the contrary, in my passion not to flub, I kept all my shots as passive and pattycake as possible, never dared the slightest variation.

Avoidance of error was not the main thing, it was the only thing, and so metronomic was the thud of ball on wall, I might have been marking time.

In the face of such utter futility, the mildest of men and divinity students seemed goaded beyond enduring. With time I acquired a regular gallery of hecklers, beseeching me, just once, to give the ball a free and hearty whack. But I never did. The very soullessness of this unending putt-puttery was its perverse pleasure. One afternoon, half-way through my seventh hundred on the forehand, Tiggle keeled over in mid-imprecation, belly-up and purple-headed at my back, with the palest pink froth about his lips like the lees of lemonade sherbet. There were murmurings of manslaughter, and these I took as a compliment.

For years the ceremonial never varied by one beat. Then I came out into The Strand, observed the snake and later, safe back in the sanctuary of Magee, I went down directly to the outhouse wall. Even though it was pitch dark, I grabbed up a rusty coal shovel, whirled it like a shillelagh; and I began to smash the balls at random.

I hit out, blindly, possessed. Exploding all about me like so many hand grenades, balls ricocheted into my face and eyes, my belly; knocked me backwards, drove me to my knees. Ball the wall, indeed I did; and the tarmac beneath me, and the air, and all of the darkness, too.

I didn't quit till every last ball I owned had been splatted or for ever lost. Then I hurled the shovel as far as my mean strength could launch it, and I never played that game again.

NIK COHN, *Ball the Wall: Age of Rock*, 1989

ONE EARLY AFTERNOON – IT WAS A SATURDAY – in May 1932, I was walking home from my aunts' house in Miller street, when I heard the unmistakeable sound of an aeroplane engine. It wasn't the deep, sonorous roar of the RAF flying boats, but a lighter higher pitched sound, and I gazed skywards, trying to spot it. Then I saw it – a little red monoplane. Because of my boyish interest in flying, I knew what a Gypsy Moth, or a Bristol Bulldog was like and I was quite familiar with the square, angular shapes of the stately Vickers Virginia bombers which sometimes flew across from Aldergrove, but this was different, the shape was puzzling. The wheels were enclosed in streamlined 'spats' and it flew much faster than the few machines I had previously seen in the skies over Derry. By this time, I was at the top of the Long Tower and I had observed the small shape come in from over the Inishowen mountains. Swiftly it sped across the sky, banked over the Waterside, and slanted down towards Pennyburn. I didn't realise it, but I was witnessing the final stage of one of the most dramatic of all trans-Atlantic flights – the first solo crossing by a woman pilot, Amelia Earhart.

Then aged thirty three, Amelia Earhart was no foolhardy, flighty female. A University graduate, an accomplished linguist – she spoke five languages – and was noted for her welfare work among the poor of Boston, Mass.

At about 1.30 p.m. the tiny Lockheed Vega aircraft circled the farm of Robert Gallagher at Springfield, Ballyarnett. Selecting a wide meadow, the pilot turned the machine into wind, and put the machine gently down on the lush, green grass. An amazed farm worker stood and watched as the cabin door opened, and a tall, lithe, fair haired figure jumped down. 'Is this Londonderry?' she asked. He could only nod, speechless. Miss Earhart walked over and introduced herself to an equally amazed farmer, who had hurried out of his house on hearing the sound of the aeroplane flying low over his rooftop. There followed a flurry of telephone calls, and soon a guard of hastily summoned policemen was placed around the machine, and within a short time, the press wires of the world were humming with the news.

Meanwhile, in Derry, by that afternoon a rumour had spread around that a long-distance flyer had landed at Culmore. The *Belfast Telegraph* for that evening confirmed it in picture and story.

Next day – Sunday – the newspapers really went to town with graphic details of the record breaking flight, including many interviews with the lady herself. The trip was not without drama, bad weather and low cloud en route, and in those days no oxygen supply to enable the pilot to fly above the weather, and then near disaster when an exhaust manifold burnt out, and naked flame from the engine licked back close to the fuselage for the final hours of the flight.

With several companions, I set off about one o'clock on the three mile walk to Ballyarnett. As we approached the field where the machine was picketed down, hundreds of people and scores of bicycles were to be seen, lining its perimeter. I managed to squeeze in through the hedge, and cautiously made my way closer to the aircraft. The police on duty were kindly, but firm. 'No touching. Stay back' was the order, but I managed to get close enough to see the name of the makers, and the type name Lockheed 'VEGA' stencilled in gold on the red fuselage. Slowly walking around the nose, I was able to peer in at the powerful, neatly cowled, air-cooled radial engine. In the same field was a tiny bi-plane – a Gipsy 'Moth' – which the *Daily Sketch* newspaper had chartered to bring over one of its reporting staff to cover the occasion. Whilst I was there, two leather clad figures with helmets and goggles – pilot and passenger – climbed into the machine. The propeller spun, the engines started with a roar, and the frail-looking craft trundled across to the far hedge, where it turned and paused for a moment. The engine was throttled back, then opened up, and with gradually increasing speed it accelerated across the grass, bumping and swaying, until daylight appeared beneath its wheels, and it climbed out over the hedge.

Gaining height, it circled the motionless aeroplane on the ground, and headed out towards Lough Foyle. A few hours later, the reporter, Mr V. Barton, and the pilot, Mr Colin Clark, lay dead in the wreckage of their machine, which crashed into a cloud-shrouded mountainside, near Stranraer.

CHARLES GALLAGHER, *Acorns and Oak Leaves*, 1981

IN THOSE DAYS DERRY CITY had not spread much beyond its walls and the 'New Free Grammar School' (as Foyle College was then called) stood in open country outside. The school grounds were large, and covered all the area between the present Northlands Road and where the Asylum used to be. There were one hundred and ten pupils of whom half were boarders, and they were all taught in one large schoolroom without any divisions between classes or age groups. The college was described in its charter as 'Primarily a Classical School', and pupils were shown on the college roster as being either 'at Latin', for those aspiring to become university graduates, or 'at English' for all others. Robert was 'at Latin' and so also was John Lawrence (later Viceroy for India) though neither of them ever went to a university. There were five Lawrence brothers (Alexander, George, Henry, John and Richard) at Foyle College and it was there that the Lawrence-Montgomery association began and continued during their lifetime; all five Lawrence brothers will appear in this book as no account of my grandfather's life would be complete without them.

The three elder Lawrence boys had arrived at the school, as boarders, in the winter of 1816, and were very soon involved in the 'school battle'. This was a perpetual war waged between the boarders and day-boys for possession of an ancient fortress which stood high on a hill behind the school building. A year later the three were joined by Robert Montgomery and John Lawrence in defence of the earthwork against raids made day and night, summer and winter, by the day-boys. Both sides challenged the other 'to come out and fight now'. The contest was hard and savage with a variety of weapons like cabbage stalks (kale runts), empty whisky barrels rolled down on the attackers during their night assaults, and hurley sticks for hand-to-hand combat. It was astonishing that serious injuries were apparently few and far between, which can only mean that the boys on each side were extremely tough and vigorous.

In school the Headmaster, the Reverend James Knox (he was an uncle of the Lawrence brothers), was a stern disciplinarian, and flogging was the order of the day. In addition there was very strict religious training, both in and out of school hours, from which there was little hope of escape. The Headmaster's sister had this part of the education as her special charge; she used to send for the boys every two or three days, one by one and always during their spare time, in order that she might read and pray with them. The Lawrences, being nephews as well as pupils, got a double dose of this treatment, and Robert Montgomery recorded how they used to slink by their aunt's room, on tiptoe, in the hope of escaping. But it was of no avail; for the door would open and their aunt would pounce out on them and carry them off to a lecture – on their great need of prayer and repentance!

Years later, it was Christmas Eve 1851, three Foyle College old boys, Henry and John Lawrence and Robert Montgomery, all then in their early forties, were dining together at Lahore, where the two Lawrences, with Robert, were jointly responsible for government of the Punjab. After dinner Robert said to the other two: 'I wonder what the old Simpsons are doing in Derry. I suggest we send them a joint Christmas present; I will give £50 (a large sum by any standards in those days) if you two will do the same.' Both agreed at once, for the Simpsons were twin brothers (William and Robert) who had been masters at Foyle College and had taught the three men. The twins were famous in their day, but very simple people, risen as it were from the ranks with virtually no educational training, and probably a butt among the boys in their classes; but they were fanatical in their loyalty to Foyle and their regard for its pupils. Later George Lawrence, then Political Agent in Rajputana, also contributed £50, so a joint letter from the four old boys, with a cheque for £200, was sent to the Simpson twins. After many months an answer came in a delightfully naive reply, which began: 'My dear boys' – then 'boys' was scratched out and 'friends' substituted. They thanked them for the generous present and added: 'We see you write from a place called Lahore. We have looked in the old school atlas but we can find no such place. But we hope that you are none of you up to any mischief.'

BRIAN MONTGOMERY, *Monty's Grandfather: A Life's Service for the Raj: Sir Robert Montgomery GCSI KCB LLD, 1809–1887*, 1984

SUMMER SUN AND WINTER SNOWS: days of rest and enjoyment on the warm turf of Holywell Hill above the city; days of paddling in the sun-flecked waters of Lough Swilly at Fahan, nine miles from home; days of shovelling away snow from our doors; of sliding and sleighing and snowballing, and of making snowmen and snowhouses that melted, alas, like our dreams too soon.

Mr Monaghan stood before us conducting as we sang:

> *Where are the scenes on which love used to beam*
>   *Long, long ago? Long, long ago?*
> *Vanished, alas, like the lines of a dream!*
>   *Long, long ago! Long ago!*

And as the examination for candidate monitors drew near he increased in severity and plied us with work, so that most of our evenings were spent poring over our books. I now developed a most uncomfortable feeling: I felt that, in spite of the work, I was unprepared for the ordeal, and I began to wonder how I could escape sitting for this examination. Sometimes I surprised my father watching me intently as I laboured at the table with an exercise, and my heart smote me that my failure should cause him pain and disappointment. I thought not of my mother in this way; nothing but her own tears could make me grieve for her, or touch me to the quick where she was concerned.

Of late, Monaghan had taken to casting up at me that I was not of the same good material as my brothers. 'Your brother Patrick would have solved that in half the time,' he had snapped at me when I was dilatory with an answer; and he shook his head ominously many times as he examined my various exercises. I read in his severe countenance strong disapproval, deep disappointment, and very often rank incredulity. Since the day he had taken my little hankie from me he had learned more about me; and I now felt that, had he not been carried away by my father's 'high ideals' talk, he might not have acted as he had done on that occasion. It would not have surprised me in the least if he had sent for me and flung the hankie at my feet, for every word that he now spoke to me savoured of that. He found fault with my best work and continually lamented the absence of John and Paddy. They had always been counted clever and there were many books in our house which they had brought home as prizes for excellent results in their examinations. On the other hand, the only one that had come my way had become mine by accident; I had won it in a penny raffle on the day of the holidays.

Then the gods spoke. Four days before the appointed day, the paper in front of my eyes became blurred and the table began to spin like a wheel. I woke up in bed and Dr McLaughlin stood over me. He was telling my mother that I must remain in bed for the next fortnight. The miracle had happened, but I was too ill to enjoy missing the examination; though I was conscious of the comings and goings of my mother, and later, when a week had passed, of the attentions of Annie and Kathleen, both of whom came and sat with me and read to me.

But my most constant visitor was Paddy, whose efforts to please me both flattered and amazed me. Quiet and reserved – and always with a book in hand – he was the most undemonstrative member of the family. Still pining in idleness, he may have found my presence a comfort in his enforced loneliness. He brought me grapes and did me the honour of reading long extracts from a large thick volume that he was interested in at the time. To please him I assumed an interested pose and tried to look as if I were really enjoying the book as much as himself; but I am afraid my resolution failed at length, for once I awoke to find him gone from the room.

The specified fortnight had passed and I was beginning to enjoy my illness when a note arrived from Mr Monaghan. He had (very kindly, my mother said) arranged that I should not be penalised for my illness. He had had a long talk with Mr McQuillan, the inspector, who had consented to examine me in papers of similar difficulty to be set in his own house at Prehen outside the city. When that note came in the door, my peace of mind flew out the window. I prolonged my sickness – for the coward was always deep in me – and I lay awake at night trying to devise ways and means of circumventing Monaghan, the maniac, in his mad desire to enter me for this examination.

HUGH McVEIGH, *Oft in the Stilly Night*, 1957

DERRY IN 1942 SEEMS OCEANS DISTANT and centuries away. I gaze through the smoke of my pipe into the past, and try to raise the nebulous ectoplasm that was myself. Those were the green years and nothing in Ireland was greener than I. Magee was inhabited by the Navy and the lawns were soon submerged in Nissen huts. Beyond the huts were allotments with ancient graduates digging, seriously raising cabbage and cauliflowers as part of the war effort.

Magee itself was shuttered and dark. Black-outs were rampant and the library was musty and rusty with non-usage. Barrage balloons festooned the horizons and the sound of the air raid sirens was heard over the land. The river was a busy thoroughfare for warships and many a ship limped into the Foyle after a mauling in the Atlantic. To me Magee seemed a pocket of calm in the midst of a storm, and my struggles with Latin, Greek, Philosophy and Physics were ephemeral and evanescent.

We had lectures for a time in the Model School, and as I look back now all I recall is an incident whereby a hen was projected through a lecture room window in the middle of a lecture. It was an operation ill conceived and execrably executed, for I still bear the scar on my hand as the window shattered. I remember the faces of friends and the drone of voices in that dark backward and abysm of time; but I found neither understanding nor rest at that time and after the examinations in March, I escaped for a season. Bewildered and terrified of war, yet looking to it as an escape from the urgent need to think seriously, I blundered on like a drunkard trying to walk the white line.

Four years and forty ages later I was back at Magee – a Magee closer to the Magee of to-day. The Nissen huts were still in place, but the black-outs were down. The library was open again, and the effervescence of thought took over from the mediocrity of activity. About this time lectures began to penetrate, and the fizz which was generated then has persisted to this moment. For this and for all that I received from the Faculty I shall be for ever grateful.

I still recall Professor Marshall being as caustic as Chaucer about Chaunticleer and Pertelote, and his discussion of predestination! 'But what

God for-woot moot nedes bee.' His elucidation of 'The Winter's Tale', and 'The Tempest' opened windows in the soul of at least one silent student which he had not known even to exist. I see him towering over the lectern with his poet's eyes glinting and his legal brain dissecting – analysing and synthesising at the same time – and ourselves faint but pursuing. It was a memorable and exciting experience. We who were privileged to sit at his feet owe him a debt which cannot be repaid.

Equally stimulating for me was my introduction to Kant. Professor Robinson – alias Tommy Logic – threw me in at the deep end with the *Critique of Pure Reason*. 'That all our knowledge begins with experience there can be no doubt' – so it opens and thus began what was to be the most intellectually satisfying experience of my hitherto sheltered life. As I read on with the help of my Professor, Kant's vast architectonic reared itself in my imagination, and the mind boggled at its sublimity. My thoughts whirled in tune with the master, and the harmony was that of immortal souls.

I was a lone student in this class and I well remember Professor Robinson lecturing to me from his sick bed. He wore a night cap, and set up a card table for my note taking. I still hear his chuckle and relish his jokes. I can see him painting a fence on a warm summer afternoon holding the paint brush in one hand and a large black umbrella in the other. It was too warm for a hat and he wanted to protect his balding pate from sunburn. It was a fine and glorious sight.

Memories crowd in upon me now – of Logic and Latin and Mathematics and Physics – of lectures and lecturers; Professors Finnegan and Guthrie and Ferguson, Messrs Orr and Nichol and Brown: attending Debates and SRC meetings: of rugby at Duncreggan and football at Assemblies: snatches of lectures and the faces of friends: dances and damsels: ideas and ideals. It is all a kaleidoscope of personal reminiscences of interest probably only to myself.

Perhaps Lord Morley's verdict on Burke best describes my impression of Magee at this time – 'the wide illumination from the great principles of human experience, the strong and masculine feeling for the two great political ends of Justice and Freedom, the large and generous interpretation of expediency, the morality, the vision, the noble temper' – all this, and more, we received from Magee in the forties.

I and my contemporaries have much to thank her for, and our debt is huge. 'Abeunt studia in mores.'

JAMES KINCADE, 'In the Forties', *Acorn* 9, Autumn 1965

I HAVE BEEN CALLED A MYTH – which I suppose is a fact to many – but how much more nowadays is VHS [Victoria High School] to the majority that read the Magazine, and for that reason I am going to recall a few of the things that stand out in my mind as a boarder. For my last year 'Vanity Fair' was my dormitory, and my room-mates were the three Laws, Mary Beare, my two sisters and myself. It was a big room, with wash basins next door, and the one dormitory that was nearest to the dining room, as we could get down to breakfast before the door closed quicker than most, and with less clothes on than anyone else, at least I was lazy and never got out of bed until the last moment, but I always managed to get inside that door and always dressed when we got back to the dormitory. Then there was the Gym at night after study, where we danced for half-an-hour so that we went to bed warm and how well we all learned to dance, even the girls whose parents frowned on dancing, it was all so enjoyable and we were so carefree.

Then there were the Sunday afternoons for the Grecians, Teutons and Celts in Miss McKillop's drawing room, and how wonderful she was with all of us. We never looked forward to these affairs, yet what foresight she had when one remembers the great changes that war brought into the home-life later on, and even in school life. We were encouraged to knit on Sundays because the work was 'Comforts' for the soldiers, and what comforts they were, helmets and mufflers, some of which were miles long, but we felt we had a hand in helping. Gracious what a time it was, and lastly those lovely hours before the holidays when we had packed all our belongings and jumped up and down to close our trunks which were taken away the day before we left school, and finally when we were in the train and the excitement of opening our 'train notes' according to the instructions on the envelopes. I wonder does the girl of to-day have these notes from their friends.

With those days in my mind last August when I was in Derry, I drove round Crawford Square and on out the Northland Road, looking for some landmark that I could recognise, and was saddened to fine none. Then I saw a familiar figure walking on ahead of me, the sight of which whisked me back to a junior class room, until I realised I was now well ahead of that. I drove on quickly to see if I was right in recognising one of my old teachers. She was a Girton scholar, and in my eyes was rather a fearsome person, but when I stopped and spoke to her I felt that at last I had recaptured something of my schooldays. Yes, can you guess who it was – Miss Bolton. To all of you who live in and around Londonderry, she is someone you see and hear of quite often, but to me who came from the far south, it was something more, and a link that no one else could forge.

GRACE ARMSTRONG, 'Thinking Back' in
Londonderry High School Old Girls' Association Magazine, Summer 1961

MATHS CLASS
November 1951

EVERY MORNING, at nine o'clock sharp, he came rushing into the room, his soutane swishing, his face reddened as if in anger, his features oddly calm. We would be ready with the thick tome of algebra open at the right page and as many questions as possible prepared in advance. He spoke nasally but smilingly. He had tight curls and glasses; but for the redness, he could have looked harmless. His name was Gildea.

He sat at the high desk, raised on a platform above the class. He lifted his chin, closed his eyes and chanted:

'Mental algebra. Ground rules. Well-known, but must be repeated, first for the sake of the brain-dead and the memory-less, who are in the usual staggering majority; second as a warning to those more fortunately endowed, but who take a litigant's pleasure in claiming that they have not been told, that they do not know, that the rules are not clear. I lie awake at night, imagining for these creatures a condign punishment; yet I have failed. Does this bespeak in me a failure of imagination, or in them an unanswerable corruption? You may answer the question, McConnellogue.'

'I'm afraid I cannot, Father,' replied McConnellogue automatically. This was routine.

'Your sorrow is touching. Perhaps you do not realise the importance of the question. Harkin, be so good as to inform McConnellogue what a litigant is.'

'A litigant is a person who creates disturbances by abuse of the rule of law, Father.'

'Do you agree with that superb definition, McConnellogue?'

'Absolutely, Father.'

'You are not litigious, McConnellogue, are you?'

'No, Father.'

'I shall test you in that statement. Are you more literate or more numerate as a consequence of my loving care, five times a week, forty minutes per time, McConnellogue?'

'I am equally blessed in both respects, Father.'

'Would you say that McConnellogue will go far, Heaney?'

'I would, Father.'

'Under what conditions would you say so, Heaney?'

'Under the conditions imposed by the question, Father.'

'Are you conversant with these conditions, Duffy?'

'I am, Father.'

'What's your name, Duffy?'

'Duffy, Father.'

'Glad to hear it. Now, ground rules. We have here, in this venerable textbook, forty simple sums in algebraic form, to each of which there is only one correct answer. There are, in this room, forty boys. One sum for each. The coincidence is pleasing. We begin with Johnson, the strange-looking creature in the left-hand corner of the front row. He gives the answer to number one in no more than two seconds. If he takes longer, he will be deemed to have given a wrong answer. McDaid, the object next to

Johnson, takes number two, and so on throughout the whole zoo-like assemblage we, in our politeness, call a class. However, if Johnson is, in McDaid's considered opinion, wrong in number one, he, McDaid, does number one over again and gives the correct answer. If the person next to McDaid happens to believe that Johnson was right in number one, and McDaid wrong to correct him, he skips number two and does number three; whereupon McDaid must, if he agrees with this verdict, re-do number two. Equally, the person next to McDaid also has the choice to believe that both Johnson and McDaid were wrong in number one; if he takes this choice, he does number one over again. And so on. The choice enriches as one proceeds, so that by the time we reach that evolutionary cul-de-sac named Irwin at the back of the class, the choice will be veritably kaleidoscopic. If any sum is done wrongly by any preceding student, whether that be immediately or more distantly preceding, the student who observes this must do that sum correctly. If a sum is done incorrectly, the punishment is a mere two strokes. If a sum done correctly is incorrectly corrected, the punishment is four strokes. If the whole class misses a sum incorrectly answered, homework is doubled. If it misses more than one sum incorrectly answered, homework is doubled for the number of nights corresponding to the number of missed incorrect answers. If every sum is answered correctly, the sun will stand still in the heavens, and I will take up the teaching of a secure and sure subject, like religion. Right. Johnson, proceed. Two seconds from now!'

SEAMUS DEANE, *Reading in the Dark*, 1996

GLENDERMOTT WAS AN IDEAL PLACE for children to grow up in. The Manse stood on the side of a hill, looking across the wooded Faughan valley to the distant mountains; there were trees round it, a garden with very fine beech hedges, laurels, and other shrubs. As in most families, the children all had little gardens of their own and can look back to the flowers that grew in them as the most beautiful and fragrant ever known. On one side of the house was a tennis-court, dug out and levelled with much labour by the boys themselves; on the other, above the kitchen garden rich with gooseberries and currants, was a summer-house, also built by one of the brotherhood with his own hands. At the back, a field sloped up and overlooked a deep sunk road; from this attractive spot you could hurl insults, and possibly missiles, at passing carters, with no fear of being caught. There were six acres of land attached to the Manse, and, though a man worked in the garden and fields, all the boys were expected to lend a hand, so that 'old John' sometimes complained they would soon leave him without a job.

Greatest attraction of all was the river – the Faughan – whose rushing stream one could hear on quiet nights from the Manse windows. The boys never tired of it, and in the long summer days they learned to swim, bathed, and boated, in boats also of their own making, battled triumphantly with the young 'Watersideys' (urchins from the town, the Waterside of Derry), and generally enjoyed themselves as healthy boys will.

EDITH CORKEY, David Corkey: A Life Story, c.1925

'AND THE FOLLOWING PREPOSITIONS take the ablative,' said Dr McCafferty, wrinkling his brow humorously and smiling down at the class.

Absque, a, ab, abs and *de,*
Coram, clam, cum, ex and *e,*
Tenus, sine, pro and *prae.*

Write them down and learn them off for tomorrow. The rhyme should make it easier.'

Colm's books, fastened in a strap, were at his feet. His Latin grammar and the small blue Caesar were on the desk in front of him, but he was not paying attention. He was thinking of Gerry, Gerry and Judith, and the row at home.

Gerry had given up his insurance job two years ago to go on tour, singing professionally. First Belfast and Dublin, then New York, Boston, Philadelphia, over to San Francisco, on to Australia and now, at last, back home, singing in triumph in the Guildhall.

Mr and Mrs O'Kane, Anna and Colm had all been there and Gerry sang all the old favourites. 'I hear you calling me', 'Because', 'The Lark in the Clear Air', 'The Clown's Song' from *Pagliacci*.

But he was not the only artist on the bill. Judith Thompson sang too, fairytale beautiful and exquisitely blonde, singing in pure, clear, sympathetic notes. Warmth and happiness flowed from her. Colm was entranced, worshipping her.

'Who is this Thompson girl?' his mother whispered. 'She's not from Derry, is she?'

'Indeed she is,' his father answered. 'You know the bakery? That family. You know the house on Culmore Road?'

Mrs O'Kane nodded.

'A Protestant! That's why I never heard of her. She wasn't in the Feis. But very nice people. And a lovely voice. A charming girl.'

The grand finale was the Love Duet from *Madame Butterfly*. They were not in costume. Gerry was in evening clothes, his crisp, black curls shining. Judith was in a gown of pale blue silk. They looked in each other's eyes, proudly, defiantly in love, and smiled and sang with such pleading passion that the women in the audience sought their handkerchiefs. When it was over, the crowd rose and cheered and clapped and whistled. There must have been a dozen curtain calls while they held hands and bowed.

Afterwards the family went proudly back stage to see Gerry, but they did not stay long. Gerry said that he was bringing Judith home for supper and Mrs O'Kane had to rush home to bake and set out the best cloth and china in the dining-room.

Once they got home, she took her hat and coat off, patted her hair and waded in, fussing around, talking and working, organizing the others.

'Anna, not those spoons! The good ones from the box in the sideboard! Very well off, the Thompsons! But Gerry is well able to stand up in any company. Colm! Tidy the hearth! No! Not that way! Here, give me! Or would you do it, George?'

She turned to her husband.

'I'm afraid he'll burn himself.'

'Don't get in a fuss, Margaret.'

'I'm not fussing. They could be here at any minute. Anna, spoon the jam out into the dish, there's a good girl. I know the house. Just at the bend in the river, isn't it? I'm sure they have a couple of maids and maybe a gardener.'

'Who?'

'The Thompsons!'

'For God's sake, Margaret! The family isn't coming, only a young girl.'

'She's used to the best, George. But I won't let you down.'

Colm knelt at the fire, holding a newspaper in front of it to give it life, reading the advertisements. At last he took it down and lapsed into his thoughts.

Gerry was late as usual. It was almost one o'clock in the morning by the time the taxi arrived at the door. He and Judith came into the house, sparkling strangers from a different world.

WALTER HEGARTY, *The Price of Chips*, 1973

ON THIS OCCASION THE ANCIENT STRIFE broke out in a very marked way. An Irish Marquis, who was an enthusiastic Harrovian, began it by calling on his fellow-travellers to contemplate that rotten place on the river – Eton.

In response to this unprovoked assault, a famous Etonian – a Field-Marshal – asked the company to contemplate that workhouse on the hill – Harrow.

The Marquis most unfairly then observed that the Field-Marshal's belt had been turned wrong side uppermost, during the entire ceremony. This raised the temperature to boiling-point.

The wife of the Marquis, by way of throwing oil on troubled waters, asked me if I had been at Eton or Harrow. I replied that for financial reasons I had not been at either, but that I had been at a school much superior to these over-lauded institutions – Foyle College, Londonderry.

'This school,' I continued, 'educated five of the greatest men the British Empire, or any other Empire, had ever produced. Four of them had preserved India for the Crown: Lord Lawrence, Sir Henry Lawrence, Sir Robert Montgomery, and the great General, John Nicholson.'

The first three had really been educated at Foyle College, but Nicholson had been a Dungannon boy. However, in the stress of the moment, I thought it well to borrow him from Dungannon for once.

'But who was the fifth?' shouted the combatants.

I said that he had no connection with India and that his name had slipped from my memory for the time. After a little reflection I exclaimed triumphantly:

'I remember him now – *it was myself!*'

Upon this modest assertion the battle was extinguished in laughter and was not renewed.

The Headmaster of Foyle College in my time was the Rev. William Percy Robinson, afterwards warden of Trinity College, Glenalmond, a fine classical scholar who had had a distinguished career in Trinity College, Dublin.

He introduced the rules of honour into the school very much after the manner of Dr Arnold in Rugby. When anything of a culpable character had occurred, the Head on the following morning announced the fact and called on the offender to stand up. This never failed, though the punishment that followed was often inflicted with no sparing hand. Even in this respect he showed great wisdom and discrimination. On one occasion I had kicked a football through a window, right into a class, that was receiving instruction from a master whom we disliked.

The act was done under the inspiration of the Devil. I was summoned to the Headmaster's room. He began by saying that the broken window must be paid for, and that it was very stupid and thoughtless to kick footballs so near the building. He inflicted a sharp imposition. I remember it was to learn by heart a considerable passage from Demosthenes' *de Corona*. It was a terrible moment. If the truth were told, it meant probably expulsion and the end of everything. But it had to be told.

'I did it intentionally!'

'What?'

'I meant to do it!'

A solemn voice said:

'You may go!'

This was much more terrifying than corporal punishment. I hardly slept for a week, always expecting to hear of the dreadful letter, requesting my father to withdraw me from the school. But none came, and nothing happened. The window was paid for, and the *de Corona* passage learned, but never called for. The subject was not mentioned again, but the culprit had suffered a torture quite adequate to satisfy the sternest tribunal.

The Headmaster was the first to inspire me with a passion for the classics which has been, and remains, one of the greatest pleasures of my life. The *Philoctetes* of Sophocles was the first Greek play I read with him, and since it has remained my favourite to be read and re-read many times.

The mathematical master was Mr Andrew Johnston, a very fine type of Trinity man. In teaching English History, he gave us a knowledge of the world and of the science of politics which was of infinite service to me in after life. We had an excellent French master in Monsieur de Bovais but, as usual spent our time in playing tricks on him instead of taking advantage of his teaching, a folly for which we had all to pay heavily in later years.

One boarder, a strong youth, was looked upon as the bully of the school; it is right to say that in after life I found him a very good fellow.

One day, in a fit of arrogance, he came into the ball court and flung my ball over the wall. I at once went up and struck him. A circle was formed for a fight. My backers were few in number and in poor heart, as I was much slighter and smaller. The proceedings opened with my being twice knocked down, amid the applause of the enemy's backers. This seemed to bring me strength and resolution to go on with the fight to the bitter end. It lasted a long time, but in the end, blackened, bruised and bleeding, I came out victorious amid wild cheering.

I have had many triumphs in my life – the most of them unexpected and undeserved. None of them ever brought me the ecstasy of that moment.

SIR JOHN ROSS, *The Years of My Pilgrimage*, 1924

A S A BOY, I OFTEN HAD TO LISTEN to the praise of things past and people long dead. What, I used to wonder, had it to do with me? I was interested in sex and Hollywood movies, not in all these old wives' tales of conflict. My aunts and mother might have been talking of the early Christians being thrown to the lions for all I cared. Their anecdotes of their own early lives I found just as boring. Now they, too, have passed into history and it is too late for me to take notes.

What can I remember of those first five or so years of my life in Derry? I can see myself at the age of three or four, in the early 1920s, standing in Bennett Street, where Dr McCurdy had delivered me, looking through my legs at a fascinatingly topsy-turvy world. Another image of myself is of stroking a grey horse that pulled a bread cart, and marvelling at the size and beauty of the animal, and wanting yet fearing to touch its smartly-groomed tail.

I recall, too, being taught to say 'Logan's Loaf' and rendering it as 'Ogan's Oaf' to an amused feminine audience. 'L' and 'r' were as difficult for me to master as they proved for Japanese students I was to teach several decades later. I used to proclaim my name, with some pride, as 'Lobelt'. I was taught a few simple Bible stories and I think the hope existed that this only child might one day feel 'the call' to the Presbyterian ministry. These stories I was encouraged to repeat in my lisping accents and I soon realised that a storyteller can capture and hold an audience.

I was particularly addicted to the story of Moses, with variations on the theme. The Old Testament for us was as real, perhaps even more so, than the New. Jews were respected as the people of the Book, not thought of with contempt or hatred. So it proved that bulrushes, wilderness, rock, children of Israel, were colourful props for an exhibitionistic little boy. I liked to emphasise the length and tedium of Moses' journey using repetition – ' ... and he go-ed and he go-ed'. This, I sensed, would bring the house down.

How many years I spent in Derry I cannot accurately remember, but an old directory lists my grandmother's name until 1925, so I think it must have been five. I have not forgotten, however, the sensation of being, as I believed, deserted by my parents and left in the care of my maternal granny and her two daughters. I cried bitterly for my mother. When I asked for her, granny said: 'She's gone away for a wee while.'

'Where? Where?'

'To a big, big city called Belfast.'

'What for?'

'To earn pennies for her Robbie.'

This news was not comforting. It alarmed me, saddened me. I felt betrayed. It was as if the sky had fallen on my head. It could not be. She could not have left me. Nothing would console me, not even the grey horse to which I once delighted to feed lumps of sugar. Nor the recital of that story about some old Jew called Moses. No, I did not want granny or my two aunts – kind and loving though they were.

Aunt Annie begged me to look at the man in the moon. Man in the moon, indeed! Had I but known the words, what obscenities I would have uttered! But small children know only the language of yells and sobs. They know betrayal, too. The parting, as it happened, was not final by any means, yet the relationship with mother never fully recovered. She lived to be nearly ninety and we were on loving terms – and yet ...

Time and again, I have made an effort to re-establish the early sense of harmony, oneness, completeness. Time and again, I have endeavoured to re-enter the lost paradise. Is it like catching a soap bubble and holding it in one's hand? The Belfast novelist, Forrest Reid, the first writer I ever met, put forward in his autobiography, *Apostate*, the suggestion that a certain kind of creative artist finds his motivation in discontent, so that, as Reid puts it, 'his art is a kind of crying for Elysium'. He may well have revealed the reason why, as a grown man, I have felt the necessity to write poems. Poetry is the antidote for hurt and frustration.

But I often think back to those Derry days. Aunt Annie, kind soul then and in later years, apart from attempting to make me believe in the reality of the man in the moon – a ploy I stubbornly resisted – used to take me out for what she called 'air'. She could ameliorate yet not dissolve the bitterness in my infant heart. The giants of the adult world, I felt, were not to be trusted. Kindness might mask betrayal.

Throughout my life, when I hear the bitter-sweet strains of the 'Londonderry Air' – as haunting a melody as has ever come out of Ireland, north or south – I think of my native city and of being taken out for 'air'. I recall with affection, not unmixed perhaps with some shame, of this good aunt of mine and her long perambulations with a fractious, self-willed, dreamy little boy along Shipquay Street and the Waterside. And I have sometimes wondered how my life would have turned out had I spent my boyhood on the banks of the River Foyle in Colmcille's 'beautiful Derry'.

ROBERT GREACEN, *The Sash My Father Wore*, 1997

FRIDAY NIGHT WAS GREAT. My father would bring home his wages in a brown envelope, sit in his armchair in the corner and open it with solemnity. We would always ask, and he would never tell us, how much he earned. 'Enough,' he would say.

This was deeply reassuring, but as I grew older, worry crept in. If there was enough, why did my mother have to go round the shops every week handing over her debt-books and a few shillings? She used to let me look at the amounts pencilled in and they were enormous. They would never be paid off. Every time the debt reduced, she'd order something else and the bill would soar again. I suggested we walk into town and save money on the bus and she laughed and repeated the story to my father and he laughed too. 'You have to enjoy yourself as well,' they'd say to me.

Sometimes, on the debt day, my mother would take me into a tea shop and order lemon pancakes sprinkled with sugar for us both. Sweet food became a symbol of stability. If my parents were poor, we'd hardly be dining like royalty downtown.

And they wouldn't be flinging money around on fish and chips, which they always did in Derry on Friday nights, which is why I loved Fridays – so did my sisters and brothers. We fought for the privilege of going to buy them. It was understood that you could open the parcel on the way home and give yourself a little snack to make up for the work of fetching them. The fish supper was wrapped in brown paper and further insulated with a sheet of newspaper. Even then, the tang of vinegar and salt seeped through and the smell would kill you with longing. You'd walk more and more slowly, holding the warm packet against your chest, sniffing and tempting yourself until you couldn't hold out any longer.

Eventually, you'd poke your finger through the wrapping and extract a long, golden chip. I always waited until I got to the gable wall of McLaughlins' house before I did that. The heat from their coal fire came through the wall at a certain spot and you could park yourself there, your bum and chest warmed, back and front, and have a solitary, magnificent feast. It was always agony, calculating just how many chips you'd get away with taking out of the family mouth.

Eventually, there came a Friday night when my parents gave me enough pocket money to buy my own chips. This was delicious torture. How long could a person make a bag of chips last? Our gang devised a solution. We'd sit in the chipper and order a plate at a time and share them out. A plate of chips cost the same as a bag. The man who owned the place gave us one plate and six forks and let us sit in the booth as long as the money lasted. Every time the plate emptied, he'd fill it up again. I have no memory of fighting over the amount of chips consumed per person. We ate one each at a time, going round the booth in strict rotation.

In the background, adults played records on the jukebox, five for a shilling. This used to worry us too. How long would the shillings and the music last? It lasted forever. It was Friday night; they had wage-packets and money to burn. Rock and roll and Elvis Presley had just begun. Though I fell in love with everything American, I felt sorry at the same time for the Yanks. According to Elvis, 'It's Saturday night, I just got paid ...'. Clearly, they had to work harder and longer over there before they could afford a plate of chips. I stopped worrying about my father's wages and became a happy Irish teenager.

Now I've a monthly salary and twenty years still to run on the mortgage. When the interest rate goes up, I take the bus into Dublin town, order lemon pancakes with sugar, have a bag of chips on the way home, and murmur 'Enough.' Have you noticed how very difficult it is these days to find a coal-fire-heated gable wall against which to park your bum?

NELL MCCAFFERTY, in *Those Were the Days: Irish Childhood Memories*
(ed. Seán Power), 1995

THE BISHOP LIVED IN A BIG HOUSE across the wall from our boarding school. On slow summer evenings we'd peep over and watch him playing croquet by himself, sometimes muttering and hammering the mallet into the ground when he missed a hoop. The grass on his side was as neat as a bebop haircut, and his shiny black shoes moved over it in tidy steps that never picked up any dirt. When his tea was ready, the housekeeper would stand outside the front door and ring a small handbell. Even if he had the mallet drawn back between his legs, poised to hit, he would drop it immediately and move at a smart pace to the house. Tweetie Downey claimed that on Sundays during the summer term the Bishop had a bowl of beans for tea. Then when we were in study hall, he would come out and zoom round the hoops like a balloon losing its air.

On Saint Patrick's Day every year he visited our boarding school. If he'd wanted, he could have opened a small door in the wall and simply walked through to us. Instead he entered through the front gates, a plump little figure half-lost in the back of a chauffeured Bentley. Among cushions he'd sit, smiling out at us with his little baby teeth, one white hand in midair sending blessings through the car's closed windows. With a March breeze whipping our Brylcreemed hair, we would line the sloping driveway to clap and cheer as his car crunched slowly past. Behind us, knees bent and head low, the Dean trotted up the line abreast with the car. 'Now boys – clap! Quick, quick before he's gone past on you.' And if he thought we weren't enthusiastic enough, he'd prod the backs of the nearest boys and hiss, 'Applause! Applause!'

Then, on Saint Patrick's Day, 1958, somebody booed. Nobody could tell where it began. When we looked up and down the line everybody seemed to be still clapping, everybody's mouth was still open apparently cheering. But there was a boo. A travelling boo that started somewhere near the entrance gates and moved like a gnat-cloud up the line in time with the Bishop's car. You felt rather than heard it pass over you. To this day I don't even know if I booed myself.

Mercifully, sealed in the back of his car, the Bishop couldn't hear a thing. All through the heresy he went on smiling and blessing us. But the Dean heard it. There could be absolutely no doubt about that. The problem was, stumbling along, he couldn't tell *who* was doing it. If the Bishop hadn't been around, the Dean'd have waded in with strap flailing and made it his business to find out. But then if the Bishop hadn't been around, there'd have been no booing. So the Dean, poor man, went staggering up the line, his little groans of frustration mixing in with the boos and the clapping.

JUDE COLLINS, 'Booing the Bishop', *Booing the Bishop and Other Stories*, 1995

Stroke
City

D URING RECENT DARK DAYS, when people were randomly killed or
seriously interfered with because of their religious affiliation, one
can see the importance of hedging one's bets and the desirability of
having a sporting chance.

Picture a lonely road in the dead of night. A man is driving wearily home
only to observe ahead the sinister outline of shady figures in the middle of
the road wielding bobbing flashlights. He stops and winds down his
window ... he has little choice. It could be a legitimate check-point. But
maybe not.

A shadowy figure asks him where he is from.

His life may depend on the answer. If the interrogators are looking for a
Protestant to work out on, a reply of 'Derry' may be enough to be granted a
welcome gruff 'Off you go, then.' If it's bad luck to be a Catholic that night,
a 'Derry' could be enough to seal a man's fate.

To circumnavigate this formidable obstacle, the BBC mandarins decreed
that presenters on radio and television, faced with the onerous task of
having to articulate the name of the city, should at first utterance use
'Londonderry' and thereafter, in the same broadcasting segment, the
abbreviation 'Derry'.

I, numbed by the complexity of this, took to naming the city Derry
Stroke Londonderry until ultimately settling for the more natural, user-
friendly 'Stroke City'.

To my surprise, this new usage rapidly caught on and became a handy
get-out for those challenged by thuggish strangers to name their native
city. And so I managed to make enemies of all those who thought that the
choice of the pointed use of 'Derry' or 'Londonderry' as a matter of principle
at all times was of great importance.

For supplying sensible people with an alternative I was heartily disliked by
a sizeable and dangerous proportion of Stroke City and beyond.

But I wasn't on the radio to be liked by everybody. I knew that now.

GERRY ANDERSON, *Surviving in Stroke City*, 1999

C ONVERSELY, I HAVE OPTED ON MOST OCCASIONS to use the name 'Derry' for both the city and county rather than the more politically correct 'Derry/Londonderry', except when the context dictates otherwise. I do so in the knowledge that County 'Londonderry' is technically more correct, since the county only came into existence after the seventeenth-century Ulster Plantation and was called after the London companies to whom it had been transferred. More than any place name, this one traditionally singles out Catholic from Protestant, for Catholics consider the ancient monastic site of Derry (Doire) as peculiarly theirs and seldom use the 'London' prefix. But since I am writing about the Catholics, it makes sense to adopt their terminology. Besides, I am beginning to tire of those mental contortions required before saying anything about Northern Ireland. We would like to believe that it is because we do not wish to offend. But there are equally valid and less complimentary explanations, including an effort to disguise our own background or to fathom that of others.

MARIANNE ELLIOTT, *The Catholics of Ulster*, 2000

Fountain Street's neat red white and blue. Wall-paintings,
freshened annually, show the Relief, King Billy
white-horsed, purified into primary colours.

'Our only trouble is we're too loyal here.
These lads would die for England. No one in England
cares, for us, or England, anymore.
The Fenian rioters get the sympathy,
and the army I served years with sent to help them.
Though now they stone the soldiers. So do our lads.

Things weren't so bad. I mind four years ago
I had a Catholic friend, lived up in Creggan.
Now, I do decorating round these streets,
some of these paintings. Well, I went up there
to set and paint the railings for my friend
round one of these wee saints they put in their gardens.
And his wife knew who I was, and didn't like it,
and got the neighbouring womenfolk who came
and threatened me, their weans all throwing stones.
And he jumped the fence, the fence was brave and high,
and hit her to the ground, and she stayed down,
and with a spade he warned the others off.

He was my friend. There was more tolerance then.
Though my Lodge didn't care for what I'd done, and warned me.
But nothing would get me up to Creggan now.'

ANDREW WATERMAN, 'Derry Images 1968–71', in *Collected Poems*, 2000

WHILE STATIONED IN DERRY, I was also gaining an awareness of the complicated political and religious divisions within Northern Ireland. During my twenty-six months there, I witnessed two incidents that to me reflected more than anything else the dichotomy of views about the British monarchy in Northern Ireland. The first occurred on 6 February 1952, when I was on beat duty, standing on the walls of Derry City and overlooking the Catholic Bogside housing estate. Immediately below were the roof-tops of old Victorian terrace houses. All at once, through the upper half of a sash-corded window, a woman's head emerged. Although a Catholic, she was sobbing uncontrollably when she called up to me, 'Constable, the King's dead!' She had just heard the wireless bulletin about the sudden death of King George VI, and I found her emotion as moving as the content of her message.

The second incident, the following year, was no less memorable. I was again on duty, standing this time in a small confectionery and tobacconist shop. As I was chatting to its owner, a young woman came in, asked for a bar of Fry's chocolate cream, and put two pennies on the glass-topped counter. The shopkeeper duly took the bar from a shelf. She picked it up, but then abruptly threw it into his face. In a raised, excited voice she snapped, 'I asked for chocolate, not for the Union Jack!' Grabbing her two pence from the counter, she rushed out of the shop and was gone. The shopkeeper and I looked at one another in amazement. But as my gaze fell on the rejected chocolate bar, I saw that the paper wrapping bore the red, white and blue of the Union flag in celebration of Queen Elizabeth II's coronation.

SIR JOHN HERMON, *Holding the Line*, 1997

IT IS A PITY TO HAVE TO SPOIL this lyrical note with an unpleasant fact; but I cannot leave Derry without pointing out that a religious bigotry rules here with blatant savagery. Figures cannot easily lie, so I leave the reader to judge for himself. The Derry City Council has twelve Unionist Members and eight Catholic members. The Catholics, however, make up over nine thousand voters, while the Unionists only number over seven thousand. The Catholic voters represent over twenty-nine thousand people; whereas the Unionists voters represent only eighteen thousand people. Yet the

Catholics have only eight representatives and the Unionists have twelve! That is as pretty an example as the North may offer of the manner in which the constituencies have been gerrymandered, without scruple, by the bosses in Belfast – who, I need hardly mention, have likewise long since abolished Proportional Representation.

SEAN O'FAOLAIN, *An Irish Journey*, 1940

B Y SHIPQUAY GATE I CLIMBED UP THE STEPS above the crowds shifting around the market stalls and on to the famous walls, which divided the central sloping oval of the fortified city from the housing estates, greenswards and spanking new shopping centres that now surrounded it. They were, I was to discover, the best preserved city walls in Europe, and they gave the old city both focus and character, as well as a great place for bored teenagers to hang out. From on top they were even more substantial than I'd imagined, the ramparts between the parapets being wide enough to drive one, if not two, cars along.

From up here you could see it all. Looking inwards, steep Shipquay Street running up to the central Diamond. Looking outwards, well, here, beyond the graffiti-plastered black cannons (Roly Majella! Michelle! Ciara! Our day will come!) was the brick-floored square outside the ornate Guildhall. In its centre, the upbeat tourist map saying 'Welcome to Londonderry, an historic city,' had had the 'London' blocked out with green spray paint. The Protestants, you see, prefer the official 'Londonderry', which dates back to the charter granted to the London companies who built the walls and the fortified city from 1600; the Catholics prefer the shorter 'Derry', which comes from the Irish *Doire*, meaning 'place of oaks', which is what the settlement's founder, Colum Cille, called it in the sixth century. Hence, to worn-out local cynics, London/derry is known as 'Stroke City'.

MARK McCRUM, *The Craic*, 1998

L ET US NOW TURN TO OTHER PHASES of Derry's lumpiness. Your rambles through the streets reveal them to you. Here is a Catholic seminary; here is a Presbyterian one. Here is the Orange Hall; here is St Columcille's Hall. Here is a street in which live militant Catholics; here alongside, radiating from a common centre, is a street in which live militant Orangemen. Here is a newspaper office from which issue periodical challenges to Croppies; here is another newspaper office from which said challenges are hurled back with interest. Here are the old seventeenth-century walls of the city which were manned by Cromwellians in 1648. Here are the historic gates slammed by the 'prentice boys in the face of the Catholic army of James forty years later. Here are the landmarks left by Columcille; here is the trophy statue to the soldier-pastor who made Derry one of the strongholds of Protestantism.

There was a day when this religious feud seemed near its end; and when the Presbyterians of Ulster were tending toward the highest idea of nationhood; but that was before Pitt arose to kindle anew the flames of religious rancour which have burned so banefully through all the nineteenth century, and whose lurid tongues are reddening the sky of the twentieth. It was a sad day for Derry and for Ireland when Irishmen of all classes and creeds forgot that they had a common country to love. Think of all that is implied by such an oversight. Think of all the blood spilled in fratricidal strife over religious rancour, and not a drop for Ireland. Think even of the brave old Protestant Walker and his brave Catholic assailants wasting blood and powder over the Stuarts! Where did Ireland come in? Think of Orange and Green to-day heaving paving-stones and scraps of iron at each other! For what; alas! for what?

The political and social animus arising out of this religious strife is written large all over Derry, as it is over most of Ulster. Near one of the gates in the old walls three or four streets converge. Right in front of the street openings, stands a large shop. When a politico-religious shindy takes place between the opposing factions that inhabit the converging streets, this shop's front is generally mutilated in the most destructive manner. The flying paving stones and other missiles play havoc with windows, and gilding, and signboard, and the furniture on the upper floors. The owner of this shop is a pacific citizen. He has no quarrel, I was told, with anybody. He takes no part with either Orange or Green. And yet his shop front is periodically wrecked. It is simply because his house is on the battle-ground of the mobs. Ireland is, more or less, in the same position; and if there is a difference at all, it lies in the fact that she pays the piper. The Derry shopman is compensated for his windows. But who or what compensates the nation for the ruinous expenditure of energy on internal strife?

WILLIAM BULFIN, *Rambles in Eirinn*, 1907

As a child in Derry I heard the shots
And the crackle of burning timber
That signalled the ancient quarrel
Of Prod and Papist, that mindless feud
Lingering on in a lost province
Where memories of long-ago battles
Are as fresh as today's headlines.

Memories of siege and horror, of Lundy,
The Apprentice Boys and God-knows what
Fag-ends of ill-digested history
Make a stirring tale for children
But light the fuse in the bitter heart.

Tales of blood and sectarian thunder
Lead to a coarse and brutal logic
Where my side is whiter that white
And yours black as a raven's wing.

Once more the pogrom and police baton,
The mob's thick urgent cries,
The pool of blood in the doorway,
The incandescent blaze of hate.

Yet I who have gone away
To safe and easy exile
Cannot quite write them off
As simply ignorant thugs.

I too am involved in their crimes.

ROBERT GREACEN, 'As a Child in Derry',
in *The Wearing of the Black* (ed. Padraic Fiacc), 1974

DERRY CONTAINED SEVERAL SHOCKS for me as a teenager. I had never
lived anywhere before where I was warned about going into certain
areas. I was not forbidden, but I received instructions to take care.
Thankfully, I never found myself in any difficulty. I walked the Walls. I
read Mackenzie's *Siege of Derry* and saw Walker's account for what it was.
More importantly, from the first I knew the Siege to be an European battle
between the Hapsburgs and the French fought on Irish soil. I saw in Derry
there were two communities living in opposition to each other not because
of what were doubtful interpretations of historic fact, but because of the
continuation of a seventeenth-century attitude of mind. This was carried
even into Church relationships. If one went into First Derry Presbyterian
Church, St Columba's Cathedral, or St Eugene's Cathedral, one could
sense it. It appeared in two forms – the Protestant/Roman Catholic and
Presbyterian/Anglican. Sadly, Orangeism and Nationalism both used their
religion as a political weapon. I do not say their Christianity. The religion of
each was a caricature.

THE REVEREND JOHN M. BARKLEY, *Blackmouth and Dissenter*, 1991

LIFE EQUALS WHITE-HOT LIGHT, white wings, white robes washed in the blood of the Lamb, soaring choirs sweet as thrushes.

At twenty, she still believes it, though the child of thirteen had spoken of it and had been laughed down by a classroom full of scornful girls – *God will not let us destroy ourselves in civil or nuclear war.* A debate on nuclear war and weapons. Her uncle, a brilliant physicist, whom she trusted, had worked at Aldermaston then. *God will not let us be destroyed ...*

Her eyes unfocus, drifting out beyond the immediacy of her round-rimmed glasses, beyond even desks and chairs. *God will not let us ...*

Unconscious of all but sight, she misses the slight scratch of fountain pens, the rustle of paper, the click of a cigarette lighter, the rise and fall of the old man's voice.

Her eyes pass down the row in front of her. Arrow-straight black hair. Coal black and glossy. *Catholic.* A long, narrow face and jutting chin. Pale eyes. Sandy brown hair and sunken cheeks. *Protestant.* Bright, freckled cheeks and a freckled snub nose. Tangle of red curls. *Catholic.* Thick, untidy flaxen hairs – a thatch in County Donegal. Rounded shoulders and a cigarette between thin lips. *Catholic.* Straw-colored hair. Long face. Gray eyes that catch hers without expression. *Protestant. No. Catholic?* She hesitates, staring a little longer than usual, but then her eyes waver and skip across the room. Pale skin except in the cheeks. Wavy, reddish-blond hair. *Catholic? No. Protestant? No ...*

The old man steps out from behind the podium, his voice changing as he opens the window with a laugh. 'Ireland doesn't know we have to work.'

The breeze rushes in and blows a flurry of papers from the podium. He stoops awkwardly to retrieve them, then continues. From beside the wooden platform, the flag of the province ripples out above his head. The bloody hand appears and disappears into its folds.

'Dorothea Brooke, we see, is so proud that she's completely blind. She's almost literally blind. Notice the repeated mention of short-sightedness. She's also metaphorically blind. Notice her refusal to see Casaubon for what he is, her inability to recognize love when she sees it in a real, fleshly form.'

The words filter through Kate's consciousness. She grasps them – the first she has heard in the forty-five minute lecture that afternoon. Her eyes jump back to the thick Penguin paperback in front of her. With a black ballpoint, she heavily underlines a few phrases of George Eliot's description. In the thin margin she sketches an open eye, reminding herself to notice the symbol as she reads the rest of the novel. 'You'll never learn anything if you don't keep your eyes wide open,' her father had always told her. Right, as usual.

Now her eyes rest on the lecturer's thinning hair and the polished scalp beneath. His eyes spark fiercely, even behind the thick pince-nez. *He's short-sighted himself,* she notices. The mouth is a thin line, the skin leathery and sallow. The hands, fluttering occasionally like white birds, are clean and long-fingered. *Catholic. Definitely Catholic.*

A gust of wind flings the window back hard against the side of the prefabricated building and slaps the flag against the wall so that the red hand stands out again. *God will not …*

ELIZABETH GIBSON, The Water is Wide, 1985

I SIOPA WOOLWORTHS BA GHNÁCH leis na cailíní Protastúnacha bheith ar paráid agus buachaillí Protastúnacha ag bolaíocht thart. Is iad a bhí ina theideal ach chuala mé á rá go raibh cuid de na cailíní chomh fiosrach faoi na buschaillí Caitliceacha is a bhí muide fúthusan. D'éirigh liom labhairt le duine acu lá. D'fhiafraigh sí díom an raibh mé ag freastal ar Choláiste Cholmcille. Dúirt mé go raibh mé ag dul chuig ranganna oíche sa *Tech*.

'You're not an apprentice, are you?' ar sise agus d'imigh léi.

The Protestant girls used to parade around Woolworths and had the Protestants lads sniffing around. They were entitled – but I had heard it said that some of the girls were as curious about Catholic boys as we were about them. One day I managed to talk to one of them. She asked me if I were at St Columb's College. I told her that I was going to night classes at the tech.

'You're not an apprentice, are you?' *she said and stalked off.*

AODH Ó CANAINN, Tearmann na gColúr (The Pigeon Sanctuary), 1998
(VERSION BY SEAN McMAHON)

WE RETURNED TO DERRY by the first train on the following morning. During the journey we had an interesting conversation with a young Irish shopkeeper from Letterkenny, who, like most of the better class population we met, was convinced that Home Rule would drive capital from the country. He was a Presbyterian; but he did not think that the Unionist party in the North would go to the length of actual warfare in resisting the establishment of a National Parliament, though he believed that extensive rioting would accompany the change. He said that the Irish people had still many grievances; and that, in various branches of the administration, large reforms were urgently required; but these wants could all be satisfied without the necessity of conceding a separate legislature. The best way to serve Ireland was to introduce capital into the country, and to open out her mines and develop her resources generally, thus providing employment for the wretched peasantry who, in the vain attempt to thrive upon an unkindly soil, resorted to agitation as a remedy – a remedy that was worse than the disease, and only intensified the evils from which they were suffering. A large number of people in Donegal, he said, were of the same opinion. He also informed us that he had been partially boycotted, the edict having gone forth that the people of Letterkenny were to refuse to buy anything at his shop; but he had simply taken no notice whatever of the decree, and, in a short time, matters resumed their usual course.

ARTHUR BENNETT, *John Bull and His Other Island II*, 1890

Or were you the Francis Farrelly that often used to say
He'd like to blow them Papishes from Darry walls away?
The boy who used to bother me that Orange Lodge to join,
And thought that history started with the Bottle o' the Boyne. –
I was not all with ye, Francis, the Pope is not ma friend,
But still I hope, poor man, he'll die without that bloody end. –
And when yer quit from care yerself, and get to Kingdom Come,
It's no use teachin' you the harp – you'll play the Orange drum!
Och! man, ye wor a fighter, of that I had no doubt,
For I seen ye in Belfast one night when the Antrim Road was out!
And many a time that evinin' I thought that ye wor dead,
The way them Papish pavin' stones was hoppin' off yer head.
Oh! if you're the Francis Farrelly who came from North Tyrone –
Here's lookin' to ye, Francis, but do leave the Pope alone!

PERCY FRENCH, 'The Four Farrellys', *Plays, Poems and Parodies*, 1929

M AGNANIMOUS IN VICTORY, he walked me to the end of the road. It was a fine November day and Harvey Terrace was at its most distinguished, an imposing Victorian cul-de-sac on the side of a hill, its single uniform row of houses looking down on a wooded embankment. But its days of grandeur were numbered. It too would have to suffer its tragic destiny. At the bottom of the hill was a burgeoning Catholic ghetto and on its summit was a new Catholic estate already a legend for barbarity. Protestants had abandoned Harvey Terrace long ago, the professional Catholics more recently, leaving to the impoverished genteel the thankless task of imposing standards on Catholic nouveaus and worse. At the city end of the street several houses had been converted into flats, let to what John described as 'problem families', and in the end house, the one with the large fenced garden, was a Chinese family, or rather community, since, as John explained, it was owned by the proprietors of the China Garden and housed a constantly changing population of kitchen staff and waiters.

The social mix was precisely that of the terrace I grew up in. Here again it was genteels versus nouveaus and both of these versus the problem people, with a foreign household too far off the end of the social scale to be measured, my analogue for the Chinese the Indian proprietors of a drapery business prominently advertised as 'the House of Quality' but universally known as 'the Black Man's'. It pleased me that so many familiar dramas were being acted out afresh. Harvey Terrace, too, was reliving an old story.

MICHAEL FOLEY, *The Road to Notown*, 1996

The walk, march, shuffle; the flute, fife and pipes.
There is no common ground, only islands.
Stepping over the seabank of one you
Step over into the rest of the world.
The crossing here is three dimensional.
Overhead, the dangerous sky is empty.

SAM BURNSIDE, 'The New Bridge, Londonderry –
Travelling East', *Walking the Marches*, 1990

DERRY WAS A BAD PLACE TO BE BORN. Although it was a majority Catholic and Nationalist city, it was controlled by the Protestant Unionist minority by gerrymander, the unfair redrawing and manipulation of electoral boundaries. That situation was not going to last for ever and I was born in time for the bloody change. Catholics either rotted in Derry without work or emigrated to find it elsewhere, so it is not surprising that my four brothers and one of my sisters left Derry while I was still quite young; my younger brother left while I was in prison; I am the only male of the family in Northern Ireland now.

SHANE O'DOHERTY, *The Volunteer*, 1993

AN EARNEST PILGRIMAGE BEGAN. But it did not prove easy going. For Protestant Derry, homeplace of the Apprentice Boys, and Rock 'n' Roll were mutual poison. The Teddy Boy riots over *Blackboard Jungle* and Bill Haley in England had triggered a panic all over loyalist Ulster. It was not merely as if a teenage rebellion loomed but as if the massed forces of Satan had been unleashed, threatening to wipe out all sanity, ditto sanctity: 'Civilisation as we know it', in the words of the *Derry Sentinel*.

For quite some time, all Rock shows, artifacts and films were outlawed. And anyone who challenged this suppression was in for a bumpy ride. Mary Fadden, a comely fifth-former at Northlands, the local girls' school, was expelled for secreting a picture of Jerry Lee Lewis in her desk; discs and posters fuelled bonfires; and Elvis himself was ceremonially torched in effigy at the Brandywell Football Grounds, nailed to a flaming cross. Only Catholics, since idolatry was their nature, were free to devil-worship in peace.

What to do? There seemed only one solution. So my feet took a turn for the worse. In reality, I had ceased to frequent Dinty after a session at which, suggesting that I might benefit from being fitted with metal instep supports, he insisted on taking my inner-thigh measurements. For public consumption, however, I now increased my visits from weekly to almost nightly and, with the freedom thus gained, I went exploring.

Across the river, in Waterside, there was a disused funeral home at which, three nights a week, at 6d a shot, contraband Teen movies could be sat through and sometimes seen, according to the state of the projector. One drawback was that a cross-pollination of embalming fluid and scented wax flowers still hung in the air, an intimation of mortality sickly sweet enough to turn the most fanatic stomach. Still, hunched in the suffocating dark, I drowned myself in *Don't Knock the Rock*, *The Girl Can't Help It* and *I Was a Teenage Werewolf*, had a crush on Eddie Cochran but chose to marry Sheree North.

The Crypt, as it was aptly named, was just the start. At the gatehouse in Donegal I discovered that by perching myself atop a step-ladder, then balancing the family steam-wireless on a stack of *Encyclopaedia Britannica*, 1911, in thirty-four volumes, I could jam my left ear up tight against the soundbox, four inches below my bedroom ceiling, and so receive the faintest static-riddled crackling of Radio Luxemburg, a thousand miles away across Europe; at Thos. Mullen, Tonsorial Artist, on Ferryquay Street, back copies of *Titbits* and *Men Only* tutored me in the hit parades, also in anatomy ('Petunia, 19, is an artists' model and this is one pulchritudinous petal that any Old Master would be proud to pluck'); and at last one night at the Palace, the first cinema in town openly to dare show an Elvis film, half-way through the 'Teddy Bear' sequence in *Loving You*, I heard a siren shrieking above, looked up from my lair in the back stalls and saw the balcony overhead shaking, literally buckling, from sheer humping tonnage of wet-knickered nymphs. 'Earthquake!' the inevitable alarmist hollered and a minor stampede ensued, cravens of all persuasions scrabbling wholesale for the exits, like so many extras from *The Last Days of Pompeii*.

But I myself failed to budge. For this, I knew well, was no earthquake or even holocaust – it was the end of the world. Or leastways, of civilization as we knew it.

NIK COHN, *Ball the Wall*, 1989

DODDS: Middle-class people – with deference, people like you and me – we tend to concentrate on the negative aspects of the culture of poverty. We tend to associate negative values to such traits as present-time orientation, and concrete versus abstract orientation. Now, I don't want to idealize or romanticize the culture of poverty; as someone has said, 'It's easier to praise poverty than to live in it.' But there are some positive aspects which we cannot overlook completely. Present-orientated living, for example, may sharpen one's attitude for spontaneity and for excitement, for the appreciation of the sensual, for the indulgence of impulse: and these aptitudes are often blunted or muted in people like us who are middle-class and future-orientated. So that to live in the culture of poverty is, in a sense, to live with the reality of the moment – in other words to practise a sort of existentialism. The result is that people with a culture of poverty suffer much less from repression than we of the middle-class suffer and indeed, if I may make the suggestion with due qualification, they often have a hell of a lot more fun than we have.

(*DODDS goes off left.*

The dressing-room door is flung open. SKINNER *is dressed in splendid mayoral robe and chain and wears an enormous ceremonial hat jauntily on his head. At the door:*)

SKINNER: You're much deceived; in nothing am I changed. But in my garments!

(*He comes into the parlour carrying robes and headgear for the other two. LILY gives one of her whoops.*)

LILY: O Jesus, Mary and Joseph!

SKINNER: Through tattered clothes small vices do appear; Robes and furred gowns hide all.

LILY: Mother of God would you look at him! And the hat! What's the rig, Skinner?

(*SKINNER distributes the gowns.*)

SKINNER: Mayor's robes, alderman's robes, councillor's robes. Put them on and I'll give you both the freedom of the city.

LILY: Skinner, you're an eejit!

SKINNER: The ceremony begins in five minutes. The world's press and television are already gathering outside. 'Social upheaval in Derry. Three gutties become freemen.' Apologies, Mr Hegarty! 'Two gutties.' What happened to the Orphans' Orchestra?

(*He switches on the radio. A military band. They have to shout to be heard above it.*)

MICHAEL: Catch yourself on, Skinner.

LILY: Lord, the weight of them! They'd cover my settee just lovely. (*To MICHAEL*) Put it on for the laugh, young fella.

SKINNER: Don the robes, ladies and gentlemen, and taste real power.
  (*LILY puts on her robe and head-dress. MICHAEL reluctantly puts on the robe only. SKINNER has the Union Jack in one hand and the ceremonial sword in the other.*)

LILY: Lookat-lookat-lookat me, would you! (*She dances around the parlour.*) Di-do-do-da-di-doo-da-da. (*Sings*) 'She is the Lily of Laguna; she is my Lily and my –'. Mother of God, if the wanes could see me now!

SKINNER: Or the chairman.

LILY: Ooooops!

SKINNER: Lily, this day I confer on you the freedom of the City of Derry. God bless you, my child. And now, Mr Hegarty, I think we'll make you a life peer. Arise Lord Michael – of Gas.

LILY: They make you feel great all the same. You feel you could – you could give benediction!

SKINNER: Make way – make way for the Lord and Lady Mayor of Derry Colmcille!

LILY: My shoes – my shoes! I can't appear without my shoes!
  (*MICHAEL takes off his robe and sits down. LILY joins SKINNER in a ceremonial parade before imaginary people. They both affect very grand accents. Very fast.*)

SKINNER: How are you? Delighted you could come.

LILY: How do do.

SKINNER: My wife – Lady Elizabeth.

LILY: (*Blows kiss*) Wonderful people.

SKINNER: Nice of you to turn up.

LILY: My husband and I.

SKINNER: Carry on with the good work.

LILY: Thank you. Thank you.

SKINNER: Splendid job you're doing.

LILY: We're really enjoying ourselves.
  (*SKINNER lifts the flowers and hands them to LILY.*)

SKINNER: From the residents of Tintown.

LILY: Oh, my! How sweet! (*Stoops down to kiss a child.*) Thank you, darling.
  (*SKINNER pauses below Sir Joshua. He is now the stern, practical man of affairs. The accent is dropped.*)

SKINNER: This is a the case I was telling you about, Sir Joshua. Eleven children in a two-roomed flat. No toilet, no running water.

LILY: Except what's running down the walls. Haaaaa!

SKINNER: She believes she has a reasonable case for a corporation house.

LILY: It's two houses I need!

SKINNER: Two?

LILY: Isn't there thirteen of us? How do you fit thirteen into one house?

SKINNER: (*To portrait*) I know. I know. They can't be satisfied.

LILY: Listen! Listen! I know that one! Do you know it Skinner?

SKINNER: Elizabeth, please.

LILY: It's a military two-step. The chairman was powerful at it. Give us your hand! Come on!

SKINNER: I think you're concussed.

> (*She drags him into the middle of the parlour and sings as she dances.*
> SKINNER *sings with her.*)

LILY: As I walk along the Bois de Boulogne with an independent air,
> You can hear the girls declare, 'He must be a millionaire'
> You can hear them sigh and hope to die and can see them
> sink the other eye
> At the man who broke the bank at Monte Carlo.

> (*LILY drops exhausted into a chair.*)

LILY: O my God, I'm punctured!

SKINNER: Lovely, Lily. Lovely.

LILY: I wasn't a bad dancer once.

SKINNER: And now Lord Michael will oblige with a recitation – *If* –
> by the inimitable Rudyard Kipling. 'If you can keep your
> head when all about you/ Are losing theirs and blaming it on
> you ...' Ladies and gentlemen, a poem to fit the place and
> the occasion – Lord Michael of Gas!

BRIAN FRIEL, *The Freedom of the City*, 1973

O N LEAVING SCHOOL, I studied for three years to be a priest, but eventually decided to give it up. For my degree I studied French and History at Maynooth College in County Kildare. While at university, I spent my summers in France. I first visited St Malo in Brittany in 1960 and then the following year I attended classes at the *Institut Catholique* in Paris where I learned to speak French fluently. Until this time I had never been out of Ireland, not even to visit England.

My European experience allowed me to study Irish history in an objective way and influenced my subsequent thinking very heavily. Once I was able to see the tradition of attitudes which prevailed in Ireland I could grasp the real nature of the problem, which eventually became my central political thesis.

After university and my studies in France, I came back to Derry an educated man and lived in our family's rented council house, which had two bedrooms and an outside toilet. My parents were still very poor, so, naturally, when I secured my first job as a teacher I would turn over my wages to my mother, and she would then give me back something from them for myself.

Our street was still poverty-stricken, with very high unemployment, and, as one of the lucky ones, I was anxious to be able to give something back to the community and do something about the problems of those who were less fortunate.

One of the first things I did after my return to Derry was to involve myself in the foundation of the Credit Union movement. We modelled this on information supplied to us by the enormously successful US Credit Unions. The Bogside in Derry had the first Credit Union in Northern Ireland, of which I was the treasurer, responsible for collecting the money on Friday nights and Saturday afternoons. My wife, Pat, is also from Derry and we were married in 1960, and every Sunday she would read out the Credit Union slips to me and I would fill in the ledgers.

We founded the Derry Credit Union on 30 October 1960 with four people and seven pounds. Today it has fourteen thousand members and twenty-one million pounds.

The people involved with me in founding the Credit Union – all voluntary work at that time – were young teachers like myself, clergy and members of the local community such as Paddy Doherty, Paddy Joe Doherty, Michael Canavan, Seamus Bonner, Dr Jim Cosgrove, John Bradley and Father Anthony Mulvey. It was these same people who were later to encourage me to go into politics.

We were a very small group at the start, but we called public meetings and gradually persuaded people of the benefits of joining. Eventually, I would travel all over Northern Ireland and further, giving lectures on how Credit Unions worked and encouraging other communities to set them up. By the time I was twenty-seven years old, I was president of the Credit Union movement throughout the whole of Ireland – the Credit Union League of Ireland – and international vice-president of the movement throughout the world. At my first international Credit Union meeting, in Dallas, Texas, in 1962, I met Senator, soon to be Vice President, Hubert Humphrey when he addressed the meeting. If I did nothing else in my life other than my involvement founding the Credit Unions, I would be a happy man.

Only a third of the population of Derry in the early 1960s was Protestant, but they were able to govern the city through a process of gerrymandering. This was achieved by dividing the city into three wards, and, since they controlled public housing, they were able to put all the Catholics into one ward and then give that ward just eight seats while the other two wards had six seats each. In this way, even though there were more Catholics in the city, the Protestants always won the elections by twelve seats to eight.

Nationalist politics at that time was understandably based in the negative – complaints about discrimination, about the shortage of housing, lack of jobs and the partition of Ireland. My response was to question the validity of always complaining and to encourage action – after all, weren't our heads and our hands as good as theirs any day, so why didn't we use them? The founding of the Credit Union provided, I felt, a shining example of what could be achieved by working together for ourselves. Self-help was the way forward.

The next step along the self-help road was our decision to attempt to build our own houses instead of asking the politicians to do it for us. So, in 1965, I helped to set up the Derry Housing Association, the founder of which was Father Anthony Mulvey. I became chairman, and we started the slow process of housing our own people. This was facilitated by having our office open during the week and inviting people to come in to discuss their problems.

The outcome was that, upon analysis of the situation, we found that there were three different kinds of housing problem. First, there were those people who could afford to buy their own house, but who did not know how to go about it. When buying a house, it was necessary to borrow from a building society, but first you had to have a deposit. So we organised methods by which these people could save in the bank for when they would need a deposit in order to buy their own house.

The second group of people were those who would have been able to afford to buy their own house but for the fact that their rent was so high, due to landlord exploitation of our housing problem, that they could not manage to save a deposit. In this instance, we took over some terraced buildings, turned them into apartments and let them out to people at double an economically reasonable rent. After two years, we gave them back half the rent as a deposit to buy a new house of their own.

The third group consisted of those who would never be able to afford to buy a house, and our solution here was to build good houses for them to rent at a fair rate. In the first year, in the mid-sixties, we housed one hundred families while in the same year the public housing authority, Derry Corporation (the city council), housed none. However, when we subsequently applied to build seven hundred more houses, the same corporation refused us permission. It was patently clear that our application was turned down because we were building houses in the wrong area, thus upsetting the gerrymandered voting pattern. At this point, we decided that we had no choice but to voice our protest in terms of civil rights.

JOHN HUME, *Personal Views*, 1996

GUARDING ITS WESTERN EDGE, where the Free State impinges on Northern Ireland, the City of Londonderry occupies a commanding position on a hill round the base of which the tidal Foyle sweeps in a broad curve. Its name has always been associated with the Oak (*Dair*); its ancient designation was *Daire Calgaith*: then it became *Daire Columchille* (St Columba's oakwood); and it obtained its present title when the Irish Society of London received grants of land in the time of James I. A deep valley on the inland side of the city, only slightly above tide-level, completes the magic circle of its virginity. With its defiant walls still intact, decorated with 'Roaring Meg' and other ancient pieces of ordnance, its Protestant Cathedral set high on the hill-top, with soaring spire and chapter-house full of keys and cannon-balls and letters of Schomberg, it seems to typify its history: the very street names – Artillery Street, Magazine Street, Lundy's Lane, Mountjoy Street, are redolent of 1689; while Cowards' Bastion and Hangman's Bastion are full of grim suggestion. There is a grimness, too, about the squatting skeleton on the city's coat of arms; but that commemorates a much earlier episode. As is characteristic of Ireland, the dead past is not allowed to bury its dead: and Derry's Prentice Boys and Closing of the Gates and drumming and marching seem natural there. But the memory of the siege and of the gallant resistance of its burghers appears to satisfy it: Derry shows none of the desire to perpetuate political and religious warfare or intolerance to the extent of outrage and murder such as has so frequently in Belfast aroused the reprobation of all right-thinking people. In the working-class areas, which now spread across the valley and far up the opposite slope, the distribution of the emblematic signs placed on the doors at the time of the Eucharistic Congress in Dublin shows that an intimate mixing of creeds and politics need not of necessity constitute an explosive compound. At the same time, the establishment of a 'frontier' a couple of miles out, where the Free State begins, is wholly deplored, for it causes heavy loss equally to the city traders and to the Donegal farmers to whom Derry is an essential market. The city lies on the Donegal side of the Foyle, it should be noted; but the 'Liberties of Londonderry', some twenty-five square miles of land surrounding the town, push back the Free State border.

ROBERT LLOYD PRAEGER, *The Way That I Went*, 1937

FOR 105 DAYS, FOODLESS, and apparently forsaken, they had maintained the struggle; and, at last, their heroism met with its guerdon; and the 'Prentice Boys and the Maiden City became the glory of the North, and the story of their bravery one of the grandest in all the annals of warfare.

Some such thoughts as these stole through my mind as we glided quietly up the river, the maze of houses and streets and monuments and spires enlarging every moment, till the iron bridge which unites the city to the suburb of Waterside appeared, and we were safely moored along the quay. Stepping ashore, we sauntered through the lower streets, and presently we reached the nearest gate, and passed beneath the walls. Everything seemed peaceable enough now, and, as we ascended the steep slope of the main thoroughfare, towards the square Town Hall, with its adjacent monument, and, continuing our course in the same direction, drew near the Cathedral, and paused at the Imperial Hotel, it was difficult to realize that this seemingly quiet locality had once been thronged with famishing soldiers, experiencing all the horrors of a cruel siege; that, even now, a spirit of antagonism lay smouldering in the breasts of the rival populations who inhabit it; and that, only two days before, on the anniversary of the Relief, the curate of the Cathedral had been wounded by a heavy stone, and a bottle containing gunpowder with a burning fuse attached, had been flung in the track of the procession which had been organized to celebrate the event. And, though everything looked so peaceful, the streets were paraded by a large number of soldiers; and an exceptional force of constabulary had been drafted into the city until the Relief Processions and the Catholic festivities in honour of Lady Day were over. Much as we both admired the courage of the people of Derry in the days of old, having regard to all these circumstances, we could not but regret that their posterity should see fit to commemorate it by party displays which, however innocent in themselves, were, to some extent, of the nature of an insult to the local Catholics, and provocative, not merely of rival demonstrations, but of dastardly outrages such as those I have described.

ARTHUR BENNETT, *John Bull and His Other Island II*, 1890

WHEN I WAS A VERY SMALL BOY we used to sing at passing Protestants:

> Proddy, proddy dick
> Your ma can't knit
> And your da
> Won't go to bed
> Without a dummy tit.

We might meet Protestants on the way to school because our school was outside the Bogside. No Protestant lived in the Bogside. The Unionist Party had seen to that. Not that the absence of Protestant neighbours was regarded by us as any deprivation. We came very early to our politics. One learned, quite literally at one's mother's knee, that Christ died for the human race and Patrick Pearse for the Irish section of it. The lessons were taught with dogmatic authority and were seemingly regarded as being of equal significance. Pearse ranked high in the teeming pantheon of Irish martyrdom. There were others. They had all died in the fight to free Ireland from British rule, a fight which had paused in partial victory in

1922 when twenty-six of our thirty-two counties won their independence. It was our task to finish the job, to cleanse the remaining traces of foreign rule from the face of Ireland.

EAMONN McCANN, *War and an Irish Town*, 1974

THE NAME OF THE CITY I WAS BORN IN IS DISPUTED. At the time of my birth it was called Londonderry. Now the majority of its people simply call it Derry. If people in Ireland ask me where I was born I can, if wishing to be politic, say 'The Maiden City' or use the more recent coinage, 'Stroke City'.

I was delivered by a Dr McCurdy. Of that gentleman I know nothing else, but, to me at least, his name is blessed except in fits of depression. It seem I was not expected to live, but I have always delighted in confounding the expectations of others. Father came from further south in Ulster, Co. Monaghan. My natal year saw the start of partition when the island of Ireland was divided into Northern Ireland and what, for some years, was called the Irish Free State.

As every Irish schoolboy knows, or used to know, Derry/Londonderry is often referred to as the 'Maiden City' because of the fight for survival of the Protestant inhabitants during James II's siege in 1689. G.M. Trevelyan, the great historian, wrote: 'The burghers of Londonderry endured the famous siege, facing starvation in the spirit that the citizens of Haarlem and Leyden had shown in like case against the Spaniard.'

The city – whatever name you care to give it – was and is a place steeped in tradition and continuity. Even today, one finds there readily enough a reminder of the brutal facts of history – the walls that have been celebrated in ballads, the River Foyle that leads to the ancient city on the hill and the two cathedrals, not to speak of the British Army presence.

History – or what passes for history – for the Irish has a reality that can be frightening and which can perpetuate ancient feuds. As a boy, from my aunts and mother I heard many a story of the suffering endured by the defiant Protestant citizenry, and in language no less eloquent than that of Trevelyan. I heard of the so-called traitor Lundy who had the same significance for us as Quisling for Norwegians during the Second World War. These tales of heroism and stoic endurance were, it was true, told me in Belfast to which my family had moved. Derry indeed was in decline. The Protestants were moving east as the city became more and more populated by Catholics. But even in true-blue, loyalist Belfast, the hearts of my mother and her sisters were still in the Maiden City of their youth when their lives had centred round the Presbyterian Church in Carlisle Road.

Derry for them – they said 'Derry' in conversation but used 'Londonderry' officially – meant Protestant Derry. History meant

Protestant history. Suffering and heroism meant that undergone by Protestants. There was never a whisper of the sixth century Derry that had become a great centre of missionary zeal, long before we Scots-Irish had settled there – along with some English – sword in one hand and Bible in the other.

Nobody told me of Colmcille who founded a monastery on the hill overlooking the wide tidal river. Nobody spoke of how, in 563, now named St Columba, he created a great Christian settlement in Iona, so spreading the Gospel through pagan Scotland and northern England. Nor did I know of how Irish monks brought Christianity to western Europe after the fall of Rome and of how the saint wrote of his beloved place:

> Were all the tributes of Scotia mine,
> From the midland to its borders,
> I would give all for one little cell
> In my beautiful Derry.

No, not a syllable of all that history was uttered, for the very good reason that my mother and aunts knew nothing of it. Theirs, I repeat, was the Protestant version of history – the near-disaster of the 105-day siege before the boom was broken and ships sailed up the Foyle with food the gallant Protestants. And of course they were gallant and determined, but no more exclusively in the right than their opponents. The past in Ireland, especially in the north, hangs round people's necks like a gigantic albatross.

None of us could foretell that history had not finished with the Protestant city which was so rapidly turning into an Irish Catholic city. Nobody guessed that one day this place would erupt violently, that television would bring names like Creggan and Bogside into English living rooms. It could not be foreseen that on January 30th, 1972, British paratroopers would shoot dead 13 Catholics and that this 'Bloody Sunday' would lead to the burning down of the British Embassy in Dublin. History, God knows, has scourged Ireland for centuries. The pity of it is that it has struck so frequently at elegant, beautiful Derry.

ROBERT GREACEN, *The Sash My Father Wore*, 1997

NOTHING IS MORE AMUSING or instructive than to lounge about a port. We were paddling in the black coal-dust mud of the quays of Derry, refreshing ourselves with the sight of their maritime activity, when a decent man in a sailor's garb addressed us, and gave as an excuse for the liberty, that hearing us speak, he had understood we were French. John Cassidy had in fact sailed a good deal. He knew Havre, Marseilles, and Bordeaux. He was now a boat builder, and the father of ten children. I remarked that it was a heavy charge. He replied simply, 'Sure, and it is, but it is a blessing from heaven. And when God sends the children they must be fed.' A Catholic and Nationalist, John Cassidy questioned us discreetly as to our religion; on learning that we were members of the same Church, he asked permission (which was willingly given) to shake our hands.

Thanks to gentler manners, the religious hatreds that once subjected the country to fire and sword now slumber so deeply that they are thought extinct for ever; but the spark smoulders beneath the ashes, and would be rekindled by a breath of the storm.

MARIE-ANNE DE BOVET, *Trois Mois en Irlande* (*Three Months in Ireland*), 1891
(TRANSLATION BY MRS ARTHUR WALTER)

NOT ONLY WERE THE CITY'S electoral boundaries gerrymandered, houses were built and rented to consolidate unionist political power. Efforts to have a non-unionist deputy mayor came to nothing. The Presbyterian Church did not necessarily agree with this, but said little.

THE REVEREND JOHN DUNLOP,
A Precarious Belonging: Presbyterians and the Conflict in Ireland, 1995

GER AND HIMSELF SPENT A LONG TIME that afternoon outside the Mackey's front gate. The Crescent was quiet, for Protestants didn't play games on Sundays and many Catholics considered that was a good example to follow. Peter Bentham, accompanied by his mother and father, passed them with scarcely a nod. This was no surprise, even though Peter was their friend and played with them every day: Prods were different on a Sunday and you'd get used to that. The good suit and the peaked cap pulled down over the eyes and the big Bible under the arm were declarations of that difference.

'I don't think they're in the house at all,' Ger said impatiently. 'Come on round their back lane and peep over the wall.'

Richmond Crescent houses had been built into the slope of the hill, looking down towards the factory and the Strand Road: beyond that was the Lough Swilly railway station, separated from the river Foyle by the shipyard. The high back lane of the Crescent meant that one could see over the wall at the bottom of Mackey's sloping garden, right into the kitchen. It was a simple matter for an adult to glance in as he passed along the lane, but it was much more difficult for children, who did not have the necessary height.

Sean gave a little leap in the air as he passed and tried to see as much as he could of Mackey's kitchen in the fraction of a second that he was airborne. Ger was smaller, but a better jumper, so they both had about the same short time to ascertain if their true loves were at home. Even if they were, there was no hope of actually talking to them on a Sunday, but even a distant glance of a half-second's duration was worth risking a lot for. Both lads knew that they had to be subtle about it too, as if they were casually walking by and giving two equally casual leaps in the air. One wouldn't like anyone to get suspicious, least of all Mr Mackey, who was in the RUC.

But a half-second look was not enough to let one's eyes get accustomed to the indistinct view through the window. They continued their walk right along the back lane, turned round into the front of the Crescent and completed the circle by aiming for the back lane again: it was all low-key and casual, so that no-one would be any the wiser. Another pair of jumps at the back of Mackey's let them know that there was definitely someone at home, but they had to do the full round of the Crescent again before they could venture another look. As they performed their next despairing leaps, completely disregarding subtlety so as to get a longer view of the kitchen, they were left in no doubt that someone was there: they recognised their true loves' father, making unmistakeable signals to them to be off – and quick about it! They ran.

TOMÁS Ó CANAINN, *Home to Derry*, 1986

ACCIDENT
June 1948

ONE DAY THE FOLLOWING SUMMER I saw a boy from Blucher Street killed by a reversing lorry. He was standing at the rear wheel, ready to jump on the back when the lorry moved off. But the driver reversed suddenly, and the boy went under the wheel as the men at the street corner turned round and began shouting and running. It was too late. He lay there in the darkness under the truck, with his arm spread out and blood creeping out on all sides. The lorry driver collapsed, and the boy's mother appeared and looked and looked and then suddenly sat down as people came to stand in front of her and hide the awful sight.

I was standing on the parapet wall above Meenan's Park, only twenty yards away, and I could see the police car coming up the road from the barracks at the far end. Two policemen got out, and one of them bent down and looked under the lorry. He stood up and pushed his cap back on his head and rubbed his hands on his thighs. I think he felt sick. His distress reached me, airborne, like a smell; in a small vertigo, I sat down on the wall. The lorry seemed to lurch again. The second policeman had a notebook in his hand and he went round to each of the men who had been standing at the corner when it happened. They all turned their backs on him. Then the ambulance came.

For months, I kept seeing the lorry reversing, and Rory Hannaway's arm going out as he was wound under. Somebody told me that one of the policemen had vomited on the other side of the lorry. I felt the vertigo again on hearing this and, with it, pity for the man. But this seemed wrong; everyone hated the police, told us to stay away from them, that they were a bad lot. So I said nothing, especially as I felt scarcely anything for Rory's mother or the lorry driver, both of whom I knew. No more than a year later, when we were hiding from police in a corn field after they had interrupted us chopping down a tree for the annual bonfire on the fifteenth of August, the Feast of the Assumption, Danny Green told me in detail how young Hannaway had been run over by a police car which had not even stopped. 'Bastards,' he said, shining the blade of his axe with wet grass. I tightened the hauling rope round my waist and said nothing; somehow this allayed the subtle sense of treachery I had felt from the start. As a result, I began to feel then a real sorrow for Rory's mother and for the driver who had never worked since. The yellow-green corn whistled as the police car slid past on the road below. It was dark before we brought the tree in, combing the back lanes clean with its nervous branches.

SEAMUS DEANE, *Reading in the Dark*, 1996

THE APPRENTICE BOYS' SOCIETY was set up in 1823, and its twice-yearly commemorations in August and December have been occasion for trouble, including serious rioting, ever since, the degree of trouble depending on the volatility of the political situation at the time. The society has a fine collection of Derry artefacts and documents in its huge Victorian Gothic hall inside the walled city. A senior Boy, William Coulter, showed me around.

'There's the lock of the old magazine where they kept the guns during the siege. Solid brass and it still works perfectly. This is a banner from the Independent Order of Good Templars, a temperance movement led by old Mr Hamilton who ran one of the factories. It's the derelict building at the end of the bridge now. That's a photograph of a demonstration against home rule – and there's one of the guns smuggled in in 1912, a German Mauser.'

There were photographs of Roaring Meg, one of the cannons still to be seen on Derry's walls. The City of London Guild of Fishmongers had supplied it. 'Historically, the charter for the city was Londonderry. The council dropped the name out of prejudice.' The nationalist council had dropped the 'London' part of the name in 1984. David Dunseith had told me that at that time he got a call from an English broadcaster who explained that his newsroom had received a fax from an organisation called the Apprentice Boys of Derry. What puzzled them was that the Apprentice

Boys of Derry were objecting to the fact that the local council had changed its name to Derry City Council. Could Dunseith explain?

Protestants have traditionally called the city Londonderry, and many who didn't have started to do so since the council's action. Some will point out that whereas there was a city called Doire before the London companies arrived, there was no county, so that the county *must* be called Londonderry. Soldiers manning UDR checkpoints would routinely challenge drivers who said they were going to Derry: 'You mean Londonderry?' A response in the negative could well result in a full-scale search of the car. Coulter agreed that the Apprentice Boys called it Derry, and that he did so himself. But if he was writing, he used Londonderry. A member of the District Partnership for Peace and Reconciliation, set up after the ceasefires in 1994, told me proudly that in their efforts to create a 'shared city' this had been the first problem. In the end, he said proudly, they had reached agreement. The partnership's headed paper ended up with 'Derry/Londonderry/Doire', followed by the postcode.

It is common in nationalist areas to see signposts for Londonderry with 'London' painted out. In Limavady, a predominantly Protestant town, there was a signpost for Londonderry and Dungiven. Dungiven, a nationalist town, had been painted off the sign entirely, and Derry had been painted out of Londonderry. The signpost was left indicating that London was just fifteen miles up the road from Limavady.

SUSAN MCKAY, *Northern Protestants: An Unsettled People*, 2000

The Donegal mountains, sitting out there
Blue, blunt heaps of lignite, sad hinterland
To a burning city; and the heavy stone walls
And houses, shops and factories, fronts erased,
Sag into the bog-ground while light title-deeds
Change hands in the silent communion of commerce.
The city's odd shop-keepers, sour and mean enough,
Clang their rat-trap tills and keep the doors guarded.
For there are those who disregard limb and life
Who blast and bomb with red-eyed, mad-dog malice;
Then again there are those who disregard even that,
Who live only for profit and tomorrow's gain.
If things were different there'd be no buts but
Life goes on, has, and somehow always will,
Despite the bombs and assassinations.

We are successful in ignoring these things,
And carry on, forming – from the old twin cultures –
Some new kind of human resistance and bloody-minded calmness.
In a hundred years it will warrant a paragraph
In some history book: the common people they'll call us,
(Our fathers, they'll note, paid a shilling for a rat,
And ate quartered dogs to live), and they'll not know
Or not reckon the fear in pubs, in shops,
The daily bumping over ramps, the body-searches,
The tension of fire-sirens singing in darkness.

SAM BURNSIDE, 'In and Out of Derry', *Walking the Marches*, 1990

ALTHOUGH WE HAD NOT BEEN ABLE to learn anything definite in reference to the Lady Day celebrations, it was evident that something was in the wind, for, at every corner, were stationed small groups of constabulary, and a Highland regiment had just gone down the street with swinging tread, as if they meant business. The *Derry Journal*, the local Home Rule organ, had strongly discountenanced the processions, as being likely to lead to disturbances; and all the better class inhabitants, of both parties, seemed to be of the same opinion, for the place was still in a very excited condition, and the incident which had occurred on the day the Relief was commemorated was fresh in everybody's mind. Descending from the tower, we at last succeeded in ascertaining that, to avoid the chance of conflict, it had been decided that the Catholic bands should not parade the city, but should march directly down to the railway and take the next train for Buncrana. Now, our great fear had been that, by having to leave early, we should miss the procession; but, as we had ourselves arranged to go to Letterkenny by this very train, we found that we should have an opportunity of seeing it to the best advantage; and so we hurried to the station, where already a considerable crowd had assembled in order to watch the start.

We had waited for perhaps ten minutes when we caught the distant strains of a band. The music grew gradually louder, and at last we discerned a number of men and youths attired in showy uniforms, and followed by a ragged multitude, turning the corner of the nearest street and making towards us. The procession was headed by an enormous flag, bearing the motto 'Erin-go-bragh', and, on each side of this, marched a man with a flag that bore the American stars and stripes, the Union Jack being conspicuous by its absence. Among the various insignia which were held aloft by the processionists was a golden harp without a crown, in curious confirmation of my words upon the previous day. There was no disorder, and the procession was not nearly so large as we had expected, though this was doubtless chiefly owing to the feeling that, at the present juncture, it would be unwise to do anything calculated to rouse the passions of the rival sections of the populace.

ARTHUR BENNETT, *John Bull and His Other Island* II, 1890

IN 1689 THE PROTESTANT APPRENTICE BOYS shut the gates of Derry to keep the Catholic army of King James out of the walled city. In 1999 Catholics made a sport of throwing stones from the ancient walls down onto the Protestants outside, and two young Protestant mothers nightly locked the gate of a fence which separated their area from the Catholic city. All's changed in Derry, Protestants so alienated from the city that, although they had 'fought for Derry's walls', they had come to hate the name. The Catholics had captured Derry.

That was how it seemed to the people in the Fountain estate, anyway. An ugly concrete enclave, partly incorporating the old city prison, the Fountain clings to the outside of the ancient walls, separated from the Catholic Bogside by what is, in effect, a peaceline, though that term is only used in Belfast. The peaceline here is a low wall with a high fence rearing over it. Someone had written on the Catholic side of the wall, on Bishop Street: 'Boris Yeltsin is a Prod.'

The young people in the Fountain's thriving youth club were definitely Prods, and they believed they were being punished for it. 'The Catholics think it's their city,' said Carly, whose mother was one of those who shut the gate at night. 'They say, go back into your cage.' It is the last working-class Protestant area on Derry's west bank, known as the cityside. There had been a large migration of Protestants across the River Foyle to its east Bank, known as the Waterside. That is where the big loyalist housing estates are. (It is also where the hospital, the railway station, the port, the city's main industrial area and some of its flashiest houses are to be found.)

We met at the youth club, temporarily using the local primary school while a new one was being built. The school was modern and bright, with lots of children's art on the walls, and a big gym where the younger children at the club were making Easter baskets and cards to give to local old people. 'We're stuck in here and we can't get out. There's nothing to do only the youth club. We've no park nor nothin',' said Carly. She and her friends were all aged between twelve and fourteen.

'The ones in the Waterside can't come over at night cos they'd be scared,' said Lorraine. 'We don't speak to Catholics. Certainly not. Would you speak to people that has broke twenty-eight windows, broke into your cars, stolen them? Them people just demolish everything they see. In town it's Spot the Prods. You get chased. I got a kickin' on my birthday. A gang of girls done it.'

'We do fight wi' them,' admitted Scott. 'But there's not enough of us to go after them. There's a whole swarm of them. They call us Orange bastards and they shout chuckey ar law.' (*Tiocfaidh ár lá* – 'our day will come' – is Sinn Féin's slogan.) 'Aye, there's too many of the fenians,' said Ian. 'On Bloody Sunday about 30 of them naw, 300 – tried to come over. It was a full-scale riot.' He was referring to the annual commemoration of Bloody Sunday. The Fountain is only about a quarter of a mile from Free Derry Corner where the annual commemoration is held.

Exchanges of hostilities were commonplace: 'Brickin', throwing bottles and paint bombs. My brother is eight and he throws bricks. He has to defend himself,' said Ian. 'You can't go to football. Them brickin' and you brickin'. We can't go to St Columb's park across the town – you get spat at. There used to be a big green place and you could run mad. Now we've nothin' only a car park, a school football field, and two wee poky parks, wee square things with rotten logs and rusted ladders.'

The young people said that when they were 'down the town', they knew who was Catholic, and Catholics knew who was Protestant. 'They know to look at us. They have a different accent and they're called things like Majella and Kevin,' said Craig. Linette nodded. 'And the girls have their hair up like a pineapple.' However, just to make it easier for each other, young Derry people wear uniform. 'I went down town in a Rangers top and I got beat up by these boys in Celtic stuff,' said Kyle. 'We were afraid to go down the town at Hallowe'en,' he said. Others agreed. Elaine didn't. 'Youse are lying,' she said. 'We went down the town and no one said a word.' 'I threw a banger at a boy,' boasted Andrew. 'We give them what they give us.' They did, it turned out, spend a good bit of time with Catholics. 'We go on school residentials. Twenty of them from St Brechin's and twenty of us from Clondermot. There's people fight with us on the bus and we get blamed,' said Linette. 'I got called in for "racial language". For defending ourselves.' 'We were forced to make friends with them,' said Ian sourly.

'I keep to my own,' said Emma. Then she said something else. 'See if you talk to Catholics, you get a beating. Some of them are nice.' They talked about a video they'd seen called *Across the Barricades*. 'It's class,' said Emma. 'It's about a Catholic and a Protestant who fall in love.' I asked them if they'd go out with a Catholic. 'My da would beat the life out of me,' said Ian. 'My ma said to me, "Don't you EVER go out with a Catholic",' said Linette. 'I went out with a Catholic,' said Rebecca. 'My mother wouldn't say anything to me.'

'Youse must admit,' said Linette. 'The only ones I'd speak to is half-Jaffs. They're half Prods and brought up as Prods. Even my ma brought one of them into the house and she wouldn't let a Catholic in.' 'I wouldn't trust them,' said Kyle. 'Jaffs' are Jaffas, as in oranges. Young Protestants were often known to young Catholics as 'Orangeys'. 'My ma said, before the fenians burned her out, she'd burn them out,' said Andrew. 'They are just greedy. They don't want our marches but they have hundreds of marches with their oul' priests and all. We're the last Protestants in Derry.'

SUSAN McKAY, *Northern Protestants: An Unsettled People*, 2000

MARY O'CONNELL TOOK JAMES and Major and me to see the burning of a traitor. His name was Lundy. In the time of King James and King William of Orange, Lundy had very grievously offended the City Apprentices. They were never able to forget it. Every year they hung him out from the high Walker Monument and burned him. Walker was the governor of the city at the time of Lundy – so his statue must have got a good deal of pleasure out of the destruction of Lundy's effigy.

At the time of the afternoon when we were accustomed to return from our walk, Mary O'Connell took us out. She turned down the little side street past the grocery shop, which had an uncle who was a monsignor, and instead of going through Bishop's Gate we went directly upon the City Walls, at their widest place, where the Monument was. It was twilight and the cold air was sharpened for frost. There was a great crowd packed around the monument railings. Mary O'Connell put me upon one of the obsolete cannon which always kept their noses out of the gaps, waiting, as black as boars, to snort at the invader. Major got upon the cannon too, behind James who kept telling Mary O'Connell that he wanted to see. Major and I had no desire to see. It got worse and worse, darker and darker, and there was something in the atmosphere that filled you with terror. It was an hour of gloom and doom. When it was almost dark enough for the moon to come out, the people crushed in together and let out an awful roar. They wanted Lundy – the way another crowd had wanted Barabbas. It was so dark that you could hardly see when one person ended and another began. And then, high up in space where the poor stuffed man swung on his gibbet, a star appeared. It stayed poised, waiting for the wind to swing Lundy towards it. As soon as his feet touched it it went off like a meteor and the blaze began. The traitor hung in the heavens like a lantern. He burned from his feet upwards. All his joints went off with cracks and explosions, and rags and tatters fell down in awful, ghostly wisps upon our faces. The more he burned, the more he exploded. It was pure terror to hear and wonder what part of him it was. Everybody cheered, except Major and I. Everybody seemed delighted, but we were delighted when it was all over, when the sparkle stopped and the night was as black as pitch. It was a relief when we got off the Walls, down into the streets where lamps were lit and all was in its customary position.

James pestered Mary to tell him more and more about Lundy. All that she would say was that: 'Lundy had opened the Gates and that he was actually a hero.' He was certainly a hero when he was upon the gibbet. You forgot all about Mr Walker who had the Monument. Father wished to take us up the Monument by the spiral staircase which wound and wound inside it. Mother forbade him to do it. I told him quite politely that I had no wish at all to go up so far to see the view over the city. It was quite enough to peep over the noses of the cannon or, at the worst, over Waterloo Gate or down over Shipquay Gate where you saw the Guildhall and the river and the Ferry Landing. The Gate I liked best was Ferryquay Gate where you could see right down into the pastry cook's where Mother bought buns and chocolates. The cook looked as small as James when you saw him from the top of the Gate.

KATHLEEN COYLE, *The Magical Realm*, 1943

A Green Hill
Far Away

There is a green hill far away,
  Without a city wall,
Where the dear Lord was crucified
  Who died to save us all.

We may not know, we cannot tell
  What pains He had to bear,
But we believe it was for us
  He hung and suffer'd there.

He died that we might be forgiven,
  He died to make us good,
That we might go at last to Heav'n,
  Saved by His precious Blood.

There was no other good enough
  To pay the price of sin;
He only could unlock the gate
  Of Heav'n, and let us in.

Oh, dearly, dearly has He loved,
  And we must love Him too,
And trust in His redeeming Blood,
  And try His works to do.   Amen.

CECIL FRANCES HUMPHREYS (later Alexander),
Hymns for Little Children, 1848

ST EUGENE'S CATHEDRAL

UNA HAS VIVID CHILDHOOD MEMORIES of the cathedral. She recalls the sun streaming through the stained-glass window at the top of the church, making very impressive patterns on the marble columns. She particularly remembers a ceremony called 'Tenebrae' which was held during Holy Week. It was extremely solemn and very theatrical. The books the priests held were slammed shut all at once. It made a frightening yet exciting sound. And then all the lights would go out for a few seconds. The whole feeling was very thrilling and dramatic.

She also remembers trying to disguise her voice at confession since most of the priests were regular visitors to her home in Francis Street opposite the church. However, her bluff was called when a certain priest told her when she'd finished confession to tell her mother to put on the kettle, he was on his way down.

Donal Doherty's present-day church choir gives her a real feeling of confidence. It produces clear, clean, secure singing with enormous control and respect. She thinks his presence as cathedral organist has done a lot to enhance the atmosphere in St Eugene's. A recent performance of Fauré's *Requiem*, for example, was truly wonderful.

ART BYRNE, *Church, Chapel, Meeting House*, 1992

HAVING DIRECTED US to the Catholic Cathedral, this 'terrible asthmatic' bade us good-morning; and, descending into the hollow which lies on this side the city, without the walls, we passed through the poorest part of it, the streets crooked and disorderly, and the houses of the lowest class. It was, we found, the Nationalist quarter; and its slovenliness and poverty confirmed the opinion which, from our talks with various people, we had already been induced to form that, in Derry, at least, the men who were against an Irish Parliament were those who had a stake in the country, and the men who were for it were those who had practically none. Near the monument a Union Jack was waving, to commemorate the Relief; and we observed another flag, of a vastly different significance, its colour green, and inscribed upon it in white letters the words 'Home Rule', which floated triumphantly, as if to bid defiance to the flag upon the walls, from the classic roof of a slaughter-house, an arrangement in which some people would doubtless have discovered a certain appropriateness. Passing the latter, we reached the Cathedral, a large and handsome building, but sadly lacking a tower and spire. The tower had, it is true, been commenced, but never completed, principally, we understood, because it was considered that the foundations would not bear the weight of the superstructure. We were rather early, and, as we waited for the door to open, we chatted with some of the people assembled near it, among whom was a young man who did not hesitate to avow his belief that Home Rule would not benefit the working classes; and that, so long as things were being continually unsettled, as of recent years, good trade was quite impossible, an opinion which, coming from this quarter, somewhat surprised us, for we had been led to believe that the whole of the Catholic inhabitants of the city were in favour of the scheme, an assertion true, no doubt, in the main, but subject to more exceptions than the Parnellites are willing to admit.

The interior of the Cathedral is spacious, and, though not very gorgeously decorated, has a solid and graceful appearance. Large as it was, it was crowded in every part; I was much impressed, not only by the size of the congregation, but by their devout behaviour. Unmistakably, to them, religion was something more than a matter of custom, and church-going something far higher than a conventional habit which it would have been bad form to neglect. Everybody seemed to feel the presence of a sacred influence, to which the distant thunder of the organ, and the lights upon the altar, and the ascending incense administered; and to realize that this was 'none other but the house of God' and the very 'gate of heaven'.

ARTHUR BENNETT, *John Bull and His Other Island II*, 1890

My hand is weary with writing
My sharp quill is not steady
My slender-beaked pen juts forth
A black draught of shining dark-blue ink.

A stream of the wisdom of blessed God
Springs from my fair-brown shapely hand:
On the page it squirts its draught
Of ink of the green-skinned holly.

My little dripping pen travels
Across the plain of shining books
Without ceasing for the wealth of the great –
Whence my hand is weary with writing.

ANONYMOUS, 'St Colum Cille the Scribe', probably 11th century,
in *Ancient Irish Poetry* (ed. and translator Kuno Meyer), 1911

AD 1162

A separation of the houses from the church of Doire was caused by the successor of Colum Cille, Flaithbhertach Ua Brolcháin, and Muircheartach Ua Lochlainn, King of Ireland: and they removed eighty houses, or more, from the place where they were: and Caiseal-an-Úrlair was erected by the successor of Colum Cille who pronounced a curse against anyone that should come over it.

AD 1163

A limekiln measuring seventy feet every way was made by the successor of Colum Cille, Flaithbhertach Ua Brolcháin, and the clergy of Colum Cille in the space of twenty days.

AD 1164

The great church of Doire which is eighty feet long was erected by the successor of Colum Cille, Flahertach O Brolchain, by the clergy of Colum Cille and Muirchertach O Lochlainn, King of Ireland.

AD 1175

Flaherty O'Brollaghan, successor of St Columbkille, a tower of wisdom and hospitality, a man to whom, on account of his goodness and wisdom, the clergy of Ireland had presented a bishop's chain and to whom the presidency [headship] of Hy [Iona] had been offered died in righteousness after exemplary sickness in the Dubh Regles [Black Church] of Columbkille; and Gilla Machiag O'Braonan was appointed in his place in the abbey.

JOHN O' DONOVAN (editor and translator),
The Annals of the Kingdom of Ireland by the Four Masters, Vol. 2, 1856

AD 1173

Murragh Ó Cobhthadh [Coffey], Bishop of Derry and Raphoe, died. He was a man of pure chastity, a precious stone, a transparent gem, a brilliant star, a treasury of wisdom and chief conservator of the canons of the church; after bestowing food and raiment on the poor and needy, ordaining priests, deacons and clergymen of every degree, repairing and consecrating many ecclesiastical establishments and cemeteries, building many monasteries, performing every clerical duty and gaining the victory of devotion, pilgrimage and penance, his spirit departed to heaven in the Black Abbey church of Columcille at Derry on the 10th day of February.

A great miracle was performed on the night of his death viz. the dark night became bright from dusk till morning, and it appeared to the inhabitants that the adjacent parts of the globe were illuminated; a large body of fire moved over the town and remained in the south-east; all the people rose from their beds, for they thought it was day; and it [the light] continued so eastward along the sea.

MacEtigh, one of the people of Keenaught, robbed the altar of the great church of Derry Columkille, and carried away with him the four most valuable cups in Ireland, which were called the Mac Riabach, the Mac Solas, the cup of O'Maoldoraidh, and the crooked cup of O'Dogherty. He broke them to pieces, and took off their valuable ornaments. In three days after the robbery, these precious ornaments and the robber were discovered. He was hanged by Flaherty [O'Maoldoraidh] at the Cross of Executions to avenge St Columkille for having profaned his altar.

OWEN CONNELLAN (editor and translator),
The Annals of Ireland from the original Irish of the Four Masters, 1846

H E WONDERED ABOUT THE THIRTY DAYS PRAYER: it might solve his problem. He scanned the conditions: '... by the devout recital of which, for the above space of time, we may hope to obtain any lawful request.' The world 'lawful' was the snag. Would God think that his prayers for Sue Mackey's conversion were lawful? Praying for a red-haired Protestant girl with freckles to become a Catholic so that she could marry him didn't seem quite right, particularly when she appeared happy enough in her Protestant state. A terrible thought came into his mind: why shouldn't he become a Protestant and marry her? It would certainly be a more practical solution. Protestants seemed to get on a lot better than Catholics in Derry. He was shocked at his own daring in toying with such thoughts. He looked guiltily across at his mother, in case she had somehow divined what was in his head. But it was nice to be thinking of Sue Mackey: the way she ran – as fast as any of the lads – or her speed off the mark in rounders. They said she was good at school, too: he liked that about her.

The thirty days prayer was all of five pages long and didn't offer any indulgences. Sean took that as a good sign of its efficacy: it seemed to be just a straight contract between God and himself, with the Blessed Virgin Mary as a go-between. He had never tried a five-page prayer before, but then he had never in all his life wanted anything with the same intensity that he wanted this. He'd start tomorrow in Portstewart.

Fr O'Loughlin was reading out the stipends now: everybody was listening carefully – far more carefully than they listened to his sermon. He was a soft-spoken man and owned a big St Bernard dog which had knocked Sean down one day as he passed.

'Mrs B. Kane, 9 Barry Street, two shillings and sixpence.' It was a bit above average for Barry Street and sixpence more than last year, though his mother couldn't really afford it. The Culmore Road people who headed the list always gave a pound, but they were in a different world.

'Mr and Mrs J. McCarron, 13 Barry Street, one shilling.' They had more money than his mother, but seemed to have no great interest in advancing themselves. Some people were like that ...

TOMÁS Ó CANAINN, *Home to Derry*, 1986

THE POOR AND THE MARGINATED are here all around us; in the homeless, the suicidal, the unemployed; in the adult (young and old) steeped in bigotry and sectarianism, in the pregnant fifteen-year-old whose boyfriend is in police custody for pushing ...

No more are there enough 'exclusive Sisters' to dedicate themselves exclusively; and so, we work shoulder to shoulder *with* (and not just *for*) all of the other labourers in the vineyard, irrespective of creed, class or colour. The shared satisfaction and achievement of our labours enriches and dignifies *all* of us as children of God, and is a natural healer and reconciler here in our divided and suspicious society ...

As far as I'm concerned, Mother McAuley is alive and well and living in Derry and even, if I may be so presumptuous, in Londonderry!

ANGELA BOLSTER RSM, 'The Story of Mercy in Derry' in
History of the Diocese of Derry (eds Henry A. Jeffries and Ciarán Devlin), 2000

BISHOP JAMES MEHAFFEY OF DERRY AND RAPHOE had been vicar of Kilkeel for several years and therefore knew all there was to know about the Needhams. Dark and slight with a captivating smile though sometimes very sad, he was a powerful example to his fellow Anglican clergy. I never heard him raise his voice, I never saw him angry, I never met anyone who had anything other than good to say of his judgement, his intellect or his character. He should be a paradigm to those who bellow instructions from the pulpit.

There was another remarkable bishop in Derry, in some ways more so, for Bishop Edward Daly stood for the majority nationalist community as God's representative against atheistic terror. It was he who had to console those who had been beaten and threatened; it was he who had to counsel the families of the young men sent to the Maze, many of whose parents would never have dreamed that their children had been seduced into terrorism. He will forever be remembered as the priest pictured waving the white but bloodstained handkerchief while leading a group carrying a dying man towards an ambulance following the infamous and, in my opinion, despicable behaviour of some members of the Parachute Regiment on Bloody Sunday.

There are some reasons for being critical of how the Catholic Church has handled the divisions in Ulster, but Bishop Daly was an inspiration. He saw all sides, he listened, and he interjected always with the greatest politeness. He saw good wherever he could, and he never failed to be where there was trouble or grief or anger. Over many years he was a granite rock which saw the city through. He once told me how, dressed in a sweater and slacks, he had gone down to the Strand Road police station to chat to the new RUC commander over an informal lunch only to be met by the chief superintendent in full dress uniform bedecked with braid, wearing gloves and clutching a cane, who greeted him with a formal salute and an icy glare. Bishop Daly had a very long war and in the end, with his health broken, he was forced into early retirement. I only wish he had been allowed more happiness and more joy.

RICHARD NEEDHAM, Battling For Peace, 1998

Regis regum rectissimi
prope est dies domini.
dies irae et vindictae,
tenebrarum et nebulae,
diesque mirabilium
tonitruorum fortium,
dies quoque angustiae,
maeroris ac tristitiae,
in quo cessabit mulierum
amor et desiderium,
hominumque contentio
. mundi huius et cupido.

The day of the lord, the king most just of all kings, is near; the day of wrath and retribution; the day of darkness and clouds, of wondrous mighty thunder; a day, too, of inescapable grief and sorrow. The love and desire for women will cease as will the battling of men. Love of this world will pass.

ST COLUM CILLE (attrib.), 'Dies Irae' (Day of Wrath)
in Altus Prosator (Great Progenitor), 6th century
(VERSION BY SEAN McMAHON)

All things bright and beautiful,
   All creatures great and small,
All things wise and wonderful,
   The Lord God made them all.

Each little flower that opens,
   Each little bird that sings,
He made their glowing colours,
   He made their tiny wings.

The rich man in his castle,
   The poor man at his gate,
God made them, high or lowly,
   And order'd their estate.

The purple-headed mountain,
   The river running by,
The sunset and the morning,
   The brightens up the sky; –

The cold wind in the winter,
   The pleasant summer sun,
The ripe fruits in the garden, –
   He made them every one;

The tall trees in the greenwood,
   The meadows where we play,
The rushes by the water
   We gather every day; –

He gave us eyes to see them,
   And lips that we might tell,
How great is God Almighty,
   Who has made all things well.   Amen.

CECIL FRANCES HUMPHREYS (later Alexander), 'Septuagesima',
Hymns for Little Children, 1848

> Dowse! Dowse! You're a dirty louse,
> And ye'll never sit in the Commons House.

This was the chant ringing round the streets of Derry from the rougher of those Tories opposed to Mr Sergeant Dowse, the Liberal candidate in the 1868 election. A less refined kind of poetry than Fanny's, the roar just outside her drawing-room window may have made her wince, not only for its literary deficiency, but also for the coarseness shown by her fellow Conservatives supporting Lord Claud John Hamilton. It was no consolation that the Liberals' hooligan element sounded even worse with the cry

> Dowse for ever! Claud in the river!
> With a skivver [skewer] through his liver.

The tranquillity of field and wood and water surrounding her previous homes had vanished. Although today's Bishop of Derry and Raphoe lives outside the city in a desirable suburb, Fanny and William moved in the autumn of 1867 into the heart of town to the then-official residence known as the Bishop's Palace. Except for the cathedral itself, the old palace (still there but no longer associated with the Church) is at the highest point in the city, and its front door opens almost directly onto the important thoroughfare of Bishop Street. Straight across the road is the elegant court-house dating from 1813, and beyond the court-house is William's Cathedral of St Columb, only a minute's walk away. The famous walls of Derry run past what was the bishop's stabling and some servants' quarters, and extend round the back of the palace. There was once a garden of two acres between the great residence and the broad walk on top of the walls. No account exists of this green oasis as it was in Fanny's time, but we do know what it was like in the early part of the twentieth century. Then, another new bishop and his wife found laid out for their pleasure a tennis court, a nine-hole pitch-and-putt course and a cricket pitch. The house had no central heating, and during the winter shortages of World War I the mistress sat in front of a very small fire at one end of her vast double drawing-room wearing a fur coat. That chatelaine had three or four women servants for the house and a man to drive the car. Fanny and William, not very long before her, had cook, butler, page-boys, housekeeper, governess and several maids, as well as men for the garden and the horses and carriage.

They were now wealthy people. William had a crest on his carriage doors and a seat in the House of Lords. The Athenaeum in Pall Mall invited him to become a member – under club rules, an invitation was automatically extended to senior figures in the Church, the Civil Service and the universities – and he thus avoided the ordinary members' usual waiting period of fifteen to twenty years. His income was in the region of £10,000 a year from lands and fisheries, and his palace and garden were rent-free.

VALERIE WALLACE, *Mrs Alexander*, 1995

S T COLUMB'S CATHEDRAL in Londonderry was built by William Parrott (or Parrat or Parratt), who contracted with The Irish Society to erect the structure for £3,400 (its final cost was £4,000). Parrott was closely connected with the Merchant Taylors' Company, and contributed to the development of their settlement at Macosquin. In 1638 he carried out works at Dunluce Castle, Co. Antrim, and was Mayor of Coleraine in 1642. However, Parrott appears to have worked under the general supervision of Sir John Vaughan, who is commemorated in an inscription in the western vestibule under the tower. It reads:

AN DO

1633

IN TEMPLO
VERVS DEVS
EST VEREQ(UE)
COLENDUS

CAR REGIS

9

IF STONES COVLD SPEAKE
THEN LONDONS PRAYSE
SHOVLD SOVNDE WHO
BVILT THIS CHVRCH AND
CITTIE FROM THE GROVNDE
VAUGHAN AED

JAMES STEVENS CURL,
The Honourable The Irish Society and the Plantation of Ulster, 1608–2000, 2000

I N THE MORNING I WALKED up through the deserted town centre to church at St Columbs. (Well, after all, the cathedral was Anglican.) But in my blue moleskins, brown GAP jacket, and open-necked shirt, I felt distinctly out of place. The men were all in dark suits and ties, the women dressed up in Sunday best. Not just out of place, but out of time, for the service took me straight back to my childhood in the 1960s. Even then there had been a hapless attempt at trendiness; here the choristers were firmly in their white surplices and red collars, there was no gregarious 'peace', and the liturgy was the old James I text, in which we beseeched our God to defend all Christian Kings, Princes and Governors, 'and especially thy servant Elizabeth our Queen, and under her we may be godly and quietly governed. *And grant unto her whole Council, and especially Ms Mo Mowlam, that they may truly and indifferently administer justice.*

Above us, high in the nave, hung a series of incredibly faded Union Jacks, with regimental coats of arms in their centres; the one right above me was so old the fabric was falling off. I tried not to think they were symbolic.

On the walls, in a prominent position, was a memorial to Colonel Henry Baker, 'A Governor of the City During the Siege of 1689' (he had taken over from Lundy) and 'Michael Browning, Captain of the Ship Mountjoy of this city, chosen to lead the relieving vessels'. The rest of that glorious resistance was celebrated in the little museum to one side of the entrance. Here, in glass cases, were the very padlocks, rusty now, with which the rebellious Apprentice Boys had locked the gates. Here were fragments of the French flags captured from the Jacobites on 5 May 1689. The original rods were proudly displayed by the altar; holding replacement flags, but with the original fleurs-de-lis.

MARK McCRUM, *The Craic*, 1998

THE GREATEST INFLUENCE, HOWEVER, was MCD which I entered in September 1929. As a student for the Ministry, I was received by the Presbytery of Derry on 20 May 1930, in the Session room in Fahan Church. The events of that evening were to make a deep impression on me. A student, considerably my senior, had to deliver a sermon before the Presbytery. This he did with his hands in his trouser-pockets. When he had finished, before the content was discussed, 'his insulting manner' in addressing the Presbytery with his hands in his pockets was considered on the proposal of the Rev. William Ross of Burt. His manners were not those of a gentleman. He might even behave in this way in the pulpit. The members of Presbytery clearly held that they had a responsibility in this regard. Sadly, there are those today who appear to be ashamed of the Genevan preacher's gown. While not being a great one for dressing up, from that evening I have believed that there is a great deal to be said for treating one's congregation or a Court of the Church with respect.

In my time MCD was a small College consisting of seven professors and five lecturers, with approximately 130–140 students. It was friendly and homely. Each professor knew every student personally. All the students knew each other. In many ways it resembled a family. Everyone was interested in the welfare of his fellows. It also had a distinguished academic record. Each year the majority of the *respondentes* in the Bachelor of Arts degree examinations were Mageemen and women. Each year, they also provided a fairish quota of honours graduates. In many ways the Academic staff resembled personal tutors. While one might have a closer relationship with some fellow students than others it would be unfair to think of anyone not being an acquaintance or a friend. Most of the male students were students for the Ministry of the Presbyterian Church, but there always was a number preparing to be teachers, medical doctors, or candidates for the legal profession. They were drawn from various backgrounds – farms, manses, Saorstat Éireann, teachers, missionaries. The MCD motto probably fitted us, *Fac et Spera* (Do and Hope). Of course some of us excelled in *Spera*, because there had not been enough *Fac*.

THE REVEREND JOHN M. BARKLEY, *Blackmouth and Dissenter*, 1991

Were all Alba mine
From its centre to its border,
I would rather have the site of a house
In the middle of fair Derry.

It is for this I love Derry,
For its smoothness, for its purity,
And for its crowd of white angels
From one end to another.

It is for this I love Derry,
For its smoothness, for its purity;
All full of angels
Is every leaf on the oaks of Derry.

My Derry, my little oak-grove,
My dwelling and my little cell,
O living God that art in Heaven above,
Woe to him who violates it!

Beloved are Durrow and Derry,
Beloved is Raphoe with purity,
Beloved Drumhome with its sweet acorns,
Beloved are Swords and Kells!

Beloved also to my heart in the West
Drumcliff on Culcinne's strand:
To gaze upon fair Loch Foyle –
The shape of its shores is delightful.

Delightful it is,
The deep-red ocean where the sea-gulls cry,
As I come from Derry afar,
It is peaceful and it is delightful.

ANONYMOUS, in *Ancient Irish Poetry* (ed. and translator Kuno Meyer), 1911

P EOPLE KEEP TELLING ME that Derry is different from the rest of Northern Ireland. I am told this is partly due to the size of the city and to a strong sense of local identity. This is the city which was traumatised by the killing of thirteen demonstrators by the army in January 1972. I have neither lived nor worked there, so I went to find out what has happened to the Presbyterians since 1968.

STRAND CHURCH

In 1968 Strand Church on the city side was on the crest of a wave; full of confidence and hope, with a packed church for Sunday worship. Their much-loved and respected minister Dr Montgomery had retired and a new minister, the Reverend Maurice Bolton, had been installed.

The intervening years have been a story of courage, struggle and disappointment. The congregational size has fallen from 500 families to 182. A member of the congregation, RUC Inspector Norman Duddy, was murdered by the IRA in the street outside the church after the morning service in March 1982. While this brought the people closer together, it profoundly shocked the congregation.

One has to understand the nature of a Presbyterian congregation in a place like Derry. It does not consist of a group of strangers who gather on a Sunday for worship, thereafter to scatter. A congregation is a closely knit unit of service and fellowship; with congregational life packed with organisations run by the members; the leaders and the committee are elected by the people and the minister has been called by the people. It is difficult to quantify the effect upon such a fellowship when one of their number is efficiently targeted and murdered outside the church after a service. Such an attack is experienced as an attack upon the church community as a whole as well as an attack upon an individual. People stand by stunned and powerless; a triumph of savagery.

CARLISLE ROAD

When the Reverend Richard Graham came to Carlisle Road, again on the city side of the River Foyle, in 1965, it was to a thriving congregation of four hundred families. It was possible for him to do nearly all of his pastoral work by walking round the parish, for most of the people lived around the church. By 1994 the congregation was reduced to 280 families with only 50 remaining on the city side; the rest have moved across the river to the Waterside. Those who have remained on the city side are mainly elderly. The Sunday School has been reduced from 240 to 80 children. Like Strand Church, it is an aging congregation with few children and increasing leadership problems.

The reduction in the size of the congregations is paralleled in what happened to the overall Protestant population on the city side of the river, which fell from 18,000 in 1968 to 2,800 in 1994. Between 1968 and 1994 13,000 Protestants left the city side; another 2,100 were lost through natural death.

THE REVEREND JOHN DUNLOP,
A Precarious Belonging: Presbyterians and the Conflict in Ireland, 1995

IN CIVITATE VOCATA HIBERNICE *Daire Coluim-cille,* (latine dici potest Boscus Sti. Columbae, Angli autem eam nominant 'Londonderry', nomenclaturam dantes huic loco a sua regia urbe, Londinio in Anglia), quae constructa est ad maris ostium in quod descendit flumen Cladius, vulgo Cláid [*recte*, Foyle], erigi fecit excellentissimus princeps Dominus O'Donnell, ex regio sanguine legitime ortus, conventum magnifice constructum ac bonis multis praeditum, petente R.P. Fr. Reginaldo eundem principem per litteras S. Patris nostri Dominici datas expresse ad illum. Cum hae litterae custodirentur sollicite et reverenter apud hanc familiam usque ad tempus Cromwelli, nugatorium omnino est quod aliqui asserunt de fundatione hujus conventus facta anno 1274. Notum est enim, quod Ordo Praedicatorum, stabilitus a magno Patriarcha D. Dominico, confirmatus sit ab Honorio III in vigilia S. Thomae Apostoli, anno 1216, et quod S. Pater noster obierit 1221; unde concludendum est hanc domum inceptam fuisse inter confirmationis tempus et mortem S. Patris, aut cito postea; ita ut haec fundatio censenda sit facta ante vel intra decennium post mortem S. Dominici. Praeterea vulgaris traditio, custodita in praedicta familia et apud vicinos magnates ac plebem, astruit fundationem istam non esse tam seram; et ab infantia mea audivi a multis, tum saecularibus tum etiam ecclesiasticis fide dignis, hunc conventum esse antiquissimum totius Ordinis nostri in regno Hiberniae.

De filiis autem illius non possum reddere rationem, nisi de valde paucis, etsi indubie plures fuerint quam potuerim invenire.

R.P. Fr. Joannes O'Laighin (*sic*), ex isto conventu, prior Derriensis, post longas carceris aerummas et diuturnam inediam, spretis ingentibus haereticorum pollicitationibus, si fidem desereret Catholicam, mori praeelegit. Retulerunt de ipso concaptivi seipsos vidisse illum sub fervore orationis cubiti altitudine in aëra elevari, et quod ipse tunc fassus sit se vidisse coelestem gloriam ne acerbitati tormentorum succumberet, finalis perseverantiae corona jam praevisa. Strangulatus in patibulo caput ei detruncatum est, et sic martyrio coronatus est.

R.P. Fr. O'Colgan, ex eodem conventu, studuit fructuose in Hispania. Redux in patriam religiose vixit in suo conventu et praedicavit lucide et ferventer usque ad regni debellationem, anno 1691, quo transmaritavit in Galliam; indeque profectus Romam, philosophiam docuit in conventu S. Xisti. Deinde repatriavit, captus autem ab haereticis, biennii integri carcerem sustinuit in civitate Derriensi, obiitque pro fide Jesu Christi in eodem carcere, anno 1704.

Ex hoc Conventu vivunt adhuc:–

R.P. Fr. Dominicus O'Doherty, qui studuit in Hispania cum laude, et in patria delitescit adhuc prior Derriensis, et est probus religiosus.

Fr. Dominicus Columbanus O'Donnell, descendens legitime ex recta linea fundatoris hujus conventus, spreto ac relicto militari vexillo, professionem emisit in conventu S. Crucis, Lovanii. Studet modo in collegio S. Jacobi, Parissiis, estque juvenis magnae spei.

Fr. Petrus Mac Sweeney, professus Lovanii, studet Pampilonae in Hispania.

Fr. Gelasius Dominicus Mac Davett, pro eodem conventu professus Lovanii, studet ibidem.

In the city called in Irish Daire Colum-cille, that is, the Oak-grove of St Columba (though the English call it Londonderry, after the City of London in England), which is built on an estuary into which the river Foyle flows, the most excellent Prince O'Donnell, of royal lineage, raised an endowed and well-appointed abbey at the solicitation of Friar Reginald, who brought a letter specially addressed to him by St Dominic. As this letter was carefully and reverently preserved by this family until the time of Cromwell, what is alleged about the founding of this abbey in 1274 is quite absurd. For it is well known that the Dominican Order, established by the patriarch St Dominic, was confirmed by Honorius III, on the vigil of St Thomas the Apostle, in the year 1216, and that Our Holy Father died in 1221: from which we must conclude that this house was begun between the confirmation of the Order and the death of Our Holy Father, or soon afterwards; so that this foundation should be considered as having been made before the death of St Dominic or within the ten years following. Besides, the general tradition, preserved in the same family and among the neighbouring chieftains and people, holds that this foundation was not so recent; and from my childhood I heard from many, both lay people and ecclesiastics worthy of credence, that this abbey was the oldest of our Order in the kingdom of Ireland.

Regarding its members, however, I cannot say anything except of very few, although without doubt, there were many more than I could get information about.

Father John O'Luinin, of this community, prior of Derry, after long imprisonment and starvation, despising the tempting promises of the heretics, if he would desert the Catholic faith, preferred to suffer death. His fellow-prisoners related that they saw him when in prayer raised in the air a cubit from the ground, and that he afterwards confessed he had beheld a vision of Heaven, vouchsafed lest he should give way under torments, the crown of final perseverance being already in sight. Having been hanged on a gallows, his head was cut off and thus he received the martyr's crown.

Father O'Colgan, of the same community, studied with success in Spain. Returning home he lived piously in his convent and preached with clearness and fervour till the conquest of the kingdom in 1691, when he crossed over to France; and thence having gone to Rome, taught philosophy in the convent of St Sixtus. Again he returned home, but having been captured by the heretics, was imprisoned for two years in Derry and died for the faith of Jesus Christ in the same prison, in 1704.

Belonging to this community are still living:–

Father Dominic O'Doherty who made a brilliant course of studies in Spain, is now prior of Derry; he is still in hiding at home and is a good religious.

Father Dominic Columban O'Donnell, a descendent in the direct line from the founder of the abbey, having spurned and abandoned his military career, made his profession in the college of Holy Cross, Louvain. He is at present studying in the convent of St Jacques, at Paris, and is a young man of great promise.

Father Peter MacSweeney, professed at Louvain, is studying at Pampeluna in Spain.

Father Gelasius Dominic Mac Davett, professed at Louvain for the same convent, is now studying there.

JOHN O'HEYNE OP, 'De Fratribus Derriensibus' (The Friars of Derry),
The Irish Dominicans of the Seventeenth Century, 1706
(TRANSLATION BY AMBROSE COLEMAN OP, 1902)

Fair City, whose long hallowed name,
    Enshrined in history's page,
Shines brightly in the light of fame,
    Through each succeeding age,
When radiant on some sunny morn,
    No lovelier scene than thine
Among the cities that adorn
    The waters of the Rhine!
Thou art the 'Maiden City' still,
    For none has ever won thee;
Enthroned upon thy stately hill
    From childhood I have known thee.
And often when, in later years,
    O'er vanished pleasures mourning,
I've felt the thrill – the joys, the tears
    Of early days returning.
But earlier scenes than these now claim
    The burden of my song,
When monarchs played life's highest game,
    And fought for right and wrong.
The right to worship – to believe –
As conscience guides, and so to live:
For this our forefathers contended,
With this the deadly struggle ended.

And we, their children, now enjoy
What tyrants threatened to destroy –
That faith which makes its votaries free,
And seals a nation's liberty.

'NEMO' (THE REVEREND G.V. CHICHESTER), 'Lines on Derry Cathedral', 1887

1718

JULY 2 My Primary Visitation.

" 5 Goeing (wth ye Dean & Mayor of Derry &c.) to dine at Fawn, we took our way by ye Top of Greanan-Gormely; whence we could see ye Outlets of the two great Loghs of Foyle and Suilly. The word signifies the place where (Queen) Gormely bask'd herself in ye sun. This Lady is s^d to have been wife to Neal o Neal a Quondam-King of Ulster; who kept his Residence at ye Castle of Elagh in this neighbourhood. She was daughter to a prince of ye Highlands in Scotland; and is suppos'd to have gone ye oftner to ye Top of this Hill to look towards ye Countrey where she was born, ye point of Cantyre being to be seen hence. Here are Remains of a Fort of Stones, like that of Maiden-Castle upon Stanemore, around wch are Cavities or Lusking-Holes. Not many Raths (or Danish Forts) in this Countrey.
NB. The Mountain of Sleaver-Snaght (ie Snowdon) is the highest in Inchowen; on the Top whereof, saies M^r McManus, there are Beds of Shells (of Oysters, Cockles, and Muscles) wch have laid there since Noah's Flood, and have alwaies a moisture on 'em at High-water. Qu.
The Isle of Inch, in Logh Suilly, is in ye parish of Temple-Moor. The Oysters here as good as at Colchester.

JULY 27 I held an Ordination at Londonderry for ye necessary occasions of ye Diocese; wherein Two Dublin-Batchelours (Mr Cha. Vaughan and Mr Gustavus Hamilton) and three Scotch Masters (Mr John Egleson, Mr Ralph Davenport and Mr Sam. Law) were ordain'd: The two former Deacons, and ye other three priests. No Licences, pending ye L^d primate's Inhibition.

AUG 1 I read prayers (first and second Service) at Londonderry; Col. Michelburn's Bloody Flag being hoisted, ye first time, on ye steeple. p.m. Great Guns & Volleys. Even'. Spendid Treat in ye Tolset, Fireworks & Illuminations.

" 2 Saturday, in ye evening, Mr Dean and I met (with a coach & four) Dr Wye ye Primate's single Commisioner; ye expected B^P of Down excuseing himself in a L^r to me. The next day (Sunday) we carry'd him to Church; treated him at Dinner &c. The next morning (Munday) he put on his Scarlet Gown in ye Vestry; where his commission was read and ye B^P Dean & Chapter visitted, wthout any ones sitting down. Thence I follow'd him to my Throne; and (Dr Ward's excellent Sermon ag^t Free thinkers ended) the Clergy were call'd, and generally appear'd. The Church-wardens had Articles given, to wch they were to answer immediately. The Visitation was adjourn'd till Nine on Tuesday-morning – But ye comm^r left us about that hour, & (from the Confines of ye Diocese with that of Rapho) sent me a Relaxation. NB. The Visitation (of ye Clergy) was open'd with a public Reprimand of ye AB's Apparitor for his Rudeness, in offering to serve me with an Inhibition two days before my own Visitation.

WILLIAM NICOLSON, BISHOP OF DERRY, Diary, 1718

SUNDAY MORNING. HOLY PICTURES, crucifixes, statuettes of the Blessed Virgin, mass cards, and other religious paraphernalia abound in Creggan houses, but attitudes toward the church vary. One mother of thirteen who has a son inside and has been deserted by her husband says, 'I'm a great believer in prayer.' One Republican mother of eight says, 'I go to mass and I believe in God, but I don't need the local clergy. They're all behind the peace people, the do-gooders. They refuse to come to grips with the problem, which is alien rule.' A local community worker says, 'The church took away some of our responsibility. A priest would walk into a room with pink wallpaper and say, "That's lovely green wallpaper," and no one would tell him different.' A Sinn Féin supporter says, 'Even if we beat the British, we'll never beat the church; people do what the priests tell them.' Some who have grown up in the Creggan talk of the dependencies here, on Britannia's dole and Rome's religion and – perhaps first and foremost – on their mothers, primal centers of the home, bearing children, bringing them up, cleaning, cooking, granting or withholding sex, even working part-time, and of course making sure their brood go off to church to learn of sins venial and mortal and the possibilities of hellfire – the faith.

And even if, as some believe, the church has less influence than it did, it still dominates the Creggan's social life through the Parochial Centre, with its gym and hall; and the most conspicuous structure on the estate is St Mary's Church. Here the Creggan's rites of passage occur. Here take place baptisms, first communions, marriages, and funerals. This is where on February 2, 1972, the funeral service was held for the thirteen – six from the Creggan – who were killed on Bloody Sunday. Here four priests, who live in a comfortable residence behind the church, take turns saying mass (three masses each weekday and six on Sundays) and hearing nightly confessions in old-style confessionals or – the new style – private rooms. The church is a gaunt concrete-beam and granite-block building, painted a chilly grey-green. Father James Doherty, the youthful, go-ahead administrator of the parish, wants to alter the pre-Vatican II layout in order to bring the priest into the congregation and the congregation around the priest. The church seats 1,500 people and is crammed at the Sunday-morning masses.

At the 10 A.M. mass, which Father Doherty is celebrating, the congregation is mostly women and children. The junior choir is giving its inaugural performance at a mass. Several dogs have got in and are wandering around, as in Dutch churches in the seventeenth century. A few babies are burbling or crying. Today's gospel is Saint Matthew 18, verses 21–35, the parable of the talents. How often should I forgive the man who injures me? Seven times? No, seventy times seven, said Jesus. Father Doherty preaches on this theme, the game of resentment: a feud is between families; between nations it is a war; a new game is needed called forgiveness – a tough game to learn, but it is the only game which everyone wins.

The mass is in English now, and the priest celebrates it facing the people. For the creed the congregation rises; they pray that 'we may heal the wounds that mutual intolerance has inflicted upon us.' Lord hear us. There is a chance for private prayer for the departed, the sick, for a better house or the means to pay the savage fuel bills. The Lord's Prayer is said, and then the congregation is encouraged to offer one another a sign of peace. Some, mostly those up front, exchange hand clasps. At communion there is a rush for the altar rail; half the congregation goes up, and Father Doherty needs the help of the other priests to lay the hosts upon the outstretched tongues. A prayer for peace is said by all, robustly, and in the calm that follows there are announcements: This is the twenty-ninth Sunday of the year; at the preceding Sunday the collection amounted to £770. Father Doherty speaks the last words: 'This mass is ended. Go in peace.'

ANTHONY BAILEY, Acts of Union, 1980

A NEW ROMAN CATHOLIC CHAPEL at Waterside is in contemplation. Subscriptions towards its erection are collecting by the priest in England and Scotland. Before the erection of the chapel in Ballyshasky the

Roman Catholic congregation attended divine service in the townland of Ardmore and in Fincairn glen, in situations admirably adapted for concealment during the time of the Penal Laws.

The Ardmore Altar, as it is called, which is adjacent to Mr Smyth's house, stands in the depths of a thick wood, on a green platform about 20 feet in length and on the brink of a fearful precipice overhanging the Faughan. The altar, on which mass was celebrated, is a wall about 8 feet long with a projecting table of loose stones and 2 flags forming steps; above it is a birch tree.

The Fincairn Altar is an accidental stone which the priest elected as being well adapted for his purpose.

DAY, McWILLIAMS, ENGLISH, and DOBSON (eds),
Ordnance Survey Memoirs of Ireland, Vol. 34: Clondermot and Waterside (1831–8), 1996

THE MOST POPULAR PAGE at Mrs McCreadie's was the one – or sometimes two – that contained the *In Memoriams*. It made me think that there was a sort of cult of death in Ulster. There certainly was one in Derry. It was not merely a list of obituaries saying 'So-and-so died yesterday' – it was a sheaf of tributes to people who had died years ago. '11th Anniversary', one read, and another '15th Anniversary', and I saw one that commemorated the twenty-second anniversary of a parent's death. And with each tribute was a poem:

> The mother is someone special, patient, kind and true,
> No other friend in all the world will be the same as you.

Or,

> Sweet are those memories, silently kept,
> Of a mother I loved and will never forget.

Or,

> We never fail to think of you
> We never cease to care
> We only wish we could go home
> And find you sitting there.

There were hundreds of these in the paper every day, often a dozen or so to the same person, invoking the prayers of St Columba – the sixth-century Irish missionary – and 'Mary, Queen of Ireland'. The Virgin Mary had been elevated to the Irish throne. Mothera God, as Mrs McCreadie said.

PAUL THEROUX, *The Kingdom by the Sea: A Journey Around the Coast of Great Britain*, 1982

I HAVE LATELY ASCERTAINED FROM the Very Rev. Neal Devine, PP, Cumberclaudy, that Dr M'Davitte, after his elevation to the episcopacy, resided for some time in the parish of Lower Moville, in the townland of Ballybrack, in the house now occupied by a man named Clyde. The penal laws were often wielded with terrible severity during those times, and, owing to the persecutions the good bishop received from the Carey family, who owned considerable property on the banks of the Foyle, he was obliged to leave Moville, and take up his residence at Claudy, on the banks of the River Finn. Father Devine derived this information from the Rev. Dean M'Cafferty, who was a contemporary of Dr M'Davitte. He founded a little seminary at Claudy, on the banks of the Finn, and became president and principal professor. The house in which it was held is still standing, but has been long since converted into a farm-house. It is a plain, thatched building not unlike the farm-houses of Ulster. The only thing that seems to recommend it is the great beauty of the locality. A number of young men were soon collected under its roof. Thanks to the old hedge-schoolmaster and the classical teacher, many such young men could be easily found anywhere in Ireland, even during the worst of the penal days. A logic class was formed, consisting at first of about twelve students. One who was present on the occasion, and wrote a short account of what passed, tells us that 'on the first day the logic class met, and as the good bishop began to deliver his first lecture, his big heart was filled to overflowing, and the warm tears came trickling down his cheeks. They were tears of joy. Twelve students in a logic class in Ireland, during the last quarter of the eighteenth century, was a great event. It evoked the Irish history of bygone days. It reminded the worthy prelate also of the schools, and the colleges, and the many happy days he had spent in "lovely France."' The little seminary has its sunny memories and its hallowed recollections. It formed the nucleus of the priesthood of the diocese in which it was situate, and furnished some worthy priests to a neighbouring diocese besides. The good bishop has long since been gathered to his fathers. He sleeps in his native parish, and the mountains on which he walked in youth overlook his grave. Of late, a worthy successor in the see of Derry, the Right Rev. Dr Kelly, has erected a tablet to perpetuate his memory in the Church of the Long Tower, Derry.

THE REVEREND JAMES McLAUGHLIN, *The Bishop of Derry*, 1879

She appears tired, though dressed in fresh, white stone,
And bows the bandaged snowdrop of her head –
Pleadingly to the bus – which hurries on
And leaves her stranded in my childhood,

Mother of small contritions, great hopes
And the lyric boredom of the rosary
When miracles seemed at our fingertips:
She is much younger now than formerly,

And in her narrow, girlish hands, she weighs
Not holiness, but a frail, human idea
That might accomplish anything – dismiss
An army – or, like childhood, disappear.

CAROL RUMENS, 'Passing a Statue of Our Lady in Derry',
Selected Poems, 1987

Robad mellach, a Meic Muire,
 dingnaib rémenn
ascnam tar tuinn topur ndílenn
 dochum nÉirenn.

Co Mag nEólairg sech Beinn Foibne
 tar Loch Febail,
airm i cluinfinn cuibdius cubaid
 ac na helaib.

Sluág na faílenn roptís fáiltig
 rér seól súntach
dia rísad Port na Ferg fáiltech
 in Derg Drúchtach.

Rom lín múich i n-ingnais Éirenn
 díamsa coimse;
'sin tír aineóil conam tharla
 taideóir toirse.

Trúag in turus do-breth formsa
 a Rí rúine –
Uch! ní ma-ndechad bu-déine
 do Cath Chúile!

Ba ma-ngénair do macc Dímma
 'na chill chredlaig
airm i cluininn tíar i nDurmaig
 mían dom menmain:

Fúaim na gaíthe frisin leman
　　ardon-peitte,
golgaire in luin léith co n-aite
　　íar mbéim eitte.

Éistecht co moch i Ros Grencha
　　frisin damraid;
coicetal na cúach don fhidbaid
　　ar brúach shamraid.

Tréide as dile lem for-ácbas
　　ar bith buidnech –
Durmag, Doire, dinn ard ainglech,
　　is Tí Luigdech.

Ro grádaiges íatha Éirenn
　　deilm cen ellach;
feis ac Comgall, cúairt co Cainnech,
　　robad mellach.

*It would be delightful, Son of Mary, in strange journeys to travel over the
sea, the well of floods, to Ireland.*

*To Mag nÉolairg by Benevanagh across Lough Foyle where I would hear
fitting harmony from the swans.*

*This host of the seagulls would rejoice at our swift sail if the dewy Derg [his
ship] were to reach welcoming Port na bhFearg.*

*Sorrow filled me leaving Ireland when I was powerful, so that mournful grief
came to me in the foreign land.*

*Wretched the journey that was imposed on me, O King of Mysteries – ah,
would that I had never gone to the battle of Cúl Dremne!*

*Lucky for the son of Dímma in his pious cell, where I used to hear westwards
in Durrow the delight of my mind:*

*The sound of the wind playing music to us in the elm-tree, and the cry of the
grey blackbird with pleasure when it had clapped its wings.*

*To listen early in Ros Grencha to the stags, and the cuckoos calling from the
woods on the brink of summer.*

*I have left the three things I love best in the populated world – Durrow,
Derry, the high angelic homestead, and Tír Luigdech.*

*I have loved the lands of Ireland, I speak truth; it would be delightful to spend
the night with Comgall and visit Canice.*

ANONYMOUS, 12th century, in *A Golden Treasure of Irish Poetry AD 600–1200*
(eds David Greene and Frank O'Connor), 1967

THE CHURCH'S INSISTENCE ON controlling the education of Catholic children affected not only those directly at the receiving end. Through the parish Building Fund it involved the whole community. The price of opting out of the state system was that the church authorities had to find thirty-five per cent of the cost of school buildings. In a depressed community with a high birth-rate and a thirst for education this was a considerable problem. It was answered with sales-of-work, jumble sales, Christmas bazaars, lotteries, Sunday night concerts, silver collections on the third Sunday of each month, pantomimes, door-to-door collections, and much else besides. All these required volunteer workers with high motivation. For some, the parish Building Fund became not so much a spare-time activity as a way of life. The collection of money and articles for sale and the selling of tickets for weekly functions kept every household in almost daily contact with the church, provided the occasion for constant, repeated renewal of commitment to it.

The intellectual diet served by the church, the schools and the Nationalist Party was supplemented by the local paper, although not to the extent of providing any variation. Everyone in the area read the *Derry Journal*. The *Journal* appeared thrice weekly until 1958, when it became a biweekly, published on Tuesdays and Fridays. The harmonizing voices of the church and the Nationalist Party spoke to us from its editorial columns. These were couched in a curious, florid style which may be peculiar to Irish provincial newspapers. The word 'forsooth' was commonly employed to indicate emphasis. The *Journal* was, and is, bitterly anti-Unionist, passionately pro-Fianna Fail, reverently Catholic and hysterically anti-communist. It never wrote 'Northern Ireland', always '"Northern" Ireland'; never 'Londonderry', always '"London" derry'. Even the punctuation was patriotic.

EAMONN McCANN, *War and an Irish Town*, 1974

FROM DERRY SUSAN MONTGOMERY sent a letter to John and Margaret Willoughby in England through William, one of John's brothers, with her impressions of her husband's diocese, of which an extract is printed below.

Derry
8 October 1606

We are settled in the Derry, in a very pretty little house built after the English fashion, but somewhat small for our company; but we shall make it bigger if you and Piggy [i.e. Margaret] will promise to come and dwell with us. I doubt not if you were here but that you would like the country well enough. I thank God I like it indifferently well [i.e. well enough] thus far and I am made [to] believe that we shall like it everyday better than [the] other. We have our fat cattle and fat sheep brought in by our tenants as fast as we can use them, and we need [i.e. lack] no good company, as my cousin William can show you, to help eat it up.

I find Derry a better place than we thought we would, for there are many of our [English] country folk, both gentlemen and gentlewomen, and as brave they go in their apparel as in England ... The most thing that I mislike is that the Irish do often trouble our house [for alms], and many times they do lend to us a louse, which makes me many times to remember my daughter Jane who told me that if I went to Ireland I should be full of lice. I pray [to] see the poor soul sometime ... I wish her with me now, but I hope in God it will not be long before she shall see her and all our other good friends in England.

... Mr Montgomery ... has many thousands [of] acres of as good land as any in England: ... he has great suit made unto him by diverse [persons] for it. If my cousin William does dispraise the country believe him not, for truly it is a fine country.

HENRY A. JEFFRIES, 'George Montgomery, First Protestant Bishop of Derry, Raphoe and Clogher (1605–1610)', in *The History of the Diocese of Derry* (eds Henry A. Jeffries and Ciarán Devlin), 2000

AT LAST, ON AUGUST 18TH, 1856, four-and-a-half years after the Lord Chancellor sanctioned the scheme for the College, the foundation stone was laid.

For the Trustees and friends of the College this was an important day and the occasion was attended with appropriate ceremony. Mr Dill read the 132nd Psalm and some verses from the fourth chapter of Zechariah; Dr Brown gave an address covering the history of the enterprise and outlining their hopes; and the Governor of the Hon. the Irish Society laid the stone. 'A large portion of the landlords and gentry of Derry and the surrounding country' attended with the Mayor and Aldermen, and a great crowd and 'the greatest enthusiasm was manifested throughout the proceedings.' Dr Brown, whose views on matters concerning Magee were not always perfectly objective and impartial, was in his best form. 'Having visited all the Scotch Colleges and the Queen's Colleges in Ireland,' he claimed, 'and also the Colleges that compose the University of Oxford, and many Colleges on the Continent, I am happy to say that in point of site the Derry College will excel them all.' And once again the catholic vision of its founders was affirmed. 'No surly janitor shall stand at the gate to say to men of any denomination, "Here is a fountain of science and piety at which you may not drink." On the contrary, men of every creed and no creed, if they conform to the laws of order and decency, may attend its lectures and share its literary distinctions.'

Victorian rhetoric easily seems pompous to us to-day, but the satirist was there too, and a somewhat irreverent account of the proceedings from the pen of a contemporary rhymester. 'The Hermit of Derry,' has survived:

> Bright was the morn, unclouded was the sky,
> When Presbyterians with their heads on high,
> Repaired beyond the Maiden City's walls
> To found a College with its lofty halls
> And stately domes, that all the world might see
> The princely bounty of defunct Magee.

And according to the 'Hermit,' not all were overwhelmed by the solemnity of the occasion:

> Some laughed and others flirted, but in fine
> The major part were itching for the wine.

THE REVEREND R.F.G. HOLMES, *Magee 1865–1965*, 1965

THE INCOME OF THE PARISH PRIEST is properly at the discretion of the laity, but the following are the parochial rules. Every head of a family pays annually in the following proportion: gentleman 1 pound, farmers 10s, artisans 5s, cottiers and servants 2s 6d. In addition to the above, they receive fees for marriages, christenings, funeral services etc. The several remunerations are thus regulated: marriage of a gentleman, farmer or grazier 1 pound 10s; marriage of a tradesman, cottier or servant 16s; christenings for the rich 10s; christenings for the poor 2s 6d; station, office etc. 5s; funeral service 5s.

The above are cheefully paid, the stipends reluctantly and in many cases not paid at all, especially by the lower classes. The richer farmers give seed-oats to the clergy, a barrel or half-barrel annually, the poorer, butter, yarn, eggs, fowl etc.

DAY, McWILLIAMS, ENGLISH, and DOBSON (eds),
Ordnance Survey Memoirs of Ireland, Vol. 34: Clondermot and Waterside (1831–8), 1996

16 July 1782

Yesterday evening in consequences of an invitation the different Volunteer Companies of the city marched to the review ground where they were politely entertained by the Rev. Mr Lynch, the Roman Catholic clergyman of Londonderry. The Rev. Mr Black (who so eminently distinguished himself in favour of toleration at Dungannon) was also present. This act of hospitality is a pleasing instance of the liberal spirit of the times leading us to charity and brotherly love, the genuine fruits of the Christian religion.

3 September 1782

On Saturday last the Rev. Dr McDavitt the Roman Catholic Bishop of the diocese of Derry, the Rev. Dr O'Donnell titular dean of the said diocese, the Rev. John Lynch, the Rev. Laurence Regan, the Rev. Eugene O'Callahan, the Rev. John McKane, the Rev. James McFeely, the Rev. John McLaughlin, with several other persons of the Romish persuasion appeared before the Honourable Mr Justice Lill in open court and took and subscribed the oath of allegiance as prescribed by the late Act of Parliament for that purpose.

17 September 1782

A liberal subscription is now raising among the Protestant gentlemen and inhabitants of the parish of Glendermot in order to enable the Roman Catholics of said parish to erect a place of worship for themselves. Surely such frequent instances of generosity and benevolence must beget in the minds of our Catholic brethren a sincere disposition to banish all religious prejudices and, by cultivating every social affection, render the people of Ireland a united and happy and a powerful nation.

London–Derry Journal, 1782, printed in
Aspects of Irish Social History 1750–1800 (eds B. Trainor and W.H. Crawford), 1969

LOOKING BACK IT IS SAD TO THINK that clergy of all denominations working in Derry, although serving the same Lord Jesus and entrusted with proclaiming the Gospel message of reconciliation, made no attempt to get to know each other. We remained in our own little ghettos and it never once occurred to us that by failing to reach out to our fellow Christian priests or ministers we were falling short of the teaching and example of the One Lord whom we all professed to serve. Church of Ireland clergy occasionally met Presbyterian and Methodist ministers at weddings and funerals and from time to time might exchange greeting on the streets, but, since marriages between Protestants and Roman Catholics were frowned on by both sides and funerals were single-denominational affairs, no such opportunities were available for even a brief encounter with Roman Catholic priests. Among the Roman Catholic clergy I knew only Bishop Farren, Monsignor Doherty, whom I met on the Education Committee, and Father Jim Coulter, later Head of St Columb's, a large Roman Catholic college in Derry. In those days he was Roman Catholic chaplain to Magee University College where I lectured part-time in philosophy. Jim Coulter was a light-hearted man with a choice sense of humour, about the same age and build as myself. During long discussions which we had in the hostelries of Donegal and in the rectory we discovered we had much in common, in particular the vision of a united community in Derry, free of sectarian bitterness and sterile political strife, with all working together to realise the full potential of our historic city.

Shortly before I left Derry he invited Daphne and myself to a farewell meal in Roneragh House Hotel, on the shores of Lough Swilly, to recall past times together and to wish us well as we set out for Dublin and St Patrick's. Being a pipe smoker himself and no doubt thinking it would make a suitable gift for another contented pipe addict, he presented me with a very large, most unusual reddish-amber pipe ashtray. As it sits on my table that ashtray is a daily reminder of a genial companion and a very good man who has since died, tragically, of cancer.

It was Jim Coulter who introduced me to a young teacher who shared our hopes for change in Derry and with whom I have remained on friendly terms ever since. His name was John Hume. A moderate socialist with no tincture of sectarianism, John was happy to work within the prevailing political structure in the North to achieve a fair deal for all. Latterly it has been said he has become more Nationalist in his thinking, doubtless in view of the failure of the power-sharing executive which seemed to rule out the possibility of an internal solution. He felt there must be an all-Ireland dimension and this was later enshrined in the Anglo-Irish Agreement.

(DEAN) VICTOR GRIFFIN, *The Mark of Protest*, 1993

W E FOUND R.J. BLACK IN A corner among the sailors at Derry. He always took a back seat. Alas, I always found myself pushing forward to the front, a Peter rushing ahead, where angels fear to tread. But that is why I appreciate my sainted brother Black all the more, because, had he lived in apostolic times, they would have called him *John*. He was the Apostle John of Londonderry. We saw him many a time push weaker and unworthier men forward, and he would take a back seat, sit in a *corner with the sailors*.

Ireland has given us some great sinners, but it has given to the world greater saints. In the higher natures of the Irish race there is a combination of gift, grace, and genius, often unequalled and seldom surpassed by any people. Statesmen, senators, soldiers, and other servants of the Queen – as Ambassadors, all of Irish blood have stood in the very front rank. Irishmen have their weaknesses and limitations, and they know it. But, we are not thinking so much of her sons eloquent to speak, gifted to write in prose, or poetry, brave to fight the enemies of the Queen, but rather humble saints, such as R.J. Black, of Derry. I came into touch with this great personality in connection with the work of the British and Foreign Sailors' Society. I was led to expect great things from our missionary deputation, William Lyons, of Belfast, who had a genius for finding out in town and ports visited, both men and women, good and true. The impression, however, made on my mind by this unique character is ineffaceable. It was good of God to permit association with such a man in happy service for his sailors. Providence placed him in a little corner of the Maiden City, but Grace brought him out, broke the *boom* and sent him, as it were, careering over the oceans of God: 'for the King had at sea a navy of ships.'

THE REVEREND E.V. MATTHEWS, 'Mr R.J. Black in a Corner with Sailors' in
R.J. Black: His Life and Work, 1901

W<small>E WERE NEAR FIVE HOURS</small> going fourteen miles, partly on horseback, partly on foot. We had, as usual, a full house at Londonderry in the evening, and again at eight on Sunday morning. In the afternoon we had a brilliant congregation. But such a sight gives me no great pleasure; as I have very little hope of doing them good: only 'with God all things are possible'.

Both this evening and the next I spoke exceeding plain to the members of the society. In no other place in Ireland has more pains been taken by the most able of our preachers. And to how little purpose! Bands they have none: four-and-forty persons in society! The greater part of these heartless and cold. The audience in general dead as stones. However, we are to deliver our message; and let our Lord do as seemeth him good.

JOHN WESLEY, *Journal*, Thursday 20 May 1769

S<small>T COLUMB'S CHURCH,</small> (*Duibh Regles, or Duv Regles,* i.e. 'Black Abbey Church', so called to distinguish it from the next,) stood near the monastery in the dense part of the grove. The ruins of it were to be seen in 1520.

Teampull Mor, (Temple More or great Church,) erected in 1164, was one of the most distinguished ecclesiastical structures built in Ireland previous to the settlement of the Anglo Normans, in the twelfth century. It was erected under the superintendence of Flahertach O'Brolchain, (Hibernicè, O'Brollaghan, Anglicè Bradley or Brolley,) *Coarbe* (successor) of Columbkille, assisted by Muirchertach O'Loughlin, a Chieftain: 'eighty houses' or huts were removed to make room for it and the accompanying buildings. This Church gave the name of Templemore to the parish in which the City of Derry is situated, and which sometimes went by the name of Termonderry.

The long or round Tower was adjacent to the Temple More; both stood without the space occupied by the present city, on the ground now allotted to the Roman Catholic Chapel and Grave-yard, and with the exception of the belfry, they were partly destroyed by Sir Henry Docwra's troops, in 1600, for the purpose, it is stated, of employing the old materials in the construction of *his* city.

The Tower survived till after the Siege, being marked on the maps or plans of that time as the 'Long Tower or Temple More', and in the Charter of Derry, it is called 'St Columbkille's Tower'. The street or lane leading from Bishop's-gate to the Roman Catholic Chapel, was its site, and still bears its name.

The Dominican Monastery and Church were founded in 1274. The number of friars in this Abbey previous to the suppression, was generally 150, and a convent of the same order was maintained in Derry till a late period, and which, in 1750, contained nine brothers. It is supposed to have stood on the north side of the City, without the wall.

The Monastery and Church of the Franciscan or Begging Friars stood according to the inquiry of 1609, 'on the North side of the bog', on the ground now occupied by Abbey-street, William-street, and Rossville-street; there were three acres of land attached to these buildings.

The Convent and Church of St Augustine were situated within the limits of the present City. The Abbey occupied the site of the See-house or Bishop's Palace, and its church in the rear, in the space now enclosed between the Palace and the City Wall. Both are supposed to have been erected in the close of the thirteenth century, and not sooner; so that St Columb's Monastery could not have been of that Order. The Augustinean Church seems to have been the only religious house preserved on the erection of the City. It was repaired and used by the Londoners previous to the erection of the Protestant Cathedral, which was finished in 1633, and on ground never before occupied by any other religious house. On the completion of the Cathedral, the Augustinean Church was ever after known as the 'Little Church'. The Chapel of Ease is not the same.

In times of fierce contention and furious zeal of the neighbouring chiefs and their tributary clans, each to establish his claim to usurped domination, or to repel, with ruthless courage, the predatory incursion of the lawless intruder, Derry was considered a sanctuary by the oppressed and unoffending, as well as a place of refuge to the vanquished. On such occasions the principal religious houses served as depositories for the moveable wealth – cups, goblets, rings, jewellery, &c. of the fugitives, who, as might be expected, were stripped of their property by every rapacious plunderer.

ROBERT SIMPSON, *The Annals of Derry*, 1847

HAVING RECEIVED, MOREOVER, the very noble and very honourable order of priesthood, and having been chosen against his will as the abbot of the black monks in that settlement of Derry, and having blessed it and made his dwelling there, he took it in hand to feed a hundred poor people every day for the sake of God. And he had a particular person to give that food to the poor. One day, after all the poor had been fed, another poor man came begging. But Colum Cille's servant said that he had already fed the customary number, so he told the poor man to return on the following day when he would get alms like the rest of the poor. But he did not come on the following day until after all the poor had been fed, and again he begged alms. He got nothing from the servant but the same answer. And he came begging a third day after the poor had been fed but only got the same answer from Colum Cille's servant.

At that point the poor man said: 'Go to Colum Cille and tell him that unless it be from himself that he gets what he gives to the poor he should not decide just to provide only for a hundred each day.'

The servant went to Colum Cille and told him what the poor man had said to him. When Colum Cille heard this, he rose suddenly, not staying for his cloak or shoes, but he pursued the poor man and overtook him eventually at the place that is called An t-Impodh Deisiul ['The Righthand-wise Turn'] on the southwest side of the Tempoll Mór ['The Great Church'] of Derry. He recognised that it was the Lord that was there and he fell on his knees before Him and he spoke with Him face to face, and was filled with the grace of the Holy Spirit. Among all the gifts that he got from God that time, he received knowledge of all the mysteries in the scriptures ... And from then on he provided not only for a hundred, but the great gifts that he got without measure from God, he gave them out without stint for the sake of God.

BRIAN LACEY (ed.), *Maghnus Ó Domhnaill: Betha Colaim Chille, 1532*
(*Manus O'Donnell: The Life of Colum Cille*), 1998

COLUMBA WAS NOW A PRIEST twenty-five years of age; and he began to think of founding a church in his native territory. The *Annals of Ulster* record the founding of Derry by Columba in the year AD 545; and it was brought about in this way. The first cousin of St Columba, Ainmire, son of Setna, who succeeded to the throne of Tara later on, was in AD 545 prince of Ailech and the neighbouring territory. His eldest son Aedh, was then a boy of ten years; but it seems, according to O'Donnell's *Life of Columba*, the king in the name of his son Aedh, offered the fort in which he then dwelt on the site of the present city of Derry to his cousin in order to found his church and monastery. Columba, however, was at first unwilling to accept the gift, because his master Mobhi had not yet given him, as was customary, permission to found a church – doubtless thinking him too young and inexperienced. But Mobhi himself was taken sick, and died of the plague in AD 544, shortly after Columba had left him; and before he died he retracted his prohibition, and sent two of his disciples to Columba with his girdle as a sign to give him full permission to act as he pleased. These messengers had just then arrived; and so Columba gladly accepted the gift of his cousin, and founded his church on, what was called then and long after, the Island of Derry. It was a rising ground oval in shape containing 200 acres of land, surrounded on two sides by the Foyle, and on the third by low marshy ground since know as the 'bog.' The slopes of the hill were covered with a beautiful grove of oak trees, which gave its name to the place. In ancient times it was called Daire Calgaich, but after the tenth century it came to be more commonly known as Daire Columcille.

Columcille's original church, called the Dubh-Regles, was built close to the site now occupied by the Roman Catholic Cathedral; and hence it was outside the walls of the modern city. Nigh to it were three wells anciently known as Adamnan's Well, and Martin's Well, and Columba's Well. One of them is, it appears, now dry; and the others are called simply 'St Columb's Wells'. Near to the church there was also erected a round tower, which in like manner has completely disappeared. So anxious was Columba to spare the beautiful oak-grove which covered the hill, that he would not even build his church with the chancel towards the east according to custom, because in that case some of his beloved oaks should be cut down to make room for the church. It was probably for the same reason he built on the low ground at the foot of the hill, instead of on its slope or summit, where the modern city stands. He strictly enjoined his successors to spare the sacred grove, and even directed in case any of the trees were blown down by the storm to give a part to the poor, a part to the citizens, and to reserve another part as fuel for the guest-house. In later ages a cathedral called Templemore was built on the slope of the hill; the Dominicans, Augustinians, and Franciscans had each a church and a monastery in the city of St Columba. It also seems that a Cistercian convent was founded there, but not a trace of any of them now remains; so effectually did the imported colonists change the physical as well as the religious aspect of the city.

We know very little of the history of Derry during the period that Columba ruled over his monastery in person. He always loved it dearly, and many a time his heart turned fondly from his lonely island in the Scottish main to his beloved Derry.

> The reason I love Derry is
> For its peace, for its purity,
> And for its crowds of white angels
> From one end to the other.

My Derry! mine own little grove!
My dwelling, my dear little cell;
O eternal God, in heaven above,
Woe be to him, who violates it!

THE REVEREND J. HEALEY DD LLD, Bishop of Clonfert,
Ireland's Ancient Schools and Scholars, 1890

MRS BIGGER, TOO, SOON FOUND a congenial sphere of work in Derry. As the wife of a professor she delighted in assisting her husband in every effort for the welfare of the students. She soon found herself at home in Great James Street church, and was welcomed into the Sabbath School, where she took a class. Derry is a city with fine Sabbath Schools, in which there are great classes for both young men and young women, and one of the greatest of the girls' classes soon gathered under her teaching. There are several ladies' school in the city, and young girls come from many parts of the country to be educated there. Most of the Presbyterian boarders in these schools became members of her class, and they found in her a friend as well as a teacher. Thus her influence extended to all parts of Ireland, and in after years, when travelling and addressing meetings on behalf of the Zenana Mission, she found some of her old pupils everywhere, as mistresses of manses and centres of life and influence in many homes and families. There were also in her class many girls employed in the public works and business houses of the city. All the study and training of her past life, and the experience gained in teaching in Belfast and Lisburn, were fully used by her now in illustrating Scripture, in teaching and applying its lessons, and in winning young lives and precious souls for the Saviour. Her own sweet personality, her bright and happy manner, her kind and loving heart, endeared her to all; and the fragrance of her life and work in Derry still lingers in many hearts and memories.

Life was brightened by much pleasant intercourse with friends, for the Bigger connection was a great one. Many little trips and excursions were made by the professor and his wife on Saturdays to the beauty spots around the city, as far as to Castlerock, with its great strand and rolling waves. Wet or stormy weather never prevented these excursions.

THE REVEREND ROBERT BARRON DD, *Mary Barron – A Biography*, 1915

BEDE SAYS THAT COLUM CILLE left Ireland 'to preach the word of God to the provinces of the Northern Picts', but Irish sources are divided as to whether he went as a form of penance or simply to find a 'desert' place for prayerful contemplation. Most modern historians, as indeed the earliest evidence, would emphasise the latter. Tradition has it that he and his companions left from Derry, sailing down Lough Foyle and across the northern channel. The legends make out of this departure one of the great dramas of the saint's life, indeed, of the history of Ireland. Later poets put words into the mouth of the saint.

> The great cry of the people of Derry
> Has shattered my heart into quarters.
> Derry of oaks we are leaving,
> Tearful with gloom and with sorrow,
> Leaving here broken-hearted,
> To go to the land of the strangers.

BRIAN LACEY, Colum Cille and the Columban Tradition, 1997

THE MITCHELBURNE WELL, an excellent spring in Gobnascale, cannot be ranked as holy, being indebted for its sanctity to the colonel himself, to whom that townland belonged. In a shed adjacent to the well his coffin was deposited for the 7 years previous to his death; and hither he used to walk every morning along the Foyle from his house in the Waterside (on the site of which Mrs Brown's now stands), in order to pray. A number of little boys were employed by the colonel to keep the pathway free from grass, and his piety led to the belief that some healing virtue resided in the water. It is accordingly the resort of a few superstitious old women, who drop pins into it and tie rags on the bushes about it. Stations have even been held here.

DAY, McWILLIAMS, ENGLISH, and DOBSON (eds),
Ordnance Survey Memoirs of Ireland, Vol. 34: Clondermot and Waterside (1831–8), 1996

DURING THE FORENOON MY FATHER was usually found in his study, and in the afternoon it was his custom to visit some members of his widely scattered congregation, every family of which he visited at least once a year. I have seen him set out in the afternoon in a wintry day with a plaid shawl over his shoulders to visit one of the outlying families of the congregation at the top of Warbleshinney Hill, more than three miles away. This particular family had at one time been engaged in the weaving industry, but when the British Government in the eighteenth century passed laws which destroyed the sale of woollen goods in Ireland this family had to find some other means of subsistence and they rented a small patch of mountain land upon which they built a cottage. After much laborious toil the family brought into cultivation a few acres that had hitherto been covered with heather. Here they eked out a meagre existence and by their fine Christian character set an example to their neighbours, most of whom were in better circumstances. My father would partake of the simple evening meal with the family, and shortly afterwards the neighbours would gather in from far and near for the prayer-meeting which my father would conduct before starting on his long journey home in the moonlight, for such visits were usually made during the week when the moon, known in the country as the 'village lamp', was shining. Such visitations were carried out regularly in each district and were announced from the pulpit beforehand so that when he called at the home the members of the family would be assembled, and he could hear the news about those members of the family at home and also about any members who might have gone abroad or into Derry City to find work. He shared their sorrows and spoke such words of comfort and counsel as might seem to him fitting and advisable. He did not catechise the children who were well taught in school, but it was his custom before leaving a home to read a portion of Scripture and commend in prayer the members of the household to the care of our loving Heavenly Father. This unostentatious work of bringing help and comfort to the individual members of the Church in their own homes was considered by my father to be one of the most important and helpful duties connected with his ministry. 'I am visiting the congregation at present' he wrote to Alex in 1902 'and have happiness in the work. Some of my people are much scattered, far away from the Church and careless. I have to keep a connection by visiting, and trying to stir them up.' Through such visitation he enjoyed the friendship and confidence of each individual member of his congregation.

THE REVEREND WILLIAM CORKEY MA DD, *Memories of an Irish Manse*, n.d.

Carlisle Road on
a Saturday Night!

CARLISLE ROAD ON A SATURDAY NIGHT! The *paseo*. Girls in threes and fours and fives, parading in their best clothes, arms linked along the footpath. The boys, prowling, watching, choosing, making bold forays, confrontations. Voices raised, singing, laughing, arguing.

Bosco was there with Eddie Carlin and Jack O'Dea. They stood outside Reid's furniture shop, lounging against the wall, dragging on cigarettes, motionless but alert.

'There's three. Come on! The blonde for me!'

'I'll try the dark one,' said Bosco.

They crossed the road and stood on the footpath, boldly waiting. The girls stopped.

'Out of the road! What do you think youse are doing? You don't own the place.'

'I seen you before. The Rialto, maybe?'

'You could have. I don't remember. You're easy forgot.'

Bosco cornered the dark one.

'What's you name?'

'Sadie! What's yours?'

'Bosco!'

'Bosco! What kind of a name is that?'

'It does me all right. People don't forget it, nor me neither.'

'Gimme a chance. I'll try to forget you.'

'Aw, come on! A bit of fun won't hurt you. Chips in the Continental, maybe? If we get away from this lot I can afford it.'

'And what's the price of chips with you?'

'No more than usual! I'm a bit slow.'

WALTER HEGARTY, *The Price of Chips*, 1973

Where the Foyle sweeps round you will find the town
    that's the diamond crown of old Erin's Isle.
Its pleasing climate would ease your mind
    and its towering spires would your heart beguile.
This ancient place with its ageless grace
    has achieved such fame and such high renown;
Not El Dorado nor Shangri-La would
    excel the grandeur of Derry Town.

Its Walls so high are the city's pride
    that defied besiegers that did assail.
Though they sought to breach them – could not defeat them
    though it cost them dear each attempt did fail.
Not bold Britannia nor noble Grainne
    could hope to harm them or pull them down;
They'll proudly stand so sound and grand
    to surround the heart of old Derry Town.

ANONYMOUS, 'Derry Town', in *There Was Music in the Derry Air*
(ed. A.M. Murray), 1989

THE BUS WAS FULL. It was one of those long narrow buses that do the slow run around Donegal twice a day. During the daytime the seats have a strictly serviceable aspect, crammed behind each other, dark green baize and stiff-backed where labourers sit in black jackets, unmoved by the scenery and smoking the miles away, the women with their chainstore shopping in plastic carriers slumped on their knees. The girl was almost surprised, as she stood expectantly in the narrow aisle, not to smell the sweat and dust on clothes, or fresh food in paper bags. But this was long past the end of the working day, and the wishful heavy scent of cigarettes and shampooed hair and bottled beer and aftershave went to her head in an overwhelming confirmation of her most secret longings. All she could see in the smoky fog was a sward of hair and a crowd of faces, pale and raucous. She could feel the excitement, it was tangible, like the warm sweat of breath condensing on the windows.

    There were no seats at the front, so the girl shoved and clambered down to the back of the bus, where a skinny youth in denims sprawled with his legs on the seat and his head against the grimy windows. He had the face of a plucked chicken, with a few hairs on his cheeks and chin, and milky blue eyes looking nowhere. There was a torn six-pack between his legs, and a bottle lolled and tipped in one hand. She hesitated, wondering whether to risk safety by interrupting his reverie, or dignity by standing for the rest of the journey, until an attentive clean-shaven man in a tight grey suit jumped to his feet and gave her a capable grin.

'Come on, Skinner,' he said, delivering a smart clip on the ear for emphasis. 'Shift yer arse and give the lady a seat.'

ANN McKAY, 'Paper Roses' in The Wall Reader, 1979

THE DISTINCTION OF SCORING Derry's first goal in competitive football went to Peter Burke. It came after half an hour and the cheer greeting it resounded throughout the Brandywell area. That goal separated the teams at half-time and the visions were bright of a splendid debut victory.

But the more cohesive and rather fitter Glentoran lot got on top after the interval and their 6 feet 5 inches centre forward Fred Roberts equalised after 60 minutes, and notched the winner 15 winners later. Nevertheless, Derry had performed creditably against one of the top sides in northern football.

Derry's next outing was at Portadown, where they were beaten 6-5 after being 5-1 down at half-time. Then at Brandywell they got their first League point, Sammy Curran scoring in a 1-1 draw, against Balllymena.

Next on the agenda was the first visit to Brandywell of the famous Blues. Linfield had won their three league games to date in impressive style and were already being hailed as the likely team of the season. They were a side packed with talent and experience, including internationals Jack Jones, Willie Gowdy, Joe Bambrick and Norman McCaw. Derry, with a single point from their three fixtures were very much the underdogs in this Gold Cup first round tie.

From the moment the draw was made for the knock-out competition, the game was the main subject of talk and anticipation among the Derry public. On that balmy autumn night of September 5, nearly 12,000 people crowded into Brandywell, paying £360 in gate money, the equivalent of about £10,500 now.

After only 7 minutes, the deadly Bambrick, who scored six goals against Wales in one Windsor Park game, an Irish international record never likely to be emulated, slipped in the first score, and it looked as if pre-match predictions would be borne out and that City would have to wait at least another match for their first win in senior football. But the occasion seemed to inspire the home players. Two minutes after Bambrick's strike, Brandywell erupted as Curran nipped in alertly to flick in the equaliser.

It was Curran, too, who put Derry in front, and then Crozier made it 3-1 with a goal that people talked about for years.

He picked up the ball at the half-way line and with a mazy dribble that left a succession of Linfield defenders floundering, cut through and gave Blues keeper Black no chance with a neat cross shot.

Linfield tried gallantly in the second half to pull back the deficit but the Derry defence, with Hilley outstanding, kept them at bay. When the final whistle sounded, hundreds of excited fans rushed on to the field to chair the Derry players off.

Derry fielded: Fitzroy, Mason, Bowie, Stewart, Reed, Ray, Kirby, Crozier, Curran, Hilley, Senior.

Linfield: Black, Brown, Frame, Moorhead, Sloan, McCleery, Housten, McCracken, Bambrick, Matthews, McCaw.

Two weeks later, the drawing power of Derry was illustrated again when another 12,000 plus crowd paid £376 in gate receipts to see Glentoran in the second round of the Gold Cup. Alas, there was no double over two of the Belfast big clubs. Man mountain Fred Roberts got the only goal of the game.

Thus, Derry's first four home fixtures had been seen by a total of about 36,000 people!

FRANK CURRAN, *The Derry City FC Story*, 1986

THE CLAYTONS LIVED IN a furnished house in Carlisle Road. They had no children of their own but Mrs Clayton was very fond of young people. She invited us to a Christmas party. It was during the holidays when James was at home. He drove us in and we put the trap up at the hotel. Elizabeth, who had a special flair for parties, was too impatient to wait. She went on in advance and was the first guest to arrive. She said her greetings very prettily, Mrs Clayton recounted later to Mother, and then she added casually: 'The juveniles will be along presently.' Mrs Clayton was enchanted with the phrase. She mistook it for a pure Irishism. She never knew that Elizabeth must have derived her juveniles from a Latin grammar. It was a word nobody used and it must have fallen upon her in pure inspiration – a word in a party dress to match its occasion.

KATHLEEN COYLE, *The Magical Realm*, 1943

In Derry we learnt to love before
we could talk, foxtrotting the floor,
nibbling earlobes
under the spinning crystal globes.
In the ballroom in Bishop Street
the educators of our feet
were James McCafferty's swinging
band and Mick McWilliams singing.

JAMES SIMMONS, *from* 'Dickie Wells Said: Variations', in *Poems 1956–86*, 1986

WHEN I WAS AT LONDONDERRY there was there, exhibiting himself, a Polish dwarf who called himself Count Boralosky. He may have been two and a half feet high. This is a most extraordinary little being. He speaks four or five languages, and has been very well brought up. His age is put down as between fifty and sixty years, and he has travelled much in Great Britain, where there are few towns which have not made his acquaintance. It is said that his wife, who is of ordinary stature, in a matrimonial quarrel, one day lifted him and set him on the mantelpiece. There was also in the same town a certain learned man, whose opposition to femininity was such that I have seen him throw his glass into the fire because, without his knowledge, it had been filled in order that he might drink to the health of the ladies.

The bishopric of Derry is one of the best of Ireland. They say it is worth £12,000 per annum. Oh, what a lovely thing it is to be an Anglican bishop or minister! These are the spoiled children of fortune, rich as bankers, enjoying good wine, good cheer, and pretty women, and all that for their benediction. God bless them! Oh, if I could one day wear the *philibeg* of black satin – how much better than being exiled that would be! Lord Bristol, besides his bishopric, has a fortune of fifteen to twenty thousand pounds sterling per annum. He is a man of talent, a learned man, but of singular habits. He travels nearly all the time in foreign countries, and spends nearly his whole income in superb houses, which are of use to the country through the money they cost.

It is rather singular to remark how in Ireland there is so little ceremonious politeness in pubic, while there is a great deal of it in private houses. In the inn at which I stopped there was given a grand ball. When the supper was announced, it was not without interest for me to observe how the whole company ran to table, everybody hurrying for a place without regard to others. It happened one day that Lady ——, who was queen of the ball, by not hurrying enough, was left without a seat. The same thing happened to me on this occasion, for, while I was philosophically regarding the spectacle, all the places were filled, and it was only with some trouble that I found a seat at the end of a form. I do not cite this as peculiar to Londonderry, it is an amusing moment at the public balls in Ireland when supper is announced.

CHEVALIER DE LATOCNAYE, *Promenade d'un Français dans l'Irlande*
(*A Frenchman's Walk Through Ireland*), 1798, translation by John Stevenson 1917

THE DIAMOND IS THE HEART of the town, and from it four arteries radiate, running to the four original gates; other smaller streets zig-zag away in various directions, and everywhere is the vigorous flow of life and trade. The shops are bright and attractive, and that evening crowds of girls, freed from the day's labour in the factories, were loitering past them, arm in arm, staring in at the windows and chattering among themselves. They were distinctly livelier than the factory girls of Athlone, and I judge that life is easier for them and that they are better paid.

We walked about for a long time, and then, for want of something better to do, went to a moving-picture show. I have forgotten all the pictures but two – a meeting of the Knights of the Garter at Windsor and a review of a body of English cavalry. In the former, King George and Queen Mary twice passed slowly before the audience; in the latter, the king, on a spirited horse, cantered down the field and then took his station in the foreground while his troops galloped past. It was a stirring scene; but the audience watched it in stony, almost breathless silence, without the shadow of applause – and this in 'loyal Derry'! I am inclined to think that, with reference to England, the north of Ireland and the south of Ireland are 'sisters under their skins'.

BURTON E. STEVENSON, The Charm of Ireland, 1915

WHEN LAST WINTER'S SNOW lay deep on Ulster, an English visitor travelled to the North by train, and was surprised at the remark of a home-going Derryman, who laid down his newspaper and said:

'I see they are slaying in Darry.'

'What's that you say?' – the Briton asked.

'Aye, they are slaying on all the hills inside the walls of the city and on the roads that run down to the Foyle.'

John Bull recalled all that he had heard of the party riots in Derry and demanded what the police were doing.

'The police,' said the native, reading from the paper, 'have cautioned several of the slayers.'

Cautioned! – John Bull realised that he was travelling in Ireland where (so he had been told) crime was the order of the day. He shuddered and asked to see the actual report.

'Och,' says the Derryman, 'there's only a wee paragraph at the foot of a column. I'll read it for you: "Slaying to an extent unrivalled for many years was indulged in in Derry during the past few nights –"'

'Slaying was indulged in!' cried the Englishman, aghast at the callousness of the expression.

'Aye,' said the Derryman, and he read on thus: '"On Saturday night the police took the names of a number of slayers in Chapel Road." I'm thinking they'll be fined sevairly,' he added.

At this, our visitor could not contain himself. A fine as the punishment for slaughter! He snatched the newspaper to read for himself the news of bloody riots to which mere cautions or fines were the mild reply of the Law. He found the paragraph, and read this heading:

'SLEIGHING IN DERRY'

His five minutes of bewilderment and alarm would have been spared if the Derryman had pronounced *sleigh* 'toboggan'. In Ireland once it was alleged that killing was no murder. In Derry to-day, at any rate slaying is no slaughter.

Winter after Winter, in that bleakest of the towns of Ireland, the young folk watch for snow and frost; for in the icy season Derry is the tobogganists's Paradise. There is not a lad but can put runners under a board or a box and go Winter-sporting on the slopes of that steep city – rushing through the freezing air, with his nose cutting the wind. Often I heard my Dad describe the sleighing in Derry as he knew it when he lived a while there as a young man long ago; and it still goes on, to keep the police and the people warm in raw days by the Foyle.

AODH DE BLÁCAM, 'Slaying No Slaughter', *The Black North*, 1938

Her voice like an instrument new set in tune,
Her cheeks are like roses that blow sweet in June,
Her eyes are like dazzling stars, you may see,
She's the bright star of Derry, my lovely Mary.

Of this sweet, gentle creature the praises I'll tell,
Above all other fair maids she does them excel,
She is neat and she's slender in every degree,
She's the bright star of Derry, my lovely Mary.

It happened one morning as I'm telling you now,
This sweet little creature was milking her cow,
Her lovely bright eyes they have quite ruined me,
She's the bright star of Derry, my lovely Mary.

When out in the evening this fair maid doth go,
And she on the footways her person doth show,
All young men around her do stand as you see,
She's the bright star of Derry, my lovely Mary.

Her teeth are like ivory, her eyes like the sloe,
Her skin is like lilies that in summer do blow,
She's a beautiful creature, if you could her see
She's the bright star of Derry, my lovely Mary.

And now I am going to finish my song,
I hope all good people I've said nothing wrong,
For I'm sorely wounded by that lovely she,
She's the bright star of Derry, my lovely Mary.

ANONYMOUS, 'The Bright Star of Derry',
in *More Irish Street Ballads* (Colm Ó Lochlainn), 1965

THE FIRST MAJOR BAND TO GET off on Good Vibrations was *The Undertones* from Derry, with Feargal Sharkey (vocals), Damian O'Neill (lead guitar), John O'Neill (rhythm guitar), Mickey Bradley (bass guitar) and Billy Doherty (drums). Formed in 1974, they paid their dues in the local rhythm and blues youth club. Their founder member, Billy Doherty, noticed Feargal Sharkey in a local competition which the latter had won for his sweet renditions of traditional songs. When they got together the group immediately had that rare musical magic of a unique sound, a sound whose strongest quality was Sharkey's goldenly-pitched vocal chords. Their greatest impetus came from the release of the *Pistols'* 'Anarchy in the UK', which put a stamp on the kind of music they would play – fast, hard-driving, punk rock, with a touch of pop melody thrown in for good measure. The release of their debut four-track single, 'Teenage Kicks' (1978) on Good Vibrations, shot them into the public consciousness, especially as it caused the most credible disc jockey in England, John Peel, to become their biggest fan. Well known as a staunch supporter of the punk movement, Peel adopted the group as his favourite band of all time and never tired of enthusing about their aggressive pop sensibility. It wasn't long before other DJs picked up on the band and the general consensus was that John O'Neill's lovely lyrics and Feargal Sharkey's delectable voice were some of the best things to come out of the punk scene.

Even when they charted their early singles, the group found it difficult to dive into the world of stardom. They were such individualists, believing so strongly in the forcefulness of punk ideology that they insisted on holding down their day jobs in Derry whilst performing their music on the BBC's *Top of the Pops*. After doing the usual slog of profile-making tours and continually entering the British record charts, *The Undertones* went fully professional and signed to a large international record company. John Peel continued to support them as his favourite 'underground' group and would play their records three at a time back-to-back, whenever he could get away with it.

MARK J. PRENDERGAST, *Irish Rock*, 1987

BRIDGE STREET MUST HAVE BEEN one of the most convenient streets in Derry to enter or leave, simply because you had the GNR station at the bottom of the street and the town shopping centre at the top of the street. And you could enter, or leave the street from several different directions, for example through Orchard Street, Sugarhouse Lane, John Street, Mattie's Lane, Foyle Alley or Rookery Lane. When people came to Derry to shop or on holiday, all they had to do was cross Foyle Road and John Street and walk up Bridge Street and they were in the town centre. It seemed that all the world passed though that street and it was always full of life.

In summer time, it was great, all we did was lie about and sit in the sun relaxing. Or we would watch the pig lorries pulling into Bigger's back and unloading their cargo for slaughter. The highlight of this would be when one of the pigs fell off the lorry and everybody would run up and down the street trying to catch this screaming pig and lift it back up on to the ramp beside McCloskey's on Sugarhouse Lane.

On Saturdays young girls, who worked in the factory all week, would start their day by helping their mothers to clean up the house and do the washing, blacken the range and whiten the habs, they even scrubbed the door step. For us Saturday was matinee day, provided you had the price of the Hall. On special days we would hire a bike from Barbers on Sackville Street, for half a crown a day, and head down to Buncrana.

When we were older finding some way to pass the time was very easy for us, especially at night. What we often did was look at the Journal and find out if there were any wakes in the area and we would head to them. It was not a nice way to pass the time, but we were young and had little sense. Failing that we would just stand at the corner talking until the early hours of the morning, or we would congregate at someone's house and tell ghost stories. The other thing was playing cards in someone's house, or on summer nights we would play out on the street. There was always some form of gambling going on, a toss pit or throwing up to the babs, anyone in the 60s or 70s will know what I mean.

We had simple needs in Bridge Street, like most of Derry at that time, all we wanted was a warm house, a clean bed and food on the table. People were always visiting one another and they always shared. If one family was having a rough time their neighbours would help them out, all they had to do was ask. If you wanted a drop of sugar, or half a loaf, all you had to do was ask. They were a poor race of people, but they were kind and generous, no matter how hard they were getting it, they always seemed to put on a smile.

DESSIE MOORE, 'Growing Up in Bridge Street', *Derry Journal*, 25 April 2000

SINGING AND STAMPING, the busload swung into the carpark of the dancehall. It was a long building like a Dutch barn, illuminated on the outside by a lowslung line of coloured light bulbs. Music glared into the night like the searchlights on the coast beyond, with Scotland on the east and on the west, America.

The three bouncers, in pink shirts and red dickie bows, flexed and watched with arms folded as the bus emptied before the door. One of them, the smallest, stood just beyond the ticket desk, wiping a flap of fair hair back onto his forehead. It flapped back. He licked his lips. The other two stood hulking and chewing gum on either side of the entrance, kicking with stacked heels at a cardboard placard, *No Denims*. They looked as if they meant it.

The men from Derry took the hint and started pulling ties from the pockets of their good suits, but Skinner in his Wranglers was apprehended at the door and steered in a no-nonsense manner back towards the bus. Encouraged by the sympathetic jeers of his mates, he made a token resistance, crestfallen and clowning, upstaging his disappointment with half-hearted gyrations and muttered blasphemies. The bouncers left him with a paternal shove, and Skinner stood his ground, brandishing a full bottle of Mundies, head tilted like a fire-eater, he poured the wine down his throat from a showy height. But the commiseration was non-commital, and no-one noticed, as they all shifted and shuffled into an orderly queue, in pairs and packs and dressed to kill.

Once inside, the girls all headed for the ladies' cloakroom. Coats off, they jostled for places at the mirror. Below the level of the wash-hand basins, a row of swingy skirts, gunsmoke grey tights and brogues. Above, a row of eager faces all tinged by the same ghastly neon strip-lighting. There were earrings and beads and the odd scarf, but only one bunch of purple rosebuds. The girl suddenly felt that she would be conspicuous and looked anxiously in the mirror for approval. It took her a few moments to find her own face among the others, because the smooth complexion, the eyes startling and compelling and the glossy lips were like all the other faces copied from magazines. Only that peculiar expression, set and impassive, and the paper roses were hers and hers alone. She wanted to check her smile, but didn't dare. Decisively, she clicked her handbag shut. Then apprehensively, but affecting nonchalance, she pushed open the mauve door of the cloakroom and, with shoulders back and legs swung from the hips, she made her way to the bar.

ANN MCKAY, 'Paper Roses', in *The Wall Reader*, 1979

WINTER, WITH ITS ATTENDANT PROBLEMS of heating, and warm waterproof clothing, may have brought worries to many a Derry parent, but not to many children. From early December on, they scanned the skies eagerly for sign of snow, and looked forward to the traditional sport of tobogganing – or 'sleighing' as it was known to one and all. Built on hills, as it is, and in those days with the minimum of vehicular traffic after 6 p.m., the city provided the ideal conditions after a snowfall, for young and old alike to indulge in an activity which many people now travel hundreds of miles to experience.

The Corporation Surveyor's Department didn't spread the roads and streets with grit and salt, as is done nowadays. Horses were provided with 'cogs' on their shoes to give a grip on snow or ice, but this was about the only official concession made. Householders in the steeper streets, such as Fountain Hill, Creggan Road, or Rosemount Hill, might spread the contents of their ash-pits (few had bins in those days) on the footpath, to give passers-by a footing, but in the main, nature took its course. If there was a good 'lie' of snow, after six in the evening, the streets would literally come alive with hundreds of 'sleighers' of all ages, coasting along on all types of primitive, or sophisticated sleds, ranging from sheets of corrugated iron, to proper toboggans with swivelling runners to steer by. The most usual vehicle, however, consisted of a flat wooden platform with supports, to which were screwed steel runners, or 'shoeings'. Steering – or Guiding – was accomplished by the 'guider' using two six inch nails, or old chisels, to apply a braking effect either left or right, and the application of this retarding force which caused the sleigh to turn either left or right depending upon which side the weight was applied, and the degree of turn determined by the amount of weight applied by the 'guider'.

Moments of embarrassment occurred when the 'guider' lost one of his implements, or perhaps was even thrown off by an unexpected bump, in which case, the unlucky passenger, trying to steer with his heels, would have vast quantities of wet, slushy snow thrown up his trouser legs. It was not uncommon to see a sleigh hurtling along, suddenly broadside, spilling its occupants onto the frozen snow, across which they would slide, sprawling, as their vehicle careered riderless up onto the footpath, scattering spectators and passers-by alike while the following sleighs would be forced to take violent evasive action, collisions would take place, or be avoided by a hairsbreadth, shouts, shrieks of laughter ringing through the frosty air as individuals, striving to regain their footing, pulled down companions in the process. Black figures, muffled against the penetrating cold, outlined against the white snow as they toiled up the hills dragging their sleighs, breaths rising like steam, whilst a brilliant moon illuminated the scene with its silvery light, made an unforgettable impression which I can instantly recall across the arches of the years, when I see a sparkle of frost on rooftop or street.

The more courageous, or skilled, trudged to Todd's Hill, with its sweeping bends, but the awesome slope of Creggan Hill, ending in the blank wall of Watt's Distillery could daunt the bravest heart. Shipquay Street had the hazard of the Gate to be negotiated, and it was not unknown for some souls to tear across Guildhall Square, hurtle over the quayside, to finish up with a tremendous splash in the icy waters of the Foyle. A more gentlemanly, sedate run was Caw Brae, but nonetheless pleasurable for all that.

CHARLES GALLAGHER, *Acorns and Oak Leaves*, 1981

THE WINTER I TURNED ELEVEN I came upon a certain snake in the street. This was in Londonderry, Northern Ireland, where I grew up and where no snakes should have been.

Time has blurred the context. Exactly what led me to the snake in question, how I even happened inside its neighbourhood, I can't now imagine. All I remember is walking by myself on an empty backstreet after dark and this street was dim and shuttered, curfew-silent, the way that all good Protestant streets in Derry were meant to be. It must have been a Thursday, the day we ran cross-country at school, because my feet ached. Anyhow. At a given moment I turned a blind corner, and I blundered on the snake.

It didn't register right away. Just at first I was dazzled by bright lights, and by the enormity of what I'd done, where I was. For my feet had brought me out into the one place in town where no soul that hoped to be saved must ever venture – Waterloo Place, at the downtown end of The Strand, on the borders of Bogside, the Papist war zone.

What made it such a plague-spot I had no idea. I only knew that a plague-spot it was. Tiggle, the janitor, said as much. So did McAlee, the man who did the drains. In the walled fastness of Magee, the college at which my father taught French, it was freely referred to as an MKS, for Mobile Knocking Shop.

And here I was, smack dab at the heart of it. After dark. By daylight, on the few furtive occasions I'd glimpsed it before, it had only looked shabby, terminally depressed. But by night it was transfigured into a style of place I hadn't dared to dream existed.

Directly across the street from me sat a perfect neon Inferno, as brightly lit and self-contained as any stage-set: Rock 'n' Roll blasting from the open doors of coffee bars; beehive blondes with sky-blue or scarlet glitterskirts and bright-orange lipstick; sailors hunting in packs; leather boys, motorbikes, the reek of diesel.

Nothing had prepared me, not remotely. Derry in that era, before the Provos and long before Bloody Sunday, was very much a backwater, some thirty to fifty years adrift of the moment, and proud of it. As for Magee itself, its isolation was almost monastic. Nobody owned a TV, precious few a gramophone and, though my father read the *Irish Times* each morning in the college library, my own grip on reality was confined to what I might glean from *Dandy* and *The Eagle*, Dan Dare had landed on Mars, Wyatt

Earp was Sheriff in Tombstone and Desperate Dan had made himself ill by devouring a box of six-inch nails, believing them to be sweet cigarettes.

Once when I was four I'd caught a whiff of 'Put Another Nickel In', Teresa Brewer, courtesy of a passing bus, and my mother had had to drag me off the street by main force. But at the moment I stumbled on to The Strand, at the turn of 1957, the only Pop singer I'd heard of was Ruby Murray, and then only because she came from Belfast.

I froze. If I'd been transported here by time machine, I could not have been worse out of place. Instinctively, I understood that my role was as voyeur, a worshipper at one remove, and I snuck back inside an unlit doorway, from which safety I could watch unobserved – see, and not be seen.

Only then did I notice the snake. From deep inside the chasm of the Roseland Café, a jukebox let loose with 'Tutti Frutti', Little Richard, and on the pavement outside an impromptu jitterbug broke out. Teenagers in fancy dress, whom I later learned were Teddy Boys, began to jive with each other, males with males, in a craze of flashing fluorescent socks and shocking-pink drapes, drain-pipes and blue suede shoes; and as they whirled they kept passing the snake, which I took at first to be a whip or a length of elasticized tubing, back and forth between them like a baton.

When the music died out, so did the dancing. But the snake remained in view, dangled beneath a streetlamp, neatly framed and backlit by the Roseland's plate-glass window; and now I could see it clearly.

From across the street, seen out of darkness into light, it appeared to be about two foot long, with a tapering greenish coil for its body and a great black-hooded skull. Something between a cobra and a python, I guessed, and it twirled and corkscrewed, stretched and contracted in rhythm, twined around a blue mohair sleeve with a purple velvet cuff.

It didn't seem a discovery, exactly. That was not the right word. Rather, my main feeling was simply of recognition. It was as if there was something I had always known deepest down, only I'd forgotten or misplaced it, let it escape me, and now the snake, and everything that went along with the snake, had restored it.

The something in question had no name, of course. And I did not try to give it one. All that I thought consciously was that I now possessed a secret, and this secret made me powerful, in some way superior.

NIK COHN, *Ball the Wall*, 1989

DERRY, SATURDAY 18 JANUARY 1964

A college student gets a surprise phone call from the leader of one of Ireland's top showbands. The Capitol's Des Kelly has a proposition for Phil Coulter, who is home for the weekend from Queen's University, Belfast. The band want to record his song 'Foolin' Time' as their first single. Coulter agrees. He puts down the phone in the hallway at Abercorn Terrace, and only then does reality sink in. 'I couldn't believe that this was actually happening,' he said of the call that changed his life. 'It was a day I'll never forget. That call ranks alongside selling out Carnegie Hall, winning the Eurovision Song Contest, having a hit with Elvis Presley or a number one in America. It started a whole chain of events that led me to where I am right now. Make no mistake about that. In this business, there is no standard laid-down procedure for becoming a songwriter, a record producer, an arranger or whatever. You see a gap in the hedge and you go through it like a ferret. Des Kelly gave me the gap in the hedge.'

VINCENT POWER, *Send 'Em Home Sweatin'*, 1991

EVERY YEAR IN EASTER WEEK, they may be spotted in great numbers, that breed indigenous to Derry City – the feis mother. Abandoning their spouses to a diet of chips and the housework, they congregate in large flocks at the Guildhall, where they spend a week twittering, squabbling and grooming their young.

As a species they are easily recognisable – generally having the well developed calf-muscles of the early Irish dancer, immensely strong kidneys and the iron digestion of a City Council refuse truck. Also stoicism of a high order to sit unfazed through seventy-eight infant renditions of 'Baidin Elemi', with the critical certainty that their wane is the best.

The feis mother pays for one seat but occupies three. This is necessary since she carries her temporary nest-building materials with her at all times.

These consist of a capacious handbag containing throat lozenges, Junior Disprin, kaolin-and-morphine mixture, half a toilet-roll and three emergency pairs of split-new dazzling white ankle socks. Her even larger holdall is crammed to capacity with mousse, gel, lacquer, pins, clips, rollers (foam and spiked), tailcombs (steel and plastic), brushes (various), bobbles, toggles, ribbons, hairslides, a battery-operated hairdryer and a gas-powered hot-brush.

Over her other arm are draped two or three coats or cardigans, while from her index finger is suspended the zippered portable wardrobe-bag containing 'the feis frock'.

The feis frock used to be a relatively simple garment. Now it would take the eye out of you. Lined in satin, stiffened with buckram, it's a riot of quasi-Celtic motifs picked out in fluorescent thread and further embellished with little bits of mirror glass. Despite the exquisiteness of its artistry, it is always too short, giving rise to ribald remarks from the louts in the lower balcony when its wearer has passed the age of puberty.

The feis mother is generally accompanied by one or more small children whose enormous knobbly heads are swathed in pink nylon scarves. You see, feis children are not prepared for competition in the comfort of their own homes where every modern facility is available. Not at all – they are garbed, titivated and rehearsed in the main thoroughfare of the Guildhall known as 'the corridor'. In the corridor, we witness the wholesale destruction of the ozone layer. A palpable fog of hairspray hangs in the air. The aroma of cheese and onion crisps permeates the atmosphere. Every second adult inhales deeply and thankfully on a cigarette. Giggling clusters of teenagers are strenuously ignoring the fellows they will have 'got off' with by the time the next competition's over. There is barely room to stand; the noise is deafening and little boys in mustard-yellow kilts are sliding merrily through the melee on the shiny parquet floor shuttling empty Coke cans as they go.

In the midst of this bedlam, the feis mother has set up her temporary nest. Every available nook and cranny is choked with children being tweaked and teased into perfection. God be with the days when it was all done with a pocket-comb and spit – though the serious feis mother 'it was said', used a secret recipe of sugar and water to stiffen petticoats and hairstyles to a uniform rigidity. It was also said (with whatever truth) that Ursula Doherty won every competition on the strength of her totally symmetrical ringlets, which bounced like bedsprings in perfect unison as she danced.

For the twenty-second time the pianist breaks into the 'Rakes of Mallow'. On stage a tiny figure, arms clamped to the concrete folds of her feis frock, points a pre-pubescent toe. Under her chair, the feis mother's feet dance every step with her child.

I walk down the Guildhall stairs with the feis mother and her friend. 'See thon adjdikkitter!' snorts the friend '– all he's tist's in he's mouth so it is! He's fer nathin! Our Sharon got two seconds and a first in Moville so she did. What about your Dona!' The feis mother shakes her head. The friend's mouth turns down – all sympathy. Then she rallies – 'Ach sure it gets ye outta the house so it does.' She turns to me. 'Does your wee girl not do nothin'!'

ANITA ROBINSON, 'Rare Birds', in *Feis Doire Colmcille Souvenir Book*, 1999

LONDONDERRY ACADEMICAL INSTITUTION FOOTBALL CLUB

Club Ground – School Grounds.   *Colours* – Scarlet and White.
Captain – A. L. Horner.
Hon. Secretary – J. K. Blackwood, Academical Institution, Londonderry.
Hon. Treasurer – J. C. Dick (Resident Head Master).
Committee – A. L. Horner, J. K. Blackwood, J. H. MacLaughlin,
W. A. Russell, J. Stewart.

The matches were fewer in number than usual, owing partly to the want of interest in games throughout the district, partly to the weather. If the Ulster Branch of the Northern Union could prevail on the railway companies to afford more facilities for schools meeting schools, the annual competition for their Challenge Cup would be much stronger. As things are, the Academical Institution was the only school in the North-west of Ireland that entered for it; and as they had to contend against great traditions, good play, and a strong team, the match *versus* Armagh Royal School went against them. However, notwithstanding defeat and the muddiness of the ground, the match was very pleasant. As this was their first trial for the 'Cup', they hope to do better next time.

[The railway companies of Ireland generally do afford facilities to travelling football teams, such as return journey for single fare, provided ten tickets are purchased. The Irish Rugby Football Union will be happy to negotiate any such arrangement, if reminded, next season. – EDITOR.]

RICHARD M. PETER, *The Irish Football Annual*, 1880
(reprinted by Ulster Historical Foundation, 1999)

Some people like to have a drive
Whilst others like a row,
Young people getting up in life
A-courting they will go.
But if the evening does keep fine
And does not threaten rain,
Sure I'd prefer a trip to Fahan
On the Buncrana train

For Crockett he's the driver,
And Bonner is the guard,
And if you have a ticket
All care you can discard.
Let you be fop or summer swell
To them it's all the same,
For every man must pay his fare
On the Buncrana train

For localists, provocalists,
And those that like to sing,
I'm sure McGarvey he'll be there
To play the Highland Fling.
As for singing or for dancing
To them it's all the same,
For he's the sole 'musicianer'
On the Buncrana train.

We pass Bridgend, reach Burnfoot,
And there we give a call
To view that ancient city
And its Corporation Hall.
The King of Tory Island
Is a man of widespread fame,
His Royal Carriage is attached
To the Buncrana train.

We go to Fahan to have a dip
And stroll along the strand,
Then up the road to have a cup
Of coffee at the Stand.
The barmaid she is charming,
With her you can remain
Until it's time for to go back
On the Buncrana train.

ANONYMOUS, *Derry Journal*, 1898

WHEN WE ARRIVED IN DERRY, we drove past The Guildhall, an architectural hodgepodge; and streets were running up, excitingly and steeply on our left, to The Diamond. Then we were in Shipquay Place, and part of the great wall of fortification was on our left, and five guns peered over the top, the oldest being presented by Queen Elizabeth I and bearing her monogram of The Tudor Rose. Buses were swirling in past the public lavatory which sprouts a strange affair that may be a ventilation shaft, and a loud speaker was blaring out of a smart car demanding 'Are you among the chosen?' and sailors were walking in the streets and looking at the girls in cardigans, and newspaper vendors were shouting and striking attitudes like figures in a newsreel of disaster, and shop people were standing at their doors engaged in what seemed to be rather mysterious conversations. It wasn't the Ulster town as we had come to think of it, and it didn't seem to be of today. It seemed – and may Derry forgive me – a rather grubby continental town during the reign of Queen Victoria; and, for the moment, the splendid old walls might have been part of Victorian viaduct architecture.

We walked up to The Diamond; and, for the first time in Ulster, we were accosted by a pimp. 'You boys want to see the old country, do you?' he muttered as he jerked his head towards two rather raddled ladies who might quite conceivably have been called 'old country'. Feeling rather like the apprentices who slammed the gates, we rushed away past a chapel with a poster that announced a 'Thought For The Day': 'I used to complain of having no shoes till I met a man who had no feet.' A policeman walked by hugging a large box of chocolates.

In the side streets, we found a pub called 'Hong's Bar' and one called 'The Electric Bar'. A house that was shivering apart held the headquarters of 'The Home Repair Service', and a pet shop had an emblem of a sheep carrying a twig of birds. The old offices of *The Sentinnel* had a figure of a soldier over welded moons.

OSWELL BLAKESTON, *Thank You Now*, 1960

A S WE APPROACHED THE IRISH COAST, the captain called me into the cabin, and I gasped with amazement when the Dublin airport came into view. As we flew over the terminal building, I could see thousands of people waving. Banners and a flags welcomed me home on every side as we glided to a halt. I had a crazy desire to run and hide under one of the seats or lock myself in the loo, but somehow I managed to pull myself together, dawdling over packing my hand luggage so that I was last out of the aircraft behind the reassuring back of my mother. The cheers broke like the roar of the sea over my ears, and I found bouquets of glorious flowers thrust into my hands as I acknowledged the wonderful welcome. It seemed even more like a state visit by royalty when Dublin's dignitaries stepped forward to give the official welcome. Then we squeezed a way through the clamouring press reporters to a reception room where there were speeches and interviews for fifty minutes before starting the last leg of the journey home. Fresh cheers went up as we mounted the steps and turned to wave goodbye.

It was a short flight to Ballykelly Airport outside Derry – just long enough for me to wonder what on earth the welcome would be like in my own home city. But I couldn't have been prepared for the wildly cheering crowds which surged across the tarmac to meet the plane, nor the reception which was waiting for me in the city. Brian Morton, Chairman of Derry City Commission, extended the official welcome, but his words were soon drowned by the chants of the crowd for The Song. The Nazareth Céilí Band struck up the tune of 'All Kinds of Everything' and out of the air someone produced a microphone, right there on the steps of the plane, and put it in my hands in place of the huge bouquets and baskets of fruit I was clutching as if my life depended on it. But for the first time, it all became too much for me. Halfway through the song, the lump in my throat grew so big I could hardly breathe, and I broke down and wept. Then I caught sight of my father. In seconds I was down the gangway steps and into his arms. Tears rolled down his face too as we hugged each other and the band played on with the crowd clapping and cheering. Then, gradually, the officials managed to steer us into the huge limousine which was to carry us in triumph on the fifteen mile journey to the city centre.

All along the route, thousands of people turned out to wave their flags and shout congratulations and love. It was just too amazing to be real. I'd left here just an ordinary schoolgirl and now I was hearing 'Dana, Dana, we love Dana. Congratulations!' on every side. I clung on to Dad's arm. He was definitely real. Every now and then, the motorcade was actually halted as the excited crowd overflowed across the road. Even so, my heart nearly stopped beating with shock at the sight which met us as we turned into the Guildhall Square.

It was awash with a vast sea of cheering, swaying people. You couldn't see the ground. They even seemed to be hanging off the buildings which lined the square, and all around brightly coloured streamers and flags waved in the chilly evening air. Somehow our car managed to nose its way to within about twenty yards of the Guildhall steps, but the officials and troops were having no success in clearing a path for us to the door. This is it, I thought. 'EUROVISION STAR CRUSHED TO DEATH IN WELCOME HOME.' But suddenly the amused face of an army officer appeared through the car window.

'Sorry, miss, but there's only one thing for it. I'm afraid you'll have to climb on the car roof and we'll try and carry you in!'

The whole scene had degenerated into the sort of weird dream you have when you've eaten too much cheese late at night. I wouldn't have been surprised if it had been a white rabbit poking his head through the window. As the door of the car was forced open, I found myself being lifted bodily into the air and on to the roof. From there I was passed from shoulder to shoulder above the heads of the rolling crowd. Dad was also borne shoulder high and in a few moments we were safely deposited inside the door of the Guildhall. Mum and Granny soon joined us.

There was no escape. The hall was buzzing with hundreds more excited well-wishers, but at least the chaos seemed a little more ordered, and I realised that many of the people stepping forward to hug and shake hands with me were friends and relatives, including some nuns from Thornhill and dear Sister Imelda. Pop went the champagne corks as yet another official welcome was given by a host of awesome dignitaries, but there was nothing formal or intimidating about their manner this evening. There were broad smiles on every face, and the speeches of the Chairman of the

Council and both the RC and Church of Ireland bishops were full of warmth and friendliness. From outside, we could still hear the roar of the crowds continuing their own celebrations and a couple of times I slipped out on to the balcony to wave to them, feeling ridiculously like a head of state.

After two hours, my speech was becoming distinctly slurred – not from the champagne but from total exhaustion – and my jaw was aching from so much smiling. Also, once again, I hadn't managed to grab anything to eat, and my tummy was beginning to rumble embarrassingly loudly, especially, it seemed, when I talked to the bishops, so I was relieved when my parents suggested we pressed on back home.

Once more we were carried like carcasses of meat back to the car. Before I got in, I thanked the crowd for all their kindness, and then we began to edge our way through the festive streets of Derry. It was like Christmas, and so beautiful to see the city alive with celebration and happiness instead of violence. Bonfires sparkled brightly out of the darkness and tonight the Bogside flats were decorated with bunting.

Getting into the flats was as difficult as breaking into Colditz, but eventually we managed to fight our way upstairs and found the fifth floor looking like Kew Gardens with flowers and fruit hanging everywhere. It was wonderful to be with all my closest family again, but I didn't forget my one remaining goal – to find something to eat. Mum knew my appetite of old, and in a few seconds a plate of food appeared. I fell on it like a vulture. When my hunger had been satisfied, I began to feel more sleepy than ever. It was about midnight and outside the crowd still chanted and sang. If anyone was to get any sleep that night, it was up to me to do something so I stepped out on to the verandah and said another heartfelt thankyou before singing a couple of verses of 'All Kinds of Everything' which they sang with me.

That seemed to do the trick. After a few more minutes of wild cheering, the crowd began to disperse with cries of 'Good night, Dana' floating up on the clear night air. I groped my way to the bedroom, feeling as if I would never be able to wake up again if ever I got to sleep. Moments later I was dead to the world.

DANA, *Autobiography*, 1985

THE DESIGN OF THE FEIS MEDAL is the work of Mother Clement Hogan, Loretto Abbey, Rathfarnham, a daughter of the eminent Irish sculptor, the late Mr John Hogan. It is a Celtic Cross, a symbol of our country's suffering.

On the front, in a centre oval panel, is a landscape typical of Ireland, of mountain, field, and water – a round tower reaching heavenwards in mute appeal appears in the foreground whilst over the mountain top the rays of the rising sun burst forth in splendour, dispelling the clouds of darkness and gloom, and sending in their stead a bright message of hope, peace and gladness, o'er water and land. A ring – symbol of eternity – encircles this panel. On the foreground of panel appears an Irish harp – emblem of our country and of music – this harp partly frames the panel picture, symbolically overshadowing the entire scene. Radiating from centre, and along each arm of cross, is scheme of Celtic interlaced tracery, and at end of each arm of cross are found the oakleaves of Doire Colmcille. The circle of cross bears the inscription:– Feis Doire Colmcille.

On left, at extreme end of arm of cross, is shown a dove – symbolic of St Colmcille – whilst opposite, on extreme right, a harp appears; also an open book – symbolic of learning. On extreme base of perpendicular arm is an Irish tower, with a vista of hill and valley showing in distance. Festooned on the circle of cross is the shamrock – emblem of St Patrick and of our land. The centre of reverse side of medal is reserved for inscriptions. Framing the space and extending far out into arms of cross, winds a chain – shown by Celtic circular inter-lacing, which chain is broken asunder, on upper part of perpendicular arm of cross by a church triumphantly crowning all – emblematic of Faith and Colmcille. The medal is thus designed to stand at once for music and learning – Doire and Erin – Colmcille and God.

ANONYMOUS, 'Feis medal', in *Feis Doire Colmcille Souvenir Book*, 1999

I LIKED DERRY AND THE SURROUNDING HILLS, its handiness to Fahan and Inch, Grianan and Burt. I liked its quays and the fact one might often be treated to coffee by the crews of trawlers and shown over the ships. I could hear of other lands – Spain, France and Greece. I liked the river and on a Saturday would go walking with friends along the bank of the Foyle to Culmore, take out a boat, and in the evening wander home. Or perhaps it would not be the Foyle, but the Faughan, where, entering at Glendermott, we would wade up the river bed looking for somewhere to fish. The environs of Derry were more attractive than the city itself.

Derry had an excellent Philharmonic Society and perhaps for me its highlight was the year they sang Handel's *Messiah* with Elsie Suddaby as one of the soloists. Sometimes, still, when listening to the work on records, I close my eyes and I can still see her standing there – I'll not say dressed, but rather robed – in spotless white. Her singing of 'I Know That My Redeemer Liveth' filled me with apocalyptic fascination. Here too, I studied the organ with Morgan Cartright, and music theory with Marie Longwell. Playing duets with Marie was great fun, especially when she finished and I had several notes left over.

THE REVEREND JOHN M. BARKLEY, *Blackmouth and Dissenter*, 1991

The next day I came to Londonderry; it was market-day, and there were stage-players and rope-dancers in the market-place, and abundance of people gathered. The Lord's Spirit filled my heart, his power struck at them, and his word was sharp. So I stood in the market-place, and proclaimed the day of the Lord among them, and warned them all to repent ... but the stage-players were sore vexed that the people left them, and followed me: whereupon they got the mayor to send two officers to take me to prison: so they came and took me; but the sober people were angry that stage-players should be suffered, and a man that declared against wickedness and vanity, and taught the things of God, must not be suffered, but hauled to prison. The gaoler put me in a room that had a window facing the market-place, where I had full sight of the people. I thrust my arm out of the window and waved it, till some of them espying, came near, and others following apace; so that presently I had most of the people from the stage-players, which vexed them much. Then they got the mayor to cause the gaoler to keep me close; so he bolted me, and locked my leg to a place where he used to fasten condemned persons. There I sat in much peace of conscience, and sweet union with the Spirit of Truth.

WILLIAM EDMUNDSON, *Journal*, 1715

T HE PRINCIPAL STREETS WERE CROWDED, especially with the younger portion of the community, of both sexes. Evidently the good folks of the city were addicted to an evening promenade and, in fact, as there are no regular places of amusement in it – for the citizens are 'unco' guid', and somewhat heavy – their only resource was either to sit indoors or go for a ramble, the latter of which alternatives, on this beautiful August night, they very naturally preferred. I noticed that the mashers of the Maiden City, unlike their prototypes in England, did not appear to consider that tobacco was essential to their adequate equipment for the conquest of hearts. Rarely did we meet a fellow with either a pipe or cigar, or even a cigarette in his mouth; and yet, strange to say, the Derry girls appeared to appreciate their attentions, and to imagine that 'a man's a man for a' that'.

To escape the bustle, we repaired to the walls, which, curiously enough, were well-nigh deserted, although a lovelier promenade it would be difficult to picture, for they are, in places, as wide as the streets themselves, and afford delicious glimpses of the river. The city which they enclose dates back for centuries. So long ago as the year 546, an abbey for regular canons of the Augustine order was founded here by St Columbkille; in 1218 Furlogh Leinigh instituted an abbey for Cistercian nuns; and a Dominican friary was established in 1274 by the request of St

Dominick. The walls are about a mile in circumference, and have six gates, one of which is a triumphal arch erected in 1789 to commemorate the centenary of the raising of the siege. It was a treat to tread the spacious paths which crossed the gateways, and to pause above them and survey the laughing crowds that filled the sloping streets; or to stand in the shadow of the few sickly-looking trees that still survive out of the thirteen that were planted on the walls in 1689; or look at the cannon which surmount them, prominent among which is Roaring Meg, said to have played an important part in the struggle, and the Memorial Hall, and the Cathedral, with their several relics of the same eventful time; or to gaze upon the lofty Doric column on the top of which the statue of the Rev. George Walker stands, with an arm extended over the city he had saved, an arm which grasped a sword that is said to have fallen on the very day of the passing of the Catholic Emancipation Bill. The scene was fascinating to-night, for the moon was almost at the full, and, beneath her consecrating beam, the meanest object assumed some form of beauty; and the irregular roofs of the quaint old houses, and the spires of the city, and the noble monument were steeped in the glamour of Fairyland; while, as we stood at the base of that mute reminder of the past, a thousand lights were twinkling just below us in the humbler homes that lay beyond the walls, and, on the broadening river, further still, a silvery lustre shimmered as it softly rippled to the sea.

ARTHUR BENNETT, *John Bull and His Other Island II*, 1890

DERRY. THE LEAFY BOWER OF ST COLUMBA. The surroundings of this city are most attractive, with fine country houses standing in wooded demesnes on the banks of the Foyle, and Donegal at the doorstep, but the city itself would do better to remember that a lot of water has flowed down the river since the *Mountjoy* rammed the boom. At present it has the air of one of those rather blousy old ladies whom one meets at tea-parties in Irish country houses – all past, and quite unable to remember that the mere act of continuing to exist entails its obligations. I, for my part, remember the city as a place where I once served as a subaltern of infantry in Ebrington barracks; that and the memory of certain sunsets witnessed from the barrack square, when the spires and pinnacles across the water went climbing up into a blood-red sky, for at the hour of sunset, and seen from the Waterside, Derry has all the romance and drama of a mediaeval city – at any rate the romance and drama traditionally associated with mediaeval cities, since if the truth were known we inhabitants of the twentieth century would probably have been bored to death with them in a month, if we hadn't first been sickened by their stench. Nevertheless, Derry remains a city of dramatic contrasts, a border fortress set over against the Gael, as I discovered for myself one winter's night when walking round the walls. A murmur of voices from a lighted window attracted me, and looking over the parapet I saw through a chink in the curtains a room crowded with men whose faces bore an expression of passionate enthusiasm and conviction. They were all looking towards the curtained window, and soon a single voice, proceeding from someone who stood with his back to me, facing his audience, took up the tale. The speech was in Gaelic, but from the expressions on the faces of the audience and the impassioned conviction of the speaker, I knew at once that I was witnessing a gathering of Irish patriots – the first mutterings of the storm that was to break two years later in O'Connell Street, Dublin; and as one who both understood and failed to understand, I thought it best to turn up the collar of my British great-coat and disappear in the darkness.

So much for my memories of Derry. But now that I come to write them down, I find that I have inconsequently left out the pleasantest of the lot. It concerns an encounter, in fact a whole series of encounters, with a charming young woman in a fortunately very much wooded glade on the banks of the Foyle ... so charming, and the glade so well wooded, that ...

DENIS IRELAND, *From the Irish Shore*, 1936

A PUBLIC LIBRARY AND NEWS ROOM, commenced in 1819 by subscription and established on its present plan in 1824, by a body of proprietors of transferable shares of 20 guineas each, is provided with about 2,660 volumes of modern works and with periodical publications and daily and weekly newspapers: it is a plain building faced with hewn Dungiven sandstone, erected by subscription in 1824, at an expense of nearly £2,000, and, besides the usual apartments, contains also the committee-room of the Chamber of Commerce. The lower part of the building is used as the news-room, to which all the inhabitants are admitted on payment of five guineas annually. A literary society for debates and lectures was instituted in 1834, and the number of its members is rapidly increasing. Concerts were formerly held at the King's Arms hotel, but have been discontinued. Races are held on a course to the north of the town. Walker's Testimonial, on the central western bastion, was completed in 1828 by subscription, at an expense of £1,200: it consists of a column of Portland stone of good proportions, in the Roman Doric style, surmounted by a statue of that distinguished governor by John Smith, Esq., of Dublin: the column is ascended by a spiral staircase within, and, including the pedestal, is 81 feet in height, in addition to which the statue measures nine feet. The city is in the northern military district, and is the head-quarters of a regiment of infantry which supplies detachments to various places: the barracks are intended for the accommodation of four officers and 320 men, with an hospital for 32 patients, but from their insufficiency a more commodious edifice is about to be erected, for which ground had been provided in the parish of Clondermot.

SAMUEL LEWIS, Topographical Dictionary of Ireland, 1837

THE MAN ARRIVED at two o'clock in the afternoon to take my dog away. The whole street came out to watch. There was no pretence about it. Rags was paralysed, his kidneys gone. I knew he was being taken away to the gas chamber, there to die. Why my parents allowed me to sit on the doorstep, sobbing, watching the man take Rags away to his early doom, I do not know. I was glad even then, and I am especially glad now in retrospect, that they let me keep vigil over his last hour on earth. It gives me a sane, calm perspective on TV violence today – children know what's going on. I was well able for it, though of tender years; about nine, I think. Afterwards, my mother insisted that I go to the pictures as a treat. I knew she was buying me off, wanted my misery out of her sight; I protested nobly that nothing would console me; and I went off anyway, making a sacrifice for mammy's sake, in the sickening, pious way that children do.

My Aunt Nellie received me with full honours at the Rialto cinema. Years later I realised she was secretary to the manager, not the manageress. She gave me popcorn, ice cream, a bag of sweets and my choice of seating, all free of charge. I cried a little, ate a lot – oh, Rags, what can I say? Life must go on – and was soon lost in the wonderful world of *The Wizard of Oz*. By the time I emerged, the day still young, my dog was well and truly dead and gone and buried. I sang songs from the movie all the way home. It was a great wake.

NELL McCAFFERTY, 'From Rags to the Rialto', in Here's Looking at You, Kid
(eds Stephanie McBride and Roddy Flynn), 1996

DERRY HAS ALWAYS BEEN KEEN on public entertainments and has had its full share of every variety. I can think of many in my early days, but for me outstanding among them all was that of 'The Jubilee Singers'. They were of the Negro race, and came in the interest of 'Fisk University', then being built that the Negro race in the matter of higher education might have an equal chance with that of the whites. Their appeal was for £5,000 from this freedom-loving country to complete the scheme, *and they got it*. Most people to-day know something of the awful experiences through which these people were called to pass even as late as the 19th Century. Common everyday occurrences were husbands being sold and dragged from their wives, never to be seen again; similarly children sold away from their mother without any hope of meeting again, while men and women, for little or nothing, came under the whip-lash of the master. The 'Jubilee Singers' who came to this country had not themselves suffered in this way, but were the sons and daughters of *those who had*. Strange though it may seem, this race has a special musical gift, while the peculiar wording of their hymns and songs, together with the plaintive character of their music, is evidently the outcome of the cruel sufferings of this slave-ridden people in the days of slavery. This party came here backed by well-known men in America, and London, and in appearance were such as any nation might be proud of. Entering 'First Derry', which had been placed at their disposal, on the night of the concert they made their way to the platform specially erected for the occasion, and seated themselves in a semi-circle, the people looked on in wonder and admiration. Words fail me to describe the programme that followed. The music was charming, and it did not fail to affect the congregation, who were sometimes smiling and the next moved to tears. Speaking from memory, and this must be 75 years ago, the following are the titles of some of the pieces they sang:– 'Swing low, sweet chariot', 'Roll, Jordan, Roll', 'Turn back Pharaoh's Army', 'Steal Away', 'Nobody knows the trouble I see, Lord', &c. Those who in these days have heard Paul Robeson can with little difficulty realise the wonderful melody produced by twelve voices of a like character singing in harmony. Those present that night can never forget the treat they had. It is pitiful to think that in more than one place in England these people were turned out of an hotel on account of colour. This sort of thing dies hard, to wit, the fact that the Maori Concert Party from New Zealand which visited this country a few years ago was treated in the same way in one town in Cornwall. I had something to do with the visit, but do not think any hotel in Derry would treat them in this way. However, when they visited Derry the Committee in charge of local arrangements took no risks, but had the whole party of 20 placed in a number of private homes where they were made heartily welcome, and spent a happy week-end.

C.W. GORDON, Reminiscences of Derry in the Last Century, n.d.

T HE GROWTH OF KNOWLEDGE deriving from sources of ancient native culture, and manifested by efficiency in music, in speech, and song is being demonstrated throughout the country (notwithstanding the impediments of disturbed and restricted social conditions) in quite a remarkable manner.

Yesterday for instance, Feis Doire Colmcille was launched upon what promises to be a highly interesting and entertaining career in the Guildhall of this city. It is to continue daily up till next Saturday night. As the report in another column indicates, a bounteous programme of great variety – well calculated to test the capacity of competitors in Gaelic readings, recitations, storytellings, and in musical renditions, vocal and instrumental – has been provided for the information and delectation of the public, and a very large array of competitors have been attracted.

The promoters have been at much pains to provide in this Feis an extended series of popular and most instructive competitions, and it is but reasonable that they are counting upon the patronage of the general public in city and district bestowed in liberal measure. We believe that this patronage, well deserved, will be forthcoming right through till the close of the Feis on Saturday night.

The only thing racy of the soil that has been unstintedly praised, even by Ireland's greatest enemies, is Irish music. Few men, for instance, wrote more venomously about Ireland than Froude, the historian, few slandered her worse, and to judge from his writings, few hated her more, but yet he had to acknowledge the supreme beauty of her music.

For a long period that rich mine of harmony lay unworked by those who cultivated the art because it was the fashion, in this as in other lands to 'boost' and study the less lyrical and more scientific productions of alien origin. It is not blameworthy, but quite the reverse to cultivate that generous breadth of taste in music which refuses to restrict itself rigidly to native themes but in this, as in other affairs, charity ought to begin at home, and in practice, the native art should have the prominence to which its merit and its beauty entitle it.

It is certainly gratifying to witness many evidences in recent years that the chill of neglect has been dissipated, and that native music, speech and song are being steadily restored to their rightful place in the esteem of our people. In the 'forward movement' of instruction and of friendly rivalry, competitions like those which will have the attention of competent adjudicators during the present week in Derry Guildhall must play a very helpful and inspiriting part, and in addition to the recreation they afford to audiences while the tests proceed, they cannot but exercise on the minds of participators and of attentive listeners a beneficial influence that will abide to mould individual taste in days to come.

It may, in passing, be observed that the annual Feis Tirconaill started nearly a quarter of a century ago in the neighbouring Diocese by his Grace Archbishop O'Donnell, and by him all along ably supported, takes place tomorrow in Fanad and it is likely to repeat in every respect its success of proceeding years.

Mighty monarchs in the realm of musical composition – Beethoven, Mendelssohn, Mozart, Schubert, Chopin, Wagner, Rossini and the rest – have bequeathed musical treasures which will continue to delight informed mankind for ages to come and they will have their hosts of admirers in Ireland as elsewhere.

Those claiming to be authorities have indeed declared that this country has no masterpieces of genius to show such as have left the hands of the composers named and other 'big men' of their time. Be it so; cruel compelling circumstances which need not be dwelt upon here, have submerged Irish genius in the past but the reign of wrong and repression is ended and we all hope brighter days of high achievement are ahead.

Meanwhile we are entitled to contend without fear of contradiction that there is no music on earth that appeals with the same power to the hearts of our people as their own. There is no other that expresses, as Irish music does, their joys and their sorrows, their hates and their aspirations, their passionate devotion to their own kith and kin and their undying love for the land of their birth.

ANONYMOUS, 'Gaelic in Music, Song and Story',
Derry Journal, 28 June 1922, printed in *Feis Doire Colmcille Souvenir Book*, 1999

A S WE GREW OLDER we went on to even grander things. When I was seventeen I took part in a three-act mystery play called 'The Creaking Chair', which was put on for a week in the Derry Opera House by a group of local amateurs who called themselves the Derry Repertory Company although they had no other plays in their *répertoire*. Looking at the programme to-day I see some well-remembered names. The butler was played by Dudley McCorkell, soon to be Mayor of the city and to receive a knighthood. Donald Shearer, the idol of the Derry citizens because he played brilliantly at centre forward for Derry City, the only amateur in the side, was Philip Speed, a journalist who turned out to be the murderer, and half way through the run had to take over the main part when Jack Towers went down with 'flu. I played the part of John Cutting, a reporter, the hero unjustly accused of murder, and the local paper, the *Londonderry Sentinel*, kindly commented that 'even professionals often make such a hash of the part of a reporter that it was pleasant to see Mr Macrory acting in such a natural manner as to achieve considerable success.' I had been given the part simply because I was the only male member of the cast tall enough to stand alongside the heroine without looking ridiculous for she was a girl of great stature. I dreaded the moment at which I had to say to her in a thrilling voice 'Sylvia, don't you care for me at all?' and then embrace her, and night after night our clumsy attempt at a kiss was greeted with cheers, hoots and whistles from the gallery.

PATRICK MACRORY, *The Days That Are Gone*, 1983

IN A BAR BY THE GUILDHALL GATE the Red boxer told James and Jeff and myself where exactly we would find the vagrant master of Magheracolton.

'If you want to live like an animal,' shouted the captain, 'live with the animals.'

'Boxer,' Jeff said, 'this is no place for you to be in. You're in training. The pride of the city depends on you.'

'I'm drinking orange crush.'

He held up the sickly drink. It was the same colour as his high-necked sweater.

'Shaka, the great Zulu,' said Jeff, 'trained his warriors for battle by enforced chastity and by making them jump barefooted on thorns. When they stamped their feet the earth shook.'

You know it all, Mister Macsorley.'

There was an uncanny, underground intimacy between asthmatic Jeff with the hooked nose, sparse sound teeth, lisp and croup-like cough and the stolid, unsmiling, red-faced boxer whose yellow hair, for battle, had been cut in a close prison crop.

'You don't stamp on thorns, boxer?'

'No reason to.'

'But you practise chastity. No visits to Fountain Lane while you're under starter's orders.'

'I live up that way, Mr Macsorley. A lot of decent people do. You'll find a pal of yours there now. Drunk as a lord.'

'Mr Chesney, no less?'

'No names, no pack-drill, Mr Macsorley. He asked me the way to where Maggie the Jennet lives.'

'Zulus,' said Jeff as we climbed the Diamond Hill, 'were a curious people. The boxer's bald head reminded me of them.'

'You shouldn't fool with a boy like that,' James said. 'He might misunderstand you.'

'Not me. He respects intellect, James, my dear.'

With the forceful stride of explorers James and myself swung west out of the Diamond, passed the jail, swung north-west out of a wide, well-lighted main street, strode, our heels echoing metallically, under the dark arch of a narrow gateway, followed the curve of the walls down thin alleys steep enough at times to need steps. In soft soles, stooped, trotting with shorter paces and talking all the time, Jeff travelled with us.

'They had one most interesting custom,' he said. 'The Zulus, I mean. They had many interesting customs. They impaled their enemies, for instance, anus foremost on high, sharp-pointed stakes and allowed them to settle down at leisure.'

From the lighted streets on the slopes beyond, where the happy road ascended towards the past and Bingen, the cathedral bells chimed Ave, Ave to Maria our Lady of Lourdes. Below us in the dusky, dimly-lighted grid-iron of lanes, a pub at each corner vociferous with singing sailors and soldiers, Alfred was with the animals. Or he was deep down among the wriggling eels, the only sexual symbols left in the blessed island from which the censor Patrick had banished the snakes. He smelt of them. He was coated with their slime. Far from the dry, redolent hazel woods where he had hunted the imbecilic nymph, Alfred was in the swamp studying life.

'Another custom they had,' said Jeff, 'should interest you, Kinnear, holder of medals, captain of victorious teams, beloved of women.'

Behind us in the dusk, hopping sideways and with great caution from jagged step to step, he was talking literally over our heads. The alpine alley shot down dizzily to the black dirt surface of Fountain Lane. On steps by dark doorways women sat and gossiped and screamed occasional admonitions to active children. From a stenchy hallway a young girl, glorious in imitation Hollywood finery, came stilted on high heels, met us, swept past in perfume, ascended perilously towards the old walls and the first evening stars. From one lighted room came sounds of singing and a melodeon.

'After the Zulu killed in battle he could have no social life, he couldn't even drink milk, until he had wiped the axe. The Zulu phrase if the two of you are interested was *sula izambe*.'

'Not interested,' James said.

'Ah, but James, you will be. To wipe the axe meant to have intercourse with a woman. Life after death. Do you follow me?'

'We follow.'

'The attractive aspect of the ritual was that any unmarried woman if (the book I read says) she was accosted by any warrior for this ceremony was morally bound to agree.'

'Morally,' said James, 'is good.'

'Any unmarried woman,' said Jeff. 'It opens up vistas.'

'Maggie Paterson, bless the girl,' he said, 'has in her time helped many a fusilier to wipe the axe. The phrase might be different for sailors.'

'The marlin spike,' said James.

There never was a woman who looked less like what she was than Maggie the Jennet. Yet, by the far-from-Paris ('Faraway is France,' said the doctor) standards of our city, she was our principal courtesan, supreme even above the beauties known to our *demi-monde* as the Bluebottle, Black Maddy and, because of unfettered opulence of bosom, Jingle Bells. Behind a black tin shed by the weighing bridge at the bottom of the city's cattle-market yard it was said she was at home every Saturday night to a dozen or two, one at a time and at threepence a head. A popular song of that halcyon, pre-inflation period went: 'We'll count the hours and kisses, and things that we may do, when I'm in the market for you.' It was publicity. It was her theme song. She greeted the derisive whistling of the melody or the singing of the words with a bony, vacuous smile, for when her own interests were not threatened (as they had been in the case of the rival who had tried to steal her fusilier) she could be as pacific as any shy village maiden. She was straw-haired, tall, fleshless, big-boned ('Strong scaffolding,' Jeff said. 'She needs it') and her freckled face and blue eyes gave her the lost, abstracted air of a middle-aged spinster of a schoolmistress who realized that all hope of a husband was past and that she might as well enter the convent. Her husband, in fact, had withdrawn from the unequal battle to the security of the mental hospital, where there was neither marrying nor giving in marriage, and had left his chair by the tiny, black-leaded kitchen range in her one-storeyed dwelling to be warmed by many a stranger. But not, as it happened on that evening of our quest, by Alfred Conway Chesney. Over the half-door she said: 'If you've money you're welcome. Even you, Jeff Macsorley.'

BENEDICT KIELY, *The Captain with the Whiskers*, 1960

THE WORD 'FEIS' in the Irish language means a Festival, usually a musical festival. The Londonderry Feis had for many years carried, and maintained a tradition of musical competition and interest in the city. It had operatic, lieder, oratorio and ballad competitions, as well as those for vocal trios, quartettes, and choirs. On the instrumental side, there were piano, violin, viola and cello competitions. However, life being what it was in Derry amongst many Catholics, the Londonderry Feis was considered an Establishment function.

The Irish literary and cultural renaissance of the early 1900's sparked off interest in Gaelic sports, pastimes, and in particular, music and dancing. When the country settled down following the Anglo-Irish Treaty of 1921, a small group of music enthusiasts decided to establish a Festival whose prime function would be to revive and sustain interest in the native songs and dances. The principal architects of this Festival – Feis Doire Colmcille as it was named – were Mrs E.H. O'Doherty, a gracious lady whose name is revered by the many hundreds of aspiring singers and musicians whom she taught and encouraged, myself among them, and Father John McGettigan, a tall gaunt cleric with fierce flashing eyes, surmounted by shaggy eyebrows, set above a bony beak of a nose, a fresh complexion, and a hair-trigger temper.

This Feis followed a similar pattern to other Feiseanna, with competitions for singers, choirs, and instrumentalists, but with the emphasis on Irish composers and arrangers. In fact, in the singing sections, of two set pieces, one in the Irish language was obligatory. This led to problems for aspiring competitors who couldn't speak the language, but soon a flourishing 'trade' in phonetic spelling developed, and soon everybody – including the adjudicators – seemed satisfied.

These adjudicators were men and women of considerable reputation in their respective fields, and I personally recall Sir Richard Terry, J. Turner Huggard, Philip Dore, Professor T.H. Weaving, Eamonn O'Gallchobair, Cormac McGinley, and George Leonard delivering their verdicts from the Guildhall stage.

The standard in all the competitions was exceptionally high. In the vocal sphere, the two major competitions were the McDaid Cup, and the McGettican Cup – the first donated by Father McDaid, Pastor of North Platte, Nebraska, a cousin of mine – who, incidentally was an assistant to Father Flanagan when he founded his famous orphanage 'Boys' Town' in Omaha, Nebraska.

The McGettigan Cup, presented by Father John McGettigan already referred to, had, as part of its requirement, a sight test. This was usually one of the last competitions of Feis Week, and what a finale it provided.

All of Derry's best known vocalists were entrants, as well as many from surrounding towns, and there was normally a capacity – and highly critical – audience in the Large Hall of the Guildhall. Imagine about twelve hundred knowledgeable people hanging on every note and phrase uttered by the competitors. Not for nothing was it one of the most coveted trophies of the Feis. The names of the competitors must inevitably evoke nostalgic memories for an older generation of Derry folk – John McCabe, Patsy Lecky, Willie Bryson, Willie John McDaid, James McCafferty, Josephine O'Doherty, Bridie McGuiness, Leo McCormick, Eileen McIntyre, Michael Cutliffe (Buncrana), Kathleen Murray (Kilcar), Vera O'Doherty (Carndonagh), Kathleen Casey, Sammy Burke, John Kyle, Tom Stone, John Judge (Castlederg), Edward Henry O'Doherty, Lily McNally, Angela McGovern, Len Callan, Harry Leavy, Afric McGinley, Eddie Mount (Moville), Eileen McGeehan – some who have gone to their eternal reward. Such a wealth of talent ensured that it was on a par with some celebrity Concerts. On occasions the musical disputants were engaged in their duels until the early hours of the morning, and I have known McGettigan Cup competitions to finish at 1.30 a.m. It says much for the intense attention with which the competitions were followed that one might have heard a pin drop when the adjudicator was delivering his verdict at that ungodly hour of the morning. About 1937, there was an upsurge of interest in Irish dancing and from that year on, some of the dancing competitions numbered the entrants in hundreds. During Easter Week – traditionally Feis week, children in their white and saffron, and green and black costumes, with intricate designs woven into cape, skirt or blouse added a gay touch of colour in the Spring sunshine as they made their way singly, or in groups, to the Guildhall.

The doyen then of Irish dancing teachers was Miss Nellie Sweeny – although her position was soon to be challenged by various of her more talented pupils, and soon the name – and fame – of teachers like Brendan de Glin, Lillian Moore and Eugene O'Donnell spread far beyond the confines of Derry.

If the rivalry in the singing competitions was intense, amongst the dancing competitors it was so fierce as to be almost frightening, and some of the Hornpipes, Slipjigs, and Reels attracted up to 145 entrants, and almost degenerated into marathons. How dancing adjudicators kept their sanity, never mind making subjective judgements after seeing scores of children of varying degrees of skill, was a never failing source of wonder to myself and dozens of others.

The nett result of all this dancing activity was the virtual domination of the entire Irish dancing scene by Derry trained dancers.

The first Season Tickets admitting the holders to all the Sessions of the Feis, was a simple cardboard badge worn in the lapel, and costing about 3/6d for children and 5/- for adults – a not inconsiderable sum for those days. Soon the more impecunious persuaded their more fortunate friends to enclose their badges in a matchbox or something similar, which was then thrown down from a lavatory window to eager hands below, quickly transferred to the buttonhole, and then the young boy or girl casually strolled past the ticket collectors, who were practically submerged under the press of youngsters. During the day, the corridors of the Guildhall were a seething mass of children and parents. Schoolboy and schoolgirl romances flourished, and moonstruck glances were exchanged at long range. The dancers were particularly attractive in their costumes, and the Guildhall echoed to the crash of adolescent hearts breaking as the eternal feminine wiles were employed – who can ever forget the grace and skill of girls like Tess Carson and her sister Nancy, the Box sisters Mona and Gerry, Dorette Given, Celine O'Donnell, Bridie Gallagher, Anna Kavanagh, and their male counterparts, Ted Kavanagh, Seumas Kerrigan, Myles Doherty, Paddy McIntyre, Hubert Gurney, and Harry Duffy.

The stewards who attempted to maintain some semblance of law, order, and decorum amongst the milling crowds of excited, energetic, youthful extroverts, were mature cheerful individuals who regarded the children with a benevolent and paternal eye, but who, at the same time, were firm and responsible. These included Big Pat McCafferty – himself a bass singer of no mean ability – and Jimmy Duffy. For many of us, they will be indelibly associated with the Feis in its golden Heyday.

For the hundreds of children, and adults, who participated annually the months and weeks of practice preceding the event provided educational and cultural amusement at the minimum of expense.

CHARLES GALLAGHER, *Acorns and Oak Leaves*, 1981

IN A RUN-DOWN AREA near the centre of town stood a ramshackle shop of sorts that stayed open until five o'clock in the morning. It was part pawn shop, part second-hand clothes-sorting area, but, most importantly, a café that sold no food. One could, however, purchase a fetid cup of tea served in a dangerously grimy cup with semi-solid sediment oozing from its base.

The place was owned and operated by Peggy, who made little or no money for her pains but seemed to receive her reward in other ways. She held court behind a shop counter piled feet-high with assorted dingy crockery, pots, pans, dusty books, extinct magazines, musty items of clothing, second-hand rat-traps, rubber hot-water bottles, worn shoes, damaged lampshades, detachable pick-ups for electric guitars, the occasional battered fiddle, old Thermos flasks and a large, surprisingly agile, ginger tomcat called Pinky.

Elsewhere there were wardrobes, washboards with glass fronts, hand-operated mangles, a dented trumpet, half of a trombone, and a cast-iron objected that I swear was a ploughshare.

Everything was for sale, though I never once witnessed anything being sold.

Amongst this triumph of variety and pointlessness stood the imperious Peggy.

Her own grubby clothes habitually smelt of stale piss, and she loved to talk.

Not just any old talk.

Not just any old gossip.

She preferred good, stimulating, difficult talk.

She was particularly fond of discussing Darwin's Theory of Evolution and its effect upon the perceived truths of the Roman Catholic Church. She also had a soft spot for Einstein's Theory of Relativity and the subsequent possibility of time travel. Endless hours were spent discussing hypotheses purporting to explain why a stick appears to bend alarmingly when it is immersed in water, or why the sky is blue.

This was what the night-wanderers wanted, and this was where they gathered.

Nobody knew what the fuck they were talking about, but it somehow felt good, almost intellectual.

Peggy's was an escape from the empty darkness of their lives.

I discovered Peggy's at a relatively tender age, whilst I was reeling home drunkenly after fruitlessly groping a girl called Dympna who worked in a shirt factory.

I had walked her back from a dance hall and, grossly over-estimating my personal charisma due to a surfeit of cheap, potent wine, had invested much time talking to her before making an ill-judged lunge at her person. Forcibly repelled, I staggered away at the pointed slamming of her front door.

Fending off a puke, I found myself staring through a dimly illuminated shop front, surprised to see people not only still up, but engaged in animated conversation. I lurched in, mumbling about needing something warm to lean against, and was given leave to stand unsteadily within the confines of the emporium, where I saw and heard enough to want to return sober at a later date.

I subsequently returned frequently to Peggy's talking shop. Nights well spent.

It's all gone now, of course. An anonymous shopping centre now squats on the site.

But the ghosts still linger.

I see Blind Eddie peer inquisitively over the top of the newspaper that he told two inches in front of his face in a doomed attempt to render the headlines more clear to his almost sightless eyes. He is wearing a long, shapeless, moth-eaten Crombie coat and his hedgehog-grey-flecked hair is on back-to-front.

Thin John leans awkwardly on the counter, toying with his germ-ridden cup of tea. A felt cap is pulled almost halfway down his face and he is wearing surprising trousers that dangle too far above a pair of steel-capped hobnail boots. He sports a huge white plastic hearing aid on his left ear and wires trail from it to some battery-powered device secreted in the vicinity of the lapel of his soup-stained jacket. A stilted conversation is therefore going on between Peggy, a man who can see very little, and a man who can't hear much at all.

If we include Peggy's severe limp, I am the only person present who is more or less functioning normally.

GERRY ANDERSON, *Surviving in Stroke City*, 1999

LAST YEAR, ON HALLOWE'EN one hundred men marched down from Creggan, through the Bogside, and into Derry city square. Unarmed police officers and unarmed British soldiers cleared traffic for them.

The men were Roman centurions. Those who posed as cops and soldiers where also in fancy dress. They were all adults. The centurions had made and silver-sprayed their own armour and helmets, and their own laced-up boots, and their own short skirts – as men do. It is taken for granted that adults in Derry will dress up for Hallowe'en, that they do so voluntarily, and that they make their own costumes.

The phenomenon began with adults about 15 years ago – nobody can adequately explain why or how – and now children too have joined in what is confidently claimed as the biggest street festival on this island; and in Europe, probably, in the sense that the festival depends entirely on voluntary participation.

Derry City Council has weighed in with formal festivities such as fireworks and bands on platforms, which cater to the overflow of people who cannot get into the pubs, or into the city centre. The city centre, which can hold thousands, just isn't big enough any more.

The festival has now expanded to four days – it started yesterday and will end as dawn comes next Wednesday morning. Unless you know someone with floor space, it's too late for outsiders to join in – the council reports virtually 100% occupancy of beds in the city for the duration.

Visitors come from the continent, from Belfast, from Cork – locals feel like visitors as they throng the late-night streets looking for one public place or pub or fast food emporium that does not have a queue outside. Some participants have been forced to return to their Derry homes to refuel with tea and sandwiches before heading into the breach once more.

Although there will be a formal competition this year for best-dressed etceteras, starting off from Derry's walls at 6.30 pm, the rest of the citizens take their own time. Students are usually on the streets by late afternoon, threading their way to the pub of their choice, utterly unself-conscious in their elaborate gear.

'It's the ones who don't dress up who stick out,' say Paul, who strolled about one year in daylight as a dandy. He borrowed the flowing white wig from a relative who is a hairdresser, the leather belt from a schoolteacher, the shirt from an art-college student, and the jacket from a hip London friend. The breeches were his own white ski pants tucked in under his velvet jeans. Years later, on their June honeymoon in Egypt, he and his wife bought native clothes specifically for the coming Hallowe'en, 'turbans, djellabas, the lot'. It was the only time they ever wore them. It was worth it, he says.

A social worker now, he wonders if the wholescale engagement in fantasy was an escape from the warfare which consumed his teenage youth. 'You could avoid it a bit when you were a child, dressing up and knocking on doors, and then you passed out of that and suddenly everybody in the world was having a great time at Hallowe'en and you were just a Derry fellow, and there was no way to stand outside what was going on. Every night of your life there was a war.'

He wonders if it began with a craze, then sweeping the north, called Murder Mystery. You sent away for the game, followed instructions and dressed up according to the assigned character. The rich, he noticed then, used to book into hotels for a Murder Mystery weekend, dress up and drink wine. Paul and his teenage friends began to play it at home, as did others.

Gradually, they brought the dressing-up out to the discos; then onto the streets, at Hallowe'en. The real cops and soldiers never interfered with the make-believe armed forces who usurped them on the streets, on that one night in the year. 'They seemed as relieved as us to have a night off.'

Then the Council weighed in with a fireworks display and parents brought their children along to watch the darkness light up. Over the years, the parents began to dress up as well as their children. It was no longer enough to be a witch.

Kylie Minogue, aliens, priests, skeletons and politicians were lampooned.

Imagination took over. A young woman constructed a sofa around herself as a couch potato and her friend came as a TV set. The centurions last year put Creggan as an entire community on the map. One hundred men spent weeks on the project. There are things that defy explanation. 'I was enjoying myself,' Paul finally comes to the point. 'There wasn't much enjoyment around then.'

He was a dandy on a Derry dancefloor the night loyalists played 'trick or treat' in a Greysteel pub, a massacre which reduced John Hume to public tears.

Derry is divided by a river on either side of which nationalists and unionists live apart. The Hallowe'en festival is called the Banks of the Foyle festival, a discreet attempt to suggest that both communities are included.

Perhaps they are. 'How would you know a Protestant in a mask?' liberals ask cheerfully. Paul's memory of the beginning of things is that local paramilitaries were not involved.

The whole point, he emphasises, was that this was a night off from all of that. Whatever the truth of the matter, the crowds are now such that the council had to provide entertainment on both sides of the river anyway, to cater to demand. City centre crowds had spilled into car parks, onto the bridge, taken over the Walls, seeking space.

This year, shops have decorated their windows, shop workers will dress up, school-children will visit the city museum to hear ghost stories, and a Haunted Walls tour will run over the four-day period. On the night, copy-bands will play Elvis, Tom Jones, the Corrs and Robbie Williams.

The council budget is £70,000, with extra contributions from pubs, clubs, radio and newspapers. There will still not be room indoors, which is why the entire festival depends on people parading about outdoors.

The mayor is expected to give a lead. Last year, Pat Ramsey was Mickey Mouse by day, and a clown by night, complete with mayoral chain. He was utterly at ease. Ramsey is an otherwise dedicated party politician.

There were those with well-founded worries that commercialism will kill the spontaneity of Derry's Hallowe'en. Not this year – the council has yet to put the subject onto a website.

It is possible – just possible – that you can get a cancelled booking (IR £50 for two nights) by ringing 048 71267284, or visiting the impossibly slow website 'info@Derryvisitor.com'.

Or you can do what famous Derryman Dermie McClenaghan does. 'I pay no attention whatsoever to Hallowe'en. Next Tuesday night, I will go home from work, change into my wife's frock as usual and sit and watch the telly.'

NELL McCAFFERTY, 'As Derry Lights Up', *Sunday Tribune*, 29 October 2000

A Lumpy,
Uneven Kind of City

DERRY IS A LUMPY, UNEVEN KIND OF CITY, may it please you; and it is lumpy and uneven from various points of view. It is hilly to begin with; nay, it began on a hill – the hill of the oaks, where the sacred grove was, from which trees the city takes its name. Derry is a rough, rugged, craggy, precipitous place politically, socially and religiously, as well as physically. It began life, as one might say, under the auspices of a precipitous, lumpy, combative sort of man – St Columcille. The Apostle of Alba was one of the greatest Irishmen of any time – scholar, poet, artist, and statesman, as well as saint. But in his hot youth he was a man of fiery pride and passion, and during the first years of his priesthood be became the chief firebrand of the sixth century. Derry-Columcille, his own city – for that is the right name of Derry and not Londonderry – took after its founder in one way. It started life with a hot temper and it has never cooled down. It has been something of a storm centre all through the ages. And it is a storm centre to-day. You cannot look upon it without a quickening of the pulses. Something of its rugged history speaks to you out of its quaint old streets. It sits there squarely astride of the Foyle under wild Inishowen, the weather-beaten citadel of the fighting North.

It slopes sheerly down to the river after climbing several hills, which give some of its causeways the appearance of trying to stand on end. During the frosty weather all vehicle traffic ceases in several precipitous thoroughfares, and the popular sport of sliding begins. You may call it tobogganing or sleighing or anything you please. It consists of sitting on a board or in a basket and flying down the slippery gradient at the rate of several miles per minute. There are certain arrangements made by which the sliders shall not be dashed to pieces, or across the river into Tyrconnel; but this is a matter of detail. With Bowden brakes you can ride a bicycle down one of those Derry streets; but you would require a ten horse-power engine to work your cranks in the upward direction. If you want to see Derry you must go to work on foot. Go over the bridge and climb the hills on the off side of the river when evening comes, and you will appreciate the situation. Tier over tier of lights shine out from the steamers and electric lamps along the water front right up into the sky. Shops, clubs, long lines of factories, depots and private houses – all contribute something to the illumination. They are perched at different altitudes on the slopes of the hills, some of them having their foundations many feet over the level of the tall roofs of others.

WILLIAM BULFIN, *Rambles in Eirinn*, 1907

I LANDED IN DERRY THE NEXT night in the pitchy darkness of a coal-hole black-out, which was unfortunate; for the journey up the river is a very pleasant one, and Derry is, to my mind, the loveliest of all Northern cities, and in normal times looks lovely at night from the fortifications, with all the little lights of the valley below you to the west, and shining across the river below you to the east. As for Connaught, I would willingly live only in Ballina, for the North I would willingly live only in Londonderry. Its river is noble. The town has antiquity and dignity. It has some very fine houses – such as The Deanery. Its main shopping district is bright and busy. Its size is about right, fifty thousand people – a little on the small side, perhaps, for a city but perfect for a large town.

I think that what makes me so fond of Derry is that it reproduces the pictorial effect of Cork – river, quays, hills, deep valley – and it has behind it the hinterland of the lovely Inishowen peninsula and all Donegal, just as Cork has the mountains to its west. If one took Cork, and bent it up in the middle, like the fallen-in cone of a volcano, or a great sombrero, that would be Derry. And when I got up in the morning and strolled around the ramparts, the Walls as they call them, wide enough to let forty men march abreast, and looked down over Bogside, towards the Clay Pits of Templemore and to the cathedral at Brooke Park, and saw all the little threads of morning smoke rising from the thousands and thousands of little houses far below, it was just like being up on Patrick's Hill, in Cork, and seeing the smoke rising from the little homes of Blackpool and Barrack Street. The walls are hemmed in by houses and streets, so that one could drop a pebble from the gravel at one's feet down a Bogside chimney, and see into the top-floor windows.

SEAN O'FAOLAIN, *An Irish Journey*, 1940

Glow black in the rubbled city's
Broken mouth. An early crone,
Muse of a fitful revolution
Wasted by the fray, she sees
Her *aisling* falter in the breeze,
Her oak-grove vision hesitate
By empty wharf and city gate.

Here it began, and here at last
It fades into the finite past
Or seems to: clattering shadows whop
Mechanically over pub and shop.
A strangely pastoral silence rules
The shining roofs and murmuring schools;
For this is how the centuries work –
Two steps forward, one step back.

Hard to believe this tranquil place,
Its desolation almost peace,
Was recently a boom-town wild
With expectation, each unscheduled
Incident a measurable
Tremor on the Richter Scale
Of world events, each vibrant scene
Translated to the drizzling screen.

What of the change envisioned here,
The quantum leap from fire to fear?
Smoke from a thousand chimneys stains
One way beneath the returning rains
That shroud the bomb-sites, while the fog
Of time receives the ideologue.
A Russian freighter bound for home
Mourns to the city in its gloom.

DEREK MAHON, 'Derry Morning', *Selected Poems*, 1991

MARY (OR 'MOLL' TO AVOID CONFUSION with her mother after whom she was named), began her narrative: 'We left Brownhall and St Ernans and all our dear friends on the 8th August, Monday'. Her first detailed description – written at Derry where the family was due to sail to Glasgow – gives a good indication of what was to follow:

We came to Derry crossing the pretty white wooden bridge in the evening and walked on the ramparts, a thick wall goes all round the town and on it is a broad gravelled walk, and on it there is the Pillar of General Walker who defended Derry when James 2nd besieged it. The ramparts were not at all like what I expected them to be but were broader and more hilly, I saw cannons there for the first time.

DERMOT JAMES, *This Recklessly Generous Landlord: John Hamilton of Donegal 1800–1884*, 1998

FAMILIARISED AS THE AUTHOR had long been with all the recorded particulars of that momentous struggle which forms the main subject of the following pages, she was overwhelmed with wonder when the first view of the maiden city broke upon her from that direction whence Lord Antrim's forces approached to meet the unexpected repulse of the gallant apprentices. Abruptly rising from within a bend of the beautiful Foyle, terminating, as it seemed, in a point, and that narrow summit crowned with a single church, Derry, the Derry of 1688, appeared, girt with the dark zone of her impregnable old walls, and occupying a space so limited, that when by an effort of imagination the numerous additions of more modern date were swept away, and their places supplied by the lines and batteries of an investing army, it did really seem like a vision of wild romance, rather than a simple fact of history, that the defenders of such a narrow fortress should have held their besiegers at bay during eight months of unsuccoured distress, and finally have driven them from the scene of their unparalleled discomfiture.

But when passing through the Ship Quay Gate, the visitor found herself actually within the boundary where no Papal foe was ever permitted to set up his banner – when, with a swelling heart, she paced the still unbroken round of those glorious ramparts, and from the cathedral's tower took in at once the whole compass of the scene, wonder and admiration rose into awe; for never in the varied history of the Church's deliverances was the finger of Omnipotence more clearly revealed than in the preservation of this diminutive casket, where the Lord had enshrined the jewel of true Protestantism, and by the word of His power had declared that no spoiler should rend it thence. He alone, who, for the promotion of His own glory, and to abase the pride of man, hath usually chosen the weak things of the world to confound the strong, could have given the victory to the enfeebled handful who remained, after a protracted period of inconceivable suffering, to maintain that post, of which the limited space, and more limited supplies, were less remarkable than its helplessly exposed situation, commanded by surrounding hills, the broad outstretch of which afforded such favourable positions to the assailants, that every battery they chose to mount could tell with certain effect on the city. In tracing the occupation of the ground by the French and Irish army, and glancing down upon the straitened space within the walls, computing the density of an imprisoned population, and the inevitable effects of an incessant bombardment upon the dwelling-houses, the streets, the walls, the inhabitants, there was but one conclusion to which the mind could satisfactorily come, – 'This was the Lord's doing, and it is marvellous in our eyes.'

Memorable and honourable as the defence of 1688–9 has rendered the name of Derry, it is far from constituting her sole claim to distinction. Many circumstances of much earlier date distinguish her among the interesting spots of a most interesting country. The extreme beauty of the situation, added to its peculiar value as a seaport, seem to have recommended it from the earliest time as a desirable post.

CHARLOTTE ELIZABETH (Mrs Tonna), Preface to *Derry – A Tale of the Revolution of 1688*, 1839

L ONDONDERRY IS SITUATED on a height over the river which runs on the east & north sides of it; it is something like the Situation of Guildford, commands a view of a well improved hilly country, of the river & the narrow part of the Lough or rather the mouth of the river: From the Situation of two or three Churchyards, where there were old Churches, I concluded that the old town of Derry was situated on the side of the windmill hill to the North west & perhaps extended down to the Valley below, as I was informed it did. When this estate was granted to the Companies, it was on Condition that they should fortifie it, which they did as it now remains in the modern way, but without any subterraneous works, so that on that account & being encompassed with hills it is by no means a strong place, nor can it possibly be made strong: The walk round the ramparts is very pleasant. The Society also built a handsome Townhouse, & a church at the first Settlement, which is an handsom parish Church; something like many Churches in large country towns in England with an organ & Gallery at the west end. The Bishops & Deans seats are pointing to the west, on each side of the opening to the Chancel; & the stalls of the Prebend are to be in a line with them. There is a monument in the church of Mr Elvinope of the first inhabitants who died in 1676 – 102 years old. The bass of the pillars are of oxes heads, which I take to have been an old Roman altar cut in two pieces, brought probably from Scotland or the North of England – The present Primate gave a new organ to the church, who was first Dean & then Bishop of this church. There is a foot Barrack in the town for a Regiment, & a Magazine for powder, & an arsenal for their old Cannon. They bombarded & played ye Canon on the town from the windmill hill & from another height to the South west; & it is said that when they began to batter the town, the besieged sent to 'em not to hurt the town which would be their own, & that they need not batter, as the gates were open for them to come; & it is said that a Colonel of a Regiment offering his service to try if he could enter the gates which were actually left open; they having notice of it, plated canon one over another, gave them a terrible fire, sallyed out & cut the whole Regiment to pieces. Below the town about three miles is Culmore fort at the mouth of the river, across which a chain was drawn to prevent any relief coming to them; but a Ship went against it under full sail, broke the Chain, & brought them provisions when they were in great distress. In the church are two of the Standards which the besieged took from the enemy. The Governor is styled Governor of Culmore & Londonderry & has a sallary of £600 a year. The Commanding Officer is Deputy Governor, & when no troops are in it the Mayor, who is the returning Officer of Members both for this town & the County, as I was informed. They have here a great market every Wednesday for linnen & flaxen yarn; Colerain, Newtown Limne Vaddy & Strabane having linnen markets on the other days of the week for the same purpose, to which the Merchants go round & buy up the linnens & yarn, the latter is sent to Manchester.

On the 12th I spent the day with the Bishop, who on visiting him, insisted on my coming to his house, & sending my horses to his Stables; I walked round the ramparts with Mr Bernard, preached, & in the even walked round the town & to Windmill Hill.

(ARCHDEACON) RICHARD POCOCKE, 1752,
in *Richard Pococke's Irish Tours* (ed. John McVeagh), 1995

COMPARED WITH PREVIOUS VISITS I had made, few political slogans were scrawled on Derry's walls and gables. I only saw the occasional 'Release the Prisoners' (a reference to political prisoners then held in Belfast's Crumlin Road jail). In several places people had written in white paint 'Give us a university' – a decided improvement on the old type of slogan of disparaging remarks about the Pope or the Queen.

While jotting a few observations down in my notebook by the famous Roaring Meg cannon a 5-year-old boy stood to watch me.

'What are ya writin', mister?'

'A story,' I said.

'What story?'

'A story about soldiers,' I answered.

My new friend paused. He pulled a face, as though he did not think much of stories about soldiers. Then he said 'My da's a *sailor*. See that boat down there?'

I saw it. It was a white one with a red and black funnel, lying below us in the harbour.

'That's my da's ship.'

His da's ship was one of many in Derry's harbour that day. Four Canadian warships were also tied up there, trim and clean in their coats of light grey paint. Canadian sailors swarmed through the town to the delight of young boys for whom the sailors never failed to 'put 'em up' when the children shot at them from the walls. The sailors had returned to the city because one of their shipmates had to face a murder attempt charge against a woman he had met on a previous visit. But not even the fact that the sailors were standing-by in case they were called as witnesses could keep the women from responding to the flashing eye and homely charm of the New World.

I had left my camera, I thought, on the bus from Strabane. But it had not been handed in at the bus depot and I was taken to read the notice-boards outside the police station where there were lists of lost property given in to the authorities. My camera was not amongst the 'screw drivers, babies' panties, spare wheels, rosary beads, ladies' dressing gowns' that crowded the lists. Fortunately, I found the camera later back in Omagh where I had left it.

A lady who I am sure never lost her dressing gown in a public place was Princess Macha of the Golden Hair, whom I much admired. Holding a bird, she sat in state in front of Altnagelvin Hospital outside the town. The fine bronze statue depicted this legendary princess who gained her reputation by reputedly being the first person to establish a hospital in Ireland at some time around 300 BC.

Her hospital, I am sure, had nothing in common with the cloud-capped towers of the new Altnagelvin building. I much preferred the sculpture to the architecture. The princess was made by F.E. McWilliam, the distinguished Ulster sculptor. He is only known in Northern Ireland for this Princess Macha and a recent work at Queen's University. The Princess of the Golden Hair is very upright and very formal as befits a royal lady who is only a legendary one. She is also in a highly-stylized form which probably has caused eyebrows to be raised at the hospital by people who may well have preferred a conventional, realistic statue of Florence Nightingale and her lamp rather than the princess with her bird.

Still, the girl of the golden hair is there now and those responsible should be congratulated. Official taste in Ulster is not always so enlightened. Belfast Art Museum has another work of McWilliam's, the second copy of his bronze bust of the Ulster painter William Scott. The first copy of this is in the Tate Gallery, London, where it is paired with Scott's wife. To have the one bust without its mate seemed to me to be a curious acquisition for Belfast to have made.

Cathedral bells were ringing the hour when I woke next morning and looked from my hotel window at the broad walk along the top of the east wall. As I sat down in the dining-room to my snap-crackle-pop, I could not help thinking about the beleaguered citizens of 1689. What would they have said, on sitting down to their dinners of horse blood and boiled rat, if they had known that in three centuries' time the bells of their own Protestant cathedral would sound across the city with those of the Catholic one?

ROBIN BRYANS, *Ulster: A Journey Through the Six Counties*, 1964

SEVEN MILES:- AT LENGTH turning suddenly a corner, Derry is there to the south of us, close at hand; rising *red* and beautiful on elevated hill or 'bluff' (it must have been once). – Foyle moderately supplied with ships, running broad and clear past the farther side of it. The prettiest-looking town I have seen in Ireland. The free school; a big old building in fields, to right of us before we enter. Two or three *mill* chimnies (*not* corn-mills all of them, a linen-mill or flax-mill one at least visible); coal-yards, appearance of real shipping trade; suburbs, gate; and steep climb by the back of the old walls; Imperial hotel in fine – 'one of the best in Ireland,' says report; one of the dearest, and not the best, says experience. Very indifferent bed there (wretched French bed, which species may the devil fly away with out of this British country!); and for lullaby the common sounds of an inn, augmented by a very powerful *cock* towards morning.

A D^r McKnight (editor, pamphleteer &) warned by Duffy, came to night; led us thro' the city wonders, the old cannon &; gave us, unconsciously, a glimpse into the raging *animosities* (London companies *versus* Derry town was the chief, but there were many) which reign here as in all parts of Ireland, and alas, of most lands; – invites us to breakfast for monday; an honest kind of man, tho' loud-toned and with wild eyes, this McKnight; has tobacco too, and a kind little orderly polite wife (a 'poverty honourable and beautiful.') Surely we will go.

THOMAS CARLYLE, *Reminiscences of My Irish Journey*, 1849

LEAVING RAPHOE, WE CONTINUED OUR JOURNEY towards DERRY. Road rough, and more hilly, till we joined the great tract leading to STRABANE, which we saw at some distance to the south, at the extremity of a fine vale, watered by the River FOYLE. Pass ST JOHN'S-TOWN, and at two miles from DERRY, descend towards the river, from whence the city, pleasantly situated on a verdant knoll (under which the FOYLE takes a most magnificent curving sweep), opens to great advantage; road very bad near the town. There are two inns in BISHOP'S STREET, adjoining the city gates; MURRAY'S on the left, WALKER'S on the right, at the former of which, we found good accommodations, and post horses. The same kind of tillage prevails between RAPHOE and DERRY, with an occasional field of wheat.

The females were busily employed in their flax harvest, which emits a most nauseous smell when spread on the ground to dry.

The evening was employed in surveying the town, cathedral, &c. &c. The city is walled, and its elevated terrace affords a dry and pleasant walk: it has one handsome street, leading down to the port, with the Exchange in the centre. The Cathedral is a large and neat building, partaking of the castellated as well as ecclesiastical architecture, being turretted and embattled at the eastern angles: its style is that which was in vogue about the reign of K. Henry VIII. A tower is at this time building, in order to support a steeple, which, on account of its threatening appearance, was prudently taken down. The only inscription, worth recording, is the following:

> If stones could speak, then London's praise would sound,
> Who built this church and city from the ground.   1638

Some renovated white or French banners, recording the bravery of the citizens of DERRY, in the year 1689, are suspended on each side of the altar.

SIR RICHARD COLT HOARE (BART), *A Journal of a Tour in Ireland: AD 1806*, 1807

In the June heat, distant
glass and metal shiver.
By train we come to fix
our posed and easiest memories,
views, over blurring hedgerows,
beyond wide water, sliding
past to be photographed.

Strands run out to gold
invisibility. The line twists
inland through parched foliage;
a rotting pier, warehouses
matt with creosote, boarded shops –
all heap in our returning's frame,
driftwood to fuel the memory,

to kindle smouldering times
when we lay listening to
the swell of bomb blasts
lap at our shaking windows,
or watched across the city
the tall flame at Dupont's
burning waste. A place, she says,

appropriate to ending,
as we drink again
in a family bar, in Derry
where we met. Now we arrange
to part. Three years on,
we make the same small shapes
at this table, blurs

beyond focus of the public lens
tilted to arrange the clear
wrenched angles: William Street,
Rossville Flats, the walls.
All landscape is disfigured
to proclaim the vivid ignorant signs
our foregrounds hold –

misted pastoral for love,
for authentic hurt
dark dessications, random
trajectories of stone
collapse, slow
crush of plaster.
Leaving now, under an

intractable sun, eyes
narrow to old perspectives.
As ever, it seems the rails
shrink behind us, the future
rises like a ladder.
Behind hot glass,
exhibited like fish

or miniatures, we stare out
from our unmoving frieze,
drawn here as if to see
the Foyle's sun-blazed curve
arc through our splintered past,
a flaring match's path, one
glare of sulphur

used, extinguished.

PAUL WILKINS, 'Returning to Derry', *Pasts*, 1979

HEALY TOOK THE FIRST HIMSELF and filled it up again for me, but I insisted on Moore taking it as I had had two between Gweedore and Crolly. We then had turn about, and had the bottle finished by the time the train slowed down at Pennyburn Station.

When we came out on to the street there were a lot of jarveys there, and when they saw the policemen and a prisoner they thought they were on a 'dead cert'.

'We will take no car,' said Healy, 'we will walk it, as we are in no hurry.'

We walked up the Strand, and when we came to the Guildhall, Moore said: 'We will go in here and see what kind of stuff they keep.'

We went into the pub which is right opposite the Guildhall on the corner of Foyle Street – I think the name at the time was McCool. We went into a snug in the corner and got plenty of meat pies and drink and remained there until half-past nine. The bartender told the police they were taking too much drink, and the jail would be closed at ten o'clock.

'Damn the jail; we will never hand Mr Gallagher in. I do not care if I am dismissed in the morning,' said Healy.

'Right!' said Moore. 'I am with you every time. Put them up again!'

Their friendliness made me want to go straight into the jail to safeguard them. After some argumentation we went staggering up Shipquay Street and along Bishop Street. As we came up to the big gate of the jail there was a warder going in by a small door in it.

I don't remember it all very well. I know I was taken into a room, and I know my pockets were turned out. I am clear enough about a big man dressed in civilian clothes who entered. He held the warrant in his hand. I staggered a little and one of the warders shouted at me: 'Stand at ease!'

The big fellow said: 'You are not to speak to this gentleman like that! He is not the ordinary type of prisoner, he is one of His Majesty's Justices of the Peace.'

'Well, sir, he was handed into me like any other prisoner,' said the warder.

He began to search my pockets again calling to the man with the book: 'A metal watch, have you that down? Six shillings and eightpence – have you that down?'

'Yes,' said the other fellow.

That was all they found on me. (When I was leaving home Sally made me take a pound, but when I left the pub I had only six shillings and eightpence.)

Then the big man said to me: 'Mr Gallagher! Surely there must be some mistake somewhere. I see by the committal warrant that you can get off if you give bail. I think you should not come in here amongst the criminals.'

I tried to answer, but he saw I was not in a fit state to give an explanation. He then turned to the warder and said: 'Give him the best cell you have, and something to eat.'

The warder hooked me off to the cell.

'Your Worship,' said he, 'what would you like to eat?'

I told him that I was full enough. My bed was a plank about a foot from the ground, and an army blanket folded at the foot of the bed. It was not long until I was fast asleep. Next morning the warder told me that the big man was the Governor.

On Wednesday I was called out to do some exercise, but I felt too bad to stir. I was only three days in jail when I was told the Governor wanted to see me. I was brought to his office. He was sitting at the table when we went into the room, but when we entered he jumped to his feet, and picking up a telegram from the table, he read:

'Dublin Castle sixty-one. To the Governor, Derry Jail. Release Patrick Gallagher, JP, of Dungloe immediately. By Order of the Lords Justices.'

He then reached his hand to me and congratulated me on my release. I marched out.

PATRICK GALLAGHER, ('Paddy the Cope'), *My Story*, 1939

SAINT COLUMB'S CHAPEL, the walls of which still stand picturesquely in Sir George Hill's park, and from which that gentleman's seat takes its name, was here since the sixth century. It is but fair to give precedence to the mention of the old abbey, which was the father, as it would seem, of the town. The approach to the latter from three quarters, certainly, by which various avenues I had occasion to see it, is always noble. We had seen the spire of the cathedral peering over the hills for four miles on our way; it stands, a stalwart and handsome building, upon an eminence, round which the old-fashioned stout red houses of the town cluster; girt in with the ramparts and walls that kept out James's soldiers of old. Quays, factories, huge red warehouses, have grown round this famous old barrier, and now stretch along the river. A couple of large steamers and other craft lay within the bridge; and, as we passed over that stout wooden edifice, stretching eleven hundred feet across the noble expanse of the Foyle, we heard along the quays a great thundering and clattering of ironwork in an enormous steam frigate which has been built in Derry, and seems to lie alongside a whole street of houses. The suburb, too, through which we passed was bustling and comfortable; and the view was not only pleasing from its natural beauties, but has a manly, thriving, honest air of prosperity, which is no bad feature, surely, for a landscape.

Nor does the town itself, as one enters it, belie, as many other Irish towns do, its first flourishing look. It is not splendid, but comfortable; a brisk movement in the streets; good downright shops, without particularly grand titles; few beggars. Nor have the common people, as they address you, that eager smile, – that manner of compound fawning and swaggering, which an Englishman finds in the townspeople of the West and South. As in the North of England, too, when compared with other districts, the people are greatly more familiar, though by no means disrespectful to the stranger.

The rest of the occurrences at Derry belong, unhappily, to the domain of private life, and though very pleasant to recall, are not honestly to be printed. Otherwise, what popular descriptions might be written of the hospitalities of Saint Columb's, of the jovialities of the mess of the –th Regiment, of the speeches made and songs sung, and the devilled turkey at twelve o'clock, and the headache afterwards; all which events could be described in an exceedingly facetious manner. But these amusements are to be met with in every other part of Her Majesty's dominions; and the only point which may be mentioned here as peculiar to this part of Ireland, is the difference of the manner of the gentry to that in the South. The Northern manner is far more *English* than that of the other provinces of Ireland – whether it is *better* for being English is a question of taste, of which an Englishman can scarcely be a fair judge.

WILLIAM MAKEPEACE THACKERAY, *The Irish Sketch Book*, 1842

DERRY SITS IN TIERS steeply banked up the hillside from the edge of the River Foyle, which runs through the centre of the city, dividing it in half: Bogside and Waterside, Catholic and Protestant. Its spires and rooftops gleam in the summer sunset as one approaches it from the south. It is a unique town, with a character and atmosphere very much its own, unlike any other place in Northern Ireland – like a little city-state tucked away in a foreign land.

The first time I visited there was in 1978, and at that time so much violence had taken place in the preceding decade that it looked like a city at war. There were bombed-out houses and office buildings, bunkers on the streets, soldiers on foot and on Saracens, crowding its citizens off the public ways. This time, in the spring of 1987, it looked bright and bustling, and except for the ever-present truckloads of soldiers, it had repaired its physical wounds.

Straight rows of apple trees, white-blossomed and fragrant, line the road approaching the city. The sidewalks and streets were crowded with men and women: students, shoppers, workers, kids on bikes, young women with baby carriages. Babies, babies, more babies! The whole city looked like a nursery on an outing!

I found the Bogside, a warren of tiny, twisting, steep roads and lanes lined with neat row houses, snowy white lace curtains and shining brass knockers attesting to proud homemaking. Clusters of small children were playing in the empty streets or sitting in twos and threes on doorsteps. On corners, little girls fastened a rope to the top of a streetlamp and made a hoop seat on the end of the rope. They could then sit in the hoop and swing each other around and around the lamppost. They had a song that they sang while they swung, but when I approached them they were too shy to sing it for me.

There is something so tribal about the Bogside, so incestuous in its relationships, that even a stranger feels in some mysterious way 'at home' there. I suppose otherwise you would feel instantly alienated. I felt engulfed as I drove into its narrow, closed-in streets, but the feeling was warm and friendly, not ominous or frightening.

ELIZABETH SHANNON, I Am of Ireland, 1997

WE HAD BEEN WONDERING, during the final reel, how we were going to find our way back to the hotel through the dark and unfamiliar streets, for it was nearly ten o'clock; and we came out into them with a start of astonishment, for it was still quite light, with the street lights not yet on. So we loitered about for half an hour longer; and then, from the balcony in front of our window, sat watching for an hour more the fascinating life flowing past below us.

One feature of it was a boy quartette, – one of the boys with a clear, high soprano voice, – which sang very sweetly, 'It's a long way to Tipperary'; and then, just as we began to think everybody had gone to bed, there came a blast of martial music down the street, and the tramp of feet, and a company of men swung past, going heaven knows where; but the fife-and-drum corps which marched at their head was making the windows rattle with

> The Maiden on her throne, boys,
>   shall be a Maiden still!

It was the first of many such processions we were to see during our remaining weeks in Ireland.

BURTON E. STEVENSON, The Charm of Ireland, 1915

THE GENIALITY AND FILTH OF DERRY, and its state of siege, made the city an interesting muddle. Here were old geezers being shifty and jaunty in an Irish way, and over there the British soldiers were tense and watchful and stiff with starch. They crouched in doorways, peering, rifles poised, while the women gathered at Foyle's Pork Store (nothing but sausages and hams) and the men strolled into the betting shop. The soldiers meant business. They wore helmets and face masks and they travelled in armoured cars; they moved singly, covering each other; all their vehicles had wire skirts beneath the chassis so that fire bombs could not be rolled under them.

PAUL THEROUX, The Kingdom by the Sea: A Journey Around the Coast of Great Britain, 1982

THE PUBLIC BUILDINGS of Derry are, I think, among the best I have seen in Ireland; and the Lunatic Asylum, especially, is to be pointed out as a model of neatness and comfort. When will the middle classes be allowed to send their own afflicted relatives to public institutions of this excellent kind, where violence is never practised – where it is never to the interest of the keeper of the asylum to exaggerate his patient's malady, or to retain him in durance, for the sake of the enormous sums which the sufferer's relatives are made to pay? The gentry of three counties which contribute to the Asylum have no such resource for members of their own body, should any be so afflicted – the condition of entering this admirable asylum is, that the patient must be a pauper, and on this account he is supplied with every comfort and the best curative means, and his relations are in perfect security. Are the rich in any way so lucky? – and if not, why not?

WILLIAM MAKEPEACE THACKERAY, *The Irish Sketchbook*, 1842

There's burnt ground
and a cindertrack
all along the ridge
between the shops
and the railway bridge,
like it's occupied territory
with no one around
this cold snap.
Here's a wet sheugh
smells like a used sheath,
and here's frogspawn
and a car battery
under a screggy hawthorn.
They're having a geg
chucking *weebits* and *yuk*
and laughing at the blups –
kids turned fierce
on a tip,
little hard men in boiler suits
locked in a wargame.

Yesterday I stared
at this girl with cropped hair –
a grandpa shirt on her
and lovebites on her neck,
little pinky bruises

like a rope had snagged there.
Ah shite, the bitter joy
as the plunged head gets born! –
a March wind
hits the main street
of a village called Convoy
and I'm starved
by the first screech that's torn
from out the guts of the blind poet.

★

Something in the air,
too-quiet-altogether
on the back road that slips
down into Derry.
Where that open pasture
slopes from a close wood
to a file of chestnuts
there's a counterfeit sense
that unsettles me just now.
It might be the landlord's absence
from a version of pastoral,
or the hidden scanner
that has to be somewhere.

Over the ramp
the light that bangs back
from the fieldgrey screens
has a preserved feel to it,
like radio silence
or the site of an accident.
I wind down the window,
pass proof of myself
and match
the copper stubble on his chin
with the light green
of his shirt –
may God forgive me
this parched gift of sight.

★

This hereness is to loiter
by a quay in Derry
and gaze at the spread river,
the pigeons and the pigeon-cowlings
on a stained flour mill,
until a voice whispers
in the balmy sigh of a lover,
'who's in the wrong county
like the maiden city?'

★

'Would you give us a lift, love?
It's that late n'scary ...'
I was only half there
like a girl after a dance,
wary, on the road to Muff.
We might've been out after curfew
in the buzzy *deux-chevaux*,
slipping past the chestnuts
on a street in provincial France.

It stuck close to me, though,
how all through the last half
a helicopter held itself
above the Guildhall –
Vershinin's lines were slewed
by the blind chopping blades,
though Olga looked chuffed
when she sighed, 'Won't it be odd
with no soldiers on the streets?'

TOM PAULIN, 'S/He', *The Liberty Tree*, 1983

DERRY IS THE TRUE EMBODIMENT of the plantation spirit; it is the real capital of that Protestant community which is spread over all Ulster, mixed but not blended with the native Catholic stock. Belfast and its outliers from Portadown to Ballymena are a different development. They belong to the nineteenth century, Derry to the seventeenth; they live on their present, Derry to a great extent on its past. Even in politics Derry looks on Belfast as a centre of unsafe and revolutionary ideas. It is in Derry that you can study the contribution which the Ulster plantation made to the development of Ireland.

As a town Derry is without beauty, except that which comes from its situation on rising ground beside a very noble river; it possesses no building of architectural beauty, no trace of sculptor's work that a trained eye would rest on with pleasure. But – and this is no small matter – there are few places in it that would offend the eye.

As a whole, it is clean, tidy, well-kept, prosperous-looking, with many signs of well-doing and comfort, few of wealth and luxury. There are good serviceable shops, but not the shops of expensive wares that one sees, for instance, at an English watering-place. It is primarily a county town; the county town in reality of Donegal as well as of its own county; supplying the wants of a gentry not rich but numerous, and of a farming population which, using the plough, brings a good deal of custom to traders.

STEPHEN GWYNN, *The Famous Cities of Ireland*, 1915

THEY ARE THE PEOPLE, too, who keep calling Derry 'Londonderry'. That's a name that's not used by any indigenous Northerner, not even the Protestants, for they'd be too self-conscious. The right name for the city is Derry from the Irish *Doire Cholm Chille* – meaning the oak-grove of Colmkille. It got the name Londonderry from a company of swindlers that were founded in London, in the seventeenth century, to drive the native Irish off the land and to settle the place with English and Scots.

It's a lovely city, Derry, and the people are all very kind and generous – as they are all over the county. I remember being up there once with my wife and we went out for a picnic. We had cold meat, tomatoes, hard-boiled eggs and bread and butter, but the one thing we needed was a drink, but being Sunday the pubs were shut. I passed a chemist's shop, however, that was open for a couple of hours, and like many other chemist's shops, there was wine for sale in it. Usually it's Australian Burgundy sold medicinally for the amount of iron in it, for it turns your tongue and teeth black when you drink it. There was an old woman behind the counter and I asked her for a bottle of wine.

'I'm sorry,' she said, 'but it's Sunday and I couldn't sell it. In the first place, it's against the law and in the second place, it would be against my principles, for I'm a teetotaller and I only sell it as medicine.'

'Well, ma'am,' I said, 'it's against my principles to drink anything else but wine. I'm not a Presbyterian but a Calathumpian'.

'Oh!' she said, 'I never heard of them. What are they?'

'Well,' I said, 'they're a religion that would sooner eat the stalks of cabbage than the leaves. But another important part of our faith is founded strictly on the Bible and, as a good Presbyterian, you know that wine was almost the only thing they drank in Biblical times.'

'What,' said she, 'about milk?'

'It interferes with my digestion,' I said; 'I'd be going against my doctor's orders if I drank milk, and I'd be going against my religion if I drank tea or coffee, and I'm just about to have something to eat and I need something to drink with my food.'

'Well,' she said then, 'I won't interfere with any man's covenant with God for the sake of any man-made law,' and she gave me the bottle of wine, which was drunk by my wife and myself with humility and pious gratitude.

BRENDAN BEHAN, *Brendan Behan's Island*, 1962

THIS BLOODY PAST HAS NOT PREVENTED DERRY from prospering more than any other Irish town; it affords a unique instance of a population of 30,000 having been tripled in the last fifty years. It is built in the shape of an amphitheatre, upon the rising ground which borders the left bank of the Foyle, where it opens into the bay of the same name. Clean, with wide streets and pretty houses, its appearance rather reminds one of Lausanne. The only historical monuments possessed by this very unwarlike town are the ramparts, which have been turned into a public promenade. Here there still remains a battery of old cannon, one of which in particular – Roaring Meg – attained some notoriety in the siege. In one of the bastions a monument had been erected to the memory of George Walker. It consists of a statue on the top of a very ugly column. It is an extraordinary form of madness that leads people in British countries to immortalize their heroes in the semblance of parrots on their perch. The rev. gentleman must have taken a liking for war, since he was killed at the Battle of the Boyne.

Derry has an Episcopal cathedral, built in the seventeenth century on the site of Tempal More, crowning the highest point of the town, with its lofty embattled tower flanked with bell-turrets. The palace of the Protestant bishop is a gloomy edifice of brick, built on the site of St Columba's Abbey. There is not a single old stone to gladden the heart of the antiquary or the eye of the painter. Modern though Derry be, all the same it has a dreary appearance, more especially in the higher parts, where the chief streets meet in the central market place, called by the Irish a 'diamond'. The port, on the contrary, is very lively and well filled with vessels of large tonnage, though, pending the enlargement of the channel, the big Atlantic steamboats anchor at Moville, at the mouth of Lough Foyle.

While the traveller, sitting in his immense room in the great dark Hotel Jury, is consulting his guidebooks with that fever of perpetual movement that in a few weeks turns to monomania, he jumps up suddenly at the sound of a growing tumult of steps, shouts and yells, which disturb the quiet of the silent street. It sounds like the clamour of a riot. Can it be another St Bartholomew, a massacre of Catholics or Protestants? In this troubled land, you must be ready for everything. Thanking the providence that has contrived for your benefit a sight so full of local colour, you run to the window.

But no! It is nothing but a big flock of geese being taken through the town to the port, where they will be shipped for Great Britain to fulfil their destiny, which is to be fattened up for Michaelmas. If they happen to meet a flock of frightened sheep at some turning, or some cattle petrified by fear, or pigs squealing as if their throats were already being cut, the confusion and disturbance become indescribable.

MARIE-ANNE DE BOVET, *Trois Mois en Irlande*, 1891
(TRANSLATION BY MRS ARTHUR WALTER)

THE EMOTIVE DETAILS OF THE SIEGE of Derry slipped easily into folk memory. I was regaled with them as a child, the zeal of the apprentice boys, Lundy's treachery, Walker's unappetising shopping list ('a dog's head 2.6, a cat 4.6, a rat 1s ... a mouse 6d'). My mother possessed a small table reputed to have belonged to Governor Walker.

No symbolism could have been invented that was more potent than the myth of defiance of the overwhelming forces of Catholicism led by the shifty Pretender. The champions of Protestantism were, like William himself, irreproachably colourless. The clergyman, Walker, writing his diary and Michelburne with his bloody flag (whose scarlet colour is remembered in the uniform of the Apprentice Boys) are dim figures compared to James. The last Stuart king emerges as an easy villain for those who continue to find emotional sustenance in the conviction that the exertions of their forebears preserved a perpetual small corner of the earth for the Protestant faith.

Such thoughts occur without much prompting in Derry. So do ideas about its alien atmosphere. De Latocnaye felt that the city 'had no appearance of being an Irish city – a degree of industry and activity reigns there unknown in any other parts of the country'. Of course it appealed to Carlyle – 'The prettiest looking town I have seen in Ireland.' 'Every man in it is "town proud",' wrote Samuel Bayne in 1904.

No one could be town proud about Derry today and the inroads which the IRA have made on the old civic arrogance have been a dubious achievement. Past walled-up houses, vanished houses and shuttered houses with security screens on the windows I made my way to St Columb's Cathedral, built in 1633 by the Irish Society in the design of a very large English parish church. Among the military monuments, the cannonball from the siege and other militaria that even more than usual in Protestant ecclesiastical buildings suggest the siege mentality, I found two monuments to members of my mother's family. They appeared to be average Establishment figures, a judge in Bengal and a general.

The Scott family has lived in the neighbourhood of Derry since around the time of the siege. An early Reverend Scott was a chaplain to King William and received a watch. King William seems to have given timepieces to a number of clergymen. I have an idea of him on that day at the Boyne mounted on his white charger surrounded by his chaplains in their robes like a flock of birds, all murmuring blessings. And later that evening they line up while he dips into the huge trunk full of watches.

The wind blew in cold gusts across the Foyle, scattering rubbish. There are no hotels in Derry at present; the violence has seen to that. I retired to a café in Ship Street darkened by steel grilles before going down below the Diamond and the city walls to the bus station. Two small boys were inside a bus breaking up the seats. It took time for Ulsterbus to find me an unvandalised vehicle and I was driven out of Derry along another smooth highway. Southerners tend to sneer at the splendid roads in the North and claim that some of the money spent on their upkeep could go on urban renewal. It is envy.

Near the turn-off for Eglington was the defunct Courtauld factory, a reminder of all that was wrong in Ulster. At Eglington the riots and burnings in Derry and the unemployment represented by the demise of Courtaulds could be easily forgotten. Many people who lived there worked in Derry. In the evenings they hurried out to the tree-lined Georgian village built by some London Livery Company in the days of plantation. The mock Tudor pub and the cricket ground where teams in white flannels play on summer weekends stressed the English connection. No bombs, no graffiti, no torn black gaps in the lines of pretty houses. And Derry less than eight miles away.

PETER SOMERVILLE-LARGE, *The Grand Irish Tour*, 1982

DERRY IS ALSO ONE OF THE FEW TOWNS that still jealously preserves its walls, and it is not surprising that a deep-seated sentiments attaches to these bastions, which still mount the cumbrous artillery used in the famous siege. Within their hilly *enceinte* as little has been changed as possible; the small squares and tree-fringed streets preserve much of the character of a thrifty old North of Ireland town, and indeed the curfew is still rung each evening from the spire of the cathedral on the hill, to which the Companies of London subscribed for the building in an interesting but belated version of Perpendicular. Eighteenth-century houses rub shoulders with dignified civic buildings of a hundred years later, and I would like to draw your attention to the jail which, on the outside at least, is one of the most delicious specimens of Georgian 'castellation' that I know. But perhaps the most charming architectural feature is the gates which, with their classic proportions and carved trophies, have an air of eighteenth-century France that it is strange to find in Ulster.

Outside the walls spreads the new town, and every year a little more of the landscape across the Foyle gets filled with slate roofs. But one must commend Derry for doing the opposite to most towns nowadays and keeping its core intact, however much this may interfere with modern traffic requirements. The place is growing outwards at a great rate, nevertheless, and already fills a good slice of the valley which sweeps southward in wood-mantled loops to Strabane. But to the south-east the pastures end in the high moorland massive of the Sperrins, and among these gauntly rounded hills, which always remind me a little of the fells of Southern Scotland, you can feel, I think, as solitary as anywhere in Ireland. Only the piled turves by the roadside, or the sight, perhaps, of a shepherd leaning on his crook in the distance, remind you that human life has established a footing here. The chief way through the hills is by the Glenshane Pass, an austere thousand-foot defile threaded by the infant Roe, from the crest of which there is a tremendous view across the lower country to Lough Neagh, and in good weather, I believe, to the far-distant Mournes beyond.

MICHAEL FLOYD, *The Face of Ireland*, 1937

IN THE PRAISE OF DERRY I cannot go quite so far as its local historian, Mr Hempton, who asserts that, 'whether it be regarded in relation to its singular picturesqueness, or to its historical associations, Londonderry is, perhaps, equally superior to any other city in the British Empire.' The assertion is characteristic, for the inhabitants of Derry are, to borrow an expressive word from the north of England, 'town-proud'.

And it cannot be denied that they have a right to be. Their walls stand as the monument of a siege, more famous than any other which has been conducted in Great Britain; of a resistance as obdurate as Saragossa's, and more fortunate. Moreover, in peaceful modern times the town has thriven and gained a considerable commercial importance, chiefly from the success of its shirt factories.

As to its picturesqueness, Derry is totally devoid of any architectural beauties, but its situation lends it a certain charm. It stands on the left bank of the Foyle, where the river is tidal, and at all times a noble stream, over 300 yards wide. The ground on which it stands is a sharply rising knoll, in old days practically an island, for the north of the town – still called the Bog Side – was an impassable morass. Both banks of the river are richly wooded and rise into hills; and from whatever point you see the town you will discern its acropolis, the cathedral stretching up to the sky. The cathedral has been altered greatly since the days when two guns were posted on its roof (then flat), to answer the fire of Hamilton's army; but, as Macaulay observes, 'it is filled with memorials of the siege.' Over the altar are draped captured French colours, with their silk indeed renewed, but the poles and tassels were wrested from the hands of besiegers; in the vestibule is a huge shell that was flung into the town, containing conditions of surrender. But the main feature of the town is its wall, on whose top a walk runs, wide enough in places, the inhabitants will tell you, for a carriage and pair to drive along it. On the wall are still mounted the guns that were fought in the siege; one of them retains its name to this day, Roaring Meg, given from the loudness of its report. And on the west side of the wall rises a column, ninety feet high, topped by a statue of Walker, to whom history (in the person of Macaulay) has given the chief credit for the famous defence.

Close to the cathedral is the central square of the city, 'the diamond', from which the streets fall sharply away north, east, and south. Here are gathered the principal public buildings, which, however, have little interest for a stranger. In the centre of the Diamond stands the Corporation Hall, now changed to other uses, which replaced the original wooden one knocked to pieces by the bombardment. The street running west leads to Bishopsgate, a triumphal arch erected in 1789 to commemorate the raising of the siege. On the north side of this street is the palace, a huge red-brick building, constructed by the Earl of Bristol, and more suitable for a prelate whose revenues reached £12,000 a year than for the modest salary with which a disestablished church rewards its divines. The cathedral has been modernised, and nothing in the town, except the walls, speaks even of a moderate antiquity, much less of a Celtic origin; yet Derry, unlike Belfast, has a history stretching far back into the past.

STEPHEN GWYNN, *Highways and Byways in Donegal and Antrim*, 1928

THE MODERN GUILDHALL faces a battlemented wall with old cannon appearing from the bastions, each provided by a merchant company of London City. The Walls are laid out as a promenade, and, by walking along them to the right, one comes to the Walker Monument with its statue looking out to the estuary. On the hilltop within the walls stands the Protestant cathedral of St Columba, a plain Gothic building erected by the City of London in 1628–33. The Catholics have a cathedral, too, but it is modern and not centrally sited.

My private interest in Derry springs from an instance of unprecedented hospitality with which I was favoured. A casual inquiry of a young lady out with her baby and pram led to an invitation to her house and introduction to her husband. Perhaps it was not quite so surprising when I mention that the couple were country people living in town because of housing difficulties, and following afternoon tea and high tea I was taken by car to the farm of Mr H. three miles away near the border, where an ailing cow had to have attention. But it still astonishes me that such a queer vagabond as myself should have been entertained so royally when quite unknown to the couple. There are nature's gentlefolk in England as well as Ireland, yet each time I think of that cordial reception in Derry I say to myself 'It couldn't happen here.' So much for Ulster Protestant dourness!

I stayed the night at the home of Mr and Mrs H., and could have remained longer, but I had rested well at Rathmullan, and it was now my intention to go by bus inland to Claudy and then walk over the peaty Sperrin Mountains that roam along the Londonderry–Tyrone border, attaining 2,240 feet on Sawel. It was not to be. Heavy rain returned with the morning, and after looking round the old walled city where it clings to its hill above the Foyle's left bank I crossed the river and made for the Northern Counties station. (The line terminating here was then the property of the British LMS Railway, but now belongs to the Ulster Transport Authority.)

JOHN WOOD, With Rucksack Round Ireland, 1950

FROM DUNGIVEN I SET OUT for Londonderry, passing through a beautiful country, and over a succession of undulating hills generally cultivated to the summit. From a circumstance which had taken place only the night before, I heard a little more on the subject of elopements. The daughter of a farmer whose house I passed had fled with her suitor; and the person who gave me the history of the affair remarked that the custom was getting gradually into disuse. The young men, he said, not satisfied with voluntary elopements, had latterly been guilty of everything but manual violence. Having fixed upon a girl whose parents were sufficiently wealthy for his purpose, the aspirant took care to meet her and her friends at a fair; where, assisted by his accomplices, he prevailed upon her to drink away her caution. In the confusion of the crowd, and the obscurity of the twilight, he found little difficulty in separating her from her party, and carrying her off, whether conscious or unconscious of her destination. After this, if the father did not choose to comply with his terms, he sent his victim home, with a ruined character. In this recital we have distinctly before us the connecting link between an odd but generally harmless custom, and the violent and brutish abductions in other parts of the country. The interested nature of the transaction, even in this district is proved by a remark of my informant, that the farmer's daughter mentioned above ran no risk of being sent back, having taken the precaution of carrying a fifty pound bank note with her.

I passed another of O'Cahan's castles by the road side, but rudely built, and uninteresting. The scenery, however, became still more picturesque as I approached Londonderry; and at length the city appeared, in its finest aspect, that of an island (as it seemed from this distance) in the midst of the Foyle, surrounded by battlemented walls, and piled up with houses, rising towards the centre, the whole surmounted by a single lofty spire. The view annexed is taken from a different point; but it exhibits distinctly a very important feature in the picture, the long and very handsome wooden bridge. The fortifications consist of an earthen rampart faced with stone, and strengthened with bastions. Within there are four main streets, with lanes diverging; the main streets being entered through archways. Outside are suburbs of a less distinguished character, for inside the walls, the greater part of the town is built on a scale of high respectability.

Londonderry is a thriving town, and the inhabitants have just the appearance which might be expected. They are business-like people, and have the air of knowing what they are about. I observed, with a little amusement, the desolate condition of a showman, who, by some unfortunate mistake, had here pitched his caravan. In vain he shouted, in vain he thumped his drum, in vain he paraded his corps dramatique: no one even turned his head to look as he passed by. At eight o'clock in the evening, I walked round the ramparts, a delightful promenade, rendered at the time as light as day by means of numerous lamps, but I did not encounter a human being. Londonderry is in fact a very respectable town, and its inhabitants are very respectable people; but, since I have, on the present occasion, but little to do with business details, I may be excused for continuing my journey with as brief delay as possible.

LEIGH RITCHIE, *Ireland: Picturesque and Romantic*, 1838

I REACHED DERRY ABOUT 9 O'CLOCK, and put up at the Imperial Hotel, just opposite the Bishop's Palace. Here I met with bishop's prices, though not, unfortunately, with bishop's fare, which after my long walk would have been very acceptable. I was received by a showily-dressed handsome waiter, who began immediately to take a great interest in my day's journey. Now this I thought did not look hopeful, for according to my experience of hotels, whenever any person connected with the establishment begins to talk about individual matters not connected with the inn, there is sure to be a deficiency somewhere. Such remarks are intended to put the traveller in good humour, and to serve as a kind of antidote or counterpoise to something very disagreeable. However on this occasion the boots, when he brought up my hot water, said that the waiter was doing the best he could for me, which looked cheering. On coming down, the waiter in the blandest manner, as if I had been a bishop at least, ushered me into the room opposite the coffee-room, as it would be cooler and less noisy, and pointing to the table, said with an air of great self-satisfaction, 'There's your dinner, sir.' I looked and saw before me that sight which is so familiar to the frequenter of English country inns, the half-consumed joint of roast beef, without any potatoes, although there had been ample time to cook them, or any other accompaniment; and, as if to make matters worse, I ordered a bottle of claret, which turned out vile stuff. That joint seemed to haunt me during my stay at Derry. I saw it next morning in the coffee-room at breakfast, and again when I came in at lunch time. I could not help speculating on the fortunate traveller who first put the knife into it, while hot and steaming, then the succession of travellers who at different stages partook of this substantial joint. My imagination then descended to the kitchen, and I saw a party of maids and waiters assembled around its remains and talking gossips, and finally I could see, in the mind's eye, some dog munching the bone with evident satisfaction. My bedroom here, also, was ill-ventilated. Some addition had been made to the hotel, and two or three rooms thrown up, regardless of the fact that the only look-out was a high wall opposite. The chambermaid, however, the next day when she brought some things I had directed to be washed, apologised for the room, and promised me a better one if I remained. Perhaps she had become impressed by the cold water I had used, for I heard her observing to a fellow-servant at the end of the passage about the quantity of water she had taken into that gentleman's room, evidently referring to myself. But there is one thing I must say in favour of the Imperial Hotel, the clothes were beautifully washed, so the bishop has at least taught this lesson, that 'cleanliness is next to godliness.'

Monday, August 21. – After breakfast I sallied forth to see the famous city of Londonderry, called for the sake of brevity, Derry. I went in the first place to visit the cathedral. It has a fine spire, which I had seen for miles along the country side. The church consists of a nave simply, which is certainly a novelty, but it looks very well. The pews are good and comfortable. There are painted windows. The East window is of the date of the church, 1633; the others, I believe, are more recent. The cathedral has been renovated, but the original pillars remain unaltered. There are monuments to Dr Knox, the last bishop but one, and to Dr Ponsonby, the last bishop, both highly complimentary. The present bishop is Dr Higgin. I had observed the palace, which is a large brick building, and so remarked to the sexton, an official who showed me over the cathedral. He replied, with some emphasis, 'The bishop lives in a stone house.' It is considered in Ireland a distinction to live in a stone house, as distinguished from one of mud, wood, or thatch. I ascended the tower of the cathedral, from which a fine view is obtained of the city and its suburbs, and the river Foyle and the surrounding country. A great part of the city, indeed the greater part, now lies beyond the walls. The ascent of the tower is very difficult, and ultimately up several ladders. The sexton told me that ladies frequently ascended, which, in these days of crinoline, must be rather a feat to accomplish.

I then ascended to the ramparts by the steps at the Bishop's Gate and walked round the walls, those walls rendered so famous by the celebrated siege of Londonderry. In a rough garden along the ramparts there are now to be seen six large guns which were used at the siege. One of them has the inscription, 'Vintners, London, 1642', and is placed on a stone stand. Another, 'Mercers, London 1642', on the ground. Another on an iron stand or carriage, two more on the ground, on one of them 'E.R. 1590', and on the other some figures and letters which are indistinct. But the most famous of all the six guns is one called 'Roaring Meg', from the great noise caused by its explosion. It bears the following inscription: 'Fishmongers, London 1642. Vita Veritas Victoria. All worship be to God only.'

That which had been the scene of so much bloodshed and of such a glorious struggle was now peaceful enough. Some pretty little girls were playing about the guns and using them as stands for making rough sketches of the adjoining houses. They pronounced their words so well that I took them for English children, but one of them, on my asking her, replied 'No, I have never been out of Derry, except to a few places,' meaning not out of Ireland. Their little dog, however, kept snarling away, the only interruption to the serene quiet which prevailed.

I then walked along the ramparts until – I mean no pun here – I reached Walker's monument. On two sides are the names of Mitchelburn, Baker, Murray, Cairnes, Leake, and Browning, and in the centre there is the following memorial:–

> This monument was erected to perpetuate the memory of the Rev. George Walker, who, aided by the garrison and brave inhabitants of this city, most gallantly defended it through a protracted siege, namely from the 7th Dec. 1689 to the 12th of August following, against an arbitrary and bigoted Monarch heading an army of upwards of 20,000 men, many of whom were foreign mercenaries; and by such valiant conduct in numerous sorties and by patiently enduring extreme privations and sufferings, successfully resisted the besiegers, and preserved for their posterity the blessings of civil and religious liberty.

To the right of the monument there are three guns, two on the ground and a large one on a carriage; and to the left also three guns, two on carriages, one large and one small, and another on the ground. The city of Derry seems to cherish the old walls with just pride; and where they have given way a new rampart has been added, as much as possible resembling the original structure. At the entrance of the cathedral there is a cannon-ball which during the siege was thrown into the church, but I was informed by the sexton that so far as he was aware there was not now to be met with any other cannon-ball or shell in any of the gardens or enclosures along the ramparts.

I now take my leave of Londonderry with my own actual experiences there. The reader perhaps may be surprised to find that I have not related at some length an account of the celebrated siege, borrowed from Macaulay and others. What an excellent opportunity for padding! But this is not my plan of writing. My desire is simply to relate the results of my own observation and experience during my travels in Ireland.

I left Derry about the middle of the day, intending to walk to Strabane, about fifteen miles, before nightfall. After leaving the town the road winds through a pretty avenue of trees, which proved welcome enough, as there came down a heavy shower of rain just at this time. Seated quite in the dry, under a large and wide-spreading tree, I had the satisfaction to watch a boat with some gentlemen rowing towards the shore, to obtain nature's friendly shelter from the dripping storm. I observed some fishermen in two or three places with nets catching fish. I saw some salmon come out, but they looked small. The country between Derry and Strabane is rich with quiet scenery. A peasant said a great part of the country hereabouts belongs to the Marquis of Abercorn and is let in farms of from seven to sixty acres, at from twenty-five to thirty shillings an acre.

'AN ENGLISHMAN', *A Walking Tour through Ireland in 1865*, 1867

AS THE TRAIN PASSED DOWN from Victoria Bridge to Derry on the west side of the Strule, I could see the road on the east side by which we went to Derry on our way to America; and when in sight of Derry I could see the bridge over which we crossed from the east side of the river into the city, on that occasion. On leaving the train and securing a luncheon at the Jura Hotel, I set out for the old walled town of historical celebrity. I knew the direction to find Bishops gate in the city wall near which we had lodged long ago, and had not far to go till it appeared in view. I remembered it well and that an old woman sat beside it at a stall selling penny's worth of the nutritious sea weed called *dulce*, and candies. And there now was the gate all the same as I had left it; and sure enough an old woman, the counterpart of the one I had left there sixty-four years ago, and with the very same kind of stand and merchandise. After buying and tasting some of her wares, in memory of former transactions of the same kind at her stand when with me half pennies were scarce, I sought and mounted the stone steps to the top of the wall, which I again traversed as when a little boy led by the hand of my father, feeling very much the same as then, only my thoughts now were tempered more with sadness. I could still remember the cannon and other important objects. I made my way around the entire wall, stopping and inspecting each old gun and the date of its manufacture. Here they remain and are kept in reasonably good condition; but still time has produced heavy pock-marks upon them, notwithstanding the repeated coats of paint. They are in their positions to rake an enemy and protect the ramparts, just as in the time of the memorable siege; and to all appearance Roaring Meg and her sisters could open fire and do good service on an enemy yet. She would have to be elevated considerably however, or would play havoc on the surrounding buildings; because more of Derry is now outside than inside the walls. Captain John Walker, a stubborn Presbyterian preacher and indomitable fighter who commanded the besieged, still keeps one hand on the open Bible whilst he grasps a sword with the other, on the summit of his tower: a shining example of the former force of religious opinion.

The wall is about twenty feet high and a little over forty feet wide on top, with parapets or breastworks on each side. Its circuit can be made at an easy walk in an hour and a half. After making the circuit and descending from the wall, I obtained admission into the ancient Cathedral of Derry and made my way up into the steeple, where hang the celebrated old Joy Bells of Derry, whose chimes, morning and evening, had so delighted me when a child during our stay in the town. Ten of these are the same which were presented to the cathedral by King Charles; two are of the same metal, but were smashed by a cannon ball during the siege and recast afterwards.

From the balcony of the steeple I had a splendid view of the city inside and outside the walls, and of the Loch and surrounding country. On leaving the church, old memories were again aroused by strains of music produced by a blind man on the streets. The air came to me like an old friend long absent; easily recognized but the name forgotten. From the child in whose plate I put a few pennies I learned the air was 'Derry Walls Away'. Produced as this blind man produced it on his pipe, no music that I have ever heard could excel it in exiting the passions or putting 'life and metal in the heels' of those inclined to dance. Those old Irish and Scotch airs have their origin in the wild depths of human feeling, and are eloquent of the history and sentiments of their time.

But I had now seen all I cared to see of Derry; indeed, all I cared to see of Ireland. I had seen again the places and people near and dear to me as old friends, around whom my early memories clustered. All else were unrelated to me, and strangers: so at three o'clock I was again on the train for Belfast.

MATTHEW T. MELLON (ed.), *Selections from* Thomas Mellon and His Times,
by Judge Thomas Mellon, 1976

A
Maiden Still

Where Foyle his swelling waters
    Rolls northward to the main,
Here, Queen of Erin's daughters,
    Fair Derry fixed her reign;
A holy temple crowned her,
    And commerce graced her street,
A rampart wall was round her,
    The river at her feet;
And here she sat alone, boys,
    And, looking from the hill,
Vowed the Maiden on her throne, boys,
    Would be a Maiden still.

From Antrim crossing over,
    In famous eighty-eight,
A plumed and belted lover
    Came to the Ferry Gate:
She summoned to defend her
    Our sires – a beardless race –
They shouted 'No Surrender!'
    And slammed it in his face.
Then, in a quiet tone, boys,
    They told him 'twas their will
That the Maiden on her throne, boys,
    Should be a Maiden still.

Next, crushing all before him,
    A kingly wooer came
(The royal banner o'er him
    Blushed crimson deep for shame);
He showed the Pope's commission,
    Nor dreamed to be refused;
She pitied his condition,
    But begged to stand excused.
In short, the fact is known, boys,
    She chased him from the hill,
For the Maiden on the throne, boys,
    Would be a Maiden still.

On our brave sires descending,
    'Twas then the tempest broke,
Their peaceful dwellings rending,
    'Mid blood, and flame, and smoke.
That hallowed grave-yard yonder
    Swells with the slaughtered dead –
O brothers! pause and ponder –
    It was for us they bled;
And while their gift we own, boys –
    The fane that tops our hill –
Oh! the Maiden on her throne, boys,
    Shall be a Maiden still!

Nor wily tongue shall move us,
    Nor tyrant arm affright,
We'll look to One above us
    Who ne'er forsook the right;
Who will, may crouch and tender
    The birthright of the free,
But, brothers, 'No Surrender,'
    No compromise for me!
We want no barrier stone, boys,
    No gates to guard the hill,
Yet the Maiden on her throne, boys,
    Shall be a Maiden still.

CHARLOTTE ELIZABETH (Mrs Tonna), 'The Maiden City', 1835

The Lord of Argile to Lenthall

[31 Aug 1646]

One of the printed ordinances of this parliament of England published 1641, inviting all well affected Christians to the relief of the Protestant Garrisons in Ireland vzt. Dublin, Caricfergus Londonderry &c came to the hands of Tho: Smart, citizen and merchant in Danzick in Prussia. He laded a ship with wheat and rye, delivered at Londonderry, whereby that and other Protestant garrisons were relieved in 1643, when poor people were dying in the streets. The ordinance promised payment in 30 days, but Smart is still unsatisfied.

Two several letters from 'the Lords of Dantzick' in his behalf have been presented by his servant and read in both houses without receiving answer.

He came over himself in May last with a third letter which was presented to the House of Lords and read and was referred to the Commons, yet has had no answer, notwithstanding a letter of request from the Comm^{rs} for Scotland.

He desires such speedy answer 'as may cause his sudden and happy return with his money in his purse', which cannot be more welcome than those corns were to the distressed Protestants thereby relieved.

[Fo. 519/328].

The Tanner Letters, 1943

To Louis XIV, 12 May 1689:

Matters are not going too well in the north. M. de Pusignan [French general] was wounded by a musket shot in the body which could have been cured if there were one good surgeon in the whole army. But I do not expect him to live, and he is dying as much by dismay at seeing himself abandoned in his plight and illness as by the actual wound.

To Louvois [Louis XIV's minister of war], 18 May 1689:

I am informed that, contrary to the express orders he has been given, M. Hamilton [Richard Hamilton, Jacobite Commander] is allowing 150 people to leave Londonderry almost every day. These orders will be the only way to starve this city which is short of many supplies, and this will also make many of the people turn against the most stubborn among them and force them to surrender.

To Louis XIV, 27 May 1689:

The siege of Londonderry drags on and matters are getting worse rather than better. I do not believe that M. Hamilton knows enough to be able to manage such a large affair. I have urged strongly that the engineers which Your Majesty has sent to this country should be dispatched up to him together with a good number of junior officers and troop reinforcements, as well as cannons, bombs and supplies. That is what should have been done from the beginning.

To Louis XIV, 10 July 1689:

As for the siege of Londonderry I see few signs that it will succeed unless the besieged give up soon through lack of food. The besiegers lack everything – that is to say that at the moment they have only thirty picks or trenching tools for digging trenches and not a single cannon since the few they do have are devoted to preventing the relief forces from entering the city; and most of the soldiers have deserted, not having been paid.

Letters from COMTE D'AVAUX (Louis XIV's special ambassador to James II),
in *Negociations de M le Comte d'Avaux en Irlande, 1689–90*, 1934
(VERSION BY FRANK D'ARCY)

THE CITY WALL WAS BUILT to keep Catholics out. Its original purpose, one historian wrote, was 'to assist the inhabitants in repelling any attack from the surrounding Celtic population, who were supposed to cherish anything but friendly feelings toward their neighbours.' Living among the people they had dispossessed, the new settlers had reason to be fearful. Londonderry was not the only Protestant community to protect itself by walling out 'the Irishry', nor did this happen only in the North. For a time in the seventeenth century, for instance, the town of Bandon, in County Cork, was also enclosed by a large wall. One of its gates is said to have borne the inscription 'Turk, Jew or Atheist may enter here; But not a Papist.' A local wit replied: 'Who wrote it, wrote it well; For the same is written on the Gates of Hell.' That wall, however, was largely dismantled in 1688.

The following year, Londonderry's city wall achieved a sort of immortality. An army loyal to the Catholic King James II of England was approaching the city, and the Protestant officer in charge of the garrison – whose name has been preserved in Protestant tradition as 'the traitor Lundy' – showed little inclination to deny entry to the King's troops. The troops in question, however, were Catholics themselves, as well as being loyal to a Catholic king, and the Protestant citizenry feared that the notorious massacres inflicted during a Catholic uprising 47 years earlier would be repeated. Lundy was planning to give away the city, they said, 'for a bap', a bun, nothing. At the last moment, thirteen apprentice boys, acting on their own, rushed down and closed the gates in the face of the approaching army. The gates remained closed, under siege, for 105 days, until forces of the Protestant William of Orange, whom Parliament was to install as monarch in place of James II, came to the city's relief.

Today, the fraternal order known as the Apprentice Boys commemorates the closing of the gates each year by burning Lundy in effigy on the section of the city wall above the Bogside. It is an occasion for fireworks, drums and 'the shrill ululation of fifes'. At times, the Bogside community also marked the occasion by piling debris on its fires, in the hope that the outpouring of ashes would smother the finely dressed celebrants. Until recently, Lundy's effigy was always hung from a column atop the wall honouring George Walker, a firebrand clergyman who suffered no Lundy-like ambivalence in his feelings toward Catholics. Walker's statue used to glower out at the Bogside from the top of the column, a Bible in one hand and a sword in the other. But it is recorded that on the night the Catholic Emancipation was signed in 1829, a strong wind rose and blew the sword out of his hand. The statue itself continued to stand, disarmed, until 1974. One Catholic writer described it to me as 'a symbol of thralldom, a constant reminder of the triumph of Protestantism over Catholicism'. In the renewed troubles of the 1970s, the column finally toppled in what a Bogsider described to me, with a smile, as a 'strong wind'.

ALEN MacWEENEY and RICHARD CONNIFF,
Ireland: Stone Walls and Fabled Landscapes, 1998

AYE, BUT DERRY WALLS – DERRY WALLS. What have we to say about that siege of Derry in 1689 which is commemorated every year with processions, drums and angry speeches?

It was in the defence of Derry against the Jacobites that the slogan 'No Surrender' first was uttered. King James II had come from France to Ireland with an ill-equipped army, hoping to win back one of his three kingdoms easily, since the great bulk of the Irish people then favoured the Stuart cause. Derry was the strong place of the North (for Belfast still was of little consequence) – the sea-gate through which Dutch William might come. To Derry, James marched. The civic chiefs were asked to surrender, and agreed; but a blundering display of force alarmed those townspeople who had been inflamed by fanatics, and the gates were closed, the King defied. It was April 18th – the siege was begun.

Within the city, there were eight regiments, numbering over 7,000 men. Volunteers brought the fighting force yet higher. There were 30 guns and plentiful ammunition. A strange, impassioned leader, the Rev. Mr Walker, suddenly arrived and took command, working up fears of the Papists and a dark religious enthusiasm, while he imposed discipline and civic order. Outside the city was the Jacobite army, numbering at most 6,000 men, possessed of only a few cannon, and with less than 400 muskets. The situation was that of a boy with a catapult attacking a barrack in which several strong policemen have shut themselves, heavily armed. So disproportionate was the struggle, that the Jacobites had the chief cause for fear. They set about digging trenches to protect themselves from the Williamite cannon, and had only 30 shovels for the task, among 3,000 men. If the besieged forces had mustered enough courage to make a sally, they could have driven James and his army out of Ulster then and there, but they preferred hunger to wounds and waited behind the impregnable walls for some weeks until, on the 105th day of the siege, the boom across the river was broken and English ships got through to land two regiments. The feeble Jacobites, who had invested Derry so long, could not hope for equal success against the seasoned fighters now brought against them, so they struck camp and marched away.

Those who favour Dutch William against Scots James in that civil war which brought in its train the usual consequence of an age-lasting feud, make much of the tenacity of the garrison. They seldom tell – they seldom know – the story of that garrison's ultimate fate. When James was dead in France and William was safely King – when civil and religious liberty had been duly established by the breaking of the treaty of Limerick and the rivetting of the Penal chains on the Catholic masses – how fared the heroes of Derry, those stubborn Ulster farmers? Their landlords raised their rents and persecuted them for their refusal to accept the Anglican religion. Multitudes of these Presbyterians, these settlers, planters, Derry-defenders, fled to America. One leader in the migration was the Rev. James McGregor, minister of Aghadoey, in the County of Derry, who preached mightily to his congregation on the evils from which they were to seek a refuge in the newer, freer world. In New Hampshire, the exiles of Aghadoey founded a city which they called Londonderry, and there the remains of the Reverend McGregor, forty years after the siege, were borne to the grave by men who had stood with him in Derry on the Foyle, when it was beleaguered by the supposed foes of freedom. From the tower of the cathedral in 1689, the Reverend McGregor had fired the great cannon. Now, in 1729, he was buried in exile, by fellow exiles whom the rule of King William's parliament had driven forth in anger and sorrow, never to see Ulster again.

Fooled! – the men of Derry had been fooled, and they knew it then, though they have forgotten about it now. They had held Derry for William, and he had broken faith with them as he broke faith with their fellow-countrymen on the other side at Limerick, and as he broke faith with MacDonald of Glencoe, whose whole clan he massacred. Over in New Hampshire, the exiles of Ulster remembered Derry to effect. Fifty years after the Reverend McGregor's death, Washington was in arms against England, and Londonderry, New Hampshire, sent more troops to his service than any other town. The grandsons of the defenders of Derry struck for the free Republic of America. At home in Ireland, the Presbyterian synod declared its sympathy. It condemned England's war against the colonist as 'unjust, cruel and detestable', and rejoiced that their kindred 'composed the flower of Washington's army, being carried by a native love of liberty to encounter every danger for the safety of their adopted country.'

Forget not this, O men of modern Derry: that your kindred achieved in the Republic of the West that freedom which they fondly thought that they were serving when at home they allowed themselves to be arrayed against their fellow-countrymen – their natural brethren. If the exiles of Derry were right to strive for a free America, you living men of Derry are wrong to resist a free Ireland.

AODH DE BLÁCAM, 'The Walls of Derry', *The Black North*, 1938

The time has nigh come round, boys,
Two hundred years ago,
When rebels on old Derry's Walls
Their faces dare not show.
When James and all his rebel band
Came up to Bishop's Gate,
They nobly stood upon the Walls
And forced him to retreat.

For blood has flowed in crimson tide
On many a winter night,
They knew the Lord was on their side
To help them in the fight.
They nobly stood upon the Walls,
Determined for to die,
Or fight and gain the victory
And raise the crimson high.

At last with one great broadside
King William sent them aid,
The boom that crossed the Foyle was broke
And James he was dismayed.
The banner, boys, that floated
Was run aloft with joy,
The dancey ship that broke the boom
And saved the Apprentice Boys.

The cry is 'No Surrender!'
And come when duty calls,
With heart and hand and sword and shield
We'll guard old Derry's Walls.

ANONYMOUS, 'Derry's Walls', in
There Was Music in the Derry Air (ed. A.M. Murray), 1989

Monday, 5th; Tuesday, 6th

These two days past several eyewitnesses have come hither from Enniskillen, and do assure us that there was a great slaughter of the enemy, that on our side we lost not fifty men. They say that the day after the battle, the country people killed many hundreds more of the enemy, who hid themselves in the woods, and also brought eight or ten Commission officers more to Enniskillen, prisoners.

The Major-General we now hear has embarked all the heavy luggage, and sent the ships with the man of war about to come to this town. He has made Capt. Barber, Governor of Inch, and has ordered all the forces to march tomorrow [by the] strand.

Wednesday, 7th

This day arrived our three Regiments with the Major-General. The city drew out their forces into the field, gave them three huzzas as they passed, with a salute of all their small shot and great guns. After dinner a Council of War was held of only the Field Officers, about the regulating the town regiment and the civil government of the town, with several other necessary things, as touching the market and cleansing the town. Tomorrow is ordered to be a day of Thanksgiving.

Thursday, 8th

This day was spent with a great deal of joy and merry-making by the triple discharge of all our cannon and small arms, the whole garrison being posted round the walls. Nothing of notice besides, hath happened. We hear only that the enemy is at Coleraine, where they are fortifying themselves.

Friday, 9th; Saturday, 10th; Sunday, 11th

This last Saturday our Fleet came in from Inch, and brought the rest of our provisions. I have now received orders from the Major-General to mount five guns at Culmore, which the enemies have blown up; Captain Collier is Governor of it: and also eight upon the quay: and to mark out a camp for the town soldiers, for here in garrison we find it a hard matter to make them rendezvous and do duty.

THE END

COLONEL GODFREY RICHARDS, *The Diary of the Fleet*, August 1689

AN CORP –

'Óró, a Thomáis, och, och, ó,
Ná fág anseo mé, ná fág anseo mé;
Óir tá mac dearthár athara domh thíos i nDoire,
Mar is cóir m'adhlacadh, mar is cóir m'adhlacadh.'

Tógadh an corpán ar mhuin Thomáis,
Mar bhí roimhe, mar bhí roimhe,
Le dul go fálta, tréithlag, cráite,
Síos go Doire, síos go Doire.

Ar theacht don áit sin domh go fágtha,
Is mé gan mhisneach, is mé gan mhisneach,
Bhí na geataí sparrtha romham go láidir,
Is thug mé preab dóibh, thug mé preab dóibh.

'Defend your walls,' Sir Walker calls,
'Or they'll be taken, or they'll be taken;
Why knock so hard? Each to his part,
Come, dead, awaken! Come, dead, awaken!'

D'éirigh cnámha is cónraí 'n airde,
As an talamh, as an talamh,
Is do shuigh gan spás i bhfíoch gan tlás
Ar mhaoil an bhalla, ar mhaoil an bhalla.

'Céad puilliliú!' ar gach aon díobh,
'What's the matter? What's the matter?'

Tomás –

'Níl ach aon de bhur gcairde do dhul chun báis,
Sé seo a Róimh-adhlacaidh, seo a Róimh-adhlacaidh.'

'Tá a ghaol san áit, is maith mar tá,
Is bíodh sé agaibh, bíodh sé agaibh.'
'Who of his people is buried here,
To claim admittance, to claim admittance?'

Tomás –

'Níl fhios agam féin cá treibh an léice,
Ar dhroim na beatha, ar dhroim na beatha,
Ach tá preab is éamh ann, labhraíg leis-sean,
Is fiafraíg desean, fiafraíg desean.'

The corpse: 'Thomas, I beg you, don't leave me here! Don't leave me here! My cousin is buried down there in Derry and it's there I should be laid, there I should be laid.'

The corpse is hoisted on Thomas's back, just as before, just as before, to make the journey, in long drawn-out agony, down to Derry, down to Derry.

As I reached that place in dire misery, sore of heart, sore of heart, the gates were sternly locked against me, till I roused the people there.

'Defend your walls,' Sir Walker calls, 'Or they'll be taken, or they'll be taken; Why knock so hard? Each to his part, Come, dead, awaken! Come dead awaken!'

Bones and coffins rose on high, out of the ground, out of the ground, and seething with rage they quickly covered the top of the wall, the top of the wall.

Each raised a horrible hullabaloo: 'What's the matter? What's the matter?'

Thomas: 'Only one of your kindred, now no longer alive, seeking Christian burial, seeking Christian burial.'

'His kin is buried here and right that they should be. Let you accept him; let you accept him.'

'Who of his people is buried here, to claim admittance, to claim admittance?'

'I do not know where on earth, where on earth, is this burial place but amidst all this racket speak to his spirit; ask him, ask him.

[The excerpt is from an old song, the text of which breaks off at this point. The unfortunate Tomás is ensnared by an unburied corpse and is forced to carry it on his back to graveyards all over Ulster seeking Christian burial. This part of the journey takes them to Derry during the Siege.]

ANONYMOUS,
'Aistriú Thomáis Oíche Shamhna' (The Portage of Thomas on Halloween Night),
in *Céad de Cheolta Uladh* (*A Hundred Ulster Songs*), (ed. Énrí Ó Muireasa), 1915
(VERSION BY SEAN McMAHON)

A FTER TWO OR THREE DAYS of sullen firing of guns, the enemy raised the siege and decamped from Derry, burning many Protestant farm houses, and savagely devastating the country on their way south.

It took some time of course to restore the city to anything like order. A proclamation was soon issued that all persons who had fled to Derry during the siege should leave at once, not taking anything with them.

Abel Keene, still weak with his healing wound, but well enough to travel the short distance necessary, lay down his musket and left with the other country people. On his way home he passed the Browning's house, which was as he had left it, deserted, but not pulled down.

His heart beat more quickly as he approached his own dwelling. The cattle had gone, but the house and its inmates were the same: more than all, Fanny was there, with a blush on her pale face, and you may be sure that the meeting between them was such as I shall not attempt to describe.

A week after, they were sitting together on the west bank of Lough Foyle in the morning sunshine. Abel had in his hand a copy of some of Shakespeare's Plays, from which he was reading to Fanny. When he was tired of reading, or of the author, he would put his head back on his hands and gaze into the sky, or at the rocks beyond Magilligan, while Fanny went on with her sewing.

'I think he's come to no harm, Fanny,' said Abel, resuming the thread of conversation which they had been having earlier in the morning.

'I hope not, Abel, dear,' said Fanny, putting down her work and pondering. 'It would be hard to think we shall never see him to thank him for what would never have been done without him. How he managed to rescue me is a mystery to me.'

'And a great mystery to me,' said Abel. 'He kept it a mystery from me,' and Abel recollected bitterly that last time they had spoken of Fanny. 'He didn't wish to disappoint me, you see. He was a mystery himself, Fanny. Every one in Derry said it was a mystery where he came from. Some said he was a waif from the ships that came up to the town in April: but he always kept the mystery to himself. He had no relations in the town, and nobody he could exactly call an intimate friend till I came: and though he was always with me, he was just as much a mystery to me.'

'And it's a mystery where he's gone,' said Fanny.

They were both silent for a while, and Abel went on reading aloud.

By and bye, Fanny interrupted him.

'Abel, dear, I feel as if I can't rest till I know what that white thing there is,' and she pointed to a place in the rocks about a hundred yards down the Lough.

'I'll go and see,' said Abel, and he was on his feet and away to the place.

He came back in a few minutes with a very grave face, and moistened eyes.

'Fanny,' he said, in a broken voice, 'it's a very sad sight. Can you bear to see it? I think it will be better than for me to tell you.'

Fanny rose firmly to her feet, and walked to the place with him.

Abel had lifted it carefully and placed it higher up the bank so that Fanny recognized it at once, and was on her knees beside it with a pitying moan. It was Tommy's dead body. He lay with filmy eyes wide open, and a wondering smile upon his face.

There was a bullet-wound in his side, and it was a mystery whether he had died of drowning or of loss of blood.

But it was no mystery to them now where that little soul had gone.

R.W.K. EDWARDS, *Unchronicled Heroes – A Story of the Siege of Londonderry*, 1888

A BAND of youthful Heroes, within our Maiden Walls,
Once dar'd a Tyrant's mandates, as history recalls;
Despising threats and shackles, that would have seal'd their woes,
They thunder'd forth defiance against insulting foes.

CHORUS

Huzza, then, for the Crimson Flag, that floated brisk and gay!
And wav'd defiance to the foes – Huzza! Huzza! Huzza!

A Monarch once, in martial mood, our Walls in state approach'd,
Demanding entrance, but he found his presence had encroach'd;
A burst repugnant to his ears saluted from within;
He wheel'd about, and fled through fear, in spite of 'shame or sin'.

CHORUS

Huzza, then, for the Crimson Flag, &c.

Away went James with whip and spur, and foremost drove his steed,
Nor look'd behind, but wistfully Mountgavelin sought with speed;
To Dublin next he sped his way, and sorely did he rue,
To Derry e'er he set his face, its 'rebels' to subdue.

CHORUS

Huzza, then, for the Crimson Flag, &c.

A ruthless host surrounded had our City – doom'd, they thought,
But soon they found their false hopes had gained less than
    they sought;
A corps of dauntless heroes – our sires in days of yore –
Rush'd boldly out upon the foe, and scorn'd the cannon's roar.

CHORUS

Huzza, then, for the Crimson Flag, &c.

When gallant Browning led the van, each pulse beat high
    with praise,
Rever'd the Power that rul'd their fate – their drooping hearts
    to raise;
Whilst famine, fever, raged within, the savage hordes around,
Foil'd, took a hasty moonlight flight and left the tented ground.

CHORUS

Huzza, then, for the Crimson Flag, &c.

Let tyrants rule with infamy, and serfs and slaves trepan;
Religion, life, and liberty are dear to every man;
Victoria reigns supreme with us – let others dare say, nay,
Who snarl and puff, or proudly boast – Britannia bears the sway.

CHORUS
  Huzza, then, for the Crimson Flag, that floats so brisk and gay!
  And waves defiance to our foes – Huzza! Huzza! Huzza!

ANONYMOUS, 'The Crimson Flag of Derry' (Air – 'The Bonnie Blue Flag'),
in *The Crimson Banner Songbook*, n.d.

IT MUST HAVE BEEN A TINY PLACE at the time of the siege, since the walled city, whose entire circuit is perfectly preserved, does not measure a quarter of a mile across at its narrowest, and considerably less than half a mile at its widest. Across the river, Waterside looked equally charming – the river pale, smooth, and motionless, reflecting the houses rising up Fountain Hill, or fading out into greenery beyond the barracks to the North. I climbed the cathedral tower, over the Ferry bastion, and got a glorious view over the whole width and stretch of Lough Foyle with the hills of Inishowen shining faintly beyond. In the vestibule is the bombshell which contained the terms of surrender offered by General Hamilton during the famous siege, and which received the historic reply of 'No Surrender,' ever since the watchword of the North.

In no other spot in the North did I feel the surge of pride which an Ulsterman must feel as he thinks back over his own local history. Had I met an Orangeman as I stood on Walker's Bastion I would have wished to take his hand and shake it. If I were an Ulsterman, I felt, I could never forget Derry, any more than, being a Munsterman, I can forget Limerick. Its siege was a magnificent example of heroic endurance, from the 18th of December 1689, when the gates were closed against King James's Irish Army, to 12th August when the relief ships that had for seven weeks been blocked on the Foyle by a boom, having burst through at the end of July, relieved the city and ended its torments. (Had it been some other king I might have felt regret that the city had not fallen, but King James was *such* a fool! As well as a coward.) The men who starved in Derry, and the woman who fought with broken bottles to defend Limerick the following autumn, have left us the two most stirring memories of the last campaign that the old Ireland fought before she was swallowed up in the darkness of the eighteenth century. To go from Derry, five or six miles out off the Buncrana Road, to the great concentric forts of the Grianan of Aileach – appropriately in Eire – the seat of the O'Neills when they were Kings of Ulster, is to run the gamut of that ancient Ireland's story.

SEAN O'FAOLAIN, *An Irish Journey*, 1940

July 2

The Enemy drive the poor Protestants, according to their threatening, under our Walls, Protected, and Unprotected, Men, Women and Children and under great distresses. Our Men at first did not understand the meaning of such a Crowd, but fearing they might be Enemies, Fired upon them; we were troubled when we found the mistake, but it supported us to a great degree, when we found that none of them were touch'd by our Shot, which by the direction of Providence (as if every Bullet had its Commission what to do) spared them, and found out and kill'd three of the Enemy, that were some of those that drove the poor People into so great a danger. There were some Thousands of them, and they did move great Compassion in us, but warm'd us with new rage and fury against the Enemy, so that in sight of their Camp we immediately erect a Gallows, and signified to them we were resolved to hang their Friends that were our Prisoners, if they did not suffer these poor People to return to their own Houses.

We send to the Enemy, that the Prisoners might have Priests to prepare them after their own Methods for death; but none came. We upbraid them with breach of Promises, and the Prisoners detect their barbarity, declaring, *They could not blame us to put them to death, seeing their People exercis'd such Severity and Cruelty upon our poor Friends, that were under their Protections.* They desired leave from the Governor, to write to L.G. *Hamilton*; they had a much better opinion of him than we cou'd be perswaded into; yet we allow a Messenger to carry the following Letter to him from their Prisoners.

My Lord,
Upon the hard dealing the Protected (as well as other Protestants) have met withal in being sent under the Walls, you have so incens'd the Governor and others of this Garrison that we are all condemn'd by a Court Martial to dye to morrow, unless those poor People be withdrawn. We have made application to Marshal General de Rosen; but having received no Answer, we make it our Request to you (as knowing you are a person that does not delight in shedding innocent Blood) that you will represent our condision to the Martial General. The Lives of 20 Prisoners lye at stake, and therefore require your diligence and care. We are all willing to die (with our Swords in our hands) for His Majesty: but to suffer like Malefactors is hard, nor can we lay our Blood to the charge of the Garrison, the Governor and the rest having used and treated us with all Civilty imaginable. We remain

Your most dutiful and dying Friends, Netervill,
Writ by another hand, he himself has lost the Fingers of his Right hand.

To L.G. Hamilton. E. Butler, G. Aylmor, – MacDonnel, – Darcy, &c. In the Name of all the rest.

July 27

The Garrison is reduced to 4456 Men, and under the greatest extremity for want of Provision, which does appear by this Account taken by a Gentleman in the Garrison, of the price of our Food.

	l. s. d.
Horse flesh sold for	0–1–8
A Quarter of a Dog	0–5–6
A Dogs Head	0–2–6
A Cat	0–4–6
A Rat	0–1–0
A Mouse	0–0–6

per pound. fatned by eating the Bodies of the slain *Irish*.

A small Flook taken in the River, not to be bought for Mony, or purchased under the rate of a quantity of Meal.

A pound of Greaves	0–1–0
A pound of Tallow	0–4–0
A pound of salted Hides	1–0
A quart of Horse blood	0–1–0
A Horse-pudding	0–0–6
An handful of Sea wreck	0–2
of Chick-weed	0–1
A quart of Meal when found	1–0

We were under so great Necessity, that we had nothing left unless we could prey upon one another: A certain Fat Gentleman conceived himself in the greatest danger, and fancying several of the Garrison lookt on him with a greedy Eye, thought fit to hide himself for three days. Our drink was nothing but Water, which we paid very dear for, and cou'd not get without great danger; We mixt in it Ginger and Anniseeds, of which we had great plenty; Our necessity of Eating the Composition of Tallow and Starch, did not only Nourish and Support us, but was an Infallible Cure of the Looseness; and recovered a great many that were strangely reduced by that Distemper, and preserved others from it.

THE REVEREND MR GEORGE WALKER, RECTOR OF DONAGHMORE IN THE COUNTY OF TIRONE, AND LATE GOVERNOUR OF DERRY IN IRELAND, *A True Account of the Siege of London-Derry*, 1689

BEHOLD the crimson banners float
O'er yonder turrets hoary;
They tell of days of mighty note,
And Derry's deathless glory;
When her brave sons undaunted stood,
Embattled to defend her,
Indignant stemmed oppression's flood,
And sung out, 'No Surrender!'

Old Derry's walls were firm and strong,
Well fenced in every quarter,
Each frowning bastion grim along,
With culverin and mortar;
But Derry had a surer guard
Than all that art could lend her,
Her 'prentice boys the gate who barred
And sung out, 'No Surrender!'

On came the force in bigot ire,
And fierce the assault was given;
By shot and shell, 'mid streams of fire,
Her fated roofs were riven:
But baffled was the tyrant's wrath,
And vain his hopes to bend her,
For still 'mid famine, fire, and death,
She sung out, 'No Surrender!'

Again, when treason maddened round,
And rebel hordes were swarming,
Were Derry's sons the foremost found,
For king and country arming:
Forth, forth they rushed at honour's call,
From age to boyhood tender,
Again to man their virgin wall,
And sung out, 'No Surrender!'

Long may the crimson banner wave,
A meteor streaming airy,
Portentous of the free and brave
Who man the walls of Derry:
And Derry's sons alike defy
Pope, traitor, or pretender;
And peal to heaven their 'prentice cry,
Their patriot – 'No Surrender!'

CHARLOTTE ELIZABETH (Mrs Tonna), 'No Surrender', 1835

BY THAT TIME, SOME COMPANIES of Antrim's regiment had arrived at the Waterside; and two of their officers, a lieutenant and an ensign, were ferried over, bringing with them a special warrant, addressed to the Deputy-Mayor and Sheriffs, to demand quarters for their men. One of the Sheriffs (Mr Horace Kennedy) intimated to them his intention of lodging the soldiers that night on the other side of the water, (in order that the inhabitants might be better prepared to oppose their entrance the next morning;) but, whilst he and the officers were in conversation, the Irish soldiers having had, it is supposed, some intimation of the Sheriff's design, crossed the river as fast as possible, and came to a landing place at the foot of Ferryquay-street about 300 yards from the gate. The youths of the town perceiving this, and animated by enthusiastic ardour, instantly determined to maintain their city, to the last, or perish in its ruins, when the following thirteen APPRENTICE BOYS, viz.

> Mr Henry Campsie, Wm Crookshanks, Samuel Hunt, Robert Sherrard, Daniel Sherrard, Alexander Irwin, James Stewart, Robert Morrison, Alexander Cuningham, James Spike, John Cuningham, William Cairns and Samuel Harvey.

armed themselves, and being joined by several others, ran to the main guard, seized the keys of the garrison, locked Ferryquay-gate, raised the draw-bridge, and secured that approach, at the moment their enemies were advanced within a few paces of it; from thence they rushed to the others, of which they possessed themselves in like manner, and placed proper guard upon them. This roused the valiant spirit of the inhabitants, the greater body of which immediately declared for a resolute defence. Thus by the courage and intrepidity of a few young heroes, the City of Londonderry was preserved from an insolent and designing foe.

JOSHUA GILLESPIE, *A Revised History of the Siege of Londonderry*, 1823

PRESENTLY TELEMACHUS STROLLED forth and spent an hour or so, viewing the sights of the historic Maiden City. He climbed up Ship Quay Street and marvelled at its steepness, – called at sundry shops and purchased picture postcards for Helena. Next he scaled the walls and walked around them, from Bishop's Gate to Walker's Monument, inspecting with interest the famous old cannon, 'Roaring Meg', which played a notable part, 'tis said, in the siege. He next visited the Cathedral, and in the churchyard by the grave of the Apprentice Boys he met an intelligent citizen, who without much pressing gave him a vivid description of the rigours of the siege.

'Ah, sir!' he concluded, 'they were hard pressed and no mistake; that siege of Ladysmith was a flea-bite to it. There were twenty thousand men before the gates for a hundred and five days, and the garrison of ten thousand was reduced to four. Close on six hundred bombs were thrown into the city. You saw that big one in the Cathedral; it weighs 275 pounds. Before it was all over they were eating anything they could get, dogs, cats, rats and mice. As for the real heroes of the siege, Walker whom you saw on the top of the Monument was not amongst them, a man who never struck a blow, fired a gun, or led a sorti. Baker, Murray and Mitchelburn it was who conducted the defence, but this Walker who was a clergyman wrote the history of it all, and gave himself most praise, and so he got stuck up on the pillar.'

Telemachus got back to his hotel in good time for dinner, and later adjourned to the lounge, ordered some coffee, and lighting up an Owl, seated himself beside a stout elderly clerical gentleman, with close trimmed sandy whiskers, who was slowly turning over the leaves of a lengthy type-written document, while he smoked a thick Egyptian cigarette.

'The gospel missionary from 23 for a dollar,' surmised Telemachus. 'He'll be the guy who's lecturing to-night in the Guild Hall, according to those posters I saw stuck around.'

'Bully sort of evening, sir!' he commenced, 'guess I'll introduce myself, Telemachus Noailles DuQuesne's my name, I'm from the States. Better try one of my Owl cigars instead of the coffin tack you're smoking, they're Sumatra wrapper, pure Havana filler, and I have inside information that the price will soon go up to ten cents.'

The stranger politely refused the proffered cigar, and handed Telemachus his card on which was inscribed, 'The Rev. Erasmus Ebenezer McClurg, DD'. 'I have not at present a charge,' he explained, 'but I manage to occupy my time to excellent advantage. I've just returned from a grand tour through Canada and am now starting out to lecture through the north of Ireland on the magnificent opportunities afforded to those who emigrate to our great Dominion overseas. There lies the true land of promise, a Canan flowing with milk and honey, the granary of our Empire, sir, and the predestined refuge of the virile Ulster Scot, if this nefarious Home Rule Bill should eventually be adopted.' So speaking he produced from a capacious pocket a batch of pamphlets which he handed across to the American.

ALICE W.H. MILLIGAN, *The Dynamite Drummer*, n.d.

COLONEL SARSFIELD MORE THAN FULFILLED the promise he had made. Seeing that Dorothy had set her heart upon joining her friends in Londonderry, he had accompanied her part of the way himself, and had provided her with an escort for the remainder of her journey. To Gervase he had shown unaffected kindness. He had provided him with a horse and apparel befitting his condition, and at parting had wrung his hand with an appearance of great warmth and friendship.

'It is right, perhaps,' he had said, 'that we should be on different sides of this quarrel, but we can part with mutual good-will. I have but one hope and one thought – to see my country once more a nation, great and free. I would that all our people were of one mind, and were striking together for their fatherland. But it is still our curse to be divided – torn and rent by civil feuds. But believe me when I say that Patrick Sarsfield has only one desire on earth, and that is that his country should have her own laws and her own government, and freedom for the meanest. I think I shall meet my fate on the field of battle, but I hope not before I have seen that splendid day. Think well of us, Mr Orme, and though you do your duty on your own side, remember that there are among us those whose cause is sacred in their eyes, and whose country is dearer to them than their lifeblood.'

They never met again, but Gervase felt in after days that there was one man in Ireland who might have saved his cause, had he not been checked by narrow prejudices and the bitter envy of those who did not understand his proud and chivalrous nature. At Limerick that fiery spirit blazed out for a while in all its native strength, but his cause was already doomed.

When Gervase had reached Londonderry in safety, and had seen Dorothy placed under the protection of her aunt, he returned to his old lodgings over a linendraper's shop in a small house near the Bishop's-gate.

In the meantime, memorable events had transpired in his absence. The Irish army, breaking through the defences of the Bann, had pressed on toward Londonderry, and having crossed the Finn, had closed upon the city. Colonel Lundy, whether through vacillation and cowardice or from deliberate treachery, had made no effort to oppose their approach, and had done his best to secure the surrender of the city. At the very moment when he was about to carry out his designs, the citizens awakened to his intentions, and took the authority into their own hands. They seized the keys and took possession of the walls; a new government was established in the city; the garrison was divided into regiments, and preparations were made to stand a long and stubborn siege.

A great change had taken place in the city and in the spirit of the citizens since Gervase had ridden out of the gate, a fortnight before. The old look of dejection and irresolution had disappeared; one of unbounded enthusiasm and zeal had taken its place. Every able-bodied man carried arms and bore himself like a soldier. Swords clanked on the causeway; rusty muskets had been furbished up, and gentlemen and yeomen alike were filled with the same ardour, and wore the same determined air. Every regiment had its post. On the ramparts the guards were posted at regular intervals; little knots of armed and resolute men were gathered in the great square, and companies were being drilled from morning till night in the Bogside. A spirit of unyielding loyalty filled the air. The paving stones had been raised from the streets and were carried to the walls: blinds had been erected to screen the men on the ramparts. From the grey Cathedral tower two guns looked down on the Waterside, and on every bastion were others ready for use. At the Market house also cannon were planted to sweep the streets. At every gate there was a great gun.

The siege had indeed commenced. Yonder beyond the Foyle lay Lord Lumley's command, three thousand strong, the white tents catching the last gleam of the sunset as the evening mists crept up the river. At Brookhall and Pennyburn Mill was a strong force that shut off communication with Culmore. Away towards St Johnston's and Carrigans was the main army of the enemy under Eustace and Ramsay. From the heights of Clooney one could see at long intervals a swift leap of flame, and hear the sullen roar of a great gun breaking on the evening air. All thought of compromise or capitulation was at an end; here the citizens must make their last stand, and show the world how dearly they held their faith and freedom.

At first sight resistance might have seemed a midsummer folly.

On both sides of the river the high ground looked down upon the city, and that within the range of cannon. The streets clamb up the gradual slope toward the square-towered Cathedral; the walls were low and might be easily breached. Still, there were seven thousand men of the imperial race within those walls, and while one stone stood upon another they had sworn to make good their defence.

S.R. KEIGHTLEY, *The Crimson Sign*, 1894

ALL THINGS BEING FIXED AND EVERY ONE POSTED, we weighed anchor about eight o'clock in the morning, and came to an anchor within cannon-shot of Culmore, and expected they would have charged us, with their cannon, but [they] did not, which at first made me believe what the people told us the night before. But looking in my telescope, I could perceive them very thick behind their walls, and found they were a hammering a great gun, which with one more was all we could see in the fort. We therefore charged them first with a broadside, and they discharged theirs and by what we could observe one of their guns split.

We lay pelting thus for above three quarters of an hour, in which time from the maintop I discovered where it was the enemy had made their Boom, viz., over against Charlesfort a little above Brook-hall. There I perceived something that extended from side to side: and several boats at a small distance from one another lay just by it, as if they buoyed it up. At the same time I saw some horse on the inner side of the fort drawing some great weight, as I judged by the slowness of their pace, but I could not see what, by reason of the rising ground that hid all but the horses' heads and a little of their backs. I guessed it to be cannon they were bringing into battery against us. Wherefore having seen what I could, and found that we were not of a sufficient force to attempt the breaking or cutting of this Boom, we weighed anchor with design to go and anchor below.

But most unfortunately as we had gotten the anchor up, the wind shifted and shrunk two points to the northward, so that ship not fitting time enough, with the narrowness of the channel we struck on shore on the south side. We endeavoured to get her off by carrying several anchors and warps; but the tide fell so quick from us, that all hopes were laid aside till the next tide. About twelve o'clock at noon, the enemies had brought into battery several great guns, some to the northward of the fort, the rest on the other side of the water which flanked us on our starboard side. The whole number we computed to be about eleven, some whereof were twenty-four pounders, eight pounders, and three pounders. There also appeared three or four battalions of foot; which made me send for forty soldiers and a lieutenant, that were on board of a ketch sent with me. For we [were] now laid almost dry, and heeling so much on our starboard side, that we could not make use of any one great gun, so that our enemies might have attacked us as we lay. But we kept so good a fire with about 120 small arms, that they made no attempt of this nature, but spared us no great guns; which did very great damage to our ship, so that in eight hours they shot seventeen shot under water, [and] above fifty in her upper works, masts, and rigging. Whoever should see in what condition we were, would hardly believe our loss of men to be so few. There were but two killed; one belonged to me, the other to Capt. Guillam. The Captain was wounded in several places, and about fourteen men more, some with splinters and some with small shot from the South shore.

COLONEL GODFREY RICHARDS, *The Diary of the Fleet*, June 1689

A MAIDEN pined by Derry's Walls,
Where want did life destroy;
Her lover rush'd to shut the Gates,
A gallant 'Prentice Boy.
Her last death-sigh was breath'd to him –
'Weep not my early grave,
Live free, or like a freeman die,
Not like a Popish slave!'

A Young Wife wept by Derry's Walls,
Her babe was dead and gone;
His father now was all she loved,
Beneath the blessed sun.
He stood upon the rampart high,
She cried to him, 'Oh! brave,
Stand to your gun, or nobly fall,
Not like a Popish slave!'

A Widow droop'd by Derry's Walls,
Her hair was grey with grief,
Her only boy had left her side,
To aid the Town's relief.
She prayed his sword like Gideon's,
In victory might wave,
Or like a freeman fight and fall,
Not live a Popish slave!

Bright is the Hero's path to Fame,
With Victory smiling down,
When beauty points the glorious path,
And wreathes the laurel crown;
Oh! her fair bosom, shrine of love,
Where soft emotion heaves,
Shall nurture Freedom's rosy boys,
Not suckle Popish slaves!

ANONYMOUS, 'A Maiden Pined by Derry's Walls'
(Air – 'The Slave'/'I Had a Dream, a Happy Dream'),
in *The Crimson Banner Songbook*, n.d.

THE APPROACHES TO LONDONDERRY are charming, and indicate the wealth of a great city. The borders of the pretty river Derg are cultivated and cared for like a garden, and dotted with country houses. The city itself, situated on an eminence, is seen from afar, and has a fine appearance, which is increased by the tall spire which Lord Bristol (Bishop of Derry) has had built by subscription.

The city enclosure, proper, is not very much, but the suburbs are very fine. The old walls exist and are used as an agreeable promenade, disfigured very little by an *arc de triomphe* which has only the look of a large door or gate; on the keystone is cut the date, 1689, in large figures, being the year in which this city was besieged by King James. There should, at least, be a stairway made to allow of communication between the two ends of the promenade. As these ramparts are of no present utility, it seems to me that if they were put out of existence and used as material to extend the hill platform on which the city is situated, it would be infinitely better for the place, and would allow the air to circulate in the streets. However, the inhabitants are jealous of attempts on their walls, and still recall the memorable siege the city sustained against King James. Certainly the walls would be of no use now in resisting an attack.

I went to visit the place of James' camp, as well as the different French posts. These latter seem to me to be cleverly chosen, but what astonished me was, how it was possible for the English frigate to force a passage in spite of the chain which barred the river, and the batteries which were on the banks. It was known that the city was almost on the point of surrendering, and that the English fleet had been obliged to retire to Lough Swilly, where it had waited nearly six weeks, without finding means of conveying succour to the besieged. Knowing, however, the extremity to which the inhabitants of the city were reduced, it was resolved to take the risk of forcing the passage by a frigate, accompanied by two or three transport vessels.

As the surrender of the place depended on the success or non-success of the enterprise, it can be imagined what interest this excited for both parties. The frigate, carried by a good breeze and by the tide current, struck the boom with violence, and by the rebound was thrown so far out of the channel as to be stranded; but, happily, the captain, profiting by the rising tide, freed his ship by the expedient of firing the whole of the cannons on the side on which the vessel had touched ground, and the tide carried the ship through the boom, which had been broken by the first shock. When the frigate had passed through, the captain and crew cried 'Huzza, huzza!' (called here 'three cheers'), and had the misfortune in commencing the third 'huzza' to have his head carried off by a cannon ball.

CHEVALIER DE LATOCNAYE, *Promenade d'un Français dans l'Irlande*
(*A Frenchman's Walk Through Ireland*), 1798, translation by John Stevenson 1917

[JULY] 26 –

An experiment was tried on a cow at Ship-quay. She was tied and smeared with tar, and tow stuck to it, which was set on fire to make her roar, thinking that the enemy's cows which were grazing in the orchard would come to her. But she was not tied fast enough for when the tow took fire and was blazing about her, she made off, and was going to the orchard. But our men shot from the wall and killed her; she belonged to Mr Gravet.

– The Council thought fit to release Ensign Cartie and the other two, who were much hurt with the powder, and incapable of doing us much hurt this campaign.

27. – This morning we heard the great guns at or near Inch. The wind is SW which I suppose hinders our ships from coming up to us, and, God knows, we never stood in so much need of a supply; for now there is not one week's provisions in the garrison. Of necessity we must surrender the city, and make the best terms we can for ourselves. Next Wednesday is our last, if relief does not arrive before it.

– This day the cows and horses, sixteen of the first, and twelve of the last, were slaughtered; the blood of the cows was sold at fourpence per quart, and that of the horses at twopence. Two of our men were killed at Butcher's-gate from the orchard. The soldiers got one pound of meal mixed with Dutch flour, and next morning one pound and a half of horse beef per man. There is not a dog to be seen, they are all killed and eaten.

28TH OF JULY, 1689!

A day to be remembered with thanksgiving by the besieged in Derry as long as they live; for on this day we were delivered from famine and slavery, and the great deliverance, which from Almighty God we have obtained. In the evening all the regiments in the garrison were placed in a rank round the walls. They fired thrice, and thrice the great guns were discharged. A proclamation was issued forbidding any to take goods out of the city without licence, and that all who were not enlisted and had formerly resided in the country should repair to their respective habitations before Monday next.

[AUGUST] 9 –
Governor Walker went on board a ship at Derry bound for England.

10. – A proclamation was made that all who expected pay for the good service they did in defending this garrison, should appear in their arms on Monday next at 10 o'clock.

CAPTAIN THOMAS ASH, *A Circumstantial Journal of the Siege of Londonderry*, pub. 1792

IN THE BURYING-GROUND a pause was made, as by general consent, each individual seeming disposed to take one more survey of the beloved temple in which they had been wont to meet their God, and of the lowly resting-places where so many of their kindred reclined – far removed from the troubling of the wicked. Leaning upon tombs and grave-stones, or upon each other, for a momentary support, they gazed in solemn silence on those objects long familiarised, but, by every human probability, soon to be shut out for ever from their view. Then might be seen the dilated eye, deep sunk indeed within its socket, but still beaming forth the high resolve of unsubdued devotion to their righteous cause, and fleshless lips, livid as those of a corpse, compressed as though they would forcibly imprison the struggling sigh of famishing distress. Walker, still robed as in the pulpit, paced slowly among the scattered groups, his gaunt frame and hollow cheek presenting a personification of suffering as acute as had been undergone by any one. Arrived at an eminence, formed by the recent interment of several bodies beneath one mound, he looked for a moment at the crimson flag, whose folds fell languidly over the battlements of the church tower, then cast his eye around upon the patient sufferers, who met it with something approaching to a smile, so full of melancholy endurance, that his tears well-nigh overflowed while once more addressing them in the tones of soothing encouragement. 'Nay, doubt not, my faithful, my true-hearted fellow-Protestants: the Lord has heard – the Lord will assuredly answer – the united appeal of His poor perishing creatures. Doubt not, for when did He reject the prayer of faith? when did' – A sound, sudden and strange, and wildly joyful, came from the direction of the water-side: it produced a singular effect upon the hearers, and occasioned, even in Walker, a sensation of such choking emotion as cut short his address. That sound – dare they believe it? had they heard it aright? Yes, again it was repeated, and again the shout was raised; and again in articulate words was the transporting intelligence borne to their ears. 'The fleet, the fleet approaches! – The ships are in the Lough!'

It was as in a death-struggle that the greater number of those emaciated beings rushed to the walls. Husbands carried their dying wives, mothers their expiring children; and, by efforts that seemed supernatural, they gained the height, to witness what to their eyes appeared a celestial vision – the broad sails of three stately vessels, filled by a favouring gale, whitening upon the curling waters, and steadily approaching, with the undoubted purpose of anchoring beneath the walls. In the besiegers' camp all was bustle: a desperate resistance would no doubt be made; and the boom that stretched across the Lough menaced destruction to the coming deliverers. The fort of Culmore was manned, and its batteries opened with thundering fury upon the advancing ships; while volleys of musketry from either bank poured upon their sides. The fire was returned, and evidently with considerable execution, upon the wretched instruments of Romish aggression; while, comparatively unharmed, the gallant vessels made good their passage past the fort.

'The boom! the boom!' was breathed in gasps, and whispers of unutterable agony, by the terribly interested spectators on the walls. 'Will they venture to pass? – Can they break it? – Oh NOW, NOW, OR NEVER! – God give them resolution! – Still they approach!' Such exclamation burst from the parching lips that had so recently moved in united prayer; while a party of the townsmen mounted the cathedral, firing as a knell their minute guns of distress, and combining the efforts of their trembling arms to wave the crimson flag, in mute yet touching appeal to the hearts of their compassionate deliverers.

The *Mountjoy* had taken the lead: her captain was a native of Derry, and within its walls were his wife, his children, and his friends. The boom was right before her, and she swerved not; but rising upon the flowing tide, impelled by a lively breeze, she bore with all her force upon the sturdy barrier. It broke: – alas! the shock was too severe for the vessel; she recoiled, rolled deeply in the waters, and striking into the shallow stream, was instantly aground.

A shout, or rather a yell of rapturous exultation, resounded from the hostile banks; and boats were rapidly pushed off for the purpose of boarding the *Mountjoy*, while a groan, a deep, low, scarcely uttered groan, seemed to issue from the walls of Derry, with now and then a shriek of woman's agony, re-echoed by terrified children. There was a horror on the minds of those devoted beings, compared with which all their preceding sufferings seemed light and trifling: but there was also many a prayerful spirit wrought into that intenseness of supplication, which cannot fail of entering into the ears of the Lord God of Sabaoth.

The *Mountjoy* lay upon her side, seemingly a helpless victim, within reach of the foe: but the stake for which her captain fought was too precious to be trifled with. He fixed an earnest gaze upon the crowded walls of Derry, then raised his eyes to heaven as in passionate appeal, and, drawing his sword, sprang forward to the most commanding station upon deck, cheering his men to a determined resistance. His shout was answered by a general huzza from the crew, each gunner applying his ignited match, and a tremendous broadside instantly enveloped the combatants in a cloud of smoke.

This was indeed the climax of agonised expectation to the gasping spectators, who clung to their rampart-walls for that support which their own trembling knees refused to yield. Mothers strained their infants as in the very grasp of death, and joined their little hands together, lifting them between their own in mute supplication. Some were actually fainting under the conflict of hope and terror; not a few of whom had mounted the walls by that strength alone which desperation gives, to sink exhausted into the arms of bystanders somewhat less enfeebled. And the voice of trembling affection was heard in anxious whispers, imploring some loved one to revive, and hope, and pray for the issue of that fearful hour. It was a scene to mock description: a reality before which all the powers of imagination fade into contemptible nothingness.

The few seconds that elapsed before that cloud of smoke rolled away, leaving the *Mountjoy* once more fully visible – those few seconds seemed long indeed to the breathless gazers. They passed, and the gallant ship reappeared, not lying in stranded helplessness upon the bank, but, majestically floating in deep water, she ploughed the dancing tide right onwards towards the town.

'That broadside saved her!' shouted Walker. 'She has bounded from the shore – she has passed the boom! Derry and Victory!'

CHARLOTTE ELIZABETH (Mrs Tonna), *Derry – A Tale of the Revolution of 1688*, 1839

Then the foemen gather'd fast – we could see them marching
    past –
The Irish from his barren hills, the Frenchman from his wars,
With their banners bravely beaming, and to our eyes their
    seeming
Was fearful as a locust band, and countless as the stars.

And they bound us with a cord from the harbour to the ford,
And they raked us with their cannon, and sallying was hot;
But our trust was still unshaken, though Culmore fort was taken,
And they wrote our men a letter, and they sent it in a shot.

They were soft words that they spoke, how we need not fear their
    yoke,
And they pleaded by our homesteads, and by our children small,
And our women fair and tender; but we answer'd, 'No
    Surrender!'
And we call'd on God Almighty, and we went to man the wall.

There was wrath in the French camp; we could hear their
    Captains stamp,
And Rosen, with his hand on his cross'd hilt, swore
The little town of Derry, not a league from Culmore ferry,
Should lie a heap of ashes on the Foyle's green shore.

CECIL FRANCES ALEXANDER, *from* 'The Siege of Derry', 1891

HMS *Marlborough*
Will Enter Harbour

THEY WERE LIGHTS ALL RIGHT – but what lights? The one that Adams had first seen was not Butt of Lewis: the other two did not seem to fit any part of the chart, either Lewis or the mainland round Cape Wrath, or the scattered islands centred on Scapa Flow and the Orkneys. He checked them again, he laid off the bearings on a piece of tracing-paper and then moved it here and there on the chart, hesitatingly, like a child with its first jigsaw puzzle. He even moved it up to Iceland, but the answer would not come – and it was an answer they *must* have before very long: they were running into something, closing an unknown coastline which might have any number of hazards – outlying rocks, dangerous overfalls, minefields barring any approach except by a single swept channel. Sucking his pencil, frowning at the harsh lamplight, he strove to find the answer: even at this last moment, delay might rob them of their triumph. But the answer would not come.

Presently he opened the chart-house door and came out again, ready to take fresh bearings and to make doubly certain of what the lights showed. Both the doctor and the Chief were now on the bridge, talking in low voices through which ran a strong note of satisfaction and assurance. The Chief turned as he heard the step, and then jerked his head at the lights.

'Finest sight I've seen in my life, sir.'

The Captain smiled. 'Same here, Chief.'

'Is that Butt of Lewis, sir?' asked the doctor.

'No.' He raised his glasses, checked the number of the flashes, and bent to the compass to take a fresh bearing. 'No, Doc, I haven't worked out what it is yet.'

'It's something solid, anyway.'

'Enough for me,' said the Chief. 'All I want is the good old putty, anywhere between Cape Wrath and the Longships.'

To himself the Captain thought: I wish I could guarantee that.

'Another light, sir!' exclaimed the signalman suddenly. 'Port bow – about four-oh.'

The Captain raised his glasses once more.

'There it is, sir,' said the signalman again, before the Captain had found it.

'It's a red one this time.'

'Red?'

'Yes, sir. I got it clearly then.'

Red ... that rang a bell, by God! There was a red light at the end of Rathlin Island, off the north coast of Ireland: it was the only one he could remember, in fact. But Rathlin Island. He walked quickly into the chart-house, and moved the tracing-paper southwards. The jigsaw suddenly resolved itself. It *was* Rathlin: the light they had first seen was Inistrahull, the others were Inishowen and something else he could not check – probably an aircraft beacon. Rathlin Island – that meant that they had come all down the coast of Scotland, over two hundred miles farther than he had thought: it meant that they must have been steering at least fifteen degrees off their proper course. Those bloody compasses! But what did it matter now? Rathlin Island. They could put in at Londonderry and get patched up, and then go home. Northern Ireland instead of Butt of Lewis – that would look good in the Report. But what the hell *did* it matter? They had made their landfall.

He walked back to his chair, sat down, and said, in as level a voice as he had ever used:

'That's the north coast of Ireland. We'll be going to Derry.'

It was a peerless morning: the clean grey sky, flecked with pearly grey clouds, turned suddenly to gold as the sun climbed over the eastern horizon. There was now land ahead: a dark bluish coastline, with noble hills beyond. The Captain's stiff stubbly face warmed slowly to the sunshine: the ache across his shoulders and round his heart seemed to melt away, taking with it his desperate fatigue. Not much longer – and then sleep, and sleep, and sleep ... Bridger handed him the morning cup of cocoa, his face one enormous grin. But all he said was: 'Cocoa, sir.'

'Thanks ... We made it, Bridger.'

'Yes, sir.'

'Who won that sweepstake?'

'The Buffer, sir – I mean, Petty Officer Adams.'

The Captain laughed aloud. 'Bad luck!' For the ship's company that must be the one flaw in an otherwise perfect morning. There were a lot of hands on the upper deck now, smiling and pointing. He felt bound to them as closely as one man could be to another. Later, he wanted to find some words that would give them an idea of that. And something about *Marlborough*, too, the ship he loved, the ship they had all striven for.

'Trawlers ahead, sir,' said the signalman, breaking in on his thoughts. 'Three of them. I think they're sweeping.'

Back to civilization: to lights, harbours, dawn mine-sweepers, patrolling aircraft, a guarded fairway.

'Call them up, signalman.'

But one of the trawlers was already flashing to them. The signalman acknowledged the message, and said: 'From the trawler, sir: "Can I help you?"'

'Make: "Thank you. Are you going into Londonderry?"'

A pause, while the lamps flickered. Then: 'Reply "Yes", sir!'

'Right. Make: "Will you pass a message to the Port War Signal Station for me, please?"'

Another pause. 'Reply, "Certainly", sir.'

The Captain drew a long breath, conscious deep within him of an enormous satisfaction. 'Write this down, and then send it to them. "To Flag Officer in Charge, Londonderry, v. *Marlborough*. HMS *Marlborough* will enter harbour at 1300 today. Ship is severely damaged above and below water-line. Request pilot, tugs, dockyard assistance, and burial arrangements for one officer and seventy-four ratings." Got that?'

'Yes, sir.'

'Right. Send it off ... Bridger!'

'Sir?'

'Ask the Surgeon-Lieutenant to relieve me for an hour. I'm going to shave. And wash. And change. And then eat.'

NICHOLAS MONSARRAT, '*HMS Marlborough* Will Enter Harbour',
in *Depends on What You Mean by Love*, 1947

Officers Mess
3rd R. Innis. Fus,
Ebrington Bks
Londonderry
20-2-1917

Dear Mother,

Had your letter this morning along with ones from George and Uncle David.

My cold got better very quickly. The wild weather on the ranges cured it. I passed in musketry as a 1st class shot. I missed being a marksman by a couple of points.

We had great fun after a big flock of wildgeese before we left the ranges on Friday. Four of us crawled down a railway embankment and got within about 200yds of 1000 of them but only knocked feathers off one. They are hard to hit with a bullet.

I got my teeth today, they are a good fit. They cost £8-8-0 but they are all plated and strengthened with gold. I thought I might as well get them good when I had a few pounds to spare.

It is hardly worth while for Maud to knit another cardigan. Who are you going to give the photos to?

The big push must be coming off soon. All hospitals are being cleared and extended as far as possible.

I am sure David is still gassing about pigs. If he does not watch himself he will lose money on his squad. Geo. has no special news.

I have had no word about going on a course yet. I am parading with the men who are in the final stages of instruction now.

I have not too much to do. Like the others I earn my ten 'bob' a day easily enough.

No more news.

Jack [John Samuel Carrothers]

Londonderry
23-2-1917

Dear Mother,

I have got sudden orders for France. Four of us are going from this battalion and seven from the 4th. We are to be in Dublin on Saturday, London on Monday, and cross from Southampton to Le Havre on Tuesday. I will drop you an odd line on the way.

The train from L'derry goes via Portadown to Dublin. I was lucky in having my teeth finished and I was ready to move as I was expecting a sudden call. I will be out with a very big crowd of chaps I know. We will be well tired when we land in France. We stand all the way over with life-belts on.

There is no other special news. I will drop you p.c any time I get a chance.

How is Miss Oldcroft and Aunt in Shanco?

I may have time to get a photo in Dublin. If I do the proofs will be sent to you and you will have to decide what to get.

There is no other special news here.

It will be some time before I am able to give you an address that will find me.

I am sending you by rail my handbag, (key enclosed), also a chair and bed.

I asked Jim Boyle to drop a note to his father at Le Havre. I am sure I will find it hard to work the 'parley-vous' with the French. Hope everyone and everything are well and doing well.

Jack

Compiled by D.S. CARROTHERS, *Memoirs of a Young Lieutenant (1898–1917)*, 1992

O N EASTER TUESDAY 1941, DERRY PAID THE PENALTY.
Near mid-night, the Air Raid Sirens moaned their grim warning, and hurriedly the ARP services mustered at their Posts. Mine was at Church House on the corner of Queen Street and Great James Street. After thoroughly checking our vehicles, stores etc., we sat down to await developments. Was it to be another alert because German aircraft were over the Irish Sea, or was it to be for real this time?

The usual rumours – or buzzes – went the rounds. Then the shrill insistent ringing of the telephone, and everybody jumped. The operator answered, and had a monosyllabic conversation with the person at the other end in ARP Headquarters.

'Belfast is being hammered again' she said laconically, as she replaced the receiver.

A total of 180 Junkers 88, and Heinkel III German bombers belonging to Kampfgeschwader 54 and Kampfgeschwader 55 had taken off from the airfields of Evereux and Druex, in occupied France, whence they flew up St George's Channel at a very low level to avoid being seen by the Radar Stations on the English and Welsh Coasts, and the station at Kilkeel on the Co. Down coast. After making their landfall at Dundalk, they made a turning point at Dromore Co. Down, from where they ran in to their target areas. However, the leading aircraft dropped their flares in the wrong place, mistaking the reservoirs of the Waterworks on the Antrim Road for the docks area, and the main force of over 100 machines dropped a total of 203 tons of bombs in a concentrated attack on what was a built-up section of the city, destroying thousands of homes, killing an estimated 745 men, women and children, and interrupting communications over a wide area by destroying telephone cables and telegraph circuits.

One bomber was shot down by a fighter from Aldergrove, flown by Squadron Leader John Simpson.

Suddenly a member of the group who had gone out to have a look, tumbled in at the door. 'Flares' he shouted, and almost immediately there came the rapid crashes of the anti-aircraft batteries, and several tremendous thudding detonations which seemed to rock the building. For a moment there was an almost incredulous look on everyone's face, and complete silence, broken by the calm voice of Miss O'Neill of Ardowen House. 'Let us,' she said simply, 'pray for those who may die tonight,' and with one accord everybody in the room bowed their heads. Then the telephone again, and this time the operator's voice sounded strained.

'Numbers One and Two Ambulances and crews to incident at Messines Park.' I was number Two and sprinted for the door. My Ambulance – a Talbot – started on the button, and with a screech of tyres we were off down Gt James Street, round the corner into Strand Road, and through the gears watching the speedo needle climbing. It was a night with a full moon and broken cloud, a perfect night for bombing. As we swung left into Buncrana Road, we could see floodlights and what we took to be fog, but turned out to be dust. Suddenly we were driving over earth and clay, and for a moment I felt disorientated. Surely I hadn't driven into a field? Then an ARP Warden appeared. 'Corner of Messines Park,' he said, 'direct hit on two houses. There's a Naval rescue team there, that's their floodlights. Standby for their instructions.'

It seemed that several parachute mines had been dropped by the Germans, possibly intended to disorganise the shipping in the Foyle, but some had drifted a few hundred yards from their target area and burst in the vicinity of Messines Park, completely demolishing two houses. All the homes in the immediate area – St Patrick's Terrace, Collon Terrace, Balmoral Avenue, Maybrook Terrace etc., – had their windows blown in by the blast, others had their roofs partially stripped of slates. In many cases ceiling and plaster work fell down.

In the craters, water cascaded from the burst mains and sewers, telephone cables were exposed and hung loosely. The sailors of the Rescue Team worked frantically. Many of them were veterans of the Blitz on naval ports such as Chatham, Plymouth and Portsmouth, and their expertise was evident in the smooth way they functioned. 'Stretcher here' one called, and I scrambled down with a standard light metal ARP stretcher. 'Give us a hand.' Under the wreckage – a mass of timber and brick – I saw an inert figure in a blood-stained nightdress. Tenderly the body was withdrawn. One glance was sufficient, and I quickly drew a blanket over the corpse. 'Off to the morgue, now' was the next instruction, and my companion and myself were silent, acutely aware of the still form in our vehicle which a short time before had been a living, sentient being, but who now with almost her entire family had been called before the Judgement Seat of God. Altogether about twelve people were killed in this incident, with several dozen treated for cuts and shock.

CHARLES GALLAGHER, *Acorns and Oak Leaves*, 1981

B Y THE SPRING OF 1941, the first signs of a serious challenge to Doenitz's fleet had begun to emerge. The round-the-clock working in British shipyards (conspicuous among them Harland & Wolff's) was breaking all records in warship construction. Sixty Flower-class corvettes, the sturdy little ships which were to be at the forefront of the anti-submarine operations for the next few years, were scheduled for completion by the end of February. This achievement was accompanied by improved convoy management and underwater detection methods. In the air, too, RAF Coastal Command was demonstrating its ability to harry the U-boats along the eastern stretches of the convoy routes when the miserable weather permitted.

These early, if modest, successes can in large measure be traced to operations from Londonderry and the Foyle Estuary which became the base for an ever-increasing number of warships. Even before hostilities commenced, it had been obvious that the Royal Navy would need a base as far west as possible. Britain's historic anchorages at Cobh, Berehaven and Lough Swilly, which she had retained by virtue of the treaty concluded with the newly-formed Dublin government in December 1921, were ceded to Eire in April 1938. There were no proximate substitutes for the loss of the two first-named ports but in the north the Foyle Estuary was a natural successor to Lough Swilly. In light of the unexpected deterioration in Britain's circumstances which set in after the fall of Norway in April 1940 the Royal Navy gratefully availed itself of the use of it.

The benefits accruing quickly became apparent. Escorts were able to accompany convoys that much farther west and also give incoming convoys a similar amount of added protection.

As to the waters of the lough itself, the potential for a dispute in international law existed which could have had serious consequences on a practical level. The respective rights of the two states over these waters which came into being on partition were not clearly defined by the Boundary Commission set up by the British government but in the event legalities were quietly ignored.

Plans to create all the services associated with a major naval base were implemented. New berthing spaces were created and maintenance and repair installations established, including the refuelling facilities which were to prove so indispensable to Allied navies for the duration of the war. The entire project was tackled energetically and throughout 1941 the number of escort groups using the base increased to the point where it assumed a pre-eminent position in the Battle of the Atlantic. The thousands of shipwrecked seamen landed at the port was grim evidence of this importance.

The base at Londonderry had as its first Naval Officer in Charge Captain Philip Ruck-Keane who was responsible to the Flag Officer in Charge at Belfast. In a report dated 3 May 1941 he spelt out another advantage which the base had in addition to its westernmost dimension: Its relative invulnerability to air attack.

The point was apropos and one which Doenitz was already painfully aware of. The Luftwaffe had no trouble in reaching British naval bases in southern England but Londonderry's comparative isolation was something that more directly jeopardized the safety of his boats.

Elsewhere in his report, Ruck-Keane predicted:

> The Battle of the Atlantic is the crux of the war and even if the battle is won in the near future it will certainly be a hard struggle until the end of the war. Londonderry will therefore remain of the highest importance throughout the war.

The accuracy of this prediction can be seen in the fact that a total of twenty-seven escort vessels, including anti-submarine trawlers, were already based there as of 1 January 1941.

The use of air power in an anti-submarine role had been well recognized before the war and when hostilities began aircraft were utilized not only to supplement the surface units but to constitute an effective offensive weapon in their own right. The area adjacent to Lough Foyle provided excellent sites for these maritime operations. At Limavady, development had taken on added urgency in the summer of 1940 and at the turn of the year Whitleys of No. 502 (Ulster) Squadron began flying anti-submarine operations from the base. Construction at Eglinton and Ballykelly also commenced in 1940, the latter destined to provide Coastal Command with another of its renowned bases. Luftwaffe aerial photographs of Ballykelly and Eglinton, both taken on 28 April 1941, show the stage reached in construction and have detailed annotations giving accurate estimates of the dimensions of buildings in course of erection. They are an indication of German concern at what was going on there and, at the same time, of their inability to do anything about it. Coastal Command's advantage in having its bases left unmolested is in stark contrast to, for example, I/KG/40's parlous tenure of Bordeaux-Merignac which was regularly attacked by RAF bombers.

After the entry of the United States into the war, the status of the Foyle base as a major terminal for Allied naval operations was progressively consolidated but it was never more important than it was in the formative days of 1940/41. Winston Churchill, writing after the war, said that the shipping losses became most grave during the twelve months from July 1940 to July 1941 '*when we could claim that the British Battle of the Atlantic was won*'. The ships and aircraft from Londonderry and the north-west carved their own niche in the history of that momentous time.

TREVOR ALLEN, The Storm Passed By, 1996

THAT WAS MY FIRST DEFINITE WAR IMPRESSION, a backward glance from a carriage window at a group standing in the sunshine on the platform of a seaside railway station and a most uncomfortable intuition that we in the train were doomed. But it was too late to do anything about it now. And so the group melted from the platform in the mellow September sunshine, back to the golf links and the beach, the gentle fair-haired beauty with the eyes (but by no means the destiny) of a Madonna being the last to leave. A curve in the line told me that: she was still there on the platform, fluttering her handkerchief, and the next time I would see her she would be a well-known London actress and I should be prematurely grey about the sides of the head ... and the hands of the clock could never be turned back again to the sunlit railway station beside the sea, and probably a very good thing too.

So the train puffs on through the September sunshine to Derry; then a drive on jaunting cars, very conscious of our new uniforms, to the whitewashed barn that is the terminus of the Londonderry and Lough Swilly Railway. We are fairly launched now into a new world; the platform here is crowded with soldiers shouldering white canvas kit-bags, and there is a most embarrassing business of saluting and being saluted ... Then the little narrow-gauge train puffs out on its leisurely journey northwards, past back gardens, across roads; Lough Swilly reflects a heavenly blue on the left, Slieve Snaght raises its snout to the right; the train climbs puffing away from the lough into darker regions of rock and heather ... and Inishowen and the business of being young officers of the Special Reserve begin to close round us, fortunately extinguishing the worlds we have known.

DENIS IRELAND, *From the Irish Shore*, 1936

BUT IT WAS AT LONDONDERRY that Northern Ireland's new status was most clearly defined. By February of 1942, more than eighty naval escort vessels were moored in the Foyle, up which Captain Browning's *Mountjoy* had sailed in 1689 to relieve the besieged Protestants of the Maiden City. And in one sense, the Royal Navy's arrival in the Second World War represented an almost equally momentous delivery for the Protestants of Northern Ireland. Londonderry's strategic role meant that the six counties were now essential to the prosecution of the war and could no longer be used as a tempting bait for de Valera in return for the restricted use of the Treaty ports or the premature entry of British troops into Eire. De Valera's very refusal to hand back Eire's Atlantic harbours now served only to emphasize the loyalty of Northern Ireland's Unionist population whose six small and generally poor counties had become a defensive bridgehead to America. The province was now not just a willing armourer, but a bastion in the Battle of the Atlantic. 'Here, by the grace of God,' Churchill later wrote, 'Ulster stood a faithful sentinel.'

Craigavon would have approved of the sentiment although he thought that Britain's good fortune was owed to Unionist loyalty rather than divine intervention. He above most others realized in the autumn of 1940 that by a happy combination of Germany's victory on the Continent and de Valera's stubborn neutrality, Northern Ireland had been placed in a new and unprecedented relationship with Britain, one which apparently proved the intrinsic worth of his Protestant Government in Belfast. Asked in November about de Valera's refusal to lend the Treaty ports to Britain, Craigavon replied that:

... all the sacrifices Ulster has made in the past have been fully justified by having secured for His Majesty's Forces a *pied à terre* in Ireland from which they can successfully combat the dangers which confront us by land, sea and air. What has happened is a complete vindication of the Government of Northern Ireland since it took office.

ROBERT FISK, In Time of War, 1983

WARTIME

THE WAR BROKE OUT IN SEPTEMBER 1939. I was still at school at the time and it had little or no effect on us kids at all, we were too young to understand what was going on. Our first introduction to war was the sight of gas masks and the air raid shelters being constructed. At school we were shown how to put on our gas mask and where to go when the sirens sounded. When the air raid sounded myself and all the pupils of St Patrick's had to make our way to the inner play ground, put on our gas masks and wait for the all clear. The people in Bridge Street would go to one of the four air raid shelters, one outside Johnny Kilkie's shop, one outside Kennedy's house and one on the battery. In the school itself as a precaution, there were two fire buckets on every landing, one filled with water and one with sand.

The Americans used to have parties for the kids at Christmas. I remember a grey bus pulling up outside the school and we were told to get on board and taken to one of the American camps outside the city. We had a great time, there were American comics, chewing gum and candy as they called it, there was turkey with all the trimmings, there was ice-cream and things we had never dreamed of. It was a great thrill for the children of Derry.

At one stage during the war we were evacuated to Cookstown. Before leaving we were taken down to Shipquay Street to the wvs where we were given a siren suit and new shoes. But all we wanted was to come back to Derry. I still remember getting off the bus in Foyle Street after the long trip home from Cookstown and walking up Foyle Alley. It was great to be back with lads, going into Nellie Clifford's shop for a wing's worth of sweets.

DESSIE MOORE, 'Growing Up in Bridge Street', Derry Journal, 25 April 2000

DERRY WASN'T QUIET FOR VERY LONG because the Yanks arrived to set up bases for the invasion of Europe. We didn't know it then but that was the long-term plan. The Japs bombed Pearl Harbor in Hawaii which brought the Americans into the war and one day we awoke to the sounds of a lot of American civilians coming up Duke Street from the railway station. Some were dressed as cowboys with holsters and guns slung at their waist, cowboy boots, chaps and big hats and others wore check shirts like lumberjacks. I had never seen a real live American before let alone a cowboy, and on top of that I had never seen so many big men. It was a great exciting time in my life. Their job was to build the camps for the fighting forces to follow. They threw us children fistfuls of money and I scrambled as good as the rest. There were chocolates and chewing gum which was all brand new to us – even before sweet-rationing our chewing gum looked different – and some of them started to shoot their guns in the air but looking back now I think they may have been using blanks, for I didn't see anybody fall.

Watching old Pathé newsreels of the war in Europe, I could identify with the people of the wee towns in France and Italy as the Yanks started to liberate them, for that was how they behaved with us that first day in Duke Street. The only difference was: this mob were civilians. Some of the Royal Navy were still in Derry and although they were supposed to be allies somehow the Yanks didn't like them, so naturally the fights started and on that particular night in Duke Street it was like a scene from the Barbary Coast. I myself had a ringside seat down Mill Street when a Yank squeezed a wee sailor to death in a bear hug and then threw him away from him like a ragdoll. He was a very big man, possibly twenty-four stone, and the sailor a normal ten or twelve stone, a perfect mismatch if ever I saw one. I still see that big hunk in my mind being led away by his buddies to Ebrington Barracks and story has it he went back to Sing Sing where he came out of.

The story also going the rounds at the time was that when America was so rudely pulled into the war on that infamous day in December 1941 a lot of the prisoners in jails throughout the States got an offer they couldn't refuse: help the war effort or stay in prison; so I'll leave it to your own imagination. This is a verse from a parody on the US marines' march 'The Halls of Montezuma'.

> From the halls of Montezuma to the huts at old Springtown
> You can see them in their uniforms go marching up and down.
> First they took them out of Sing Sing and dressed them up in green;
> Then they sent them here to Derry as United States marines.

JOHN DORAN, *Red Doran – The Story of a Derryman*, 1996

A WINTER NIGHT IN DERRY. Huddled in my Irish Fusiliers greatcoat I was walking round the walls. Flush with the parapet was a lighted window, obscured by curtains, with the blind pulled down to make certain. From behind blind and curtains came a voice speaking in Irish, a high insistent voice, interrupted by bursts of frenzied applause.

No place for newly-joined second-lieutenants in British greatcoats. I stood back from the window, moved into darkness. With me moved my maternal grandfather, invisible, but present in the frosty night. I never heard him discussed in the family, not with Carsonite rifles in the attic. If he figured at all, he figured as a sort of disreputable relative from the Australian outback, never to be mentioned in polite Belfast society.

Actually he was a Presbyterian minister, and somewhere about the middle of last century he preached from the pulpit of a small Presbyterian church in county Louth – in English one Sunday, in Irish the next. No wonder we kept quiet about him on the Malone Road. At the height of Carsonite 'Ulsteria' grandfathers who preached in Irish were pushed in behind the historical background, and kept there. Yet without my knowing much about him, he was there the night I stood by the lighted window on Derry's walls; there when, in a mood of black infantry man's despair, I wrote a sketch about another 'lighted window', this time a hatch for serving drinks. I was sitting, in mufti, in the snug of a combined public-house and grocery store in the shadow of Inishowen mountains, drinking stout and at the same time watching, through the hatch, a beautiful girl at the grocery counter:

> Unconscious of her beauty, she stood directly under a paraffin lamp, her shawl flung back, laughing and joking with the storekeeper, a prim pince-nezed young woman from Derry – the pair of them oblivious of male attention, surrounded by stacks of groceries.

DENIS IRELAND, 'Grandfather Preached in Irish', *From the Jungle of Belfast*, 1973

E VERY CITY HAS ITS MOODS. Londonderry, by the exile from a friendlier climate, is allowed only one. It is Ulster's Manchester, veiled, to the eye of unsympathetic memory, by perpetual drizzle. This is the Derry of a grey cowl of cloud, a bend of rain-darkened water and streets that pencil thin, dull lines down to the riverbank.

This mood asserted itself with the war, in the short winter days and the narrow, blacked-out streets. Across the river from home, the dumpy corvettes lay eternally in the rain-pocked Foyle, seeming to crouch for unattainable shelter against the dock sheds.

Behind them the clock tower of the Guildhall pointed sombrely at the weeping sky. The utility buses – 'futility' buses as they were called – swished fitfully to a halt for the queues of dripping passengers in the square.

Every day the tiny ferry took me across the river to school, while I hoped for a fault in the ramshackle engine and the consequent excuse for a late arrival in class.

The misery of rotating slowly down the Foyle, hunched against the soaking gusts of wind and listening to the ferryman's vituperative address to his engine – this was a bargain price for the vaguely romantic effect of entering class late, heroically wet, and explaining with the air of a reluctant Ulysses that the ferry had broken down again.

Towards the end of the war the small ferry was replaced by quite a large steamboat, built originally for pleasure trips at Brighton or some such resort. This was to transport considerable numbers of seamen from the Waterside barracks to their posts on the city side. It was much more comfortable, but somehow less satisfying. It never broke down.

This feeling of a wartime Derry inextricably associated with rain may give an impression of cheerlessness. That would be most misleading. To begin with, it doesn't, of course, rain any more there than elsewhere in Ulster. In addition, the influx of nationalities brought with it a most stimulating cosmopolitanism.

Once we even had some Russian ships in port. Anticipation varied. Some expected unscrubbed Bolshevists in obsolete ships officered by brutal incompetents. Others visualised clean-limbed youth conversing in Marxian dialectic.

In the event they were distressingly normal. We saw them at a concert in the Guildhall. I was then, with many another, an enthusiastic Russophile, appealing in most of my school essays for a 'Second Front now'. I had also begun – it never went beyond a beginning – to learn Russian. The situation seemed appropriate, and I made a few remarks in Russian to my companion.

The words penetrated, as intended, to a rather dyspeptic-looking Russian sailor in the next row. Turning round, he spoke to us fluently, incomprehensibly and with every appearance of ill-will. As we were leaving, he pointed us out to his friends.

It has remained a mystery how I gave such offence by saying, in the only Russian I knew: 'How do you do, comrade? It is a frosty night. Cabbage soup.' Possibly cabbage soup has the same significance for a Russian as rice pudding for a boy at a boarding school.

Outside the smoky warmth of the hall the night, I remember, was starless. On its impenetrable purposes, an occasional searchlight cut a narrow clearing through the black sky, illuminating casually the fins of a barrage balloon, then letting the grotesque shape drop back into the void. Opposite the Guildhall the walls were a darker rectangle, Shipquay Gate a blurred cavity against which moved dim silhouettes.

It recalled my fancy of a city barricaded in on itself by war, palisaded by sky and river, the easy contacts of peace only a memory. Within the defences, as in Boccaccio's city cut off by plague, the inhabitants accepted the infrequent hour's amusement.

Then came return to the ships, the aerodromes, the canteens, the hesitant bustle of the streets, the wireless with its news of defeat and victory. In our wars, nowhere is wholly isolated. The palisades were in fact not barriers, but means of communication with the vast and inescapable struggle.

D.E.S. MAXWELL, 'A Reminiscence of Wartime Londonderry', *Acorn* 5, Autumn 1963

TED LATTA, A TECHNICAL SERGEANT AND A CREW CHIEF – head mechanic – on the P38s of 82nd Fighter Group, wrote a short account of his time at Eglinton with his impressions of the area and the food available when the group arrived there.

> ... our barracks were Quonset Huts down both sides of a company street. At the far end was the Airman's Ablutions (bathhouse) and the latrine.
>
> We settled into a semblance of camplife on a British air station to await the arrival of our P38s ... Our first mess call on the RAF base happened to be Tea. We were served fresh bread, jam and margarine and tea laced with milk and sugar. Not bad for a bunch of hungry GI's, but it was all downhill from there.
>
> ... In my own ramblings I came across the post gym with a sign over the door. 'You must be wearing Plimsoles to enter'. It took me a while to decipher that plimsoles were gym shoes. Ah – the colourful English language! A boot was the trunk of a car, a spanner was a Crescent Wrench and a Green Grocer sold only vegetables.
>
> Next door to the gym was the NAAFI, the English version of the USO. In the hut the local women sold tea and cakes. I ... ordered a pot of tea and proceeded to load my plate with cookies and cakes. I settled down to enjoy myself only to find that they all had the flavour of GI laundry soap. I found out they had used sheep tallow for shortening. So much for the NAAFI.

To improve the food situation Ted Latta and his friends bought up the meagre stock of a local grocery shop and then raided a potato field by moonlight. The plants were dug up, 'depotatoed' and replanted.

They were allowed leave passes to 'Eglinton, Limavady, Ballymena, Portrush and Londonderry' and travelled by double-deck bus to towns where they were able to see how the civilian population was fighting the war.

> We located ... the American Red Cross in downtown Londonderry on the second floor of a building on the main street. We were able to buy a cup of coffee and a doughnut there and to get directions to the various sights in the area.
>
> I remember some of us found an Irish Pub that served meals. The meal consisted of a bowl of potatoes about the size of golf balls. They

228

were cooked in their skins and served with margarine. The spuds were peeled with your pocket knife and garnished with that muton tallow margarine coloured to resemble butter. Another dish served was sausages made from sawdust and a plant called bloodroot. This was the first ersatz food we had. Our dreams at night were of ham and eggs, steak and real butter.

Even for Thanksgiving Day, when the Americans had hoped that a special meal might be provided, the treat consisted of 'a boiled kidney on a china plate surrounded by a yellow liquid'. Then, at last, an American Mess was set up and US rations became available as sufficient supplies were arriving in the UK. When the Mess opened and the group's men had their first American food in months 'C rations never tasted so good'. Any complainers were threatened with banishment to the British mess; 'no-one was so exiled'.

RICHARD DOHERTY, Key to Victory: The Maiden City in the Second World War, 1995

N OR WERE THE PEOPLE TROUBLED MUCH by any restrictions on their food supply, as, outside Dublin, these were observed in a very casual manner. I remember seeing in Derry a little framed menu which always hung on the porch outside one of the hotels, giving the day's dinner. On this was the announcement, in large capitals, that it was a 'Meatless Day', but following this, under the head of 'Fish', there appeared 'Boiled Mutton, Caper Sauce', and under 'Joint' there was a blank, so as to convey to all and sundry that, notwithstanding the piscatory boiled mutton, the management realized its obligations in regard to the meatless day. Outside the hotel, lazily basking in the sun, a policeman was leaning against the porch which bore the announcement conveying to the diners this legend of meatless mutton.

SIR HENRY ROBINSON, Memories Wise and Otherwise, 1924

W E TOOK A PILOT ABOARD and sailed up the River Foyle for the first time. Through lush green Irish fields, trees and meadows, we slid quietly and gently between the river banks up to the city of Londonderry. On we sailed until we passed the Guildhall and tied up almost under the parapet of the bridge. We had left the unrelieved cold grey monotony of the Atlantic behind and taken a journey through some delightful country before arriving in the centre of a city.

The transition was difficult to assimilate; it was also difficult to appreciate, for our thoughts were concentrated on the protracted and time-consuming journey which faced those who were entitled to leave.

The city of 'Derry' did not hold many attractions to lads who had recently experienced three visits to the flesh-pots of Liverpool.

Libertymen from the watch aboard went ashore in search of whatever delights Derry could offer. Some of us found a dance hall which gradually assumed a dual role as the evening progressed. Brawls broke out from time to time and then it became a battlefield; some of them spilled out into the forecourt.

A diminutive and extremely drunk Irishman loudly denounced the Royal Navy and everything British. His avowed intent was clearly to destroy them all single-handed, starting there and then; with arms swinging wildly in all directions he was bound to make contact sooner or later with anyone who stood before him.

When four matelots retired hurt in the face of his unrelenting aggression we decided there were better places to spend our evening despite the loss of our admission fee to the dance.

Our opinion of Londonderry and its welcome was not enhanced by the experience, yet on our return to the ship we discovered there were some who had apparently fared rather better than we had done. They did not return until morning.

One of them brought a varied assortment of dresses and ladies' underwear which he had removed from the wardrobe of the 'lady' with whom he had spent the better part of the night. At the first opportunity he declared he would 'pop' them at the nearest pawnbrokers in order to recover some of the money his lady had stolen out of his pockets.

Others became withdrawn and said little about their escapades. We were left to draw our own conclusions when they put in a request for the Roman Catholic priest to be called. It was a request which was granted automatically and the Captain had to make his cabin available as a confessional when the priest arrived on board.

Abject and troubled creatures suddenly became carefree and happy within the space of a few short minutes as their sins and misdemeanours were absolved.

Our Canadian friends, tied up alongside and outboard of Polyanthus, had arranged things differently. One or two selected ladies of the town had been smuggled aboard for the night. Their departure on the following morning was witnessed by our quartermaster, 'Darby' Allen.

'Could I help you ladies?' he enquired solicitously, 'You look absolutely worn out.'

'Some other time, Jack, m'darlin',' they replied as they stumbled across our deck in order to get ashore.

Derry's image was receiving some very rough treatment.

FRED KELLETT, *A Flower for the Sea – A Fish for the Sky*, 1995

THE CROWDED CITY STREETS, with the throngs of people and the various figures in uniform, were indeed a constant source of interest to the little country girl. She grew to love the old grey city, with its ancient walls and gates, and she learned as so many others have learned, to lift up her eyes and find even in its closest and most congested quarters a flash of beauty – tall trees against the skyline, a hillside vivid with gold and green, or a glimpse of the blue shining waters of the Foyle.

The shop windows, too, were a never-ending delight to her, and she studied them with great care, hoping that some day she might make Miss Elton's modest establishment look as prosperous and up-to-date.

The very posters fired her with enthusiasm. Isolated as she had been in the country, she had never realised what war meant and had thought little about it. Now her sole desire was to help in any way she could. She became a diligent collector of salvage, every scrap of paper was saved, a special box was kept for rags, another for rubber, while the smallest piece of bone was immediately carried to the nearest collection.

But this she felt was not nearly enough, and her heart jumped with delight when Miss Elton remarked one evening: 'This is my night to work at the Canteen, Jemima Jane; would you like to come along and help?'

ISOBEL MARSHALL, *A Jack and His Jill*, 1944

IN THE TRAIN FOR DERRY. Somewhere amongst grey clouds over the grey entrance waters of the Foyle a seaplane zooms like a noxious insect. *Boom-p, boom-p*, two dull thuds from out at sea rattle the carriage windows. An English petty officer on leave from the naval base at Derry explains that the seaplane has probably caught sight of some dark shadow in the water below, and just to make sure is bombing it. The hawk-men are at work blowing the lights out of the fish-men. Thank God I am a civilian! I happen to know those *boom-p*'s from the last war.

The train plunges in and out of rock tunnels below the once episcopal estate of Downhill and the pavilion on the edge of the cliffs overlooking the Atlantic and the dark mountains of Inishowen that Augustus Hervey, Bishop of Derry, built for some particular Vanessa of the period. To-day it is, I suppose, an *Aussichtspunkt* for an entirely different kind of coastwatcher, and the broad sands below, where the bishop used to amuse himself by organising horse races with neighbouring clergymen as jockeys, are intersected by rows of posts and aprons of barbed wire.

The grey Atlantic, with its occasional plumes of black smoke from distant warships, recedes; the train flashes past Bellarena and its wooded mountain; past the barbed-wire-defended sand dunes of Magilligan, the green, well-tilled farmlands of the Roe Valley; past Limavady Junction and the field at Broighter where a stumbling ploughman unearthed the gold ornaments that caused an international lawsuit and now dully glitter in the National Museum in Dublin. *There is a grey eye looks back to Derry*, wrote Columba centuries ago. Derry of the leafy oak shade, the spires and pinnacles against the sunset, the rusty key that must be turned, not forced, before Ireland is a nation once again. Beyond the Foyle the green curve of the Inishowen hills flattens; the wooded point, famous in the siege, projects like a rampart into the mirror-like surface of the river; across the lagoon the steeples, smoke-smudge, and uninspiring gable-ends of Derry suddenly line the water's edge, appearing as if by magic from behind the woods on the farther shore. Bevies of grey-painted, camouflaged ex-American destroyers lie at anchor in the river, or cluster thickly by the wharves, and a thick crop of silver-grey barrage balloons has sprung up above the spires and pinnacles in the cloudy grey sky. Twentieth-century was has come to the Maiden City.

In the bar of the hotel the hawk-men are relaxing after their patrols over the grey wastes of the Atlantic; the atmosphere is pure tin-shanty West translated into terms of the flying services, with machine-guns substituted for six-shooters and quickness at the bomb-lever the mark of a living man. The frontier has rolled back from North America, eastwards in time and space to Europe, then westwards again to this city on the Foyle where Irish Protestantism first issued its battle cry of '*No Surrender*'. Just another little drink for the road, say the uniformed frontiersmen in the bar, and please God the next time the fog comes down, we shall win our way back to land and safe anchorage, back from the unsettled wilderness of the Atlantic rolling in from the West. If not, then a short life and a merry one.

It is a good manly philosophy, but somehow it is foreign to the atmosphere of Derry, with its roots plunging down below its famous siege into a past that has seen not only darkness in Europe but dawn and the beginnings of the worship of God in man. Foreign too to the soft wind, almost syrupy in its treacherous sweetness, that blows out of the dark boglands and along the winding roads from Donegal. The soft, sweet wind whispers of the ecstasies of knowledge, of the life that begins when life is forgotten, of the almost delirious pleasures awaiting the man who can cease to be himself and become instead a channel for eternal truth. It is a wind for saints and scholars, and not for hawk-men, who have delirious pleasures of their own.

DENIS IRELAND, 'The Road to the Isles', in *Northern Harvest*,
(ed. Robert Greacen), 1944

OUR SHIP WAS THE *USS HURST* and we made many trips into the little port outside of Londonderry (Lessinhally?).

When we arrived in Derry we would go to the CB base to play basketball and softball.

I had many good experiences in Derry and met quite a few nice people. One family invited me into their home for tea. They live across the street from the university. The husband worked in the Guildhall.

One of the photos is of Father McCully [Cauley]. He was pastor of St Patrick's Church. I would bring him cigars and cigarettes. He would treat me to beer. He knew an American Navy chaplin [sic]. That's how he got the beer.

Also there was a group of young children with a cart pulled by a goat or pony (I'm not sure which) they would take us around town in the cart. We would give them American money and candy.

Ernest Garynutes, Wilmington, Delaware

My ship the *USS Hurst,* DE-250, one of a division of six US Coast Guard destroyer escorts, accompanied several convoys to Londonderry. In fact we made so many trips to Northern Ireland that we dubbed ourselves 'The Londonderry Ferry'.

Our first visit was in March of 1944, when we rendezvoused with 101 tankers and freighters at Gravesend Bay, off the coast of New York and shepherded them across the North Atlantic, then steamed down Lough Foyle to Derry. There is no doubt in my mind at that time that Ireland was the loveliest piece of terra firma I'd ever seen. Of course, at the time I was in a debilitated psychological state. Let me explain ...

The voyage was my first experience on the 'bounding main' and I had been seasick every foot of the way. I think that even the Sahara would have looked beautiful to me. Land – any land – was a haven from the incessant heaving and pitching of the deck. I'd gladly have changed places with any soldier, sailor or marine stationed in Ireland for the privilege of not going back to sea.

I'm engaging in a bit of wry levity, of course: even now 50 years later, I remember vividly the beauty of Ireland. As a native of the northeastern United States (I was born in New Jersey), I was accustomed to verdancy; nevertheless, I was dazzled by Ireland's incredible greenness. Seeing, I comprehended for the first time why it's called 'The Emerald Isle'. I always thought it was just an affectation on the part of the Blarney-tongued Sons of Erin.

I was very young in those days ... young and inexperienced. I remember being astonished on my first visit to Derry when I saw Jewish-owned business establishments. I guess I was pretty naïve. It had never occurred to me that there might be Jewish Irishmen.

Another thing that surprised me occurred on a July evening, when a buddy and I went to see a movie in Londonderry. When the film ended and we left the theatre, we discovered that the sun was still shining ... at nearly eleven pm. I guess I really was pretty uninformed; I should have known how far north Derry is and how long the summer days are at latitude.

Warren F. De Louise (Former RM-1/C, USCGR),
Culver City, California

First, and most of all, I remember the children. Each Liberty several shipmates and myself would carry a large grocery bag of chocolate candy ashore and we felt like the pied-piper as the children would follow us while we emptied the bags ...

I also remember the churches ... We attended worship services, and we gave a pint of blood ... so maybe a spot of my blood is coursing through some Irishman's veins.

I remember rain! Believe it rained on every Liberty I made in Londonderry. One of the few places I had the opportunity to wear my navy raincoat in lieu of the proverbial 'Pea Jacket'.

I also remember Londonderry had no 'suburbs' at that time. When you passed the last house on the block, you were in the country ... as evidenced by the cows strolling into a Londonderry street ...

Robert L. Hines CLU, Richmond, Virginia

Letters written in 1994 to RICHARD DOHERTY,
a military historian, by retired US naval officers

RESENTMENT HAD BEEN BUILDING UP ever since the Americans had moved into Londonderry. They had constructed the naval base off Strand Road and their hospital at Creevagh. Compared with the Canadians and ourselves they had more of everything, food, facilities, mouths and money, particularly money, and the money pulled the girls.

We went up on deck to see groups of lads from the Canadian ships heading out of the base without a thought for liberty boats or other restrictions. Their shipmates who remained aboard passed on varied and probably exaggerated reports of ambulances collecting the injured and blood flowing in the streets. Like the flames of a forest fire the news spread throughout the ships and kindled our curiosity. We awaited the return of our libertymen and hoped they would provide a more reliable account of the situation.

The quartermaster returned later to impart some news he had picked up from one of our family of Canadian corvettes.

'The Canadians and Yanks are having a battle royal at the Corinthian Hall. A lot of the Canadians are going ashore to help out but none of our lads are involved, as far as I know.'

FRED KELLETT, *A Flower for the Sea – A Fish for the Sky*, 1995

I joined up with the Territorials on the fourth of April 1939
and we were called up to service in September 1939.
We were kept at home here for about a month or so.
We were moved away in November.
They put us on board trains
and we went right through France down to Marseilles
and we got the ship down there,
the *Etterick*,
for Egypt.
We landed in Egypt round about the end of November.
Then we went down through the Sudan,
down to Aden.
I do remember, on one occasion,
there was a fellow –
we were in Port Sudan.
We went up with McLean,
he was an officer, a captain,
and coming down again we saw this figure coming along.
And he says to me, 'Who in under goodness is that?'
He was coming along with his full pack and all.
I says, 'I don't know till I get down his length
to see if I know him.'
And when we got down the length of him
I recognised him.
Of course the captain says, 'Stand man!'
He says to him, 'Where are you going, man?'
He says, 'I'm goin' home,
I've had enough of this carry on!'
He says, 'Get on man!'
That regiment, Twenty-four, Twenty-five Battery

were all Derry men, part Strabane, Limavady –
land's sakes alive,
when we left there must have been
a thousand left the City.
The first one we lost
was a fellow called Tommy Porter –
shrapnel in the stomach –
poor Tommy,
he was an inoffensive fellow.
It killed him in no time at all.
Jim Gilmore was killed in Italy
when the bomb went into the gun-pit.'

ANONYMOUS, in *The Fountain* (ed. Leon McAuley), 1993

ON JUNE 30 [1941], THE FIRST BODY of 362 United States technicians arrived in Londonderry to begin work. During the next five months, their numbers gradually rose, another four hundred at the end of July, more in September and over two hundred more in October. Supplies, too, began to pour into Northern Ireland, mainly into Londonderry but some through Belfast for Lough Erne, where work had begun at Ely Lodge. Londonderry itself served as the clearing house for the schemes both in Scotland and Northern Ireland, so that not all the men and materials which arrived stayed long in the vicinity of the walled city. But it meant that the quayside and hotels of Londonderry hummed with excitement and buzzed with rumour. The city seemed from time to time to be crowded with the 'visitors', as indeed it often was. They were still housed in Ebrington Barracks. As a whole they were a good type; their food, brought from the United States, was superior to the rationed diet of the local population and their wages were higher than those of their colleagues, recruited mainly in Northern Ireland. They worked hard, ten hours a day, and six days a week. What they needed were better facilities for recreation and especially the opening of cinemas on Sundays. It was not all smooth going. There were difficulties with the local inhabitants: aloofness and curiosity, more particularly because the Americans were rightly disinclined to discuss their work. There was envy at the relatively high wages which the 'visitors' earned. There were the local gold-diggers. The Americans themselves did not find the weather congenial:

The first contingent arrived unsuitably clad, with no waterproof coats and no tools. They wandered about in the rain for days, bought up shovels and picks and tools locally and started clearing the ground. The inclemency of the weather and the lack of amusement drove a number of them to drink, and the licensed premises did and are still doing thriving business.

Even so, everyone was impressed with their high output and their powers of concentration. When machinery and materials arrived, they settled down to work with 'a concentration of effort not familiar to this country'. The fact was that progress both at Londonderry and Lough Erne was rapid. Starting in the city of Londonderry, where they began to resuscitate part of the old shipyard as a repair base, they quickly extended the area of construction. As the work proceeded, the British and United States authorities were jointly concerned in avoiding wastage, overlapping and developments at cross purposes; the Londonderry Harbour Commissioners in dredging various sections of the river; the Ministry of Commerce in dealing with applications for priority supplies; and the Works Branch of the Ministry of Finance in requisitioning property, both houses in the city or parts of estates along the east bank of the lough. In November, the United States authorities intimated that they would like the Royal Navy to make full use of the base facilities built or building by them in the United Kingdom, provided that in the event of need part or the whole of the bases would be turned over immediately to themselves. But this modification of the initial scheme did not materially affect the rate of progress on the sites. At Lough Erne, where work did not begin until August, the whole of the original programme was completed within five months, and extra accommodation for a marine battalion had been started. At Londonderry, the achievement was even more impressive. When the United States entered the war in December 1941, the radio station was ready, the repair base in the harbour was almost ready, and a timber jetty at Lisahally, one thousand feet long and sixty feet wide, supported on round larch piles and designed for unloading and the fuelling of escort vessels, was also almost ready. In addition, the following works were far advanced: an ammunition depot at Fincairn Glen; hutments for personnel at Beech Hill; extensive storage facilities at Lisahally and close to the city repair base; and the conversion of the Talbot House area, centrally situated in relation to all the other projects, into a vast underground operational and administrative headquarters.

JOHN W. BLAKE, *Northern Ireland in the Second World War*, 1956

ON WASTE GROUND BETWEEN THE BLOCKADES and the Foyle, enormous temporary buildings were springing up. A large party of flamboyant American technicians had arrived to prepare the way for their troops. One couldn't help noticing the bright clothes they wore, even at work. Sean was sure that Derry people did buy new clothes now and again, since shops up the town were selling them, but Derry dress was not bright and it never seemed to change: you'd always recognise people at a distance by what they wore. The American technicians changed the fashion-face of the city and increased the pace of its life. For them, speed was everything.

A Derryman whom they had employed to help in the work was doing his best to loosen a tight nut. It was his first job in some twenty years of signing the dole. The 'Yank' looked at his struggles for a few moments before he spoke.

'Hi, buddy,' he said, in a not unfriendly voice, 'shit or get off the pot!'

Life was never the same again after the American Forces landed in Derry. The town was jammed with lorries and jeeps full of happy people. They did not have the heavy boots and clicking heels of the English 'Tommies', but were more relaxed and friendly: they certainly made much closer contact with the people of Derry – particularly the girls.

It wasn't that Derry girls had disliked the seduction style of the English Tommies, but most of them found the American technique irresistible: it included unheard-of delicacies like mouth-watering Herschey's chocolate, so different from the dark brown wartime chocolate they were used to. Cigarettes came in new exciting packets and whole cartons of them could suddenly appear if the job was right. The 'Camel' was more potent than the 'Player'.

As if that were not enough to seduce the 'Maiden City', the Yanks hit poor Derry with their chewing gum. Sean and his friends scrambled for it and for coins and sweets thrown to them from passing jeeps. They had no defence against succulent American confectionery, after the tastelessness of wartime rationed sweets and chewing-gum that became bland rubber after a dozen chews. Who would blame Derry girls for succumbing to their other awful temptations? What hope had virtue against the novelty of nylons?

Even the holy nuns of St Eugene's fell under their spell: the Yanks organised a big party for the girl's classes and the nuns responded by teaching the students to sing the 'Star-Spangled Banner'. Sean learned it by listening to Brid and Jenny.

'Then conquer we must, when our cause it is just and this be our motto – in God is our trust.'

To have the 'conquered' singing those lines with swelling hearts and feeling like conquerors themselves was no bad trick.

TOMÁS Ó CANAINN, Home to Derry, 1986

THE AMERICAN TECHNICIANS – and later the USN personnel – brought a colourful note to the otherwise drab lives of the people in the war-time atmosphere of food rationing, clothes rationing, black-out, and the ever-present threat of a visit from the Luftwaffe.

They were buoyant, vigorous extroverts, loving life, and living it to the full. There were the inevitable romances, and many Derry girls married eligible bachelors from amongst them.

At Christmas time, and the great American holidays of Thanksgiving and Independence Days, their generosity and affection for children was very much in evidence in the lavish parties they arranged for school kids and orphans, and many a Derry child ate its first banana or orange, and tasted its first ice-cream at one of these functions – luxuries which they only knew of by hearsay from their parents or grandparents.

The weather was a never failing source of discontent to most of them, who were used to a much drier climate. On one occasion I was ploughing through the sea of mud which then constituted Pennyburn Navy Yard. It had been raining for about forty-eight hours without a let-up, and was still teeming down. As I passed the Quonset hut I saw Les Fieldhack leaning over the half-door of the building gazing morosely at the rain. The balloon barrage had been hauled down until the balloons were flying just under the cloud base, which was not more than about three hundred feet. 'Hey! Kid,' he called, as I splashed past. 'I got a theory about those things,' he gestured towards the balloons. 'Yes, Les,' I said, 'What's that?' 'Well' he retorted, 'I think they keep this Goddam place from sinking.' Another quip was that 'Six months of the year, Lough Foyle is in County Derry, the other six months County Derry is in Lough Foyle.' 'Nine months Winter, and three months bad weather make up the year here', was the opinion of several others, but the pièce de résistance came from a disgruntled, frustrated Chief Petty Officer. 'Lough Foyle,' he said 'is the ass-hole of N. Ireland, and Derry is fourteen miles up it.'

CHARLES GALLAGHER, *Acorns and Oak Leaves*, 1981

MY LORDS COMMISSIONERS OF THE ADMIRALTY had many decisions to make and our fate was not high in their list of priorities. I was able to visit Londonderry and look up my friends Mr and Mrs Bell, but the Longwell family were on holiday in Portrush. I found it hard to reconcile being in Derry as an officer, it was almost as if I were another person from the AB. I had been when I had left Polyanthus there in 1943.

Arrangements were made for advice on release and resettlement to be available during our enforced idleness. Tables were set up in a long, glass-fronted building which might have been a conservatory at some stage and we attended in batches at appointed times. It was a hastily-organised affair which provided us with some useful information but the venture was limited for obvious reasons and we spent quite a lot of our time browsing around rather aimlessly once we had discovered the things that interested us most.

One or two educational types moved about behind the row of tables and with the help of some Wrens did all they could to stir up interest. I sensed that I was under scrutiny, a Wren was appraising me with a steady gaze; her face was familiar but not one that I could place readily.

Slowly she leaned back on her chair, her eyes, unfaltering, never left mine as she tapped her teeth gently with a pencil. And then the faintest trace of a smile crept into the corners of her eyes.

'Well hello, Polyanthus.' She spoke softly, in a voice as smooth as Irish cream.

Then I remembered; I had last seen her in Captain 'D's' signals office in Derry. I stood, open-mouthed, captivated by her smiling Irish eyes.

She eventually broke the silence: 'So you made it.'

Spellbound, I continued to stand, oblivious of everyone in the room apart from this girl whose name I had never known, the girl who, two years earlier, had handed me the signal that had saved my life.

'Yes.' I answered quietly. 'Yes, I made it.'

FRED KELLETT, *A Flower for the Sea – A Fish for the Sky*, 1995

Derry is Different

SIEGES APART, DERRY'S HISTORY goes back to the dawn of Irish Christianity. In 546 St Columba founded his first abbey here on a tree-crowned hill; the Irish word 'Doire' means 'a place of oaks'. And one quickly becomes aware of Derry as a city where – despite centuries of discrimination and discontent – the Catholic and Protestant strands within Irish Christianity have in some subtle way become interwoven. At present the city's population of 51,000 is about 60 per cent Catholic and 40 per cent Protestant and within hours of my crossing Craigavon bridge at 8.30 a.m. I had been told by seven citizens that 'Derry is Different'. By which they meant that Derry people, whatever their religion or politics, are not temperamentally inclined towards Belfast's brand of implacable sectarianism.

DERVLA MURPHY, A Place Apart, 1978

MOODY AND SANKEY

THESE NAMES, HITHERTO UNKNOWN, came, in the last century, to be associated in the minds of British people with American evangelism of a high order. After a time a suggestion that they might visit England was warmly welcomed, and this was looked forward to with great anticipation. This was about 1873, and in due course they arrived in London, where, I think, the campaign opened. People flocked to hear them, and the largest buildings were too small for the crowds who came. Requests poured in from the large provincial towns, where success followed success. This was not merely in a matter of numbers, but the result as seen in changed lives. In 1874 Belfast opened its arms to receive them, and the crowds seeking admission everywhere were such that eventually a huge tent was erected to serve the purpose. Derry folk had been following with interest their progress across the water, and encouraged by the enthusiastic reports from Belfast. I think it was the autumn of 1874 that these men began their work in Derry – Moody, the preacher; Sankey, the singer. The first meeting here was announced for Sunday morning, 8 o'clock, in the old Corporation Hall in

The Diamond. Going sharp to the time I was rather surprised to find seating accommodation taken up, but with many others was soon provided with a seat on the platform, where I had a good view of the celebrated missioners. That meeting, though the smallest of the series, stands out prominently in my mind. From my position on the platform I could see the faces of the people – alert, eager, solemn, expectant. Mr Moody, in view of the services to come spoke with fervour, and the people hung on his words. As Mr Sankey moved towards the little harmonium which always accompanied him on these missions, I could see the deepening interest on the part of the people evidenced as they leaned forward lest they should miss a word. The words, 'Hold the fort for I am coming', as Mr Sankey then sang them, were new to Derry people then, but very familiar for long years after, though almost forgotten in these latter days. Withal, that hymn has still something to say for itself. While sitting at the harmonium Mr Sankey spoke of the origin of the hymn. It had a link with American history. He said that an isolated group of men in charge of a fort in danger of being wiped out had a message flashed from a General who with his men was hastening to their rescue and couched in these words, 'Hold the fort for I am coming.' Mr Sankey as a singer had his critics in those days. His anxiety was to get the message of the words through, and so sometimes sacrificed the music to some little extent in favour of elocution.

The night meetings that ensued, Sundays and week-days alike, were held in 'First Derry', and were always crowded. It had been arranged that on the opening Sunday, and as often as seemed desirable, the Methodist Church, then on East Wall, would be available for any overflow. I was present at the ordinary 7 o'clock service that first Sunday evening, and at 8 o'clock as the preacher was about to conclude a stir was heard outside and people began to pour in. The minister in charge did not expect any so soon, but rose to the occasion by a quick change over, announcing a popular hymn in which all could join. A little later Mr Sankey came along to the great delight of a crowded house. Meantime Mr Moody held the crowd at 'First Derry', where he was later joined by Mr Sankey. These meetings went on for several weeks nightly without any slackening of interest. A great impression was made on the city, and this could be seen in the transformed lives of many of its citizens. I can think of many of those whom I knew personally, but they seem to have passed on. This series of meetings was continued by Professor Drummond, author of 'Natural Law in the Spiritual World'.

These great evangelists paid one or two return visits to the city before they left for America. They were always given a great welcome and left many pleasing memories behind.

C.W. GORDON, *Reminiscences of Derry in the Last Century*, n.d.

So now, when Lenten years
Burgeon, at last, to bless
This land of Faith and Tears
With fruitful nobleness,
The poet, for a coin,
Hands to the gabbling rout
A bucketful of Boyne
To put the sunrise out.

'Ulster' is ours, not yours,
Is ours to have and hold,
Our hills and lakes and moors
Have shaped her in our mould
Derry to Limerick Walls
Fused us in battle flame;
Limerick to Derry calls
One strong-shared Irish name.

We keep the elder faith,
Not slain by Cromwell's sword;
Nor bribed to subtler death
By William's broken word.
Free from those chains, and free
From hate for hate endured,
We share the liberty
Our lavish blood assured.

One place, one dream, one doom,
One task and toil assigned,
Union of plough and loom
Have bound us and shall bind.
The wounds of labour healed,
Life rescued and made fair –
There lies the battlefield
Of Ulster's holy war.

THOMAS M. KETTLE, *from* 'Ulster', in *Poems and Parodies,* 1916

WHEN MY FATHER HAD BUSINESS IN Derry City on a Wednesday, a market day, on which the farmers around Glendermott visited the City, it was almost impossible for him to get his business done as he was stopped every few yards along the street by one or other of the members of his Church who, when they met him, wished to consult him on some problem on which they desired guidance. I can vouch for the foregoing from my own experience as I happened to accompany him on some of these visits to the City of Derry and as we walked along I can remember him remarking to me 'People who think I have not much to do should just follow me around for a day.'

He was always ready to give a helping hand to any person, and more especially to any member of his Church who was in trouble of any kind. Even if the call for help was what some people would consider beneath the dignity of a Minister yet it was not ignored, as the following incident will shows. One afternoon a farmer on his way home from the market in the City of Derry called at the Manse. He was an addict of alcohol at that particular period of his life and was slightly intoxicated when he called. He said he had called to ask my father to accompany him to his home as he was afraid he would not be able, if he were alone, to resist the temptation to go into the one public house which he would have to pass on his way home. Without hesitation my father took his arm and accompanied him all the way to his home.

The journey was not in vain for in after years that man became attached to his Church; and was a sober worthy citizen, and able by God's grace to overcome the temptation of strong drink.

There were many homes in the countryside where some individual member of the family had become an addict of strong drink and my father had to witness many sad tragedies which were caused by over indulgence in alcoholic liquor. But of many such cases two come to my mind as I write. One was in connection with a young man of splendid physique, the only children of excellent and well-to-do parents. This young man brought disgrace to his home and discredit to himself through his drinking habits. He spent much of his time driving behind a fine high stepping horse from one public house to another and was accustomed to call for drinks for all and sundry who happened to be on the premises. One evening he called at the Manse in a tipsy state and produced a gallon jar of whiskey. My father was from home but my mother found him in a penitent mood and anxious to give up his drinking habits. She encouraged him to make a new start and he decided to leave the jar of whiskey at the Manse where it went down the drain next morning. Before he left that night in token of gratitude he said to my mother that he could give her a useful hint. 'If you are ever in jail' he said 'and put on the tread mill be sure to choose a position next the wall!'

On another occasion I saw this jovial youth driving smartly past the Manse, standing up in a light cart, dressed only in his shirt and trousers. At the local public house he happened to meet a fife and drum band out on a practice parade. He raised his hand, stopped the members of the band and invited all the young men into the public house for a drink. As the crowd following also gathered into the bar the publican was soon overwhelmed and men began to help themselves. In the bedlam that ensued the publican sent a message for help to a local barrister who lived a short distance away – a Dr Todd. When he arrived he took in the situation and, raising his hand, he called for silence. He then brought a paper from his pocket and read what purported to be 'the riot Act' with the terms of which he was familiar. The mob speedily retired from the pub, the band reformed and the instigator of all the trouble remained to pay the bill for drink and damages. All my father's and mother's efforts to help him were in vain and he died of alcoholic poisoning while still in early manhood.

THE REVEREND WILLIAM CORKEY MA DD, *Memories of an Irish Manse*, n.d.

TO ME, DERRY WAS A CITY of women. They gave it character and bustle as they streamed to and from the shirt factories, scattered within and without the old walled city. They took their work home, where they sheared collars of their surplus threads to earn a few extra pence. In the evenings, released from work by the factory horns, they filled the cinemas and dance halls. They prided themselves on making the finest shirts in the world. They married early and would temporarily stop making shirts to produce the next generation of stitchers, cuffers, button-holers and collar-makers. They were the colour in a community of grey, unemployed men. Their passion for clothes sustained a network of credit houses and their agents all year round, and climaxed in a magnificent fashion parade as the annual religious retreat came to a close in May. At one retreat the unemployed men, their drabness relieved by white flowers in their buttonholes, loudly renounced 'the world, the flesh and the devil', prompted by a visiting missionary who preached about 'an honest day's pay for an honest day's work'.

PADDY DOHERTY, *Paddy Bogside*, 2001

VERY LITTLE OF NOTE HAD HAPPENED in the Northern Catholic community in the decade after the Second World War. One year followed another and differed little from it. In Derry the male unemployment rate hovered around twenty per cent. Over a fifth of the population of the South Ward lived in houses where there were two or more persons per room (1951 census). The Nationalist Party maintained its grip, while the Republican movement began to wither away. Some may have taken vicarious pleasure from the *Journal*'s eager recording of further British reverses in international affairs ('British bluff called on Argentine meat' – 27 April 1951) or raged against the successful (allegedly British) plot to stop the Catholic General Douglas MacArthur dropping atom bombs on the Chinese Communists ('MacArthur takes hero's leave of

Japan. Emperor Hirohito's precedent-breaking gesture' – 16 April 1951). There were minor riots after Nationalist parades in 1951 and 1952, but the local event which raised the Bogside's spirits highest was, necessarily, symbolic. Late on Easter Saturday, 24 April 1951, a local Republican, Manus Canning, climbed to the top of Walker's Pillar, which was set on the city walls and towers over the Bogside, and fixed an Irish Tricolour to the flagpost. The *Journal* report conveys the effect perfectly:

NATIONAL FLAG FLIES FROM WALKER'S PILLAR

... Small groups of people assembled in adjacent streets approaching midnight and stared in amazement at the unique spectacle ... Our reporter says that by the time the sky had cleared and in the light of the full moon the Tricolour could be quite clearly seen. It had been perfectly raised to the top of the tall vertical flag-pole and fanned by a slight breeze from the south-west it floated fully spread out and presented an impressive sight. It was right over the head of the Orangemen's hero, Rev. George Walker.

(In August 1973 the Provisional IRA blew the pillar up.)

EAMONN McCANN, *War and an Irish Town*, 1974

It's the high high walls of Derry looks dismal and grey,
Since my beloved Johnny he has gone far far away.
He has gone away to England strange faces he will see,
May the Lord protect poor Johnny till he comes back to me.

The first place we courted it was very well known,
It was in her father's garden in the County Tyrone.
It was there he said he loved me above all womenkind,
Oh! come tell me lovely Johnny what had altered your mind.

The next place we courted it being in the wild wood,
Where the green berry bushes grew around where we stood.
Then you threw your arms around me for to shade the cold wind,
Oh! come tell me lovely Johnny what has altered your mind.

If I were a scholar and could handle a pen,
I would write my love a letter and I would let him ken.
I would write my love a letter and I would let him know,
It was the high high walls of Derry that made me so low.

ANONYMOUS, 'The High Walls of Derry', in *My Parents Reared Me Tenderly*, (eds Jimmy McBride and Jim McFarland), 1985

There used to be a big man
sat in The Diamond.
I never knew what his name was,
but we never knew him as anything else
but 'Snuffytrunk'.
He used to sit
with a big snuffy trail
down his waistcoat
and he used to sit there
snuffing it up,
a half ounce every time.
But The Rabble was in The Diamond,
Spring and Autumn,
and it lasted to about five o'clock –
a two day fair –
and they sold everything in connection with farming –
ropes, anything at all –
and as well as that
there were all these itinerant people came,
fortune tellers
and Tie-the-boy.
Tie-the-boy
was one of these characters,
I don't know where he came from,
but they used to come in
from far and near,
these come-all-ye singers, as we called them,
singing their own songs –
that was the first time
ever I heard
The Gallant Forty-twa,
that's the first time I heard it.
It was an itinerant there
and he had made up the song himself
and he sang it himself.
This was the whole beauty of it.
They made up their song
and they sang it
to try to sell you the sheet,
and it was great.
And these boys –
oh, they could talk.

They would have sold you everything –
monkeys on sticks –
they had even the wee bird,
like a canary,
to tell you your fortune.
I think it was a penny or something
you gave them
and they opened the cage
and they had a wee stick,
and the canary hopped on up
and they brought it up
and they pulled out a drawer
and they had a wee fortune card
and the canary lifted a card
and that was your fortune –
whether it ever came to pass or not
I don't know.
I know that there was the hiring fair –
they were used mainly for that,
they came in and they hired them
for six months or a year,
whatever it might be.
And when it went on into the evening –
the horse fair was held in Butcher Street
and Magazine Street,
this is at The Diamond there,
that's where the horses were bought and sold,
and always –
there were plenty of pubs about there –
then there was the fight at night,
you know,
the coats trailed,
as they called it,
then there would be the odd battle there.
And that went on every year
without fail.

ANONYMOUS, 'The Rabble', in *The Fountain*
(ed. Leon McAuley), 1993

AS PETER HAD RECEIVED AN URGENT LETTER from Glasgow on business, he had been forced to end his holiday suddenly. There was not, therefore, much time to spare, for he had taken a berth on board the

Thistle, which was to sail in the evening. Miss Ferryquay took him, after they left the Ferry, along the Prehen Road – 'the finest walk,' she said, 'in Derry.' They walked until the view opened, and a scene of surpassing loveliness was obtained of the upper reaches of the Foyle. Miss Ferryquay became sentimental. She quoted poetry.

> Sweet Derry loveliest city of the North
> How can I leave thee and go forth.

Fortunately for herself, she fathered these verses upon an acquaintance, the usual mode of getting rid of bad poetry. The fact is, ever since Peter came to Derry she had been 'setting her cap at him', and now it was arranged that the 'affair' would come off at Christmas, in Derry. Peter accepted his fate like a philosopher.

As they passed over Carlisle Bridge, Miss Ferryquay drew his attention to the beauty of its structure, and how admirably it was kept in repair. 'There have never been any accidents on this bridge of ours,' she said, 'since it was built, but it will probably be widened by the time the Queen's successor reaches his Jubilee, by which time also, by a process of development on the Darwinian principle, the Corporation at that date will have gained what their predecessors lacked.'

'And now, Peter, here we are in Ferryquay Street, founded by a namesake of my own. This is Pump Street, so-called from the fact that there are two newspaper editors in it, constantly pumping out of 'wells of English pure and undefiled' for the public consumption. But I must take you into the Colportage Society's Shop, and give you a present of an album of North of Ireland Views, as a memento of your visit. *Forr-e-ster*-ling article you could not enter a better shop.'

They then went home.

After tea and a confidential talk, Miss Ferryquay – there being an hour until the time of Peter's departure – took her cousin a visit to Gwynn's grounds. 'These,' she explained, 'are open to the public so far, but it is only through courtesy. I am inclined, and so are others, to believe, that they would make an excellent public park for Derry, but there, what is the use of talking, the people of Derry, as I told you before, do not require a public park.'

After coming out of Gwynn's they visited St Eugene's Cathedral, which Peter declared had only one fault in point of architecture, and that was, lack of a-*spire*-ation. From the grounds, Miss Ferryquay pointed out a Derry industry.

It now neared the time of Peter's departure, and they wended their way down to the quay. Miss Ferryquay was pensive a little, but she brightened up, when Peter, with great modesty, produced a poem, and read it to her.

It was as follows —

> Let fortune smile on fair Derrie
> An' bring again prosperitie.
>
> May wisdom rule the corporation
> An' common sense the administration.
>
> Let landlords practice moderation
> An' try and reduce taxation.
>
> Let industry wi' wealth be crowned
> An' health an' cleanliness abound.
>
> Till paupers purchase railway shares
> An' carpets line the Bastion stairs.

Peter blushed at this unusual effort, which had cost him and *another* author not a few nights in the composing. He bade his cousin good-bye, and as Miss Ferryquay turned homewards, after watching the steamer out of sight, she hummed —

> Oh, where an' oh where is my Gleasca laddie gone,
> He's gone to bonnie Scotland, etc.

'Ah, well,' she added, 'he'll be here again at Christmas, and then I'll no longer be Miss Ferryquay.'

ANONYMOUS, *Miss Ferryquay's Grand Tour*, 1887

> Fair Londonderry! in thy very name
> A spell is found, which renders thee a theme
> For bards in each succeeding age to sing,
> And touch with vigorous hand the vocal string.
> How pleasing is thy aspect to behold,
> Thou celebrated city, fam'd of old!
> As on a height, the flowing Foyle beside,
> On whose broad bosom stately vessels ride,
> Supreme thou sittest, with proud trophies crown'd –
> The queen of all the lofty hills around.
> What strange events in thee have taken place,
> Since Columbkille, sprung from a royal race,
> Thy site from Aidan as a gift obtained,

And, being by celestial grace sustained,
An Abbey founded northward on the hill,
That he his holy mission might fulfil,
And preach the Gospel of salvation free,
To all who would to Christ for refuge flee,
And seek redemption earnestly to gain,
Through Him, the Paschal Lamb for sinners slain,
Whose death for Adam's guilt atonement made,
And for believers hath the ransom paid.
'The wood of oak' had been thy title then,
Thy people but a few rude, valiant men,
Who had not learn'd the rules of polish'd life,
But, sway'd too oft by sanguinary strife,
The strong the weak inhumanly opprest,
And peace here seldom found a place of rest.
But when the British settlers hither came,
And Londonderry had become thy name,
Prosperity on thee began to shine,
And freedom, faith, and fortitude divine
Inspired thy sons fair liberty to shield,
And scorn but with their latest breath to yield.
Meantime, a wall encircled thee around,
Which rendered thee soon afterward renowned.
When James the Second thought thee to subdue,
And subjugate the British nation too,
Thy gallant youths their gates against him clos'd,
And, though but few, a mighty host opposed –
Mounted thy ramparts – made their cannons roar,
Which caus'd their foes, in terror and uproar,
Far from the walls to hastily retreat,
And but return to meet renewed defeat;
For many months a hard-press'd siege sustain'd,
And William's cause undauntedly maintain'd;
Through pestilence and famine raised their cry
Of 'No Surrender – here we'll bravely die,
Or civil rights triumphantly secure,
And to posterity religion pure,
And freedom constitutional hand down –
The glorious bulwark of the British Crown.'
And thus they stood till succour to them came,
And baffled foemen, full of rage and shame,
Retreated from the city far away,
Nor dared again their colours here display.
These scenes of strife and war have long since ceas'd,

Peace on a sure foundation has been plac'd.
And liberty of conscience gain'd for all,
Secur'd for ever by the Stuarts' downfall.
Thy citizens, of every class and creed,
To make thee more exalted now proceed –
Extending streets around on every side,
While all in friendship feel an honest pride
At thy prosperity, which onward cheers
To brighter prospects through succeeding years,
When thy resources shall develop'd be,
And, in a very eminent degree,
Thou, as a mart of trade and commerce nam'd,
Shall through the land deservedly be fam'd.

ROBERT YOUNG, 'Address to Londonderry', *The Poetic Works of Robert Young*, 1863

T HE SIGNS OF THAT RELATIVE PROSPERITY are obvious. Thus in the neighbourhood of Derry (we say Londonderry, but the natives all say Derry), you observe with pleasure a line of tramcars moved by steam machinery, which puts remote places in communication with the railway. The carriages are of superior make, divided into three classes, towed by an engine heated with petroleum. Coming, as you do, out of Mayo and Galway, that steam tramway puffs in your face a breath of civilisation. You seem to enter a different world.

Derry, with its active traffic, its elegant iron bridge over the Foyle, the fine, new buildings which attest its wealth, justifies that impression. It is the capital of the famous 'Ulster plantation' of James I, entrusted by him to the 'Honourable Irish Company', which included twelve guilds of the city of London. For a century or two those grants of land did not answer as had been expected. But they have ended, in the course of time, by being prosperous. The municipal estates of Coleraine and Derry are accounted now the most flourishing in the island.

PASCHAL GROUSSET, *Ireland's Disease: The English in Ireland*, 1887, 1980

A HUSH FELL OVER GUILDHALL SQUARE as Clinton's motorcade crawled into view. Two identical limousines broke from the convoy; the decoy car going left, and the one carrying the Clintons turning right. It made for a back door of the Guildhall and rolled under a canopy, which had been built on security advice to block a potential gunman's line of sight from across the Foyle. Patrol boats buzzed up and down the river to guard against any eventuality. 'Anybody could have left Libya and come round the coast of

Ireland and down Lough Foyle,' superintendent Sheridan of the RUC commented. 'You could've easily had a Middle East crackpot who could see this as an opportunity to launch an attack. It was a big concern to them. We had a Royal Navy destroyer off the coast monitoring shipping in the lough for days in advance.' Security concerns didn't stop there. The First Couple were entering a building which, in the paranoid world of the Secret Service, had been practically taken to pieces and reassembled in the preceding 48 hours. Guildhall superintendent Colin Sharp revealed: 'The police and army moved in and virtually pulled the building apart on five occasions for different checks. They even took the boiler in the basement apart. The first big check was for Semtex. They gave each of the staff a pair of cotton gloves to rub themselves down from head to toe. You took the gloves off and they were analysed by a computer for traces of explosives.'

The Guildhall's labyrinthine, six-level interior was broken down into one-metre-square zones and bomb disposal experts donned gloves to painstakingly dust every centimetre. Hi-tech scanners were also deployed to sweep behind antique oak-panelling, a feature of the building. The square around the Guildhall was also combed. A US source said: 'On the morning of the visit a truck drove around, blasting out radio frequencies to trigger any bombs that had been set. We had to turn off all the bank machines and pay phones. It was a very intense and unpleasant part of the trip.'

Inside the Guildhall, Clinton dashed to the toilet and then went to the Mayor's parlour where he and Mrs Clinton spent five minutes with the Kerrs. The President munched on one of the apples he'd bought on the Shankill Road and declined an offer of a shot of Irish whiskey. 'They were extremely exhausted,' said Kerr. 'At one stage the President put his head down on Hillary's shoulder. He was very tired.' Emerson knocked on the door and told Clinton: 'Mr President, the crowd's ready for you.' The retinue left the parlour and was directed down a darkened corridor. Clinton's friend Jim Lyons said: 'We were walking towards the front door and you could hear the people's cheers grow louder. When we got to the steps the daylight hit us and we saw there were thousands of people in that tiny square. It was an overpowering experience. He was touching people's lives here. I talked about it later with the President and told him he wouldn't be as well regarded in some places in Arkansas. He said, "Yeah, you're probably right."'

Keanie was sent as advance man to the stage, which had been built only a few metres from the door. It was surrounded by red, white and blue carnations intended for inside the Guildhall until staff were told Clinton was allergic to them. 'Emerson gave me a shove and said, "Go for it, buddy,"' Keanie said. Emerson then began briefing Clinton on what was to follow. 'Clinton was totally focused, trying to get himself fired up,' the advance man remembered. 'I had my hand on his chest literally trying to keep him back from going out too soon. The crowd was so out of its mind he was charged up to get out there.'

Keanie had barely uttered his first welcoming words when Clinton could wait no longer and started marching to the stage ahead of schedule. Once he went they all went. The crowd was in raptures. Recalled the Town Clerk: 'When I hit the platform there was a surge of noise. We had twenty-five thousand watts of a personal address system that day but I had to roar at the top of my voice to be heard. It worked like an absolute dream.' Said Emerson: 'The second John Keanie spoke the President started walking. I couldn't hold him back he was so excited. Clinton was actually coming up on stage before John had finished the introduction. It wasn't exactly as we'd planned it, but John was great. He just nailed that introduction.' Amidst the cheers could be heard the distinct rustle of thousands of tiny Stars and Stripes which the crowd waved almost in rhythmic unison. Derry City Council staff had scoured Britain and Ireland, snapping up every available flag. 'We phoned everywhere looking for flags,' said Clare Lundy. 'It was like buying shares on Wall Street. Somebody would discover a company in England had so many to sell and we would all shout, "Buy, buy." We bought every Stars and Stripes available. We ended up with five thousand of them, costing two thousand pounds.' Hundreds of them had pointed tips and that morning American security ordered they be broken off. A source joked: 'It would've been quite poignant if the President had been stabbed with a plastic Stars and Stripes.'

Clinton gazed in wonderment at the adoring crowds, as one by one, Keanie bellowed out the names of the platform party, which included John Hume and his wife Pat. The President later revealed to the authors: 'I was honoured to share a dais with John Hume and I know that added to the warm greeting we received. Derry was wonderful. Every part of the steps, the square and the street was filled with the songs and the spirit of the moment.' Clinton's regard for Hume was such that he was the only politician invited to share a stage with the President in his own right. Kerr, in mayoral chain, took to the podium. To his right stood a large Christmas tree and, above him on the Guildhall's façade, a light display depicted Santa's sledge being pulled by reindeers. At a pause in Kerr's speech, spectators began chanting: 'We want Bill, we want Bill.' Clinton leaned nearer to Hume, who was seated beside him, and asked: 'Why are they saying, "We want bull?"' The Derry accent was clearly troubling him.

TREVOR BIRNEY and JULIAN O'NEILL, *When the President Calls*, 1997

L ILLY McCAFFERTY IS A WELL-KNOWN and respected Bogside citizen. Pithy, witty, warm, and outspoken in her political views, she is loved by her family with the special passion that the Irish reserve for their mothers. I know one of her daughters, Nell, in Dublin. She is a gifted journalist and commentator on current affairs in Ireland, both North and South. Nell grew up in the Bogside, and her childhood memories are of the staunch camaraderie that surrounded the children in that enclave, but the images of her teenage years are of marches, confrontations, riots, shootings, firebombings, and civil disorder. Although she now lives in Dublin, her family (and, I suspect, her heart) are still in the Bogside.

Lilly and another daughter, Nuala, a secretary in the town government, live in a small row house where the key is always in the front door lock, a symbol of Bogside hospitality. When a stranger goes into the McCaffertys', sits down, and has tea, it is impossible for her to feel like a stranger for long. It is as if the first and second acts of friendship were performed off stage, and now it's the third act and strangers are effortlessly relating to each other in a way that usually takes many days or weeks to establish.

We sat down around a table in their small dining room while Lilly prepared a tea of rashers and eggs, toast and tea. Nuala had to eat in a hurry in order to attend a political meeting. Her mother's eyes twinkled behind her glasses as she teased Nuala about her political affiliation.

'Nuala belongs to a wee party. When she goes to a meeting, there'll be two members there: herself and the other one.'

Anti-British feeling runs deep in Lilly McCafferty's heart, and nothing will ever change that. Despite her stories of wrenching poverty when she was young ('My mother died, and I had to help raise my brother and sister. We had to do that on two pounds ten a week'), she gives no credit to the British government for its generous welfare system that in recent decades has created a much better, healthier life for Derry citizens.

'Listen,' she said, 'that Mrs Thatcher is a reptile of a woman, and you can quote me. Things are better now, but there is still massive unemployment. What's here for the children? Nothing. Nothing.'

'Things are quieter now,' Nuala said. 'I can't believe it's been eighteen years since the Troubles started. There were barricades here. You had to be searched coming and going. You took it in your stride, but it was objectionable. I had a wee dog, I remember. It sat under my desk at work and didn't bother anybody. Once when we were being searched, my dog barked and all hell broke loose. I was arrested and taken to a detention center. They accused me of hitting the policewoman who had searched me – she was six feet tall and I'm four feet eight!

'We'd go to the cinema in those days and crawl home on our hands and knees to miss the bullets! People got used to it, I suppose, and took it all in their stride. Things are much better now. Women have come into their own. They got involved and realized that they had to speak up. They had to become the breadwinners. It gave them more independence.'

Nell's view of this newly won independence is more jaded. 'The situation in Derry removed the social structure of the neighborhoods. The women did become more independent, perhaps, but they also lost the structure which formed their behavior. With so many husbands and sons away in prison, they went wild. Unmarried pregnancies became common; lots of the women played around while their boyfriends or husbands were in prison. I remember once when Martin McGuinness (an IRA leader) came back to the Bogside to visit his mother. He saw what was going on in his old neighborhood, and he was horrified.

'He said, "This fucking has got to stop!" And the women just laughed.'

Lilly and women of her generation probably will never change or soften their views about the Troubles. But her daughter Nell has had second thoughts.

'One saw the need for an armed struggle then,' she said. 'There were injustices inflicted on the Catholic population. We had goals. The IRA had goals. But too many civilians have been killed. We're all war-weary.'

Lilly was eager for me to meet as many women as I could while I was in Derry, and she went to her telephone directly to make a wee list for me. 'Talk to them all, luv,' she advised. 'You'll hear a different story from each one.'

ELIZABETH SHANNON, *I Am of Ireland*, 1997

THE TOWN, IF SUCH IT MIGHT THEN BE TERMED, consisted originally of a few humble, straggling huts, of a conical shape, constructed of mud or wood, in conformity to the scanty means, and more to the modes of life of its inhabitants; which modes closely approached those of wild uncultivated nature. And, with respect to the system of religion practised, it was nothing else than Druidism, which they inherited from their ancestors and brethren of the Celtic race in Britain; but, after the introduction of Christianity into it, and the erection of religious houses and habitations for the monks and the clergy, in times less remote, the town began to assume a habitable appearance. In those days every *stone* building, no matter how rudely constructed, was called a *Castle*; and the only one of this kind recorded to have been erected in Derry, was a small *square tower* built by O'Dougherty, Chief of Inishowen, in the middle of the sixteenth century, for a citadel or place of defence; or as it has been supposed, for the purpose of imprisoning O'Donnel, Chief of Tirconnell (Donegal,) on a spot of ground purchased for that purpose from the *Erenach*, Mac Loughlin. The same was repaired by Sir Henry Docwra, on his arrival at Derry, in 1600. Of this castle some remains are supposed to have existed in the old Magazine lately pulled down, which stood in Magazine-street, opposite to the platform or demi-bastion, a little above the Butter market. The site and some of the old materials are now occupied by a tobacco-store. But of none of the original ecclesiastical buildings is there a vestige to be found. They have all shared the fate of the venerable *Oak grove*, in the midst of which they were erected, and which had been preserved through successive ages with equally religious veneration.

In times long past there were in Ireland many *Derries*. Even from a lingering traditionary remembrance of their former condition the name would be entitled to attention. When crowned with oaks, they were distinguishable from the dense forest of firs, skirting the marshy plains around them, and the abundance of ancient timber found in the districts surrounding the town of *our* Derry, is now evinced by tradition and public documents as well as by frequent observation. The vast quantities of pine found in all the bogs; of yew at Magilligan; and the immense number of huge fossil oaks and firs in the mosses, even in the most exposed situation, are a sufficient proof. But *Derry-Calgach* or *Derry-Columbkille* stood pre-eminent over every other *Derry*.

ROBERT SIMPSON, *The Annals of Derry*, 1847

THE MOST SIGNIFICANT ADDITION TO Derry's street pattern in Victorian times was caused by the proposal to replace the 1790 timber bridge by a new steel structure 200 yds upstream. Plans and estimates for this had been prepared in the first year of Victoria's reign, 1837. In 1852 it was reported in *The Builder* that the work was to begin at a cost of £60,000, a third being paid by the Londonderry and Enniskillen Railway Co., but it was not until 1863 that the project was finally realized and the bridge declared open at a ceremony performed by the Lord Lieutenant, the Earl of Carlisle. The cost was £100,000. The bridge with its approaches opened up the area at the foot of Wapping Lane just below the cathedral precinct, and it also led to the construction of two new roads in Waterside, Duke Street and Spencer Road. On the city side Carlisle Road, running in a dog-leg from the bridge end up to Ferryquay Gate, replaced the older Bridge Street as the thoroughfare into the town. In the same year, 1863, a new line of quays was completed, extending from the old bridge end to the Strand opposite the mental hospital. The city's rail connections were now extensive, with lines via Strabane, Omagh, and Enniskillen to Dundalk and Dublin, and via Coleraine and Antrim to Belfast. One was also in course of construction to Buncrana, 'a fashionable watering place on Lough Swilly'.

ALASTAIR ROWAN, *The Buildings of Ireland: North West Ulster*, 1979

THE CENTENARY OF THE SHUTTING OF THE GATES — 7 December 1788 — was ushered in with the ringing of bells, the beating of drums, and the discharge of the cannon used in 1689; the red flag was displayed on the cathedral. At 10:30 a large procession left the Ship Quay, consisting of the corporation, the clergy, the naval officers and the 46th regiment, the Volunteers, the merchants and principal citizens, the merchants' apprentices, the tradesmen's apprentices, the young gentlemen of the Free School and the masters of ships and the seamen. Orange ribbons were universally worn. Anniversary sermons were preached in the cathedral by the Rev. John Hume, the dean of Derry, and in the First Presbyterian meeting-house by the Rev. Robert Black. At 2:00 p.m. the Volunteers and regular soldiers paraded, the gates were ceremonially closed, and there were *feux de joye* in the Diamond before a dinner in the town hall. Festivities continued the following day with the distribution of meat, bread and beer to the poor, and a ball. Another elaborate spectacle was staged to mark the raising of the siege in August 1789, when the first stone of a triumphal arch, paid for by the corporation and the Irish Society, was laid.

These civic entertainments followed the pattern of the Glorious Revolution centenary in England, where great cities and county towns had witnessed similar displays of Orange ribbons, banners and flags, fireworks, pageantry, bell-ringing, speech-making and gunfire. In the Irish context, however, two aspects of the siege centenary deserve particular notice. On the hundredth anniversary of the shutting of the gates the official procession was imitated by 'the lower class of Citizens', who carried an effigy of Lundy through the streets and burned it in the market place 'with every circumstance of ignominy'. This was the inauguration of one of the most vital rituals in the liturgy of Ulster loyalism which, unlike Guy Fawkes Night, has retained its political edge to the present day. In the later nineteenth century, when parades were banned under public order legislation, the Apprentice Boys Clubs would go to extraordinary lengths to conceal the effigy from the authorities until it could be despatched to the flames at dusk. The ritual was even observed on the western front towards the end of 1915, when members of the Ulster Division held a torchlit procession, accompanied by Orange music, and set fire to two straw figures of Lundy.

IAN McBRIDE, *The Siege of Derry in Ulster Protestant Mythology*, 1997

LONDONDERRY CITY ELECTION, 1885
Chas. E. Lewis Q.C. (C.) 1824
Justin McCarthy (P.) 1795

To the black North, to Derry fair, a great 'Historian'
came,
Backed by the strength of all his clan, by Parnell's
mighty name,

His was the task, by wiles or force, to wrest the Virgin
  Crown
From the proud city by the Foyle, of siege's great
  renown.
In vain the Separatist force, for naught their trumpets
  blown,
Derry has shown that she prefers a 'history' of her
  own!

Coblentz, December 1885

LONDONDERRY CITY ELECTION, 1913

Hogg (N.) 2699
Colonel Pakenham (C.) 2642

Flow, Foyle, full of tears, not water, on to the main,
  Past the wreck of the Boom, past Culmore, past
    MacGilligan,
Take to the ocean, wind-swept and wave-tossed,
        Our story of pain.

Close gates, so heavy and ancient, brave Prentice boys,
  Shut out the sea, shut off England, shut out the
    Union.
Shut out all links with our Empire, our trade and
  communion,
        Our hopes and our joys!

Blow, black from the North, cold wind from Malin
  Head!
Take to our comrades in Leinster, in Connacht, in
  Munster,
The tale of our struggle, our work, our disaster
        Our honour is dead.

January 31, 1913

C. E. DE LA POER BERESFORD, *A Happy New Year and Other Verses*, 1913

ASSUREDLY OUR DERRY DOESN'T LOOK TOO PROSPEROUS. And the
Irishman of at least the Nationalist side agrees that it isn't, and finds his
own explanation. He says that Derry in the old days was the business town
of half Ulster; it was the market-place and manufacturing city and office and
port of the whole north-west of Ireland, and there were great fortunes made

out of Derry. But now, he says, the Border has stopped all that. All County Donegal would once trade with Derry, and now there is a Customs barrier. The county belongs to the Free State, and the city is left rather high and dry in the Six Counties.

Then the place differs in another way from Belfast. There always would be a Belfast of sorts, I suppose, much in the same way as there would always be a Liverpool of sorts. But the ancient Liverpool was really a sort of hanger-on to the ancient parish of Walton-on-the-Hill; and ancient Belfast was only a kind of hard-up second-cousin to the now forgotten port of Carrickfergus. The great modern Belfast did not really begin its history until about the end of the seventeen hundreds. But Derry had been a city ever since the early sixteen hundreds. Derry had a start of at least a century and a half of history; and that in Northern Ireland means that Derry has enjoyed an extra hundred and fifty years of hatred. You may think that party feeling runs high in Belfast; but the place is a Quakers' meeting-house of contented peace as compared to Derry.

JOHN GIBBONS, *Ireland – The New Ally*, 1938

THUR. 27 – I WENT ON TO Londonderry. Friday, 28. I was invited to see the bishop's palace (a grand and beautiful structure), and his garden, newly laid, and exceeding pleasant. Here I innocently gave some offence to the gardener, by mentioning the English of a Greek word. But he set us right, warmly assuring us that the English name of the flower is not Crane's bill, but Geranium!

JOHN WESLEY, *Journal*, 27 June 1773

THE DAYS OF THE 'HORNY-DICKS'

PRIOR TO 1868 THE CITY HAD A LOCAL POLICE FORCE with a rather quaint uniform and something of a tall headpiece. They were commonly spoken of as 'Horny Dicks': Every night sharp at nine o'clock a company of them, perhaps twenty in number, marched from the gaol, two deep, down Bishop Street, past Mulholland's and on the right-hand side of the Corporation Hall which stood there then. One of the old lamp-posts which many may still remember stood alongside the path adjoining the Hall and opposite Ferryquay Street. By way of a practical joke some of the city wags tied a strong cord at what they regarded as a fitting height from the lamp-post to the railings, with the result that as the 'Horny-Dicks' passed along they were suddenly and ignominiously left without any headdress to the intense delight of an hilarious group that stood expectantly at a safe distance. It was about this time that this force was disbanded and replaced by the RIC – men of a smarter and more fitting type.

I remember the demolition of the old Ferryquay Gate at the time of which I speak. Shortly after this the Mayor had an intimation of a Royal Visit which was to the effect that in a few days Prince Arthur, Duke of Connaught, was to come to the city. There was consternation as the entry of the Royal Visitor was to be by Carlisle Road and Ferryquay Gate, and it looked as if it was impossible that the Gate which was then not half up could be completed in time. Judge of my surprise when on the morning of the visit a friend came in and said that they had rushed the work through at the Gate during the night and that it had been completed and looked splendid. I ran up the Diamond to the corner of Ferryquay Street to see for myself and there it was sure enough – finished, but not with stone and mortar. The workers during the night had fallen back on Nature for such assistance as she could give and right well it served the purpose. The sidewalls were carried up and the arch gracefully finished with evergreens, plants, flowers and bunting. Nothing could have looked better and everyone was delighted. Unfortunately a day which passed over so well was followed by an orgy of rioting after dark. On my way to school the next morning I saw signs of the previous night's work in the blood-bespattered streets. When I think of such scenes as this which were not unfamiliar seventy to eighty years ago I rejoice in the more tolerant spirit that prevails to-day, and this is not confined to any one party.

That reminds me of an improvement in another respect. It was not an uncommon sight to see two men in a brutal and bloody struggle with each other – not a party fight, but something of a drunken brawl. Such a thing so far as my observation goes, is seldom seen to-day. Long may this continue.

C.W. GORDON, *Reminiscences of Derry in the Last Century*, n.d.

JOHN HUME AND I AND SOME LIBERAL UNIONISTS wanted to break away from the traditional stagnant Nationalist-Unionist party politics and engage in joint action which would benefit all the citizens of Derry, particularly in the area of unemployment which afflicted the whole community, Protestant as well as Catholic. It seemed to us that Stormont was pursuing a deliberate low key policy in order not to threaten the status quo. The lion's share of new industries seemed to be concentrated in the North East. No infrastructural developments such as motorways were being planned for the North West. Instead a new town, Craigavon, was built not very far from Belfast. Derry's increasing isolation was made more acute by the closure of the Great Northern Railway line which ran via Strabane, Omagh and Portadown to Belfast and Dublin and served the interior of the province. The Derry Corporation refused to consider extending the city boundaries, a move which would have allowed more space for much needed new housing. The Unionist line was that to upgrade Derry significantly would result in an influx of more Nationalists from across the nearby Co. Donegal border and this in time would mean the end of Protestant and Unionist rule in the city. I actually heard a prominent Derry Unionist declare, 'We don't want any more industry here because if we upset the apple cart the RCs will come in and swamp us.' Everything was nicely arranged. The Unionist majority was assured. So why upset the status quo? Change spelt danger.

In my sermons I tried to bring the Christian Gospel to bear on the situation in Derry. What was wrong? Why was it wrong and what changes should be made? Not long after the decision to close the GNR railway I preached a Christmas sermon in Christ Church, on the lines from the carol:

> The star drew nigh to the north west,
> O'er Bethlehem it took its rest.

'The star never draws nigh to the north west in this benighted province,' I said. 'We are the forgotten people. The star in Ulster is always drawing nigh to the north east.' The sermon received a fair amount of media coverage and, while I received some very critical letters from extreme Protestants who told me not to preach politics from the pulpit, the majority of messages which I received were favourable and encouraging.

A further blow came when Derry was not chosen as the site for Northern Ireland's second university, though common sense pointed to developing what was already there and centred on Magee University College. But the university went to Coleraine, a decision which at least in the early years of the university's life proved no more enlightened than the disastrous choice of Craigavon as a new centre for population and industry. These actions not only sharpened Nationalist discontent but also annoyed many moderate Unionists. Before the decision in favour of Coleraine was announced we held a great public meeting in the Guildhall, attended by people and political representatives from both sides of the community, whose enthusiasm to work together for the good of Derry was wonderful to behold. Roman Catholics and Protestants together drove in a long motorcade through Strabane and Omagh to Stormont to lobby the government in Derry's cause, a government which included our MP, Mr E.C. Jones, Attorney General of Northern Ireland.

Unknown to us the decision had already been taken. Although most Unionist leaders in Derry were outwardly in favour of a university for the city, some of them had reservations, and it was widely accepted that the confidential message to Stormont from a group of influential Unionists was, 'Don't bring the university to Derry.' Word got round that certain 'faceless men of Derry' had stabbed the city in the back. Teddy Jones, the Unionist MP for Derry, well aware that feelings were running high in Derry in support of the university, nevertheless submitted to the Stormont

Whip and voted against the city. Some diehard Unionists in the city defended Jones, saying he had no choice because his political career was at stake!

I wrote an article at the time for the Christ Church parish magazine, which was subsequently taken up by the local press. I pointed out that according to Holy Scripture the high priest said of Our Lord's crucifixion that it was 'expedient that one man should die for the people'. But nowhere in Holy Writ was it ever recorded that all the people should die for one man, yet this was what we were being asked by some to accept, to let Derry and its people die, in order to ensure Mr Jones' political survival!

(DEAN) VICTOR GRIFFIN, *The Mark of Protest*, 1993

IT SEEMS THERE HAS NEVER BEEN much foreign influence in Derry though at first the People's Democracy Movement attracted (having itself been inspired by) left-wing students from many countries. The media tended to exaggerate this student solidarity until it became – to some newspaper readers – of Sinister International Significance. I was told a glorious true story which is well-known but still seems worth writing down. To Derry during the thick of The Troubles came a keen young English press photographer, intent on a scoop. A Provisional told him that for a substantial consideration this could be arranged and next day the two met at a place from which the photographer was driven (blindfolded) to a field above the Creggan. There he spent an ecstatic hour photographing *very* sinister 'Foreign Influences' training local boys. When he had been reblindfolded and driven away his Provo friend took the rifles from the Chinese waiters' nervous hands, helped them to remove their unfamiliar paramilitary uniforms, paid them a meagre percentage of the scoop fee and sent them back to their restaurant in the city centre.

DERVLA MURPHY, *A Place Apart*, 1978

THE MOST DEMANDING VISIT WAS AN OUTING to Londonderry with Julian Amery and Sir John Biggs-Davison. I had been asked by Julian to pick him up and take him to the airport, but I did not realise this would require me to pack his 'smalls' into an old, battered, leather hold-all while he drank half a bottle of good claret with his breakfast.

I had warned Paddy Doherty that he would be receiving high-ranking Tory grandees, and he had grumbled. But before meeting Paddy's team, we had lunch with the Honourable the Irish Society. The society was founded by the City of London to raise the finance to plant settlers in the north-west of Ireland, hence the 'London' prefix to 'Derry'. By the 1980s most of its wealth and power had long since gone, but it still had a wonderful Georgian house next to the cathedral and right by the army barracks within the walls of Londonderry. Its secretary, Peter Campbell, brother-in-law to the duke of Abercorn, gave us a spectacular lunch, at which Julian, Sir John and others reminisced about the Empire. After brandies and with large Havana cigars clamped between our teeth, we strolled down Shipquay Street to discover how the other half lived.

Paddy had arranged a slide presentation of the work he was doing with the unemployed. He had also brought along the unemployed, a considerable number of whom had pink Mohican haircuts, rings in their ears and high-laced Doc Martens. They looked in astonishment at the cigar-smoke-shrouded, astrakhan-coated grandees before them.

Paddy invited us guests to sit down while the punks lined the wall at the back of the room. The slide show started. Julian Amery decided that he would prefer to be facing the enemy rather than have his back to them. So he swivelled his chair and stared at the mob while sucking on his cigar, and the mob stared back. Paddy continued with his presentation, which grew progressively more anti-British as the slides moved from one bombed-out building to the next. Mercifully, both sides seemed so shocked by the appearance of the other that no words were spoken.

As soon as Paddy had finished I suggested we take a short tour of one or two of the sites themselves and visit the city walls. Paddy set off with Julian on one side and Sir John on the other. Julian, who had been parachuted in to help Tito's partisans in the Second World War, could recognise a fellow 'resistance' fighter when he saw one. He immediately started to question Paddy about his part in the Troubles in the early seventies. Paddy whispered to me that if he had known who I was bringing he would have organised a different sort of reception, and then explained to Julian how the Walker monument had been bombed. (Walker conducted himself heroically during the Siege of Derry in 1689 and his statue dominating the skyline over the Bogside had long been a source of irritation to the nationalist community.) 'There,' Paddy said as we got to the wall, 'Walker was blown up and he fell down the slope without dislodging a roof tile or breaking a window. It landed within six inches of where it was expected to. Who says Paddies can't do a proper job.' Julian, who had spent much time blowing up Germans in Serbia, looked on admiringly. Within minutes they were friends, swapping jokes and stories. On the way back Julian said, with a twinkle, 'We should have locked up Paddy years ago.' I said I was sure the Germans would have liked to have done the same, or worse, with him.

The remains of Walker's statue are still held in store by the Department of the Environment, and from time to time over the six and a half years I was the minister, I received requests to put him back and rebuild his column. I always found reasons for delaying, as history in Ireland generally repeats itself.

RICHARD NEEDHAM, *Battling for Peace*, 1998

It cheers an honest 'Prentice Boy,
Above all other joys,
To act an independent part
With comrade 'Prentice Boys;
And, O, we prize that sister link
Of lovely living pearls,
Right joyously we rise and drink –
To Derry's 'Prentice Girls.

Though thoughtless flirts and dainty dames,
Of Irish birth and blood,
Look coldly on the hopes and aims
Of our dear sisterhood;
We'll have their sympathy to cheer
Their sweethearts through all perils,
To us your doubly near and dear –
Old Derry's 'Prentice Girls.

Their mothers proved long, long ago,
Fit mates for gallant men,
And if their daughters are but tried,
They'll prove as true again;
They scorned to fear their fathers' foes,
And smiled through all their perils,
And such is still the faith of those –
Old Derry's 'Prentice Girls.

Through every struggle for our cause
Since famous Eighty-eight,
We've had fair woman's sweet applause,
Our hearts to stimulate;
And still no matter what's the odds,
We fear nor foes nor perils,
We'll act our part, and look for praise –
From Derry's 'Prentice Girls.

With hopeful hearts we pledge once more,
Our gentle sisters here,
We've now received their Crimson Flag,
We'll guard it never fear –
Yes, comrades, it shall proudly wave,
And safely through all perils,
We'll die ere caitiff hand shall grasp –
The Flag of the 'Prentice Girls.

ANONYMOUS, 'The 'Prentice Girls', *The Crimson Banner Songbook*, n.d.

WELL, THEN, LET ME INFORM YOU, that this place has its own peculiar features. In the first place, all the larger towns in the south and west have, besides the country neighbourhood that surrounds them, a certain sprinkling of gentlefolk, who, though with small fortunes and not much usage of the world, are still a great accession to society, and make up the blank which, even in the most thickly populated country, would be sadly felt without them. Now, in Derry, there is none of this. After the great guns – and *per Baccho!* what great guns they are! – you have nothing but the men engaged in commerce – sharp, clever, shrewd, well-informed fellows; they are deep in flax-seed, cunning in molasses, and not to be excelled in all that pertains to coffee, sassafras, cinnamon, oakum, and elephants' teeth. The place is a rich one, and the spirit of commerce is felt throughout it. Nothing is cared for, nothing is talked of, nothing alluded to, that does not bear upon this; and, in fact, if you haven't a venture in Smyrna figs, Memel timber, Dutch dolls, or some such commodity, you are absolutely nothing, and might as well be at a ball with a cork leg, or go deaf to the Opera.

Now, when I've told you thus much, I leave you to guess what impression our triumphal entry into the city produced. Instead of the admiring crowds that awaited us elsewhere, as we marched gaily into quarters, here we saw nothing but grave, sober-looking, and, I confess it, intelligent-looking faces, that scrutinised our appearance closely enough, but evidently with no great approval, and less enthusiasm. The men passed on hurriedly to the counting-houses and the wharfs; the women, with almost as little interest, peered at us from the windows, and walked away again. Oh! how we wished for Galway, – glorious Galway, that paradise of the infantry, that lies west of the Shannon. Little we knew, as we ordered the band, in lively anticipation of the gaieties before us, to strike up 'Payne's first set,' that, to the ears of the fair listeners in Shipquay Street, the rumble of a sugar hogshead, or the crank of a weighing-crane, were more delightful music.

CHARLES LEVER, *Charles O'Malley*, 1841

DERRY IS CLUSTERED ROUND A HILL rising above the River Foyle, which soon broadens into a lough to meet the sea. Beneath the walls of Derry the Foyle changes from a sweet country river and becomes a thoroughfare for ships, though it has none of the ugly excrescences and effluents which have ruined the approaches of most great rivers in England. From the opposite bank, Derry can be viewed complete before the bus turns sharply and runs across the long bridge over the Foyle, finally darting into the city's narrow streets.

Like most cities once small enough to be contained within an encircling wall, Derry has since spread beyond its earlier confines. But the wall itself, artillery-proof and wide enough to drive a carriage round, remains complete to this day. I found a small hotel on the east wall, and before lunch did the grand tour. I went up to the top of the wall by Coward's Bastion, buying the day's edition of *The Londonderry Sentinel* on my way. The front page headline was 'NEW BRA. FACTORY OPENS IN DERRY, *City chosen because female skills are renowned.*'

ROBIN BRYANS, Ulster: A Journey Through the Six Counties, 1964

B ACK THEN, EVERY OTHER BUILDING on Magazine Street was in ruins. The First Derry Presbyterian Church, bombed out and restored at a cost of £122,000, had just been burned again, a victim of the cardinal law of real estate: location. There was nothing between Magazine Street and the Bogside but the wall, surmounted by an additional 30-foot height of chain-link fencing, and that was apparently not enough.

When I returned to the city in the 1990s, it had undergone a stunning transformation. Catholics had gained political and economic power in the city, which they now called simply Derry. (The surrounding county, in which Protestants predominate, is still called Londonderry.) Within the city walls almost everything had been rebuilt. The place was awash in craft and heritage centres. The First Presbyterian Church School was about to become the Verbal Arts Centre. The gates of the city no longer closed at night, and three separate agencies were offering tours of the city walls. One evening in the Diamond, the heart of the city, I heard thumping and pounding coming from a place called Gymnasia. An aerobics teacher barked encouragement at his class, 'Come on! Forty seconds! Let's hear it in the back row. Yo! Yo! Yo!' They were working out to a disco version of the *West Side Story* song 'There's a place for us'.

But even now, as the Northern Ireland peace process attempts to draw people together, the walls continue to keep them apart. In Belfast, the so-called Peace Line stands 20 feet high, built of corrugated metal and concrete block. It closes off streets connecting the Falls Road and the Shankill Road, so that these two working-class communities of opposing denominations can pretend that they are not neighbours – a classic Irish response to inbred animosities. In Derry, the Protestants I talked to said they no longer felt comfortable inside the city walls. Many now shopped on the other side of the River Foyle, where Protestants remain a majority. The Catholic powers in the city centre 'say they invite people to come over', one Protestant community worker told me. 'But it isn't enough to be "invited over".' He recollected venturing back inside the walls for a city festival. As in a bad marriage, every casual phrase evoked bristling and ill-feeling. 'People said, "What are you doing here tonight?" Or "We wouldn't have been here 20 years ago." It was made perfectly clear to me that this was a Catholic city.'

My enduring impression of the Derry city wall still comes from the 1980s, and an evening when I stopped by several houses that opened onto the walltop promenade. They had been abandoned, evidently in a hurry. Coats still hung on hooks in the hall. A boarded-over window was marked with religious epithets. To the left, a seventeenth-century sentry post with arrow slits and a corbelled roof looked out at nothing. To the right, above Bishop's Gate, a modern sentry post of concrete blocks, enclosed in chain-link fencing and barbed wire, also looked out at nothing, an empty street. The post was unmanned; a monitor camera there relayed the scene to soldiers at a less vulnerable location. Not far from the two sentry posts, on a parapet, a graffito inquired: 'Who the fuck are we?' Looking at the two sentry posts, the slogans and the abandoned houses, I felt that the people here have developed far too finely tuned a sense of who they are separately, and no sense at all of what they might become together – a remarkable waste of 300 years.

ALEN MacWEENEY and RICHARD CONNIFF,
Ireland: Stone Walls and Fabled Landscapes, 1998

O N AUGUST 12, 1970, ON ONE OF my 'information-finding' visits to the North, I had an unpleasant experience in Derry. As I wrote shortly afterwards:

> In the afternoon there was to be an Apprentice Boys rally at St Columb's Park on the outskirts of Derry across the Foyle and remote from the Bogside. This was a substitute – a highly unsatisfactory one from an Apprentice Boys point of view – for the usual triumphal parade. It was also an important occasion however as it was to be addressed by William Craig, the hard-lining former Minister for Home Affairs, who was then making a bid, supported by the whole unionist right, to be the next Prime Minister in Northern Ireland. We decided to attend this rally.
>
> This was not quite so imprudent as it might appear. On July 13, 1969, I had walked with the great Orange March in Belfast to Finaghy Field, had been recognized several times and without any unpleasantness. But that had been a happy occasion for the Orangemen: they had held their march with full traditional pomp. The Apprentice Boys, on the other hand, were forced to use maimed rites. No one minds onlookers for triumphs; humiliations are another matter.
>
> We arrived late at St Columb's Park. It was dark and rainy, adding to the misery of the day. I was wearing a heavy raincoat. I bought

some literature from a stall at the entrance to the grounds: two sets of prison messages from Dr Paisley, dating from different periods of incarceration, and a booklet with the title, *The Pope is the Devil*. To keep the booklets from the rain I shoved them inside the front of my white trenchcoat. When we reached the fringe of the crowd of about 5,000, Mr William Craig was speaking. A sign over his head said simply 'Welcome'. At each side of the covered speakers' stand were Union Jacks and the plain crimson flag which is the emblem of the Derry Siege.

Mr Craig's theme was law and order. The government had failed to maintain law and order and had betrayed Ulster by disarming the Royal Ulster Constabulary and disbanding the B Specials. The RUC must be re-armed – whether they wanted to be re-armed or not – and the Specials reconstituted. There would have to be a new government which would do all this and generally restore order by all means necessary, possibly including 'the use of methods that might make me shudder'.

A young man who had been behind me stumbled against me, stood beside me and asked me what was inside my coat that made it bulge. I told him books. He asked to see the books and I produced them. The book on top was *The Pope is the Devil*. He looked puzzled, relaxed a little, smiled and said: 'Sorry, I thought you might be the reporter for the *Derry Journal*' – the local Catholic and Irish Nationalist paper.

Mr Craig reiterated his point about re-forming the B Specials. Most of the audience clapped but a good many did not. Ulster Protestants are an undemonstrative breed. The young man who had bumped against me asked me why I didn't clap. I said I didn't clap because I didn't agree with a lot the speaker had said (by this time I had a fair idea that I was going to get a beating and on the whole preferred being beaten without having clapped to clapping and then getting beaten as well). The young man told me I was to clap. I told him – speaking within the context of the emphasis on law and order – that it was my lawful right to decide whether to clap or not to clap at a public meeting. This was an unsatisfactory reply.

The substance of Mr Craig's remarks was inflammatory, but his manner and delivery were quiet. He was succeeded by a 'Free Presbyterian' (Paisleyite) minister who said the same sort of thing, but in a scream. The temperature went up. The applause became more frequent and several young men moved in around us clapping frequently and vigorously and nudging us with their elbows as they did so. Then they started kicking our legs quite gently from behind. None of these was an Apprentice Boy.

We moved away from them in order to leave the ground, slowly.

For the moment they did not follow. As we moved away a big man in Apprentice Boys regalia came up. He suggested we should leave the grounds immediately. We said we asked for nothing better and moved away with him. As we were doing so several of the young men who had been jostling us came up and struck us. I got a bloody nose and lip; Séamus MacEntee – Máire's brother who was with me – a lump on the head. The Apprentice Boy told them to go away and was joined by two other Apprentice Boys with the same message. They drew back and we went on with our Apprentice Boys. One of them said it was foolish of us to come. We could not very well disagree, and he did not rub the point in. The other said he believed in defending Ulster but didn't believe in this kind of violence. He pointed out that our assailants were not Apprentice Boys.

At this point we had got about halfway across a large meadow, following a route that was intended to take us clear of the crowd toward the police ranks. (Police were at the exits of the ground, not on the ground itself.) A large group of young men now came running toward us from behind. They were more purposeful this time. An identification had occurred. They wanted 'to get O'Brien'. They hit me several times and I fell down, then they started kicking me. An Apprentice Boy said: 'Is it murder ye want?' After a short while they stopped kicking and went away. I was shaken and sore but not badly hurt; Séamus – who had been trying to pull back my main assailants but who had not been attacked by them this time – said that the long wet grass got in the way of their boots.

We walked away through the long wet grass with the three Apprentice Boys for about a quarter of a mile. At the edge of the meadow we met a Royal Ulster Constabulary man who took us over to a police car. Our Apprentice Boy guides disappeared at this point. As we got into the police car a small crowd – it was near the exit to the grounds and near the end of the meeting – took notice of us and began to shout. One man said: 'Ye didn't get half enough.' There was nothing personal in this anger; our former assailants had not followed and nobody in this crowd recognised me. It was just that I was bleeding from the nose and mouth, I had obviously been beaten up at the Apprentice Boys rally, and was therefore clearly a troublemaker and enemy of Ulster. As the police car drew away the crowd began to hammer with fists and umbrellas on its roof and windows.

Not long after this episode I got a postcard from Omagh: 'I see you got a Protestant beating-up in Derry. If you come to Omagh I promise you a Catholic beating-up.'

CONOR CRUISE O'BRIEN, *Memoir: My Life and Themes*, 1998

PEGGY'S HUSBAND PATSY DEERY had an even more hardy rearing. His family came out of Walker's Square, site of the most legendary tenements in the history of the city of Derry. The square abutted onto, and below, the city walls. Above the huddled Catholics, and planted firmly onto the ramparts, was a vast pillar and atop that was a statue of Governor Walker, the Protestant who defended the city against the siege of the English Catholic King James in 1690. Governor Walker was fighting for representative democracy, an ideal which became lost in the mists of time in the North. Once a year, until the IRA blew up the statue in 1973, members of the Protestant Orange Order used to gather under the pillar and throw pennies to the Catholics below. Catholic children such as Patsy Deery grew up gladly gathering those pennies. He was one of ten sisters and brothers. Surviving members of his family remember that one room of their small tenement in Walker's Square was in such dangerous condition that the children were forbidden to enter it, lest they crash through the ceiling.

After the Second World War, when the Allies pulled out of emergency billets in Derry, the more desperate of the citizenry squatted into the abandoned camps. Patsy Deery's family went first to the British Army nissen huts on the outskirts of town. A reconnoitre of the area later showed that Springtown Camp was a slightly better proposition. The American Army had erected Springtown, and the Yanks were known to appreciate luxury.

Hundreds of Catholics, including the Deerys, and some Protestants, swarmed into Springtown Camp. There was no electricity in the tin huts; there was no indoor water supply; the people used two communal taps and a communal latrine; some families shared a hut, marking the division of property with a curtain.

Springtown Camp was an improvement on their condition.

The Ministry of Health and Local Government for Northern Ireland made the squatters sign a licence in order to become legal tenants. The licence declared that:

> the occupier will use the premises for residential purposes only and will not carry on or permit to be carried on therein any trade or business and will not do, or permit to be done, any act or thing which may cause discomfort or annoyance to other occupiers of the said premises ... and will at all times during his or her occupation keep the said premises in a clean state and condition..

Springtown Camp did not close until 1968.

NELL McCAFFERTY, *Peggy Deery*, 1987

CLIMBING AGAIN, SHE SAW ICE FORM on the windshield and felt it weighing down the plane. For the next ten hours she fought to stay low enough to prevent icing but high enough to use her instruments. All through the night she felt the vibrations of the flaming manifold, and tried not to look at it while the rudder bar throbbed under her feet. The cabin stank of gas fumes, increasing the stomach contractions she always had on long flights. To retain her strength and stay alert she forced down part of the chicken soup in the thermos and drank the tomato juice from the tins, which she pierced with an icepick. When she reached up to turn on the reserve fuel tank she discovered the gauge was broken. Gasoline was dripping down the back of her neck. She no longer knew how much fuel remained in her tank.

Shortly after dawn she spotted a ship, then a fishing fleet. She knew she was off the coast of Ireland and would have to land. 'Paris was out of the question.' Because the waves beneath her indicated a northwest wind, she decided she was south of her course and turned north. Actually she was already north of the course to Paris and by flying even farther north she almost missed the northernmost tip of Ireland, beyond which there was nothing but open sea. After sighting the coast, she flew inland, following some railroad tracks while she looked for an airfield. There was none. She landed in a meadow, 'frightening all the cows in the neighborhood', and for a brief moment sat in the plane, looking out at the green hills.

Dan McCallion, herder of the frightened cows, approached the plane as she climbed out, her face smeared with grease. 'Where am I?' she asked him.

'Sure, you're in Derry, sir.'

'In Derry? Oh, Londonderry.' She pointed to a farmhouse across the field. 'Whose house is that over there?'

'It belongs to the Gallaghers.'

'Could I stop there?'

'Yes, sir – I mean, Ma'am. And have you come far?'

'From America.'

'Holy Mother of God' McCallion muttered as she walked toward the house.

At the James Gallaghers she washed her face and drank two cups of tea but insisted she was neither hungry nor tired. A few minutes later she hailed a passing car and rode into Londonderry to telephone G.P. [George Putnam – her husband]. She spoke to him for six minutes, then returned to the Gallaghers to watch her plane until arrangements were made to guard it – a wise procedure, for it might well have disappeared, a piece at a time, in the clutches of souvenir hunters. The plane secured, Amelia returned to Londonderry and placed five three-minute calls to G.P. When she returned a second time to the Gallaghers, she was mobbed by crowds until 10 p.m. when she retired.

DORIS RICH, *Amelia Earhart*, 1989

THE 'WALLS OF DERRY' ARE STILL to the good. They enclose a diamond-shaped area in which stood Derry of the sieges. The modern city spreads all round the walls and the walled town, and is to the Derry of to-day what the New York of 1907 is to New York of 1860. The population of Derry is now over 40,000. In the stormy days of the sieges it was little more than a fortified village. The space enclosed by the historic walls appears to be smaller than many a square or plaza in modern cities. The walls are immense ridges of masonry. Two waggons could meet and pass each other on the top. They are proportionately wide at the base. Their height seems to vary, but is in places over thirty feet above the street. There are parapets, loopholes, bastions, lookouts and other details of engineering, all of which had their uses in the days of short-range artillery and small arms. The gateways are arched, and the principal ones have a due share of architectural ornamentation. I do not know what has become of the gates which refused to open. I enquired, but discovered no antiquarian in Derry who could give me the desired information.

The walls were built in 1617–18, at a cost of £8,500, a sum which represented a great deal more in those days than it does in ours. They were found to be impregnable by the Royalists, who besieged the Cromwellian garrison for four months in 1648. But the most memorable siege took place in 1688, when for 105 days it held out against the army of James II. The beleaguered city endured the most terrible privations, and behaved with a heroism which Catholic as well as Protestant cannot but admire. The brunt of the fight fell on the 'prentice boys, and they won. King James was obliged to raise the siege. His generals may or may not have been incompetent, and the elements of attack inadequate. Be that as it may, James was worsted. Derry held her own against him, and he was obliged to leave her in peace.

> In short, the fact is known, boys, she chased him from
> the hill,
> For the maiden on her throne, boys, would be a maiden
> still.

The hero of the defence was the Rev. Mr Walker. Derry raised a great monument to his memory on the walls which he made famous. There it stands yet, overlooking the city. The sword which the right hand of the statue held aloft fell with a mighty crash on the night that Catholic emancipation for Ireland became law. The prominence given to this circumstance in Irish history of the nineteenth century shows that in neither religious camp was it regarded as a mere coincidence at the time.

On the rampart facing the river are a few ancient pieces of ordnance presented to Derry by various guilds of London. Clan London has always been ready to make presents of anything which would contribute to the work of keeping the Irishry down and squelching them, and protecting the warriors who were doing the trampling down and the squelching. Each gun bears an inscription giving the names of the donors and the date of its manufacture. Several of these had pet names in the fighting years. 'Roaring Meg' was one of them. 'Roaring' was a favourite adjective used in connection with cannon in the seventeenth century. And in reality those 'roarers' made more noise than destruction. The rusted 'roarers' on the walls of Derry are kept there now merely as historical landmarks. Like the walls on which they stand, they are useless as elements of defence – a half battery of modern field guns would blow all that stone heap and old iron into ruin in a few hours from any of the hills around the city. But the historic ramparts and ordnance are not there for defence. They are merely symbols speaking from the past.

WILLIAM BULFIN, *Rambles in Eirinn*, 1907

I HAD NO IDEA THAT DERRY was so beautiful. Its sandstone walls reminded me of St Malo in Brittany. An asphalt roadway runs along the top of the walls which, speckled with white chippings, gives one the impression of a woodland pathway on which the hawthorn petals of autumn are forever falling.

Looking down from the walls, one sees the cemetery where the Catholic dead fill the sloping riverside fields above the Foyle; nearer one's point of vantage is the Bogside, the story of which would fill many tomes and superficial comment on which would constitute an impertinence.

And yet despite its many superficial contradictions this lovely old city conveys a sense of Irishness as valid as that of Dunquin in Kerry or Cashel in Tipperary.

Latter-day gates pierce old walls as if to mimic Quebec and the Heights of Abraham. Here cannon mouths appear to gape across the centuries while below the walls the Foyle flows seaward to join the exiles' 'bowl of tears' so that one hums a line of an old ballad: *As down the Foyle, the waters boil, an' our ship stands out from the land.'*

In Derry the women are the breadwinners: linen and shirt-making are responsible for this domestic inversion with its resultant social repercussions. In Derry, too, the dirtiest word one can utter is 'Hong Kong', as cheap shirts from that city sorely harass the city's economy.

Founded by St Colmcille and loved intensely by that holy man even in his exile of Iona, Derry was primarily a monastic foundation. Its location close to the northern sea track resulted in its being recurrently attacked by the Danes. Later it attracted the unwelcome attentions of the Normans. The medieval city was accidentally blown up and subsequently fire-destroyed. After the suppression of an O'Doherty rebellion it was granted in 1613 by James I, together with an enormous tract of land, to the citizens of London who planted the area and enwalled the town.

The highest point of its history was the siege of 1688–89. Attacked by Jacobite forces, the citizens, spearheaded by the city's apprentice boys banged out the weak-kneed governor Lundy and, inspired by the Reverend George Walker, held out until, after 7,000 citizens had died, three relieving ships sailed up the Foyle to sever the boom of floating beams which had blocked the river. Thus was raised an epic siege.

BRYAN MACMAHON, Here's Ireland, 1971

NAME – DERRY, IN IRISH DOIRE – the popular name of the place – means literally a 'place of oaks', but is also used to express a 'thick wood': it is so explained by Colgan (1645) – an Irish topographer of the highest authority – in his *Acta Sanctorum*: p. 566 [*rectè* 562]. This word, however, was not topographically used by the ancient Irish without the addition of some distinctive epithet, as in Doire Broscaidh, Doire Lóráin, &c.: thus the original Pagan appellation of this place was Doire Calgach, or Derry-Calgach – the 'oak wood of Calgach', – *Calgach*, which signifies a 'fierce warrior', being the proper name of a man in Pagan times, and rendered illustrious as *Galgacus* in the pages of Tacitus. In support of this etymology may be adduced the high authority of Adamnan – abbot of Iona, in the 7th century – who, in his Life of his predecessor, St Columbkille, invariably calls this place '*Roboretum Calgagi*', in conformity with his habitual substitution of Latin equivalents for Irish topographical names. For a long period subsequent to the 6th century, in which a monastery was erected here by St Columbkille, the name of Derry-Calgach prevailed; but, towards the latter end of the 10th century, it seems to have yielded to that of Derry-Columbkille – no other appearing in the Irish annals after that period. In subsequent ages, when the place had risen in importance above every other *Derry*, the distinctive epithet *Columbkille* was dropped as no longer necessary; and such is the effect of long established usage that the English prefix *London* – imperatively imposed by the original charter of James I, and preserved with pride by the colonists for a long time after – has likewise fallen into popular disuse. Indeed this mode of abbreviation is usual in Ireland, whenever the name of a place is compounded of two distinct and easily separable words: thus, in the counties of Antrim and Down, Carrickfergus is shortened into *Carrick*, Downpatrick into *Down*, Iniscourcy into *Inch*, &c.

It may, perhaps, not be unworthy of remark that the English prefix *London*, and the original Irish name *Derry*, are equally traceable to a Celtic – or, more correctly, Scythic – origin; and that, by a curious coincidence, the word LONDON seems as graphically descriptive of the modern locality as DERRY was of the ancient. By LLUYD, and other British etymologists, it is interpreted the 'town of ships', from *long* in British, and Irish, 'ship', – and *dinas* in British, or dún in Irish, 'fortress', – (the *dunum* of the Romans,) which is the root of the word 'town'. This derivation is, however, merely conjectural; and the Celtic compound Lonn-dún, signifying a 'strong fortress', is as likely to have been the original signification of LONDON. Either explanation is, however, curiously applicable to Londonderry, or Lonndún-doire, which would mean in Irish what the English have really made the city – the 'ship town', or 'fortified town, of Derry'; and it may be added that an etymology similar to the former may be found in the name of an ancient fortress, a few miles higher up the river, called Dún na long – 'fortress of ships', or 'town of ships', as it has been preserved to the present time.

THOMAS COLBY (Colonel, Royal Engineers),
Ordnance Survey of the County Londonderry, 1837

'You had the coats – maybe you had pockets –
some people had a wee bag ...'
' ... or under your skirt –
we never wore trousers, girls never wore trousers.'
'You wore skirts, and maybe you wore a heavier skirt,
and you had like an apron, and it all in pockets,
and you had it tied around your waist
underneath your skirt and your petticoat,
but in case you had been caught,
you always kept something handy,
which you didn't care whether they took off you or not.
As long as they didn't take the tea
and the sugar off you, you know, or the cigarettes.
When my grandfather was alive he was a chain smoker
and I used to bring him cigarettes.
You had to –
when the things like that were rationed.
You had certain shops that you went into
and whenever the things came in, you got your supply.
But you couldn't have gone to a shop in the Waterside –
and they would have had their supply in,
they wouldn't have given it to you.'
'These were for the regulars.'
'That was for their customers only.'
'And you're talking about the men in the factory,

the way they were considerate –
we never got fruit, or tinned fruit,
they were all rationed.
Well sometimes
somebody would have come in to the factory
and said, "There's stuff up in – wherever ..."'
'Lynn's.'
'The Man would have let the women go out,
because you had to queue,
or maybe he would have let two or three women
go out to bring in – maybe you only got two tins each,
it's all there was –
but just to have got those two tins or whatever –
and the managers would have let
a few girls out to bring stuff in for everybody
so as you would get your share of it
when there was fresh fruit and stuff like that ...'

ANONYMOUS, 'How to Smuggle', in *The Fountain*, (ed. Leon McAuley), 1993

[Published in the local Papers at the time]

ON THE DERRY WATER-SUPPLY

A LULLABY

Suggested by the following recent letter to the City Engineer from the City Analyst regarding the City and the Waterside water-supplies:–

6 COLLEGE AVENUE, LONDONDERRY,
October 21st, 1905

DEAR MR ROBINSON – I enclose the result of the analysis of samples of water from the City and Waterside supplies. Of course, there is a good deal of vegetable impurity present, but the waters are really better than I expected them to be, considering the low state of the reservoirs. After filtration any of the samples is a clear and pleasant drinking water. Without filtration none of them is desirable to drink, but I would not class either of them as unsafe or injurious. – Yours very truly,

J.R. Leebody

Hush! Hushaby! Hush!
          Derry Councillors all!
Through your waters injurious bacteria crawl;
And of matter malignant, of course, there is plenty,
For your reservoirs now might be labelled as empty;
But be thankful and calm – for I boldly maintain
That their emptiness comes of inadequate rain;
And, perhaps, if the water you carefully strain,
Your efforts may not be teetotally vain
(If your filters be choice ones – the cheap never buy!),
Unless in the meantime of typhoid you die.
But the waters unfiltered are exellent, too,
And may, possibly, never do damage to you;
For while I describe them as being impure,
I likewise regard them as safe, to be sure.
So now fill up with water your bowls to the brink,
That your own and the citizens' health you may drink;
And you then may securely repair to your couches,
Content with what Analyst Leebody vouches!

M.C.H. (One of the Councillors – subsequently one of the
Aldermen of the Corporation).

DERRY, *November 5th,* 1905

MAURICE C. HIME, *Christmas Roses,* 1920

So FREDERICK WENT TO DERRY – or as the *Dublin Evening News* announed, 'We can assure the public that the Right Hon. and Right Rev. Dr Hervey, Bishop of Cloyne, is translated to See of Derry.'

With him went Mrs Hervey – regretting somewhat that she must exchange the sleepy air of Co. Cork for the harsher climate of the north, but otherwise well content – and their children, Mary, John Augustus, who was destined for the Navy, Elizabeth and the baby Louisa.

Gone were the days when an increasse in their family was a matter for financial concern. Frederick was now, as he wrote to a French acquaintance with naïve satisfaction, 'un Évêque de cent-vingt et quartre mille livres de rentes.'

But though he frankly revelled in his sudden affluence his enjoyment of it was not entirely selfish.

The same wish to do good, to be a public benefactor as had animated him at Cloyne and had won him so much popularity there, filled him with enthusiastic energy at Derry, only now he had the means to gratify his benevolent intentions on a large scale.

He had hardly arrived before he had made a rapid tour of the diocese, arranged for new parsonages to be built, and started a fund for the assistance of superannuated curates. 'If he goes on as he has begun,' someone wrote, 'we shall not grudge him the monstrous income of his Bishopric.'

This was nothing – a mere beginning. He was astounded to find that the inhabitants of Londonderry had to cross the Foyle by ferry. They must have a bridge. They must certainly have a bridge. He contributed £1,000 towards the project, a further sum towards the development of local coal mines, and at his own expense constructed the magnificent highway across the mountains from Downhill to the Strand which was to be known as 'the Bishop's Road'.

The citizens of Londonderry, bedazzled by his munificence, conferred on him, within a year of his arrival, the Freedom of the City, an honour which no previous Bishop had enjoyed.

His benevolence overflowed on to Roman Catholics and Dissenters alike, as well as on to members of his own flock. He allowed the former to use any empty chapels in the neighbourhood, and even offered the Roman Catholic Bishop of Derry a donation from his private income that he might build himself a church.

To those who remonstrated with him, he merely replied, 'The rights of humanity demand an unlimited and general tolerance at all times.'

Busy, benevolent and beloved, even his most spiteful enemies were hard put to it to find fault with him at this stage of his career.

MAGDALEN KING-HALL, *The Edifying Bishop*, 1951

DERRY
County Derry

O N SUNDAY EVENING LAST THIS CITY and its neighbourhood were visited by a storm of extraordinary violenceJohn H. Gebbie (ed.), *An Introduction to the Abercorn Letters*, 1972 ... The two previous days a considerable quantity of snow had fallen at intervals, and throughout Sunday the air was keen and penetrating, but there was no indication whatever of the coming tempest.

About midnight the strorm broke out, the wind blowing south-easterly, from which point it gradually veered round to the south-west. It blew long and heavy gusts, between which the intervals were very brief, and brought with it rain which descended in deluges, and did not subside until about six o'clock in the morning.

So noisy was the elemental strife, that it must have banished sleep from every eye. In the morning there was not a street or lane in the city that did not exhibit proofs of its violence ... The Court-house was much damaged, the glass in the windows of the Grand Jury Room having been shattered to pieces, and one of the scales in the hand of the figure of Justice in front of the building carried away.

We have heard of some providential escapes, owing to the roofs of the houses being sufficiently strong to support the stacks of chimnies which fell immediately above the beds where they lay. Mr George Foster's rope-walk was blown into the river; but it would be vain to particularize the losses. In the neighbourhood a vast number of stately trees were torn up, and some of the roads, particularly the one to Muff by Brook hall, were rendered impassable ... For many miles around, in all directions, according to accounts we have received, the damage done has been very great, the thatch, and even the scraws of the houses of many poor people having been whirled into the air ... (LJ) [*Londonderry Journal*]

Many of the huts of the peasantry have been unroofed or entirely prostrated, and in not a few cases ... totally consumed by their thatch taking fire. (DS) [*Derry Standard*]

PETER CARR, *The Big Wind*, 1991

HIGHLY SPICED, AROMATIC MINCED MEAT has always been a great delicacy in Derry. Each butcher usually had his own recipe, which was displayed as 'Special'. Many children, in fact, thought that 'Special' was a variety of meat, such as steak, mutton, or beef. The ordinary variety was known simply as mince and was the principal ingredient in stew, or fried with onions, and served up with boiled potatoes made a nourishing dinner. In fact it was tasty, easily cooked, lent itself to a wide variety of dishes, but most of all, it was cheap. Nevertheless, I know many Derry exiles who, when they hear of people returning for holidays to the city by the Foyle, ask the travellers to bring them back some 'Derry Mince'.

Black puddings were also very popular, and once again, many butchers evolved their own recipes. Perhaps the doyen of these pudding makers was George Doherty – better known as George the Brad – whose shop was on Creggan Road, near the junction with Windsor Terrace, and to this shop, customers trekked from all over the city for his delicious black puddings. George was a local wit, and also had a reputation for being a practical joker. There is a story that, following a joke played by the 'Brad' on the late Ned Ramsay, who lived nearby in Marlborough Terrace, Ned bribed a young lad to enter George's shop late on a Saturday night, when it was crowded with customers, carrying a dead cat wrapped up in a parcel, so arranged that the animal's tail stuck out of the wrapping, making the contents evident. The lad slapped the parcel down on the counter in front of the startled customers, and said, on Ned's instructions, 'There now, Mr

Doherty, that's the last of the half dozen' implying that these were the ingredients in some of George's products. There was a moment's hushed silence until with a roar, George seized the nearest implement and tore round the counter after the boy, who by this time was wisely putting as much distance as possible between himself and the outraged butcher.

CHARLES GALLAGHER, *Acorns and Oak Leaves*, 1981

W E HAVE YET HARDLY RECOVER'D OURSELVES from our consternation occasion'd by one of the most daring and inhuman acts of violence that I ever remember, I mean the murder of Miss Knox by Mr McNaghten: I see by the English papers you have already had some account of it but as the particulars have never yet been truly given to the public and as your Lordship may possibly have some curiosity to know them, I will just mention some of the most remarkable ones which I had from Captain J. Hamilton and an other person who assist'd in taking examinations. McNaghten has been lurking about this country in disguise for these five months past, and by his address found means to conciliate to his interest many persons, whom one wou'd hardly have suspected. They agreed with him that he was highly injured by having his wife detain'd from him and listen'd with pleasure to his declarations that he wou'd recover [her] by force, bind her father and mother and consummate the marriage in their presence: this scheme was applauded by many and in particular by several ladies whose knowledge of it will be proved and some of whose letters will be produced in court. It seems however that this was only a feint and that his real plan was to murder the whole family in the actual execution of which he had engaged three desperate assassins formerly his servants, whose names are known, and one of whom I hear is taken since the Proclamation, offering five hundred pounds reward for apprehending each of them. He had besides many spies and letters particularly two Irwins of Lisdivin within a few miles of Strabane, and one Winsley who I believe is your tenant. These persons procured information that Colonel Knox was to pass that way on Tuesday the 19th of this instant which was ascertained by a letter from Mr Knox in answer to one from Mr Hamilton of Dunamanna who desir'd a place in his coach to Dublin, falling into the hands of one of the Irwins, in what manner will be known in a few days. It appears already from Mr Hamiltons examinations that he knew of McN's being in that place with the Irwins for several days before, and though it is also proved he apprehended something dangerous was there contriving, he gave his friend Mr Knox no account of it, but desir'd Mr Tyrel the collector of Strabane the very morning of the assassination to use his influence with the Irwins to drive McN. from their house. Now cou'd Mr Hamilton who is their landlord stand in need of such influence? Sums of money have been discover'd to have been lodged for the service of intelligence of Mr Knox's motions, and some of his servants were actually bribed and one particularly now in prison, who was entrusted to load the arms and which he did in such a manner as to make them inoffensive, except the gun of one servant whose cowardice they thought made that precaution unnecessary. The 10th, one of the Irwins set out upon the business of setting the coach, and when it had passed, rode after it, looked into it and then went on briskly about a mile to the wood where McNaghten and his accomplices were posted, who upon the coach's coming up, immediately rushed out on foot, as I believe they all were. The coachman was call'd upon to stop and fir'd at but without effect. Mr Knox was attended by two persons on horseback, one with a Blunderbuss, the other with a gun; three shots were immediately fired at the former, as he was the only one they fear'd, though the servant I mention'd who was not in company had previously taken care to shake out the priming of the Blunderbuss, which he snapped twice upon their first coming up and must have prevented the whole mischief had it gone off; the poor fellow was totally disabled though not mortally wounded. McNaghten then stept'd up to the coach and with a long gun shot Miss Knox in the side below her stays, who immediately cried out, I am kill'd; the other servant who was indeed timorous had retir'd behind a turf stack and fir'd at the very same instant and lodged three bullets in McN's back whose position was such that they glanced up instead of going to his body as they must have done had he been standing upright. McNaghten snapp'd a pistol at him, which did not go off; he then ran round to the other side of the coach and two shots were immediately fired into it through the wooden blind which was drawn up but they did no hurt.

Mr Knox then fir'd his second pistol close to him and was surprised to find it had no effect. McN finding himself weaken'd by the wounds he had received, thought proper to make his retreat and was assisted in getting over the brook and help'd upon his horse by the same Irwin who set the coach; he then went to Winsley's house and concealed himself in the hay loft not being able to ride any farther. Mr Knox's son upon his sister's being wounded rode in all haste to Strabane and return'd in a very short time with Dr Law and a party of the light horse; a reward of 100 guineas being offered to who ever shou'd take McNaghten, they separated and began the pursuit. The Corporal and Knox the innkeeper at Strabane went to Winsley's house and not seeing any horse began to despair of finding him there, but Winsley's daughter passing then in the yard with a teapot in her hand, they question'd her what she had been doing with it, and not getting a satisfactory answer they renew'd their pursuit. The Corporal immediately rush'd up into the hay loft, and having had two shots fir'd at him without effect, McNaghten apprehending a return surrendered himself and was tied upon a car and convey'd to Lifford Gaol; it was thought at first his wounds would prove mortal, but he is in no danger from them.

His design at present is to starve himself having refused to take any sort of food for these three days. Judge Scot and Baron Mountney are to be at Strabane on Saturday the 5th December to try him and his accomplices there. As he has too many well wishers, it is thought necessary to keep a very strong guard over him. I forgot to mention that the poor young lady died about five hours after she receiv'd her wound. I have most likely tired your Lordship with this long detail.

JOHN H. GEBBIE (ed.), An Introduction to the Abercorn Letters, 1972

BUT, WHATEVER TRADITION DERRY MEN choose to stand in, or, to use an Ulster expression, whichever foot they dig with, they are the kind of people who have a way of their own in most matters and they clearly think that 'No surrender!' is a sound slogan.

And since we have been talking so much about Derry men, it occurs to me that it may be well to mention that there are also some women in Derry.

> The sweet girls of Derry are comely and merry;
> They've lips like the cherry and teeth like the snow;
> But 'tis not in nature to dwell on each feature
> That every sweet creature in Derry can show.
> Och anee, so pleasant, so pleasant and merry,
> They quite captivate me, the sweet girls of Derry.

And at the present day a large proportion of them are employed at making shirts. It was the sweet girls of Derry who kept shirts on the backs of the British Armed Services during two world wars.

Yet there are parts of the world where Derry and its ways and traditions are not well known. I was told recently about an experience of a well-known Derry man who was travelling in France with his wife. They were sitting in a café at a French holiday resort. The place was rather empty and the little band was playing rather drearily. The manager of the establishment made himself particularly gracious to the few people who were there, inquiring if there was anything he could procure them, any kind of further food or drink that madame would like, and, finally, anything they would like the band to play. Since his graciousness was a little fatiguing, our visitor from Derry pricked up his ears at the suggestion about the band and said, 'Let's have the Londonderry Air!' The manager went and consulted with the leader of the band. There were shrugs and shakings of the head. Finally he returned to the Derry visitors and said: 'I am very sorry. The band cannot play you the "London Derrière", but they can play you the "Black Bottom".'

HUGH SHEARMAN, Ulster, 1949

WE FOUND THE HOUSE OF THE INVENTOR of Hervey's Sauce, The Bishop of Derry and Earl of Bristol, almost opposite The Court House; and we thought that it might serve for a minor embassy but not for such a mighty man. We were not surprised that Frederick Hervey had taken to building palaces elsewhere. This small palace was clearly not enough for a real over-life size, eighteenth-century character who figured in the most fantastic stories. A very beautiful and extravagant piece of garden architecture, The Casino, which the Earl Bishop had himself designed, has, to the irreperable loss of Derry, been demolished.

A man who lived with a roar and a shout like Frederick Hervey inevitably created legends that may or may not be true. Nobody quite knows which contemporary wit said: 'There are men, women and Herveys.' He certainly did dabble for a time in Irish politics, and it may have been from a genuine wish to relieve oppression or it may have been that Irish politics gave the great man an opportunity for ostentation. Some people tell the story that he appeared with a gorgeous cavalcade in Dublin, dressed in a uniform of his own devising that was stuck with gold tassels and priceless gems, and proposed that he should be made monarch of an Independent Kingdom of Ireland. It is feasible; for we know, from sober chroniclers, that towards the end of his life he was constantly writing to Prime Ministers proposing that some crisis in some country could expeditiously be solved by appointing him the English plenipotentiary or ambassador or viceroy. He felt that he was made for summits. 'When it is my pleasure to receive distinguished company,' he said, 'I shall have my house full no matter where I live.'

Deans and rectors and curates had to do the best they could to live up to him. He would invite them to dinner and present them with a banquet, for heaven knows what The Bishop of Derry would have said to the Queen of Sweden who, for the sake of economy, made her ladies eat the bones in herrings and boasted that she never had bleeding gums. The clergy would be surfeited with the richest foods and then intoxicated with Madeira under chrystallised chandeliers, and then ordered to jump and run races. Promotion would be preferred by the smiling Bishop on the winners. The fat and unathlectic were made to mount horses, and Hervey would roar with mirth when they came to grief. He'd force them to place bets; and then he'd preach a sermon in church the next day about the evils of betting, making a special reference to the scandalous clerical steeplechase of the previous day. Their bishop's world must have seemed as strange to the poor clergymen as that of winged bulls.

But the Earl Bishop often could tolerate downright honesty. He admired a curate who had the temerity to propose a toast, 'A rot among the rectors.' He made the curate a rector; and waited gleefully to see whether the honest man would say, 'A rot among the bishops.' Once he feigned illness and called in all the doctors; and listened scornfully to their sympathetic words until one young doctor said, 'Get up, my lord, you know perfectly well there is nothing the matter with you.' The Earl Bishop made this doctor his personal physician. It was a wise stratagem. When the Bishop was ill with quinsey, this doctor came to a secret agreement with the cook. So, when the cook himself brought up the porridge for the illustrious invalid's lunch, the doctor pretended to be outraged by the thinness of the gruel and snatched the plate and threw its contents over the cook's head; and My Lord Bishop laughed so much that the quinsey burst and he was cured.

Yes, one sadly has to admit there was a streak of cruelty in all the grand living which Hervey inspired; but it was, in a sense, the streak of sadism which was in the age rather than particularly in the Bishop. It was an age which let a man, in the position of the Earl Bishop, make his own laws, his own politics and his own religion.

He was, for instance, most unorthodoxly fond of consulting fortune tellers; and he would dress himself in all manner of disguises so as not to be recognised by the witches he consulted. Once he went in a false beard to a seer in a very poor hamlet in County Down, and the woman gazed at him with terror. 'Ah sure,' she moaned, 'you are The Devil himself – or else you are The Bishop of Derry.' They say he was cured of his desire to look into the future when a certain book was placed in his hands. There was a tradition that St Columbkille had left behind him, when he fled to Iona, a volume of prophecies which had been lost; and Frederick Hervey commissioned scholars to search for them; and one day they brought him a sealed box. The Bishop broke the seal, and many vipers came hissing out of the box; but there was the book, and the Bishop opened it, and he went white and sweat poured off him. Like our old man in Pomeroy who had never wanted to hear the end of the story about the ghost in the bottle, the Bishop never looked at the book again.

Had he learnt that he, the Prince of Priests, was to die in an outhouse? That he was to fall from his horse, while journeying from Albano to Rome, with an acute attack of gout in the stomach, and that peasants in the near-by cottages were to refuse to allow a heretic prelate to die under their roofs? Could St Columbkille have told the Earl Bishop that his body was to be brought back to England in a packing case labelled, in order not to offend the superstitions of the sailors on *The Monmouth*, 'Antique Statue'? So much, in fact, was to happen; and some believe, too, that the packing case was lost, and that in the end a statue was actually buried at Ickworth instead of the Bishop's remains.

OSWELL BLAKESTON, *Thank You Now*, 1960

A RCHDEACON FREDERICK HAMILTON, Grafton Street, Dublin to the
Earl of Abercorn.

I am thinking of going to the North very soon, and shall pass the summer at
Derry. It is my duty to acquaint your Lordship of my being soon to be
married to Miss Daniel: her father is a clergyman: if a want of fortune can
be compensated by merit and every good quality I may expect to escape
censure, but I fear these are little esteemed in this provident age ... There is
nothing talk'd of here but the great victory of the King of Prussia [invasion
of Bohemia], the Papists being promis'd a total revolution are much dejected
and in some places have fasted for three or four days successively.

JOHN H. GEBBIE (ed.), *An Introduction to the Abercorn Letters*, 1972

A Place of
Wheels and Looms

By day a place of wheels and looms
That struggle in a narrow space,
A shout of children in the slums
And girls with labour-stained face.

By night a queen with victory crowned,
For all her years of loud turmoil.
She spreads her beauty all around,
Reflects her glory in the Foyle.

FRANCIS LEDWIDGE, 'Derry', in *Complete Poems*, 1997

THE FIRM I WORKED FOR HAD THREE BRANCH SHOPS, so, when they hadn't the shoe in one shop, I would have been called to take the shoes to wherever. It was great, this, and the shops were within walking distance of each other, so it broke the monotony to get out, to see what was going on in the outside world. The manager of my branch, John Bradley, was ancient, probably about twenty-seven and there wasn't a lot of conversation. It was also better than fitting some old farmer whose boots were sometimes still 'leggard' with cow manure. John Bradley – still alive at time of writing – was cute enough to leave that kind of customer to me. The firm also had a boot-and-shoe repair place, and after six months I got a transfer there. My mother was elated. I was in my fifteenth year then.

That period was very happy, for I was in with three others known as journeymen; I was a first-year apprentice. There was also a second-year apprentice called Jim Nicell, and he and I struck it off together. The crack was good for Jim and myself re-enacted all the movies of the day, and our shoot-outs and death scenes were real Hollywood classics. Cecil B, eat your heart out! All this would take place during working hours, and the old journeymen – they were in their forties – thought we were crazy. If only things could be as simple nowadays.

Big Johnny McKeown, my boss, stood about six feet six inches to my five feet four inches, so can you imagine me wearing his raincoat. Well I did, for it was raining one day and as I was about to go home for my lunch Big Johnny says: 'Ginger, take my coat; it'll keep you dry.' God bless us! it would have kept half of Derry dry, it was that big, and greasy to boot. I walked over the bridge looking like Dopey the dwarf in *Snow White*, with the greasy coat trailing the ground and the sleeves six inches too long. To crown it out, the factory girls were just getting out for lunch and whilst I hadn't yet started going out with Agnes my wife there was a good chance I would see her and she me. That's the way romance blossomed in those days. I made sure always to bring my coat in future. I was sixteen and the war was just over.

JOHN DORAN, *Red Doran*, 1996

THE AVERAGE FACTORY GIRL was also relatively unsophisticated, in fact, it might be true to say that to the majority, smoking represented the acme of sophistication. Social drinking was seldom indulged in, probably because of the tradition that public houses – or pubs – were masculine territory, and only females of dubious character or morals, would frequent such places. Make-up was restricted to a narrower range of cosmetics than is available today. The technique of application was also rather rudimentary, and cheeks tended to be over-rouged, against a dead white background, with a slash of vivid red lipstick. It was not uncommon to see girls going to work with their hair a mass of steel, or tape, curlers, if they had an important 'date' for the evening, or if they intended going to a dance.

Girls usually commenced their working lives in the factories as soon as they were legally permitted to leave school. Their jobs were usually secured by being spoken for by a sister, or other relative already employed in the firm, or by recommendation from a teacher. Many began as 'message girls' e.g., those who ran inter-departmental errands etc., or as 'Clippers' removing superfluous threads from the semi-finished parts of the product. Depending upon opportunity, they then progressed to various other departments or finishing trades – smoothers, buttonholers, examiners, etc. The office girls were usually those with a higher standard of education, or clerical skills such as typing or bookkeeping.

Factory girls seldom suffered fools gladly. They were quick to detect the sham character, and were scathing in observation and comment. Woe betide the would-be Romeo who tried to impress, or who tried to patronise them, he would like as not be told 'Away an' lick wur leg', or 'For Christ's sake, catch yourself on'. A favourite Derry adjective was 'Wild'. It could be 'Wild wet', 'Wild warm', or 'Wild coul'.

The Divine name was invoked with monotonous regularity, to such degree that most girls were unaware that they were using it. – 'Jesus! Who does he think he is' or 'Jesus! Luk at her', 'Jesus! Where d'ye think ye're goin' or simply 'Jeeeesus'. The advent of the sound film had introduced a measure of American slang, but in the main, the vernacular expressions showed strong traces of Donegal sayings.

'It's no odds' meaning 'It doesn't matter', 'She's not herself' meaning 'She's unwell', 'He got the quare gunk' meaning that he had been disappointed. 'She's a clashbag' – a talebearer. 'She has a notion of him' meaning that she is in love with him. 'Don't let on' – do not tell anyone. 'Her man's well-mended' – her husband's health is much improved. 'She's awaiting on', meaning that she is on the point of death. Of a person having a limb amputated, 'He/she is wanting an arm'. 'She stood forenenst him' – she stood opposite him.

There were expressions which were peculiar to the world of the factories. 'Ah'll blind ye wi' a dozen o' work' – shirts, or their components were usually counted in bundles of twelve for costing and pricing purposes, and were known as 'dozens' – hence this expression meant 'I'll strike you across the face (eyes) with a bundle of cloth, or components'. Derry women, and girls, made tremendous sacrifices for their menfolk – brothers, fathers and husbands. Many gave up the opportunity of a home and marriage, so that their contribution, earned at 'speedbench' or ironing table, would make possible the further education of a male member of the family, enabling him to become a schoolteacher, solicitor, or clergyman.

Expectant mothers worked as long as possible before their confinement was due, to maximise their earnings, and to ensure that as little time as possible was spent away from work. Grandparents also played their unselfish part in the economic life of the family, by taking responsibility for the 'rearing' of little ones in the case of larger than usual families – and families of five and six children were the rule rather than the exception! For these reasons, family ties and kinship were very important in Derry, and these ties were further strengthened and reinforced by shared experience, and economic necessity.

When it came to subscribing to a charity dear to their hearts, the girls were exceptionally generous, and Derry churches, of all denominations, have benefited from the donations of thousands of factory workers of several generations. These gifts have included plate, furnishings, linens, etc.

Departmental managers were normally male, and such an individual was known simply as 'The Man' – perhaps a contraction for 'The Manager', 'There the Man' indicated his approach. The toilets were known as 'Parlours', and were a favourite spot for the surreptitious smoke.

CHARLES GALLAGHER, *Acorns and Oak Leaves*, 1981

I AM ALLOWED AN EGG FOR BREAKFAST. I have my breakfast in the kitchen, when Mister and Missus have finished theirs in the dining room and when he has gone to work. I like best being alone for breakfast but often she is in with me, heating milk for the child and telling me all I should do and how I should do it.

She is very small. I am like a giant beside her. She likes this, that I make her look even smaller than she is. My mother liked it too. Small women are usually very proud of being small, I have often noticed – as if being small means that they are very clever and good babies, who normally could not be expected to do a single thing for themselves. 'And the size of her!' my father would say proudly when my mother had given a hand with the hay, or baked a big stack of scones for a *meitheal* – something as ordinary and easy as buttermilk scones, that size had no bearing on one way or the other. And she'd smile, as full of herself as a bonny boychild after a bowl of poundies, all thirteen stone of her, wee pet!

That's what himself calls the missus. Sometimes I am beside her in the kitchen when he comes in in the evenings. And over he comes and kisses her and says, 'My wee wee wee pet.' Three wees, like the three wee piggies. And gives me a look as if to say, You big ould heifer, you. And this even through the missus is expecting and has a huge tummy on her like a turnip. But all that does is make the rest of her look tinier. And to be honest, the rest of her is very slight and thin, not swollen up at all. I believe she's delicate, although they'd never let on.

She wears nice clothes – a dark blue skirt and a frilly blouse, snow white, starched (by me), a fresh blouse every second day. She sits in the kitchen and chats. 'Don't you miss your family?'

'Sometimes.'

'How many brothers and sisters have you?'

When I tell her – twelve – she gasps and smiles.

'Are they all still at home?'

They are. I'm the eldest.

'It must be strange for you, living in the city.'

'It's different.'

It is different. Every single thing about it is different, so that when I first came to Derry, first got off the train, first came into the McCallums' house, different from any house I had ever been in, I felt completely lost and very tiny, like a little spider or a fly. But I was still myself. I was myself, only smaller. That is the thing that I have found out. And after a few days I began to grow back to being my big self again, and the strange things all around me shrank back to being their own size.

'It's exciting,' I added. 'But you get used to it.'

'Exciting?' She could be as nice as you like when she was interested in something.

'Yes. It is all so different and that makes it exciting.'

'Maybe it is like going to a foreign country, where people speak a different language, and wear different clothes, and where everything looks strange?'

That's it to a tee. It was just like that. Foreign. Foreign language, foreign clothes, foreign place. But, you know, I don't think she knew what she was saying. When she said 'like a foreign country' she was laughing; she meant it was not, of course, really a foreign country. That's where she's wrong. She didn't seem to know at all that at home we speak a different language and that the houses are different and even the people look different. If she knew this, she thought it was unimportant, that they were differences that didn't count. She had never been to Gweedore. Or, maybe, anywhere.

'Have you been to a foreign country?' I asked.

'Och no. We go to Portrush on our holidays. That's it.' She wanted to go to France. Her friend had been there last year, staying in Paris. And she wanted to go to London. That's what she meant by foreign. 'No harm in dreaming,' she said. 'I'll never see further than Portrush. Or Dublin, if I'm lucky.'

I wondered what Portrush was like. She tried to tell me. There is the sea and a beach and a place for men to bathe and women to bathe. There is a promenade and a lot of hotels, and brass bands playing along the seafront in special stands, like merry-go-rounds. (What is a stand? What is a merry-go-round?) And people on holiday, walking about. There are children making sand castles and old men paddling. Sometimes I thought it sounded like Derry, sometimes like Gweedore. Sometimes I just could not picture it at all. I hoped she'd say, You'll see it yourself when we go in the summer, but she never did. It was January when I started with them, and I thought she would be having the baby at maybe Easter, if not sooner. Maybe they would not go to Portrush at all.

I had to do everything in the house. Clean everything, scrub everything, cook everything, wash everything, and also mind the baby. Missus did nothing, really. Nothing worth mentioning. She was too small, too delicate, too tired. At first I was tired too, very tired. I felt homesick because I was so tired. I would lie on my bed, when I finally got there at about eleven o'clock, and cry from tiredness. It was, I thought, as if I had come into a lovely place, a place like the Eastern world, the shining kingdoms I knew about from old stories, but had to work so hard there that the magic world turned into a nightmare.

After a while I became accustomed to the work and managed it better. And I must say that from the start I loved the house. It astonished me. The storytellers never described the insides of the castles and palaces the princes and princesses lived in at the end of the tale. They just said they were full of good things to eat and drink, and fine golden goblets and cups of silver. But they must have had other things in them. Lace cloths, silver vases of carnations, brass bowls with green plants growing in them, cabinets full of white china painted with roses. Mirrors, curly-legged tables and chairs. They must have had beds covered in silk sheets or snowy linen trimmed with crochet. Mrs McCallum's house was so cluttered up with such things that I felt I would never get to know them, and I could hardly imagine that she had ever had the time or the strength, let alone the money, to get them all.

ÉILÍS NÍ DHUIBHNE, 'Gweedore Girl' in *The Inland Ice*, 1997

ABBEY STREET DISTILLERY, LONDONDERRY
SOLE PROPRIETOR, ANDREW ALEXANDER WATT

IT WAS ALMOST WITH REGRET that we once more entered the train, as we realised that with the next stoppage our pleasant Irish Distillery Tour would come to an end. On leaving Limavady Junction, the rail runs close by the shores of Lough Foyle, and we were soon in sight of the Donegal Mountains. The tops were cloud-capped, here and there broken by a conical peak which appeared as though it had detached itself from the mass; the shadows of the setting sun were falling on the slopes, and the whole range had a mournful and oppressive look. On the right we caught glimpses of gentle hills, covered with plantations; here and there a village, and anon some ancient church, with its tower rising above the trees. All too quickly we found ourselves gliding into the station, and as we neared we had a view of Derry, the ancient city, and the prominent chimney-stacks of the Abbey Street Distillery. On emerging from the station we drove across the fine bridge, which is an ornament to the river and city, and sought our hotel for rest and refreshment.

The old-established Distillery which heads this Chapter, is the largest in Ireland; the buildings alone cover eight acres of ground. It is situated in the heart of the picturesque old city, the chief town of the county. The original name of the city was Derry, and it still retains its popular title. The name is from the Irish 'Doire', which signifies a place of oaks. About the year 1613 the English prefix of London was imposed upon it by the Irish Society, incorporated by charter of James I; the name of Londonderry was retained for many years by the colonists, but has now fallen into popular disuse. The town is of ancient date, and was many times besieged and plundered by the Danes. In 1689 occurred the famous siege of Derry, and the gallant struggle of the besieged, and how they were relieved, are matters of history.

The Distillery is close to the walls of the city, which are in a perfect state of preservation, and the ramparts thereon afford a fine promenade all round the town. 'Roaring Meg' is still there, but let us hope she will never be called upon to frighten another enemy. But to return to the Distillery. It would be impossible to describe fully the shape and position of the buildings, as they cover such a large area of ground. They are erected on the slope of a hill, and have, from time to time, been added to by the grandfather and the father of the present proprietor. At the end of the last century, it is recorded in the statistics of that period, that it was then used as a Distillery. In 1826 it came into the hands of Mr Andrew Alexander Watt, grandfather of the present proprietor, who was a leading merchant and alderman of the city, and head of most of the principal charitable institutions.

The water used in the Distillery comes from the Glashaugh Hills, and is collected in reservoirs on the Distillery property; besides this supply, there are wells in the yard for reducing and cooling.

The Wheat and Maize Stores are of immense proportions, as the following figures will testify: – No. 1 Building consists of three floors, 200 feet long by 150 feet, and contains 2,000 tons of wheat and barley; No. 2 Building is 200 feet long by 60 feet broad, and contains 1,000 tons of maize; No. 3 Building is also 200 feet long by 80 feet broad, and holds 2,000 tons of maize; No. 4 Building has four floors, each 150 feet long by 60 feet wide, and at the time of our visit contained 1,600 tons of grain. On the opposite side of the way there are two lofty Barley Floors, connected by a bridge. The floors are 200 feet long and 160 feet wide, and contained 2,000 tons of home-grown barley. Adjoining this is another four-storied building, 150 feet long by 60 feet wide, which contained 1,600 tons of barley, oats, and maize. The corn is elevated to the various floors and buildings by a steam-hoist. There is a Flour Mill in connection with the premises and business, the property of the proprietor, where a large trade has been carried on for some years past.

ALFRED BERNARD, *The Whisky Distillers of the United Kingdom*, 1987

LONDONDERRY HAS NOT THE AIR of an Irish town. There is there an activity and an industry which are not generally to be found in other parts of the country. The principal trade consists in linens, of which there is a market once or twice a week. It is surprising to note the speed with which the linen merchants examine the cloth. They stand on a sort of platform with a little desk before them, while the peasants carry their webs past and stop for just a moment. The merchant looks, and immediately mentions a price; if it is accepted, he marks it on the cloth, and the peasant goes to the office for payment. There is one merchant who, on every market day, buys in a single hour cloth to the value of three or four hundred pounds sterling.

It is very strange that, although the flax from which this linen is made grows in the country, they have never been able to save seed, and are obliged to bring it from America. The first manufactures of linen were established in Ireland by the Protestants who quitted France under the reign of Louis XIV, and carried their industry to another country. The exportation of this linen is a source of immense profit to Ireland. According to the researches I have been able to make into the subject of the exportation of linen, salted beef, and grain, it would appear that in the last ten years (in spite of the great number of absentee rich who draw away enormous sums) Ireland has received annually about two hundred thousand pounds sterling more than she has paid out of the country. If such a state of affairs can be continued for some time, this country will soon reach a pitch of prosperity which few nations can hope to equal.

CHEVALIER DE LATOCNAYE, *Promenade d'un Français dans l'Irlande*
(*A Frenchman's Walk Through Ireland*), 1798, translation by John Stevenson 1917

A LONGSIDE THESE REMARKABLE MEN were many others from the city council (the first to share power), commerce, industry and voluntary groups, and above them all towered Northern Ireland's only internationally recognised statesman, John Hume. He is a man of prodigious physical and intellectual capability. He smokes too much, he eats too much, sometimes he may drink too much. He does not sleep enough and he does not exercise enough, but he works like a man possessed. He drives tens of thousands of miles from Aldergrove to Derry to Dublin to Donegal. How he has ended up in the ditch only once is a miracle. He has no protection because he does not want it and because any young RUC officer would, in John's judgement, be more at risk than he. He and his family therefore are enormously courageous in the face of loyalist threats and Sinn Féin blackmail. Like all great men, behind him stands a great woman; his wife Pat has looked after him and his constituency and maintained his morale when the black dog of depression has threatened to overwhelm him.

He has a vision of bringing the two cultures together through respect and understanding, and he has promoted that vision in Northern Ireland, London, Dublin and Washington with consistency, conviction and flair. Like every really good schoolteacher, he can explain and illustrate in ways that even the most hardened sceptic can find difficult to resist. By his reason and his force of personality he has dominated and dictated both the Washington and the Dublin approach to the problems of the North. Single-handedly he has wrested the initiative towards his corner and kept the arguments to his agenda, despite the relentless opposition of the unionists, the distrust of the Northern Ireland Office and the ambivalence of the Foreign Office.

He can infuriate the British by his refusal to be specific, by his use of generalities, by his change of tactics, venues or times, by what they perceive as his inconsistencies. But John knows what he wants. It is power-sharing in Northern Ireland acceptable to both sides, underwritten by both governments, with as many cross-border institutions as possible, which one day, with the support of unionists, could lead to a political system covering the island of Ireland. He has all the attributes to succeed. He is the one political leader in Northern Ireland capable of forging an acceptable way through for both communities. But sometimes, at the crucial moment, he fails to go that extra inch with the unionists. Somewhere in the recesses of his psyche there is a nationalist Derry reflex that gets the better of him, and sometimes he appears ready to risk offending his colleagues and losing his supporters by courting Sinn Féin while he temporises on attracting even moderate unionists to his view.

For years he had been demanding a bigger input into attracting investment to Derry and harnessing his contacts in America to that cause. No one had better qualifications, yet he was left by the Industrial Development Board to struggle on his own. But as always with John, the struggle intensified the effort. The beginnings of the regeneration had begun in the early eighties with the building of the Richmond shopping centre (to a design which did little to flatter the city's remaining historic architecture) and the opening of the Foyle Bridge. But whenever I went to Londonderry or deputations came to see me, I was always reminded of what was happening in Belfast and how little Derry received in comparison.

I knew that regeneration in the north-west of the province would provide the SDLP and their leader with the proof they required to show their people that co-operation with the British government could bring results and that economic and social improvement could bring opportunities denied them by violence and deprivation. We also observed that the IRA were finding that a bomb in Derry brought a very much stronger reaction from their own community that one in Belfast city centre, and if we could halt the bombs in the north-west it would become more difficult to justify destroying 'economic' targets elsewhere.

RICHARD NEEDHAM, *Battling for Peace*, 1998

GRANDMOTHER WAS THE YOUNGEST in a family of eleven and not one of them, she remarked, ever came out deaf and dumb from anything. She was not entirely *for* the family doctor. She did not condemn him as Father condemned him but she diffused a great and sincere doubt about his efficiency. This was not the doctor who had a daughter named Valetta. He was the doctor with the ten children and a beautiful wife, who, for some reason, which was never gone into, 'was destroying herself'. There were only the two doctors available. Mother would have had the other doctor, she said, 'if it were not for his wife'. I was made conscious of the fact that there *were* doctors' wives, even if they never came with the doctors. They were doctors' problems which were kept at home.

Mother paid her doctor by the year. No matter who was ill in the household it was understood that he could be sent for at any hour of the day or night and in any sort of weather. She had a lawyer on the same system, but the lawyer could only be seen when it suited him.

She took me to the lawyer's. His name was written backwards upon a frosted door. All his books were the same size, and all in mourning. They were bound in black with funeral cards for the titles. He had a very hungry clerk who ate his moustache – and put it out again.

Mother was in great trouble, she told the lawyer. She was demented because Mr Tilly would neither answer letters nor call upon Mr Dawlay. The lawyer said that Mr Tilly was a robber baron and that the only thing for Mother to do was to beard the lion in his den. Mr Tilly, it appeared, was the owner of the factory at the beginning of Carlisle Bridge. When you drove down Carlisle Road, past the doctor's house where his car and coachman were always standing, you saw the square factory. It had very clean windows in which stacks of shirts moved and from which sewing machines whirred like beehives. When you drove over the bridge and got exactly to the middle you saw that there was almost as much of the factory below the bridge, level with the riverside, as there was on top. It always affected me like a dog that you hadn't expected would bite. It was a very bare building, very cold and *closed*. It held itself together like a set of clenched teeth.

Mother said she would take me with her when she went to Mr Tilly's.

We drove there through the town and up towards the new cathedral and out along the high Creggan Road. It was a windy day. Every time we passed a garden all the flowers were nodding. When we got to Mr Tilly's gate Mother said that I was to stay with MacDaid. MacDaid was to drive me up and down the road. I didn't mind at all not having to see Mr Tilly. It was very brave of Mother to see him alone. She said that she would be out again presently.

KATHLEEN COYLE, *The Magical Realm*, 1943

IN WINTER, THE MEN TOOK WHAT CASUAL WORK was available in Derry, and Nellie and Peggie worked in the shirt factories, the staple local industry for women. The family income was supplemented by the mother, Maggie, who was famous in the Bogside for her toffee apples. She boiled up vats of toffee in her kitchen, dipped the apples into them, and left the delicious confections to dry on a tray that poked appetisingly out of the front window of her house. Queues used form on a Friday night outside Maggie McIntyre's house as children arrived to spend their pocket-money. Out of season, she sold toffee squares in wax paper. The kitchen was regularly examined by a government health-inspector, anxious to ensure that the Catholic subjects of Her Majesty were eating only the very best fast food.

Maggie also tried to augment income by a daily gamble on the horses.

Her grandchildren were a familiar local sight, betting slip and coins in hand, as they trotted a well-worn path between her home and the betting shop, which was located in a back lane. It was Maggie's money which paid for headstones for those babies born dead to her daughter Nellie, who had seventeen miscarriages and still-births as well as five children.

NELL McCAFFERTY, *Peggy Deery*, 1987

DERRY WAS A BREEDING GROUND for showbands. Three factors contributed to the boom. Firstly, a strong musical tradition already existed: there was a proliferation of brass and reed bands; boys learned to play the trumpet as early as fifteen or sixteen. Secondly, unemployment was rampant: the notion of converting music into money, even while on the dole, was widespread. Men were out of work; women were the breadwinners, and many got jobs in the shirt factories. By night, unemployed men dabbled in bands. Thirdly, dance-band musicians were always in demand in Derry because of the British and American bases, whose presence fuelled the growth of bands and orchestras. Sit-down bands played Jimmy Lally orchestrations – or 'orcs', as they were popularly known.

The business was non-sectarian: if a band needed a trumpeter, nobody asked whether the applicant was a Catholic or a Protestant. Every Derry youngster with any musical ability wanted to play in a showband. There was a time when 'You couldn't throw a stone without hitting someone who sang or played in one,' Coulter explained. 'To me there was never a problem utilising my music to make money. Looking at my long-term goals, I was aware that music could be a means to a livelihood.' To this day, he makes no apologies for his strong sense of commercialism. Critics try to dismiss him by saying he's trivial and geared to trying to be too popular. He retorts: 'Well, if it was that easy to appeal to such a wide audience consistently, then everybody would be doing it.'

VINCENT POWER, *Send 'Em Home Sweatin'*, 1991

THE HIRING FAIRS, OR 'RABBLES' as they were called, were held twice a year in May and November and covered a period of three weeks. The period of contract was six months. If the twelfth of May or November happened to fall on a Wednesday, that was release day. If the twelfth happened to fall on a Thursday, as it often did, release day didn't occur until the following Wednesday, so the farmer had a free week. The first 'rabble' then was release day, when all the wee boys and girls who had been hired would come home and spend a week with their families. The following Wednesday would be the hiring fair proper when farmers would be looking for new servants, and wee boys and girls for new places.

The third 'rabble' would take place the following Wednesday but it was never popular. Only those farmers who had failed to get someone suitable the previous Wednesday, and boys and girls who had failed to get a suitable place, would attend.

It was the first time I had been to Derry and I found the place a bit bewildering. Everyone seemed to be in a great hurry. The place where the hiring took place was at the top of the Bogside in an area called the Diamond. There was a big crowd there that day, mostly wee boys and girls who like myself carried a pathetic little bundle under their arms, which was just a change of washing. Strange farmers were looking us over. Soon a prosperous-looking gentleman approached and, addressing my father, inquired: 'What are ye esking for the wee boy?'

'Six pounds,' my father replied.

'He's a bit wee. How old is he? Can he milk? Is he any good with horses?' the man wanted to know. At last a bargain was struck for five pounds and ten shillings. The stranger took my bundle, gave me a shilling and told me to meet him back on the Diamond at four o'clock sharp. Then he and my father went off to the nearest 'snug' to clinch the deal over a bottle of stout. Taking the little bundle from you, once the bargain had been struck, was a cute move by the farmer because, as long as you were in possession of it, this was an indication that you were still not hired. So, by taking it from you, the farmer was guarding against anyone else making you a better offer. Also it was a kind of assurance that you would turn up at the appointed place later.

I went looking at shop windows; I'd never seen so many shops before. I found an eating-house and had a great blow-out, and still had thruppence change from my employer's shilling. I wandered down to the quayside and watched boats being unloaded. Derry was a busy seaport in those days. I was fascinated by the dray-horses as they took their heavy loads up the steep incline at the trot, their drivers having to run to keep up with them. Back in the Diamond I met my father again; we both agreed there was no point in him hanging around any longer. The tears weren't far from the surface on either of us as we said our brief farewells, particularly me as I watched him disappear down the Bogside to catch the train home. But I was a big man now. I was hired. Promptly at four o'clock my boss returned and took me down a street to where a horse and trap were waiting and being loaded with groceries. There was a lady present but she didn't speak. When all the groceries were loaded, I was told to get in the back. It was now almost dark, the streetlamps were coming alive, and it was very cold as we set off at a brisk trot southwards. It had been a long day and I was beginning to feel tired and miserable, knowing that each clip-clop of the horse's hooves was taking me a little bit farther away from home.

PATRICK J. DEVLIN, *That Was the Way of It*, 2001

She delivered them here, and down in The Bog,
she delivered wains down in The Bog,
and many's a time all she got was a glass of whiskey.
But I remember hearing a story
that one night the door went at two o'clock in the morning
and it was some man from down the Lecky Road.
Now this was at the time of the Black and Tans
and there was a curfew and all the rest of it in the streets,
and he said,
'Nurse, my wife's in labour, could you come down?'
And she said,
'Go on you down, son, I'll get dressed and come down.'
And apparently always put on the nurse's uniform,
almost like a clergyman or a priest –
she went into her professional role –
so the uniform went on to deliver the baby
and she was going down Fahan Street,
the old Fahan Street then.
And the police patrol – the Black and Tans –
apparently they *did* shoot on sight –
or beat you up on sight –
whatever it was happened.
So she had to show them
what she was carrying in her bag
was actually the nurse's tools.
So that must have been very frightening –
that was a woman, maybe thirties, forty,
but headed off herself
because my granda or the big daughter Nellie
would have been in to watch the rest of the wains –
and heading off into the night yourself
with the political turmoil ...
But I remember another story
of her going down
to deliver the wain in the middle of the night.
And it came eight o'clock in the morning,
she wasn't back, and – you know the men –
Billy McGahey,
he wasn't about to get
six or seven youngsters ready for school.
So my granny's eldest, my Aunt Nellie,
was sent down to the house,
'Go you down
and see what's happening with your granny ...'

(there was a lot more interchange then
between The Fountain and The Bog).
So Nellie ran down to see how long she would be
and apparently it was a particularly difficult labour.
And the man lived down the Lecky Road
next door to a pub.
And Nellie went in, and the man was sitting –
he was actually sitting at the kitchen table –
sleeping.
And she says 'Where's my mother?'
'Oh,' he says, 'Nurse McGahey's up with ...'.
So Nellie went up the stairs
and my Grannie was lying, either tired
or tired and emotional,
actually in the bed
with the woman that was having the baby.
So just at that time
the woman started to go into the last stages of labour.
So my granny got up,
up all night exhausted,
did the business
and the baby was delivered ...

ANONYMOUS, 'Deliveries', in *The Fountain* (ed. Leon McAuley), 1993

WILLIAM SCOTT
Founder of the Derry Shirt-Industry

IN THE AUTUMN OF 1831 an elderly gentleman carrying a parcel of hand-made linen shirts boarded the steamer *Foyle* for the twenty-hour voyage from Derry to Glasgow. William Scott was already sixty-six years old but he was a man of great energy and enterprise and far from planning a peaceful retirement he was about to put a new business idea into effect. William Scott, born in Balloughry in County Derry, had spent all his working life as a weaver in the city, first as an apprentice to Mr Gilmour of Artillery Street and then in his own business in Weaver's Row.

He was part of the great linen-industry for which Ulster was famous. For generations farmers had grown and bleached flax which was spun into yarn by their wives and daughters and then sold to weavers who produced linen cloth. The cloth was in turn sold in drapers' shops and made up by housewives, domestic servants or professional seamstresses. This was the traditional way in which clothes and household linens had been made for hundreds of years.

But in the early decades of the nineteenth century enormous changes took place which affected people's lives not only in Ireland but throughout the world. The industrial revolution meant that goods which had traditionally been made in the home were now being produced in factories. The invention in 1825, by James Kay, of a new wet-spinning method led to the collapse of the domestic spinning-industry and women who had earned their livings as spinners had to seek other means of livelihood. Many of them turned to sprigging or flowering, a special sort of white embroidery on white linen. In counties Derry, Donegal and Tyrone there were thousands of spinners, all expert needlewomen, looking for work. The growing populations of large industrial cities, and of America and the colonies, wanted to buy ready-made clothes. Men in particular wanted inexpensive, ready-to-wear shirts which could be bought without delay in a drapery shop or man's outfitters.

These new shirts, however, were not the old style linen or flannel garment. Previously for the fashionable Regency Buck, a shirt had been an item of underwear and was hardly visible. The space between the waistcoat and neck was filled with an enormous stock like those worn by King William IV. The new nineteenth-century look dictated a lower-cut waistcoat, a smaller tie, a stiff collar and a starched white linen shirt-front. A man's shirt was now an article of fashion.

GERALDINE McCARTER, *Derry's Shirt Tale*, 1991

B EING A PROFESSIONAL MUSICIAN IN STROKE CITY meant that one did not have to sign on the dole as often as one did when one was not a professional musician.

A professional musician was one who derived the bulk of his income from the playing of music, buoyed by a small but essential weekly financial supplement gleaned from the Government by making par-for-the-course false criminal claims at Casual Box 6; one was not a professional musician if the reverse applied ... a fine distinction, but it seemed important at the time. This practice has marked me for life to the extent that modern talk of dole fraud goes right over my head. Why not defraud a Government funded by money collected from English people? Nobody I knew paid taxes, and rightly so.

The starving began when one clinched a permanent job in a musically decent band that had been together for some time. The first inkling of the Great Hunger usually came when bands were forced to tour Irish clubs in England.

This bold move was necessitated by the onset of the annual season of Lent, when showbands fled Catholic Ireland like rats from a trap; religious tradition having decreed that all dancing must cease during that

Holy Time ... Dust Bowl time for musicians.

The season of Lent is the period of forty days lasting from Ash Wednesday to Holy Saturday, observed as a time of penance and fasting, commemorating Jesus's fasting in the wilderness.

God was obviously not a deity keen on fasting alone. Many musicians joined Him, though for different reasons. Starving during Lent was but a harbinger of what was to come ... a useful introduction.

Six weeks of traipsing around England and Scotland (no Wales; the Irish don't like Wales ... too much like home), financial welfare depending on the caprice of a usually demagogic bandleader who would frequently disappear for days on end with big-titted Irish nurses from Galway, was a surefire method of losing weight.

Many a carefree day was spent staring penniless through the scuffed windows of back-street Glaswegian, Mancunian or Shepherd's Bushian boarding houses, avoiding shrill, fat landladies, subsisting on a balanced diet of milk and Mars bars, waiting for news of the next gig.

GERRY ANDERSON, *Surviving in Stroke City*, 1999

THERE USED TO BE A GREAT DISTILLERY IN DERRY, but now that is closed. Modern Ireland doesn't drink what it used to drink. And incredible as it sounds to the decent English reader, there are plenty of Irishmen who will say that the country in the old days was encouraged to drink. What has England always done with any country she wished to conquer, they will ask! Has it not been opium for the East, and didn't we once force a war on China on purpose to make them take opium? And I myself do not know. Did we? And then the Irishman will go on to say that our authorities actually encouraged Irish drink. Certainly they themselves have tightened up their own drinking laws. There is Saint Patrick's Day, and in the British times it was a recognized occasion for a general argue; and to-day every bar in Eire will be closed tight down for the National Day. I only mention the point to help to show an Irish point of view.

JOHN GIBBONS, *Ireland – the New Ally*, 1938

THERE WAS GREAT TALK about what a quare place the factory was an' how ye could make a fortune an' be drivin' about in a big swanky car after bein' there for a wheen of years. The day a was sent for the interview there was this nice man called the personnel officer that asked me a lot of questions an' things like what me hobbies were an' why a wanted te work in the factory. A toul him what me hobbies were an' that a wanted te work in the factory because me ma an' da heard that there was gran' money te be made. He asked me what age a was an' could he see me birth certificate an' a showed it te him. Then he patted me on the head an' said that if a wanted the job a was te come on the followin' Monday mornin' at nine a-clock an' the wages was two poun' six an' nine pence, an' if a iver had any problems a was te come an' see him an' a said a would.

The followin' Monday mornin' a turned up an' a was sick for a'm no good at travelin in buses. A woman called a supervisor took me te a big room way a wile lot of noise in it an' toul me that it was the machine room an' a was te learn te be a machinist. Then she took me te an' office an' toul me that a had te get fitted for an overall. A girl way wile nice perfume an' make-up on come an' asked me what size a was an' a said a didn't know. She asked me what size of bra a took an' a said a didn't wear a bra. Then she made a tired sort of face an' said, a suppose a'll just have te measure ye, an' she begin' te pull out drawers an' push them in again like they were hir mortal enemies.

She got a tape measure out an' started te measure me, first roun' the waist. She said a was wile thin. Nixt she measured me hips an' said, oom, a suppose it'll have te be small woman. Then she measured me chest an' just laughed an' went an' got an overall an' give it te the supervisor an' said, it'll have te be shortened but that's your problem, an' they both laughed.

The supervisor took me te a machine an' toul me that if a was te learn how te work it the first thing a should know was how te switch it on. That didn't take long so then she showed me how te thread it an' how te work the pedals. After a while when a got the hang of it, it was great fun seein' the rows of sewin' bein' done without any trouble atall an' a allowed that me ma could fairly do way a sewin' machine.

The first real job a done in the factory was turn up the hem of me overall an' the supervisor said a done a quare good job for a beginner. Wheniver it was dinner time she took me te a canteen an' toul me that a could buy me dinner for ten shillin's a week if a wanted te. A toul hir that a had sandwiches so she said a could sit at any table a liked. A went an' set down at an empty table an' as soon as a started te ate, five ouler girls come over an' stood aroun' just lookin' at me.

Wan of them said, are you a catholic or a protestant? A said nothin'. Another of them took a cigarette lighter outa hir pocket an' lit it an' hel' the flame close te me face an' said, we only allow catholics te sit at this table. A got up an' walked away an' set at another table. They all follied after me an' kept on askin' was a catholic or protestant? In the en' a said a was a christian. Then the wan way the cigarette lighter said, we know you're a prod. A said, if ye know so much why de ye waste yer breath askin' questions? She lit the lighter again an' set fire te the side of me hair. A screamed an' beat the flames out way me han's. Then a woman from our town seen all the hullabaloo an' come over te see what was goin' on.

The girls said a was a prod but she said, what nonsense an' toul them who a was. Then all the girls said they were sorry but they were sure a would understan' that a body couldn't be too careful. They asked me what a thought of the factory an' a said it was gran'. Then they toul me that a should come te a hop way them that night because the hops were great an' all the lovely fellas of the day would be there but a said a would be goin' home.

After a had finished aten a asked the woman from our town te tell me where the lavatory was an' she showed me. When a got there a nearly passed out way the cloud of thick smoke that hit me on the face as soon as a opened the door. Inside there were twenty lavatories all in a row down wan side an' twenty han' basins in a row down the other side. Girls an' weemen were sittin' on tap of all the han' basins smokin', or combin' their hair, or puttin' on makeup. All the lavatory doors were closed an' the loudest laughin' an' wailin' an' thumpin' an' screechin' was goin' on in behine them.

A walked up the full length of the room an' seen that none of them was empty so a stood an' waited in a corner for somebody te come out because a was in a hurry. A was standin' there for a long time for as soon as a door opened an' the people inside come out, a whole rush of new wans would burst in before me.

The bell went for the en' of dinnertime before a got a chance te go an' a was just puttin' the bolt in when two weemen come an' shoved the door in me face. Wan of them said, hey you, what de ye think ye'r doin' in the ladies toilets, an' a said a had to go. She said, ye have a cheek goin' te the ladies toilets an' you a wee fella, so a toul hir that a was a girl. Then they both grabbed me an' started to rub their han's all over me chest an' say, ye'r not a girl, ye'r a wee fella. A started te cry an' tell them te lave me alone but they hel' on te me an' started te pull me knickers down. A took a bite outa wan of them an' she thumped me on the face an' made me nose bleed an' said a had no fun in me atall an' couldn't take a joke. Then they both went away an' left me alone.

FRANCES MOLLOY, *No Mate for the Magpie*, 1985

THE SITUATION OF THE CITY OF DERRY is one of striking beauty, lying as it does at a lovely curve of the splendid River Foyle. And in the old city there is much to think about, much to dream about, and lessons which will not be lost on those who have the parts to read and the grace to understand. And it is fitting that we should revere these, our noble forbears, not in any spirit of religious fanaticism, but with high thoughts of the blow which they struck for the liberties of future generations.

To-day, with a population of about 50,000, Derry is the second city of Ulster, and whilst within recent times it was an important centre of the shipbuilding and distilling trades, it is now almost entirely dependent upon the shirt and collar-making industry. This is a misfortune, for it means that whilst there is ample work for the female artisan population, employment for men is not easily come by. And a severe blow was dealt to the distributing trades of Derry by the setting up of the Border almost on the outskirts of the city. For Derry was to all intents and purposes the commercial capital of Donegal, and at a swoop that large territory was cut off by an impassable tariff wall. As a result, some of the biggest wholesale houses in Ireland have had to close their doors, but a people whose ancestors withstood the forces of James of the Fleeing could not be lacking in determination in the face of adverse circumstances, and already the commercial genius of Derry is accommodating itself to the new and untoward conditions.

Like the linen industry, the business of shirtmaking is not without its romance and interest. Until the years following Waterloo there did not exist such a thing as a ready-made shirt. Material had to be bought and made up at home, but when the cravat fell out of favour and stiff shirts and collars began to be worn, the domestic shirtmakers found that their abilities were becoming somewhat overtaxed. A good housewife might find the creation of an ornamental cravat well within her powers, but a stiff collar was also a stiff proposition. And so William Scott, a linen weaver of Derry, conceived the revolutionary idea of placing on the market professionally-made shirts and collars which could be bought over the counter. Scott made his first experiment through a Glasgow draper, and it was so successful that soon all Scotland was buying Derry shirts. Australia, a land of many womenless men at that time, was equally enthusiastic, but London did not receive the idea kindly for another five years. Eventually the ready-made shirt found universal favour, and Scott found himself at the head of a new and thriving industry. And with typical Ulster thoroughness he set himself to organise this industry on a large and profitable basis. In Derry he cut out his shirts, and for the stitching of them he set up sewing depots in the county, and in Tyrone and Donegal. And he was lucky there too, for women were everywhere out of work since the spinning of flax by machinery had rendered the old spinning-wheel well-nigh obsolete. From the country the finished shirts came back to Derry, and there they were laundered and sent out to the four corners of the earth.

With the invention of the sewing machine came one William Tillie from Scotland to set up a machine shirt factory in Derry about 1850. And to-day there are almost forty factories in Derry employing about six thousand operatives, whilst the old tradition of 'out workers' still continues and absorbs nearly ten thousand country stitchers in the Counties of Derry, Tyrone and Donegal.

RICHARD HAYWARD, *In Praise of Ulster*, 1938, revised edition 1946

THE MANUFACTURES ARE NOT VERY CONSIDERABLE: the principal is that of meal, for which there are several corn-mills, of which one erected by Mr Schoales in 1831, and worked by a steam-engine of 18-horse power, and another subsequently by Mr Leatham, worked by an engine of 20-horse power, are the chief: the recent extension of this branch of trade has made meal an article of export instead of import, as formerly; in 1831, 553 tons were imported, and in 1834 6,950 tons were exported. In William-street are a brewery and distillery; there are copper-works which supply the whole of the north-west of Ulster, and afford regular employment to 27 men; two coach-factories; and a corn-mill and distillery at Pennyburn, and another at Waterside. A sugar-house was built in 1762, in what is still called Sugar-house-lane, but was abandoned in 1809; the buildings were converted into a glass manufactory in 1820, but this branch of business was carried on for a few years only.

SAMUEL LEWIS, *Topographical Dictionary of Ireland*, 1837

I had seen nothing like it for years.
Almost a generation back, my father taught me
To tip my cap-brim at every passing
Identifiable church. Even then,
I squirmed; and when my mother died
He stitched on his overcoat sleeve
A diamond of black, so people wouldn't ask.

In Ireland now, people on my bus
Each morning passing the Pennyburn chapel
Rapidly bless themselves. I get out
And go to teach their sons
The use of semi-colons; explain Joyce's
Aesthetics; and read, with appropriate voices,
Magwitch in the graveyard, or 'This other Eden'.

And with Form Three, *Pygmalion*.
I sketch a map of London, marking in
Bow Bells; drop every aitch, that they call
*H*aitch; put on, for them to giggle at
And mimic, the Cockney sounds I make these days
Only when drunk or angry.
Professor Higgins wins his bet again.

Later, we rehearse the Nativity Play,
Sticking down tape to mark where we will set,
In blackout, cardboard walls against
Painted winter; where, in spotlight,
Sixteen and embarrassed, wired-up
In tinselled halo, the angel
Must arrive with his annual message.

When people ask, I tell
Some story of my life, each day opening
My classroom door to hear the vowels of home

PAUL WILKINS, 'Nativity Play', *Pasts*, 1979

MACDAID DROVE ME TO A PLACE where we could see the river and the
railway station where we took the train for the shore. It had the low
insignificance of a woodshed from that distance. Beyond it were the quays
where I had walked with Father, where the water *plonk-plonked* beneath the
boards and I had to catch his hand. On the slope opposite, on the Waterside,
we saw the path coming down from the military barracks. We saw the wall
of the barracks with the toy soldiers in the sentry boxes. MacDaid spat when
he mentioned them. The tiny ferryboat was pulling a silver line through the
water across to the Guildhall. We drove up the road and came back again to
the same spot. MacDaid made me look down the hill, through the trees
below us. There was a set of buildings enfolded by a wall like the picture of
Cistercian monasteries. Inside the wall there were bunches of men wearing
tam-o'-shanters. They were weeding and digging and watering – a group of
gardeners. 'Do you see them?' MacDaid said with a terrible, dire significance
in his voice. Yes, I said, I saw them. He told me it was the County Asylum
and that all these men were mad. 'Look well,' he said in the dire, ponderous
voice, '*you might see somebody you knew there!*' His voice frightened me. I
looked very intently down upon the mad gardeners and recognised none
of them. They were all wearing tam-o'-shanters.

KATHLEEN COYLE, *The Magical Realm*, 1943

IN SEPTEMBER 1951, I WAS NOTIFIED of my transfer to the County Police
Headquarters at Victoria Barracks in Strand Road, Derry City. Although
it was a routine transfer, and I should have expected it, I was disappointed at
having to leave Eglinton. I found it especially hard to take my leave of
Sergeant Grace. I did not realise for several years the extent to which he had
influenced my development as a constable in the RUC. For his part, he was

genuinely sad to see me go. Less than two weeks later, he wrote to me. His manner of expression was simple, direct and sincere. I felt unworthy of his praise, wishing I had done more and stayed longer, and yet I drew from his words a degree of confidence in my ability to be a good constable.

My arrival at Victoria Barracks was treated casually. It was the RUC's County Headquarters, and personnel – especially at constable level – were coming and going all the time. The offices, kitchen and dining-room were on the ground floor, with sleeping accommodation upstairs. I was pleased to find one large, albeit sparsely furnished, recreation-room, amongst the rows of offices and dormitories. My own room was on the first floor, at the rear of the building. It overlooked extensive cattle pens, which stretched almost the entire length of a fairly narrow, cobbled street. Beyond them lay the docks and quays of Derry's harbour. The noise and smell of the cattle awaiting live shipment filled my bedroom, especially during the warm summers of 1952 and 1953.

The windows of the spartan dining-room also looked out over the pens. Against the opposite wall of the room were our individual lockers, in which we needed to store supplementary food, as Victoria Barracks had a 'skeleton mess', producing only a cooked midday meal. The main course was predictable, with meat, potatoes and vegetables, except on Fridays, when we had fish to meet the religious obligation of Catholic officers – in truth, it was a welcome variant for us all. Other than that, men in residence were required to provide their own food for both breakfast and tea. Since wartime rationing continued through the early 1950s, basic foodstuffs were still in short supply. Hence, on my cycling trips into Donegal in the Republic of Ireland, where no rationing existed, I invariably returned with my saddle-bag full of food, and cigarettes or tobacco for those constables who smoked. Officers of the Garda Síochána (the Republic's police force) in the border area soon recognised me on my blue bicycle, and allowed me a sensible degree of immunity from search – something I never abused.

Even with such forays into the Republic, I found that my mess bill, together with the cost of extra food, totalled almost £15 each month. This was more than half of a probationary constable's net pay, then around £27 a month. After rail fares to Belfast once a month to see Jean, I had little left for personal savings towards, I hoped, our eventual marriage. Studiously avoiding debt of any sort, it was only occasionally that I could make some financial contribution to my mother.

The strictures of life in Victoria Barracks brought about a very real sense of comradeship between the constables, the majority of whom were young, with only a few older bachelors or married men 'living in'. The small group of men of varying ages who dressed neatly in suits I identified as detectives, either in the Criminal Investigation Department (CID) or Special Branch. The former was responsible for investigating routine crime, including serious assault, burglary and theft, while the latter was, and remains, responsible for uncovering terrorist crime and keeping track of subversive organisations.

Derry has had a long and turbulent history. It is not only Northern Ireland's second city, but, being so close to the border, is the main town for a substantial part of County Donegal. With reliable bus and rail services to and from the Republic, there was always a steady flow of shoppers and business people across the border. Our police Subdistrict itself was principally occupied by business premises and factories for pork processing and shirt manufacturing. Consequently, large numbers of workers from the densely populated urban parts of Derry, and the surrounding rural areas, poured in and out each working day. We found that much of the crime in our Subdistrict was committed by criminals and juvenile delinquents from outside it. Juvenile crime was a very real problem but an understandable one, when there were many children from deprived homes, in a city with high unemployment and few recreational facilities.

SIR JOHN HERMON, *Holding the Line*, 1997

IN THE AUTUMN OF 1887 ALICE WENT to Derry to take up a post as a governess at the Ladies' Collegiate School run by the Misses MacKillip. There were two other governesses with whom she made friends, Mademoiselle Cazalong taught French and Alice nicknamed her 'La Marsellaise'. In return Mademoiselle referred to Alice as 'Meeligano'.

The other governess was the young music teacher, Marjorie Arthur who was also Alice's room-mate. Alice referred to her as 'The Highland Lassie' because she was from Scotland. Her mother's people were MacDonalds from Skye.

Throughout her life Alice never suffered fools gladly. Conversely, when she gave loyalty to a cause or a person her devotion was absolute.

Alice found in Marjorie Arthur a friend who was the perfect foil for her vivid personality. Both were fun-loving and full of laughter. But Marjorie was also gentle and serene, where Alice was impelled by a more aggressive spirit. This deep friendship, through tragedy, was to be the genesis of some of Alice's finest verse.

This was in the future. The academic year 1887–88 was a happy year for La Marsellaise, The Highland Lassie and Meeligano. Alice was the only one who was in her native land and she became an unofficial guide to the countryside around. She was free at a certain time each week, whereas the other two had to alternate school duties on a two week rota.

Thus one week Mademoiselle would appear before her and stamp her foot. Years later Alice could still recall her voice: 'Meeligano! put down zat seely newspaper deer-r-r-rectly. It is only on von day in ze fortnight I ask you to valk vid me. Sacre au nom d'un chien! It vill be dark at five o'clock.

Bring me somefare today!'

So Alice would take her perhaps to Corrody Hill to look down on Derry City which, she said over ten years later: 'appeared under a frosty sky, with the wide Foyle flowing around it ... Far away on the horizon's edge, where the sky was scarlet, stood a line of mountains blue as sapphire, and the red river seemed to come like a fiery serpent all the way from there to the walls of Derry'.

Alice loved such scenery and was able to describe vividly many parts of Ireland seen in different moods, especially Donegal. Proudly she showed her two friends Lough Swilly, Glendermot, Aonach Lough, Culmore Ferry, Prehen Wood and – one of her favourite places – the Grianan of Aileach.

SHEILA TURNER JOHNSTON, *Alice: A Life of Alice Milligan*, 1994

O N SATURDAY, WAS LAUNCHED FROM THE BUILDING YARD of that enterprising gentleman, Mr William Coppin, the splendid ship named the 'City of Derry' of 450 tons register. For symmetry of model, soundness of material, and style of workmanship she is not excelled in the merchant marine of the United Kingdom. Thursday has been fixed for the imposing operations, but it was unavoidably deferred till the above day. There are many things entirely new in the construction of this fine vessel. The knees which fasten her upper and lower deck beams are made of angle and plate iron, so exceedingly strong, and occupying so little space, that it is calculated that the gain of room in the hold will be worth £100 freight on a cargo to Calcutta – a matter of serious importance to the owner. The stanchions that support her hold beams are light hollow columns of cast iron, through which from the deck to the keel run maleable iron bolts, effectually preventing the decks from elevation or depression. On looking aloft you are forcibly struck with the light and tasteful appearance of her tops, which are entirely constructed of iron by an ingenious contrivance of the builder. The rigging is attached to very strong swivels, which entirely does away with the clumsy method heretofore in use of passing the shrouds round the mast head, where water constantly lodges, and speedily decomposes the rope and mast. She is built of British and African Oak, and is put in Lloyd's books in the first class, for 12 years, the longest period allowed any British ship. Her cabin accommodation, for its extent, is of the first order, and her sleeping cabins are furnished with side lights, which serve the double purpose of light and ventilation. The style of painting is very classic, and reflects great credit on the Derry artist who executed the work.

The 'City of Derry', as we stated in our last, is the property of our much esteemed fellow-citizen, Gardner Boggs, Esq., now resident in Liverpool, and is to be in the East India and China trade. It reflects much credit on the owner having her built here, affording an opportunity of developing the talent and ingenuity of Mr Coppin in naval architecture. We understand that Mr Boggs is so much pleased with the ship that another is to be laid down for the same trade of much larger dimensions.

The novelty of witnessing a launch collected a vast assemblage of all ranks of our fellow-citizens, and we were glad to see present so many of the fairer sex, for whose accommodation Mr Coppin had erected comfortable stands, commanding a good view of the ways to the river. This presence contributed not a little to enliven the scene, and, through the kindness of Major Crofton and Captain McClintock, the bands of the 83d depot and Derry staff were in attendance, whose spirit stirring music heightened the enjoyment of the spectators.

The 'City of Derry' gaily bedecked with a rainbow variety of flags and streamers, majestically moved into the tide amidst the thunders of cannon and the cheers of the delighted multitude, the ceremony of naming her having been performed by Captain Ramsay. Soon her anchor dropped, and the bands played very appropriately, 'We'll gang nae mair to yon town.'

It will give us much pleasure to notice many a launch from the yard of the same gentleman.

ANONYMOUS, from *The Londonderry Journal*, 12 November 1839,
in *Captain William Coppin: 'Neptune's Brightest Star'*, 1992

PUPIL TEACHER

TWO DAYS LATER I WAS SUMMONED BEFORE MR MONAGHAN. He stood behind his high writing-desk with the sloping top and he was writing furiously, and very intent on what he was doing. As I stood awaiting his pleasure I thought his face was graver than usual. I could not see his steel-grey eyes, but with his face lowered slightly over the paper on the desk, he presented a good view of the sloping top of his head. He had a remarkably high forehead, and his hair was thin – a mixture of black and grey – and looked exactly like the bones of a herring that had been affixed to the middle of his head with some adhesive.

He took no notice of me until he had finished writing, by which time I had sensed that this was to be no ordinary meeting. He had an indefinable expression that boded ill for me; there was disappointment in the air, and the silence of the room, broken only by the scratching of his pen on the paper, spelt doom. At last, he stopped writing, raised his eyes and stared at me. I remained outwardly calm, but trembled inwardly. The stare told me that the result had come. He raised the sloping top of the desk, took out a large, official envelope, and removed a long white communication from it.

'This,' he said, indicating the long paper in his hand, 'is Mr McQuillan's report on your recent examination.'

'Yes, sir.' And as I said the words, I knew that I had read his face as truly as I now felt the pain in my own heart. He frowned as he studied the paper before him.

'It is, in many ways,' he continued, 'one of the most remarkable documents I have ever set eyes upon in my long experience as a teacher.'

He paused, and I managed to utter my, 'Yes, sir.'

'It is incomprehensible to me how any pupil of mine could sink so low as to obtain a mere 43 per cent in arithmetic.'

My fears were justified. My heart turned within me, and the cold winds of the world blew round it. I answered, 'Yes, sir,' and my voice was husky.

'Your geography mark is little better, 54 per cent, though I knew you had little to hope for from that subject as you have shown no aptitude whatever for it. The lowest to date was obtained by Francis McColgan four years ago when he was awarded a princely 56 per cent. Your mark beats his for the record, and I doubt whether any pupil of mine will ever challenge you on it.'

I did not emit my acknowledgement that I was still listening. Like Macbeth in the play, 'Amen' stuck in my throat and I could not say it. Mr Monaghan mentioned other papers in which I had not done so badly, but the arithmetic mark had touched his pride, for in that subject his students always excelled. Then he continued:

'There are other astounding features in this remarkable document. I was not aware that you possessed any outstanding talent as a singer, but Mr McQuillan seems to think differently. He has given you 95 marks in singing.'

'Yes, sir.'

'Your powers of expression, of which I have had little or no evidence in your English essays, are also amply rewarded in this curious document. I have consulted three of my teachers to ensure that there is no mistake in my reading of this figure, which is one hundred and eighty-six out of a possible two hundred marks.'

He coughed before commenting: 'This brings your otherwise poor total to something like normality.'

'Yes, sir.'

He stroked his chin and looked from the document to me; then he left it on the desk and began to walk to and fro in front of me, stopping at the window several times to look out across the way at St Columba's Church on a lower level. With his hands clasped behind his back he talked half to me and half to himself.

'That arithmetic mark ... it makes me feel thoroughly ashamed that a pupil of mine ... should sink so low ... it is unheard of ... never in all my experience have I ... known the like ... and the other marks are ... in my opinion ... incredible.'

The stunning shocks which I had suffered during this interview began to lose their effect; my brain was clearing and hope dawned. I found my voice.

'Did I pass, sir? Have I been appointed?' I asked.

He stopped in his stride and turned to face me.

'Of course you have passed,' he snapped. 'Your appointment dates from the first of next month. But those marks. I ... I ... really cannot fathom how ...'

My happiness must have been clearly recorded in my face. I felt like a man who had got the worst of a punching match and who is now lying bruised, but happy that the enemy has withdrawn.

HUGH McVEIGH, Oft in the Stilly Night, 1957

THE CUSTOM-HOUSE, a small and inconvenient building, was built as a store in 1805, and since 1809 has been held by Government on a permanent tenure, at an annual rental of £1419.4.6, at first as a king's store, and since 1824 as a custom-house: the premises comprise some extensive tobacco and timber yards, laid out at different periods, and extend in front 450 feet, varying in depth: the duties received here in 1837 amounted to £99,652. The markets are generally well supplied. The shambles, for meat daily, and to which there is a weigh-house attached, are situated off Linen-hall-street, and were built in 1760, by Alderman Alexander and other members of the corporation: the tolls belong to Sir R.A. Ferguson, Bart., who in 1830 purchased the shambles and the fish and vegetable markets of the corporation. The linen market, on Wednesday, is held in a hall occupying an obscure situation in a street to which it gives name, and built in 1770, by the late Fred. Hamilton, Esq., to whose descendant the tolls belong: it consists of a court measuring 147 feet by 15, and enclosed by small dilapidated houses; the cloth is exposed on stands placed in the court and under sheds; on the opposite side of the street is the sealing-room. The butter market, in Waterloo-place, for butter and hides daily, and to which three weigh-houses are attached; the fish market, off Linen-hall-street, daily; the potatoe market, in Society-street, for potatoes and meal by retail daily, with a weigh-house attached; and the vegetable market, off Linen-hall-street, for vegetables, poultry, and butter daily, were all built in 1825 by the corporation, to whom the tolls of the butter and potatoe markets belong. The cow market, for the sale of cows, pigs, sheep, and goats, every Wednesday, is held in a field to the south of Bishop-street, near the river, which was enclosed in 1832 by the corporation, to whom the tolls belong. There are also a flax market in Bishop-street every Thursday, and a market for yarn in Butchers'-street every Wednesday. Six fairs are held annually, but only three are of importance, namely, on June 17th, Sept. 4th, and Oct. 17th; the others are on March 4th, April 30th, and Sept. 20th. Custom was charged on every article of merchandise brought into the city prior to 1826, when it was abolished, except as regards goods conveyed over the bridge;

and in lieu thereof, the corporation instituted trespass, cranage, storage, and other dues. The post-office was established in 1784; the amount of postage for 1834 was £4,047.17.1½. The revenue police force usually consists of a lieutenant and twelve men; and the constabulary is composed of a chief constable and twelve men.

SAMUEL LEWIS, Topographical Dictionary of Ireland, 1837

'Half a' Derry worked in the shirt factory.
I was fourteen on the Wednesday, the thirtieth of April
and I started work on the fifth of May
because they wouldn't start me in the middle of the week.
I had to start on a Monday.
But about three weeks before that my mother –
she worked in it,
my sister, sister-in-law and aunt all worked in Welch's –
and my mother would go to her boss and say,
"I have a wee girl that'll soon be ready for work –
in about three weeks' time."
And he said, "Well,
the week before she's due t'come in let me know."
And they just said, "Bring her in on Monday
an' bring a pair of scissors."'

'That was for clipping the threads.
Everybody that went into the factory at first
went in as a clipper or a message girl,
and then after about two, three months doing that
then you started and you went to another job
until eventually you learned what was called a trade.
Now everybody said, "Always learn a trade"
because, at that time,
when the women had a trade
and then they got married and then they had a family,
well eventually they went back to work again
and they always had a trade to go into.'
'You'd always go into the same thing
or you could go into another factory with this trade.
I became a smoother –
that was a trade.'

'Well the trades in the factory were
side-seaming, front-stitching, pocketing, hemming,
button-holing.'
'Button-holing.'

'Fitting.'
'Fitting.'

'And then in the collar ...
there was the inserting,
the patent turning, the collar stitching,
button-holing again –
well then you went from that to the examining
and then the next thing, next step was the laundry
that was a trade, the smoothing –
you had to smooth and fold –
and the boxing was a trade.'

'Well I was a smoother
but sure I finished up a boxer.
And one time somebody asked me
what I did in the factory –
in fact I was away on holiday and we were talking –
and it was somebody we met
one night when we were out
and they asked me what I did.
I said I was a boxer –
and they weren't too happy –
they thought I was being funny, so they did,
so they call them now packers –
and smoothers are now pressers –
but that's what they were when I learnt ...'

ANONYMOUS, 'Half a' Derry', in *The Fountain*
(ed. Leon McAuley), 1993

LIKE BELFAST, DERRY IS A BUSY INDUSTRIAL CENTRE. There is a good deal
of the beehive about it. It has stings, but also honey. It fights, but it
makes money. It has some important industries in linen, especially in shirt
making, and in materials for the make up of linen shirts. I counted eight or
ten factories all working full time, and I could see other smaller
establishments also engaged in the linen trade as I looked southward from
the heights beyond the Foyle. Along the quays are lines of steamers loading

and discharging merchandise, and you may see bales of goods for export marked Buenos Ayres, Rio, Bombay, Melbourne, Valparaiso, Shanghai, etc. The factories give employment to thousands of hands; and after 6 o'clock in the evening the streets are crowded by the spinners and other operatives going home. I did not find out exactly how the manufacturing industry of Derry stands. But I think it as financially sound as it is in any other centre in the three kingdoms. Certainly the mills are all working. There did not seem to be many people out of employment.

WILLIAM BULFIN, *Rambles in Eirinn*, 1907

YOUTH ARRIVED – ALL THREE. Such a luxury was still possible then and of course the tiny size of the class contributed to the atmosphere of exclusivity and privilege. The names of the girls I have long since forgotten but I remember their eventual grades – *A*, *B* and *C*. *B* was the ideal convent-school product – intelligent (a mathematician), talented (a cellist), articulate (leader of the debating team), exemplary (head girl). All the staff admired her and found my own lack of enthusiasm inexplicable and churlish. What I objected to was the docility that permitted itself to be so easily moulded. There should always be an element of resistance in the medium.

A and *C* offered resistance – but *C* was a garrulous scatterbrain whose escapades revealed only that youthful energy and restlessness which dissipate as swiftly and completely as morning mist on a garden suburb. *A*, though rarely in trouble, was a true rebel angel, arrogant, dissatisfied and resentful, possessing in abundance the terrible twin gifts of Lucifer – intelligence and pride.

'Are you coming to the sixth-form party?' *C* made the ritual attempt at distraction.

I shrugged, presenting my favourite posture of disengagement and indifference.

'How about the convent dinner tonight? *We're all waitresses.*' She offered the slack mouth and large vacant eyes that had already attracted male attention. A man can drown in six inches of water as well as in the deepest of oceans.

I shrugged again. 'Probably.'

Before they could pursue the matter, I enquired about the homework, two applied mathematics problems on kinetic and potential energy. When they admitted defeat on both I turned to the blackboard with the sigh of one who has found his way back to the garden. For clever grammar-school pupils, paradise lost is the elegant closed systems – logical, consistent and complete – of Euclidian geometry and Newtonian mechanics. What does it matter if these systems are wrong? Forever insulated from the squalor and perdition of the world, their beauty is pure, incorruptible, timeless. Not only was the subject matter of mechanics eternally fixed, the A-level syllabus and even the textbook were the same as those I had studied myself.

Today's questions were weighty brain-crushers from the end of an exercise – but as usual I had not prepared answers, preferring the frisson of danger in performing on the high wire without a net. Never yet had I wavered, much less fallen to earth. Nor did today provide an appointment with destiny. Beneath the squeaky chalk an elegant solution duly appeared.

A objected to the reasoning in her usual vicious way – every discussion involving her seemed to turn bitter and personal. She was more intelligent and a better mathematician than I but as yet unaware of this. For the moment experience gave me the edge. I went over the reasoning again and when B came in on my side A ungraciously withdrew.

Leaving them to finish the second problem, I turned back to the window. The old nun had gone and in the fading light the scene was dominated by the sombre bulk of the convent house. While the senior school was a modern building, airy and bright and contemporary as befitted its ethos, the nuns inhabited a gaunt Victorian mansion which gave the impression of traditional authority exercised without concession to the age. In fact today was the only day of the year in which lay staff were permitted to cross its mysterious and slightly sinister threshold. On the last day of the Christmas term the nuns put on a dinner to 'thank' staff (and God help anyone who declined to be 'thanked'). Into the heavy dark atmosphere of the house, with its overpowering smell of tradition zealously upheld (boiled vegetables and mustiness overlaid by furniture and floor polish), came a largely female lay staff who had exchanged their decorous day uniform for evening wear that exposed arms and throats and white backs. For such colleagues to bare flesh was startling enough and for them to bare it in the inner sanctum of piety added to the shamelessness of exposure the insolence of desecration and sacrilege. Naturally the atmosphere was electric. Even the timid who stayed covered shared in the delirium of transgression. Nothing is more intoxicating than the illusion of escape from categories.

There was also the oddity of being waited on by pupils. The girls were restricted to white blouse and dark skirt but, like the sonneteers of the silver age, managed triumphs of individual expression within the strictly defined limits.

MICHAEL FOLEY, *Getting Used to Not Being Remarkable*, 1998

FROM LIMMAVADDY TO DERRY there is very little uncultivated land. Within 4 miles of the latter, rents are from 12*s.* to 20*s.* mountains paid for but in the gross. Reached Derry at night, and waited two hours in the dark before the ferry-boat came over for me.

August 7th, in the morning went to the Bishop's palace to leave my letters of recommendation; for I was informed of my misfortune in his being out of the kingdom. He was upon a voyage to Staffa, and had sent home some of the stones of which it consists; they appeared perfectly to resemble in shape, colour, and smell, those of the Giant's Causeway. I felt at once the extent of my loss in the absence of his lordship, who I had been repeatedly told was one of the men in all Ireland the most able to give me a variety of useful information, with at the same time the most liberal spirit of communication.

Waited on Mr Robert Alexander, one of the principal merchants of Derry, who very obligingly took every means of procuring me such information as I wanted; rode with me to Loch Swilly for viewing the scene of the herring fishery, and, assisted by the Rev. Mr Barnard, gave me the following particulars concerning it.

In the barony of Innishoen, the courses are, 1. Barley 8 barrels; 2. oats 10; 3. oats 6; 4. lay for 3 years.

1. Oats; 2. oats; 3. oats; 4. lay 3 years.

1. Potatoes on lay; 2. barley; 3. oats 10 barrels; 4. oats 6; 5. oats 5; 6. lay 3 years.

1. Potatoes £10. 2. barley; 3. oats; 4. oats; 5. flax 4 Cwt. Barley the principal crop, and generally worth £5 to £6. Rent of the whole peninsula to Lord Donnegal £11,000, and to the occupying tenant £22,000. The measure is the plantation acre. The bottoms of Innishoen 20s. an acre: the whole county of Donnegal not 1s. The linen is getting in but very slowly, but spinning very general, and the best yarn in all the north: they spin all their own flax, and generally into 3 hank yarn; which all goes to Derry, and from thence to Manchester. The spinners spin a hank a day: a pound of flax worth 6d. spins into 3 hanks, which sell at present at 1s. 9d. which is 5d. a day earning, but in common only 4d. Flax yields per acre scutched $3\frac{1}{2}$ Cwt. at $6\frac{1}{2}d.$ per lb. sells on foot at £6 to £8 expences per acre, scutching included, £5 14s.

ARTHUR YOUNG, *A Tour in Ireland 1776–1779*, 1780

SOME SCHOOL-CHILDREN REMAIN IN YOUR MIND, years after you taught them, and you wonder whatever became of them. It is particularly difficult to trace girls, since most of them get married and give up their original surnames.

For a long time now I have been curious about a group of teenage females who were placed in my charge, in Derry, in 1968, when I was given a three month substitute teaching job.

It was made clear to me that if I could keep them quiet, I would have achieved a great deal. They belonged to a difficult class, and showed not the remotest interest in learning. With only one year of school left, they had but one thought in mind – getting a job.

That being so, I concentrated a lot of effort into reducing them to a state of happy physical exhaustion. While other girls swotted over reading, writing and arithmetic, my lot were out on the playing field, where they engaged in everything from football to American baseball. Once in a while, I took them on a tour of Creggan Estate, where the school was situated, and got them to write down all the names of the streets where most of them lived. It was a desperate attempt to encourage them towards writing and spelling.

After a month of touring the estate, they progressed to writing out the words of rock and roll songs. The Beatles were popular, and there used to be dead silence in class while they listened to the records I played, and tried to record the lyrics.

When things got really desperate, which was usually once a day, I relied on the most untried method of all – I used to march them down the hill towards my mother's house, bring them in, and give them tea and biscuits.

In her presence, they were all well behaved as one would expect any Derry girl to be. Mothers command a respect that teachers do not.

One girl, whose mother was dead, took to hanging around our house after school closed. My mother would call her in from the street and chat with her. Years later, I met the girl's father and was impressed. He was a Republican of the old school, and heavily engaged in the fight for civil rights. Then I lost touch.

Now I know what happened to her in the interim.

A young Republican man, himself an orphan, came to lodge in her father's house. She started to date him, and became pregnant by him.

He was as young and cheerful and feckless as herself. She became pregnant. On his way to the wedding, he stopped off with the best man and bought a bottle of vodka, and had a couple of drinks. The bottle, in the paper, shows in their wedding picture.

He joined the INLA.

Their marriage deteriorated, and blows were struck, by both sides. She had two babies and he ended up in jail, serving a long sentence.

She started a relationship with another man. Her husband sued for a divorce.

Then the hunger strike of 1981 started.

The young man volunteered.

He forbade his wife to visit him in hospital.

As he lay dying, his children were brought to him. Blind by now, he could only feel the outline of their young bodies.

His wife was informed that he would not be buried, if he died, from her home, and that she would not be allowed to attend his funeral.

He was buried from his sister's house, the children followed his hearse, and his wife remained invisible.

She has since had three children by the man whom she met while her husband was in prison, but she refused to marry him and all five children now carry the hunger-striker's surname. She spends long periods in a mental home. The history of these and other pupils of the class of '68 is contained in a devastatingly sad book about the hunger strike, called *Ten men dead*, by David Beresford.

NELL McCAFFERTY, 'The Class of '68', in *Goodnight Sisters*, 1988

A Barrage of
Stones

Once again, it happens.
Under a barrage of stones
and flaring petrol bombs
the blunt, squat shape of
an armoured car glides
into the narrow streets
of the Catholic quarter
leading a file of helmet-
ed, shielded riot police;
once again, it happens,
like an old Troubles film,
run for the last time ...

Lines of history
   lines of power
the long sweep
   of the Bogside
under the walls
   up to Creggan
the black muzzle
   of Roaring Meg
staring dead on
   cramped houses
the jackal shapes
   of James's army
watching the city
   stiffen in siege

Lines of defiance
   lines of discord
near the Diamond
   brisk with guns
British soldiers
   patrol the walls
the gates between
   Ulster Catholic
Ulster Protestant
   a Saracen slides
past the Guildhall
   a black Cuchulain
bellowing against
   the Scarlet Whore
twin races petrified
   the volcanic ash
   of religious hatred

JOHN MONTAGUE, *from* 'A New Siege', in *The Rough Field*, 1989

J UST AS WE WERE ABOUT TO GET UP and move, a man moved along the gable wall of the last house in Chamberlain Street, about twenty yards from us. The house backed on to waste ground. He suddenly appeared at the corner of this house and moved cautiously along the gable. His movements were rather suspicious and suddenly he produced a gun from his jacket. It was a small gun, a hand-gun, and he fired two or three shots around the corner at the soldiers. The soldiers in this area facing the flats were stepping out in the open from time to time. I cannot recall the soldiers reacting or firing in his direction. They did not seem to be aware of the gunman. We screamed at the gunman to go away because we were frightened that the soldiers might think the fire was coming from where we were located. He looked at us and then he just drifted away across or into the mouth of Chamberlain Street. I did not see him after that nor, to the best of my knowledge, did I see him before then. I did not recognise him as someone I knew.

At this point we decided to make a dash for it. We got up first of all from our knees and I waved the handkerchief, which, by now, was heavily bloodstained. I went in front and the men behind me carried Jackie Duddy. We made our way into Chamberlain Street, along that street and then turned into Harvey Street. Soldiers challenged us at this point and we saw the BBC News camera crew with cameraman, Cyril Cave and reporter John Bierman. We then proceeded to the corner of Waterloo Street and Harvey Street. At this point Willie Barber took off his coat, spread it on the ground, and we laid Jackie Duddy on it. At that time he appeared to be dead. After being asked by us, a woman called Mrs McCloskey, who, as far as I recall, resided in the street, phoned for an ambulance. Then a patrol of soldiers appeared in Waterloo Street and told us to clear off and I asked the people to calm down and kneel down and offer a prayer. The soldiers moved away. I remember one of the women screaming down the street after them shouting, 'He's only a child and you've killed him.'

(BISHOP) EDWARD DALY, *Hi Mister! Are You a Priest?*, 2000

A strong drink, hundred-year-old
schnapps, to be sipped at, invading
the secret places that lie in wait and
lonely between bone and muscle, or
counting (Morse code for insomniacs)
the seconds round the heart
when it stutters to itself. Or to be
taken in at the eyes in small doses,
phrase by somatic phrase, a line
of laundry after dawn, air clean as

vodka, snow all over, the laundry
lightly shaking itself
from frigid sleep. Shirts, flowered sheets,
pyjamas, empty trousers, empty
socks – risen as at a last day's dawn
to pure body, light as air. Whiteness
whiter than snow, blueness bluer than
new day brightening the sky-lid
behind trees stripped of their illusions
down to a webbed geometry
subtler than speech. A fierce blue eye
farther off than God, witnessing
house-boxes huddled together
for comfort, fronting blindly
the deserted streets down which in time
come farting lorries full of soldiers.
You are a fugitive *I*, a singing
nerve: you flit from garden to garden
in your fit of silence, bits of you
flaking off in steam and sizzling
like hot fat in the snow. Listen
to the pickers and stealers, the shots,
man-shouts, women wailing, the cry of kids
who clutch stuffed dolls or teddy bears
and shiver, gripping tight as a kite
whatever hand is offered. Here
is the light glinting on top-boots, on
the barrel of an M-16 that grins, holding
its breath, beyond argument. And here is
a small room where robust winter sunlight
rummages much of the day when the day
is cloudless, making some ordinary potted plants
flower to your surprise again, again,
and again: pink, anaemic red, wax-white
their resurrection petals. Like hearts
drawn by children, like oiled arrowheads,
their unquestioning green leaves seem
alive with expectation.

EAMON GRENNAN, in 'Soul Music: The Derry Air',
in *What Light There Is,* 1987

ARCHBISHOP FLOOD OF TRINIDAD, the Dominican, whom we met before, went to Derry on the 14th of August, the eve of Lady's Day in Harvest, the Feast of the Assumption of the Blessed Virgin, a day on which the Ulster Catholics are in the habit of having religious processions and celebrations. He was hooted and mobbed in his carriage or cab by a crowd of Orangemen 'waving crimson handkerchiefs'. The mob attacked one of the Catholic Churches, where 'confessions were being heard', with the result that the 'congregation had to be dismissed and the church closed'. The windows of the priest's house were also broken, and the priest chased into the streets. Nothing could exceed the violence of the language in which the Orangemen were condemned by the Catholic press.

MICHAEL J.F. McCARTHY, *Five Years in Ireland 1895–1900*, 1901

Nowhere else for us to go
but off the bus at the last stop.
Past fierce mad-looking Macha
you say I'll look like in twenty years.
Tunnel of bone-chilling wind.
In through the portals of pain
to the temple of healing.

Here are the worried sick
sick to the stomach
the sick at heart
sick unto death
the quick and the dead.
We are not out of place.

Hot-house fit for humming-birds.
Brightest lights in town, like
mid-cruise liner, anchored.
In this house of many mansions
we skulk the aisles, loiter about pillars.

Driven asunder once by a chariot
attended by two young running women
in christly white,
old woman rearing up,
her face green as silage
*Let me out of this world, God,
let me out of this life.*

Babies petalled in rugs borne by like bouquets.
At the vending machine, knee
to knee not
quite touching.
Explain me despair.
You pull on a Gold Blend, you
grin. I see the skull beneath your skin.
Explain me faith and hope.
I finger lean white ribs of coffee cup.
O feed me squares of Caramac.
Explain me love.

Here's where they take the tar off
and pick out the bullets and bits of shops. Right?

Here the placentas are buried
of true citizens,
here on the hill's scalp, flat as a battlefield,
patrolled by crows. Yes?

Och. Ask me a proper question. Like
why do the sins of the fathers
have to get visited on us?

The flag of this place – a white and red hankie waving
or the flickering colours of daffodils in March or
a bunting of washed-out washing – which?

And tell me again
my eyes are like forget-me-not-no-nevers and
will you take my hand and
will it be sweaty and
will anything happen
if we cut down Daly's Brae?

Nothing to do but go.
Nowhere to go but the valley of night.

The Altnagelvin soars
behind us. Great glowing box
of costly precious warmth and brightness.

Beacon at our backs.

ANN McKAY, 'A Date at the Altnagelvin', in *Giving Shine*, 2000

SLOWLY CYCLING INTO THE BOGSIDE I saw a huge proud notice: YOU ARE NOW IN FREE DERRY. To prove it, lamp standards and pillar-boxes are painted green, white and orange in horizontal stripes; and there are several crude life-size murals of heavily-armed Brits with monkey heads and faces – unwitting shades of Hanuman! Many new rows of houses or blocks of flats already look irreparably neglected or vandalised and much black paint has been thrown at their walls – sometimes to deface large, carefully-painted tricolours or Easter lilies, or legends saying BRITS OUT! REMEMBER 1916! UP THE REPUBLIC! Are these paints splashes the work of the Stickies? Or the Irps? Or do Tartan gangs from the Waterside across the Foyle recklessly steal into the Bogside at dead of night? In the midst of so much sordid vandalism the memorial to those shot on Bloody Sunday stands immaculate and inviolable – the visible sign of yet another powerful myth. And nearby, painted in large letters across the front wall of the Bogside Inn – the main Provo pub – are the words INFORMERS WILL BE KILLED. For a moment I took this casually, as just another bit of swaggering adolescent graffiti. Then, with a chilly feeling inside, I realised that the slogan is nobody's sick joke. It is a statement of fact. How free is Free Derry?

DERVLA MURPHY, *A Place Apart*, 1978

RAIN HAD SET IN BY THE TIME that school was over. That was a good thing really as it meant that most people set off quickly for home and there wasn't too much mucking around.

He pulled the hood of his anorak up over his head and ran. The rain made a good excuse for running. He didn't want to be the only running person in the whole city. He ran as fast as he could, not looking to left or right in case he saw Kathleen. There was nobody much about. A few wet prams stood outside the shops under the flats. The windows of the shops themselves were steamed over. Some gardeners from the council stamped their feet with cold and impatience as they waited in the shelter of the flats for the rain to slacken off. Their spades and forks grew like plants from the newly-turned earth on the hillside. The high grey walls had seen it all before. Tragedy, comedy, guns in small boys' school bags, left them cold. He walked soberly up the steps. His trousers were all splashed with mud. His jaw throbbed dismally. There was no else at the checkpoint. The soldiers were laughing at some joke.

'You're a bit wet, aren't you son?' said one of them to Joe.

He nodded and smiled, a wide disarming smile. He tried hard to keep the smile in position as he opened the school bag and held it out towards the soldier. The man barely glanced into it.

'That's OK.' He ran his hands briefly over Joe's body and gave him a friendly shove on the shoulder.

'Tara.'

Safe. He walked quickly across the road. Almost safe. Almost. He went down a narrow street and on to the quay. Cars moved slowly, nose to tail. The cranes were motionless. A couple of dockers talked and smoked in the shelter of one of the warehouses. The seagulls on the rooftops were hunched down into themselves, like sick old men. He walked slowly along the edge of the wharf. In front of him a timber ship lay, its flags sad in the rain. He stepped carefully over one of the huge ropes attaching it to the wharf. He opened his bag and groped into it with cold, wet fingers. A man in a blue jersey leaned over the ship's rail smoking. He didn't seem to mind the rain. He dropped his butt in the river and turned away. Joe pulled the gun out of the bag and dropped it down the side of the wharf. It seemed to fall so slowly. Slower than anything before had ever fallen. He stood, rooted to the ground, waiting for it to disappear, be gone. It splashed into the water, and mesmerising circles grew out and out towards the centre of the river. He dropped the bag on the ground and, leaning out over the brown water, was sick. A white gush of water poured out from the side of the ship. There was turbulence. There was definitely no longer any gun.

JENNIFER JOHNSTON, *Shadows on Our Skin*, 1977

15 MAY 1920, DERRY QUAY
Denis Moroney D/Sgt 59644

THE DETECTIVE SERGEANT WAS THE CHIEF of the Crimes Detective Department in the city and was the first member of the RIC to be killed in Ulster since the beginning of 1919. Along with a small party of Detectives, the Detective Sergeant accompanied uniform police in a bayonet charge to disperse rioters. As the police moved along the Quay, near to the Great Northern Station, a person in the crowd shot and wounded the Detective. He was taken to the Metropole Hotel, where he died from his wounds.

Background
At 10.30 a.m. a riot developed between two crowds, one in Fountain Street, the other in Bridge Street, Londonderry. The police charged down Bridge Street and the crowd scattered in all directions at the end of the street. A portion of the crowd made its way into Rookery Lane and across Foyle Street, through Fish Lane and on to the Quay. The police followed this crowd, who fired revolvers at the police as they ran away. Once onto the Quay this crowd concealed themselves behind wagons and continued to fire at the police. Shortly after reaching the quay Moroney said to Detective Constable Patrick Kelly, 'My God,

Kelly, I am shot.' Kelly, along with Detective Constable Darragh, then helped the Sergeant from the scene. As they did so he said, 'Help me, boys! I am falling.'

Moroney lived at 16 Grove Place and at 11.20 a.m. on 18 May his remains were carried the entire distance from his home to the Great Northern Railway Station by his former comrades, with all the available police in the city attending the funeral. His body was taken to Ballinrobe, Co. Mayo, and was later interred at Roundfort, Hollymount, Co. Mayo. The body was exhumed by relations and brought to his native Co. Clare for reinterment. Moroney, from Tulla, Co. Clare, had nineteen years' police service, having been a farmer before joining the RIC.

RICHARD ABBOTT, *Police Casualties in Ireland 1919–1922*, 2000

PISTOL
January 1949

IN THAT DARK WINTER, THERE WERE two police cars, black and black, that appeared to have landed like spaceships out of the early morning light of the street. I saw their gleaming metal reflected in the lacquered window glass of the house next door as they took off with us. But first there was the search. A bright figure, in a white rain-cape, came through the bedroom door and stood with his back to the wall, switching the light on and off. He was shouting, but I was numb with shock and could see only his mouth opening and closing. I dressed within that thin membrane of silence. They were, I knew, looking for the gun I had found the afternoon before in the bottom drawer inside the wardrobe of the room next door, where my sisters slept.

It was a long, chill pistol, blue-black and heavy, which I had smuggled out the back to show to some boys from Fahan Street, up near the old city walls. They had come over to play football and afterwards we had an argument about politics. I had been warned never even to mention the gun which, I was told, had been a gift to my father from a young German sailor, whose submarine had been brought in to the port at the end of the war. He had been held with about thirty others in Nissen huts down by the docks, and my father used to bring him extra sandwiches or milk every lunch-time when he was helping to wire up the huts for light and heat. Before he went away the young sailor gave my father the gun as a memento. But since we had cousins in gaol for being in the IRA, we were a marked family and had to be careful. Young as I was, I was being stupid.

While we were gathered round the gun, hefting it, aiming it, measuring its length against our forearms, I had felt eyes watching. Fogey McKeever, known to be a police informer, was at the end of the lane, looking on. He was a young, open-faced man of twenty or so with a bright smile and wide-spaced, rounded eyes. He looked the soul of candour. He had seen me bring the gun back into the house.

I waited ten minutes and then brought it out again, wrapped in an old newspaper, and buried it in one of the stone trenches up the field. I was so sure that was enough that I had forgotten about it even before I went to sleep. But now, here were the police, and the house was being splintered open. The linoleum was being ripped off, the floorboards crowbarred up, the wardrobe was lying face down in the middle of the floor and the slashed wallpaper was hanging down in ribbons.

We were huddled downstairs and held in the centre of the room while the kitchen was searched. One policeman opened a tin of Australian peaches and poured the yellow scimitar slices and the sugar-logged syrup all over the floor. Another went out to the yard and split open a bag of cement in his ransack of the shed. He came walking through in a white cloud, his boots sticking to the slimy lino and the cement falling from him in white flakes. I was still in the silence. Objects seemed to be floating, free of gravity, all over the room. Everybody had sweat or tears on their faces. Then my father, Liam and I were in the police cars and the morning light had already reached the roof-tops as a polished gleam in the slates that fled as we turned the corner of the street towards the police barracks, no more than a few hundred yards away.

Where was the gun? I had had it, I had been seen with it, where was it? Policemen with huge faces bent down to ask me, quietly at first, then more and more loudly. They made my father sit at a table and then lean over it, with his arms outspread. Then they beat him on the neck and shoulders with rubber truncheons, short and gorged-red in colour. He told them, but they didn't believe him. So they beat us too, Liam and me, across the table from him. I remember the sweat and rage on his face as he looked. When they pushed my chin down on the table for a moment, I was looking up at him. Did he wink at me? Or were there tears in his eyes? Then my head bounced so hard on the table with the blows that I bit hard on my tongue.

For long after, I would come awake in the small hours of the morning, sweating, asking myself over and over, 'Where is the gun? Where is it? Where is the gun?' I would rub the sleep and fear that lay like a cobweb across my face. If a light flickered from the street beyond, the image of the police car would reappear and my hair would feel starched and my hands sweaty. The police smell took the oxygen out of the air and left me sitting there, with my chest heaving.

SEAMUS DEANE, *Reading in the Dark*, 1996

I HEARD the Poor Old Woman say:
'At break of day the fowler came,
And took my blackbirds from their songs
Who loved me well thro' shame and blame.

'No more from lovely distances
Their songs shall bless me mile by mile
Nor to white Ashbourne call me down
To wear my crown another while.

'With bended flowers the angels mark
For the skylark the place they lie,
From there its little family
Shall dip their wings first in the sky.

'And when the first surprise of flight
Sweet songs excite, from the far dawn
Shall there come blackbirds loud with love,
Sweet echoes of the singers gone.

'But in the lonely hush of eve
Weeping I grieve the silent bills.'
I heard the Poor Old Woman say
In Derry of the little hills.

FRANCIS LEDWIDGE, 'Lament for the Poets: 1916', in *Complete Poems*, 1997

September deepens and the nights are long
And noisy; through this autumn damp with blood
There glows the other autumn of his song,
There falls the shadow of the old oak wood
Over the broken, dusty streets that lead
Us on to death's steep brink. And there is still
That spot where the sun slants across the hill
Burning the leaves as though the branches bleed.

My childhood's magic moments shone between
These ancient walls; I will return once more,
One evening late and weary I will lean
Against that gate or knock upon that door
To find again the dusky littered room
Where the oil lamp smokes and the curtains smell of home.

FRANCIS STUART, 'Reading Keats in Derry City',
in *A Rage for Order* (ed. Frank Ormsby), 1992

WITHIN A MINUTE, A MAN, who I think was Francie Brolly, came running down William Street calling my name. I asked what was wrong, and he shouted for me to come with him quickly, as two people had been shot at the back of the march. I went with him and someone showed us to the Shields's house, where I found a teenager and a middle-aged man, both of whom had been shot. The boy had an entry bullet wound on the upper third of the inner surface of his right thigh, and a jagged exit wound over the middle third of the outer surface of the same thigh. He was pale and shocked but wasn't losing much blood externally. The boy's name was Damian Donaghy. I then examined the middle-aged man whose name was John Johnston. He had a gunshot wound over his upper inner right thigh, and a peculiar jagged wound over his left shoulder region, which I thought could possibly have been caused by a ricochet.

I was treating these two casualties with some first-aiders for approximately fifteen minutes, when I heard the sound of several gun shots in the vicinity, coming in rapid succession. The sound appeared to be coming from the Glenfada Park direction. I was very familiar with the sound of petrol bombs and nail bombs exploding. I did not hear any sounds which resembled these explosions. After a few minutes the sounds of firing ceased, and a man came into the house saying someone had been shot dead just outside. Just then Dr Kevin Swords, an old friend of mine from my Dublin days, came in and asked if there was anything he could do to help. Our two casualties were then almost ready for transfer to hospital, so I asked Kevin to check on the story outside – which I didn't really believe. Kevin came back in a few minutes to confirm the story that someone had been shot dead outside. I went outside and started across the small square. I found a man lying on the steps of the square being tended by two young boys. This man was Gerald McKinney, and on examination I found that he was already dead (Post Mortem Findings Appendix F). I told the boys to continue their efforts at resuscitation. Someone told me that several other people had been shot and were in houses across the square. I continued across the square and met Leo Day of the Knights of Malta. I asked him to contact Altnagelvin Hospital and ask them to send ambulances immediately.

In the first house I found Michael Kelly, who had an entry bullet wound just to the left of his umbilicus. I could not find any exit wound. Michael was already dead when I examined him. Lying beside Michael was Jim Wray. He had two entry gun-shot wounds on the right side of his back. He had an exit wound on the left side of his back, and another larger exit wound at his left shoulder. Jim was also dead when I examined him. Again I told the young first-aiders to continue their efforts at resuscitation. I did this mainly to keep them occupied, and in the hope that if they were kept busy they would be less likely to panic in what was an extremely horrific situation. I went next door where I found William McKinney lying on the floor. He had an entry bullet wound over his right chest, and a jagged exit wound in his left chest. There was not much external bleeding. He was quite conscious when I examined him. He was pale and shocked, but extremely calm. He said to me very calmly, 'I'm going to die, doctor, am I?' I lied a bit and said, 'You have been hit badly, but if we can get an ambulance and get you to hospital quickly, I hope you will be alright.' I saw Father Mulvey in the hall and asked him to see William, which he did. I stayed with William until he gradually lost consciousness and died.

We continued our efforts at resuscitation until the ambulances eventually arrived from Altnagelvin Hospital. I had lost all knowledge of the passage of time, but as William lay dying I had plenty of time to think. I knew the IRA were not firing and I thought to myself, 'My God, these soldiers are going to shoot us all.' I looked around the small room and realised that we were completely trapped with no way out. My first thought was that I wished I had a rifle so that at least I could put up some defence. Then I realised that I didn't know how to fire a rifle, and that we were dealing with professionals who were holding all the aces.

RAYMOND McCLEAN, *The Road to Bloody Sunday*, 1981

POLICEMEN WERE LYING AROUND all over the place – some sleeping, but most too exhausted to sleep. Their tunics were open, their bootlaces loosened and their faces blackened with smoke. They had the vacant gazes of defeated men. 'Christ! They're hammered,' said Pat Clarke. 'There is no way they can take the Bogside tonight.' I remembered the VE Day parade in London in 1945. All the armed forces of the British Empire took part in the march. The men from Northern Ireland, with their black uniforms and the harp on their caps, all of them well over six feet tall, received a tremendous ovation. All around me I heard people ask, 'Who are they? Where do they come from?' 'They're Irish,' I had answered with pride.

As I gazed at the exhausted policemen who had allowed themselves to become the stooges of the Unionist Party, I became aware of the contradictions in my own thinking. I was leading a revolt and yet respect for law and order was deeply ingrained in my character. And I knew that a society that didn't respect authority would go nowhere. But most of all, my hope of one day living in a united Ireland, where all citizens – Catholic, Protestant or whatever – had the same rights, had faded, like the morale of the shattered men lying around me. A polite greeting from a senior police officer – 'Good night, Mr Doherty' – lent a surreal touch to the scene.

PADDY DOHERTY, *Paddy Bogside*, 2001

Two of my father's brothers, William and George, took part in the Irish War of Independence. George O'Doherty later became a Lieutenant-Colonel in the Irish army, while William became a civil servant. Both lived in Dublin. The only reference I ever read in print about my father's family's involvement in the Old IRA (a term used to describe the IRA during the Irish War of Independence) was in an issue of *The Capuchin Annual* for, appropriately, 1969. It noted that the Doherty home in Waterloo Street had been an IRA contact-house during the War of Independence. I did not discover this fact until I was active in the IRA and 'on the run'. The veteran Derry Old IRA survivor, Neil Gillespie, told me in his home in the Brandywell in the early 1970s that my uncle George saved him from summary execution when he was captured as an Anti-Treaty Irregular by the pro-Treaty IRA. My aunt Lizzie played her part in the Old IRA as well, as her collection of medals proves. Unfortunately, I never sought to hear her experiences, a fact I came to regret too late when she died.

I never met my uncles George or William, and my parents' contact with the Dublin end of the family was very infrequent, being restricted to occasions of weddings and funerals. Dublin was always a long way from Derry in more ways than one, as it still is. If I ever heard my father mentioning George or William, I must have paid scant attention. He never spoke a single word to me about his family's involvement in the Old IRA or about those times, nor did he ever utter in my hearing a single comment for or against Republicanism. I almost never discussed politics with him or ever heard him state any strong party political viewpoint. He was just another of those silent supporters of Eddie McAteer's Nationalist Party until, I suppose, the advent of the Social Democratic and Labour Party, latterly led by John Hume, when he'd have become an equally silent supporter of the SDLP.

SHANE O'DOHERTY, The Volunteer, 1993

Des invited me to go with him to the Waterside on one of his community projects so Roz was put in the boot and off we went across Craigavon Bridge to a sprawl of new housing estates high above the east bank of the Foyle. Although the Waterside is often thought of as 'Protestant Derry' one-third of the residents are Catholics – or were, until very recently. There is now a two-way cross-Foyle movement because so many feel safer in exclusively Orange or Green areas. This is the sort of thing that could soon undermine everybody's proud boast that 'Derry is different.'

Certainly much of the Waterside looks Protestant. It is far tidier than the Green districts, many of its electricity poles and kerbs are painted red, white and blue and its walls say UDA RULE, UVF HERE, FUCK THE IRA. Yet its pale small children seem no less numerous than the Catholic young and have just as many sweet-rotten first teeth and lollipop-stained chins. These new housing estates were atrociously planned; they have no shops or post office within reasonable reach and no playing spaces. We listened to many complaints about the local Tenants' Association and the women seemed just as dominant and vigorous as their sisters across the Foyle. Several parlour mantelpieces were adorned by what appeared to be life-sized phallic symbols; eventually I identified them as rubber bullets mounted in brass at the relevant angle – an indication that the Waterside people either have exceptionally clean or exceptionally dirty minds. The former, Des insisted, because if the latter they would have doctored the pointed tip. It is horribly easy to see how these objects could kill a person if they hit a vulnerable spot.

All Derry's social workers are deeply worried about a problem to be found now in cities all over Europe – the psychological effects of uprooting slum communities and re-housing them in comparative luxury. People who have been 'dropping in' on each other all their lives no longer visit, or depend on each other in emergencies, though they are still neighbours. Keeping up with the McCanns has suddenly replaced the old values and countless respectable families, who before always managed to pay their way, are in debt. During times of tension neighbourly support becomes more important than ever and its weakening here has contributed to a spectacular increase in mental illness and alcoholism among women.

Des and I talked at length to an elderly widow in a hideously carpeted little room strewn with expensive broken toys and crammed with shoddy new furniture; the large television, on spindly legs, supported a variety of seaside souvenirs. Annie lives with her married daughter who works in a factory and the five children are at school all day and the son-in-law 'had to go across the water because when he was out of a job for a long while he got tangled with the UVF. They pay regular, like the Provos. Then the RUC was after him and he'll hardly come back – 'twouldn't ever be safe'. Annie is very fond of her son-in-law and was most upset when she accidentally discovered his connection with 'that lot'. She began to take a drop more than she should and when he went off and she was alone every day she only had the drop to cheer her up. 'Everything got worse for us all when there was no string on the doors.' She meant that in their new housing estate you could no longer put your hand through a letter-box, pull the key out on a string and enter a friend's house without knocking. 'No one ever needed to be worried or lonesome or in want in my old street. Now it's gone – all pulled down.' And what to some town-planner is a triumph – one slum less – to her is a disaster.

When Des had driven off to a meeting about Spastic children I cycled slowly across the Waterside to a mainly Catholic housing estate where I was to meet one of the Community Centre leaders. From this height Derry looked very lovely in the light of a cloudless summer evening. Across the

smooth, wide Foyle lay the Bogside and Creggan and the big Republican
graveyard on a steep green slope scattered with white tombstones. The clear
strong Atlantic air must contribute quite a lot to the Derry people's aliveness.
Around me were miles of unhuman new council estates and yet – somehow
– no part of Derry is depressing. It embarrasses me now to remember what I
expected to find here: a city of sullen, suspicious underdogs, slouching and
lounging through ruined streets.

DERVLA MURPHY, A Place Apart, 1978

CUIRIM 'AN RAIDIÓ AIR LE HAGHAIDH NA NÚACHTA. 'Chríost, tá siad ag
rá gur thug an tArm ruathar faoi na ceantair Chaitliceacha, ag a ceathair
a chlog ar maidin. Tharraing na saighdiúirí fir a dúradh a bheith báúil leis an
IRA amach as a leapacha agus chaith isteach sna carranna armúrtha *Saracen* iad.
Réabadh doirse tí le hoird an chéad leid a fuarthas. Cad é a dhéanfaidh mé?
Teitheadh thar teorainn? Caillfidh mé mo phost má theithim. Samhlaím
guth magúil m'athar:
Afraid you might be arrested? For makin' a few corny speeches? Don't make me
laugh.'

Caithfidh mé teacht ar bhealach thar teorainn agus imeacht ó Dhoire
chomh tiubh géar is a thig liom. Casaim an carr agus suas Bóthar Dhún
Creagáin liom arís.

Tá an manadh UA GALLCHOBHAIR, OIFIG AN PHUIST, GLEANN COMHRAIC, os
cionn an dorais i dtólamh, é scríofa sa seanchló i litreacha buí ar chúlra glas.
Tá na dathanna tréigthe, cuid den phéint ina calóga seargtha agus liath an
adhmaid le feiceáil tríthi. Gan aon mhaise curtha ar an áit ó d'fhág mé seo
anuraidh seachas doras gloine in éiric an tseandorais chláraigh. Nuair a
bhrúim an doras isteach, déantar scáthán den ghloine agus ritheann íomhá
m'éadain trasna air. Tá cuma cineál cloíte orm. Samhail eile a bhí ag na
siopadóirí díom cheana. Teanntaím mo bhéal le dreach misniúil a chur orm
féin. Níl duine ná deoraí le feiceáil istigh ach tá teilifíseán ar bun ar an
chuntar.
'Duine ar bith fá bhaile?'
Scríobann cosa cathaoireach agus ardaíonn cloigeann girsí aníos as cúl an
chuntair.
'Can I help you?' a fhiafraíonn sí de thuin na hAlban. San aois idir eatarthu
atá sí, a cúl gruaige fáiscthe le ribín, fáinní plaisteacha ina cluasa agus
headlights, mar a deirtí i nDoire, ar hob bláthú.
'Bhfuil an páipéar agat?'
'No Gaelic, sir. Will I get my granda?'
Granda go deimhin! Slusaí plámásach a labharfadh Gaeilge leat ar mhaithe
le deontas a ghnóthú. Deirim *'Derry Journal'* léi agus síneann sí cóip chugam.

Tá 'Internment' scríofa i litreacha móra ar an chéad leathanach. Tosaím á léamh agus mé ag dul amach. Tá mé sásta nár casadh airsean ná ar dhuine ar bith eile de na sean-naimhde mé. Dá mbeadh dóigh bhreá orm agus cuma na maitheasa orm ba bhreá liom siúl isteach agus a thaispeáint dóibh gur cuma liom fúthu. Agus mé ag tarraingt an dorais i mo dhiaidh feicim duine de na cairde a bhíodh agam. Tá sí ina seasamh i ndoras oifig GHARÁISTE AN GHLEANNA, agus ní aithním ar dtús í mar tá sí ag iompar clainne. Ach an t-éadan cruinn, an béal teann agus na súile bioracha sin mar a bhí riamh. Déanaim obainn casadh isteach arís lena sheachaint ach tá sí róluath agam. Bhí riamh.

'Nach tú an strainséir?'

'Bhfuil siad á thabhairt sin orm i dtólamh?' a fhiafraím, agus déanaim gáire leis an dochar a bhaint as.

Ní hí ba mheasa. Ach cá bhfuil an bolmán sin a phós sí? Is iontach nach bhfuil sé ag smúrthaíl thart.

'Tá bail mhaith curtha ar an gharáiste agaibh.'

'Níl Garbhán anseo,' ar sise, amhail is dá mbeadh sí in ann m'intinn a léamh. 'Tá sé i ndiaidh dul go Doire. Tá súil agam nach mbéarfaidh na saighdiúirí air. Dúrt mé leis gan dul ach tá fhios agat féin ...'

Tá 'fhios agam ceart go leor. Beidh sé ag caitheamh cloch leis na saighdiúirí. An buaileam sciath agus réabadh nach dtig leis a chleachtadh faoin bhaile ón uair a ndearnadh saoránach measúil de, beidh scóip aige dó i nDoire.

'Nach i nDoire atá tú féin ag obair anois?' a fhiafraíonn sí.

Aithním an dara ceist taobh thiar den chéad cheist. Ba mhaith léi a fháil amach an bhfuil mé i ndiaidh teitheadh as Doire mar gheall ar na saighdiúirí bheith ag tógáil daoine maidin inniu. An ceart aici.

'Tá mé ar mo choimhéad, más é sin atá i gceist agat. Is gearr ó d'fhág mé Doire.'

'Nach raibh saighdiúirí ar na bóithre?'

'Bóthar an Ghleanna a chuaigh mé agus bhain cúlbhealach Ghrianán Ailigh amach.

'Tá 'fhios agam é. Bealach maith smuigleála aimsir an chogaidh. Tuige nár tháinig tú aréir? Nár chuala tú an callán a thóg na mná le daoine a chur ar an eolas?'

'Níor mhothaigh mise a dhath. Tá teach s'againne i gceantar measctha agus ar chúl bhalla ard na Páirce. Folach maith.

I turn the radio on to hear the news. Christ! They say the army raided Catholic areas at 4 am. The soldiers dragged any men suspected of being IRA sympathisers out of their beds and threw them into their armoured Saracens. The breaking down of the doors with sledgehammers was the first inkling they had. What'll I do? Scarper across the border? I'll lose my job if I do. I imagine my father's mocking voice:

'*Afraid you might be arrested? For making a few corny speeches? Don't make me laugh.*'

I'll have to hit the border road and get out of Derry as quickly as I can. I turn the car and head up Duncreggan Road again.

The legend: Gallagher, Post Office, Gleann Comhraic is still there above the door, written in the old script in yellow letters on a green background. The colours are faded, the paint flaking off to reveal the grey of the wood underneath. Not a hand has been laid on the place since I left it last year other than the replacement of the old wooden door with a glass one. When I push open the door the glass acts as a mirror and the reflection of my head dances across it. I look jacked – not the sort of appearance I presented to shopkeepers in the past. I tighten my mouth to give my face a manly expression. There isn't a being to be seen inside though there is a switched-on television set on the counter.

'*Anyone at home?*'

There is a scrape of chair legs and the head of a girl appears above the counter.

'*Can I help you?*' *she asks in an English accent. She's of an in-between age, her hair tied with a ribbon and 'headlights', as they used to say in Derry, about to blossom.*

'*Have you the paper?*'

'*No Gaelic, sir. Will I get my granda?*'

Granda indeed! A cringing creep who spoke Irish strictly to get the grant. I say 'Derry Journal' to her and she reaches me a copy. The word 'Internment' is written in huge letters on the front page. I begin to read it as I go out. I am glad that I haven't met him or any of the old enemies. If I were doing well and looked it, it would be great to walk in and show them that I couldn't care less about them. As I was closing the door behind me I see one of my old acquaintances. She is standing in the doorway of the office of the Glen garage and I don't recognise her at first as she is pregnant. But the round forehead, the tight mouth and the sharp eyes are still the same. I try to go inside again to avoid her but she is too quick for me – as ever.

'*Aren't you the stranger!*'

'*Is that what they're still saying about me?*' *I ask with a laugh to take the sting out of it.*

She wasn't the worst but where was the windbag she married?

'*You've made a great job of the garage.*'

'*Garvan isn't here,*' *she says, as if she read my thoughts. 'He's gone to Derry. I hope the military don't lift him. I asked him not to go but sure you know yourself …*'

I know right enough. He'll be throwing stones at the soldiers. The swagger and the violence that he cannot indulge in at home since he was made a worthy citizen he'll have full scope for in Derry.

'*Isn't it in Derry that you're working yourself?*'

I recognise the real question that is hidden behind the first. She'd like to know if I got out of Derry because the soldiers were lifting people this morning. She was right!

'*I'm on the run, if that's what you want to know. I've just come from Derry.*'

'*Were there no soldiers on the roads?*'

'*I took the Glen Road and used the back road at Grianan.*'

'I know it – a great smuggling road during the war. Why didn't you come last night?
Didn't you hear the racket the women were making to warn people?'
'I didn't notice a thing. Our house is in a mixed area – a safe spot.'

AODH Ó CANAINN, *Tearmann na gColúr* (*The Pigeon Sanctuary*), 1998
(VERSION BY SEAN McMAHON)

5 MARCH 1793

ADDRESS OF THE TITULAR CLERGY OF DERRY
TO THEIR HEARERS

Greeting dearest brethren. At a time when the public mind seems to be much agitated, when sentiments inimical to good government, hostile to civil society and subversive of all order and regularity begin to be manifested by unlawful and tumultuous associations and to be carried into executions by riotous and unwarrantable proceedings, we feel it to be our indispensable duty to remind you of your obligations both civil and religious, a deep sense of which we have constantly endeavoured to impress on your minds from our respective altars. We think ourselves called upon to use all the authority we are invested with as Ministers of the Gospel of Peace and all the influence we may be entitled to, not only to admonish but also to conjure you by everything that is most dear to you not to let yourselves be misled under any pretence whatsoever from the line of loyalty due to your sovereign and of obedience to the laws of your country which you have hitherto uniformly pursued with no less honour and credit to yourselves and satisfaction to your rulers.

Bound by office to instruct and led by inclination to direct you always for the better and to promote your real happiness, we make bold to inform you that nothing can be more prejudicial to your real interest, nothing more hurtful both to your spiritual and temporal welfare than to let yourselves be drawn at this critical juncture by any insinuations whatever into acts of violence or outrage highly derogatory to your character as Christians and to your duty as faithful subjects. We therefore most earnestly recommend to you a continuation of the inoffensive respectful and exemplary conduct you have hitherto observed under more trying circumstances and greater hardships than you now labour under, and to wait with your usual patience and resignation the determination of your cause now pending in the hands of your most gracious sovereign and of a wise humane and enlightened legislature.

We confidently hope that you will never forget the many obligations you are under to your Protestant brethren who have generously stood forward as your advocates and protectors at this interesting period and who, by their friendly interposition and mediation with the Government and by their powerful applications to the legislature in your behalf, have justly merited at your hands every good office and every return of gratitude benevolence and affection that ye are capable of.

We cannot here omit to assure you that any individual under our care who shall be so unhappy so imprudent and so foolhardy as to deviate from the line of conduct here pointed out to him shall upon conviction be forthwith branded by us as an enemy to the community at large and shall be and is hereby declared altogether unworthy of our communion. We trust that we need not entertain the least doubt but this charitable and friendly advice will be as cheerfully submitted to, as gratefully received and as punctually followed by you as it is cordially and sincerely given by dearest brethren your most affectionate friends and most obedient humble servants the titular clergy of Derry.

Phil. McDavitt
London–Derry Journal, Mic. 60

THE BISHOP OF DERRY, *Aspects of Irish Social History 1750–1800*
(eds B. Trainor and W.H. Crawford), 1969

WE EXPECTED ABOUT FIVE THOUSAND people to turn out. There had, after all, been four thousand at Dungannon. Our calculation all along had been that a ban would encourage thousands of outraged citizens who would not otherwise have marched to come and demonstrate their disgust. Gerry Fitt arrived from Blackpool, where the Labour Party conference was in session, bringing three Tribunite MPs with him as 'observers'. Our loudspeaker van toured the streets from early morning with Hinds at the mike informing the populace that 'when you gotta go, you gotta go and we gotta go today'. Police reinforcements poured into the city, and there were rumours that there were 'dozens' of Alsatian dogs in the Waterside police station.

Commentators afterwards were unanimous that the imposition of a ban had indeed doubled the number of marchers. If this is so, then without the ban the turn-out would have been pathetic indeed. About four hundred people formed up in ranks in Duke Street. About two hundred stood on the pavement and looked on. It was a very disappointing crowd. People may have been deterred not by the ban but by the expectation of violence. And our somewhat melodramatic advance publicity had probably done little to reassure them. The march would proceed, we had said, 'come hell or high water', and the overwhelming majority of people in the Bogside and Creggan were not yet ready for either. Moreover, the whole route of our march lay outside the Catholic ghetto. We were to learn in time that when organizing a march towards confrontation it is essential to begin in 'home' territory and march out, so that there is somewhere for people to stream back to if this proves necessary.

On the day, however, numbers soon became irrelevant. Our route was blocked by a cordon of police and tenders drawn up across the road about three hundred yards from the starting point. We marched into the police cordon but failed to force a way through. Gerry Fitt's head was bloodied by the first baton blow of the day. We noticed that another police cordon had moved in from the rear and cut us off from behind. There were no exits from Duke Street in the stretch between the two cordons. So we were trapped. The crowd milled around for a few minutes, no one knowing quite what to do. Then a chair was produced and Miss Betty Sinclair got up and made a speech. She somewhat prematurely congratulated the crowd on its good behaviour and advised everyone to go home peacefully. Mr McAteer and Mr Cooper spoke along similar lines. Austin Currie, Nationalist MP for East Tyrone, was much less explicit about peace. I made a speech which was later to be characterized by the magistrates' court as 'incitement to riot'. It was an unruly meeting. Our loudspeaker had been seized by the police and it was difficult to make ourselves heard. Some of the crowd were demanding action. 'There must be no violence,' shouted Miss Sinclair, to a barrage of disagreement. But the decision as to whether there would be violence was soon taken from our hands.

The two police cordons moved simultaneously on the crowd. Men, women and children were clubbed to the ground. People were fleeing down the street from the front cordon and up the street from the rear cordon, crashing into one another, stumbling over one another, huddling in doorways, some screaming. District Inspector Ross McGimpsie, chief of the local police (now promoted), moved in behind his men and laid about him with gusto. Most people ran the gauntlet of batons and reached Craigavon Bridge, at the head of Duke Street. A water cannon – the first we had ever seen – appeared and hosed them across the bridge. The rest of the crowd went back down Duke Street, crouched and heads covered for protection from the police, ran through side streets and made a roundabout way back home. About a hundred had to go to hospital for treatment.

In the evening the lounge of the City Hotel looked like a casualty clearing station, all bandaged heads and arms in slings. In a corner Miss Sinclair was loudly denouncing the 'hooligans and anarchists' who had provoked the police and 'ruined our reputation'. Later there was sporadic fighting at the edges of the Bogside which lasted until early morning. Police cars were stoned, shop windows smashed and a flimsy, token barricade was erected in Rossville Street. A few petrol bombs were thrown. By the next morning, after the television newsreels and the newspaper pictures, a howl of elemental rage was unleashed across Northern Ireland, and it was clear that things were never going to be the same again. We had indeed set out to make the police over-react. But we hadn't expected the animal brutality of the RUC.

EAMONN MCCANN, *War and an Irish Town*, 1974

Halfway down the hill, Jack hesitated. The street was strangely empty. Alerted by Jack's stillness, Deirdre looked around; several shopkeepers were boarding up their windows.

They could not yet see into Guildhall Square; ash-gray walls and ancient cannons blocked the view, and dusk was falling. The square was always busy: buses revving and pulling in and out, people hurrying in and out of the Northern Bank, cars honking, boats in the Foyle waters blowing warning whistles, cranes whirring over the hoppers down on Prince's Quay. But the sound ascending to Deirdre and Jack as they stood in the middle of the pavement was none of these; it was the roar of a crowd.

'Wait here, Deirdre, till I see what's happening.' Jack started down the hill without her.

She glanced around frantically. 'Oh – no – please, let's turn back. Don't make me stay here by myself.'

He turned. 'I didn't mean to frighten you. Come on, then, if you want to stay with me.'

She hurried to catch up with him. 'Shouldn't we go back up and around the other way?'

A sharp bang in the Diamond made them both jump.

Jack swung round. 'Oh – it's just another board going up ... But I don't know if it'd be any better going the other way. If a riot starts down here, all Bogside'll be up in arms.' He steadied her with his hand on her arm. She had begun to shake. 'Here – would it make you feel better to take my arm?'

'No, of course not,' she flashed back. 'How would it be looking to anyone who knows us?' She set her jaw. 'We'll do whatever you think best, though ... I mean about the way we should –'

Suddenly male voices, yelling and cursing, and the tramp of feet sounded behind them, beyond the crest of Shipquay Street. Twenty or more youths, one of them displaying a small Tricolour, emerged from the darkness on the west side of the Diamond and came marching down the hill in military formation. They were gangly, wiry fellows with heavy boots. The Tricolour appeared luminous in the twilight.

Jack saw no sign of weapons, but was not going to wait for a confrontation with them. He grabbed Deirdre's arm. 'Like it or not,' he said, 'we'll be safer this way ... in the square ... more anonymous ... hurry ... let's get down there.'

They fled ahead of the small battalion under the arch of the wall and into the square. The place teemed with people. Opposite them on the lighted steps of the Guildhall and below it, Protestant crowds waved Union Jacks and chanted, 'Paisley. Paisley. No surrender.' Nearer to them, at the back of the crowd, enraged Catholic men and boys surged forward with fists raised in fury. Skirting the edge of the crowd, Jack led Deirdre along in the shadows of the city wall by the Magazine Gate and out toward Strand Road. Over the roar of the mob, he yelled, 'All we want is the British Army. Then there'll be a full-scale riot.'

Deirdre stared back in terror. She caught a glimpse of a big man in clerical garb coming out of the Guildhall with his hands raised as if in victory. Holding a bull horn in one hand, he was silhouetted in the yellow light of the wide door behind him. Below the steps, the crowd stilled somewhat to listen.

'There are one million Protestants in this country, and half a million Catholics. We will not bow to Rome.'

Again the front of the crowd shouted, 'No surrender, no!'

He went on, warmed by their response. 'We must let the agents of Rome know that we intend to stay in Ulster – and to stay in charge. ... We will not talk peace with the Scarlet Woman as long as she doesn't accept the Northern Irish Constitution. Until then, the Catholic Church is the enemy. Ulster will be Protestant! Ulster will be free!'

'Burn the Union Jack. Burn it! Burn it!'screamed a man's voice a few feet away from Deirdre and Jack. The fury erupted again.

Is Liam here? Deirdre suddenly wondered, her stomach muscles tightening in fear. If he had known Paisley was having a rally, surely he'd be down here with other civil rights men to protest. Had he truly been rehearsing for folk club – or was that just a cover? She looked around again, wildly this time, as if expecting him to rush out of the crowd toward her.

Jack pulled her along. 'Don't turn round, Deirdre.'

They had almost reached the edge of the square when a man staggered out of the crowd just ahead of them; a torn Union Jack dangled limply from his left arm. For a minute, Deirdre thought he was wounded. He clutched at his stomach with his right hand and stumbled forward in front of them, swaying, and blocked their path.

'Hey, big boy! Got a fancy little piece there, ain't ya?'

Jack stood still, holding Deirdre tightly. 'Get out of the way. You're drunk,' he said, his voice low and menacing. Deirdre hardly recognized it. Her heart thudded.

The drunk spat. 'Filthy, whoring Taigs!' He lurched toward them, his hand out to grab Deirdre's coat.

Breaking free of Jack, she dodged to the side, ducked past the drunkard, and began to run. Jack shoved the man against the wall and sprinted after her. They did not stop running until they reached the back gates of the University.

Breathlessly they leaned against the wall at the foot of the path that would lead them up to the Students' Union. Deirdre began to cry, great sobs of relief and release.

'I should've given him a good beating,' Jack gasped.

'No – no.'

'I should have,' he said between his teeth. 'No one should talk to a woman that way.'

Deirdre's crying suddenly turned to broken laughter. 'Indeed you shouldn't. What sort of a priest will you be ... if you get in a fight with a drunkard ... for wee Protestant girls mistaken for Catholics?' She looked up the wooded hill. 'But never mind, we're safe.' In the quiet of falling darkness not a sound came but the swish of a passing car.

Jack's breathing had slowed. 'Aye, for now.'

ELIZABETH GIBSON, *The Water is Wide*, 1985

SO WHEN A YOUNG WOMAN FROM DERRY said to me yesterday: 'My earliest memory of Derry is my going there to see Lundy's effigy burned,' and described the scene for me, it was a description less of fleeting and inarticulate life than of a chapter in a novel which interprets, annotates, and explains. I had heard how the citizens, every year, burn this effigy of the governor Lundy who wished to surrender the town. I had heard too how the Catholics below in Bogside, a spit's throw from the walls, pack paper, and turf, and rubbish into their fires so that the chimneys, on a level with the walls, pour stink and smoke into the faces of the Protestants upon the walls. I asked if this were a fact or a legend. The young woman said: 'I can smell it still.' Again the thing became larger than life.

SEAN O'FAOLAIN, *An Irish Journey*, 1940

THERE WERE OTHER SPEAKERS after Betty Sinclair but I didn't listen to them. The old buildings on either side of the street seemed to take on a new character. They were no longer decrepit and tired, but dark, ominous and solid, like the walls of a prison. I looked around for an open door or a space where we could shelter, but saw none. The rally grew noisier. I watched the rear line of policemen react by drawing their batons and crouching forward like runners in a race, poised and waiting for the starter's pistol. 'We don't have a chance if they charge us,' I said to Carlin. 'It's time to get offside.' About twenty yards of empty, open ground separated us from the line of policemen. We had a choice: we could rejoin the protesters, or head towards the police behind us before the balloon went up. With feigned nonchalance, Tommy and I walked the twenty yards towards the defenders of the northern statelet. Staring straight ahead, awaiting orders, the policemen scarcely noticed us as we eased our way through their ranks. Carlin and I had just got through when a tremendous shout went up from the crowd at the other barricade. I turned, to see makeshift placards flying through the air and the policemen, like young bulls stung by picadors, charging the marchers. I watched the police swing their batons, hitting heads, backs and shoulders. Private parts received short, vicious thrusts. Those still standing broke and ran. Carlin and I reached Fountain Hill ahead of the crowd; as we ran up the hill, Eamonn McCann shot by. I envied him his youth and lengthened my own stride to get as far away as possible from the police and back to the safety of the Bogside. I hoped that John L. had not been caught or injured by the RUC.

PADDY DOHERTY, *Paddy Bogside*, 2001

IT IS STRANGE TO FIND ONESELF cut off suddenly from all one's work and ordinary interests and to be projected into a new sphere where every standard of value is completely changed. Stranger still, how quickly a normal person accommodates himself to such an altered existence.

Thus it was with me in Derry Gaol. It was no avail to me there that I could draft a 'Conveyance', or that I knew something about 'Contingent Remainders' and quite a lot about the 'Law of Contracts'. But it was of vast importance that I learned the most effective way of heating my milk on the flickering cell gas-jet, and that I was able to make my wooden spoon serve all the purposes of a knife and fork. All my other accomplishments, too, paled into utter insignificance compared with the one great fact that I found that I could write doggerel about the life and humours of the prison, that passed from cell to cell and was laboriously transcribed into tattered copybooks against the day when the General Release would come and the boys go home to tell their friends all about their varied experiences.

One quickly settles down to the dull routine of prison, and all the interests and causes for excitement in one's outside existence are soon replaced by the incidents that ripple the surface of that monotonous life that makes up the sum of one's days within those dreary walls. What commotion there was if the long hours after the evening 'lock-up' were broken, say, by the step of the Governor along the corridor, and you heard him going into another prisoner's cell! What could he be coming about? Was somebody going to be released? And the tremendous interest that was excited amongst us by seeing one of our comrades going off to his Court-Martial! How we clambered round him on his return and listened to his account of the proceedings and wondered what his sentence would be!

There were sixty or so of us, untried political prisoners, in Derry at the time, representing several counties and many walks in life. We were professional and business men, farmers, artisans and labourers; but we all stood for the same ideal, and a fine spirit of comradeship linked us all together. We had the usual prison organisation that has proved so effective in many jail fights. For the British Authorities have had to accept the awkward fact that they cannot put more than two Sinn Feiners together without an organisation emerging.

LOUIS J. WALSH, *'On My Keeping' – And in Theirs*, 1921

I FELT THAT IF ANY VIOLENCE BROKE OUT, if they started attacking anyone – me, for instance – it would be serious. I felt that anyone who drew their anger could be badly beaten. I saw a photographer I knew wandering around with a group of American photographers. He told me in whispers that one of them had been kicked on the way across the bridge. I whispered to him that I thought we should get out now. He seemed anxious in case anyone would notice how worried we looked: we were out of our depth.

We moved slowly back away from where Robinson and Paisley were still greeting their supporters, and edged our way towards the bridge. The march was beginning; the music of the accordions, the pipes and drums filled the air. We moved back towards the city centre, there to get a better and safer view of the march. I felt I was stupid to have followed Robinson for so long. I wasn't going to do that again.

As they came into the Diamond, the marchers, the Apprentice Boys, removed their hats as they passed the monument to those killed in the war. Shipquay Street was blocked by RUC jeeps. Police and army stood about; they were jeered by some of the groups who passed by, especially a black soldier at whom they shouted 'Nigger', 'Blackie' and 'Darkie'.

There were bands from all over the North. Pipe bands wearing kilts, pipe bands wearing purple dickey bows, pipe bands with two little boys in front throwing batons up in the air and catching them with immense skill. There were accordion bands, too, dressed in red, white and blue. Even young ones marching, the teenagers, had a severe look on their faces.

Each band had a banner dedicated to King William himself, who had saved Ulster from Popery, or General Walker who had led the resistance to the siege, or some other figure from the mythology of Unionism, with a slogan such as 'No Surrender' and the name of the band's place of origin. Some of them came from across the border.

Each band, too, had men carrying swords, one of whom I followed along for some time, enjoying the look of pleasure, importance and pomposity on his face. Others had men carrying huge ceremonial batons, or sticks. Coleraine had a man dressed up like a general. The Sons of Ulster, Carrickfergus had a skinhead out in front with a heavy stick in his hand; as he came around the corner he let out a yowl, and glared ahead as though daring anyone to deny him his right to do so. A few boys with National Front tee-shirts stood about and watched the parade as well. A branch from Liverpool passed by. A man stuck out his tongue at the RUC.

Afterwards, I went down into the Bogside to see what our Catholic brethren had been doing while their compatriots had been celebrating their deliverance in 1689. On Shipquay Street the RUC drew their batons and went in pursuit of a few youths; otherwise it was all calm. It was even quieter as I turned left, walked past a few RUC jeeps and made my way along towards the Bogside.

My mind was on something else. I was walking along without paying the slightest attention to what was around me. I was swiftly and suddenly brought down to earth by a Derry accent: 'Get out of the way'. Right in front of me were two blokes both wearing balaclava helmets over their faces, slits for their eyes, both moving forward cautiously towards the corner. It didn't take long for me to realise that what they had in their hands were petrol bombs. I ran across the street to a cafe which had begun to pull its shutters down.

They threw the petrol bombs and ran, removing the balaclavas, so that within a few seconds it was impossible to distinguish them from ordinary passers-by. As soon as the bombs exploded the RUC jeeps careered into the street and the cafe filled up with people running for cover. I could hear the sound of rubber bullets being fired.

When the noise died down, they pulled up the shutter of the cafe again and I moved towards Rossville Street. People had come out of the houses and the flats and were standing around. Six different television crews had placed themselves at strategic points on the waste ground all around. Photographers were everywhere. I watched some children putting on balaclava helmets and leading a group of photographers up a side alley. Most of the photographers were foreign. Someone pointed out to me a man who was standing among the crowd as a senior member of the IRA, who was watching over things.

A boy, who couldn't be more than ten years of age, moved out from the crowd and threw a stone at the RUC jeep. He ran back and emerged again with another stone. He didn't bother putting on a mask. A few RUC jeeps moved around the piece of waste ground, but did not come any closer. Further down the Bogside a few kids had lit a bonfire on the street. A youth was wandering around wearing a pink balaclava helmet. A helicopter flew overhead.

The photographers in the Bogside and the camera crews who had stayed in the Bogside had not done well that afternoon. Had they ventured across the river to the Waterside they would have witnessed a battle between the RUC and the more militant of the Loyalist marchers. Such a battle would have been unthinkable before the Anglo-Irish Agreement.

A few photographers had snapped up that battle, and sat having dinner in an Indian restaurant. They were delighted with themselves. An American photographer and her French colleague were making a deal whereby she would give her photos to his agency and he would pay her. An Iranian photographer was trying to contact Paris and other faraway capitals from the coin box, and returned constantly to our table bemoaning the fact that he couldn't get through.

Later that night in the Catholic Bogside, a hijacked Ulsterbus blocked Rossville Street and groups of people stood around the flats. On the left one whole block of flats was in the process of being demolished by the authorities; everything had been cleared out except the outside walls, the floors and the walls between the flats. You could look up at this shell, and see the wallpaper, the few light fittings left, and the tiny, cramped spaces where whole families had been reared. The place resembled a giant empty book case towering over the journalists and photographers waiting for a riot to begin and the locals who were obligingly preparing to put on a show for them.

When the pubs were well shut, and everyone was assembled, a few blokes wearing masks went into the bus and covered it with petrol. We stood back and watched them douse the seats and the floor and then set the bus alight before running back into an alleyway. The bus began to burn, slowly at first, but then with increasing ferocity. As it burned, it was decided by whoever was controlling this event that more material was needed; a French journalist and a BBC journalist were forced to hand over their cars, which were driven up and down the road with enormous relish by a group of local teenagers before they were handed back, undamaged.

The burning bus revved for a while, as though a phantom driver had started the ignition. Then the fire died down. 'Now that it's gone out I'm cold,' said an American photographer. I was cold too, and decided that it was time to go home.

COLM TÓIBÍN, Bad Blood, 1994

The way I feel it coming
Is as a fire with one wing
That is already blackening
My heart;

Or as the blind hammering
Of the trapped crowd
On the closing walls
Of the street;

And the seams of the houses
Splitting in a swarm of cock-
Roaches that riot in an
Alarming silence;

And we are all running
Through a cloud, glimpsing icebergs,
Calling goodbye to disaster
And then hello;

The mirrors curl up like paper
In the rumpling fire;
Sightless we follow the blind
Whose hands

Drum fire from our brittle dread
Blow by saturating blow,
Until it hardens to a cold
Rallentando for the dead.

When it comes darkly over us
I will hold you and say
In disappointed love, 'Look
See my face in the wave?'

SEAMUS DEANE, 'Civil War: 13 August 1970', in *The Wearing of the Black*
(ed. Padraic Fiacc), 1974

A DISUSED STATION, A SMALL but once-busy terminus of four platforms, waiting- and refreshment-room, booking office, book stall and offices. Not the main station which still functioned across the river but a secondary one that had served a remote and 'backward' district and that was situated in what had become one of the 'no-go' areas of the town. This was the, at first sight, not very promising looking complex of dilapidated buildings entrusted to me by Mullen and the Committee of Five who administered this barricaded district to make into a community centre, in the hope, I guessed, that I'd think of something better both to call it and to do with it.

In case I should later think I hear you ask: What about the car drive, why did you leave that out? I'll mention that it was a unique journey, being the only one we ever took together. And there were the glimpses of holy places as we passed, windows through trees, half-hidden porches, places rooted in the motionless quietude that formed banks on each side of the swiftly-flowing road. You saw them too, perhaps before I did, but you didn't enquire why we couldn't get Mullen to stop and let us out with the suitcases, the cats' basket, the fish and their aquarium so that with the money for the Rolls and what your mother had left with you we could have looked around for a safe retreat. As you put it later in all innocence: 'Mary didn't say to Jesus at the tomb: Let's call it a day; I've a friend with a house on the lake who'll lend us the top floor.'

Just once you took my hand and held it (with Liz we were at the back, Mullen had a young man I took to be his bodyguard beside him) and with your other drew my head back when I'd turned it for a last glimpse of a thatched roof at the end of a leafy lane.

The first night in the Laggan we stayed with Mullen and his wife in a small two-storeyed house whose windows, like most of the others in the row, had been broken and were partially boarded up.

We were given the three bedrooms that made up the upper floor, Mullen and his wife moving down to sleep in the sitting room. So far so good, and even the view from the part of my window that was still glazed of a wide, desolate space strewn with burnt-out cars from temporary barricades wouldn't have worried me hadn't it been for the stray animals, dogs, cats, and a lean goat, roaming the waste ground.

I imagined you at your window before you undressed, sharing, in the way I knew of but couldn't quite grasp, their plight. That is, if yours was the other front room next to mine, Liz having been allotted the larger one at the back.

Through the dividing wall I heard a clink of glass or china and the splash of water poured from the jug that must be a replica of the one in my room standing in its matching basin on a washstand.

Had you pulled the curtain without looking out and were you tranquilly washing yourself? More likely transferring the fish from the bowl in which they'd travelled to the larger tank. What you were doing became a matter of such life-and-death concern that I listened with my ear to a bunch of wall-paper roses and louder than the watery sounds heard my own quickened heart-beat. With my chest touching the wall I imagined the echo penetrating it and that the silence that now seemed to have fallen over the next room meant that you too were listening, waiting and, perhaps, yes perhaps impatiently, for me to come to you.

Start thinking these thoughts and there's no end to them; the only end to what begins as a smouldering kind of wonder about you and soon flares into a smoky, blinding wanting is in your arms.

I took off my shoes, slipped out onto the landing, slid my feet over the boards that I could tell were creaky ones (I could tell all sorts of things in this state of heightened physical consciousness) and opened what should have been the door to ...

Liz, part-undressed, was kneeling by the bed saying her prayers. Her big face turned to me with the pallor on it that had gathered there while hidden in her hands. Better have looked on her physical nakedness than that, or was my shame exaggerated by my disappointment? Shamed and humbled at another revelation of my being subject to possession to the point where I dwell in a world of only a single street and that made up of brothels, so different to the one we share where reality is a complex mosaic of various shades of fear, love and anguish.

FRANCIS STUART, *Memorial*, 1973

A TRÍ A DEIR AN CLOG TAOBH NA LEAPA. Ní aithníonn an intinn go bhfuil réaltacht ar bith ag baint leis an chlog. Sórt síoraíochta a mhothaíos sí sin; ní aithníonn cora an choirp aon am, caite ná le teacht. Ní raibh am ar bith nach raibh mar seo, ná ní bheidh nach mbeidh. Titeann deireadh i log mór iasachta. Baineann léine agus bríste do chraiceann marbh. Amach síos atá stocaí is bróga.

De réir a chéile, ag dul staighre síos, ordaíonn an aigne an corp is ligeann an corp a scíste chrua. Siocann an gaosán le boladh an bhia fhriochta is lúbann na putóga.

'Suigh síos ansin, a Bhulaí. Beidh seo réidh i gceann bomaite. Ar chodail tú go maith?'

'Rinne. Ar mhothaigh tú scéala ar bith?'

'Dúirt an fear ar Radio Éireann go raibh trioblóid i mBéal Feirste i rith na hoíche. Cuireadh monarcha fá thine is cúpla teach.'

''Beag maith a dhéanfaidh sin do dhuine ar bith. 'nDúirt sé cé a rinne é?'

'Ní dúirt. Tithe le Caitlicigh a dódh.'

''Mhothaigh Cathal scéala ar bith?'

'Bhí sé ag rá liom go raibh scaifte maith amuigh aréir. Tá siad ag dúil lena thuilleadh don oíche anocht.'

'Níl 'fhios agam an fíor an méid a dúradh. Más fíor, beidh an oiread agus is féidir a dhíth le stop a chur leo anocht.'

'Tá Cathal ró-óg le tabhairt amach i lár troda. Beidh sé dona go leor gan páistí á ngortú.'

'Ní tharlóidh rud ar bith má bhíonn go leor againne ann. Níl i gceist ach iad thaispeáint dúinne go bhfuil cead a gcos acu sa bhaile seo – i lár an Bhogaigh féin. Déanfaidh siad iarracht siúl isteach is ní ligfear dófa.'

'Nach mbeidh gunnaí agus gás agus lorgaidí leo?'

'Ní bheidh ann ach sin. Beidh sprais cloch sa mhullach orthu sula mbíonn seans acu a theacht chomh fada le siopa an bhúistéara. Ina dhiaidh sin beidh an t-ádh leo mura dtigtear ar a gcúl orthu. Tá a fhios sin acu.'

'Ní bheidh maith ar bith ionatsa anocht i ndiaidh seachtaine ar oícheanta. Ní fiú Cathal ...'

'Tífidh muid níos moille. B'fhéidir go gcluinfimis dea-scéala ar an nuacht – beag an baol. 'Domh cupán eile tae.'

Is iontach an casadh a níonn an saol. Bhí lá ann a chrochfadh muintir Dhoire fear ar bith a shílfeadh siad bheith ina phoblachtach achrannach. Anois tá na daoine féin, daoine cosúil le muintir chairde Chathail, nach raibh baint acu ariamh le polaitíocht ná le náisiúntacht, tá siad ag smaoineamh ar an phéas a throid. Ní náisiúntacht atá ann, ar ndóigh, ach míshástracht leis an mhíchothrom, leis an leathpháirt, le bardas leataobhach Albanach.

'Cad é an deireadh a bheas leis?'

'Ag Dia atá a fhios. Seo an chéad uair le leathchéad bliain a bhfuil iomlán na ndaoine le chéile, 'bhfuil 'fhios agat. Ní poblachtaigh agus lucht náisiúnta atá i gceann na hoibre. Tá lucht gnó is tráchtála ag cur léi. Na sagairt féin, tá cuid mhaith acu páirteach ann.'

Ba rud sin a ghoill go mór, a ghoill le 'fiche nó tríocha de bhlianta, na sagairt nach gcuideodh le hógánaigh a muintire féin. Bhí siad sásta lucht achrainn is coireanna a thabhairt orthu, is d'fhág siad iad ar an trá fholamh fúthu féin. Ní oireann na smaointe sin; baineann siad le dearcadh leataobhach ar an tsaol, dearcadh a ligeadh i ndearmad lá den tsaol idir dhá dhea-chomhairle is atá á shíobadh anois de bharr an mhíshuaimhnis.

Three the bedside clock says. The mind doesn't accept that the clock has any reality. A sort of infinity it feels; body movements don't recognise any time, past or future. There was no time that wasn't like this, nor will there be that won't. The whole lot falls into a trough of strangeness. Shirt and trousers touch dead skin. Far below are socks and shoes.

Gradually on the way downstairs the mind sorts out the body, the body takes its hard-earned rest. The nose tightens at the smell of fried food and the gut churns.

'Sit down there, Willy. This'll be ready in a minute. Sleep well?'

'I did. Did you hear any news?'

'The man on Radio Éireann said there was trouble in Belfast during the night. A factory and some houses were set on fire.'

'Not much good that'll do anybody. Did he say who did it?'

'No. It was Catholic houses that were burned.'

'Cathal hear any news?'

'He was saying there was a good crowd out last night. They expect it will be bigger tonight.'

'I don't know if it's true what was said. If it is it'll take as many as we can get to stop them.'

'Cathal's too young to be mixed up in that fight. It'll be bad enough without injuring children.'

'Nothing will happen if there are enough of us. The whole point is to show us that they have right of entry in this town, into the heart of the Bogside itself. They'll try to get in and we won't let them.'

'Won't they have guns and gas and batons?'

'That's all there will be. There'll be a shower of stones on the top of their heads before they can get as far as the butcher's. After that they'll be lucky if we don't get round the back of them. And they know that.'

'You won't be much use tonight after a week on nights. There's no point in Cathal ...'

'We'll soon see. Maybe we'll hear good news on the bulletin, though it's unlikely. Give us another cup of tea.'

Life is full of odd twists. Once upon a time the Derry people would have hanged anybody they thought was a troublemaking Republican. Now the same people, people like the families of Cathal's friends, who had never had any connection with nationalism, are ready to fight the police. It's not a nationalist feeling at all but rage at injustice, at sectarianism and at the discrimination of a Protestant corporation.

'What will it all come to?'

'God knows! This is the first time for fifty years that the majority of the people are united, you understand. Republicans and nationalists are involved. Business people and commercial interests are participating. The very priests – at least a good section of them – are taking part.'

That had rankled a lot, been rankling for twenty, thirty years, that the priests wouldn't help the youth of their own flocks. They dubbed them troublemakers and criminals, and essentially abandoned them. Those thoughts don't belong; they come from a biased sense of the world, a point of view that has been pushed out a long time ago, between two common senses, and that's being blown to pieces because of the unrest.

SEÁN Ó SIADHAIL, 'Iósaf' ('Joseph'), in *Scéalta Mhac an Ghobáin* (*The Stories of the Artificer's Son*), 1981 (VERSION BY SEAN McMAHON)

O H, GOD! POOR DERRY! Or Londonderry as they so insultingly called it. No Derryman, Catholic or Protestant, called it that. The soccer team was Derry City, the cricket club, City of Derry, the walls were Derry walls. Even in Orange song, that's what they were. But Londonderry or, as the BBC would say, Londond'ry, was an insult. Still, that was the least of our injuries. It was not much more than a symptom, really, a bit of best British insensitivity.

Up until now there had been a faint hope. Labour had, at least, stood in a neutral corner letting Cameron and Hunt do the work. Now we would see the Unionists assert themselves again. A special enclave, created out of nothing except to give the Protestants safe power. Not based on the idea of Irish unity. That would have made a minority out of a group who had ruled always. Not based on a provincial basis. The nine counties of Ulster would have been fifty-fifty, and that would have been dangerous. Not based on a county basis. Fermanagh and Tyrone would have been out. Not based on electoral areas. All they would have then would be the large area around Belfast. An abomination, the original gerrymander, the largest possible area that they could safely rule. That's what it was based on. That was democracy. That was guaranteed. Protestants were superior to Catholics and should never be in a minority position to them. England was tolerant, but not that tolerant. A Protestant Queen, a Protestant established church, a prime minister who could not be Catholic. He could be a Jew or an atheist but not a Catholic. And now, after the fight, back to democracy, back to the Orange Order, back to despair and poverty under the Union Jack.

The sky was blazing red and gold, and the river at the foot of the garden was on fire as Colm made his way to bed. Even though it was summer, his feet were cold. His throat was sore from cigarettes. Cursed are the meek, for they shall never inherit the earth!

Clusters of men in little groups all over Bogside, anger in their voices. Bernadette Devlin in jail! It was outrageous. She was a daft wee girl, full of crazy notions, but she had been on the barricades. We hadn't asked her. We didn't need her. But she was there. Now she was in jail.

The B Specials who had murdered Gallagher in Armagh in front of a hundred witnesses were not in jail. The police who had batoned seventy-year-old McCloskey in Dungiven and left him to die in a doorway were not in jail. The police who had killed Sam Devenney and attacked his family were not in jail. None of the Protestant mob who burned Bombay Street and murdered a child in his own home were in jail. None of the well-photographed thugs of Burntollet were in jail. In fact, some of them had been signed up in the Specials as a reward two days later. None of the hundreds of police who had rampaged through Bogside after Burntollet were in jail. They had smashed windows, shouted obscenities, batoned and terrorized, but they were still in uniform. Who was prosecuted after the Orange rampage in Maghera? No one! Croppies lie down! Back to your kennels! Scum! Layabouts! Fenian bastards!

Christ, we'll teach them. They stopped us the last time. We shouldn't have heeded Hume. We should have burned them out.

The boys in uniform stood at their sentry boxes nervously. An army Land-Rover stopped in Waterloo Square and someone used his walkie-talkie. A few trucks arrived from Ebrington Barracks. The groups in Bogside merged and murmured. In shadowed laneways, stones were gathered.

Peter and Bosco and a group went round by the Little Diamond to avoid the barricades and joined a throng from Creggan. More soldiers gathered in Waterloo Square, young, bewildered boys who had, for months, been on a kind of holiday. Now there was trouble and they did not know why. It was not their fight. Why should they have to deal with it?

A shout. A stone flew. Then another. The soldiers flinched and raised their riot shields but did not retaliate. More stones and, of a sudden, a petrol bomb. A voice on a loud-hailer, disperse or ... rubber bullets ... water cannon ... armoured cars. A movement of vehicles and grim snatch squads, a flurry of stones and struggling bodies.

Bosco stood aloof. It was not the soldiers he wanted. It was the police. He watched dispassionately, listening to the sharp commands, the shouts and jeers, the revving engines and grinding gears, the crash of stone on metal, the thud of batons.

'Come on, Peter. This'll get us nowhere. Up Francis Street and down the other way!'

WALTER HEGARTY, *The Price of Chips*, 1973

THEN CAME THAT SATURDAY IN OCTOBER. The weather wasn't bad. Oh yes I was there. We all knew it was going to be an event, there was going to be trouble too. Like so many who claim to have been there that day, I went to watch. By the time I caught up with it the march was trying to reach the bridge. It had taken almost two hours to make a quarter of a mile from its gathering point beneath the railway clock. First it had tried its planned route up Bond's Hill, but the Royal Ulster Constabulary blocked this illegal procession there. Then an attempt to make it up Simpson's Brae was blocked. Back it went, down Duke Street, seeking the quickest retreat from the Waterside. Before it reached Archie Cassoni's cafe it was blocked again. It's rear slowly pressed on till the marchers were compacted in. They didn't stretch further than Lower Fountain Hill Street. Was it even a hundred yards? Police now sealed that end too. Here it stood, utterly blocked. This trickle of protest was going no further.

The RUC in its naivety pressed in. When the Inspector drove his baton into that protest he burst an abscess that had been festering for generations. It was an abscess whose pus came from the very heart of our society, from the very heart of each of us. The screams weren't to stop for twenty-five years.

We spectators, clustered around the junction of Spencer Road and the bridge, knew something was happening. A woman grabbed my sleeve. She spun me unto the road. 'Quick son, sit down, block its way!' I looked up at a great grey metal box of a vehicle, it's windscreen meshed. As it pushed through the crowd towards me I realised it had to be a water cannon. It looked nothing at all like the dark squat things we knew roamed the streets of Paris and other European cities. 'Don't be stupid, missus. It's the police!' I pulled free from her. Her pleading found no takers and she too fled its path.

GERARD McMENAMIN, 'King Street', in *The Waterside Book*, 1996

Shielded, vague soldiers, visored, crouch alert:
between tall houses down the blackened street;
the hurled stones pour, hurt-instinct aims to hurt,
frustration spurts in flame about their feet.

Lads who at ease had tossed a laughing ball,
or, ganged in teams, pursued some shouting game,
beat angry fists against that stubborn wall
of faceless fears which now at last they name.

Night after night this city yields a stage
with peak of drama for the pointless day,
where shadows offer stature, roles to play,
urging the gestures which might purge in rage
the slights, the wrongs, the long indignities
the stubborn core within each heart defies.

JOHN HEWITT, 'Bogside, Derry, 1971', *Collected Poems*, 1991

IT SHOULD BE EMPHASISED THAT MANY of the reported effects applied to individuals who had no part in the fighting and who were affected in their own homes. Many of the high flats became uninhabitable, as CS collected through broken windows and ventilators. No shells were shot through windows in these flats, but this appears to have resulted more from the strength of the windows and the acute angle at which the shots were fired than from any specific attempt by the police to avoid this dangerous possibility. The windows in Rossville Estates are made of a double-thickness glass. In some cases which we inspected, the shells broke the outer layer without penetrating into the flats. All broken windows seem to have resulted from stones thrown by police and their civilian supporters. Some windows had fortunately been boarded over by the residents in anticipation of the attacks. In the eighteeen most exposed flats of Rossville Estates (the lowest layer of the righthand building) five had broken windows. In some cases shells hit the front doors of flats. In one case, an elderly resident thought it was someone knocking at the door and went to open it. Her next door neighbour opened her door at the same time to see what the noise was. Both received a strong, intense dose of CS, which thereupon permeated the interior of the flats. A second case was more serious. It occurred in one of the lowest flats in the end building, so that the firing angle approached 180°. The doors of these flats are released by a Bales catch, which gives way when pushed from the outside or pulled from within. The direct hit of the CS cartridge forced the door open and sent CS streaming into the flat. A fourteen-month-old infant, resting at the very back of the flat at the time, developed an acute bronchial disorder and was taken to hospital a few hours later.

RUSSELL STETLER, *The Battle of Bogside*, 1970

THE FIRST GLIMPSE OF LONDONDERRY from the east bank of the Foyle is unforgettable: a walled city with a magnificent cathedral surrounded by Georgian terraced houses. If it were not for the barbed wire and the army pillboxes, it could compare with Windsor. In recent years the city has become deeply divided. The west bank is now over 90 per cent Catholic and only a small and poor Protestant community still hangs on in the Fountain Estate. The Shantallow and Creggan estates, neat and modern, belie a male unemployment rate of 60–70 per cent. The SDLP have a hard grip over the middle class, the middle-aged and the elderly. Sinn Féin have a worryingly high level of support among the young.

Derry's history is a roller-coaster of success and hope followed by failure and despair. Geographically a backwater, the city was strategically at the hinge of the centuries-old battle between British domination and Irish resistance. Every paving-stone has a story and the suffering of both sides requires no embellishment to convey its awful authenticity.

When St Columba founded Derry in the sixth century, he scribbled a verse:

> This is my reason for loving Derry. It is in all its width and length
> Filled with shining peace for it is peopled by God's angels only.

In July 1689, deep into the city's third siege, the defending commander, General Walker, recounted a grisly shopping list in his diary:

A quarter of a dog fattened by eating the bodies of the slain Irish	5s 6d
A dog's head	2s 6d
A cat	4s 6d
A rat	1s 0d
A mouse	0s 6d

The history of the city and its place in the pantheon of both communities are imbibed from birth. In the nineteenth century it was the port through which many of the starving passed on their way to America. Later, it became a world centre for shirt making (and still is).

Much of the latest Troubles have centred on Londonderry and by the end of the seventies the *Guardian*, in a major centrepiece article, was describing the city centre as 'Tumbledown Derry'. A BBC news correspondent described sitting in his studio waiting to do a piece on the one o'clock bulletin when a building next door collapsed with a loud thump. Determined to get a vox pop reaction to the blast, he went out and stuck his microphone into the face of a bemused onlooker who told him: 'That there was my shop. Some boy come in with a television set and dropped it on the counter. 'How long does it take to mend?' he says. 'About a week,' I said. 'Well you've got two minutes,' he says, with me running out behind him.'

RICHARD NEEDHAM, *Battling for Peace*, 1998

Purge the filth and do not stir it.
Let them out. At least let in
A breath or two of oxygen,
So they may settle down for good
And mix themselves in the common blood.
We all are what we are, and that
Is mongrel pure. What nation's not
Where any stranger hung his hat
And seized a lover where she sat?'
He ceased and faded. Zephyr blew
And all the others faded too.
I stood like a ghost. My fingers strayed
Along the fatal barricade.
The gentle rainfall drifting down
Over Colmcille's town
Could not refresh, only distil
In silent grief from hill to hill.

THOMAS KINSELLA, 'Butcher's Dozen', *Collected Poems*, 1996

TO REACH THE RUINS OF THE DISTILLERY, we had only to cross Blucher Street, go along Eglinton Terrace, across the mouth of the Bogside, with the city abattoir on our left, the street stained by the droppings of the cows, pigs and sheep that were herded in there from the high lorries with their slatted sides. There, vast and red-bricked, blackened and gaunt, was the distillery, taking up a whole block of territory. The black stumps of its roof-timbers poked into the sky. Sometimes, when passing there, I would hear the terrified squealing of pigs from the slaughterhouse. They sounded so human I imagined they were going to break into words, screaming for mercy. And the noise would echo in the hollow distillery, wailing through the collapsed floors, clinging to the blackened brick inside. I had heard that people ran from their houses as the shooting started and the police cordon tightened. The crowd in the street, at the top of the Bogside, started singing rebel songs, but the police fired over their heads and the crowd scattered. The IRA gunmen, on the roof or at the top-floor windows, fired single shots, each one like a match flare against the sky. They were outgunned, surrounded, lost. It was their last-minute protest at the founding of the new state. Then the explosion came and the whole building shook and went on fire. No one knew when or if the building would be repaired or knocked down and replaced. It was a burnt space in the heart of the neighbourhood.

The town lay entranced, embraced by the great sleeping light of the river and the green beyond of the border. It woke now and then, like someone startled and shouting from a dream, in clamour at its abandonment. Once, at the height of a St Patrick's Day riot, when the police had baton-charged a march and pursued us into our territory, we enticed them to follow us further downhill from the Lone Moor into the long street called Stanley's Walk that ran parallel with our own. We had splashed half a barrel of oil from a ransacked garage on the road surface at the curve of the slope. The police and B Specials raced down after us, under a hail of stones thrown at the cars and the jeeps they rode in or ran alongside. Advertising hoardings at the side of the street took the first volley of our missiles as the two leading cars hit the oil. A giant paper Coca-Cola bottle was punctured, along with the raised chin of a clean-shaven Gillette model. The cars swung and hurtled into the side walls, shredding stones from them like flakes of straw. The oil glittered in the sudsy swathe of the tyres, and one car lit up in a blue circle of flame as the police ran from it. The whole street seemed to be bent sideways, tilted by the blazing hoardings into the old Gaelic football ground.

SEAMUS DEANE, *Reading in the Dark*, 1996

FREE DERRY ENCOMPASSED THE BOGSIDE, the sprawling Creggan housing estate, the more compact Brandywell and a small middle-class area. The territory held by the rebels roughly corresponded to the South Ward, which had been set up by the Unionist administration to contain the Catholic population of the city. The newly liberated territory measured 888 acres and two roods, or roughly four square miles. By gerrymandering the city for over half a century, the Unionists had inadvertently created an Achilles heel for themselves. Twenty-eight thousand despised people shoved together, piled on top of each other and discriminated against, had decided that enough was enough. They were now outside the law, and their position, energy, and numbers posed a threat to the very existence of the state. In the vacuum created by the uneasy peace, we were playing a whole new game. From behind the barricades, which were now higher than ever, Free Derry proclaimed its independence to the world, and it appeared as if the whole world wanted to make our acquaintance. Congratulatory telegrams and letters flooded in. Telephones were few and far between in the Bogside, so many of the telephone messages were relayed by people in other parts of the city. The nearest telephone to me belonged to my neighbour, who was a foreman with the local Development Commission. The Defence Association desperately needed its own telephone. A GPO engineer came to install one. 'Black or green?' he asked.

'Green,' I said.

PADDY DOHERTY, *Paddy Bogside*, 2001

Lightnings slaughtered
The distance. In the harmless houses
Faces narrowed. The membrane
Of power darkened
Above the valley,
And in a flood of khaki
Burst. Indigoed
As rain they came
As the thunder radioed
For a further
Haemorrhage of flame.

The roads died, the clocks
Went out. The peace
Had been a delicately flawed
Honeymoon signalling
The fearful marriage
To come. Death had been
A form of doubt.
Now it was moving
Like a missionary
Through the collapsed cities
Converting all it came among.

And when the storm passed
We came out of the back rooms
Wishing we could say
Ruin itself would last.
But the dead would not
Listen. Nor could we speak
Of love. Brothers had been
Pitiless. What could ignite
This sodden night?
Let us bury the corpses.
Fast. Death is our future

And now is our past.
There are new children
In the gaunt houses.
Their eyes are fused.
Youth has gone out
Like a light. Only the insects
Grovel for life, their strange heads
Twitching. No one kills them

Anymore. This is the honeymoon
Of the cockroach, the small
Spiderless eternity of the fly.

SEAMUS DEANE, 'After Derry, 30 January 1972', *Gradual Wars*, 1972

ABOUT TEN YEARS LATER WE MOVED from Dublin to Derry where Dan
became the head of the mathematics department in a large grammar
school. I remember so little of those years. It's probably just as well or
otherwise I might bore you with tedious domestic details. It is a curious
reflection on more than twenty years of marriage that all I remember with
clarity was the ending of it, and even that memory is electric still in my mind
for what most people in the world would consider to be the wrong reasons.
It was shortly before Christmas in 1975 and I was alone in the house. I was
sitting in front of the fire. I could feel the heat spreading through me.
Around me on the floor were the Christmas cards. Daniel always complained that I left them too late for politeness. He was out visiting the
parents of one of his sixth-form pupils. I even remember the name of the
boy. George Cranston. His father was an Inspector in the RUC. My
shoulders had been stiff for days and the warmth was mellowing them. The
bell rang. I put the top on my pen and placed it carefully on the floor beside
the unwritten envelopes and got up and went and opened the door. A
policeman and a policewoman were standing on the step.

It's strange how immune you always feel to violence, devilry. Snow
mixed with rain feathered their caps. In the car parked in the driveway
behind them some sort of a radio crackled.

'Yes?' I said.

'Mrs Cuffe' he asked, moving his hands nervously as he spoke.

'Yes.'

'May we come in a minute?'

'Of course. It's a horrible night for standing on doorsteps.'

I moved back into the hall and they came in through the door. He took
off his cap and banged at it for a moment with his hand. Snow drops
sprinkled onto the carpet and melted. The policewoman closed the door
and they stood looking at me as if waiting for me to speak first.

'I'm afraid we have some bad news for you ...'

'I think,' said the woman, interrupting him, 'we should go into the fire. I
think you should sit down.'

'Bad news.' The words didn't have any meaning to me as I spoke them.
'What's bad news? I mean – I think you'd better tell me here. Now.'

'There's been an accident. Your husband's been shot.'

I laughed.

'Cuffe's my name. Helen Cuffe. You must have got the wrong person.'

The policewoman took me by the arm and pushed me into the sitting room. I looked at the piles of envelopes and cards on the floor.

'I was writing Christmas cards ...' I gestured towards them.

'You husband has been shot,' she said.

'Dan?'

'Yes.'

'But how? Why? Dan?'

'He was with Inspector Cranston. Leaving his house. They were ...'

'Yes. That's where he was. He went to see George Cranston's father.'

'It seems like they were trying to get the Inspector, but they got ...'

'Dan?'

'Your husband has been injured.'

'Is he ... is he all right?'

'They've taken him to the hospital.'

'Is he all right?'

'We don't know any more than that. That's all we were told.'

'Shot.'

I wanted to laugh at the absurdity of it, but I didn't think they would understand.

'Would you like to get your coat?' The policewoman touched my arm. 'It's cold out. We'll take you on over to the hospital.'

I nodded and went towards the hall again.

'Nothing like this has ever happened before. To me ... to us ... I feel a bit confused.' I pulled my coat out of the press in the hall. 'Are you sure ... ?'

'Yes. Quite sure.'

The policeman took the coat from me and held it while I fumbled my arms into the sleeves.

'I don't think anyone would want to shoot Dan.'

The policewoman held my bag out towards me.

'Is your key in this?' she asked. 'You'll need your key.'

JENNIFER JOHNSTON, *The Railway Station Man*, 1984

'WE CAN'T WASTE TIME.'

Bosco stood up and back, admitting by the movement that he had no longer any control over his son's life. Willing hands lifted Davy up and put him in the back seat. The driver got in and the engine started. The lights went on. The car swung in a tight turn back up the hill, turned left again and vanished.

Bosco slipped away while the crowd watched and, in the darkness reached McGuigan's yard. The back gate was on the latch. It swung in silently as though it had been recently oiled. There was a wall and a corrugated lean-to shed. Now, where could it have fallen? The house was silent. The yard was silent. There was no moon. Bosco suddenly shivered and wondered why he shivered. His hands groped here and there and he swung his feet this way and that to help the search. There was a scraping sound and a faint clatter. Was this it? No! It was just a yard brush. An empty bucket rattled faintly at his touch and slowly and rhythmically rocked itself to silence. The something heavy! A gun was not this heavy, was it? But it was the gun. Bosco's heart beat faster. This was the first time in his life that he had touched a gun and he was half-scared of it. Cautiously, by the stock, he picked it up. Like that, with the stock awkwardly in his hand and the barrel pointing down, he opened the yard gate and sneaked along the wall, heading for home. The street was quiet. There were watching figures crouching in the darkness but the street was quiet. He had not far to go.

At the shop door he groped for his key. His heart was pounding. It was just like the time that he had been at the foot of Grianan Aileach in McDonagh's van, and the engine would not start.

Take it easy, Bosco! Nothing can happen.

There was a sudden blare of noise and a blaze of headlights. Christ! The army! Where had they come out of? Bosco jerked up his hand to shade his eyes but he and Davy's gun were plainly visible, and he still had not found his key. There was no choice.

He raised the gun awkwardly and pressed the trigger. There was a painful thud at his right shoulder as the rifle kicked. He staggered and almost fell. The shot in the narrow street whined and ricocheted.

Two soldiers in the truck fired back.

Suddenly Bosco felt another thud, this time in his other shoulder. He spun and staggered and fell. The truck drove on, heading for the gap in the barricade.

There was not much pain. Just the darkness and the whiff of tear-gas. Bosco found his key and tried to rise. He shouldn't have tried the gun. He was no good at it. Stones, Bosco, stones: He was on his knees, straining to fill his lungs with the gas-tainted Bogside air but his legs would not lift him up. Silly, it was. The key in his hand and him at his own front door! They would all laugh at him. Lucky there was no one about.

Should he call Mary? No. Mary would laugh, too. Anyone would laugh to see a man at his own front door, with his own key, just kneeling. Better lie down easy.

It was late summer and the air was warm, as warm as blood. It was dark in the lane but she wasn't there.

'Sadie!' he called.

Mary heard his cry and came quickly down. She found him with his key in his hand, slumped on top of Davy's gun. In the light from the shop his wasted blood shone black on the pavement and dripped softly into the gutter, mingling with the sweepings of the shop – dead matches, cigarette butts, and empty packets of potato crisps.

WALTER HEGARTY, *The Price of Chips*, 1973

A Very Fine and
Broad River

THAT CITY HAS A MAGNIFICENT SITUATION for a harbour. With a lough running miles inland from the sea, and then a very fine and broad River Foyle. Down the lough there is Moville (on the Free State side), as a sort of local Tilbury, and in the old days of the American emigrant trade plenty of transatlantic liners from Glasgow or Belfast would make a call at Moville. Or Derry has its own harbour launch which would put out to meet the ships. There must be at least a mile and a half of that Derry Quayside, with berthing room for almost scores of great ships. But where are the ships? I have never in several visits seen any. There is the cross-channel steamer which so many times a week runs over to Glasgow, and there is another ship which at intervals carries cargo only to Heysham in Lancashire. That is all the shipping that I have ever seen in Derry. Except when I was last there in the December of 1937; and there were two Spanish ore-ships from Bilbao apparently moored-up permanently and deserted; I do not know whether they were officially interned or whether they just couldn't pay their harbour dues, but at all events the quay did not look bustling. It may be, for all I know, that there are millions of Derry shirts and collars finding their way out by train. But that railway from Derry to Strabane obviously used to have a double track; and now the extra metals have been pulled up for presumable lack of traffic.

JOHN GIBBONS, *Ireland – The New Ally*, 1938

TORY ISLAND TO STARBOARD. Looks like a mediaeval fortress. A road contractor and his wife, both from the Middle West, flatly refuse to believe me when I inform them at dinner that I am nearly home now, and that I intend to disembark in Lough Foyle. Know what is troubling them. They have seen me wearing a dinner jacket and watched me using a knife and fork, so obviously I can't be Irish. The Irish, in their opinion, a nation of policemen, ward politicians, hotel porters and night watchmen.

Malachi, it appears, instead of wearing a collar of gold, now wears a whistle and chain.

Inspect my fellow-countrymen and women as they huddle together on the deck of the tender in Lough Foyle at one o'clock on a cold and blustery morning. A floodlight at the gangway throws a cold illumination on the scene. Decide that though we may be a nation of poets, statesmen and heroes, we would be all the better for some new teeth. Anyhow, teeth or no teeth, we're all going home now instead of going the other way, which is all to the good.

Wait on the draughty quay at Derry while the customs men ineffectively pretend to be searching our baggage. At last a joke gets me through without any search at all. What will an Irishman not do for a joke?

Ring the front-door bell at the principal hotel. Am admitted to a bedroom the wallpaper of which, at four o'clock in the morning, and by the light of one (of course) extremely inconveniently placed electric light, reminds me of my childish ideas of Hell – that is, of dark confusion. Query: Who designed the wallpapers in the more old-fashioned English, Irish, and Scottish hotels? Answer: Martin Luther in a fit of temporary depression.

Nevertheless, an extremely good breakfast is brought to me next morning by an extremely pretty little maid from Donegal, who inquires as she dumps the tray just inside the bedroom door:

'Would you be wanting grape fruit with your breakfast, sir?'

So much for my horn-rimmed spectacles! Considering this I remain in bed after breakfast, just to prove that I'm Irish and proud of it. Inspect the wallpaper by daylight, and decide that the next time some unfortunate person or persons send me to the United States on business, I shall travel Santa Fé, 'stop over' in New Orleans – and charge the cost to the said person or persons.

After which I light a pipe of the first decent Virginian tobacco I have smoked since I landed in America, contemplate the fact that I am in bed and that nobody in the hotel, or the whole city for that matter, gives a damn whether I ever leave it, and decide that there is something to be said for being a European after all – atavistic wallpaper and absence of bedside lamps to the contrary, notwithstanding.

Fall asleep and miss the first train to Belfast ...

DENIS IRELAND, *From the Irish Shore*, 1936

Again I roam the fragrant fields that skirt the Foyle's
        calm tide,
And gaze upon its sparkling waves that seawards
        proudly glide;
Again I pluck the humble flowers that deck its winding
        shore,
And feel anew the bliss with which I gathered them of
        yore.
Again I feast mine eyes upon the hills my boyhood
        knew –
Unchang'd, familiar friends they seem when other friends
        are few.
All other streams their charms possess, but none, oh!
        none I see
Has half the charms that thou, O Foyle! hast ever had
        for me!

THE MOST REVEREND JOHN KEYS O'DOHERTY, Bishop of Derry (1890–1907),
from 'On a Distant View of Derry', in *Derriana*, 1902

HIS MOTHER WANTED TO KNOW why they wouldn't go fishing in a nice clean country river instead of in the filthy Foyle. That was when they decided to try the river Faughan out at Drumahoe. They were up early on a Saturday morning and digging worms in the far field before nine o'clock. When the cocoa tin was nearly full of good specimens, Sean threw some clay on top of them and grass, 'just to keep them alive'. They made a few holes in the lid with a nail, because they always did that: he wondered how worms managed for air when they were deep in the ground.

They took a bus to the Waterside and that gave them a great start on the journey. It seemed strange to be going beyond the bus terminus and taking the road marked 'Dungiven'. That was the way Mr McAdoo took them in his car last year when they went to Aunt Maggie's place in the country. But Drumahoe was only three miles out the road and the Faughan was supposed to be full of fish.

They fished and fished, but no fish came.

'It's too bright,' Eamonn said.

They moved to a darker spot beneath an overhanging tree.

'This is just right,' Eamonn said, giving the rod a big swing. The hook caught high in the branches and no amount of jerking would shift it. He cut the line and put on new gut and hooks.

'Are you hungry?' said Sean.

'Starvin'. Me belly thinks me throat's cut,' was the reply.

He took out the sandwiches while Eamonn set the lines, putting a big stone on each rod. He was clearly expecting a monster, thought Sean. It was a real pet of a day: they listened to the trout plopping in the river, only yards from the rods.

'Maybe the hooks are too big, Sean.'

'Aye. Maybe.'

The flies were collecting around them as they ate. Sean jumped up and shook himself to avoid them. Flies always gave him the shivers, particularly the big ones you'd find by the river.

'It might be better lower down,' he said.

Eamonn followed him towards the bridge. They could see an odd car passing on the Derry Road. An Army lorry went past and the soldiers waved to them.

'Them's salmon hooks,' said Sean, with an air of finality. 'You'll never catch trout with those big things.'

'Maybe we should get trout hooks and come back some other day,' Eamonn said hopefully.

They tidied up their gear and made their way along the bank until they reached the bridge. The evening rise was on and the fish were jumping furiously as he followed Eamonn over the barbed wire and on to the Derry Road. He heard the enormous splash of a salmon and was sure Eamonn had heard it too, but neither of them mentioned it.

They spent their last pennies on chewing-gum, so they had to walk all the way home. When they reached the Strand Road at last, they turned right to walk down the quay. It was always far more interesting then being on the main road. He'd be able to collect some grain for Gallan's pigeons too.

A dock policeman spoke to them. 'Are you naval officers?' he asked.

'No, we're not,' Sean answered. He couldn't help feeling a certain elation that a dock 'horney' had mistaken them for officers. It was some compensation for the long walk.

'Don't you know that only naval personnel and authorised people are allowed on the quay now?'

It took some time for them to realise the awfulness of the new situation. As they turned to leave, Sean could feel the utter loneliness of a quay that wouldn't belong to them anymore.

They trudged down a very lonely Strand Road.

'Well, damn Hitler anyway,' Eamonn said.

TOMÁS Ó CANAINN, *Home to Derry*, 1986

FOR THE WHOLE OF THE EVENING I could not take my eyes off the boats that lay by 'Derry Pier. Micky's Jim took no notice of them, because he had seen them often enough before.

'Ye'll not wonder much at ships when ye've seen them as much as I've seen them,' he said.

We sought out our own boat, and Jim said that she was a rotten tub when he had examined her critically with his eyes for a moment.

'It'll make ye as sick as a dog goin' roun' the Moils o' Kentire,' he said. 'Ye'll know what it is to be seasick this night, Dermod.'

We went on board, and waited for the rest of the party to come along. While waiting Jim prowled into the cook's galley and procured two cups of strong black tea, which we drank together on deck.

It was, 'Under God, the day an' the night, ye've grown to be a big man, Dermod,' and 'Ye're a soncy rung o' a fellow this minute, Dermod Flynn,' when the people from my own arm of the Glen came up the deck and saw me there along with Micky's Jim. Many of the squad were old stagers who had been in the country across the water before. They planted their patch of potatoes and corn in their little croft at home, then went to Scotland for five or six months in the middle of the year to earn money for the rent of their holding. The land of Donegal is bare and hungry, and nobody can make a decent livelihood there except landlords.

The one for whom I longed most was the last to come, and when I saw her my heart almost stopped beating. She was the same as ever with her soft tender eyes and sweet face, that put me in mind of the angels pictured over the altar of the little chapel at home. Her hair fell over her shawl like a cascade of brown waters, her forehead was white and pure as marble, her cheeks seemed made of rose-leaf, of a pale carnation hue, and her fair light body, slender as a young poplar, seemed too holy for the contact of the cold world. She stepped up the gangplank, slowly and timidly, for she was afraid of the noise and shouting of the place.

The boat's carricks creaked angrily on their pivots, the gangways clattered loudly as they were shifted here and there by noisy and dirty men, and the droves of bullocks, fresh from the country fairs, bellowed increasingly as they were hammered into the darkness of the hold. On these things I looked with wonder, Norah looked with fright.

All evening I had been thinking about her, and the words of welcome which I would say to her when we met. When she came on deck I put out my hand, but couldn't for the life of me say a word of greeting. She was the first to speak.

'Dermod Flynn, I hardly knew ye at all,' she said with a half-smile on her lips. 'Ye got very big these last two years.'

'So did you, Norah,' I answered, feeling very glad because she had kept count of the time I was gone. 'You are almost as tall as I am.'

'Why wouldn't I be as tall as ye are,' she answered with a full smile. 'Sure am I not a year and two months older?'

Some of the other women began to talk to Norah, and I turned to look at the scene around me. The sun was setting, and showed like a red bladder in the pink haze that lay over the western horizon. The Foyle was a sheet of wavy molten gold which the boat cut through as she sped out from the pier. The upper deck was crowded with people who were going to Scotland to work for the summer and autumn. They were all very ragged, both women and men; most of the men were drunk, and they discussed, quarrelled, argued, and swore until the din was deafening. Little heed was taken by them of the beauty of the evening, and all alone I watched the vessel turn up a furrow of gold at the bow until my brain was reeling with the motion of the water that sobbed past the sides of the steamer, and swept far astern where the line of white churned foam fell into rank with the sombre expanse of sea that we were leaving behind.

PATRICK MacGILL, *The Children of the Dead End*, 1914

M ANY ROYAL NAVY SAILORS had especially fond memories of the city and some of them found local wives, settling down to live in the city after the war. Most had seen Derry for the first time from an escort ship as it sailed up the Foyle towards the port. Donald Macintyre summed up their feelings when he wrote

Londonderry was a land 'flowing with milk and honey' for us, where such unheard of luxuries as steaks could be had in the restaurants and butter in lumps instead of thin slivers. After the scene of smoking ruin at Liverpool, Londonderry's peaceful air, where people would probably show you the scene of the explosion of 'the bomb', was a benison. It sometimes made going to sea to face the winter gales all the harder. As one slipped down the narrow river, peaceful little sheltered cottages passed within biscuit toss. The blue peat smoke rose lazily into the air and one envied the owners their warm fireside and quiet night ahead of them. A corner of the river would be rounded, the wind would start keening through the rigging and we knew that by nightfall water would be sloshing about between decks and we would be lashing ourselves into our bunks when the time came to turn in.

RICHARD DOHERTY, *Key to Victory: The Maiden City in the Second World War*, 1995

T HE RIVER FOYLE WITH ITS EXTENSIVE SYSTEM of tributaries drains a scenic mountainous catchment of some 1,130 square miles, in the counties of Derry, Donegal and Tyrone, into Lough Foyle. It is primarily regarded as a salmon and seatrout system. The total commercial catch for the Foyle area between the years 1979 and 1987 ranged from a peak of 83,252 fish in 1983 to a low of 18,483 in 1987. It would appear from the figures available that the River Foyle has the potential to be one of the top salmon producing rivers in the country.

The River Foyle to Lifford Bridge consists of 20 miles of tidal water. Angling is confined to a stretch reaching from a point about half a mile above Lifford Bridge and a one mile stretch downstream of the bridge. The river here is wide and shallow. It is tidal and fishes best when the tide is out and with low water conditions obtaining upstream in the tributaries. A rise of 6 inches on the River Finn or River Mourne can put the Foyle out of order.

The salmon fishing can be fair to good, depending on water levels. It is reported to produce about 20 spring fish and 100 grilse annually. The spring fishing is from March to May and the grilse run from the end of May to the end of July. There is no autumn run.

The seatrout fishing can be exceptionally good in a short stretch half a mile either side of Lifford Bridge. It fishes best at night.

PETER O'REILLY, Trout and Salmon Rivers of Ireland, 1995

WE HAD DINNER IN A FINE HOTEL which the Earl Bishop might have blessed; for, when he travelled abroad, he always did his best to raise standards by his patronage, and the many Bristol Hotels in continental towns are named after him. While we ate, two musicians played jazz rather insecurely, the pianist with his nose buried in the music, and the double-bass player trying also to have a peep and coiling round his instrument like the Laocoon. After dinner, we took a few steps down to the river and stood by a large shed marked LIVERPOOL. The lights were shining on the bridge over the Foyle, and they were grouped in threes. There was a promise of a fine day to come. We did not need a seer's crystal ball to be sure of it.

OSWELL BLAKESTON, Thank You Now, 1960

Oh I know a wee spot, 'tis a place of great fame,
And it lies to the North, now I'll tell you its name;
'Tis my own little birthplace, and it's on Irish soil,
Sure they call it lovely Derry on the banks of the Foyle.

Now I courted a wee girl, her age was nineteen,
She was the fairest colleen that ever you've seen;
For her cheeks were like roses, and her hair waved in coil
And she came from lovely Derry on the banks of the Foyle.

By those banks have I roamed, in the dear days gone by;
With my dear girl I strolled, not a tear, not a sigh;
Her fair charms without equal, from the Nore to the Moyle.
Oh, sweet maid from Lovely Derry on the banks of the Foyle.

But now cruel misfortune drove me from my home,
'Twas my fate in deep sorrow to sail o'er the foam:
And now from dark strangers, in grief I recoil,
While I pine from dear old Derry on the banks of the Foyle.

Oh, mind when I left her, for to cross o'er the sea,
For to try and make a fortune, for Mary and me,
How I cried when I left her, but my tears fell in toil
Far away from Dear Old Derry on the banks of the Foyle.

I was young, I was wild, like the rest of the boys,
I had not many sorrows nor yet many joys,
I worked hard for a living, all day I did toil,
Far away from lovely Derry on the banks of the Foyle.

I was fearing that another had a place in her heart,
And that from me my darling forever would part,
That no more would she brighten with her sweet sunny smile,
My dear home in lovely Derry on the banks of the Foyle.

For my true love was buxom, and a fine girl to see:
That she won my affection, all my friends did agree,
And I long for to wed her, on our own native soil
Though I'm far from dear old Derry on the banks of the Foyle.

But a wee bird came flying from over the sea,
And he brought me a letter from my true love to see;
Saying, 'Come home, my darling, to your native soil,
And I'll wed you in lovely Derry on the banks of the Foyle.'

Now when I make a fortune, then to home I will go,
To the dear land of my boyhood, to the sweet girl I know
I will build her a mansion, and no more need we toil.
Far away from lovely Derry on the banks of the Foyle.

ANONYMOUS, 'Londonderry on the Banks of the Foyle,' n.d.

THE QUAYS THAT UP TO NOW only had taken coal boats were hastily modified; the river was dredged or deepened to handle much larger warships like corvettes and minesweepers, and the English soldiers that we were once used to in our streets were now replaced by foreign sailors like the Free French, Norwegian, Dutch, Russian, Polish. Derry, owing to its geographical position, was strategically placed as a base for the minesweepers that protected from German submarines the armaments and food convoys from America to England and Russia. The U-boats patrolled a radius of about 400 miles, so though the ships were safe far out at sea, as they approached land, their worries would start.

JOHN DORAN, *Red Doran*, 1996

HAIL! Captain Coppin, Neptune's brighest star,
That shines with splendour and effulgence bright;
Whose buoyant spirit, like a jolly Tar,
Will yet burst forth with more effective might;
Give to mechanics full employment here,
And pay them for their labour so severe.

Hard, hard they toil, their work they finish well.
With skill and judgement they their tasks pursue;
The builders act their parts, as truth can tell,
And still they keep the glorious end in view –
To build steam vessels with a structure grand,
Which may compete with those in any land.

The Captain's worth our citizens will prize,
His value is esteemed surpassing great;
He'll build fine ships, of great enormous size,
Which shall plough Ocean's waves with pride elate,
Sail to the East, or to Columbia's shores,
Which nautic skill, with enterprize, explores.

Now may our Merchants lend their helping hand
To raise fair DERRY's fame, extend her sway;
For they have wealth in plenty at command:
Let them build ships and make a grand display.
Setting a bright example, to impart
An emulative impulse to each heart.

R. TAGGART, *from* 'Neptune's Brightest Star', 1839, in Annesley Malley and
Mary McLaughlin, *Captain Coppin: 'Neptune's Brightest Star'*, 1992

HERE IS LOUGH FOYLE RUNNING in from the sea; narrow right at its very mouth, it widens out inland and makes a regular lake, in that way being rather like the Tagus at Lisbon. Derry is a natural port. The city is built just about the extreme inner end of the Lough, so that above the Craigavon Bridge is only plain river. Over on the other side you see from the bastion the smoke of the NCC trains, and they will point out to you the site of the opposition camp in the famous siege. There is a big old muzzle-loader cannon up by that bastion, and it is the pet of the Protestant City. (I think it was the Catholics who were besieging the Protestants; or else it was the other way on.) Anyway, there is this cannon. 'Roaring Meg' was her name, and I suppose that at intervals she would drop a shot over on the enemy encampment.

There is a wonderful quay-side all along that Lough, and it is simply lined with cannon. They have them all over Derry, as if they absolutely refused to forget something that happened about two centuries and a half ago. But when you come to modern times, then that quay-side is not too active; it must have been built in the old days of booming trade, for there is about a mile and a half of it with berths for endless steamers. When I was there, exactly two steamers were tied up, the cross-channel Glasgow boat and Derry's own tender, apparently idle for want of anything to do. There is the world depression, of course, partly to account for things, but the real truth is that the division of Ireland has not exactly done the North much good. The Six Counties used to say that they had all the industries and all the operative virtues, and that Southern Ireland was in effect a picturesque loafer. But now that there is a Border, the separation has half-ruined the North, and Derry, as I say, as the Industrious Apprentice was looking a little blank with two ships to a mile and a half of quay. Waterford was nothing to it, and Dublin was positively a hive of teeming industry.

It is like that all round, and the great mansions that must have been the residences of the wealthy Derry merchants look shabby or shut up. There would be big money there in the old days when the city was the shop-counter for a whole Ireland, but those days are gone. I said that Waterford depressed me, but it is a city of gay southern laughter as compared to the bleak deadness of Londonderry. There is too much history about that place to be healthy, and whichever way you turn you hear about the 'Derry Crimson' or the 'Derry Prentice Boys' or the 'Derry Drums'.

JOHN GIBBONS, *Abroad in Ireland*, 1936

A RUSH THROUGH DERRY to the Post Office, and then to the quay to catch the ferry boat to the station for Portrush, which provokingly glided out into the stream just as we came up; a call to the nearest car-driver, for our train was almost due, and it was a long walk round by the bridge to the station; an exciting drive through the town, along a street parallel with the river, where, this being market day, a continuous succession of carts from the country met us, and persisted in getting in our way; a scamper across the bridge and up the street which leads to the railway terminus, and at last we dismounted and found that the train was about to start. We entered it, and, in a few moments, were moving along by the side of the Foyle, and had a last peep at the lofty spire and monument – at the walls and churches and colleges – at the hills and quays and houses; and then we left 'The Maiden City' behind us, and sped on towards Coleraine, along the shores of the Lough, and through a smiling land of trees and meadows and sweet villages, with gentle slopes in the distance, and, across the misty waters, the outlines of the loftier hills of Donegal, growing vaguer as the inlet widened. Past Newtown Junction, with Newtown Limavady, the clean and ancient town near which the Irish chief, O' Cahan, once abode, and still more interesting as the home of the famous 'Peg' whose charms are so quaintly commemorated by Thackeray, a couple of miles away, and across the river Roe we rode until we got amid the cliffs again, and, leaving Magilligan Point on our left, drew up at Castle Rock, a favourite watering place, where the platform was crowded with well-dressed visitors, and we could easily have imagined ourselves in England once more.

ARTHUR BENNETT, *John Bull and His Other Island II*, 1890

A FEW GUNS ARE PRESERVED in their proper positions, but the greater number are used as posts for fastening cables and protecting the corners of streets. The houses are chiefly built of brick: the entire number in the city and suburbs is 2947. The city is watched, paved, cleansed, and lighted with gas, under the superintendence of commissioners of general police, consisting of the mayor and 12 inhabitants chosen by ballot: the gas-works were erected in 1829, at an expense of £7,000, raised in shares of £11. Water is conveyed to the town across the bridge by pipes, from a reservoir on Brae Head, beyond the Waterside, in the parish of Clondermot; the works were constructed by the corporation under an act of the 40th of Geo. III, at a total expense of £15,500, and iron pipes have been laid down within the last few years. The bridge, a celebrated wooden structure erected by Lemuel Cox, an American, in lieu of a ferry which the corporation held under the Irish Society, was begun in 1789, and completed in the spring of 1791. It is 1068 feet in length, and 40 in breadth: the piles are of oak, and the head of each is tenoned into a cap piece 40 feet long and 17 inches square, supported by three sets of girths and braces; the piers, which are $16\frac{1}{2}$ feet apart, are bound together by thirteen string-pieces equally divided and transversely bolted, on which is laid the flooring: on each side of the platform is a railing $4\frac{1}{2}$ feet high, also a broad pathway provided with gas lamps. Near the end next to the city a turning bridge has been constructed in place of the original drawbridge, to allow of the free navigation of the river. On the 6th of Feb., 1814, a portion of the bridge extending to 350 feet was carried away by large masses of ice floated down the river by the ebb tide and a very high wind. The original expense of its erection was £16,594, and of the repairs after the damage in 1814, £18,208, of which latter sum, £15,000 was advanced as a loan by Government: the average annual amount of tolls from 1831 to 1834, inclusive, was £3,693. Plans and estimates for the erection of a new bridge, nearly 200 yards above the present, have been procured; but there is no prospect of the immediate execution of the design.

SAMUEL LEWIS, *Topographical Dictionary of Ireland*, 1837

The day is now approaching fast,
When thou that hast withstood the blast
Of many a winter bleak,
Shall be by ruthless hands destroy'd,
Axe, crow-bar, hammer be employ'd
Thee to asunder break.

Thy builders sage, with skill and toil,
From side to side, across the Foyle,
Thy planks securely laid,
That travellers of every class,
And vehicles, might o'er thee pass,
Soon as the toll was paid.

And long thou wert the boast and pride
Of Derry, and the highest tide
Resisted, till the frost
Of eighteen hundred and fourteen
Raised blocks of ice thy piles between,
And broke each centre post.

But soon thou wert repair'd again,
And render'd able to sustain
Of many tons the weight;
Of every tempest bear the shock,
Unshaken as a solid rock,
When waves against it beat.

Of service great thou hast been long,
And though grown old, still hale and strong,
And fit for use appear;
The credit of thy cash account,
In pounds, to thousands will amount
Thy last surviving year.

As billows to the strand rush on,
Break suddenly, and soon are gone,
As though they ne'er had been;
Thousands of those who cross'd thee o'er
Have reach'd eternity's vast shore,
And will no more be seen.

And time, which has pronounc'd thy doom,
And rais'd a rival in thy room,
Built up of iron strong,
Will also at some future day
Cause it, like thee, to pass away,
With all that round it throng.

ROBERT YOUNG, 'Stanzas Addressed to the Old Wooden Bridge of Londonderry,
Which it is Expected will be Removed During the Present Year',
The Poetic Works of Robert Young, 1863

THE APPOINTED DAY ARRIVED HOWEVER, and I was delivered over to my parents as agreed on. I remember very well our journey to Derry, which we entered by the bridge across the Foyle. We were to go aboard ship the next day but were prevented by an event of a serious nature. My father's trouble and worriment incident to the settlement of affairs and the labor of packing up and preparing to leave, had brought on a fever which did not develop until after we arrived in Derry. For a few days he had complained of pains in his limbs, and a ringing sound in his ears; but on the day we were to go on board a high fever had set in, and the ship's surgeon excluded him on the ground of illness. This was a serious disappointment; but not so serious as our apprehensions regarding the illness. Our means were not such as to justify the expense of costly board or lodging and medical treatment; and indeed, my father had become so ill that a hotel or boarding house would not have cared to admit him. The physician pronounced it a dangerous and probably a protracted attack.

My mother was equal to the emergency however; I remember going with her from place to place until she found two suitable upstairs rooms which she engaged as lodging rooms. She then had her baggage removed, and bedding unpacked and adjusted; and had my father conveyed from the lodging house where we had stopped, and placed as comfortably as circumstances would allow in this new temporary home in Derry. She then procured an attentive and skillful physician recommended by Mr Buchanan, the owner of the vessel in which we had taken passage. This Buchanan was the uncle of the late President of the United States of that name. Here my father lay in a helpless and at last almost hopeless condition for nearly four weeks. But the physician's care, and my mother's nursing, finally brought him through. At one time he was so low that the physician gave him up, and my mother wrote a letter to his father's family in America, informing them of our distress and asking their advice: whether in case of his death they would advise her to go on with me and join them, or to return to her own people at Kinkitt. The turn came however and he began to convalesce; and I remember, after he was able to walk out of doors with a cane, his usual stroll with me by the hand was along the top of Derry walls, where I thought it very strange to be able to look down into the chimney tops. And I remember of our examining Roaring Meg, and the other celebrated old guns which had done such execution in the siege of Derry. Derry must have been supplied with hydrants at that time much resembling those in present use, as I was greatly surprised at one which stood on the pavement near our lodging house. There was a pool of water at and around its base, which was the only supply visible to me; and how so large a supply of water could be obtained from so small a source, and why the water of its own accord flowed up and out of the spout, were mysteries which excited my curiosity. I remember very well also the appearance of an old woman who sat at the open gate of the city wall, beside a stand of candies and sea *dulce*. Her table afforded an irresistible temptation to my scarce half-pennies.

MATTHEW T. MELLON (ed.), *Selections from* Thomas Mellon and His Times,
by Judge Thomas Mellon, 1976

Look at the man.

Crawling along the white line on the Craigavon Bridge
instead of being
upstanding and working my way
by the railings
on the footpath
at least
under the lamplight
instead of crawling here
like a dog.

Because of the river.

And even if up to the
hills of the walled city behind and the far
hills of Donegal behind that or up to the green
hills of the Sperrins away beyond the steep
hill without
of Victoria Park and Gobnascale
I lift mine eyes,
it is the river that fills every
sense in me
drawing me in its strong arms to
its dark self
on its onward unchristian rolling charge
to the deep.

Crawling along the white line
on the Craigavon Bridge
wearing the shadow of a black dog
I cross the river with river in all
the caverns and conduits of my being
its tides tugging me like a
leash I tear at to loosen and bear
as the sign of my authority,
my black dry nose set for
some place called
home
where the heart is
fed.

Heart. What weight is
yours as you look on me here,
the man on Craigavon Bridge
along the white line
crawling –

what weight is your heart?

ANN McKAY, 'Anubis on the Craigavon Bridge', *Giving Shine*, 2000

Far out, on the west bank, petrified trees
Cling to the steep flanks of the River Foyle;
They were mere saplings when deep tenders took
The dark-clothed men and inaccessible women
Down past the sand ridges to the waiting ships.

Age, and the insistent wind from the east,
Has crooked all their limbs: they squat, crippled,
Denuded, on the brae faces, their deep-digging roots
Wringing life from the land, tippling greedily; offering,
Among that netted web, no asylum for their betrayed seeds
That must drift on the wind to flourish God know where.

SAM BURNSIDE, 'Foyle', Walking the Marches, 1990

M acDAID DROVE US DOWN TO THE Waterside Station just after
breakfast. When he dashed us to a dead stop in the Station Square the
station master's house door was open and his wife was sending her little girls
to school. Mother was introduced to them. One was dark and one was
blonde and their names were Adelaide and Madeleine. Great funnels of
smoke were blowing out of the open side of the station. MacDaid whistled
and a porter came and took out bags and ran off with them so fast that
Mother and I had to run after him. Mother said: 'Where ever did she get
their names? She must be English.' And when we were safely up in the
first-class carriage that smelt of stale cigars, she said: 'Thank heavens I never
married a station master. It must be a nightmare to keep the windows clean.'

The engine kept shunting as though it were practising. But at last we
moved off. The train slid along the lovely Foyle River, past familiar
wooded demesnes. Mother made me look at the white patch of Boom
Hall, showing like a postage stamp among its trees: 'That is where they put
the boom that blocked King William when he came up the river. William of
Orange ... in the William and James Wars. Of all places they had to fight it
out *here*!' She resented it as a personal encroachment, as something that had
interfered with her mode of living. She made it intimate to me so that I saw
the little church-crowned city that I knew waiting for the kings, whom I
never knew, to clash. They were as clear to me as Mother sitting against the
blue buttoned-down railway cushions. She was wearing a brown straw hat
trimmed with ribbon bows and bunches of red flowers that had an Alpine
name, or she gave them an Alpine name. They looked as though they were
about to become berries. They were half berries. She was wearing a new pair
of gloves. The fingers were bulged with her rings and the tips were drawn
out and pressed flat according to the law which, my grandmother said,
showed how 'a lady should wear her gloves'.

KATHLEEN COYLE, The Magical Realm, 1943

L ONDONDERRY, THE MOST NORTHERLY PORT in Ireland, had built up a
successful trade with the smaller American ports as well as with Canada
where most of the ships owned in Derry were built, usually in Saint John

and New Brunswick and Halifax. A sturdy little barque of under 200 tons was actually named the *Londonderry* and carried emigrant-passengers to Quebec, Montreal and Savannah. On one trip home from this cotton stronghold in Georgia, Captain Samuel Hatrick reported, 'I have been 57 times across the Atlantic and never encountered such severe gales. For 24 hours at a time I was forced to run under bare poles.' The winds were so bad that he was compelled to lower all his sails, and trust to God. In direct contrast in size, the huge 875-ton *Marchioness of Abercorn*, was at one time the largest in the Irish-owned fleet. Commanded by Captain John Hegarty, she regularly carried upwards of 500 Famine emigrants to Quebec during the summer, and to New Orleans in the winter. She was fast and registered a round-trip to Canada of 44 days – 25 out and 19 home. But size is not everything – a rival in this northern port was the much smaller 260-ton brig *Unicorn* which unloaded her passengers in Quebec, took on a cargo of timber and sailed home, under Captain William Allen – land-to-land in 15 days in the summer of 1848.

Another Londonderry ship owner was William McCorkell who allowed his son Bartholomew to name their 408-ton barque *Fanny* after his new wife, but the ship almost had a very short career. In a winter crossing from New Orleans, after disembarking her passengers and reloading with American grain, she lost her bowsprit and mizzen (rear) mast in a storm. The crew had to throw much of the cargo overboard to remain afloat but she made it back to Cork in February. Repairs never took very long as trade was too important, and by the spring the *Fanny* was carrying emigrants once more to Quebec. Later, in August 1848, under Captain John Quinn, she had an astonishingly brisk passage, leaving Londonderry on the 4th and arriving in New York on the 26th. Such a short westward crossing of only 22 days was a real exception, and though the wind must have blown hard to afford such speed, it was mercifully mid-summer. The *Fanny* could carry as many as 158 emigrants, but on this voyage conveyed just 69, with only 12 children in total. Thomas McKeever and his wife, Jane, travelled with their three; Bridget McHue, with six and Betty Convery with three. Were the husbands and fathers of these two families waiting on the other side?

EDWARD LAXTON, *The Famine Ships*, 1996

THE LONG WOODEN BRIDGE over the river, is a singularly striking object, particularly when you are upon it.

The following account of its construction has been given in the *Statistical Survey of Derry*: 'This bridge was constructed by LEMUEL COX, of BOSTON, in NORTH AMERICA; it was completed in the space of 13 months: in length it is 1068 feet, in breadth 40 feet: the piers consist of oak from 14 to 18 inches square, and from 14 to 58 feet long; the head of each post is tenanted into a cap piece, 14 inches square, and 40 feet long, supported by three sets of girths and braces; the piers, which are distant from each other $16\frac{1}{2}$ feet, are bound together by 13 string-pieces, equally divided, and transversely bolted; on the string-pieces is laid the flooring; to each side of the platform is affixed a railing $4\frac{1}{2}$ feet high; inside railings are also made to guard the foot passengers; 26 lamp-posts are arranged along the sides of the bridge. Between the middle of the bridge and the end next the city, a draw-arch has been constructed, of which all the machinery is worked under the floor of the bridge. The greatest depth of the river at low water is 31 feet, and the rise of the tide is from eight to ten feet.'

SIR RICHARD COLT HOARE (BART), *A Journal of a Tour in Ireland AD 1806*, 1807

THIS WAS A BUSY PLACE ONCE in the days of small ships and tall sails, creaked the wooden planks of the dockside as they moved uneasily under our loitering feet.

Through cracks in the timber we saw yellow water glazed over speckled mud. The malty smell of two mills was strong around us and one solitary outlaw of a jackdaw plotted and thieved for God knew what. Ahead of us and high up, traffic passed east and west behind the steel trellis of the one big bridge, and underneath, ten feet above the sweep of the spreading water, railway trucks were lined like chests of booty in a Cyclops' cave, and from the shadows bogeymen chatting around a brazier waved greetings to the familiar young couple. Beyond the bridge and the bogeymen there was a wilderness of rough grass and rusted, disused railway tracks and then a steep ridge, now coated with grass and flowers, that had once been slag shovelled and scraped out of exhausted engines that through seven radiant counties had chugged and pulled all the way from Dublin. Over that ridge, our lovers' bastion, we were cut off from everything except the broad movement of the water, gull cries, a car or a bus seen, but diminutive and unheard, on the southward road on the far bank, a stately sail or the humble chugging of an outboard engine. On a seat the bogeymen had made for themselves out of discarded sleepers and then, reverencing our dream, had abandoned to us, we sat side by side and hand in hand, and sometimes, in a way she had, her head rested sideways on my shoulder, close to my neck, and every hair and every breath was a sign of God. There was no dirty danger in our being alone together far away from the bulls and cows in the champing, grazing, butting, rutting herd.

That was our city and that was our dry, tender love.

BENEDICT KIELY, *The Captain with the Whiskers*, 1960

THE ADVANTAGES OF STEAM-NAVIGATION are here sensibly felt by the farmers along the whole line of coast from Derry to Dublin. Their live stock, particularly pigs and sheep, are sent to Glasgow, Bristol, and Liverpool at a very cheap rate. A firkin of butter, for instance, can be sent from Derry to Liverpool for a penny; in fact, the certainty and cheapness of steam-navigation are such, that an Irish farmer, in the vicinity of a port, is quite as well off for a market, as an English or Scotch farmer at sixty miles from Liverpool or Glasgow.

The Foyle is here about a quarter of a mile in width, and is crossed by a wooden bridge one thousand and sixty-eight feet long, with a naked wooden floor, over which the rattling noise of the cars put me in mind of that of the droskies over the Isaac Bridge across the Neva with its wooden floor; to which that of the Foyle bears a resemblance. One part of the floor draws up to let vessels pass, and the Foyle is navigable by lighters and other craft of twenty or thirty tons burden as high up as Lifford, a distance of twelve or fourteen miles, and to Strabane, with the aid of a canal which joins the Foyle. By these rivers, and the Finn and the Mourne, the produce of Tyrone and of Donegal easily finds its way to Derry, receiving in return, barilla, pearl-ashes, flax-seed, deals, coals, and iron, – the trade and the manufacture of linen thus extending over the whole county. All this business is transacted by a few established houses in Derry and Coleraine, which will, perhaps, be sufficient to account for their small increase in population. If we compare the two counties of Antrim and Derry, we shall find them stand as under:–

	POPULATION	ACRES
Antrim . .	227,934	492,000
Derry . .	263,622	405,334
DIFFERENCE	35,688	86,666

Hence it is clear that Antrim, having more land and less population than Derry, must be less agricultural and more manufacturing than Derry, and consequently more favourable to an increase of population in its towns.

The fisheries of the Foyle contribute little to the trade or the consumption of Derry. The salmon do not appear to affect this stream. In some of the branches that fall into the Lough on the right bank below the bridge there are a few taken, but of no importance. I understand, however, that there is an extensive oyster-bank in the Lough, so productive as, in the season, to be sold at from threepence to sixpence a hundred; and that a few years ago twopence a hundred was the common price, but that now they were sent, like all other articles of provision, to Liverpool.

The banks of the Foyle are not so well wooded as those of the Bann, but numerous handsome villas are seen scattered over the country both above and below Derry; and I should say, from what I have seen of the country and of this neighbourhood, that it wants nothing but more trees and some hawthorn hedges, to place it on a comparison with some of the best parts of England.

JOHN BARRON, *A Tour Round Ireland Through the Sea-coast Counties*
in the Autumn of 1835, 1836

Toll-gate

The toll-gate is annually put up to auction by the corporation and the highest and fairest bidder will then receive it on approved security, the bridge therefore becoming the private property of the purchaser. He may stipulate at pleasure with the county and city gentlemen for a certain sum, according to the extent of their business on trespass on the bridge for the current year. The proprietor must take an annual sum from all government establishments.

The bridge is crazy and old, and seems to require perpetual repairings. The heavy weight of the pipes and gas-lamps on the southern side will be probably in the end injurious by producing an unequal pressure. An instance has been known of a farmer who seriously damaged the fabric by loading his cart too heavily.

The tolls of this bridge are fully equivalent to a tax of 1,000 [pounds?] a year on each of the parishes of Templemore, Faughanvale, Clonder-mot and Cumber. The tolls of the bridge are equivalent to a tax of from 10 to 30 and 50 per cent on all purchases of small articles in the city by the poor of Clondermot. They cannot afford to purchase much at a time and are accordingly debarred by the heavy percentage of the toll, which acts in the following manner.

In buying a whitefish from the city, value 6d, the toll of 1d must be paid, which is equivalent to a duty of 16 and a half per cent; in buying a lb. of beef, value 5d, the toll is 20 per cent; in buying 10d worth of mutton the toll is 10 per cent; 9d worth of pork, 11 per cent; vegetables, 2d worth, 50 per cent; grocery, 6d worth, 16 and a half per cent; fuel, 3d worth, 30 per cent.

The above purchases are as much as the poorer orders can afford to make at one time.

However, herrings are sold at the Waterside. Other kinds of fish can only be had in the city, as the fishermen all live on that side of the Foyle and bring up their fish to be sold there.

As long as the capital of the county of Londonderry is besieged by a toll-gatherer, the advantages of a free communication will be diminished and the communication itself decreased. The city is nearly as it was when it only had the ferryboat.

There are other obstructions to improvement as well as this wooden bridge, i.e. some of the parochial landlords.

Schedule of Tolls

Painted on a board at the bridge: payable at the bridge of Derry in British currency, on the 5th January 1826.

Coaches with 6 horses: for every coach, Berlin chariot, calash, chaise or chair, drawn by 6 or more horses or other beasts of burthen, the sum of 3s; if drawn by any lesser number of horses or beasts of burthen than 6 and more than 2, the sum of 2s 6d; if drawn by 2 horses or other beasts of burthen, the sum of 1s.

Wagons [waggons] with 4 or more horses: for every wagon, waincart, dray car or other carriage with 4 wheels, drawn by 4 or more horses or other beasts of burthen, the sum of 1s. By less than 4 horses: if drawn by less than 4 horses or other beasts of burthen, the sum of 10d. Wagons with 2 horses: if drawn by 2 horses or other beasts of burthen, the sum of 6d ha'penny.

Gig or jaunting car with 1 horse: for every carriage with 2 wheels, commonly called a chaise, chair gig or jaunting car, drawn by 1 horse or other beast of burthen, the sum of 6d; if drawn by 2 or more horses or beats of burthen, the sum of 10d.

For every sedan chair the sum of 4d.

Wagons with 1 horse: for every wagon, waincart, dray car or other carriage drawn by 1 horse or other beast of burthen, the sum of 4d.

Sledges without wheels: for every sledge, slide or other carriage without wheels, drawn in any manner, the sum of 9d.

For all carriages whatever, drawn in any other manner than aforesaid, the sum of 6d, together with the sum of 1d ha'penny for each animal employed in drawing the same.

Single horse: for every horse, gelding, mare, mule or ass, the sum of 1d ha'penny.

Droves of cattle: for every drove of oxen, cows, heifers or meat cattle, the sum of 3s 4d per score and so in proportion for any greater or less number.

For every calf, hog, pig, sheep or lamb, the sum of 1d.

Foot-passengers: for any passenger passing over said bridge, except such persons as drive or shall be driven in such coach, Berlin chaise, chair, calash, gig or jaunting car, a ha'penny and every horse and man 2d ha'penny.

For every single horse 1d ha'penny.

For every person carrying or conveying any kish, basket, sack, load or package or any kind, the weight of which shall amount to 30lbs, the sum of 1d.

This last clause was strictly imposed, in consequence of a practice resorted to by the peasantry to evade the charge for cart-loads. They unloaded at the Waterside and carried the load down in moderate parcels on the human back.

The tolls were altered in 1826. Up to 1833 the charge for foot-passengers was 1d. Many individuals among the parishioners compound annually with the toll-gatherer for a certain sum, in order to obtain the privilege of walking through the gate without stopping.

DAY, McWILLIAMS, ENGLISH, and DOBSON (eds),
Ordnance Survey Memoirs of Ireland, Vol. 34: Clondermot and Waterside (1831–8), 1996

Among the great improvements which appear,
The citizens of Derry fam'd to cheer,
The handsome iron bridge conspicuous stands,
And from the muse attention due demands.
This lofty structure, pleasing to the sight,
In all beholders doth surprise excite;
While many wonder how the art of man
A double roadway bridge so well could plan –
Beauty and strength, with symmetry combin'd
Show forth the skill with which it was designed;
And engineering science, crown'd with bays,
Tends higher on the roll of fame to raise.

Contractors, who presume to take in hand
Works to erect they do not understand,
Will find both ruin and disgrace ensue,
And blight the prospects which they had in view.
But here, across a river deep and wide,
Where rises high a rapid running tide
Is seen a bridge, which may for beauty vie
With any other underneath the sky.

ROBERT YOUNG, 'Lines on Viewing the New Iron Bridge Which Spans the Foyle,
on the South-East Side of the City of Londonderry',
The Poetic Works of Robert Young, 1863

THE McKEEVER FAMILY RAN THE FERRY – an open boat driven by a paraffin-burning engine. The Ferry plied between the city and the Waterside, the city terminus being a wooden hut, with the legend GARRISON FERRY emblazoned across the fascia, while the Waterside landing stage was at the rear of Ebrington Barracks. It was a cheap and popular method of transport, particularly with the troops who were then stationed in Ebrington Barracks.

To me, as a child, the docks always seemed busy, with regular sailings to

Glasgow carrying passengers, cargo and livestock, and intermittent services to other English ports.

The coal trade was a particularly important one, and it was not unusual to see at least half-a-dozen colliers discharging their cargos for local merchants such as Lanes, Montgomerys, McDevitt & Donnells, and Kellys. The vessels were emptied by gangs of dockers working in their holds, shovelling coal into huge buckets which were hoisted out by cranes, and tipped into the waiting horse-drawn carts or railway wagons, amid clouds of coal dust. In the depths of the holds, the dockers toiled, hour after hour, the black dust caked on their sweating bodies, teeth and eyes gleaming in their blackened faces, their shovels shining like polished silver, scoured by the coal.

Usually at least one boat per week was destined for the Gas Company, or the Electricity Generating Station – Derry, incidentally, was one of the first cities in the British Isles to have its main streets entirely lighted by electric light – and on this day, there was a constant procession of horse-drawn carts from the quays, lumbering up Strand Road, Gt James' Street, Little James' Street, Rossville Street, and Lecky Road to the Gas Yard. Part of Strand Road, and part of William Street, were paved with square-setts on which the iron-shod wheels made a tremendous clatter, while the steel shoes of the horses struck sparks from the irregular surfaces of the setts.

CHARLES GALLAGHER, *Acorns and Oak Leaves*, 1981

TODAY THEY WERE BORED AND HOT and sleepy, too languid even to invent challenges for one another, too apathetic to talk. They went across Ferryquay Street and looked idly into the shop windows. The sun made mirrors of the plate glass and they stood for a while contorting their faces at their reflections. Then they shuffled on to the Diamond where black soldiers of the War Memorial towered in taut menace above them. But today they were too spiritless to cock a snook up at them. The seats around the base of the memorial were empty and in passing they kicked them. They went down Shipquay Street and across Guildhall Square and came to the quays. There the heat was even more oppressive: the smell of the river gave it body.

Three tramp steamers slept against the wooden props of the wharf. The boys looked at them without interest. In the middle of the quay lay a mountain of scrap metal, golden colored with exposure, waiting to be shipped across the Irish Sea to England. They walked around it twice, assessing it, and went away, rejecting it. They went out to the end of a jetty and stood looking down into the brown, stagnant water. Johnny spat first, then Mick. It occurred to them both to have a spitting contest but neither of them suggested it and they went back to the main part of the quay. The sliding door of one of the sheds was ajar and Mick put his head in through the opening. He whistled into the gloomy cave. 'Listen!' he said.

'What?' said Johnny.

'The echo!' said Mick. 'Listen!' He whistled again. 'There! Don't you hear it?'

A pigeon stirred in the scaffolding of the roof but did not fly away.

'You're a genius. That's what you are, kid. A genius,' said Johnny.

They followed the railway lines that ran parallel to the water, Johnny in front, Mick a few paces behind, both of them tightrope walking on the rusted track. It led them to the barrier beyond which pedestrians could not go.

On their way home, they discovered Browning Drive. Johnny had said that he knew a short cut from the quay to the squatters' huts at the outskirts of the town where they lived, but somewhere along the way they must have taken a wrong turning because now they found themselves in a district that was new to them. The drive was as wide as three ordinary streets and inclined sharply down to the river which lay cool and sparkling at its feet. On one side there were houses, each planted in a miniature field of green and on the other side was a wall beyond which stretched a wooded park. There were trees just inside the wall too, great, spreading trees which formed a long sunshade down that whole side so that the roadway beneath the houses and the park was split exactly down the middle, one half in the sun, the other in the shade. The pavement between the trees was already coated with fallen leaves, crisp and brown. But autumn had not touched the other side. The houses were bright and fresh and gaily colored and their gardens vivid with flowers and their lawns soft. Some were bungalows and some were two-story houses and the windows of all of them were slightly open to catch the breeze that came up from the river and stirred their careful curtains.

BRIAN FRIEL, 'Johnny and Mick', in The Saucer of Larks, 1962

A S THE AFTERNOON PROGRESSED, the Lough began to narrow again; and we presently caught a far-off glimpse of the spire of Derry Cathedral. In course of time, our track dwindled to a river, with a deep channel, and fertile banks, which gradually grew closer and closer together as we approached the city, and were studded with parks and mansions; and soon the city itself appeared, covering a hill, on the highest part of which the spire rose quaintly skyward, with other spires arising from the jumble of curious streets and time-worn houses, which sloped in regular gradations up to meet it, and carried the imagination back to Camelot, the mystic city of the blameless king.

ARTHUR BENNETT, John Bull and His Other Island II, 1890

The General
Witchery

IN THE EVENING WE STROLLED ACROSS the bridge to Waterside, and were astonished to discover, in the vicinity of the best houses, a large number of absolute hovels. From a distance, the whole suburb looked well-built, and almost luxurious. We were on high ground here, and had a rare view of the city, as the sun set and slowly folded it in shadow, which spread and spread until all was dusk except at one solitary point; and here the Cathedral spire uprose amid the ruddy light which vividly contrasted with the gloom that swathed all else, and, to the right, where the hills were loftier and the river broadened, grew almost black, while from the dimness loomed some ghostly mansions and a shadowy tower. But, to the left, the river curves abruptly round the city, and here the sunrays were only partially obscured, and fell upon the leaden waters, and were reflected in a dull red glare as if the flood that rolled beneath the bridge were intertwined with fire; and, just below us, in the very foreground, a forest of masts and spars and rigging was weirdly visible amid the prevailing murkiness, as if a phantom fleet had anchored in the silent stream. And then, as the mysterious afterglow left the western heavens, a light began to twinkle here and there beyond it, and within the windows of the houses at our feet; while from the city came the music of a band that, softened by distance, stole thrillingly over the water and added to the general witchery.

ARTHUR BENNETT, *John Bull and His Other Island II*, 1890

BOGSIDE WAS THE NAME OF A STREET as well as the name of the general area. It was an unlikely city street. At one end there was a large house, built in the style of a farmhouse. At the other end there was the city abattoir. The abattoir was a great place for men to gather to discuss football, horses or the news of the day. I do not know how any work got done there. There was just one pub in the street, Duddy's, and a grocery shop, the All Cash Stores. Houses of various sizes lined the street. None was similar to any other. There were single-storey, two-storey and three-storey houses of differing shapes and sizes. The area had many culs-de-sac. There was a cul-de-sac off the Bogside called Carlisle Place. On the other side Abbey Street linked the Bogside to William Street. Abbey Street derived its name from the medieval Dominican Abbey that was located in that general area of Derry.

Town gas was the main source of energy in the area. Whole families cooked on one gas ring and in some houses the lighting was also fuelled by gas. In some homes, there were hearth fires with a crook for pots and kettles, the same as houses in the country. In others there were black ranges. There were open coal or coke fires in most houses, and in the still, dark, cold days of winter, the entire area was shrouded in a pall of blue smoke, wisps slowly going up in a straight line from every chimney.

There were all kinds of men constantly doing the rounds of the streets and homes – coal men, gas men, brock men, insurance men, bread men, debt men, cruelty men, post men, rent men, milk men, bin men, dole men, football pools men, lemonade men, sanitary men, Corporation men, school attendance men, wee Indian and Pakistani men selling clothes and there was me!

'Hi, mister, are you a priest?' called a small grubby youngster amid a group of children playing in a battered cardboard box. It was my first day in the Bogside. It was a whole new, fascinating world. This was to be my home and place of work for the next eleven years.

(BISHOP) EDWARD DALY, *Hi Mister! Are You a Priest?'*, 2000

AH, raise it up –
Raise up the statue in the storied town;
Make it a sign of sorrow and renown,
Like flags that tell us where a ship went down.

Ah, raise it up –
Raise up the statue in the quiet square;
Crowning the street that rises, like a stair,
Up from the river in the gloom or glare.

And let it front
At eve or dawn, or with a nameless charm
Of mystic darkness on its folded arm,
The Foyle that brims and brightens by the Farm.

Why raise it up?
Where are the great lines there that we may seek,
As of the statesman with pale brow and cheek,
As of the senator in act to speak?

Not such are here,
If life-drawn truth have moulded it; not such,
If inspiration, by some happy touch,
Have stamp'd in bronze the presence loved so much.

Yet raise it up.
Methinks the shaggy brow speaks honest scorn,
And sharp and kindly as a frosty morn
Is the man's wholesome influence reborn.

Ah, raise it up –
Show us the rugged gentleness, the true eyes
Of him who never wrought for place or prize,
Who lack'd the golden eloquence – that lies!

Ah, raise it up –
And let it tell, as far as sculpture can,
For those who have congenial hearts to scan,
The noble quietness of an honest man.

Yet scarcely tell
The lines that gather on that kindly brow,
The cares that wither and the pains that bow –
He has forgotten them, and we will now.

And often here,
Come from the heather'd hill, where ever higher,
Summer by summer, creeps the yellow fire
Of the ripe corn right up the mountain's spire –

And often here,
When in the busy square the parted meet,
Peasant and stately gentleman shall greet
A face they know, a presence sadly sweet.

Ah me! ah me!
The souls in white, who with a single aim
Have wrought or thought for us, they may not claim
Or care to hear the echoes of their name.

They may not heed
If men remember them or not below –
Earth's bells are muffled for them as with snow,
Perchance unheard o'er the dark river's flow.

Yet raise it up –
Raise up the statue, in this land and time,
When to tell truth heads all the lists of crime,
And lives are low, and only words sublime.

THE REVEREND WILLIAM ALEXANDER DD DCL, Bishop of Derry and Raphoe,
'The Derry Statue to the Memory of Sir R.A. Ferguson, MP',
St Augustine's Holiday and Other Poems, 1886

S T COLUMBA'S PROCESSION WAS HELD as usual on the saint's feast day that year – the 9th of June. And the following Saturday I presented myself at the inspector's house at ten o'clock for examination.

It was a beautiful morning as I crossed Carlisle Bridge that spanned the majestic, broad-bosomed Foyle. I looked down into the water: a small ferry boat was steaming its way across, the passengers standing on the deck; the Glasgow boat was moored at the Scotch shed on the quays, the houses rising in tiers behind her and above her tall funnels. Large buildings that I knew to be shirt-and-collar factories stood on that bank of the river, too, one in red brick, another in grey stone. All these were on the city side of the Foyle. I turned and looked ahead at the other side of the river where I was going and there the houses rose from the water's edge in terraces in the same manner. But away to my right, and a little apart from the rest of the houses, stood several mansions on the highest ground. It was to one of these stately dwellings that I now bent my steps. At the end of the bridge I turned to my right, walked a short distance and was soon at the ornamental gates that had been described to me in great detail.

My nervousness began the moment I passed through these gates and increased as I mounted the long winding drive towards the house. Long before I came to it I could see the upper windows with their white lace curtains; the rest of the house was hidden from my view by trees and shrubs.

I stopped and looked back at the flowing river and the city on its banks. And I saw their beauty and was miserable. Father Willie had often told us that Columba preferred this spot to any other in the world. I knew by heart the words of the saint from his writings:

Were the tribute of all Alba mine,
I had rather have a house
Set in the midst of fair Derry ...

But the saintly Columba had never, I felt certain, sat for an examination as I was now called upon to do, and therefore could not possibly have experienced my present gloom. Was I the only one in this fair city condemned on this glorious summer's day to sit for a detestable examination for which I was not fit? Cars and horse-drawn lorries were passing along the roads and crossing the bridge below; the chimneys were smoking peacefully in the quiet of the morning; a train on the opposite bank was bearing its passengers joyfully away, leaving a long trail of white smoke in its wake; two rowing boats were now crossing the Foyle; and far above the city on the opposite side from where I stood, the white tombstones of the city's dead, showed clear and clean against the surrounding green. I looked; and the peace that I saw made me lonely ... as if the world and I had no connection with each other whatsoever; as if the moving life and the still life around me were cut off from me and I stood alone, having nothing in common with anyone or anything.

HUGH McVEIGH, *Oft in the Stilly Night*, 1957

I WAS BORN IN COLERAINE IN 1858, but three years later the family moved to Derry City in the autumn of 1861.

We came on the line now known as the Midland Railway and arrived at the old Waterside Station situated where the present one is to-day. I was only a child of three years, but I know that I was taken across the old Wooden Bridge which spanned the River Foyle from Walker Street, near the Waterside Station, to Bridge Street, on the other side. Bridge Street, by the way, was so named because it was the leading thoroughfare from the centre of the city to the Waterside.

Thus I have been across the three Londonderry Bridges, – the old Wooden Bridge which gave place to Carlisle Bridge in 1863, two years after my arrival in the city, and the present Craigavon Bridge. When I hear the Northern Government criticised for its little thought of Derry, I think of this gift, a matter of a quarter of a million sterling!

A first memory of my childhood in Derry is of the opening of Carlisle Bridge in 1863. The Earl of Carlisle as Lord Lieutenant of Ireland had been invited to open the Bridge. I can quite well remember as a boy of five years standing at my father's shop door in The Diamond – just where it is now – and seeing the great procession coming out of Ferryquay Street after the opening function and wheeling round The Diamond on its way to the Model School, which also was to be opened the same day. The bridge took its name from the fact that it was opened by the Earl of Carlisle, and of course the same applies to Carlisle Road.

I went to the Model School as a child of six years. The old school, with its lovely green in front, was a picture to anyone passing along Northland Road, which was then just a country road leading to Bridgend and Burt. The new building is much more spacious and better equipped for educational purposes, but it has not anything like the picturesque appearance of its predecessor, being more utilitarian in design. The Model

School, by the way, was then on the very outskirts of the city. Following the custom in those days our family lived over the business premises, and thus I was at the very hub of affairs. The Diamond was much the same as it is now except for the removal of the Corporation Hall.

C.W. GORDON, *Reminiscences of Derry in the Last Century*, n.d.

As I roved out one evening in the sweet month of June,
To view the green fields and to hear the lark's tune;
The blackbirds sang sweetly, purling streams on each side,
And the boys and girls courting down by the Bogside.

My mind bent on rambling, I crossed Bishop's Grove,
Where me and my true love did oftentimes rove;
If she had proved constant, and proved constant still,
We yet might be courting around Blue Bell Hill.

My love's tall and handsome, she lives by the Wall,
For beauty and daring she far exceeds all;
She gave me her hand that married we'd be,
Och, in sweet Londonderry, how happy we'd be.

Just two short months after, her father did say,
'Oh, Mary, dear Mary, you must go away;
To the fair land of promise where stars always shine,
And leave Londonderry and your true love behind.'

At hearing this news, she fell in despair,
To the wringing her hands and tearing her hair;
Saying, 'Father, dear father, it grieves my heart sore,
To leave Londonderry and the boy I adore.'

ANONYMOUS, 'A Londonderry Love Song', in *There Was Music in the Derry Air* (ed. A.M. Murray), 1989

DAWN OVER ROSEMOUNT. The sun turned the arch of sky from deep blue to green, gold, then white. It outlined in gold the tarnished oak and beech leaves. The green and brown ferns in the stone wall around the university suddenly showed, now vivid among the slate and mortar. In the shrubbery, rhododendrons that had drooped in the night imperceptibly lifted their leaves toward the light. A car swished by, scattering the pigeons. The cathedral bells began to ring: Sunday in Rosemount.

Above Northland Road a square of well-kept, tall Victorian houses looked out onto a railed-in area of grass and shrubs. Two of the houses, though, were more worn than the others. The first of these stood to the left of the square, the so-called Presbyterian Hostel. The second stood at the very top of the square next to a narrow alley. Its bow windows faced downhill toward the university wall and the city beyond. On its gatepost a small sign read, simply, 'McCrae'. One window on the top floor was curtained by a thin ivory-colored muslin that covered only the lower part of the sash. The glass reflected the walls and towers of the city; the room within was shadowy and dim.

The sun climbed higher, pushing long yellow bars into the shadowed room. A desk haphazardly piled with books, papers, and journals adjoined the window sill. Over a chairback, a white towel hung limp and damp. Below it, several days' worth of clothing lay where their owner had dropped them. A bulging, open suitcase spilled shirts, socks, and records onto the floor by one of the beds. The name 'Forbes' was scrawled on the suitcase in heavy black ink.

On the other side of the room, a small, neatly ordered bookshelf stood on top of a table which obviously served as a desk. The tabletop was clear of all but a mug of sharp pencils, an opened packet of loose-leaf paper, and a family photograph. Beside this desk, a spotless sink and small wall mirror above gleamed in the eastern light. Razors, shaving brushes, and a cracked china cup cluttered the glass shelf over the sink.

One of the two sleepers turned over, groaning softly. His eyes blinked open and shut. Particles of dust hung and swirled in the sunlight over the bed. He screwed up his eyes and frowned, pushing his hand through his brown hair.

Sunday, he thought, stretching. His mouth moved silently as he woke to habitual morning prayer. *Thank you, Father, for today. I need it. I don't feel ready for this term yet. Help me to rest in you, to set work aside. Communion today … I'm not ready for that, either. 'Love the Lord your God with all your heart, and with all your soul, and with all your mind.' All. Father, I haven't. Forgive me, Lord, but she's so beautiful and I do want her. Purify my love for her so that it's a small part of my greater love for you, my longing to do your will … including your will in relation to her. Also, help me if I'm elected in the CU presidency – help me to change things. Help me to have a right balance of tact and – Tact! You know I don't have much, Father – and boldness … and graciousness. Especially toward James. Help me to love him more even if I dislike him. Lord, I'd like it if everyone in the CU could be more open, less concerned about what others think and more concerned about who we are and what we need to do here … 'Love thy neighbor' … James again. I simply have to learn to love him more. Who else is my neighbor at the moment?*

He stopped, looking across the room at the form hunched under an old gray eiderdown. Jack Monaghan. Speaking of neighbors ... How strange to have lived with someone for a week, yet to know so little about him, to have seen so little of him.

He'd been at Queen's University in Belfast last year, he'd said, waiting to see if the New U would actually survive. Older than the usual second-year student, apparently. Twenty-five perhaps? Used to be a carpenter for Harland & Wolff. Here to read English – like Sheila.

ELIZABETH GIBSON, *The Water is Wide*, 1985

DERIVATION OF TOWNLAND NAMES

45 KILFINNAN: called in the Down Survey Kilfury part of Balliowen, but it is probable that fury is one of those blunders or mistakes frequently committed by the draftsmen employed by Sir William Petty to draw fair copies of that survey. The etymology is probably *Coill Fionnain*, 'Finnan's wood'. *Fionnan*, a diminutive of *fionn*, is synonymous with albin or candide and was very common as the name of men, especially of saints in Ireland.

DAY, McWILLIAMS, ENGLISH, and DOBSON (eds),
Ordnance Survey Memoirs of Ireland, Vol. 34: Clondermot and Waterside (1831–8), 1996

THE POET SEAMUS DEAN, describing the area in which he was born and reared, wrote: 'Bogside was once a street. Now it is a condition.' The condition was one of poor housing, low pay and unemployment in the swampy valley below the walled city of Derry. Bogside was the name of the main street in the swamp. The population there was and is almost exclusively Catholic.

The condition known as 'Bogside' is indelibly imprinted in the memories of those who rose up against it in 1968, pouring out of the warrens that surround the main street ... These streets are gone now, replaced by modern housing in response to the Civil Rights Movement. The former slum-dwellers are proud that they survived and overcame the worst that the Unionist Government inflicted on them.

Those streets which best evoked the condition known as 'Bogside' were called Fahan Street, Walker's Square, Nailor's Row, and St Columb's Wells. The condition was not confined to the Bogside area. It was to be found wherever Catholics sought shelter. Within the walled city, it was to be found in Magazine Street; abutting the walled city it was to be found in Bridge Street and an alleyway off it called Miller's Close; beyond the city boundary it was to be found, notoriously, in Springtown Camp.

Peggy Deery's parents were born in these streets. The parents of her husband Patsy were born in these streets. The parents reared their children in these streets. Peggy and Patsy began their marriage in a rented room in one of these streets.

NELL McCAFFERTY, *Peggy Deery*, 1987

BHÍ DHÁ THEAGHLACH INA GCÓNAÍ ag taobh a chéile ar Thaobh an Uisce i nDoire, teaghlach a raibh Ó Míocháin orthu agus teaghlach a raibh Ó Dochartaigh orthu. Bhí gasúr i ngach teach acu seo agus bhí na gasúir fán aois amháin. Bhí an bheirt ag comrádaíocht ó thainig ann díobh. Bhí siad le chéile go dtí an scoil náisiúnta an chéad uair. Ón scoil naisiunta, bhí an bheirt ag comrádaíocht go dtí Coláiste Cholm Cille. Nuair a d'fhág siad Coláiste Cholm Cille chuaigh an bheirt go Maigh Nuad le theacht amach ina dhá sagart.

Tógadh an Dochartach ag dhá aintín agus uncail dó i nDoire, nó maraíodh a athair agus a mháthair i dtaisme bóthair roimhe sin agus thóg a dhá aintín agus a uncail leo é agus thóg siad é. Ach nuair a bhí sé tamall i Maigh Nuad fuair sé scéala go raibh a uncail le bás agus fuair sé cead a theacht chun an bhaile. Fuair an t-uncail bás agus d'fhan sé sa bhaile go dtí go bhfuair sé é a fhaire agus a adhlacadh. Chuaigh sé ar ais go Maigh Nuad.

Tháinig sé féin agus an Míochánach amach ina dhá sagart sa lá amháin. Chuaigh siad faoi ord bheannaithe. Cuireadh an Sagart Ó Míocháin síos go dtí paróiste Mhaigh Bhile agus an tAthair Ó Dochartaigh go hAlbain, go dtí áit ar a dtugtar Eilistrim, taobh amuigh de Ghlaschú. Ach i ndiaidh don Dochartach a dhul anonn ina shagart go hAlbain, bhí an dá aintín fágtha leo féin. D'éirigh solas marbh sa teach gach oíche ó bheadh a haon déag go dtí a haon a chlog agus tormán mór. Ach de réir mar a bhí an t-am á chaitheamh, bhí an tormán ag éirí níba láidre agus an solas ag éirí niba soiléire. Thosaigh na daoine a chruinniú le é a fheiceáil agus a chluinstin. Chuir siad scéala anonn go hAlbain chuig an tsagart, ag iarraidh air a theacht anall agus feiceáil cad é a bhí contráilte.

Nuair a fuair an sagart an litir scríobh se chuig an Athair Ó Míocháin le linn é a bheith ina chomrádaí aige agus é a bheith de chóir baile. D'iarr sé air a dhul anonn, mas é a thoil é, agus feiceáil cad é a bhí contrailte, mar nach raibh gléas airsean an áit ina raibh sé a fhágáil.

Tháinig an tAthair Ó Míocháin nuair a fuair sé an scéala. Nuair a tháinig sé go dtí an teach, bhí slua mór daoine ann idir istigh agus amuigh. Bhí an solas le feiceáil go soiléir thuas an staighre agus an tormán le cluinstin mar an gcéanna. D'aithin an tAthair Ó Míocháin nach raibh uchtach aige a dhul suas leis féin agus chuir sé scéala chuig sagart an pharóiste sa Túr Fhada. Tháinig sagart an pharóiste agus is é an gléas marcaíochta a bhí leis, carr taoibhe, beithíoch agus tiománaí.

Nuair a tháinig sé isteach chuir sé ceist ar an Athair Ó Miocháin cad é a bharúil a bhí ann. Dúirt seisean nach raibh a fhios aige ach go raibh an solas agus an tormán ann.

'Bhail,' ar seisean, 'thig leat coinneal a lasadh.'

Sular las siad an choinneal, chuir sé ceist an raibh áit ar bith nó teach ar bith thíos a dtiocfadh leo an rud a chur isteach ann agus é a chur faoi ghlas. Dúirt fear amháin go raibh *magazine* thall giota, go raibh sé déanta de bhrící, go raibh leathdhoras iarainn air agus nár baineadh úsáid as le blianta. Dúirt sé fosta go raibh glas air ach go raibh an eochair ag cléireach an bhaile mhóir.

Cuireadh scéala chuig an chléireach agus tháinig sé. Dúirt sé leis cinnte go dtiocfadh leis é a fháil, nach raibh úsáid ar bith as an áit le blianta.

Chuaigh cúpla duíne anonn agus bhain siad an glas den doras agus d'oscail siad amach é. D'iarr sagart an pharóiste ar an Athair Ó Míocháin coinneal a lasadh. Lasadh agus cuireadh isteach i gcoinnleoir í. Chuaigh an sagart ar tús agus coinnleoir leis agus nuair a tháinig sé go dtí barr an staighre cuireadh as an choinneal. Cuireadh as an dara huair í. Ach ghlac an sagart paróiste talann feirge agus chuaigh sé amach agus bhain sé an fhuip den tiománaí agus tháinig sé isteach agus an fhuip leis.

'Rachaidh mise mé féin ar tús agus coinnigh thusa ar mo chúl leis an choinneal lasta,' ar seisean.

Nuair a chuaigh siad suas go dtí barr an staighre, chonaic siad an t-óganach i gcoirnéal sa tseomra. Bhí cruthaíocht air mar ghabhar a bheadh ag siúl ar a dhá chois deiridh. D'ordaigh an sagart dó teacht amach, anuas an staighre, síos an tsráid agus isteach go dtí an *magazine* seo.

Bhí an doras oscailte agus d'iarr sé air a dhul isteach sa *mhagazine* agus chuaigh. Druideadh an doras agus cuireadh an glas air agus bhí sin ceart go leor. Ní raibh trup ná torman ann níos mó.

Fuair an dá aintín seo bás agus tháinig daoine eile ina n-áit. Daoine Gallda a bhí iontu. Bliain na Gaoithe Móire 1926 tháinig an tormán agus an solas ann mar an gcéanna. Chuala siad go raibh sé ann roimhe sin agus gurb é an Sagart Ó Míocháin agus sagart na paróiste a chur ar shiúl é. Cuireadh scéala fá choinne an Athar Uí Mhíocháin agus tháinig sé. Dúirt sé go gcaithfeadh sé cuidiú a fháil agus chuir sé scéala chuig an easpag. Tháinig an tEaspag agus d'inis an tAthair Ó Míocháin cad é mar bhí ón chéad uair. 'Is dócha gurb é an rud céanna a bheas ann anois,' ar seisean.

Chuir an tEaspag ceist an raibh teach folamh ar bith thart mar d'imigh an díon de *mhagazine* agus sin an dóigh a bhfuair an rud amach. Dúirt siad go raibh teach úr guail tógtha ar chúl an tí agus nár baineadh úsáid as go fóill. D'iarr an tEaspag orthu a dhul amach agus an doras a oscailt. Lasadh an choinneal. Chuaigh an tEaspag é féin ar tús suas an staighre. Bhí an t-óganach ina shuí san áit chéanna. D'ordaigh an tEaspag agus an sagart anuas an staighre é, isteach i gclós agus ansin isteach i dteach an ghuail. Cuireadh glas ar an doras.

Nuair a phill an sagart isteach chuir sé ceist ar mhuintir an tí an bhfaca siad a dhath agus dúirt bean amháin go bhfaca sise.

'Cad é a chonaic tú?', ar seisean.

'Bhail, is í an tsamhailt a bhéarfainn dó, gabhar a bheadh ag siúl ar a dhá chois deiridh.'

'Bhail,' ar seisean, 'chonaic tú é cinnte.'

Ach ba é an pionós a chur sé ar mhuintir an tí, gan feoil a ithe Dé hAoine. Tamall ina dhiaidh sin, thiontaigh siad ina gCaitlicigh agus tá siad ina gCaitlicigh, riamh ó shin.

Two families lived side by side in the Waterside area of Derry, one called Meehan, the other Doherty. There were sons in each house of exactly the same age and they were comrades from boyhood. They went to primary school together and still remained friends when they attended St Columb's College. When they left there the two of them went to Maynooth to study for the priesthood.

The Doherty boy had been reared by two aunts and an uncle in Derry because his father and mother had previously died in a road accident. They had taken the boy and cared for him. After spending some time in Maynooth he learned that his uncle was dying and he was given permission to go home. The uncle died and young Doherty stayed for the wake and the burial, returning afterwards to Maynooth.

He and his friend were ordained on the same day; Fr Meehan was appointed to Moville parish, while Fr O'Doherty was sent to Scotland, to a place called Eilistrim near Glasgow. His two aunts now lived alone in the house and soon a 'dead light' was seen to shine each night from eleven o'clock until one in the morning accompanied by a loud noise. Towards the end of the period the din would grow louder and the light more brilliant. People began to visit the house to hear and see the manifestations, and word was sent to Scotland to the priest, asking him to come back and try to discover what was wrong.

When Fr O'Doherty received the letter he wrote to Fr Meehan, trusting in his friendship and because he was nearer to hand. He asked him to go and see what might be amiss since he couldn't leave his post. Fr Meehan came when he heard the news. Reaching the house he found a hugh crowd both inside and out. The light was clear to be seen and there were the usual sounds. Fr Meehan realised that he had not sufficient power to proceed alone. He sent word to the parish priest of the Long Tower, who came in his horse-drawn sidecar, complete with driver.

When he entered he asked Fr Meehan for his opionion but he replied that he knew nothing more than that the light and the noise were clearly evident. 'Well,' said the parish priest, 'We should light a candle.' Before they lit it the parish priest asked if there were any place in the house into which the spirit could be driven and secured. One of the men present said that there was a storehouse at the back. It was built of brick, had an iron half-door and had not been used for years. He also said that the door had a lock but that the key was in the possession of the town clerk. He was sent for and when he arrived said that they were welcome to the key since the place had been derelict for years.

Two men unlocked the storeroom and opened the door outwards. Then the parish priest asked Fr Meehan to light the candle. It was lit and fixed in a candlestick. The parish priest led the way carrying the candlestick but when he came to the bottom of the stairs the candle went out. When it went out a second time the priest became very angry. He rushed out, took the whip from the driver and came back into the house with it. 'I'll go in front,' he said, 'and you follow behind with the lit candle.'

When they reached the top of the stairs they saw a figure in the corner of a room. It had the appearance of a goat that could walk on its hind legs. The priest ordered it to come out, down the stairs, up the street and into the storehouse. The door was open and the thing was asked to go inside. It obeyed. The door was closed and locked – and that was that. There were no more disturbances.

The two aunts died and newcomers, who were English, came to live in the house. In 1926, the Year of the Big Wind, the sounds and the light returned. The people of the house found out that they had been heard and seen in the past and that Fr Meehan and the parish priest had banished them. Fr Meehan was summoned and when he came he said he would need assistance. He sent word to the bishop and when he came told him the story from the beginning. 'It's likely to be the same thing again,' he said.

The bishop asked if there were any empty dwelling nearby because the roof had been blown off the storehouse and that was how the thing had escaped. The people told him that there was a new coalhouse at the back and that it hadn't yet been used. The bishop asked them to go out and open up the coalhouse. A candle was lit and the bishop himself led the way up the stairs. The thing was seated in exactly the same place. The bishop and the priest ordered it down the stairs, out to the yard and into the coalhouse. The door was locked.

When the priest got back inside he asked the people of the house if they had seen anything unusual and one woman said that she had seen something. 'What was it you saw?' he asked. 'Well, it seemed like a goat walking on its hind legs.'

'Well,' said the priest, 'you certainly saw it.'

He imposed as a penance on the householders that they should not eat meat on Fridays. Shortly afterwards they converted to Catholicism and remained Catholics ever afterwards.

MICÍ SHEÁIN NÉILL Ó BAOILL, 'Taibhse Dhoire' ('A Derry Ghost'),
Lá de na Laethaibh (*Once Upon a Time*), (ed. Lorcán Ó Searcaigh), 1983
(VERSION BY SEAN McMAHON)

WATERSIDE DISTILLERY, LONDONDERRY
SOLE PROPRIETOR, ANDREW ALEXANDER WATT

ON LEAVING ABBEY STREET, we drove with our conductor, the polite and courteous distiller, to the Malt Distillery, which is situated about a mile distant, passing various objects of interest on the way. Near the Roman Catholic Chapel, outside the walls, are to be seen the St Columb's

Wells; the waters therein contained are considered by the pious country people to be a specific for diseases of the eye, but in Derry itself they are not held in much repute. Adjacent to these wells is St Columb's Stone; on each side of it are two oval hollows, of which various legends are related. It is said that the water deposited in rain in these hollows possesses a miraculous power in curing certain diseases.

The Distillery is placed on the side of a steep hill, and is within a few minutes' walk of the river Foyle. Just above the works we had a fine view of the city with its picturesque surroundings. The establishment covers three acres of ground, and the water used is derived from a huge Reservoir covering nearly three acres of ground, some little distance away from the town, and the property of the Distillery. Besides this supply, there are two deep wells on the premises, from which water containing fine properties for mashing and distilling purposes is obtained.

ALFRED BERNARD, *The Whisky Distillers of the United Kingdom*, 1987

O N REMOVING ME FROM the City and County Infirmary where my bum was slapped to evoke the first of my many protests, my parents did not have to travel far to reach home. We lived in the long downhill sweep of the wide road immediately below the hospital, Clarendon Street.

Clarendon Street and its large, Georgian red-brick houses were then almost an integral part of the hospital. Some houses had been joined inside to form large homes for nurses, and a surprisingly high number of doctors and dentists (and their families) lived in the others and even practised from the ground-floor or basement surgeries. The street also sported a chiropodist, a denture-maker, Clarendon Springs on top of which Madden's Mineral Waters business flourished, a huge Young Women's Christian Association Hostel, music and Irish Dancing teachers, and quiet houses discreetly offering full board, or, less respectably, bed and breakfast. Nearly every house bore one or more brass plates which maids (some in uniform) carefully polished with Brasso each morning, nodding or waving to each other as they did so. At the city centre end of the street, a shirt factory (Derry was famous for its shirt factories), a betting office and an Italian fish and chip shop 'lowered the tone' considerably.

The area ministered not merely to the flesh, but also to the soul: there were at least five churches of different denominations in the vicinity, including the huge and imposing St Eugene's Cathedral, where I was a choirboy for some years. Sundays saw parades of conflicting religion, all of them sprung from Jesus Christ, but few reflecting his love.

Those whom religion failed might seek refuge in the somewhat chilling Municipal Lunatic Asylum set in its own spacious grounds behind a huge, long wall in adjacent Asylum Road. In retrospect, many of the politicians and churchmen later to deface Northern Ireland might usefully have been confined there, but their futures, like my own, were hidden. Instead, the new police headquarters was fittingly built there.

The Lough Swilly Bus Company was based a street away and ferried Derry holidaymakers to Donegal and back all summer; it also carried hundreds of Catholic girls to and from the rural Thornhill College every day, a fact which came to interest me considerably as I grew older. Other large shirt factories were nearby, and so every day waves of women and girls, patients and penitents, flowed through the street more regularly than the tides. It was a busy area and I came to find the working women and girls, and the largely unemployed men and boys, the norm.

Behind Lower Clarendon Street and the commercial Strand Road was the wide and sluggish River Foyle, port and lough dividing Northern Ireland from Donegal in the Irish Republic. It sported an American Naval Base and many visiting navies, and sailors from ships and submarines. It was natural to be attracted to the quays in the evenings to stand alongside docked subs, whose sailors threw coins and notes to the gazing children – 'Give that to your sister!' they cried as the notes landed coin-laden at our feet. At eight or nine years of age, I couldn't figure out how they knew we had sisters or why they wanted to send notes to them at all. I fought all the time with one of my sisters – surely they wouldn't want to write to her!

But Clarendon Street was very respectable and quite well-off; it was fairly snobby and inhabited by Protestant and Catholic professional and business people (mostly Protestant) among whom, I always felt, my moderately-off family was a little out of place. Most families in the street owned at least one car, some two, and other kept speedboats in their garages which they raced on Lough Foyle at weekends. Ours apart, most houses had one or more maids or housekeepers to look after the children (or the bachelor doctors), and special playrooms for the kids. Well-off families, Protestant and Catholic, tended to send their children to boarding schools. We were not that wealthy.

My father, who taught for decades in the Brow of the Hill Christian Brothers' Primary School overlooking the Bogside, hadn't owned a car since his marriage. For years he had the character either to pedal a bicycle to and from school or to walk the long distance in all weathers, his winter protection being a huge, heavy trench coat, galoshes and sturdy umbrella.

SHANE DOHERTY, *The Volunteer*, 1993

THE OUTSKIRTS OF DERRY ARE especially beautiful, and the glory of Donegal lies at its doors. For the golfer there is a splendid eighteen-hole course at Prehen, and eight miles away, across the border in Donegal, the celebrated North-West course at Lisfannon. And talking of Prehen reminds me that it isn't only golf that is associated with that name, for in the year 1760 a tragedy occurred in the old manion of the Knox's, Prehen House. And this is how it was.

Sure wasn't a brave lump of a fellow the name of Macnaghten courting the daughter of the house, Grace Knox, as nice a wee girl as was ever in the County Derry, and that's no word of a lie. And mind you that's a mouthful and a half, for the Derry girls was aye famous. And what was in it but the ould fellow Knox, a curwheeble of an ould crab, took a scunner at young Macnaghten and forbade the match. But the same Macnaghten was no schoolboy, and didn't himself and Grace lay to it to run away. And the ould sepulchre got word of this and was ready for the boyoh. And an awful brawl of a gun fight started, and in the midst of it all who was killed but the lovely Grace Knox herself. Ah, that was a lesson to any crabbed parent not to affront the ways of love. Well, Macnaghten was hidden away with his burden of love and sorrow, till one day he was caught, and what fell out but he was condemned to death, for the law ones found it was himself and his wild plans was responsible for the poor girl's death. There was a terrible crowd round the gallows at the hanging, more in sympathy than anything else I may tell you, and what happened now but the rope broke, and the crowd cheered, and with the Will of God made plain to all, young Macnaghten was free to go. For no man would stand in the way of the Will of God made manifest. But Macnaghten wouldn't face that road at all, and sure didn't he take the rope in his own two hands and make it good again, and didn't he cry out to the crowd: 'Innocent though I am I would rather be dead than live without my Grace Knox, the love of my heart, to be known always and to all men as Half-hanged Macnaghten.' And before anyone could stop him hadn't he the rope round his neck, and himself off the gallows to die the death of a hero and a true lover by his own hand. Ah, that was a terrible sad end to a grand love affair, and not a word of a lie in all I've told you, as any of the Derry ones will entertain.

RICHARD HAYWARD, *In Praise of Ulster*, 1938, revised edition 1946

LATER, DERRY SUFFERED MOST OF THE CALAMITIES which befell so many Northern Ireland towns. It was seized by armies and blown up by armies and recaptured and refired, long before the settlers came from London and called the city Londonderry. Then, after the famous siege, did Londonderry fade out of history? Indeed it did not. Londonderry was to know The Earl Bishop; and his kidney-shaped desk, with drawers all round it, is still preserved in The Cathedral Museum. And Londonderry was to have the first prison in Ulster shaped in the rotunda form invented by some pious Victorian so that the iron-grilled doors of all the tiered cells could be under the eye of one gaoler standing in a central position. The plan effected great economy in prison staff; but it was condemned when psychiatrists appeared on the scene and pointed out what dreadful things it did to the prisoners' unconscious minds when they realised that so many were under the control of one.

OSWELL BLAKESTON, *Thank You Now*, 1960

ONCE COLUM CILLE WAS IN THE PLACE called Clooney in the port of Derry on the east bank of Lough Foyle, and he blessed the place and built a church there. Speaking through the spirit of prophecy, he said: 'A foreign bishop will come to this place long after me and he will demolish this church that I've made, and he will build something else with its stones at a place called Bun Sentuinne ['mouth of the old wave'?] in the same townland.' Then he made this verse:

> My fear is that foreign strangers,
> Here to Clooney, yet will come,
> And bear my church away with them,
> To Bun Sentuinne, cold and numb.

All this was fulfilled as is clear to everyone today; that is a foreign bishop called Nicholas Weston came to Derry [bishop of Derry, 1466–84], and destroyed the church in order to make a palace from it. But that palace was never finished, and I'm certain that it was because of a miracle of Colum Cille that they weren't able to complete it with the stones of his very own church.

BRIAN LACEY (ed.), *Maghnus Ó Domhnaill: Betha Colaim Chille, 1532*
(*Manus O'Donnell: The Life of Colum Cille*), 1998

I SMELT THE DRINK OFF HIS BREATH right away. Unlike Father Jack, he couldn't put it down to altar-wine that time on a Sunday morning. 'Where to?' he says.

'Father O'Kane's first,' I told him.

'But there'll be nobody in,' says he, as if I didn't know as much myself and me after leaving the wee Father and Mrs Chambers in the chapel.

Patsy – that's Father Jack's maid – had told me one time where Mrs Chambers left the key. And I found it where she says; under a stone at the front door. In my heart of hearts I was hoping the money wouldn't be there. But it was, and a lot more with it. The whole lot filled my handbag.

'Where now?' says Tim when I come out again.

'I'm catching the boat-train for England,' I says to him.

He got mad as hell. And I knew the reason why as well. The kind of Tim, it made him angry to see another person doing what he hadn't the guts to do himself.

He plagued me with question after question. The Inquisition wouldn't be in it with him. Till, in the end, he got on my nerves, for I wasn't able to put my thoughts in words the way he wanted me to. Not that I owed him any explanation. All I knew was I wanted out of there. The place was smothering me. And I says as much to him. He shut up then.

We come into Derry by Bridge-End and along the Culmore Road. The streets was deserted as was usual on a Sunday. For years now, since the Troubles started, the place was a ghost town after the shops shut on Saturday night. An army jeep crawled by and the soldier on Tim's side gave him a suspicious look. There was a light on in the Odeon in the Strand but everyplace else was shuttered and dark. In the Guildhall Square the only sign of life was some rubbish blowing in the wind which only made the place look more desolate and deserted. Barely visible behind a barrage of shutters, the Foyle Street bus-station was shut up for the day. The way things was, nobody in Derry had any business outside their own front door on a Sunday except to go to church or chapel. I took heed of a lone woman loitering at the foot of Orchard Street, like she was waiting on somebody. She stared in at us as we passed.

'Ahh,' Tim let a growl out of him. 'You're likely better out of this God-forsaken place. Do you mind it, in the Fifties,' he says, 'when you and me was growing up? You wouldn't think to look at it now. Mind – Shipquay Street teeming with life at night. Brightly lit shops and people out having a good time. Six cinemas there was, can you believe it? Not to mention the Corinthian Ballroom in Bishop Street, and the Embassy in the Strand. And Yannarelli's fish and chip shop. That was in the Strand too, do you mind? People wasn't afraid to leave their houses then.'

Tim was in a right miserable mood that day. But there was something to his story still and all. Derry was far from the place it used to be when him and me was growing up. Like me, it was worn down by strife and trouble; though I never ceased to marvel at the way it kept rearing its head no matter how many times it was flattened. At the same time, I wasn't sorry to be leaving the place. Just surviving wasn't enough for me any more.

At the checkpoint on the bridge, a policeman with a pistol signalled us to stop. He took Tim's licence across to a soldier [who] was standing on the other side of the road. They talked for a few minutes. Then the soldier come across and started firing questions at us. Was Tim and me married? What work did Tim do? Where was I going? Like it was any of his business! I worried if he decided to hold us up and search the car I'd miss my train.

The last impression I have of Derry was Tim cadging a light off a conductor on the platform. Then he drew his cheeks in till they were hollow. And I turned my face away.

KATHLEEN FERGUSON, *The Maid's Tale*, 1994

THE BOGSIDE DISTRICT OF DERRY was a strange and intriguing place in the early 1960s. It was full of interesting contradictions. Despite the fact that the population was almost one hundred per cent Irish Nationalist or Republican, many of the principal streets were named after British military icons or commemorated triumphs from bygone wars, such as Wellington Street, Nelson Street, Blucher Street and Waterloo Street. It was an area where, contrary to the norm, the workforce was predominantly female. Whilst some of the men were dockers and others worked in the BSR factory, which manufactured record players, a very large percentage of the men were unemployed. Most of them had signed on the dole for years. There was poverty and overcrowding everywhere. Despite the poverty and the dreadful housing conditons, most of the people were incredibly good humoured and kind. They had brilliant, razor-sharp wit. It was a quintessential urban community, yet even in the early 1960s there were a few people who kept pigs or chickens in their backyards, somewhat to the discomfiture of their immediate neighbours. One of the more incongruous memories of early mornings in the Bogside was that of hearing a cock crowing in the middle of a city! Despite their poverty, they were by and large law-abiding people. Few doors were ever locked. Vandalism and criminal activity were insignificant. Most children were cherished, and there were many, many children. Anyone's problem was everyone's problem. There was a powerful community network of informal support in almost every situation that needed it – considerable emotional support, and as much financial support as could be afforded. Sickness, death and other family crises were occasions when such support would be gladly offered. There were even women in the community who washed and laid out the bodies of the dead, or 'stretched' them, as it was described. It was a Christian community in the real sense of the word.

One of the major arteries of the Bogside was Rossville Street. This was a street that could provide most of the staple needs of life. There were several grocery shops, many pubs, two small bakeries, a fish-and-chip shop, a newsagent, a confectionery shop, a very busy pawnbroker's shop and a lot of residential dwellings. At one stage, before I came to Derry, it had a bathhouse. There was the city cattle-market, just off Rossville Street and occasionally in the early 1960s the street would be filled with the chaos of cattle driven by shouting drovers on their way to the market or on their way to the nearby Glasgow or Liverpool boats which berthed about a half a mile away on the quays. Rossville Street embraced seven-day opening for pubs thirty years before it became legal! There was a hall, the Rossville Hall, where older men played cards, and discussed the affairs of the day; there were several bookies within easy reach. Rossville Street was always crowded with women and girls after the factory horns sounded at the beginning or end of work each day or at lunch hour. They stopped and purchased a bap or a turnover to eat at work, or something more substantial for the family meal on their way home from work. There was a cluster of large shirt factories nearby; the City Factory, Hogg & Mitchell's and Richardson's. Little streets led off Rossville Street, like branches of a tree – Pilot's Row, Eden Place, Joseph Street and Foxes Corner on one side and Union Street, Thomas Street and Bogside on the other.

(BISHOP) EDWARD DALY, Hi Mister! Are You a Priest?, 2000

THE RAIN COMES FROM THE NORTH, driven by the gusting wind in sheets made visible by the shadow of the winter beeches beyond the road. Skirts of rain, fluttered, tangled, ragged – rain fugitive over the fields, whipped over the crest of Rosemount, spilt onto the envalleyed city, thrown against the opposing ranks of hilltops: Kilfennan, Altnagelvin, Gobnascale. I try to picture the miles of land and sea this winter gale traversed to end up here, venting its spite. I do not like the north.

But this north-facing window where my desk stands gives a good steady light for drawing by. I can see the path of my inked nib clearly. This is where I work best, facing out into the teeth of the gale, though this aspect does make me feel lonely, peeled of comfort. I am poised at this northerly corner of the house, like some mythic mariner at the forward tip of his boat, heading northwards into unknown waters: cold, storm-tossed, iceberged, with dragons coiling greyly in the depths below the hull. The light at this window is like the snowlight, cold, precise, that floods the house when the ground and roofs around are all whited out. I love that clarity. Snowlight is surgically precise.

MARILYN McLAUGHLIN, 'Aspects', in A Dream Woke Me, 1999

THÍOS AG BUN NA hurrainne tá fuadar faoi do chomhphaisnéirí. An lánúin óg ag bailiú chucu agus ag miongháire go rúnmhar le chéile. Tá sé féin ag ligean na málaí taistil nua anuas go trom ar an suíochán, rud a tharraingeann spléachadh imníoch ón sagart mór an áit a bhfuil sé ag comhrá go tionscalach leis an bhean agus an bheirt ghirseach. Feichthear duit gur Gaeilge atá ar siúl acu ón chorrfhocal a thagann chugat. Dá éagsamhalta leat é, tá an teanga sin á seachadadh, go teolaí ó bheola daoine agus go lasánta de ghob pinn; do shinsir go buan inti agus do dhúchas á rá. Leathann cuar deireanach an Fheabhail amach romhat gan choinne de réir mar a thagann maoitheán na traenach thart ar an rannaidh talaimh. Braitheann tú spuaiceanna na cathrach ina gcolgsheasamh os cionn díonta sclátaí mar a bhfuil dealramh fuar na gealaí ina luí. Airíonn tú arís an t-aer bealaithe i do bhéal, é ar maos i mboladh an gháis agus an ghuail. Na duilleoga feoite smeartha ar na leacacha dubha agus cumha an fhómhair ina hanáil síos agus aníos i do scamhóga mar bheifeá i do ghasúr scoile ag filleadh go leisciúil ar thús téarma. Láimh leis an iarnród tá leargaí glasuaine ag blgadh anuas go dtí an t-uisce agus tithe buirgéiseacha bána ina staic i lár muineacha crann; fuinseoga agus a ngéaga loma dubh le heidheann ar bharr na binne taobh amuigh de na fuinneoga thall. Is léir duit anois sraitheanna tithe gróigthe thar dhroim a chéile ar ardáin Thaobh an Uisce agus síos Taobh an Bhogaigh agus ar bharr na haille ar oileán ársa Cholm Cille. Droichead mór an ainm ghránna ina shnaidhm thar an chaolas, mar a bhfuil múrtha agus gunnaí na Plandála ina strainc os a chionn; míle siméar beag ag stealladh teolaíocht teallaigh agus daonnacht Ghael aníos in éadan an chompal cloiche a bhuail ceannaithe Londain uirthi mar Dhoire, an chathair ghiobach gheabach ghrámhar mar a bhfuil an t-aincheart ina laibhín ag coipeadh chun a phléasctha ...

Fead fhada chianach thar an abhainn agus tá sraothartach an innill ina thost. Rithfidh sibh saor leis an fhuinneamh atá libh an leathmhíle deiridh isteach chun an stáisiúin. Tá na glórtha ansin thíos go toll sa chiúineas; scolagnach na roth agus preabadaíl na ráillí fúibh amuigh ag moilliú go sonraíoch. Spléachadh agat as eireaball do shúile ar an reilig ag streachailt suas an Creagán sula dtagann crothán foirgintí idir tú agus é a bhfuil fógra déirí in airde orthu. Tá an dream thíos go léir ar a mbonna anois, málaí ag scríobadh ar an urlár acu, iad á soipriú féin i gcótaí móra agus ag greafadach i gcúinní suíocháin. Tá fothram na himeachta ina rithim réidh stuama faoi bhur gcosa. Tagann sraith de thoir ísle idir sibh agus léinseach an uisce, scuaine carráistí ar thaobhlach faoina scáth. Bogann stórais agus seantáin thart ina scaifte idir sibh agus balla na sráide, agus both comharthaí ina ndiaidh a dtig leat a ainm a léamh ina litreacha bána ar chlár dubh: *Londonderry South*. Tithe dhá stór a bhfuil ciumháiseanna bríce fá na fuinneoga orthu fán na sráide amuigh agus ina raonta ar mhala an chnoic suas. Bloc liath de mhonarchain léinte agus fuinneoga ar nós súile leathdhúnta ann. Taobh thall den abhainn tá árais scoite sa choill ag gluaiseacht thart libh chomh cianach le crócharnaid. Aill dhearg bhríce in aice libh ar chlé, monarchain *Tilly and Henderson*; agus isteach libh faoi scáth Dhroichead Chraigavon, idir a rachtaí agus a chearchaillí urrúnta. An t-ardán go tobann in aice leis na fuinneoga. Díoscán íseal na gcoscán dá síorneartú. Shílfeá nach raibh tada ag corraí sa chathair tréigthe seo. Gliúrascnach ghrusach dheiridh agus stadann sibh de gheit a chuireann an bhaicle thíos ag stangaireacht. Tá cuma bheag tíriúil ar an stáisiún faoi na soilse buí. Corrdhuine ag stárógacht chugaibh amuigh. Labhraíonn glór gíománaigh mar bheadh sé ag teacht as domhan eile. Tá an doras oscailte ag an sagart mór thíos. Éiríonn tú ar do bhonna agus d'altanna frithir. Siúlann tú anonn fá choinne an chóta bháisti atá fillte go cúramach ar an eangach os cionn na fuinneoige. Tarraingeann tú ort é agus ceanglaíonn tú an crios in aghaidh aer na hoíche amuigh, iarracht de theanntás sónta ort faoin déata seort mileata a fhágann an gabairdín buí ort. Casann tú ar do sháil le do mhála tathagach leathair a bhaint anuas. Fágann tú ar an suíochán romhat é, snapann tú an dá laistín agus leagann tú an t-úrscéal thart isteach ann idir an gheansaí cniotáilte agus an chulaith oíche fhlannbhuí, an t-úrscéal nach mó ná gur léigh tú leathanach iomlán de ach a ndeachaigh d'intinn i bhfostú ann ina dhiaidh sin. Dúnann tú claibín an mhála anuas ar phictiúr na reilige agus an seanduine i measc na dtuamaí den ghlaschloch. Tá an urrainn bánaithe ar fad. Ligeann tú síos an fhuinneog go garbh. Múrlán práis an dorais amuigh, tá sé fliuch bealaithe. Brúnn tú an chomhla uait siar i gcoinne cliathán mahogaine an charráiste. Amach leat ar an ardán crua. Tá sé fuar.

Down at the end of the compartment there is considerable bustle among your fellow travellers: a young couple snuggling together and giggling secretly. The man pulls down several new cases heavily on to the seat, an action that draws an anxious glance from the tall priest where he is engaged in serious conversation with a woman and two girls. It seems to you that the talk is in Irish from the odd word that drifts in your direction. However inconceivable it may seem to you, the language still has currency, falling easily from the lips of people and brilliantly from the nib of a pen, your forefathers forever enshrined in it as it speaks of your heritage. In front of you the last curve of the Foyle broadens out unexpectedly as the track follows the swerve of the land. You see the steeples of the city stand vertical above the slate roofs as if lit by the cold glitter of the sleeping moon. You feel again the greasy air gather in your mouth, heavy with the tang of gas and coal. There are dingy grubby leaves on the black flagstones and the melancholy breath of autumn is in your very lungs as if you were a schoolboy returning reluctantly at the beginning of term. Beside the track rich green fields surge towards the water and there are white middle-class houses climbing amidst thickets of trees. Ash, their bare branches black with ivy, reach to the top of the eaves beyond the windows. Now you can see swathes of houses piled on top of one another on the scarp of the Waterside, down the Bogside and on the summit of the rise of the ancient island of Colum Cille. The huge bridge with the ugly name is set where the river is at its narrowest, while the walls and cannon of the Planters seem to glare down at it. A thousand chimneys belch out the warmth of domestic comfort and Irish decency against the stone enclosure that the London merchants imposed on Derry, the untidy, garrulous, amiable city, with rooted injustice as the leaven that led to eruption …

A long mournful hoot over the river and the snorting of the engine ceases. You'll run the last half-mile into the station under your own steam. Voices booming hollowly in the surrounding silence; rattle of the wheels and the clacking of the rails beneath them as they are slowly retarded. A view out of the corner of your eye of the cemetery struggling up the hill of Creggan before a scattering of buildings, marked with a signboard saying 'Dairy' comes between you and it. The people at the far end are all on their feet, bags scraping on the floor, wrapping themselves in overcoats and rooting in the corners of the seats. The din of departure in a steady easy rhythm under your feet. A string of low bushes comes between you and the smooth flowing water, shadowing a line of carriages in a siding. Clumps of shacks and storehouses move between you and the street wall and now comes a signal box where in white letters on a black sign you can read: Londonderry South. Two-storey houses, their windows edged with brick, line the streets outside and in rise in terraces on the brow of the hill. The grey mass of a shirt factory, its windows like half-shut eyes. Across the river homesteads scattered about a wood, seeming to move with the melancholy of a phantom funeral. A cliff of redbrick near on your left, Tilly and Henderson's factory, and now in you go under the shadow of Craigavon Bridge, with its mighty girders and piers. The platform suddenly appears at the windows. A deep grinding sound as the brakes are applied. The city has a lost air of dereliction. A short final creak and you stop with a jerk that sets the crowd at the end chattering. The station looks quite pleasant under the yellow lights. There are a few people outside staring in. The voice of the official sounds as though it came from some other world. The priest at the lower end has opened the door. You rise eagerly to your feet and cross to get the raincoat that is folded carefully on the net-rack above the window. You put it on, tightening the belt against the cold outside, trying for an air of even naïve assurance, the sort of military bearing that a fawn gabardine imposes. You turn on your heel to bring down your bulky leather bag, place it on the seat opposite, open the two catches and put the novel inside between the knitted sweaters and the orange pyjamas; the novel of which you had only to read a full page until your mind was absolutely engrossed. You shut the lid of the case on the picture of the cemetery and the old man among the whinstone memorials. The compartment is completely empty. You let the window down roughly. The outside handle of the door is wet and greasy. You push the door outwards from the mahogany frame of the carriage and step out on to the platform. It is cold.

BREANDÁN Ó DÓIBHLIN, *An Branar gan Cur* (*The Untilled Field*), 1979

(VERSION BY SEAN McMAHON)

IN JANUARY 1849, Dr Edward Maginn, Bishop of Derry, caught typhoid fever on a visit to the city and died within a few days.

In October 1849 Dr Francis Kelly, his successor, was ordained bishop at the age of thirty-six. Unexpectedly made Bishop at this early age, Dr Kelly faced a multitude of problems as bishop. The diocese had no cathedral, no secondary schools for boys or girls, no house for diocesan organisation, or for the bishop, and no money to train students for the priesthood. The diocese was desperately poor – the last bishop had lived for some years in a small cottage near Buncrana. Even in 1860, when a levy was made on all Catholic parishes in Ireland to support the new Catholic University, Derry could only afford three pounds per parish; this was the lowest sum among all the Ulster dioceses and compares to Dublin which paid £20 per parish.

The diocese was still emerging from the shadows of the 18th century penal laws and fearful of its weak position. In 1851 the Ecclesiastical Titles

Bill became law. This Bill made it illegal for Dr Kelly to call himself Bishop of Derry; at least one of his fellow-bishops appeared in court on the charge of using his Catholic title. It is a measure of Dr Kelly's success as bishop that by 1870 every parish in the diocese had its own church and schools.

The plight of his people was also desperate. They had suffered severely in the potato famine of 1846 and 1847 – Bishop Maginn had noted in 1847 that 'at the present time there are at least fifty thousand in actual starvation' – and Derry's population had been swollen by thousands fleeing from the famine in Donegal.

Living conditions in the City were already wretched in the extreme. A statement to the Poor Law Commission in 1833 reports on an Urban District in terms that exactly described conditions in the Bogside at that time.

> The lanes and streets are filled with filth; there are no sewers; no attention is paid to the ventilation of the houses, and the poor are obliged to buy even the water which they drink; it is of the worst description and tends to promote disease as much by its scarcity as its quality. Their sufferings from want of fuel, want of water and of clothing can only be credited by those who have witnessed them. The sufferings of the poor children cannot be described; many perish and those who survive are, in many instances, so debilitated by want as to become sickly and infirm at an early period in life.

Thomas Colby wrote in the Ordnance Survey of the County of Londonderry, 1837:

> Among the labourers of Derry great poverty prevails ... The better class inhabit huts, which let for about £3 a year; but the poor frequently lodge in out-houses, chiefly in the Bogside, at a rent of about 1s. 3d. a week – and yet even in these hovels they contrive to let shares of their rooms at 6d (a week.)

An 1835 Report on Derry gives the example of a mother and daughter:

> The daughter had hurt her leg and could not work; her mother, a very old woman had hurt herself when gathering potatoes and was confined to bed; the miserable hut they lived in was so smoky it was scarcely possible to see the bed.

The 1832 Poor Inquiry referred to the many families sleeping on the floors of damp houses with no bed-clothes, and in the 1840s the Long Tower district still had people living in mud-cabins. Tuberculosis was rampant.

Public health was a matter of serious concern right through the nineteenth century. In 1831 there was an outbreak of cholera with over 1,000 cases recorded, mostly from the Bogside. Typhus was endemic: a letter to the *Londonderry Standard* in 1836, called the attention of the public to the fact that 'there are more deaths at present in the city and suburbs from typhus fever than there were at the time the cholera raged here at its greatest fierceness'. This was due to the large number of open cesspools in the Bogside.

In 1840 for example, there was no water-closet of any kind in Ann Street, Frederick Street, Thomas Street, Abbey Street and most of Fahan Street and Bogside Street.

Health Boards and sanitary inspectors' reports continually complain of the 'offensive stench' of the streets and of Corporation inaction in tackling the problem. Even in 1901 almost 2,500 houses, a great number of which were in the Bogside, were without toilet facilities of any kind. And the Recollections section of the Heritage Library in Derry records that in 1920 some houses still had open cesspools in the rear.

Conditions were particularly bad in the 1840s and 1850s with regard to living conditions and employment because of the long economic decline which Derry experienced during those years. The glass-making and the sugar-refining industries both collapsed and other industries went into recession.

(BROTHER) JOHN LEDWIDGE, *The Brow, the Brothers and the Bogside*, 1990

TOWNS: WATERSIDE

A SUBURB OF LONDONDERRY called the Waterside and a small village called New Buildings are situated in the parish, but there is no town of importance in it.

The Waterside is immediately adjoining the bridge of Londonderry on the eastern side of the river, extending along 2 mail coach roads which then work towards the north and south along its banks and also up a steep bank on the old road to Dungiven called Brae Face. The whole suburb consists of 120 houses, of which 50 are wretched cabins, and mostly [insert alternative: chiefly] situated on the steep bank above mentioned.

In the other parts there is a great proportion of very respectable houses and 2 good inns; see Table of Occupations [insert marginal note: introduce table].

The arrangements with respect to lighting, paving and watching, and other municipal regulations, are the same as in the city of Londonderry. The shops appear to be improving. In 1833 there were 6 new houses built and 1 has been built in 1834. It is under the same regulations as the city.

On Wednesdays and Saturdays, which are the market days of the city, 2 merchants purchase corn at their own stores at the Waterside from persons who thus avoid the toll of the bridge. Carriages and cars are kept for hire at the 2 inns; here also many persons coming from the east side of the Foyle leave their conveyances and horses during the time they transact business in the city.

The Waterside owes its increase to the heavy tolls of the bridge.

The reservoir which supplies the city of Londonderry with water is in the townland of Corrody. The water is led through pipes to a second and smaller reservoir in Clooney, immediately above the Waterside, from whence it is conveyed in pipes across the bridge to the town. The cost of conveying the supply, which was 1,000 pounds, was met by a loan from government not yet repaid.

DAY, McWILLIAMS, ENGLISH, and DOBSON (eds),
Ordnance Survey Memoirs of Ireland, Vol. 34: Clondermot and Waterside (1831–8), 1996

I TOOK TO TRAVELLING, INSTEAD. Of a sudden Magee no longer seemed a refuge, only a confinement, and I invented numberless excuses to be free of it, to go out scavenging.

There were, for instance, my feet. Claiming incipient droopage of the instep, I won permission to pay a weekly visit after Friday school to one Bernard Dinty, a cobbler turned foot-healer.

Dinty's office, a bare, white room above a flesher's on Shipquay Street, lay deep within the walled city, overlooking Bogside, and it hid behind drawn blinds, with a hurricane lamp for shadowing. There I would be marched back and forth across a narrow strip of linoleum, one full hour by the clock, practising posture, balance and what Dinty termed tone of gait.

This office, it was rumoured at Foyle, doubled as a front for a butter-smuggling ring. And it's true, there was something rancid and furtive in its air, a smell of dirty little secrets. As for the healer himself, a rumpled little squit of a man, all polka-dot bow tie and stained white medico's coat, he liked to soundtrack my perambulations with lectures on the evils of masturbation, also of patronizing brothels, or, as he preferred, the Temples of Venus. 'Fallen arches today, fallen women next Saturday', was his pet motto and, each time he delivered it, he would touch my bare short-trousered leg above the knee, not so much sweating as oozing, clammily steaming, like an overheated jam pudding in melt-down.

My compensation was that, by the time I won release, it would be after dark, all the streets would have changed for night, and then the straightest, safest way home would lead me directly past the Roseland Café.

The snake itself, I never saw again. But the Teddy Boys, its votaries, were regulars, and they came to embody everything I sensed, everything that I still couldn't spell.

In their daytime incarnations, I understood, the Teds were only Papist scum, the delinquent flotsam and jetsam of Bogside. As such, their life prospects were nil. Foredoomed, the dispossessed, they had traded away the

Free for the Welfare State, and now they had no work, no homeplace, no future hope whatever, unless it be the fleeting glory of an IRA martyrdom. They were, in every common sense, non-persons. And yet, here on The Strand, in the neon night by Rock 'n' Roll, they were made heroic. In every flash of fluorescent sock or velvet cuff, every jivestep swagger for Chuck Berry, every leer and flaunt of their greased pompadoured ducktails, they beggared the fates, made reality irrelevant.

NIK COHN, *Ball the Wall*, 1989

T O-DAY AS I PASS DOWN SHIPQUAY STREET and through the Gate I see a very different view before me from that which I was familiar with 'in the long agoes'. Then there was no Guildhall or Northern Bank, no GPO or Harbour Offices in the background. The former Post Office, through which I often passed, was at the far end of Castle Street, and close by the late David Irvine, sen., had his printing works. In the space now occupied by the Guildhall was a large square of buildings in their last days. One of those I remember particularly well. It was a wholesale grocery store owned by the late Robert Henderson, father of the late Dr Henderson, from out Glendermott way, who died a few years ago, and was well known in the city. Those old buildings 'had served their day and generation', so were due for demolition. When this took place, the firm, Robert Henderson & Co., moved to the building at the foot of Shipquay Street now known as 'The City Cafe'.

Turning towards Waterloo Square, my attention is arrested by 'The Golden Teapot' standing out so prominently against the sky just as it did 70 or 80 years ago, with its worthy traditions upheld as of old. Away beyond that I see the name Hugh Stevenson & Co. just as in the olden times. In this connection a boyish recollection comes to mind. In those days there was no lunch-hour at the Model School save a few minutes in the playground. We boys were glad to have at lunch-time one of Stevenson's buns known to us as 'a bap'. The Stevenson family then lived in Great James Street (the house is still standing), but later on they built a mansion on Northland Road, with a magnificent view across the river, and it was nicknamed by the jokers of the city 'Bap House'. Owned now by the O'Neill family, it rejoices in a more euphonious name – 'Ardowen'.

Speaking of Northland Road, as I look back I can think of it only as a country road. The one house before reaching Magee College was Edenmore House. There was no Crawford Square then save the four houses at the top running parallel to Northland Road. In my schooldays I often paused with interest at the space between Asylum Road and Clarendon Street as seen from Francis Street. There is a wall now hiding it from view, but then there was just a low grass rampart on which I lay looking into a green

412

valley, which was known as 'The Camp Field', land in which there was an old Icehouse. As I lay there I romanced over the possible link that may have been with the Siege times or as a Gipsy camp. To-day there is no 'Green Valley', as outhouses have been built from both sides. What space is now left serves as a mews lane. The present Academy Road was then known as 'Haw Lane', suggestive as a country lane, which it really was. A little way up there were to the left and backing on to the Model School five or six houses called as now 'Nicholson Terrace'. From that on it was pure country. 'The Academy,' now Foyle College property, had not then been built. Beyond Brooke Park, Rosemount stood, then a distinct village, and there were very few houses or streets from that down to the Lone Moor Road.

C.W. GORDON, Reminiscences of Derry in the Last Century, n.d.

Soliloquising
he stalks the larchlap battlements
eyeing
the dark hulk of the wheelie bin,
reviews the hoard of evidence within –
Captain's Table haddock portion packets,
fractured delph, Punjana tea-leaves,
Gideon Bible with exhausted spine –
evidence
of something rotten.

The mother tells him over Cup-a-Soup with croutons
not, if he really cares, to care at all,
that all manner of things shall be well
on Scene Around Six,
that the supermarket shelves will be
for all a labyrinth of self-fulfilment
one fine day.

The wicked uncle and his cronies
visit the house with no windows
and a back door only,
take poison, dance together, close
as constituent parts of a hard-boiled egg.

Ophelia has her GCEs,
needs UCCA points for having lived.
Whenever Hamlet reads, the words stir like
tadpoles coming to.
Whenever Hamlet walks about the town
footpaths convey him leaflike
to the rims of underpasses.
Whenever Hamlet calls Ophelia on the phone
beasts of the fields chew the line,
pull apart connection every time,
ruminating gently.

Hamlet decides
not to tell
the RUC
the Operatic Society
the minister
the British Army
the doctor, the dentist, the optician
the English teacher
the Rugby Club
the mother
the two friends
the driver of the Altnagelvin bus
the editor of *The Sentinel*
the binman ...

One fine day Ophelia
by way of the Good Shepherd Convent –
where she passes in
through the hatch some dirty linen
and is passed back a docket –

takes herself down to the Faughan Bridge,
plucks vetch, bluebells, Robin-run-the hedge,
dog roses, star of Bethlehem, alder catkins
wood anemones, May blossom, lesser celandine,

spreads a tartan rug
and knits a wondrous flowery gansey
which she dons.

Ophelia takes the Maiden City Flyer.

This much has come to pass:
scallions at Christmas from Mexico in Stewarts.

In Rossdowney, Hamlet remains, as heretofore.

ANN McKAY, 'Hamlet in Rossdowney', *Giving Shine*, 2000

O UR HOUSE HAD A GROUNDFLOOR front room and back kitchen, with a long hall that ran from the street to the backyard, and next floor up were two bedrooms with two attic bedrooms above that. The attic bedrooms' ceilings sloped with the roof and each had a skylight on the slates and when we as children were put to bed at night and my mother thought she had the front room to herself, the calling would start: 'Ma, can I have a drink of water? Ma, can I have ...' and so it went on.

One night everything was too quiet, so she went to the foot of the stairs to listen to the silence, when in through the door from the street burst Gerard competely out of breath, followed by Mannix. He too was breathless after running a race. The course was a semi-obstacle one which started for one runner at the top of Fountain Hill on Spencer Road and for the other at the bottom of Fountain Hill on Duke Street. The idea was that one would run up Duke Street, the other down Spencer Road towards each other to meet at Cafolla's ice-cream parlour, do one turn round the revolving doors and head for home, dressed in their birthday suits. As this had been going on for a while, they were always assured of an audience. I guess they must have been the original streakers. They were about seven years old at the time.

JOHN DORAN, *Red Doran*, 1996

DEATH OF MISS KNOX

T HE DEATH OF MISS MARY ANNE KNOX OF PREHEN, by the hand of John MacNaughten or MacNaghten Esquire, on the 10th November 1761, naturally excited much interest at the time, which length of years has but slightly abated. According to a manuscript account of this transaction, written by a female friend of Miss Knox, this ill-fated young lady, believing that her father had consented to her union with MacNaghten, a condition which she had made indispensable, went through the marriage ceremony with him in private, but on learning that deception had been practised on her, refused to live with him. He pursued her to different places under various disguises, but in vain. However, being at length informed that she was on her way to Dublin with her parents, he overtook the carriage on the road between Lifford and Strabane, and lodged a bullet in her side, which in a few hours occasioned her death. For this crime MacNaghten and an accomplice were soon after executed.

The statement from which these particulars have been derived is annexed to a few poems 'copied from Gray's works by the lovely but unfortunate Mary Anne Knox,' and preserved 'as a relique of that much and justly esteemed and admir'd lady.'

It is believed that MacNaghten, after having been for some time concealed from the officers of justice by different females of his acquaintance, was discovered by some person who had observed a lady bringing food to an outhouse in which he was at the time secreted. He suffered at Strabane, justly, although perhaps for an unintentional crime, as it is supposed by some that the bullet [crossed out: firelock, weapon] which occasioned the death of Miss Knox had been intended [crossed out: aimed] at her father.

In the church of Killygarvan in the county of Donegal is a tablet erected in the memory of the father of the present Colonel Knox, at the head of which is engraved: 'Mariana filia obiit November 1761'.

DAY, McWILLIAMS, ENGLISH, and DOBSON (eds),
Ordnance Survey Memoirs of Ireland, Vol. 34: Clondermot and Waterside (1831–8), 1996

We are north-seeking
On an express bus,
Vibrating through rain
That slants from
Ardee and Slane and Monaghan.

Faces I know
And have never seen
Surround me.
That girl with plaits
Reading 'Dublin Made Me' –
Could she be you returning to the Waterside
Remembering?

We are homing always
To the lodestone of Derry.

TOMÁS Ó CANAINN, 'Homing', *Melos*, 1987

Acknowledgements

The editor and publisher gratefully acknowledge permission to include the following copyright material:

ABBOTT, RICHARD, from *Police Casualties in Ireland 1919–1922* (Cork: Mercier Press, 2000), by permission of the Mercier Press.

ALLEN, TREVOR, from *The Storm Passed By* (Irish Academic Press, 1996), copyright holder not traced.

ANDERSON, GERRY, from *Surviving in Stroke City* (Hutchinson, 1999), by permission of the Random House Group.

ANONYMOUS, 'Aistriú Thomáis Oíche Shamhna', in *Céad de Cheolta Uladh*, (ed.) Énrí Ó Muireasa (1915), (ed.) T.F. Beausang (Bro.) (Comhlatas Uladh, 1983), by permission of Comhlatas Uladh.

ANONYMOUS, 'Colum Cille's Exile' (trans. James Carney), in *Medieval Irish Lyrics* (Dolmen, 1967), by permission of Colin Smythe Limited on behalf of Paul Carney.

ANONYMOUS, 'Derry Town', 'Derry's Walls' and 'A Londonderry Love Song', from *There Was Music in the Derry Air*, (ed.) A.M. Murray (Guildhall Press, 1989), by permission of the Guildhall Press.

ANONYMOUS, 'Feis Medal'; 'Gaelic in Music, Song and Story' (*Derry Journal*, 28 June 1922), both in *Feis Doire Colmcille Souvenir Book* (1999), by permission of the feis archivist, Pat McCafferty.

ANONYMOUS, from *The Fountain*, (ed.) Leon McAuley (Verbal Arts Centre, 1993), by permission of the Verbal Arts Centre.

ANONYMOUS, from *The Londonderry Journal*, 12 November 1839, in *Captain William Coppin: 'Neptune's Brightest Star'*, Annesley Malley and Mary McLaughlin (Foyle Civic Trust, 1992), by permission of the authors.

ANONYMOUS, 'The High Walls of Derry', in *My Parents Reared Me Tenderly*, (eds) Jimmy McBride and Jim McFarland (self-published, 1985), by the permission of the editors.

ARMSTRONG, GRACE, 'Thinking Back', in *Londonderry High School Old Girls' Association Magazine* (Summer 1961), by permission of the author.

BAILEY, ANTHONY, *Acts of Union* (Faber, 1980), by permission of the Random House Group. Copyright © 1977, 1978 and 1980 by Anthony Bailey.

BARKLEY, JOHN M. (Rev.), from *Blackmouth and Dissenter* (White Row Press, 1991), by permission of the White Row Press.

BARRON (DD), ROBERT (Rev.), from *Mary Barron – A Biography* (Sabbath School for Ireland, Fisherwick Place, Belfast, 1915), copyright holder not traced.

BEHAN, BRENDAN, from *Brendan Behan's Island* (Hutchinson, 1962), by kind permission of the estate of Brendan Behan and the Sayle Literary Agency. Copyright © Brendan Behan 1962.

BERNARD, ALFRED, from *The Whiskey Distillers of the United Kingdom* (Mainstream, 1987), by permission of Mainstream Publishing Co. Ltd.

BIRNEY, TREVOR AND JULIAN O'NEILL, from *When the President Calls* (Guildhall Press, 1997), by permission of the authors.

BLAKE, JOHN W., *Northern Ireland in the Second World War* (Her Majesty's Stationery Office, 1956; Blackstaff Press, 2000), by permission of the Controller of Her Majesty's Stationery Office and Queen's Printer for Scotland. © Crown copyright.

BLAKESTON, OSWELL, from *Thank You Now* (Anthony Blond, 1960), copyright holder not traced.

BOLSTER (RSM), ANGELA, from 'The Story of Mercy in Derry', in *The History of the Diocese of Derry*, (eds) Henry A. Jeffries and Ciarán Devlin (Four Courts Press, 2000), by kind permission of the Four Courts Press.

BRYANS, ROBIN (ROBERT HARBINSON), *Ulster: A Journey Through the Six Counties* (Faber, 1964; Blackstaff Press, 1989), by permission of the author.

BURNSIDE, SAM, 'The Field', in *The Blackstaff Book of Short Stories* (Blackstaff Press, 1988); 'The New Bridge, Londonderry – Travelling East', 'In and Out of Derry' and 'Foyle', from *Walking the Marches* (Salmon, 1990), all by permission of the author.

BYRNE, ART, *Church, Chapel, Meeting House* (Guildhall Press, 1992), by permission of the Guildhall Press.

CARR, PETER, *The Big Wind* (White Row Press, 1991), by permission of the White Row Press.

CARROTHERS, JOHN SAMUEL, from *Memoirs of a Young Lieutenant* (compiled by D.S. Carrothers, 1992), by permission of D.S. Carrothers.

CLAYTON-LEA, TONY AND RICHIE TAYLOR, *Irish Rock* (Gill & Macmillan, 1992), by permission of Gill & Macmillan, Dublin.

COHN, NIK, from *Ball the Wall: Age of Rock* (Picador, 1989), by permission of Rogers, Coleridge & White, 20 Powis Mews, London W11 1JN. Copyright © Nik Cohn 1989.

COLHOUN, MABEL R., 'Strand House School', in *Londonderry High School Old Girls' Association Magazine* (Summer 1960), by permission of the author.

COLLINS, JUDE, 'Booing the Bishop', *Booing the Bishop and Other Stories* (Blackstaff Press, 1995), by permission of the author.

CORKEY, EDITH, *David Corkey: A Life Story* (The Religious Tract Society, n.d.), copyright holder not traced.

CORKEY (MA DD), WILLIAM (Rev.), *Memories of an Irish Manse* (*Belfast News Letter* n.d.), by permission of Century Newspaper Ltd.

COULTER, PHIL, 'The Town I Loved So Well', by permission of the composer.

COYLE, KATHLEEN, from *The Magical Realm* (E.P. Dutton, 1943), by permission of Merlin Books.

CURRAN, FRANK, from *The Derry City FC Story* (*Donegal Democrat*, 1986), by permission of the author.

CURL, J.S., *The Honourable The Irish Society and the Plantation of Ulster, 1608–2000* (Phillimore, 2000), by permisson of Phillimore & Co.

DALY, EDWARD (Bishop), *'Hi Mister! Are You a Priest?'* (Four Courts Press, 2000), by kind permission of the Four Courts Press.

DANA (with LUCY ELPHINSTONE), from *Autobiography* (Hodder and Stoughton, 1985), by permission of Hodder and Stoughton.

D'AVAUX, COMTE, *Negociations de M le Comte d'Avaux en Irlande, 1689–90* (Dublin Stationery Office, 1934), by kind permission of the Irish Manuscripts Commission.

DAY, ANGÉLIQUE, PATRICK McWILLIAMS, LISA ENGLISH AND NÓIRÍN DOBSON (eds), *Ordnance Survey Memoirs of Ireland, Vol 34: Clondermot and Waterside* (Institute of Irish Studies, Queen's University Belfast in association with The Royal Irish Academy, 1996), by permission of the Institute of Irish Studies and Queen's University Belfast.

DEANE, SEAMUS, 'After Derry, 30 January 1972', from *Gradual Wars* (Gallery Press, 1972), by kind permission of the author and the Gallery Press, Loughcrew, Oldcastle, County Meath, Ireland; 'Civil War', in *The Wearing of the Black*, (ed.) Padriac Fiacc (Blackstaff Press, 1974), by permission of the author; 'A Schooling', from *Rumours*, (Gallery Press, 1977), by kind permission of the author and the Gallery Press; 'Accident', 'Pistol', 'Maths Class' and 'Fire', from *Reading in the Dark* (Jonathan Cape, 1996), by permission of the Random House Group.

DE BLÁCAM, AODH, *The Black North* (W.H. Gill & Son, 1938), by permission of Carl de Blácam.

DE LA POER BERESFORD, C.E., 'Londonderry City Election, 1885' and 'Londonderry City Election, 1913', in *A Happy New Year and Other Verses* (Eton College, 1913), copyright holder not traced.

DEVLIN, P.J., from *That Was the Way of It* (Cork: Mercier Press, 2001), by permission of the Mercier Press.

DOHERTY, PADDY, from *Paddy Bogside* (Cork: Mercier, 2001), by permission of the Mercier Press.

DOHERTY, RICHARD, *Key to Victory: The Maiden City in the Second World War* (Glendale, 1995), by permission of the author.

DORAN, JOHN, from *Red Doran – The Story of a Derryman* (Blackstaff Press, 1996), by permission of the author.

DOYLE, LYNN, from *The Spirit of Ireland* (B.T. Batsford, 1935), by permission of Wyn Fisher.

DUNLOP, JOHN (Rev.), *A Precarious Belonging: Presbyterians and the Conflict in Ireland* (Blackstaff Press, 1995), by permission of the Blackstaff Press.

ELLIOTT, MARIANNE, from *The Catholics of Ulster* (Allen Lane, 2000; Penguin, 2000), by permission of Penguin Books. Copyright © Marianne Elliott 2000.

FERGUSON, KATHLEEN, from *The Maid's Tale* (Torc Books, 1994), by permission of the author.

FISK, ROBERT, from *In Time of War* (Andre Deutsch, 1983), by permission of Andre Deutsch.

FLOYD, MICHAEL, *The Face of Ireland* (B.T. Batsford, 1937), by permission of Chrysalis Books.

FOLEY, MICHAEL, 'A Provincial Adolescence', in *The GO Situation* (Blackstaff Press, 1982); *The Road to Notown* (Blackstaff Press, 1996); *Getting Used To Not Being Remarkable* (Blackstaff Press, 1998), all by permission of the author.

FRIEL, BRIAN, from 'Johnny and Mick', in *The Saucer of Larks* (Victor Gollancz, 1962), by permission of Victor Gollancz, a division of the Orion Publishing Group; *The Freedom of the City* (Faber, 1973), by permission of Faber & Faber.

GALLAGHER, CHARLES, from *Acorns and Oak Leaves* (Dubh-Regles Books, 1981), by permission of Séamus Gallagher.

GALLAGHER, PATRICK ('PADDY THE COPE'), *My Story* (Templecrone Cooperative Society, 1939), by permission of Paddy the Cope Gallagher.

GEBBIE, JOHN H. (ed.), *An Introduction to the Abercorn Letters* (Strule Press, 1972), copyright holder not traced.

GIBBONS, JOHN, from *Abroad in Ireland* (Frederick Muller, 1936); *Ireland – the New Ally* (Robert Hale, 1938), copyright holder not traced.

GIBSON, ELIZABETH, from *The Water is Wide* (Hodder, 1985), by permission of Chrysalis Books.

GORDON, C.W., *Reminiscences of Derry in the Last Century* (self-published, n.d.), copyright holder not traced.

GREACEN, ROBERT, from *The Sash My Father Wore* (Mainstream, 1997), by permission of the author; 'As a Child in Derry', in *The Wearing of the Black*, (ed.) Padraic Fiacc (Blackstaff Press, 1974), by permission of the author.

GRENNAN, EAMON, 'Soul Music: The Derry Air', in *What Light There Is* (Gallery Press, 1987), by kind permission of the author and the Gallery Press, Loughcrew, Oldcastle, County Meath, Ireland.

GRIBBON, H.D., from *The History of Water Power in Ulster* (David & Charles, 1969), by permission of David & Charles.

GRIFFIN, VICTOR (Dean), from *The Mark of Protest* (Gill & Macmillan, 1993), by permission of Gill & Macmillan, Dublin.

GWYNN, STEPHEN, from *The Famous Cities of Ireland* (Maunsel, 1915); from *Highways and Byways in Donegal and Antrim* (Macmillan, 1928), copyright holder not traced.

HAYWARD, RICHARD, *In Praise of Ulster* (William Mullan, 1938), copyright holder not traced.

HEANEY, SEAMUS, from 'The Ministry of Fear', from 'Singing Schools', in *North* (Faber, 1975); 'In the Afterlife', from 'Bodies and Souls', and The Real Names', in *Electric Light* (Faber, 2001), all by permission of Faber & Faber.

HEGARTY, WALTER, from *The Price of Chips* (Davis-Poynter, 1973), copyright holder not traced.

HERDMAN, REX, from *They All Made Me* (S.D. Montgomery, Omagh 1970), by permission of Mark Herdman.

HERMON, SIR JOHN, from *Holding the Line* (Gill & Macmillan, 1997), by permission of Gill & Macmillan, Dublin.

HEWITT, JOHN, 'Bogside, Derry, 1971', in *Collected Poems* (Blackstaff Press, 1991), by permission of the Blackstaff Press.

HIME, MAURICE C., 'On the Derry Water-supply', in *Christmas Roses* (1920), copyright holder not traced.

HOLMES, R.F.G. (Rev.), *Magee 1865–1965: The Evolution of the Magee Colleges* (Magee College, 1965), by permission of the author.

HUME, JOHN, *Personal Views* (Town House, 1996), by permission of Town House.

IRELAND, DENIS, from *From the Irish Shore* (Rich & Cowan, 1936); 'The Road to the Isles', in *Northern Harvest*, ed. Robert Greacen (Northern Harvest, 1944); 'Grandfather Preached in Irish', in *From the Jungle of Belfast* (Blackstaff Press, 1973), copyright holder not traced.

JAMES, DERMOT, *This Recklessly Generous Landlord: John Hamilton of Donegal 1800–1884* (Woodfield Press, 1998), by permission of the Woodfield Press.

JEFFRIES, HENRY A., 'George Montgomery, First Protestant Bishop of Derry, Raphoe and Clogher (1605–1610)', from *The History of the Diocese of Derry*, (eds) Henry A. Jeffries and Ciarán Devlin (Four Courts Press, 2000), by kind permission of the Four Courts Press.

JOHNSTON, JENNIFER, *Shadows on Our Skin* (Hamish Hamilton, 1977), by permission of Penguin Books, copyright © Jennifer Johnston, 1977; *The Railway Station Man* (Hamish Hamilton, 1984), by permission of the author.

JOHNSTON, SHEILA, from *Alice: A Life of Alice Milligan* (Colourpoint Books, 1994; ISBN 1 898392 01 3), by kind permission of the author.

KEIGHTLEY, S.R., from *The Crimson Sign* (Hutchinson, 1894), copyright holder not traced.

KELLETT, FRED, from *A Flower for the Sea – A Fish for the Sky* (Dellwood Press, 1995), by permission of the author.

KELLY, OWEN, from *Hens' Teeth and Other Rarities* (Greystone, 1990), by permission of the author.

KERR, MARYANNE, from *Over the Mountain* (Michael Joseph, 1996), by permission of Curtis Brown on behalf of Maryanne Kerr. Copyright © Maryanne Kerr 1996.

KIELY, BENEDICT, from *The Captain with the Whiskers* (Methuen, 1960), by permission of A.P. Watt on behalf of Benedict Kiely.

KINCADE, JAMES, 'In the Forties', in *Acorn* 9 (Autumn 1965), by permission of the author.

KING-HALL, MAGDALEN, from *The Edifying Bishop* (Peter Davies, 1951), by permission of A.P. Watt on behalf of the Executors of the Estate of Magdalen Perceval Maxwell.

KINSELLA, THOMAS, 'Butcher's Dozen' from *Collected Poems* (Oxford University Press, 1996), by permission of the Carcanet Press.

LACEY, BRIAN, from *Colum Cille and the Columban Tradition* (Four Courts Press, 1997); (ed.), from *Maghnus Ó Domhnaill: Betha Colaim Chille, 1532* (Four Courts Place, 1998), all by kind permission of the Four Courts Press.

LAXTON, EDWARD, from *The Famine Ships* (Bloomsbury Publishing plc., 1996), by permission of Bloomsbury Publishing plc.

LEDWIDGE, JOHN (Bro.), from *The Brow, the Brothers and the Bogside* (Guildhall Press, 1990), by permission of the author.

MACRORY, PATRICK, from *The Days That Are Gone,* (North-West Books, 1983), by permission of Patrick Macrory.

MAHON, DEREK, 'Derry Morning' from *Collected Poems* (Gallery Press, 1991), by kind permission of the author and the Gallery Press, Loughcrew, Oldcastle, County Meath, Ireland.

MARSHALL, ISOBEL, from *A Jack and His Jill* (Quota Press, 1944), copyright holder not traced.

MATHEWS, E.V. (Rev.), 'Mr R. J. Black in a Corner with Sailors' in R. J. Black: *His Life and Work* (compiled by A. Irwin) (*Derry Standard*, 1901), copyright holder not traced.

MAXWELL, D.E.S., 'A Reminiscence of Wartime Londonderry', in *Acorn* 5 (Autumn 1963), by permission of the author.

McBRIDE, IAN, from *The Siege of Derry in Ulster Protestant Mythology* (Four Courts Press, 1997), by kind permission of the Four Courts Press.

McCAFFERTY, NELL, from *Those Were the Days: Childhood Memories*, (ed.) Seán Power (Gill & Macmillan, 1995), by permission of Gill & Macmillan; *Peggy Deery* (Attic Press, 1987); 'The Class of '98', in *Goodnight Sisters* (Attic Press, 1988), copyright © Nell McCafferty 1987 and 1988, both by permission of the Attic Press, Crawford Business Park, Crosses Green, Cork, Ireland; 'From Rags to the Rialto', in *Here's Looking at You, Kid*, (eds) Stephanie McBride and Roddy Flynn (Wolfhound Press, 1996), by permission of the author; 'As Derry Lights Up' (*The Sunday Tribune*, 29 October 2000), by permission of the author.

McCANN, EAMONN, from *War and Peace in Northern Ireland* (Hot Press, 2000), by permission of Hot Press Books, 13 Trinity Street, Dublin 2, Ireland (book available at €12.27plus €2.50 p&p from Hot Press Books, or from booksales@hotpress.com); *War and an Irish Town* (Penguin, 1974), by permission of the author.

McCARTER, GERALDINE, from *Derry's Shirt Tale* (Guildhall Press, 1991), by permission of the Guildhall Press.

McCARTHY, MICHAEL J.F., *Five Years in Ireland: 1895–1900* (Hodges Figgis, 1901), copyright holder not traced.

McCLEAN, RAYMOND, *The Road to Bloody Sunday* (Ward River Press, 1981; Guildhall Press,1997), by permission of the author.

McCRUM, MARK, from *The Craic* (Victor Gollancz, London 1998), by permission of Victor Gollancz, a division of the Orion Publishing Group.

McCULLOUGH, ELIZABETH, from *A Square Peg* (Dublin: Marino Books, 1997), by permission of the Mercier Press.

MacGILL, PATRICK, *The Children of the Dead End* (Herbert Jenkins, 1914), by permission of Birlinn, Edinburgh.

McKAY, ANN, from 'Paper Roses', in *The Wall Reader* (Arlen House, 1979), by permission of the author; 'A Date at the Altnagelvin', 'Anubis on the Craigavon Bridge' and 'Hamlet in Rossdowney', from *Giving Shine* (Summer Palace Press, 2000), by permission of the Summer Palace Press.

McKAY, SUSAN, *Northern Protestants: An Unsettled People* (Blackstaff Press, 2000), by permission of the editor.

McLAUGHLIN, MARILYN, 'Aspects' and 'The Tree', in *A Dream Woke Me* (Blackstaff Press, 1999), by permission of the Blackstaff Press.

MacMAHON, BRIAN, *Here's Ireland* (B.T. Batsford, 1971), by permission of Chrysalis Books.

McMENAMIN, GERARD, from 'King Street', in *The Waterside Book* (Verbal Arts Centre, 1996), by permission of the Verbal Arts Centre.

McVEIGH, ARTHUR, 'Thoughts on the Derry Riots', in *A Rage for Order* (Blackstaff Press, 1992), copyholder not traced.

McVEIGH, HUGH, from *Oft in the Stilly Night* (Robert Hale, 1957), by permission of Robert Hale.

MacWEENEY, ALEN AND RICHARD CONNIFF, from *Ireland: Stone Walls and Fabled Landscapes* (Frances Lincoln, 1998), by permission of Frances Lincoln, 4 Torriano Mews, Torriano Avenue, London NW5 2RZ. Copyright © Frances Lincoln Ltd 1998. Text and photographs copyright © Alen MacWeeney and Richard Conniff 1986.

MELLON, MATTHEW T. (ed.), *Selections from* Thomas Mellon and His Times*, by Judge Thomas Mellon* (The Scotch-Irish Trust, Ulster American Folk Park, Omagh, 1976), by permission of Dr Phil Mowat, Curator, Ulster American Folk Park.

MILLIGAN, ALICE, from *The Dynamite Drummer* (Martin Lester, n.d.), by permission of Gill & Macmillan, Dublin.

MOLLOY, FRANCES, *No Mate for the Magpie* (Virago, 1985), by permission of Gerard Brady.

MONSARRAT, NICHOLAS, from '*HMS Marlborough* Will Enter Harbour', in *Depends on What You Mean by Love* (Cassell Illustrated, 1947), copyright holder not traced.

MONTAGUE, JOHN, extracts from 'A New Siege', in *The Rough Field*, 1989, by kind permission of the author and the Gallery Press, Loughcrew, Oldcastle, County Meath, Ireland.

MONTGOMERY, BRIAN, from *Monty's Grandfather: A Life's Service for the Raj: Sir Robert Montgomery GCSI KCB, 1809–1887* (Blandford Press, 1984), by permission of Victor Gollancz, a division of the Orion Publishing Group.

MOORE, DESSIE, from 'Growing Up in Bridge Street' (*Derry Journal*, 25 April 2000), by permission of the *Derry Journal*.

MURPHY, DERVLA, from *A Place Apart* (John Murray, 1978), by permission of John Murray.

NEEDHAM, RICHARD, *Battling for Peace* (Blackstaff Press, 1998), by permission of Curtis Brown on behalf of Richard Needham. Copyright © Richard Needham 1998.

NÍ DHUIBHNE, ÉILÍS, 'Gweedore Girl', in *The Inland Ice* (Blackstaff Press, 1997), by permission of the author.

Ó BAOILL, MICÍ SHEÁIN NÉILL, 'Taibhse Dhoire', in *Lá de na Laethaibh*, (ed.) Lorcán Ó Searcaigh SP (Oriel Press, 1983), by permission of the editor.

O'BRIEN, CONOR CRUISE, from *Memoir: My Life and Themes* (Poolbeg, 1998), by permission of Poolbeg.

Ó CANAINN, AODH, from *Tearmann na gColúr* (Cló Iar-Chonnachta Teo.,1998), by permission of Cló Iar-Cnonnachta.

Ó CANAINN, TOMÁS, from *Home to Derry* (Appletree Press, 1986), by permission of the Appletree Press; *A Lifetime of Notes* (Collins Press, 1997), by permission of the Collins Press; 'Homing', from *Melos* (self-published, 1987), by permission of the author.

O'CONNOR, FRANK, from *A Golden Treasury of Irish Poetry*, (Macmillan, 1967), by permission of PFD on behalf of Frank O'Connor. Copyright © Frank O'Connor 1967.

Ó DÓIBHLIN, BREANDÁN, from *An Branar gan Cur* (Gilbert Dalton, 1979), by permission of the author and the Columba Press.

O'DOHERTY, SHANE, from *The Volunteer* (Fount, 1993), by permission of the author.

O'FAOLAIN, SEAN, from *An Irish Journey* (Longman & Green, 1940), by permission of Rogers, Coleridge & White, 20 Powis Mews, London W11 1JN. Copyright © Estate of Sean O'Faolain 1940.

O'REILLY, PETER, from *Trout and Salmon Rivers of Ireland*, Fifth Edition (self-published, 1995), by permission of the author.

Ó SIADHAIL, SEÁN, from 'Iósaf', in *Scéalta Mhac an Ghobáin* (FNT, 1981), by permission of the author.

PAULIN, TOM, 'S/He', from *The Liberty Tree* (Faber, 1983), by permission of Faber & Faber.

PETER, RICHARD M., from *The Irish Football Annual: 1880* (Ulster Historical Foundation, 1999), by permission of the Ulster Historical Foundation.

POCOCKE, RICHARD (Archdeacon), from *Richard Pococke's Irish Tours*, (ed.) John McVeagh (Irish Academic Press, 1995), by permission of the Irish Academic Press.

POWER, VINCENT, from *Send 'Em Home Sweatin': The Showband Story* (1991; Mercier, 2000), by permission of the Mercier Press.

PRAEGER, ROBERT LLOYD, from *The Way That I Went* (Hodges Figgis, 1937), copyright holder not traced.

PRENDERGAST, MARK, from *Irish Rock* (O'Brien Press, 1987), by permission of the O'Brien Press, Dublin. Copyright © Mark Prendergast, 1987.

RICH, DORIS L., *Amelia Earhart* (Airlife, 1989), by permission of the Smithsonian Institution Press, Washington, D.C. Copyright © 1989.

ROBINSON, ANITA, 'Rare Birds', from *Feis Doire Colmcille Souvenir Book* (1999), by permission of the author.

ROBINSON, SIR HENRY, from *Memories Wise and Otherwise* (Cassell Illustrated, 1924), copyright holder not traced.

ROSS, SIR, JOHN, from *The Years of My Pilgrimage* (Edward Arnold, 1924), copyright holder not traced.

ROWAN, ALISTAIR, from *The Buildings of Ireland: North West Ulster* (Penguin, 1979), by permission of Yale University Press. Copyright © Alistair Rowan 1979.

RUMENS, CAROL, 'Passing a Statue of Our Lady in Derry' from *Selected Poems*, (Chatto & Windus, 1987), by permission of PFD on behalf of Carol Rumens. Copyright © Carol Rumens 1987.

SHANNON, ELIZABETH (ed.), from *I Am of Ireland* (University of Massachusetts Press, 1997), by permission of the University of Massachusetts Press.

SHEARMAN, HUGH, from *Ulster* (Robert Hale, 1939), copyright holder not traced.

SIMMONS, JAMES, verse 2 of 'Dickie Wells Said: Variations', from *Poems 1956–1986*, (Gallery Press, 1986), by kind permission of the author and the Gallery Press, Loughcrew, Oldcastle, County Meath, Ireland.

SOMERVILLE-LARGE, PETER, *The Grand Irish Tour* (Hamish Hamilton, 1982), by permission of the author and Curtis Brown. Copyright © Peter Somerville-Large 1982.

STETLER, RUSSELL, *The Battle of the Bogside* (Sheed & Ward, 1970), by permission of Continuum.

STEVENSON, BURTON, *The Charm of Ireland* (John Murray, 1915), copyright holder not traced.

STUART, FRANCIS, from *Memorial* (Martin Brian O'Keefe, 1973); 'Reading Keats in Derry City', in *A Rage for Order*, (ed.) Frank Ormsby (Blackstaff Press, 1992), both by kind permission of Fionnuala Stuart.

TAGGART, R., 'Neptune's Brightest Star', in *Captain William Coppin: 'Neptune's Brightest Star'*, Annesley Malley and Mary McLaughlin (Foyle Civic Trust, 1992), by permission of the authors.

TANNER LETTERS, THE (Stationery Office, 1943), by permission of the Irish Manuscripts Commission.

THEROUX, PAUL, from *The Kingdom by the Sea: A Journey Around the Coast of Great Britain* (London: Hamish Hamilton, 1982), by permission of Penguin Books. Copyright © Paul Theroux 1982.

TÓIBÍN, COLM, from *Bad Blood* (Vintage, 1994), by permission of the Random House Group.

TRAINOR, BRIAN AND W.H. CRAWFORD (eds), from *Aspects of Irish Social History 1750–1800* (PRONI, 1969), by permission of PRONI.

WALLACE, VALERIE, from *Mrs Alexander* (Lilliput Press, 1995), by permission of the author and the Lilliput Press.

WALSH, LOUIS J., *'On My Keeping' – And in Theirs* (Talbot Press, 1921), by permission of the Walsh family.

WATERMAN, ANDREW, 'Derry Images 1968–71', from *Collected Poems (1959–1999)* (Carcanet, 1999), by permission of the Carcanet Press.

WILKINS, PAUL, 'Returning to Derry' and 'Nativity Play', from *Pasts* (Carcanet, 1979), by permission of the Carcanet Press.

WOOD, JOHN, *With Rucksack Round Ireland* (Paul Elek, 1950), copyright holder not traced.

Every effort has been made to trace and contact copyright holders before publication. If notified, the publisher will rectify any errors or omissions at the earliest opportunity.

Index of Authors